W9-BSL-060

MYTHOLOGY

MYTHOLOGY

The ILLUSTRATED ANTHOLOGY
of WORLD MYTH & STORYTELLING

General Editor **C. Scott Littleton**

THUNDER BAY
P·R·E·S·S

San Diego, California

Thunder Bay Press
An imprint of the Advantage Publishers Group
5880 Oberlin Drive, San Diego, CA 92121-4794
www.thunderbaybooks.com

Created, edited, and designed by
Duncan Baird Publishers
6th Floor, Castle House
75–76 Wells Street
London W1T 3QH

Library of Congress Cataloging-in-Publication Data:

Mythology : the illustrated anthology of world myth &
storytelling / general editor C. Scott Littleton.
    p.cm
    Includes index
    ISBN 1-57145-827-1
    1. Mythology. I. Littleton, C. Scott
    BL312 .M985 2002
    291.1'3--dc21

                            2002032083

Typeset in Garamond
Color reproduction by Colourscan, Singapore
Printed and bound in Singapore by Imago

2 3 4 5 06 05 04 03

Design Managers: Gail Jones, Gabriella Le Grazie and
Clare Thorpe
Editorial Managers: Christopher Westhorp and Diana Loxley
Picture Researchers: Cecilia Weston-Baker, Anne-Marie
Ehrlich, Julia Ruxton and Susannah Stone
Consultants: *Egypt's Divine Kingship:* Dr Joann Fletcher,
Harrogate Museums and Arts; *Ancient Mesopotamia:* Dr Jeremy
Black, Oriental Institute, University of Oxford; *The Glories of
Greece and Rome:* Dr Michael Trapp, King's College, London
and Piers Vitebsky, Scott Polar Research Institute, University of
Cambridge; *Celtic Deities and Heroes:* Dr John McInnes, School
of Scottish Studies, Edinburgh; *Sagas of the Norsemen:* Dr Hilda
Ellis Davidson, Lucy Cavendish College, University of
Cambridge; *India's Eternal Cycle:* Dr Stuart Blackburn,
University of London; *China's Heavenly Mandate:* Dr John
Chinnery, University of Edinburgh; *Japan's Realm of the Rising
Sun:* Professor C. Scott Littleton, Occidental College, Los
Angeles; *North America's Mother Earth, Father Sky:* Hugh
Brodie; *Mesoamerica's Gods of Sun and Sacrifice:* Dr Tim
Laughton, University of Essex; *South American Kingdoms of
Gold:* Dr Andrew Canessa, University of Essex; *The Ancestral
Voices of Africa:* Dr Stephen Belcher, Pennsylvania State
University; *The Unseen Worlds of Australasia:* Dr Chris Gosden,
Pitt Rivers Museum, University of Oxford.

Title page: The enigmatic face of the Egyptian goddess Hathor
stares from a column capital at Dendara, dating from the Old
Kingdom (*c.* 2625–*c.* 2130 B.C.).

Contents

THE MEANING OF MYTH

Above: **This painted plate depicts the Maya goddess Xmucane grinding kernels. The Maya's sacred text, the *Popol Vuh* contained a story in which the first people were made from maize.**

Opposite, left: **In a number of cultures, twins were feared and welcomed in equal measure. This 19th-century Luba stool from the Congo, incorporates twin figures, which are symbols of unity as well as representatives of the divine snake, believed to be the oldest and greatest of all animals.**

Myths can be understood as magic mirrors in which the reflection not just of our own hopes and fears, but also those of people from the earliest times can be viewed. Some of the stories are unimaginably old and were almost certainly recounted long before the birth of writing and the dawn of recorded history. Collectively, the tales form the basis of much of the world's literature, philosophy and religion, and act as a powerful document of the human imagination.

For the people who originally told them, the myths served many purposes. Not only did they provide answers to the great philosophical questions – how the universe came into being, the nature of the forces operating within it, the origins of the first people and of the human community – but they also addressed more intimate issues, offering guidance on personal behaviour, social rules and what might happen in the afterlife. In combination, they provided the mental foundations of understanding and belief on which individuals could build their lives. And, crucially, they did so in narrative form. These were stories that people could remember and identify with, that could make them laugh, cry and feel awestruck.

Because the questions they address are so large, almost universal in their outlook, myths have always had an interest that crosses cultural boundaries. Yet anyone studying the subject quickly makes a surprising discovery: it is impossible to spend any length of time reading about the world's myths without being struck by the strange similarities that link them. Many of the same images – an egg from which the cosmos hatched; a universal flood; mortality being inflicted on humankind as a punishment for transgressions – constantly reappear.

Such similarities are sufficiently marked to have attracted the attention of scholars from many intellectual disciplines who, over the years in their respective fields, have sought an explanation for them. One obvious line of enquiry lay in cultural diffusion – the idea that myths travelled from people to people through direct contact, just as trade goods might have done. In the nineteenth century, for example, great significance was attached to the discovery of the spread of the Indo-European languages across Eurasia in the Bronze Age. One group of Aryan peoples credited with transmitting the tongues went to India, while another passed through the Middle East and Greece to northern Europe. Here was an obvious route of transmission that explained how some common themes appear in Indian, Greek and Norse mythology.

The picture became more complicated in the twentieth century as Westerners learned more about the myths of Australasia, sub-Saharan Africa and the Americas – places that had no physical links in early times with the Eurasian stock of myth but whose myths nevertheless revealed common features. It turned out that there were deluge myths from Australia and South America just as there were from China and Mesopotamia, and creation stories from Africa that paralleled those from ancient Greece. Some other factor, then, seemed to be at work in the construction of such stories, bridging distances that past populations had never spanned.

The problem caught the attention of the great Swiss psychiatrist Carl Gustav Jung, who further noted that many of the themes that recur repeatedly in world myth – dark forests, abrupt transformations, monstrous creatures, abandoned children, descriptions of flying or falling – also featured in his own dreams and those of his patients. He used this connection to formulate his theory of the "collective unconscious" – a section of the unconscious mind made up of memories and images shared with all humankind. Although many people have since challenged this theory, the attendant notion of archetypes – the term he used to

Above: Japanese myth was filled with heroic warrior exploits and the all-pervasive *kami* of the natural world. Woodblock print of a water spirit by Kunimasa, 19th century.

describe universally recognized mental symbols – has passed into common currency. In Jung's view, these archetypes were the missing link between the individual mind and myth. And it is the archetypes that make the great themes underlying world mythology relevant to this day. "That's a myth," people say, implying something is ridiculous or untrue; but they also speak of those things that touch them profoundly as having "a mythic dimension".

And that is why individuals still look to the old tales to help make sense of their own lives and the world around them. The fact is that the great themes of myth parallel our own experiences – they play out on an imaginative plane our deepest hopes and fears. It is because we can identify with and be moved by many of the strands within their narratives that myths remain of enduring interest and continue to attract new audiences.

Below: Bronze ritual wine vessel of China's Middle Western Zhou period, 10th century BC. Such items offered proof of the owner's status to the deceased ancestors who were believed to drink from it.

Myths also carry a social message – they suggest that beneath the huge differences of language and outlook that separate the world's cultures, there may be a common foundation. Something still not fully explained in the structure of the human mind may cause peoples of all continents and climes to thrill to the same plotlines and respond to the same dramas. In this respect, myths utilize a universal language which recalls the world before Babel – recurring with endless variation from culture to culture, myths demonstrate the timeless and essential imaginative unity of the human race.

CRADLES OF CIVILIZATION

EGYPT'S DIVINE KINGSHIP

In 1798 Napoleon Bonaparte and his French troops conquered Egypt. They were the latest in a succession of foreign forces – Persians, Greeks, Romans, Arabs, Turks – to dominate in the wake of the pharaohs. The expedition's reports of countless temples, tombs and monuments lining the banks of the Nile – the remnants of an ancient yet sophisticated civilization – helped to spark a new interest in the region that has not abated. The power of ancient Egypt, at its zenith in c.1450BC, extended from the border with Libya in the west to the river Euphrates in the east, and from the Nubian deserts in the south to Syria in the north. But the heart of the empire lay, as it always had, along the Nile. The riverbanks were a haven from the surrounding deserts in which the Egyptians could nourish their own unique vision of the world.

A stark duality – harsh desert versus fertile river margins – was woven deeply into Egyptian thought. Even after political unification in c.3100BC, there were always two Egypts: Lower Egypt (the delta of the Nile) and Upper Egypt (from Memphis at the apex of the delta and along the river to its upper reaches at Aswan), represented by the gods Seth and Horus respectively. Religion continued to offer diversity and a variety of creation myths were to be found in different cults that flourished in the major cities, such as Heliopolis and Memphis.

Above: the pyramids of, from left to right, Menkaure, Khephren and Khufu at Giza, built *c.*2500BC.

Opposite: Mysterious and imposing, the Great Sphinx at Giza has the head of a man and the body of a lion. It dates from *c.*2500BC, but has been repaired at various times in Egyptian history.

Myths were expressed in Egyptian iconography, hieroglyphs and ritual, but no one version of a story was held to be authoritative. However, these views of the world's origins did contain certain fundamental ingredients, namely those primary sources of life that the Egyptians saw about them – the Nile waters, with its life-giving annual flooding, and the sun, whose gods were uppermost in Egypt's pantheon, with Re of Heliopolis the supreme solar deity.

The ultimate development of Egypt's belief system was the principle of god-kingship. Thought to be descended from the gods, the pharaohs linked the land, people and universal deities; Egyptian religion was a cult of the pharaohs' ancestors, with the attendant rituals conducted in temples open only to priests and the king himself. Indeed, so pervasive was the presence of the gods and goddesses in every aspect of life that there was no separate word to denote religion. The gods, the world and the planets were all part of the same cosmic order, known as *ma'at*, which humans sought to maintain.

Order out of Chaos

The Egyptians' understanding of the universe was limited by what they could see around them. According to ancient texts, the waters of chaos surrounded their world, which was separated into three parts: the Earth, the sky, and the underworld (which was known as the "Duat"). The sun journeyed into the perilous Duat at night, which was why it could not be seen. This lucid but somewhat disturbing vision raised one crucial question: how had life been formed in the first place?

In their accounts of the mysteries of creation the Egyptians were inspired by the natural world. They observed the changing levels of the Nile River and the alluvial silt that was left behind as the annual flood receded. The black silt was rich in nutrients that enabled crops to flourish. Each year, as the Nile flood retreated, the newly fertilized earth began to appear above the surface of the waters. The Egyptians concluded that creation had started in a sinilar way, with a single mound that rose from the vast expanse of the primeval waters, which contained a procreative energy that was the source of all life.

The mound was central to all Egyptian creation myths, and its existence was never disputed. The god Tatjenen, whose name translates as "Risen Land", personified this primordial feature. But the precise origins of the mound provoked debate: where had it first arisen? Every major religious centre claimed that it had emerged at its own site, and theologians spent a great deal of time debating which deity had first appeared there.

The creation myths themselves varied from place to place. At Heliopolis, in Lower Egypt, a family of nine original gods, the Ennead (or "Group of Nine"), as the Greeks later called them, was worshipped. The first god to materialize on the mound was Atum, Lord of Heliopolis, described as "he who came into being of himself". He immediately started to produce more gods: according to one part of the *Pyramid Texts*, he "took his penis in his hand and ejaculated through it to produce the twins Shu (Air) and Tefnut (Moisture)," while elsewhere in these texts Atum is said to have "sneezed out Shu and spat up Tefnut". Thus the world's atmosphere was formed. Shu and Tefnut then coupled to produce Geb (Earth) and Nut (Sky). Nut and Geb begat four children: Osiris and Seth, the opposing gods of order and disorder, and their consorts Isis and Nephthys. From these origins all other life came into being.

A statuette of Ptah, held to be the creator of the world by the people of Memphis, who believed that he brought everything into being by thought and word alone.

The Birth of the Year

Originally, the year had only 360 days. This changed when Atum discovered an illicit passion between his two grandchildren, Nut (Sky) and Geb (Earth), whose union deprived the world of its atmosphere.

A copy of the astrological zodiac (introduced into Egypt in Graeco-Roman times), based on an original carved onto the ceiling of the temple at Dendera. The Egyptian calendar was founded in part on observation of the movements of the stars.

According to a Greek version of this tale, Nut and Geb were so closely intertwined that there was no room for anything between them. This angered Atum, who ordered their father Shu, god of air, to separate them. Shu did so by standing on Geb and hoisting Nut above his head so that they could not touch each other. Nut, however, was already pregnant. In his wrath Atum cursed her: she was allowed to give birth, he announced, but she was forbidden to do so on any of the 360 days that made up the year at that time. Among the gods whom Atum created was Thoth, god of wisdom. Thoth loved Nut and decided to help her by challenging the other gods to a game of draughts in which he gambled for more time. He won five days, and by adding them to the existing year he created time for Nut to give birth on successive days to her five children: Osiris, Horus, Seth, Isis and Nephthys. Thoth's wisdom and cunning had gained Egypt a full calendar year.

Ptah, the Creator God

The Heliopolitan doctrine was markedly physical in character. Atum's act was seen as procreative even though he had no partner: the theologians ascribed female qualities to his hand, which eventually gained the status of a goddess. In Memphis, however, the creator god Ptah's act of creation was contemplative rather than physically active. Ptah was part of a triad of deities, along with his consort the lioness-goddess Sekhmet and the lotus god Nefertem, understood to be Ptah's son. Like the god Khnum (see pages 18–20), Ptah was a patron of craftsmen, and his high priest was called "greatest of the controllers of craftsmen". Ptah created by intellectual effort alone, thinking things into existence with the ideas that emanated from his heart and the names that then issued from his tongue. For the Egyptians, the heart was the seat of intellect and the source of any thought, which the tongue then spoke to make real. By uttering a litany of names Ptah was able to produce the gods and all of Egypt, including the cities, shrines, temples and nomes (provinces).

The Memphite creation myth exalting Ptah did not supersede the myth of Atum as creator, nor did it reject Atum's actions on the mound. The two myths coexisted: Atum's material presence was symbolized by the sacred hill at every religious site, while Ptah's intellectual presence was in "all gods, all people, all cattle, all creeping things that live". Some variations included both Ptah and Atum: the Ennead and Atum were thought of as the lips and teeth of Ptah. In another fusion, with the god Tatjenen who personified the primeval mound, Ptah was linked to the sacred hill.

Ptah was one of the oldest creator gods and there were temples to him all over Egypt, but he did not rise to ultimate supremacy in the

Sources of Egyptian Myth

The myths of the Egyptians were referred to by various classical writers including the Greek historian Herodotus, who visited the country in 450BC. However, most of our knowledge comes from the discovery of abundant sacred texts and images preserved by the desert sand across Egypt.

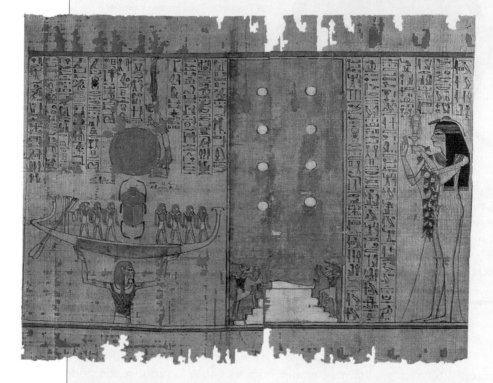

This section of *The Book of the Dead* shows eight discs, representing the four gods and goddesses of the Ogdoad. They emerged as the basic elements from the primeval chaos. The god Nun is also shown here, holding up the sun barque above the primordial waters.

The main source for ancient Egyptian myths concerning creation, the gods and rebirth are tombs, coffins and scrolls. However the principal purpose of the texts and images recorded there was not to recount the myths but to assist the dead on their perilous journey into the afterlife. The stories are therefore only implicit. Further insight into the Egyptians' beliefs is given by inscriptions on temple walls, spells, prayers, incantations and hymns.

Some of the most striking accounts of the unfolding of creation have survived on the interior and exterior surfaces of wooden coffins. Information about Atum's "divine masturbation" (see page 12) was included among the *Coffin Texts* (as they are known) found at Bersha, near Hermopolis. They were made for those who could afford an elaborate burial.

The earliest funerary texts, known as the *Pyramid Texts*, date from the early third millennium BC. They were carved onto the walls of nine royal pyramids of the Old Kingdom (2625–2130BC) and were composed exclusively for the king. However, by the New Kingdom (1539–1075BC) such texts had evolved, via the *Coffin Texts*, into the so-called *Book of the Dead*, which was reproduced individually for the deceased. Known to Egyptians as "The Chapters of Coming Forth By Day", these widely available texts were written on papyrus and could contain up to 200 different chapters, according to the wealth of the owner. The papyrus was rolled up and placed in a special container in the coffin alongside the corpse. (One copy, dating from the fourth century BC, follows a theme found in earlier *Coffin Texts* in its reference to Atum, the original "All".)

In the hearts of all Egyptians was the fear that they might fail to speak the correct words that would help them reach eternity when their heart was weighed against the feather of truth before the throne of Osiris, ruler of the underworld. A typical formula from the *Book of the Dead*, offering defensive spells for the judgement scene, proclaims: "Oh Far Strider, who came forth from Heliopolis, I have done no falsehood; Oh Fire-embracer who came forth from Kheraha, I have not robbed."

Temple libraries were repositories for a range of texts, but until the Ptolemaic period few were of a non-funerary kind.

pantheon. By the Late Period (712–332BC) he had combined with other gods, to become Ptah-Sokar-Osiris, a god of the dead. When the Greeks arrived in Egypt, they identified Ptah with their smith god Hephaistos, and one of Ptah's shrines in Memphis, called *Hwt-ka-Ptah* ("Mansion of the Spirit of Ptah"), came to refer to the whole region: its Greek form *Aeguptos* gave us the modern name, "Egypt".

The Ogdoad and Amun

In Hermopolis, further to the south in the centre of Egypt, local myth dealt as much with what had occurred before the mound was formed as with what had happened after. The Hermopolitan Ogdoad, or "Group of Eight", consisted of four pairs of male and female deities who inhabited the primeval waters before the world existed. The males took the form of frogs and the females were represented as snakes, although sometimes they were depicted as baboons.

The gods and goddesses were paired to represent four different aspects of the universe before the world was created: Nun and his consort Naunet together personified the original formless ocean, Heh and Hauhet symbolized infinity, Kek and Kauket embodied darkness, and Amun and Amaunet were the dual incarnation of hidden power. The divinities signified all that could not be seen or touched – they comprised the antithesis of life. Yet, as male and female pairs, they represented at the same time the *possibility* of life. They were also linked with the sun by their association with baboons, who greeted the dawn with howls.

Initially the Ogdoad was divided into two groups, male and female; but, at a certain point in their existence, the two sexes were driven together. Although the exact details of this cataclysmic meeting are unknown, the myths from Hermopolis describe the event as having come about at the command of Thoth, the patron deity of the city. No doubt the claim was intended to promote his status.

This relief depicts three baboons associated with the god of knowledge, Thoth. The animals were also celebrated by those who worshipped the sun god because they appeared to greet the dawn with a chorus of howls.

The violent meeting between the two groups produced a tremendous upheaval, which in turn engendered the primordial mound. The mound itself contained a cosmic egg, which hatched to reveal the young sun god. As the shell fell apart, the mound turned into an "Island of Flame", and the new-born sun god ascended the sky to his rightful position in the heavens. This event was considered in Hermopolis to be the very first sunrise. The Ogdoad had thus become "the fathers and mothers who came into being at the start, who gave birth to the sun and who created Atum".

The Hermopolitan concept, which likened the birth of the universe to a cataclysm, in some ways anticipates modern "Big Bang" theories. It is tempting to speculate that the Egyptians, who were accomplished astronomers, based this concept on their observations of the night sky. It is more likely, though, that the idea represented an especially intense example of their view that life was made up of opposites. In a clash of cosmic genders the basis for life was laid down.

The Theban view of creation was different again. In Thebes Amun was all-powerful, whereas in Hermopolis he was just one of a number of

The Wandering Eye

On his crown the pharaoh bore the protective uraeus, *the cobra that symbolized Wadjet, goddess of Lower Egypt. Wadjet was said to protect the king by spitting fire at his enemies. In the creation myth of Heliopolis we learn why the* uraeus *was so powerful.*

Atum created his children Shu and Tefnut (see page 12) to alleviate years of solitude as the only being in the waters of chaos. But they were poor companions – they drifted away and could not be found. Atum was alone once again, but he was determined to find his newly created offspring, and so he removed one eye from his face and filled it with his own power, elevating it to the status of a goddess. He then called the Eye his daughter, manifested as both Hathor and Sekhmet.

Atum then commanded Hathor-Sekhmet to scour the universe for signs of his children. Eventually, she discovered Shu

and Tefnut and brought them back to their father. Atum, weeping for joy, embraced them. The tears fell to earth and were transformed into the first human beings. As a reward for her services, Atum placed the Eye on his forehead in the form of a cobra. In this position, he promised, she would be feared forever by gods and men alike.

Hathor, shown here in her benign aspect with cow horns. She is accompanied by the pharaoh Menkaure and the personification of the province of Hu, *c.*2490–2472BC.

This 4th-Dynasty image is from a tomb at Medum. Grazing geese would have been a common sight in the Delta and the Nile valley. In Thebes they inspired a major creation myth.

original gods. The Thebans did not reject the Ogdoad altogether, but placed Amun as its sole creator: he was the "First One Who Gave Birth to the First Ones". One version of the myth depicts him as a serpent, Amun-Kamutef ("He Who Has Completed his Moment"), living in the waters of Nun. However, it is suggested elsewhere that he emitted a mighty honk, like a goose, which burst into the stillness of the universe, causing a cosmic reaction by which the Ogdoad and Ennead were formed. The bird imagery may have been borrowed from a story that described the world coming into being after a *benu* bird – a heron rather than a goose – laid its egg on the primeval mound (see box, page 30).

The Thebans developed a distinct theology in which Amun was concealed even from the gods, existing somewhere beyond the natural world. It was thought that a creator had to stand apart from his creation, and Amun, the "hidden" god, suited this role. The texts summarized Amun's mystery and power:

"He is hidden from the gods, and his aspect is unknown. He is farther than the sky, he is deeper than the Duat. No god knows his true appearance ... no one testifies to him accurately. He is too secret to uncover his awesomeness, he is too great to investigate, too powerful to know. Manifest one, whose identity is hidden ... as it is inaccessible."

Amun's identity was so secret that anyone who tried to discover his origins suffered instantaneous death. Yet he was also omnipotent, and, as part of the Ennead, he was present everywhere (despite being concealed). As one text put it, "The Ennead is combined in your body: your image is every god, joined in your person." How could Amun at the same time be separate and combined with everything? The Theban response to this paradox was to envisage every god as an image of Amun. They also invented a composite figure that included Re as the face, Ptah as the body and Amun himself as the essential hidden power.

It was at Thebes, the splendid capital of Upper Egypt, that Amun was held in greatest respect. Here, in the spectacular temple complex of Karnak and the smaller but no less impressive one at Luxor, he was worshipped daily by the priesthood and honoured by the population as a whole during his annual festivals. Such sacred mass gatherings were common, but those surrounding Amun were the most magnificent. There were two celebrations – the Festival of Opet and the Beautiful Festival of the Valley. In the latter the cult statues of Amun, his wife Mut and their son Khonsu were taken in procession from their home at Karnak across the Nile to the mortuary temples on the west bank. At the Festival of Opet, which took place during the second month of the annual flood, the cult statues were carried along the

17

Sacred Hills

The primeval mound was a common feature in creation myths. As the place where the sun first rose, or where the first divine being was created, the mound fulfilled a vital, if passive, function. Its exact location was never certain, but at each major religious site a facsimile of it was built within the temple boundaries.

Pyramids have been interpreted as replicating the shape of the primeval mound. The earliest, built in step form, was that of King Djoser, constructed at Saqqara (c.2630BC).

At its most basic, the primeval mound was nothing more than a pile of sand. At Heliopolis, however, it was a rock venerated as the *benben*, thought to be the petrified semen of the god Atum. The *benben* was the stone upon which the first rays of sunlight fell.

The Egyptians' esteem for the mound found its fullest expression in the construction of the pyramids inside which pharaohs were buried. The pyramid was a representation of the primeval mound from which the dead monarch could launch himself, like the original sun god, into the afterlife. The cap of each pyramid (the *benbennet*) was often gilded, and viewed as an extension of the original *benben*.

Hills could also harbour divine power. Atop a high mountain (called "The Peak of The West"), which overlooked the Valley of the Kings, the goddess Meretseger guarded the dead of Thebes. The daily passage of the sun was also framed by mountains: it rose above an eastern mountain called Bakhu, and, as it approached the Duat at the end of the day, it set behind a western mountain called Manu.

sphinx-lined avenue which linked the temples of Karnak and Luxor. Here, the priests celebrated the sexual union between Amun and the mother of the reigning king, which took place so that she could give birth to the royal *ka* (spirit). The proceedings culminated when the king himself entered the inner sanctum so that his physical form could receive the *ka*, whereupon he would emerge from the temple as a god.

As Thebes grew in status and wealth, Amun became the nation's supreme creator god. Apart from a brief interlude between *c.*1353BC and *c.*1335BC, when the pharaoh Akhenaten attempted to establish the supremacy of the sun god at the expense of the pantheon (see pages 31–33), Amun was worshipped up and down the Nile and in many myths appeared in combination with various other deities.

Khnum and the Origins of Mankind

The Egyptians appear to have had little interest in the origin of human beings. Occasional references here and there, such as the story of Atum-Re's tears (see pages 16 and 21), seem to have been added to the creation myths as an afterthought. However, there was one particularly strong myth concerning human creation which originated in the island shrine of Elephantine, situated by one of the Nile's cataracts just inside the border with Nubia. The priests of Elephantine worshipped a ram-headed deity called Khnum, who was closely associated with the Nile and Egypt's fertile soil.

Khnum was a craftsman. Unlike Memphis's Ptah who thought beings into existence, he created them from clay on his potter's wheel. This is suggested in the hymn to Khnum found carved on the walls of his temple at Esna: "He knotted the

At every conception Khnum fashioned two models. One represented the new human body, the other the *ka*, or vital essence (see page 66), which continued to exist after its mortal twin had died. These two entities emerged from the womb nine months later as a living child.

In this way Khnum was involved also in the union between Amun and the mother of the king, as celebrated at the Festival of Opet (see page 17). Inscriptions at Luxor recount how Amun assumed human form in order to impregnate Queen Mutemwiya, mother of the great pharaoh Amenhotep III who ruled between *c*.1390 and *c*.1353BC. According to this myth, once Amun had completed the act of procreation, he instructed Khnum to create models of the new king and his *ka*. The story underlined Amenhotep's divine status and also left no doubt as to which of the two gods was considered superior. In reality, however,

Khnum, the ram-headed god, was worshipped at Elephantine, an island in the Nile just to the north of the first cataract. His association with the flooding of the Nile, an annual event that sparked the yearly cycle of natural activity, befitted his role as a creator.

flow of blood to the bones, /Formed in his workshop as his handiwork, /So the breath of life is in everything." The text goes on to describe how he built the skull and created cheeks, "to give shape to the image". He then furnished the body with a spine to keep it upright, lungs in order to breathe, guts for digestion, and sexual organs to procreate with. Khnum did not restrict himself to the creation of Egyptians, but was responsible for all nationalities. He set in motion the worldwide propagation of the human species as an act of continuous creation, and the Egyptians believed that "without pause henceforth the wheel turns every day".

Khnum at his potter's wheel fashions a person out of clay. The god was described modelling two figures to signify each individual: one represented the *ka* (spirit), while the other represented the physical body. Both came together to create the new being.

19

Khnum was the more ancient, long pre-dating Amun. The priests of Elephantine subtly indicated his seniority by depicting him with corkscrew horns; Amun, too, was sometimes portrayed as a ram, but usually with smooth horns. (Sheep with corkscrew horns were the first to be domesticated in Egypt, whereas those with smooth horns belonged to a less distinguished breed introduced at a later stage in the country's development.)

Along the whole of the Nile valley, all the way from Heliopolis to Elephantine Island, the process of creation was constantly reinterpreted. The Ogdoad, the Ennead, Amun and Ptah were the major protagonists in creation myths, but numerous other suggestions were put forward during the course of Egyptian history. At one period

in Heliopolis, it was suggested that the sun rose as a "golden child" from a lotus flower on the eternal waters. At another time the sun was represented by the *benu* bird (see box, page 30). A further version of the Amun story claimed that as a mighty goose he had hatched an egg on the primeval mound, and as the shell fell apart it created a space amidst the primordial waters of Nun in which the world could be formed.

The Egyptians did not worship relics, but where possible each religious centre treasured a physical manifestation of divinity. At Heliopolis they guarded the *benben* stone, which seems to have been regarded as the petrified semen of Atum (see box, page 18). The *benben* was inscribed with the rays of the sun and was a symbol of both

Serpents

Snakes played a rich and complex role in Egyptian myth, but most often appeared as elemental symbols of chaos and evil – reflecting the real danger posed by their deadly bite.

Fear of snakes was especially justified in the Delta, where they were abundant. The Egyptians wore protective amulets to guard against the risk of being bitten.

The four female deities of the Ogdoad – forces of elemental chaos before the world was created – were represented as serpents. Apocalypse for the Egyptians could be brought about by the great serpent Apophis, which lay in wait to ambush the sun every night. And the sun was destined to become

a snake when the world ended (see main text, opposite).

However, the snake could also have positive attributes in myth. Wadjet, the patron goddess of Lower Egypt, was the most revered of a number of serpent deities. The cobra goddess Renenutet, whose name translated as "the nourishing

The monstrous serpent Apophis was vanquished nightly by the sun god Re, often pictured in the form of a cat. A detail from a papyrus, *c.*1250BC.

snake", was the goddess of good fortune, invoked to ensure bountiful harvests, easy childbirth and a happy future.

creation and resurrection. Its shape clearly related to pharaonic tomb construction: the pyramid came to be seen as a larger version of the *benben* and was capped with a replica of the *benben* (see also box, page 18). The first part of the pyramid to be touched by the morning sun was this pinnacle, which the Egyptians called the *benbennet*; it was also thought to have magical qualities as it provided the initial step on the pharaoh's ascension to heaven where he would join the gods. As spell 508 of the *Pyramid Texts* put it, "I have trodden those thy rays as a ramp under my feet whereon I mount up to Re."

Apophis and the Forces of Darkness

Egyptian creation myths were not exclusively concerned with life and procreation, but also acknowledged the forces of darkness. As in many other cultures, the snake, principally embodied in Egypt by the god Apophis who took the form of a threatening serpent, represented a source of evil, standing for the elemental forces the Egyptians feared. He is frequently portrayed as the enemy of Re on tomb walls and in funerary papyri.

The story of Apophis's birth was told in the second century BC on the walls of Esna temple. It describes Neith (an archer goddess of the Delta) producing Apophis by spitting into the primeval waters – his name meant "he who was spat out". In a variant of the story of the tears of Atum-Re, Neith was the first being to appear on the primordial mound, and it was she who gave birth to the sun. She called to her newborn child but, blinded by his own brilliance, he was unable to see her. As he cried for his mother, he shed the tears that formed humanity. But even as his mother found him, the concept of duality exerted itself: good could not exist without evil, and so just after the sun was created the sinister Apophis was born.

Apophis was the antithesis of the sun – an embodiment of the forces of chaos and evil that churned within Nun's ocean. His huge serpentine coils lurked in the Duat every dusk, waiting to destroy the sun god and prevent him from rising over the horizon. Every night Re had to fight and defeat Apophis, but as the serpent was indestructible, his victory was never final.

The defeat of Apophis was an important feature of most pharaohs' tomb inscriptions. Although the snake could not be killed, he was depicted being chopped to pieces, often by Re in the form of a cat, one of the many animals that were held sacred in Egypt (see pages 34–35). His defeat enabled the god-king to rise up and take his rightful place in the sun-god's barque that sailed across the sky.

The victory of the sun in this nightly battle was considered vital to the continuing existence of all forms of life, but was not taken for granted by the Egyptians. If Apophis defeated Re, the world would come to an end. However, it was also important that Apophis should not be destroyed – if either combatant ultimately triumphed, then the balance between the forces of good and evil would be altered and the world would be returned to the chaos from which it had come. As a chapter from *The Book of the Dead* prophesied: "This earth will return to the primeval water, Nun, to the endless flood as it was in the beginning. And in the end there will be no gods or goddesses. Nothing but Atum the Lord of All who made all mankind and all gods." In this final manifestation, Atum was destined to appear as a serpent.

Regardless of whether the universe was seen as springing from Atum's masturbation, Ptah's utterance, the cataclysmic union of the Ogdoad or Amun's goose cry, all the stories make it clear that the Egyptians did not perceive creation as an isolated event. It was an ongoing process that was evident in the arrival of every new day and every new season. Ma'at, the goddess who personified truth, justice and harmony in the cosmos, imposed an unchanging order, and any deviation from her divine command was thought to be profoundly damaging to the social and political fabric of Egypt (see page 36). Creation was a state of perfection perpetually re-enacted, and its cardinal force, the sun, rose above the Nile every day as a sign and guarantee of cosmic security.

21

The Sun God

For much of Egyptian history, Re was the supreme deity. He regulated the passing of hours, days, months, seasons and years. He brought order to the universe and, as an essential source of energy, made life on Earth possible. His daily emergence from the Duat symbolized the cyclical nature of creation. But Re's manifestation as the sun was merely one of his many aspects. He was simultaneously a creator, the ancestor of the pharaohs, an agent of daily rebirth and much more besides.

The royal title *sa Re* ("son of Re") was introduced by the pharaoh Djedefre in the Fourth Dynasty – a time when the worship of the sun god was particularly strong. Re was especially celebrated at Heliopolis, Greek for the "City of the Sun". His influence, however, was not limited to this period of Egyptian history – all through the Old Kingdom the Egyptian pantheon was affected by his cult. For example, the kings of the Fifth Dynasty diverted a large portion of state resources to constructing massive temples open to the sun.

Re exerted such a strong influence that most other significant gods were eventually subsumed into the sun cult by the process of syncretism (the fusion of two or more deities to become a single object of worship). For example, Re was combined with the two major creation deities, Atum and Amun, to produce the hybrid entities, Atum-Re and Amun-Re. Thus the sun god came to be worshipped as a creator. Similar amalgamations with other gods expanded Re's dominion.

Re was also the ancestor of the pharaohs, and his role in this guise was even more complex than his fusion with other gods. The Egyptians explained this link between Re and the

A gold statue of Amun from Karnak, 22nd–25th Dynasties (945–656BC). Amun became combined with Re, and Amun-Re's temple at Karnak is one of the best-preserved New Kingdom sites.

The Destruction of Humankind

Before Egypt had human kings, its ruler was the god Re. In his declining years, angered by his subjects' lack of respect, the god sent his Eye, deified as the goddess Hathor, to take vengeance. The earliest version of this myth was found in Tutankhamun's tomb (c.1323BC), but it may have originated much earlier, possibly in a year when the Nile failed to flood and thousands of people died.

Hathor, shown here in the guise of the lioness-goddess Sekhmet, was consumed by a bloodthirsty desire to wipe out the human race. Re brought an end to her vengeance by drugging her with vast quantities of beer.

Re, as a ruler of men, was past his prime. As he grew old his bones turned silver, his body gold, and his hair blue as lapis lazuli. But his age did not prevent him from hearing that men were mocking him and plotting to overthrow him. Calling the gods to a secret conference, he asked their advice. Nun, as the eldest, was the one to whom he listened most avidly.

Nun advised Re to punish the blasphemers by scorching them with his blazing heat. However, when Re did this, his victims ran for shelter to the rocks and escaped his fury. Frustrated, Re reconvened the conference. The gods were unanimous: Re should send his Eye in the form of Hathor-Sekhmet (who had previously done Atum good service in finding his children in the cosmic waters; see box, page 16), to punish mankind. "No eye is better for this task than yours," concluded Nun. "Let it go forth as Hathor-Sekhmet." Hathor did as she was bidden: she perpetrated a savage slaughter, taking the form of a lioness. By the time that she was recalled by Re, she had acquired an insatiable taste for blood and was determined to return to Earth to destroy the rest of humankind.

Re was alarmed. He had meant only to teach people a lesson, not to wipe them out.

While Hathor rested, he sent messengers to Aswan to bring back a consignment of local red ochre. He ordered the High Priest of Heliopolis to pound it. As this was done, the god ordered servant girls to brew barley beer. The two elements were mixed together to produce 7,000 jugs of an intoxicating drink that looked like blood. Re ordered the jugs to be emptied over the fields where Hathor had planned her destruction for the next day.

Hathor was taken in by the ruse. Flying over the fields, she saw what she assumed to be blood and swooped down for a drink. She imbibed too much and fell into a stupor. On regaining her senses, she had forgotten her original aim and set off home again, once more the benevolent goddess.

As a reconciliatory gesture, Re decreed that the Egyptian people could drink as much as they liked at Hathor's festivals, in commemoration of Hathor, Lady of Drunkenness.

23

king in a myth that also accounted for the origins of mankind's destructiveness and inclination to fight in wars.

Re's Ascension to the Sky

At the beginning of time, immediately after the world was created, Re was not a distant figure who dwelled in the sky: he lived on Earth as the king of all beings, including the gods. His earthly rule was a paradisiacal time, and his only task was to venture forth occasionally to inspect his domain with a retinue of lesser gods to accompany him. However, Re grew old and began to consider abandoning his duties, which led some of mankind to scorn him and doubt his capacity as a ruler. This attitude infuriated Re, who sent his Eye, in the form of the goddess Hathor, to destroy the miscreants. After avenging himself, he chose to abandon the world and reside in the sky. But his departure was sullied by evidence of further human failing: as he rose above the Earth, he saw the people below fighting among themselves, blaming each other for the loss of the sun. Mankind had fallen from grace, and warfare was now endemic on Earth.

According to the texts, the responsibility for Re's migration to the heavens lay entirely with humanity. There was no question of divine negligence. One text explained, in the words of the god, the full extent of the blessings that he had brought to Egypt and its people:

This pendant from the tomb of Tutankhamun (1333–1323BC) shows the sun god as a scarab (Khepri) on the celestial boat flanked by baboons with moon discs. The baboon was one manifestation of the god Thoth.

"Words spoken by the Secret-of-Names, Lord of the Universe: I have carried out four good deeds within the portal of the horizon. I made the four winds, that every person might breathe in his time ... I made the great flood, that the poor might be mighty like the rich ... I made every man like his fellow; I did not ordain that they do evil, it is their hearts that destroyed what I had said ... I made their hearts not forget the West [where the sun set and where the dead were buried]."

To mitigate the effects on humanity of his departure to the sky, Re did two further good deeds. First, he instructed the god Thoth to act as his deputy during the hours of night when he himself was voyaging through the Duat under the new cosmic arrangements. Thoth was given a great deal of responsibility: his duties were to maintain order and justice on Earth, to present people with the precious gift of knowledge in writing (in the form of hieroglyphs) and, above all, to create some light in the night sky (which is why the moon was first created).

Secondly, Re appointed a ruler to take his place as king on Earth. To begin with, his choice fell upon gods: his first surrogates were, in turn, the deities Shu (god of air), Geb (god of the Earth) and Osiris (lord of the underworld, associated with death and rebirth). But eventually the succession passed on to human beings, providing a convenient mythological lineage for the god-king pharaoh who gained divine status by inheritance (see box, page 51).

24

Isis and the Name of the Sun God

The Egyptians were firm believers in magic. The goddess Isis was considered to be especially potent in the magical arts (see pages 50–58), and one of her greatest coups came when she persuaded Re to divulge his secret name so that she held power over him.

An incised carving of Isis from the sarcophagus of Ramesses III, *c.*1163BC. Her healing powers were put to the service of both gods and people.

"Isis was a clever woman," explained one story, "more intelligent than countless gods ... she was ignorant of nothing in heaven or on earth." She wanted to place herself and her son Horus at the head of the pantheon of gods and the only way to do this was to discover Re's secret name.

One day Isis came upon Re when he was asleep, snoring loudly. From the corner of his open mouth hung a long dribble of saliva which gathered weight and fell to the ground. Isis pounced: scooping up the spittle, she mixed it with clay in the form of a poisonous snake. Then she breathed magic into the snake to make it come alive.

Isis had noted Re's movements and knew that every so often he would leave his palace to go for a walk. Each time, on his route, he passed a crossroads. Isis left her snake there and awaited further developments.

Re emerged for his excursion, and – as Isis had planned – the snake bit him. Re saw nothing, but he felt the poison coursing through him. In pain, he called to the nine gods of the Ennead for help. Re had a fever and was sweating and shivering, but the other gods were helpless: they could do no more that mourn the impending loss of the sun.

Isis then made a dramatic entrance. She could cure him, she said, but only if he would tell her his name. Re refused. She offered again and again, but still he declined. Eventually his agony became so extreme that he could bear it no longer, and he agreed to give Isis the secret, on condition that she should tell it to no one other than her son, Horus. Isis accepted these terms, and speaking aloud the god's true name, she removed the poison. The sun god was cured at once, and Isis and Horus attained the power that they had sought.

The Journey through Night and Day

For ancient Egyptians, night and day were clearly defined periods that each consisted of twelve "hours". This formula never varied. Should the days be longer or shorter, owing to seasonal changes, then each hour expanded or contracted appropriately. This system may have had some confusing practical implications, but at least it provided a framework around which Re's movements could be plotted.

Re sailed across the sky during the day in the *mandjet* (the day-barque), and at night he travelled through the Duat in the *mesketet*, also known as the "Boat of Millions". With him travelled a crew of lesser deities who helped to steer and defend the vessel. The barque also carried, as passengers, the countless humans who after death had risen to become the blessed dead, and among them Re's descendants, the deceased pharaohs who had joined him in splendour.

Re's daytime voyage was represented pictorially as a journey along the body of Nut, the sky goddess (see pages 12–13). Some myths then describe Re being swallowed by Nut at dusk, and, after travelling through her body during the night, being reborn at dawn – the red and pink color of the dawn was said to be represent the blood lost by Nut in childbirth. Other myths declared that he travelled through a massive snake which encircled the universe, tail in mouth.

When Re sank below the horizon at dusk, his journey became hazardous. The Duat was divided into twelve chambers or "gates" – one for every hour of the night – through which Re and his crew had to pass before they could emerge on the other side the next day. Each chamber had specific features, mostly hostile, which had to be encountered and overcome before Re could rise again.

Re's journey through the Duat was recorded in three main texts: *The Book of Amduat*, *The Book of Gates* and *The Book of Caverns*. On the precise nature of his passage all the texts differed. In *The Book of Amduat* it was said that Re's first task was to establish land rights for certain gods. According to *The Book of Gates*, Re supervised Atum's destruction of his enemies. And in *The Book of Caverns* we learn that Re subjugated three serpents. All these versions, however, were consistent in including two events: a meeting between Re and Osiris, and the subjugation of Apophis and all the enemies of Re, who dwelled in the underworld. These two episodes were essential to secure the sun's reappearance the following day.

The Meeting between Re and Osiris

Osiris was god of the underworld and the personification of resurrection and reborn kingship. His
encounters with Re took place in the Duat in the
depth of the night. Here, the two gods would
embrace as the "Twin Souls" – "Re in Osiris, Osiris
in Re" – and replenish each other's life source, to
emerge mutually empowered.

This was one important stage in the nightly
process that led to Re's rebirth in the morning.
However, the climactic event during Re's passage
through the underworld was the struggle with the
giant serpent Apophis, who represented the forces
of chaos. Although Apophis could never be

destroyed, Re overcame him each night with the
aid of spells, magic and – in some accounts – the
cunning of the god Seth.

Each of these two events had special meaning for the Egyptians. The meeting with Osiris
affirmed the ability of Re – and so of dead kings –
to rise again. At the same time, it may also have
served as a political contrivance: at one stage the
cults of Re and Osiris were in opposition and their
nocturnal unity may have been a means of satisfying both factions. The conflict between the sun
god and the serpent was a manifestation of a
continual anxiety shared by all ancient peoples:
that the sun might fail to rise. There is evidence
that solar eclipses provoked a fear that Re had
been swallowed whole by Apophis the previous
night. In the temple of Karnak at Thebes, and in
other centres, priests conducted rituals to assist Re
in his struggle. Prayers were offered, incantations
uttered, and magic spells recited using the secret
names of Apophis. Knowledge of these names was
believed to bestow power over Apophis: they

The boat that took Re on his celestial journey
each day was thought to be similar to the
ordinary craft found on the Nile, of the
type seen in this 12th-Dynasty model
(1938–1759BC).

27

The Sacred Scarab

The Egyptians always looked to nature to provide a model for their cosmic imaginings. The activities of the scarab, or dung beetle, provided an ideal allegory for the movement of the sun across the sky.

The dung beetle laid its eggs in a ball of dung that it rolled across the ground to its burrow. Safely ensconced, the eggs would then be incubated by the warmth of the sun's rays. This imagery was irresistible to ancient Egyptians: they saw in the life-cycle of the beetle a microcosm of the daily voyage of the sun emerging from the Duat to cross the daytime sky before sinking below the horizon again at sunset.

There were additional aspects to the scarab beetle's symbolism. Inside the warm casing of each dung ball was an egg, which burst open to reveal a larva, causing Egyptians to believe that the insect had created itself. The creature's first flight was also woven into myth as the common motif of the sun god rising up into the sky. In the words of *The Book of the Dead*: "I have flown up like the primeval ones, I have become Khepri ... "

Thus the scarab beetle personified Khepri, the morning aspect of the sun god – and by extension the sun's (and the pharaoh's) rebirth. Khepri is often pictured as a scarab sailing in a boat on Nun, the waters of chaos, or even as a human body with a scarab head.

Scarabs were made in various materials – stone and glazed earthenware were common – and could have a purely ornamental function, apart from their properties as amulets. In the Middle Kingdom (*c.*1980– *c.*1630BC) they were used as seals, and during the New Kingdom reign of Amenhotep III (*c.*1390– *c.*1353BC) they served to record important events in the king's reign. Their flat undersides were inscribed with designs referring to a variety of subjects according to their purpose.

Scarabs also played an important role as funerary equipment. Nearly always

Scarabs were particularly popular as symbols of the sun god from the start of the Middle Kingdom (*c.*1980BC). This is a pectoral scarab pendant from the tomb of Tutankhamun.

fashioned out of blue faience (glazed earthenware), funerary scarabs were large, winged amulets often attached to the surface of a mummy within the bead nets that covered its torso.

Another type of scarab, known as the heart scarab, was inscribed with a chapter of *The Book of the Dead* and was embedded in the bandages of the mummy.

were written in fresh ink on new papyrus which was then burned. Also, according to various texts, wax images were fashioned in the form of a serpent, to be ceremonially spat upon, mutilated and set alight to ward off disaster.

The first glow of dawn signalled a positive response to these prayers and incantations – even though, at this stage, Re had not yet returned to the world. He was in a region called the *Akhet* ("Horizon"), also known as "the place of coming into being", where his power was evident but he could not be seen by the human eye. Seeing the rosy glow at first light, an Egyptian could rejoice in the confidence that the daily cycle was still intact.

The Many Aspects of Re

During his journey across the daytime sky, Re was not represented simply as one god, but took many forms. The sun rising in the east was called Re-Horakhty ("Re, Horus of the Horizon"), an amalgam of Re with Horemakhet (who was himself a form of Horus, as "Horus in the Horizon"). In one Heliopolitan myth, Re was also envisaged at dawn as a golden child rising out of a lotus floating on the waters of Nun (the lotus, or water lily, was the emblem of Upper Egypt). More often, however, he was depicted as Khepri, "He Who is Coming into Being", who took the form of a scarab, or dung-beetle. The symbolism of both manifestations was appropriate: the lotus closed its petals every night, opening them only with the sun's appearance; and the scarab beetle emerged from its mound to meet the day. The movement of the sun from east to west was also likened to a scarab beetle pushing its dung-ball along the ground.

Re continued as Khepri until midday, when he reverted to being Re. At this time he was usually shown as a falcon, a bird suitably distinguished both for attaining great heights during flight and for its predatory power. This is Re's most common form. As a falcon, Re is usually depicted bearing a sun disc on his head – an aspect of the sun god that seems to have resulted when he was amalgamated with Horemakhet.

A gilded wooden statue of the falcon god Horus, embodiment of divine kingship. He carries on his head a large sun disc inscribed with a winged scarab representing Khepri, the morning manifestation of Re. This artefact was discovered with one of the chariots in the antechamber of the tomb of Tutankhamun (reigned *c.*1333–*c.*1323BC).

Once past his zenith at the end of his daily journey, Re became Atum-Re, the evening sun, in the form of an elderly man. Re was joined with Atum because he was about to enter a world of darkness from which he would be reborn, like Atum, the following dawn. (In some stories Re is also pictured as an ageing king whose flesh was gold, whose bones were silver and whose hair was lapis lazuli; see page 23.) And finally, in the Duat, Re assumed the shape of a ram-headed human figure known as "Flesh of Re", his bodily manifestation in the underworld.

In combination with Amun, Re remained pre-eminent in Egypt even after the country had been conquered by invaders. So powerful was this god's hold over the imagination that even the foreign settlers succumbed to his influence. Only once, during the seventeen-year reign of Akhenaten, did Amun-Re's influence falter. At one stroke this heretic pharaoh attempted to promote the sun disc, called the Aten, as a deity, to the exclusion of the rest of the Egyptian pantheon. For a while, instead of being vividly personified, the sun was perceived as a divine abstraction.

The Fiery Phoenix

According to Heliopolitan myth the sun had first risen in the form of a sacred bird called the benu, *later associated with the phoenix. In some accounts the* benu *was a form of the creator Atum, or associated with the* benben *stone that symbolized the primeval mound.*

The *benu* bird is better known to us from Greek myth as the phoenix. It was believed that the bird perished in flames every 500 years and was reborn out of its own ashes.

The *benu* was also associated with the sacred *ished* (persea) tree, which had solar significance and was protected from Apophis by the Great Cat of Heliopolis, sacred to Re.

In the *Pyramid Texts* the *benu* appeared as a yellow wagtail, a manifestation of the Heliopolitan sun god Atum. Its name translated as "to rise in brilliance". Later, however, in *The Book of the Dead*, it was represented in its common form as the grey heron. Either way, it was seen as a symbol of rebirth and a harbinger of good fortune.

In the form of a heron, it was described as perching above the waters of chaos, occasionally breaking the silence with a cry. The bird's call created a disturbance that set the creation act in motion, determining "what is and what is not to be". This myth reflected that of Amun honking like a goose on the waters of Nun, causing a similar cosmic cataclysm. When the heron settled on the primeval mound it laid an egg which hatched to produce the sun god.

Herodotus recorded it as the phoenix, a bird like an eagle with red and gold plumage that supposedly lived in the Arabian peninsula. There was never more than one alive at any time. When it died, its successor carried the carcass to the sun god's temple at Heliopolis. In another Greek story that encapsulated the *benu*'s mysterious qualities, the phoenix was supposed to set fire to itself and be reborn from the ashes.

The Servant of the Sun

In *c.*1353BC, the pharaoh Amenhotep IV ("Amun is Content") ascended the throne. Many of the surviving portraits depict him as physically distinctive: his spindly shins and weak shoulders were separated by a potbelly and massive thighs. From the top of his odd torso emerged a long, narrow neck, which supported an enormous head, ornamented with big lips and slanting eyes. This highly exaggerated portrayal of the king, with both masculine and feminine features, possibly represented an attempt to promote him as the androgynous primal sun god – "the father and mother of creation". These forms of representation were also applied to portraits of his wife Nefertiti. However unusual his true appearance may have been, he had an extraordinary mind capable of orchestrating a religious revolution.

On coming to power, Amenhotep immediately began to reorganize Egyptian religion. In place of the many gods of the traditional Egyptian pantheon, the new king made the Aten ("Disc of the Sun"), which was devoid of human characteristics, the only deity. Whereas Re had taken a variety of different forms, Aten was depicted only as a disc from which rays extended that terminated in hands holding the *ankh*, the symbol of life.

The first references to the Aten date from several centuries previously. It had become a major deity by the reign of Amenhotep IV's father, Amenhotep III, who himself was known as the "Dazzling Sun Disc". By the time of his son's accession it was widely known as a symbol of the sun and, tentatively, as yet another manifestation of Re. Initially, as a disembodied entity, the Aten continued to coexist with the other gods, albeit in an elevated position. But Amenhotep IV accorded it absolute supremacy. In the fifth year of his reign, the pharaoh symbolically changed his name to Akhenaten (which has been variously interpreted as "One Beneficial to the Aten", "Glory of Aten" or "Incarnation of Aten"). Then he built an entirely new capital on a secluded plain some 200 miles north of Thebes, in an unpopulated location which had no association with any other god. It is believed that the pharaoh drew the street plan himself. Among other buildings, the new settlement included no less than five royal palaces and

This exquisite wall carving found in the royal tomb at Amarna (formerly Akhetaten) shows Akhenaten officiating in ceremonies of the Aten, the sun disc that was elevated to divine supremacy during his reign. Here he is raising the lotus flower, popular in Egyptian creation myth, to the sun. Akhenaten is often shown with androgynous features.

31

several temples to the Aten. The king called the new city Akhetaten, "Horizon of the Aten" – today it is called Amarna.

The final stage of the Aten's ascendancy came shortly before the new capital was completed, when Akhenaten announced that all Egyptians, and all foreign subjects (predominantly Nubians and Syrians), had to worship the Aten alone.

Akhenaten was supported by his queen, Nefertiti, who was represented in portraiture as extremely beautiful. Together they instituted a wholesale pogrom against the Egyptian pantheon. The most popular sun god, Amun-Re (after whom Amenhotep had originally been named), was a particular obstacle to the virtually monotheistic new cult, and his statues were smashed and his name chiselled off monuments throughout Egypt. To hasten his downfall his priests were thrown out of office, his temples were closed and their great wealth and properties were confiscated by the crown. Anyone whose name included a reference to Amun-Re – as Akhenaten's had previously done – was required to change it. As the new ideology maintained, "Re lives, ruler of the horizons ... returned as Aten."

A few of Akhenaten's subjects resisted. In private, those who denied the Aten's supremacy continued to venerate the old ways, and even in the new capital some people wore amulets dedicated to other gods. Yet they formed a small community. Within a few years the elaborate panoply of Egyptian religion, with its multiple gods, priests and temples, had been reduced to a single cult led by one individual, Akhenaten. Only he and Nefertiti could communicate with the new sun god and interpret its will.

Akhenaten was a dictator, but he was not necessarily an evil one. In the Aten he promoted a benevolent divinity that was the creator and nurturer of humankind. The cult of the Aten also

A blue-glazed amulet in the form of an *ankh* (the hieroglyph for "life"), *c.*1400BC. The Aten is often shown holding *ankh*s at the ends of its solar rays.

brought a welcome openness to Egyptian religion. Traditionally, temples had tended to be dark, mysterious places, shadowed by huge colonnades. Those that were constructed in Akhenaten's reign, on the other hand, were built as spacious roofless courtyards that allowed light to flood in. Within them, beautifully composed hymns were sung in the Aten's honour, celebrating human equality.

Had Akhenaten been more accommodating, his revolution might have survived. However, by focusing on the cult of the Aten to the exclusion of almost everything else, the pharaoh alienated people who wanted to worship old, familiar gods such as Osiris, through whom they could attain rebirth. Inevitably, the priests resented their loss of power and revenue. It is also possible that Akhenaten neglected his role as administrator, although there is evidence of military campaigns into Asia Minor during his reign.

When Akhenaten died in *c.*1335BC, the Aten effectively died with him. Following the two-year reign of the shadowy Smenkhkare (who was possibly Nefertiti), a young pharaoh called Tutankhaten, possibly Akhenaten's son by a minor wife, ascended to the throne. Tutankhaten abandoned the new capital, restored the old pantheon and began the long and not entirely successful struggle to restore Egypt's material fortunes. As a sign of his good intentions, he changed his name to Tutankhamun. Once more, Amun-Re was in the ascendant.

Akhenaten's presence was systematically obliterated. His city was torn down, his inscriptions were defaced and the old temples were rebuilt. Meanwhile, Re was once again established in the "Boat of Millions", sailing across the heavens: Akhenaten's reign had been merely an aberration in the long rule of the gods.

Akhenaten's Art

King Akhenaten instituted a dramatic development in Egypt's art that long outlived his attempt to elevate the sun disc Aten as the supreme god. Egyptian art tended towards a flat style that showed people and animals in formal poses (as shown here). The innovations brought greater realism (as in the carving on page 31).

In art before Akhenaten, royal figures had generally been depicted not as they must have appeared but as they aspired to be – grandiose, young and god-like. The new pharaoh changed all that. He issued orders that every living thing be portrayed exactly as it was. His reasons were possibly aesthetic, possibly theological. Certainly, Egyptian art attained a new sophistication. Children were shown as youths, not miniature adults. Birds flew, instead of being stuck, motionless, in the air. Even the king was depicted with Nefertiti and his family, very much at home and with every flaw on show.

The new artistic vogue was most in evidence at Akhetaten (now Amarna), the pharaoh's purpose-built capital. Even though the city was destroyed by later rulers in an effort to stamp out all evidence of Akhenaten's heretical rule, ample evidence has survived. The spectacular painted limestone bust of Nefertiti, discovered in the workshop of the royal sculptor Thutmose, is just one of many surviving portraits of the queen. Group images of Akhenaten, Nefertiti and their six daughters (there are no representations of a male heir) are found repeatedly throughout this period. The family is often shown in procession bringing offerings to the Aten. The daughters are depicted playing on the laps of the king and queen in scenes of extraordinary intimacy.

Akhenaten's successors tried to reinstate the old style, but it was impossible to eradicate his new ideas. Ultimately, Akhenaten's contribution to art was to be the most potent legacy of his reign.

This carving on the back of a cedar-wood chair found in the tomb of Tutankhamun (*c.*1333–*c.*1323BC) exemplifies a partial return to traditionally formal poses after the realism favoured in Akhenaten's reign.

A DIVINE MENAGERIE

The ancient Egyptians were surrounded by domestic animals and wildlife. The balance of nature was seen as essential to the maintenance of order in the universe, and mythology reflects the close kinship between gods, creatures and humankind. That animals held the key symbolic role in the worship of the gods is therefore not surprising. The diversity of this animal pantheon reflects the fecundity and richness of Egypt's fauna. Creatures of the land, sea, river and air all played their part.

Right: The crocodile god, Sobek, was often shown wearing a feathered headdress that included a horned sun disc. This carved relief was found in his main cult centre, Kom Ombo. His temples often had pools where sacred living crocodiles were kept.

Below: Cattle were important in Egypt, not only as a source of food but also as draft animals, and domestic cattle were commonly included in tomb scenes. But in myth the cow was specifically associated with the goddess Hathor, in her benign aspect, who had motherly and domestic qualities. This example embellishes one of three funerary couches found in the tomb of the boy-pharaoh Tutankhamun.

Left: A dead man is praying to Anubis, in this papyrus of *The Book of the Dead* of Neferrenpet (from the New Kingdom). Anubis, the jackal god, was usually black because of his connection with the discolored mummified body and the black earth of the Nile. It was thought that by paying homage to the deity in this form, a worshipper could ward off the scavenging jackals after death.

Below: The lions in this papyrus from *The Book of the Dead* of Ani (*c.*1250BC) represent the god Aker – an earth god who was generally portrayed as two lions back to back. Because one lion faced towards the sunset and the other the sunrise, the god was associated with the journey of the sun through the underworld. Also shown in this papyrus is the *benu* bird, closely associated with the sacred *benben* stone and a possible source for the Greek myth of the phoenix.

Left: Found in a brick-lined pit in the temple at Hierakonpolis, this 6th-Dynasty beaten-gold falcon head was part of a bronze statue of Horus, the embodiment of divine kingship.

Right: The hippopotamus was revered as the protective female deity Taweret, who was particularly associated with child-birth. However, the dangerous aspect of the hippo's character is acknowledged in its inclusion as part of the hybrid creature Ammut.

The Celestial Domain

During the daylight hours the sky was dominated by Re, the sun god. At night, when he descended to the underworld, the sky became alive with stars, some of which were perceived as deities. The movement of the stars was ordered by the divine goddess Ma'at, just as she regulated the seasons and the relations between the gods and humanity.

Ma'at personified the harmony of the universe. Although she had few temples of her own, statues of her as a seated woman are often found in temples dedicated to other gods. Ma'at represented order, truthfulness and justice, and all human beings sought to live by her ethical rule. The accession of every new pharaoh was greeted as a new beginning and, however effective the rule of his predecessor, the incoming monarch was invariably credited with restoring the spirit of Ma'at to the world. While they recognized their own human fallibility, the Egyptians could always reassure themselves that they were only one aspect of Ma'at. All around and above them, on the Earth and in the sky, were the gods and goddesses who were equally part of the universal order. They were present in each new season of crops, each new human birth. They were also present in the stars which, in their serene and unchanging motions, provided visible proof of Ma'at's existence.

Observing the Night Sky

The night sky was studied by a group of priests who were known as the "Hour Priests". From observatories set on temple roofs they recorded everything they saw – the movements of constellations, the rising and setting of the sun, the paths of the planets. These priests were not in pursuit of astronomical knowledge for its own sake: what they wanted to determine, in charting the skies, were the patterns of cosmic harmony which would affect life on the Earth below.

The sky itself was venerated as the great goddess Nut, who took the form of a woman arching over the Earth. Every night she was believed to swallow the sun, and every morning she gave birth to him again. (This belief was not considered to be at odds with the myth of Re sailing nightly through the Duat in his barque: see pages 26–29.) Because she embodied the night sky, her body was speckled with the stars and constellations which filled the heavens. Nut had no temple or cult dedicated to her – although some of the stars on her body were identified with particular gods and goddesses, and therefore were worshipped as such.

The moon, the largest object in the night sky, was commonly associated with the god Thoth. Described variously as "The Silent Being", "The Silver Aten" and "Beautiful of Night", Thoth was the god of learning and wisdom, and was also

Symbolizing the vault of the heavens, the sky goddess Nut arches her body over the recumbent figure of Geb, god of the Earth. Separating the two in this papyrus illustration of *c.*1000BC is the squatting figure of Shu, god of air.

The Evolution of the Egyptian Calendar

The Egyptian year was initially based upon the lunar cycle and the timing of the Nile's annual flooding. The more sophisticated system that was adopted in due course forms the basis of the calendar that we use today.

In its earliest form the Egyptian year comprised twelve months, each broken down into three ten-day weeks. Day and night were allotted twelve hours each; the length of the hour varied according to the season (although, of course, the variation was only slight as Egypt was close to the tropics). Not until the Ptolemaic period was the sixty-minute hour introduced from Babylonia. Until then, the smallest unit of time was the *at*, or moment.

The year was divided into only three seasons, each of which lasted four months – *akhet*, the period of inundation; *peret*, the time when the flood receded and crops could be planted; and *shemu*, the harvest. Compared to our present calendar with its unequal months, the Egyptian year was a paragon of neatness. However, as soon became apparent, this orderly arrangement did not accord with the reality of the solar year. To correct the discrepancy, five extra days – the epagomenal days – were introduced at the end of the year. These were designated as the birthdays of Osiris, Horus, Seth, Isis and Nephthys, and were celebrated with gala ceremonies.

Under the revised calendar the year started with the first appearance in the morning sky of the star Sirius, whose arrival – on about 19 July, according to

the modern calendar – marked the beginning of *akhet*. But even the new system was not without its flaws, for the true solar year is about six hours longer than the allotted 365 days. As a result the calendar and the seasons coincided accurately only every 1,460 years. It was not until the Ptolemaic period that the concept of the leap year was introduced – later to form the basis of our own calendar. Until then, the priesthood adopted their own calendar based on a lunar month of approximately 29.5 days to ensure that festivals were celebrated at the right time.

There was, in addition, a further calendar which has been associated with modern notions of astrology. However, although

Written in hieratic script, a 19th-Dynasty calendar lists propitious days of the year in black ink and unlucky days in menacing red.

the priests who charted the heavens were to be credited in centuries to come as the fathers of astrology, they did not in fact have a zodiac, horoscopes or planetary houses: these concepts came to Egypt in Ptolemaic times from Babylonia. The calendars that the Egyptian priests kept were of lucky and unlucky days. These were based on mythical events, according to which, for example, a day on which a god was born was considered lucky, and a day on which two gods had fought was seen as unlucky.

Khonsu and the Princess of Hatti

In the late second millennium BC, Egypt was engaged in a long war with the Hittite empire. The conflict was ended finally in 1256BC by the marriage of Ramesses II to the daughter of the Hittite ruler, the King of Hatti.

Ramesses, sometimes known as Ramses, was captivated by the beauty of his new bride and bestowed upon her the Egyptian name of Nefrure and the title "Great Royal Wife." Shortly after her arrival, however, Ramesses was celebrating a festival at Thebes in honour of the god Amun when a messenger arrived from the King of Hatti. He brought news that Nefrure's younger sister, Bentresh, was seriously ill and the Hittites were unable to cure her. The pharaoh summoned his top physicians and magicians to ask them their opinion on what this disease might be. When they were unable to reach a diagnosis, he dispatched the royal doctor himself.

Three years later this doctor returned home. The princess, he announced, was possessed by evil spirits and only the intercession of a god could cure her. Ramesses consulted the priests at the shrine of Khonsu in Thebes, and asked them for their help. The priests in turn put the question to Khonsu, whose

A 13th-century BC statue depicts Ramesses II (*c.*1279–1213BC), wearing the false beard and *uraeus* that were familiar symbols of kingship, impassively holding an offering table.

statue nodded its head as a sign that he agreed to be taken to cure the princess.

However, there was one theological problem. In his role as protector of Thebes, the moon god Khonsu had to stay in his city. The priests therefore sought help from the other form of the god, "Khonsu-the-Expeller-of-Demons".

Protected by magical amulets donated by his more senior *alter ego*, Khonsu-the-Expeller-of-Demons set out with his entourage to the Hittite capital. Seventeen months later the statue reached its destination and cured Bentresh on the spot. Bentresh's father, however, was so impressed by the statue's power to heal that he refused to let it go and made a shrine for it in his own kingdom where he intended to keep it. For three years and nine months the statue stayed where it was until the Prince of Hatti was visited by a prophetic dream. In it the statue of Khonsu rose from its shrine in the form of a golden falcon and swooped down at the prince before rising into the sky and heading for Egypt.

The prince realized that he must return the statue, and so he sent it back to Thebes accompanied by a huge tribute. On its return to the city, the statue presented the senior Khonsu with the entire Hittite booty – without having even removed any items of treasure, as recompense for the priests of its own shrine in Hatti.

associated with night. He was linked with the waxing and waning of the moon – one of the primary means of measuring time. He was also a mediator and peacemaker, in which role he was instrumental in resolving the titanic battle between Horus and Seth (see pages 50–58).

As the god of learning, Thoth was associated with every kind of knowledge: scribes in particular saw themselves as "followers of Thoth". This body of bureaucrats prided itself on its service to the state, and in one hymn it was warned that the baboon – an earthly emblem of Thoth – was keeping its eye on errant scribes to ensure that they did not abuse their position by indulging in a little illicit freelance work during office hours.

As the god who oversaw all scientific and literary achievements, Thoth was a lunar librarian, the deity in charge of "the sacred books in the house of life". These books contained the collected scientific wisdom of Egypt. Among them was said to be *The Book of Thoth*, forty-two papyrus scrolls which had supposedly been dictated by the god himself and which covered a wide range of subjects. Four of the papyri contained all of the Egyptians' accumulated wisdom on astrology and astronomy and were required reading for every "Hour Priest". The rest comprised hymns to Thoth and treatises on philosophy and medicine, interwoven with details of religious traditions and ceremonial practices. Tantalizingly, although it is mentioned in many other papyri, no copy of this mysterious book has ever been discovered – one theory holds it that a copy was lodged at the Great Library at Alexandria and perished in the fire there in the fourth century AD.

Thoth was worshipped at Hermopolis where he was believed to be one of the forces behind creation. In Thebes they associated a different god with the moon and with medicine – Khonsu, believed by the Thebans to be the son of Amun. People flocked to his shrine to be healed of their ailments or to have evil spirits driven out. So potent was his statue that it was even carried from Thebes to cure the sick and the possessed elsewhere (see box, opposite).

The Many Facets of Horus

Horus, son of Isis and Osiris, was also a deity with many roles. Represented as a falcon or human figure with a falcon head, he was a god of the sky and god of the east. His left eye represented the moon and his right the sun. In one of the many episodes in the myths of his long struggle with his uncle, the god Seth, it is recounted that both his eyes were torn out and the goddess Hathor had to use her magical healing powers to restore them. In one variant of this story, it was only his left, or moon eye, which was lost. In this version it was not Hathor but Thoth who restored it, acting simultaneously in his various roles as peacemaker, healer and moon god.

Horus embodied the idea of divine kingship and represented the living king, while his father, Osiris, represented the deceased king. Osiris was credited with the annual regeneration of crops made possible by the flooding of the Nile (see

Shown here at approximately twice its actual size, a polychrome glass fragment that may once have served as a furniture inlay depicts the god Horus in his most common manifestation as a falcon. From the Graeco-Roman period.

39

page 78). Orion, the constellation with which he was identified, appeared in the sky just before the flood arrived in July. Among the numerous myths about the conflict between Horus and Seth, one told how Osiris was trampled to death by Seth in the guise of a bull, and was restored to life by the goddess Isis, who was both his sister and his wife. Seth, too, had a place in the heavens. In one version of the myth, Horus chopped off Seth's foreleg and flung it into the night sky where it hung as a constellation, which we know as the Great Bear.

A direct parallel to the family of Isis, Osiris and Horus was provided by the goddess Sopdet (Sothis in Greek), her husband Sah and their son Soped. Sopdet was the personification of the dog star Sirius, and had an important role in the Egyptian calendar because the appearance of Sirius heralded the inundation. Like Osiris, with whom he was identified, Sah was associated with Orion. In the Old Kingdom *Pyramid Texts* Sopdet is described as uniting with Osiris to give birth to the morning star – that is, the planet Venus.

The "Hour Priests" also observed in the night sky the "Ikhmu-Seku", "The Imperishable Stars", which never set when seen from the latitude of Egypt. These are the circumpolar stars, which the Egyptians believed to be the souls of those who had achieved perfection in the afterlife. By the Middle Kingdom, Egyptian astronomers had also identified "The Stars Which Know No Rest", a term that referred to the five planets nearest to Earth. Three of them were named after Horus: "Horus who limits the two lands" (Jupiter), "Horus, bull of the sky" (Saturn) and "Red Horus" (Mars). The other two were named "Segebu", a god associated with Seth (Mercury), and "God of the Morning" (Venus), linked with Osiris.

This stylized clay figurine (height 7in) of a woman dates from the Middle Kingdom. Similar figures have been found in excavated houses as well as tombs and are thought to have represented fertility and rebirth.

Gods of Fertility and War

A number of gods were linked with growth and fertility. Hapy, who presided over the Nile's flood, lived in the cavern at the cataracts on the Egyptian border. He was associated with the creator god Khnum, who controlled the gates which were thought to have held back the flood and who gave the order when they were to be raised to unleash the benevolent waters upon Egypt. Min, who was celebrated riotously in festivals at Coptos and Akhmim in Upper Egypt, was the god of male sexual potency. And the god Bes, with his extraordinary appearance as a bow-legged, lion-maned dwarf, sometimes depicted clad in a motley of animal skins and a feathered headdress, was a protective god of the household and of childbirth. Behind, or rather under, all was Osiris, god of the underworld (Duat). As the deity of rebirth in the Duat, he was considered responsible for each new season's crops, his spirit manifest in every green sprig of growth.

Some gods and goddesses, in attending to other aspects of life, were at the same time seen as deities of war. Among the goddesses were Sekhmet (the lioness-goddess known as the "powerful one"), Neith ("mistress of the bow, ruler of the arrows") and the two Syrian deities Astarte and Anat, worshipped in Egypt by the late second millennium BC (see box, page 49). A major Egyptian warrior god, also associated with hunting, was Anhur, whom the Greeks identified with their own war god Ares. The name Anhur means "he who brings back the distant one": he was believed to have left Egypt for Nubia and returned with Mehit, his lioness consort who was associated with Sekhmet. That Sekhmet was regarded as the daughter of Re (in combination with Hathor as the

Eye of Re; see box, page 23) served to bolster the idea that Anhur was a son of Re.

Montu was another god of war. Worshipped in Thebes, he was depicted as a falcon-headed god whose headdress bore the disc of the sun. He was seen as the conquering spirit of the pharaoh and as such was venerated at the city of Tod, to the south of Thebes. The measure of his power was reflected in the Middle Kingdom pharaoh Amenemhet II's gift to Montu's priesthood – four chests full of treasure from Syria, the Aegean and Mesopotamia, as emblems of Egypt's supremacy in foreign lands.

As Egypt came in contact with other, more martial civilizations, so it adopted some of their divinities of battle in preparation for war. One such was Reshep, a mace-wielding deity from the Levant, who rose to prominence following Egypt's conquest of Syria and Palestine during the second millennium BC. Another was Ba'al, infamous in the Old Testament because he killed and devoured human beings. He was accepted into the Egyptian pantheon as a god of thunder and the battlefield during the second millennium BC when the Egyptians were in conflict with the Hittites. At one cult centre he was associated with Seth, the Egyptian god of chaos (see pages 50–58), probably because one of Seth's functions was to be a god of thunder.

Thoth and the Eye of Horus

One account of the long battles between Horus and Seth (see pages 50–58) describes how Horus lost both his eyes; another claims that it was his moon eye that was torn out. The eye was found and restored to its original position by Thoth – an action symbolizing restoration of the cosmic order.

A bronze statuette from the Ptolemaic Period depicts ibis-headed Thoth, the divine scribe credited with the invention of speech and writing. The god was believed to play a part in the judgement of the dead, recording with his scribal palette the results of the weighing of the deceased's heart (see pages 74–75).

Horus was resting beside an oasis when Seth crept up on him in the form of a black boar. As Horus slept, Seth ripped out his left eye and flung it beyond the edge of the world. Horus awoke and retaliated by ripping off Seth's testicles. But there was nothing that he could do about his eye, which seemed lost forever. Meanwhile, deprived of its moon, the night sky sank into blackness.

Thoth came to the rescue. Ever the peacemaker during the conflict between the two gods, he scoured the chaos beyond the world's confines until he discovered the missing eye. It had been shattered by its fall, but Thoth pieced it together and restored it to its owner. The Eye of Horus was thereafter represented by the *wedjat* amulet.

The Divine Protectress

Among Egypt's female deities were goddesses of fertility, childbearing and healing, but their roles extended far beyond those of nurturers and protectors. Sekhmet and Neith were venerated as powerful and belligerent forces; Isis was the supreme magician; and Ma'at symbolized the order of the universe. Hathor was celebrated as the goddess of love, music and dance. So great was the fame of many of these goddesses that they were recognized well beyond the confines of Egypt.

The most enduringly popular of all goddesses was Isis, whose cult was adopted enthusiastically by the Greeks and Romans. Her influence in the Roman Empire reached as far as Britain, where, today, many bridges on the River Thames bear her image. Isis spanned many aspects of Egyptian culture. With Osiris, she was said to have helped to civilize Egypt, taught the people how to farm, given them the secrets of medicine and instituted the custom of marriage.

A wall painting from the Theban tomb of Nefertari, wife of Ramesses II, shows the goddess Isis leading the dead queen by the hand. From New Kingdom times Isis was often identified with the cow goddess Hathor, whose horns she wears here.

Isis may possibly have evolved from an early fertility goddess. Archaeological finds have shown that the early Egyptians worshipped a goddess whose potbelly clearly demonstrated her fecundity. During Graeco-Roman times, Isis was the most revered of female deities, and her international cult rivalled even the new Christian religion. Associated with Osiris, she was at the same time his sister and his wife. (The pharaohs themselves often married their own sisters.)

Isis helped Osiris in the struggle with their brother Seth, bringing Osiris back to life by taking the shape of a kite and flapping her wings to put breath into his body after Seth had used his trickery to kill him. As she did so, the revived god impregnated her, and in due course she gave birth to a son, Horus. Isis's act of resurrection frequently appeared on coffins, which bore the image of a bird enfolding the dead in its wings.

As the mother of Horus, Isis was regarded not only as a link between royalty and the gods, but also as having a maternal role that extended to the population at large. She became venerated as a protector of children, and her name was often called upon in magical spells to cure childhood ailments. In a typical example, to heal a scald, a plaster of human milk, gum and cat hair was applied to the sore spot while an incantation told Isis that her son was in the desert with no water to soothe him. The expected response from Isis was that she would alleviate the pain with a mixture of saliva and urine – "the Nile flood between my thighs", as it was euphemistically described.

A squatting woman goes into labour with the assistance of twin images of Hathor, one of two major deities invoked in childbirth (the other was the hippopotamus goddess Taweret). This Ptolemaic relief comes from Dendera, north of Thebes.

Having given birth to Horus at Khemmis in the Nile Delta, Isis watched over her son assiduously so that he might grow up to avenge his father. And just as the legends of Horus and Seth spread, so too did Isis's attributes grow more numerous. She was respected as the devoted wife, the ideal mother, a healer, a resurrector, a deity of children and fertility and, finally, a goddess of magic and cunning, "more clever than a million gods". Notable among her feats was the occasion when she tricked Seth into proclaiming his guilt in front of the Ennead and her discovery of the secret name of Re (see box, page 25).

Hathor, Goddess of Love and Fertility

The goddess Hathor was accorded almost as much respect as Isis and, like Isis, was given many identities: she could be shown in human form, or as a cow, or a lioness, or even occasionally a snake or a sycamore tree. She was also "Lady of the West" – the land of the dead – and a funerary goddess. As the Eye of Re, Hathor could also take the form of the destructive lioness Sekhmet. In her cow

form, she was a goddess of fertility. As such she had a special association with royal births: she, as well as Isis and Mut, was seen as the symbolic mother of each pharaoh. The pharaoh was sometimes portrayed drinking the milk of the goddess Hathor in reaffirmation of his divine right to rule Egypt. There was a further connection between Hathor and the pharaoh: Hathor was Horus's wife, and each pharaoh was considered the earthly embodiment of Horus. Each pharaoh was entitled to be described as "the son of Hathor". However, the pharaoh was equally considered the son of Isis as her cult grew in popularity. In time, the two goddesses became virtually interchangeable.

As the sworn enemy of evil, Hathor shook her favourite musical instrument, the sistrum (a kind of rattle), to drive away malign influences. Like Isis, Hathor was a healing goddess, and at her cult centre in Dendera mud-brick cubicles were con-

43

In this detail from a Theban tomb painting, a female musician entertains guests at a banquet. The "cone" on her head is believed to represent the perfumed oil worn on both hair and skin.

Hathor's associations with Re were numerous. In some rituals she was referred to as the mother of Re, and represented as a cow carrying an emblem of the sun between her horns. In others she was called the daughter or the Eye of Re. Her name means "Temple of Horus" (*Huwt-Hor*), which strengthens her identification as "lady of the sky", since Horus was lord of the sky.

Hathor's earthly renown was celebrated not only by the Egyptians but also by the Greeks, who linked her with their goddess of love, Aphrodite. In Byblos, a major centre for the timber trade, she was heralded as the "Lady of Byblos", and in the Sinai peninsula, where desert mines supplied the turquoise for much of the ancient world, she was worshipped in her temple as *nebet mefkat*, or "mistress of turquoise". Furthermore, any lands from which Egypt derived income were seen as a part of her domain. Around 2250BC an official called Harkhuf was recorded as bringing from Nubia a train of 300 donkeys laden with bounty including ebony, incense, elephant tusks and panther skins. Rather than being seen as the booty that it really was, this cargo was described as Hathor's gift to the pharaoh.

structed for the sick who came to be purified – and hopefully cured – by the water of the Nile. It was her curative powers that restored Horus's sight after his eyes had been torn out (see page 54).

Hathor's popularity was further enhanced by her role as the goddess of love and beauty, music and dance. She was described as "she of the beautiful hair", and in love poetry she is characterized as "golden", or "the lady of heaven". At Dendera it was believed that, after an episode of sensual abandon, she and Horus had produced a son called Ihy whose name was interpreted as "sistrum-player" and who, fittingly, personified musical ecstasy. Her eroticism once worked its magic even on the majestic Re. One time when he was depressed, Hathor danced naked in front of him until he started to smile. Her priests would ritually re-enact this dance by carrying her statue from the darkness of its shrine at Dendera on to the roof of the temple where, to the accompaniment of music, she was once again bathed in the glow of Re's smile.

Hathor in the Underworld

Hathor was also identified with the underworld. Her role as a funerary goddess was particularly prominent at Thebes where the necropolis on the west bank of the Nile was under her protection as Lady of the West. She was often depicted welcoming souls into the underworld with beneficent gifts of refreshing food and drink. The dying hoped that in the afterlife they would be counted as part of "the following of Hathor" so that they might receive her protection.

The Lady of the West was customarily depicted as a cow leaving the arid desert, where most pharaonic burials took place, to drink from the papyrus marshes. The everlasting life that the Egyptians hoped to achieve after death was in this way linked with the ever-renewing fruitfulness of the Nile which they could see with their own eyes.

Once the deceased had entered the underworld, Hathor offered more than merely sustenance: she was also believed to lend the worthy ones her outer robe, which would grant them safe passage through any dangers that they might face on their unknown journey.

Goddesses of Fertility

Hathor was sometimes depicted in the underworld alongside Taweret who, as a pregnant hippopotamus goddess, was a protector of women in childbirth. Taweret was one of the consorts of Seth, who could also appear in the same animal form; and in the battle between Horus and Seth, she switched allegiances to take Horus's side. When Horus cut off Seth's leg, which Seth had used in the guise of a bull to trample Osiris to death, he flung the limb into the sky. It was the magic of Taweret that prevented it from causing any further harm.

Another of the goddesses of childbirth was Heket, who would be summoned to hasten the final stages of labour. There is some evidence to suggest that midwives were known as "servants of Heket". One of the Ogdoad group of creator divinities, she took the shape of a frog. This outwardly unappealing form was, in fact, a harbinger of the Nile's forthcoming abundance, because when the Nile flooded, frogs seemed miraculously to appear from the mud.

The goddess Sopdet was also associated with the season of fertility through her identification with the dog star Sirius, whose appearance above the horizon in July heralded the coming of the flood (see page 40).

Another patron of childbirth was the goddess Meskhenet, who represented the so-called "birth-brick" on which women squatted to give birth. She was believed to be able to predict a child's destiny at the time of its nativity – although from the New Kingdom onwards this power was sometimes credited to the god Shay. Her function in helping with birth extended to the afterlife, when she would assist the dead to be reborn.

The swollen belly of this statuette of the hippopotamus goddess Taweret indicates her role as a patron of childbirth.

The Cat Goddess

One of the most popular goddesses was Bastet, whose name means "she of the ointment jar". Bastet was originally depicted as a lioness wielding a sceptre, but over time she dwindled in ferocity to become a cat-headed goddess holding the musical instrument known as a sistrum.

The cat, far from being a symbol of power like the lion, was seen as a free-spirited embodiment of household entertainment. Although most often linked with royalty, cats were favourite pets in even the lowliest household. Like Hathor, Bastet was considered to be a daughter of the sun god, and was a national deity of protection. She was celebrated at lively festivals with dancing, music and sistrum-playing at her cult centre, Bubastis.

Hatshepsut, the best known of Egypt's few women pharaohs, kneels to receive the benediction of the seated Amun-Re and the lion-headed goddess Sekhmet in this carved, 15th-century BC relief from the temple of Karnak in Thebes.

The Egyptians recognized the potential for destructive behaviour in their gods and goddesses: Hathor provided a particularly vivid example of this when she adopted the form of the leonine, vengeful Sekhmet, with a compulsion to destroy the whole of humanity. Sekhmet was also associated with plague, and was sometimes seen as the consort of Ptah, the Memphis creator god.

The opposite natures of the lion and the domestic cat are seen in the following myth, where Hathor is identified as Sekhmet until she returns to the care of the sun god. The story is also typical in encompassing the several aspects of Hathor.

Hathor, as the Eye of Re, rebelled against the sun god and fled to the deserts of Nubia. Thoth, the eternal peacemaker, was sent to find her, disguised as a baboon. But when he discovered her, she did not appear either in her normal form as Hathor, nor as Sekhmet, but as the cat goddess Bastet. Thoth used all his charm to make her homesick, recounting stories of Egypt and the life she had left behind. But all this was to no avail, and instead of being charmed, Bastet suddenly turned into Sekhmet, the furious lion goddess. Thoth redoubled his efforts – finally to good effect. Soothed by his words, Hathor agreed to return with him to Egypt, where she was greeted at the border by crowds of well-wishers.

However, their difficulties were not over and a serious danger faced them before they could return. Shortly before they reached the end of their journey, Hathor fell asleep, and Apophis, the serpent of chaos, came to attack her. Just as he was about to kill her, Thoth saw what was happening and came to her rescue by shaking her awake. They now entered Heliopolis in triumph, whereupon the Eye of Re reunited herself with the sun god.

Other Goddesses

Initially associated with funerary rites, Neith, an ancient archer goddess of the Delta, was symbolized by a shield and crossed arrows (see pages 21 and 40). She was identified with Athena by the Greeks, and with Diana by the Romans. A fearsome but righteous deity, she was a wise mediator often described as a divine mother figure, and sometimes regarded as the mother of Sobek, Isis, Re and even Apophis. In one myth, she is credited as the first being to appear on the primeval mound. At times, she could even intercede with the Ennead, and she played a judicial part in the epic battles between Horus and Seth.

Satis, a goddess associated with the island of Elephantine, guarded the southern frontiers of Egypt. But her protective role was not exclusively martial. With her cult centre situated at the point

The Festival of Bastet

The festivals held annually at the Delta city of Bubastis in honour of the cat-headed goddess Bastet were among the best-attended ones in Egypt. Colorfully reported by Herodotus, these events were widely held to be fabrications until archaeologists discovered evidence to confirm that they actually happened.

By the Late Period, Bastet's festival was one of the most popular in the Egyptian calendar. For ceremonial purposes the town of Bubastis – fifty miles northeast of modern Cairo – was best approached by water. "They come in barges," wrote Herodotus of the festival, "men and women together, a great number in each boat; on the way, some of the women keep up a continual clatter with castanets and some of the men play flutes, while the rest, both men and women, sing and clap their hands. Whenever they pass a town on the riverbank, they bring the barge close in-shore, some of the women continuing to act as I have said, while others shout abuse at the women of the place, or start dancing, or stand up and hitch their skirts. When they reach Bubastis, they celebrate the festival with elaborate sacrifices, and more wine is consumed than during all the rest of the year."

Herodotus recorded at least 700,000 people – "excluding children" – arriving in similar fashion to pay their respects at the red granite temple which had been erected in honour of the goddess. Again, according to Herodotus, "Cats which have died are taken to Bubastis where they are embalmed and buried in sacred receptacles." Thousands of the dead creatures were mummified and interred in underground galleries here and at other sites so that they might carry their owners' messages all the more swiftly to the realm of the gods.

The sheer scale of the festival seemed incredible to early Egyptologists. But in 1887 an archaeologist called Edouard Naville, excavating the site, discovered that Herodotus had indeed spoken the truth. He uncovered the site of Bubastis's main temple, the catacombs of mummified cats, and a number of pharaonic shrines which proved that even the highest born venerated Bastet.

A bronze from early in the 1st millennium BC shows the cat goddess Bastet shaking the rattle-like instrument known as the sistrum.

The Wives of Seth

Following Seth's long and unsuccessful battle with Horus for the Egyptian throne, the goddess Neith suggested to the council of gods that Seth be awarded a loser's prize: the "foreign" daughters of Re were offered to him as his wives. The involvement of these divine consorts, Anat and Astarte, may be connected with Seth's own affinity with the foreign gods Ba'al and Reshep.

One day as Seth was walking by the Nile, he came across the goddess Anat, bathing in the stream. He changed himself into a ram and raped her. But Anat could only be impregnated by divine fire, and so her body expelled his semen with such force that it struck him in the forehead, making him

With evil intent, Seth, the troublemaker of the Egyptian pantheon, approaches Anat in the shape of a ram.

dangerously ill. Seth was relieved of his punishing headache by Re, whom Isis sent to cure him.

In another myth, of which only a part has ever been found, the

gods of Egypt were in conflict with the sea god Yamm, and were coming off the worst. Yamm demanded tribute of gold, silver and lapis lazuli, which was duly brought to him by the goddess Renenutet. However, having received these treasures, he became greedy for more, and insisted on further tribute. He threatened that, if his demands were not met, he would enslave every god in Egypt. In despair, Renenutet pleaded for help from Astarte, who was famed both for her beauty and her ferocity. The messenger, in the shape of a bird, begged Astarte to carry the extra tribute to Yamm. Reluctantly, Astarte agreed. But when she reached the shoreline, her fiery nature got the better of her and she began to taunt the sea god. Alternately outraged by her impudence and bewitched by her beauty, Yamm demanded that he be given Astarte as well as the treasure. The goddess Renenutet retired to deliberate with the gods, who acceded to the sea god's demands and furnished Astarte with a dowry consisting of Nut's necklace and Geb's signet ring.

Seth, however, rebelled at the loss of his beautiful wife. Tantalizingly, the remainder of the story is lost. But the outcome, surely, was that, whether by force or by guile, Seth overcame the sea god, saved Egypt's pantheon from slavery, and returned from the adventure with Astarte.

where the annual inundation first becomes apparent, she was given a share of the credit for this event. And because of her association with the Nile's sacred waters, she was seen, too, as a purifier of the dead.

Over the centuries, the native Egyptian goddesses were joined by foreign deities. During the rule of the Hyksos – immigrants whose name simply means "rulers of foreign lands" – who appear to have entered Egypt peacefully during the eighteenth to sixteenth centuries BC from the area of Palestine, three striking deities were added to the pantheon:

the two martial goddesses Anat and Astarte, and a goddess of love, Qudshu (see below).

Egypt's goddesses enjoyed a popular appeal which the gods – for all their pomp and importance – never quite achieved. Indeed, when the closure of all the temples had been ordered by the Roman Emperor Theodosius in AD384, one continued to function – the temple of Isis at the city of Philae, near Aswan on the Egypt-Nubia border. Until around AD535 this remained the centre for a cult of Isis which had been powerful enough to challenge early Christianity for religious supremacy.

Foreign Goddesses

During the mid-second millennium BC, Egypt assimilated a wave of immigrants mostly from neighbouring countries, who added further deities from their own mythologies to the Egyptian pantheon.

Found in the palace of the Assyrian kings at Nimrud in what is now Iraq, this ivory plaque is thought to represent the goddess Ishtar, the Mesopotamian cousin of the Syrian divinity Astarte.

Of all the additions to the Egyptian gods at this time, none featured more prominently than the two warlike goddesses Anat and Astarte, and at a later period Qudshu, goddess of sexual love. Anat, a deity of battle, was – in a twist of the Isis myth – both sister and husband to the Middle Eastern god Ba'al, who was worshipped in Egypt as an aspect of Seth. She is also depicted with Min, Egyptian god of fertility – an association that emphasizes the pronounced sexual nature of her cult. In Egypt she was held to be the daughter of Re. She was also linked with Hathor, as both were associated with foreign lands, both had a potential for aggression, and both were sometimes presented in a distinctly sexual manner.

Astarte was also seen as a daughter of Re and additionally as a daughter of the creator god Ptah. She was particularly associated with horses and chariots, and is sometimes portrayed naked on horseback.

Qudshu was, by comparison, a benign goddess. In Egypt she was believed to be a consort of Min, as well as being linked with Hathor. Unlike Anat or Astarte, she carried only symbols of reproduction, such as the lotus. But the powerful sexuality she demonstrated was not to be doubted, for Qudshu rode naked on a lion.

The Conflicts of Horus and Seth

The story of Horus and Seth is set at the beginning of Egypt's long history (an early version even refers to them as brothers rather than nephew and uncle, see box, page 13). When the sun god Re relinquished his rule on Earth, he left as his successor his son Shu, who was succeeded by his son Geb, and in turn by *his* son Osiris. Following his marriage to his sister Isis, Osiris taught humankind the arts of agriculture and civilization, and proved a wise and just ruler. He brought abundance and prosperity to the land and Egypt flourished. But the golden age was all too brief. For there was terrible jealousy within the god's own family. Osiris's younger brother, Seth, burned with envy and ruthlessly plotted against him.

A Late Period bronze of the jackal-headed Anubis. The god embalmed the dismembered body of Osiris, for which service he became patron of mummifiers.

Osiris, so full of goodness, found it impossible to see evil in others, and made no effort to protect himself from Seth's malice. Stories of how Seth murdered him differ: according to Plutarch's widely told version, Seth sealed Osiris in a chest and threw it into the Nile (see box, page 56); according to another account, he turned himself into a raging bull and trampled Osiris into the dust.

In any event, Seth was not satisfied with a simple killing. Still consumed with jealous rage, he hacked the body to bits and scattered the pieces throughout the land. So it was that the soul of his brother left the world of the living and crossed into the darkness of the underworld. He was the first living thing to die; and as such, it was only fitting that in his afterlife he should command the land of the dead, the kingdom of the Beautiful West. Seth, safe in the knowledge that Osiris had left behind no son to avenge him, settled down to enjoy the kingdom he had usurped.

Isis, sister-wife to Osiris, was wild with grief. But she was also enterprising and resourceful: using all her skills of divination and magic, she scoured the land of Egypt with the help of her sister Nephthys until she had pieced together her husband's body. (In later times, cult temples all over the land marked sites where dismembered parts of the murdered god were found.)

Isis then sought out the jackal-god Anubis. He was generally regarded as the son of Nephthys, the fourth of the children of Geb and Nut; some claimed that his father was Osiris. Whatever his ancestry, Anubis sought to help Osiris by embalming the remains, the first time that such a feat had been accomplished. Anubis, as the inventor of mummification, came to be regarded as a god of great service to the dead.

Isis, using her own magic as well as the skills of Anubis, was able to resurrect her dead husband for just the amount of time needed to impregnate herself with his seed. She then sought refuge at Khemmis in the Nile Delta, where she gave birth to Horus, far from the reach of his jealous uncle. While the boy was an infant, he was cared for by Isis herself and by the cow goddess Hathor, who served as his wet-nurse. As soon as he was old

enough, Isis brought her child before the council of the assembled gods to demand the return of his birthright: the throne of Osiris.

The meeting was long and stormy. Re himself was unwilling to allow the lordship of the Earth to pass from mighty Seth to a mere boy; but most of the other gods were impressed by the evident justice of Horus's case. As Shu, god of air and the eldest son of the creator, put it: "Justice should triumph. We should give Horus his throne." The scribe god Thoth declared his agreement: "That is a million times right."

Re was not convinced by their decision, and was more than somewhat disgruntled that any other god should dare to oppose his will. Isis was also

The goddess Hathor greets King Seti I in a scene that originally embellished his Theban tomb, c.1290BC.

The Divinity of the Pharaoh

From the beginning of pharaonic times, Egypt's kings were revered not only as royal, but divine. Their godhood served as a link between the land, the people and the deities who ruled the universe.

In the hierarchy of Egyptian religion, only the king was permitted to make offerings to the gods: there could be no other mediator between Earth and heaven. Although such work might well be delegated to the high priests, it was understood that a priest only deputized for the king, having, in theory, no authority of his own.

Each pharaoh was a god from birth. While the queen mother was recognized by all as his human mother, the idea that he had been sired by Amun-Re, incarnate as his royal father, was widely accepted. When the

pharaoh had his own son, the same principle of divine incarnation would ensure that godhood was passed down through the dynasty.

The coronation rituals further reinforced this concept. And at death, the king became wholly divine: no longer taking the living form of Horus as ruler, he became one with Osiris in the underworld, while at the same time joining his father Re in his ascendancy over all things.

All this was the most natural of arrangements and a matter of simple, if wonderful, fact. None doubted the irresistible logic: "God is our king; the king is a god." The pharaoh's divinity, almost like a written constitution, established the Egyptian state as an entity sanctioned by the law of humankind and the gods.

51

Seth, Lord of Disorder

In very early times, Seth was worshipped at his cult centre, Naqada, and because he was associated with the frightening desert sandstorms of the region, it was important to appease him. He ultimately became a lord of misrule and chaos, the god of storms, the enemy of Horus and the organized world that Horus stood for. Indeed, that enmity was part of the Egyptian order, a darkness against which the divine light could flourish.

Like most Egyptian gods, Seth was often pictured with the head of an animal – usually the strange "Seth beast", an imaginary creature with a vague resemblance to an ant-eater. Sometimes he was depicted as one of the animals considered to be "unclean" by the Egyptians – such as the hippopotamus or the pig.

For all his villainy, Seth's antecedents were impeccable: as the son of sky goddess Nut, he matched in divine status his brother Osiris and his sisters Isis and Nephthys (the latter was also one of his wives). Indeed, his strength and rank among the gods gained him Re's support during much of his bitter struggle with Horus. After his defeat on Earth, he journeyed with the sun god during the hours of the night, defending him against the serpent Apophis.

Seth's immense strength and his forceful sexuality guaranteed him the veneration of at least a minority of mortals. Although rarely a popular god, he did have his good points: an appeal to Seth, the lord of chaos, might help keep bad weather away. Indeed, at one point in Egypt's history, he enjoyed a period of general worship and respect, during the Nineteenth and Twentieth Dynasties (1292–1075BC).

But Seth was always a dangerous god to venerate. The dynasties that followed characterized him as the god of harm, and late in Egyptian history he had generally come to be regarded as the personification of evil-doing.

Seth is depicted in this basalt carving with his sister and wife Nephthys at his side. For most of Egyptian history, Seth was lord of chaos, a god to be carefully placated.

proving a very able advocate. At one point in the wrangling, Seth became so angry with Isis's cunning pleas that he threatened to kill a god for each day that Isis remained at the divine court.

"Let us cross over to the island in the middle of the river," said the sun god, "and tell the ferryman to deny passage to Isis, or any who may resemble her." Nemty, the divine ferryman, duly rowed all but Isis to the island, and returned to the mainland where he waited while the gods enjoyed a meal during a break from their disputations. After a time, Isis appeared on the bank, disguised as an old crone. "Ferry me across," she begged. "I am taking food to the cowherd who has been working on the island for the last five days."

At first, Nemty refused, even though he had no suspicion that he was talking to Isis. But the bribe of a golden ring soon changed his mind, and Isis entered the camp of the gods. Once again, she changed her shape, this time taking on the appearance of a beautiful young woman dressed in widow's weeds. Seth, always a rake, at once approached her.

"Why are you here, and who are you?" he asked, in a bantering tone. "O great lord," answered Isis, "I come to seek justice. For I was the wife of a cowherd, and bore his son. Then when my husband died, the boy went to take over his father's herd. But a stranger came, and seized our cattle for himself. When my young son protested, the stranger threatened him with a beating. Please, help me restore my son's inheritance." Seth waxed indignant. "How can a stranger seize the cattle while the son is still alive?" Isis had got what she wanted. Turning herself into a kite, she flew to a nearby tree and cackled with laughter at Seth's hypocrisy. "O Seth, you have judged yourself." This time, the other gods, including Re, agreed. Together, they prepared to crown Horus as rightful lord of the Earth.

Seth, though, was far from willing to accept the verdict. He may have lost his crown, but he was still unbeaten; and to prove it, he challenged Horus to the first of a series of combats. With Re's approval, the two gods transformed themselves

In the prow of Re's solar barque, Seth leans forward to spear the dangerous serpent Apophis (see box, page 20). Despite Seth's evil reputation, his enormous strength was greatly valued by Re, who relied on his protection each night as he passed through the *Duat*. From the Hirweben's *Book of the Dead*, 21st Dynasty.

into hippopotamuses, and fought in the waters of the Nile. "He who survives three months," declared Seth, "shall be given the throne."

So the battle commenced. But once more Isis intervened – though this time to little effect. She quickly contrived a magic harpoon from a piece of copper and some yarn, and hurled it at Seth. But the churning water where the beast-gods were struggling confused her aim, and her first throw struck Horus. Instantly she used her magic to retrieve the weapon, and threw it once again. This time, the barb penetrated Seth, who rose to the surface with a cry of pain. "O sister," he wailed, "why are you always my enemy? I am your brother: let me go."

Isis could not resist her brother's plea, and at once removed her harpoon. This was more than Horus could bear. He burst from the water in so great a rage at his mother's change of heart that he cut off her head with one stroke of his copper knife. He took hold of the head, then marched to the mountains.

But Isis was, after all, the Mistress of Magic, and so, unperturbed, she turned her body into a flint statue and walked over to join the watching assembly of the gods. When Re was told exactly what had happened, he was beside himself with anger at Horus. While Isis restored herself to normal form, the gods scoured the Earth for the miscreant.

It was Seth who found him, sound asleep in the shade of a shenusha tree in an oasis in the western desert. Seth at once leaped upon his nephew and tore out both of his eyes. Leaving Horus to his terrible pain, Seth buried the eyes in the desert, where they took root and grew into two fine lotus flowers. Then Seth returned to Re – and denied he had ever seen Horus.

One by one, the other gods abandoned the search. Only the goddess Hathor, who had wet-nursed the baby Horus, refused to give up; and it was she who found the eyeless god the next morning. With milk taken from a passing gazelle, she anointed the bleeding sockets and restored Horus's sight. Then she took him with her to the assembled gods and told them about Seth's appalling deeds.

But this time, Horus had also put himself in the wrong: he had attacked Isis with extreme violence, and even though his mother had forgiven his irrational action, Re refused to show favour. He ordered a truce between Horus and Seth.

Lotus flowers blossom across the walls of the temple of Seti I at Abydos, just as they burst forth from the torn-out eyes of Horus after Seth had buried them in the desert. Shortly afterwards Horus's injuries were miraculously healed. The lotus was regarded as a symbol of rebirth.

An Intimate Encounter

Seth's hatred did not diminish, and Horus soon found himself contending once again with the older god's superior strength and immense capacity for dirty tricks. Against these qualities, Horus had only two genuine weapons: a burning sense that justice was on his side, and a mother whose cunning and command of magic proved to be enough to tip the balance.

Isis's help was especially useful on an occasion when Seth subjected his nephew to an outright sexual attack. In ancient Egypt, semen was thought to flow through all the veins of the body, and was considered both potent and dangerous – so much so that the word for semen was similar to the word for poison. A god's semen was considered to be particularly powerful.

After decades of fighting between Horus and Seth, the other gods were growing increasingly weary of the destructive rivalry, and there came a time when Re flatly ordered it to end: "Be at peace together, and cease your quarrelling."

Making a show of accepting the edict, Seth attempted to befriend Horus and invited him to his home. In due course, night fell; a bed was prepared, and the two gods settled down together. When Seth thought that Horus was asleep, he attacked him sexually to show his dominance over his younger rival.

But Horus was ready, and caught Seth's seed with his hand. At once he ran to Isis, crying, "Look what Seth has done to me!" Isis, who understood the dangers from Seth's semen, at once cut off her son's hand – and threw it into the Nile. (Of course, she quickly replaced it with another.)

Then she prepared a counter-attack. She took some of Horus's own semen and took it to Seth's garden, where she sprinkled it over the lettuces, the god's favourite vegetable. Sure enough, the next morning Seth came to his garden to pick and eat the lettuces, and in the extraordinary way of gods, he became "pregnant" with the seed of Horus.

The next time the two rivals appeared before the council of gods, Seth began to boast once more of his might and skill. He seemed to be making a powerful impression – until Horus asked the gods to call out to his seed and that of his uncle. In response, Thoth laid hands on Horus, and summoned the seed of Seth, but it answered only from the river. However, when in turn he touched Seth and called for the seed of Horus, it answered from within the god. Thoth then summoned the seed to Seth's forehead, where it appeared – to Seth's great rage – as a golden sun. This proved the dominance of Horus over his uncle.

The Final Battle

Already, the struggle between the two had lasted many decades (according to the gods' particular reckoning of time). But Seth demanded one last challenge. "Let us each build a ship of stone," he said, "and race each other down the Nile. The winner will have the crown of Osiris."

When Seth came to his garden to pick lettuces, his favourite vegetable, he was impregnated by the semen of his nephew Horus, sprinkled there by Isis.

Horus built his ship first, out of stout pine; but then he plastered it over to make it look as if it had been made of stone. When Seth saw it, he used a mighty club to knock off a whole mountain top, from which he built a much larger ship of solid stone for himself. Of course, when the two boats were launched, Seth's vessel immediately sank to the bottom. But Horus had little time to laugh: Seth at once changed himself into a hippopotamus, charged at Horus's ship and dashed it to pieces. Undaunted by this, Horus prepared to

The Chest and the Tree

By Graeco-Roman times, one at least of Egypt's goddesses had acquired a greatly expanded repertoire. Isis, mother, healer and arch-magician, appealed enormously to peoples all around the Mediterranean and beyond. Naturally, from this worship there grew a great demand for new tales of the goddess.

Plutarch, the Greek historian and biographer who lived from *c.*AD46 to AD120, was one of many writers glad to oblige. From Egyptian sources, which he mixed with a little Greek legend and no doubt a few ideas of his own, he came up with a colorful account of the trickery Seth used to murder Osiris.

In Plutarch's version, Seth ordered the making of an exquisitely crafted chest, to the exact height and width of his brother. Then he threw a great banquet for Osiris, at which he displayed the chest to the admiration of all. It should belong, said Seth, to whomsoever it might fit; and one by one the guests tried the chest for size. But none matched its measurements – except Osiris himself. And the moment the unsuspecting king lay in the chest, Seth and his fellow-plotters promptly nailed the lid shut, sealed it with molten lead, and cast the chest upon the waters of the Nile Delta.

Isis at once set off to find her husband's body. But by the time she learned where Seth had put the great chest, it had floated far out to sea. It finally came to land at Byblos in the Lebanon. There, the washed-up chest gave root to a sapling which magically grew into a vast tree big enough to enclose Osiris and his coffin within its trunk. Impressed by the size of the tree, the king of Lebanon had it cut down and used as a pillar for his new palace – with Osiris still within.

In time, of course, Isis tracked the coffin down, and to the astonishment of the king and his court, cut open the great roof-pillar and removed her husband's body.

The tree, Plutarch adds, lending credibility to his tale, was preserved for many years in Byblos and worshipped there.

Highly decorative chests were valued items of Egyptian furniture. This ornate example belonged to the Lady Meryt and was found in the tomb that she shared with her husband Kha (*c.*1400BC).

harpoon the hippopotamus-Seth. But the other gods intervened to stop him.

Thus another battle was over, leaving everything still unresolved. Despairing of a solution, Horus went to see Neith, the revered goddess of wisdom, in her Delta city of Sais. "Please," he begged her, "let judgement be made. For eighty years, Seth and I have stood before the tribunal of the gods, and we are no nearer a decision. I have won the day a thousand times, yet Seth refuses to give in, and never pays the slightest attention to what the gods say to him."

When the other gods heard Horus's plea to Neith, they agreed that he was justified. Besides, their own patience in dealing with the dispute was by now completely exhausted. At last, Thoth suggested to Re that he apply for advice to Osiris

Isis, mother of Horus, used all her skills to ensure her son's victory over Seth. This relief, depicting Isis, is from the tomb equipment of Yuya and Thuya, the great grandparents of Tutankhamun, c.1380BC.

himself, in the Beautiful West, his kingdom of the underworld. And, accordingly, a messenger was dispatched to the realm of Osiris.

After a long and perilous journey into the realm of the dead, the messenger returned with Osiris's reply. Not surprisingly, the god supported his son Horus. But he was also greatly angered that justice had not already been done for the boy: why, asked Osiris, should Horus be cheated?

Re was irked at being addressed in such a manner, and sent the messenger on his journey westwards again with a haughty answer. This time,

A tomb painting of Horus, in his customary, falcon-headed form, decorates the tomb of Ramesses I. The god wears a double crown, which represents his right to rule over both Upper and Lower Egypt. This right was finally won at the end of his long battles with Seth.

Osiris's rage knew no bounds. "Here in my kingdom of the dead, " he wrote, "there are many powerful demons: should I send them into the land of the living, to return here with the stolen hearts of evil-doers? For I am much stronger than you: sooner or later, even the gods must come to sleep in my Beautiful West."

Osiris's threat resolved the matter. In solemn conclave, the gods agreed that Horus should inherit the lordship of the Earth. Re ordered Isis to bring Seth in chains before him, which she willingly did. "Seth," asked Re, "do you still claim the throne of Osiris?" By this time Seth was ready to concede. "No, great one. Let Horus be summoned and given his father's throne."

The long dispute was finally over. The young Horus was given the crown of Egypt, and all the Earth rejoiced. As for Seth, Re had something to offer by way of recompense. "You may join me in the skies as my son, and god of storms," he told the loser. "Your thunder and lightning will terrify people for eternity."

The Divine Order

Taken as a whole, this myth was – and is – a powerful evocation of the tension and conflict between, on the one hand, the forces of order, as exemplified by Osiris and Horus; and, on the other hand, their dark counterparts, the chaos and confusion represented by Seth (see box, page 52). There were times in Egypt's long history when Seth won a temporary victory; but it was in the interests of all people, for the sake of peace and prosperity, to support the successors of Horus.

And the successors of Horus, of course, were the pharaohs. So it was that the human king of Egypt took the name of Horus (given to him on his accession) and added it to his own, which not only set him clearly among the gods, but also announced him to be the earthly representative of the forces of divine order.

The Horus-Seth myth reflects issues of kingship that were rarely discussed openly in Egypt. Young Horus is portrayed as a vulnerable candidate vying for the position of supreme ruler, who in the end is victorious over his uncle, Seth, who represents chaos. Although successful usurpations were rare, Egypt needed a central myth to discourage what it most feared – the violent transference of power. The triumph of Horus was regularly enacted as a ritual drama in temple ceremonials, so that Egypt remained united: "The white crown (Upper Egypt) is the Eye of Horus; the red crown (Delta) is the Eye of Horus."

The Earthly Power of the Pharaoh

Since the pharaoh was a god, it followed that he had absolute power on Earth. However, despite the trappings of divinity, ordinary human politics ensured that there were sometimes plots against his power. Assassinations and usurpations were rarely mentioned – such chaotic possibilities were too dangerous to contemplate – but treachery was by no means unheard of.

One famous document, *The Instructions of King Amenemhet I*, purporting to be the last testimony of the king, set out a bleak and Machiavellian view of Egyptian power-politics:

Beware of subjects who are nobodies,
Of whose plotting one is not aware.
Trust not a brother, know not a friend,
Make no intimates, it is worthless.
When you lie down, guard your heart yourself,
For no man has adherents on the day of woe.
I gave to the beggar, I raised the orphan,
I gave success to the poor as to the wealthy;
But he who ate my food raised opposition,
He to whom I gave my trust used it to plot.

Apart from the ever-present risk of treason, Egypt at the height of its civilization was simply too large and complex for one man to exercise sole power. There was the priesthood to be taken into account, for a start. When Akhenaten attempted to greatly extend the revival of the ancient cult of the sun god, and hence to remove the powerful influence of the Amun clergy at Karnak over the monarchy (see pages 31–32), he ran into resistance from the traditional religious authorities. Indeed, they eradicated his reforms immediately after his death. Then there were provincial governors (nomarchs), who with other senior officials and administrators always sought to keep as much power in their own hands as possible; and of course the military commanders, all of whom were capable of acting in their own interests before those of the king. As a dispatch from an unruly general put it in the time of Ramesses XI: "Pharaoh? Whose master is he these days?"

Senwosret III, who ruled from *c.*1836 to *c.*1818BC, was one of Egypt's most effective kings, radically reforming his adminstration and showing how authority could be successfully delegated. Other kings were less fortunate: despite the trappings of divinity, a number of pharaohs fell victim to political elements beyond their control.

The Kings in Myth

"Re has placed the king on the earth of the living for ever and eternity to judge humanity and to pacify the gods, to realize right and to annihilate wrong; he gives divine offerings to the gods, funerary offerings to the transfigured dead, the name of the king is in the sky like that of Re, he lives in elation like Re-Horakhty." This New Kingdom inscription from Thebes makes it clear how the king was thought to be at one with the gods. Myth for the Egyptians was not an account of events in a distant past or in a place far removed from Earth: kings took their place in the mythic world as soon as they assumed the throne.

In a palette relief dating from *c.*3000BC, King Narmer prepares to strike a prisoner with the royal mace. A pharaoh was generally far too august for such coarse, hand-to-hand violence: the image is symbolic of the triumph of order over chaos and of Egypt over her foes.

One consequence of according divine status to the king was that each king became the central character in his own mythology. Godhood itself was the core of the myth: a divine birth was assumed automatically with accession to the throne, and throughout his reign a king's divinity would regularly be celebrated, culminating in the funerary cult he could expect to be established after his death.

Although the king's own mythology would be woven from the actual happenings of a specific reign, it is difficult to tease out hard historical evidence from the accounts in which kings and their courtiers cocooned real events – invariably written in an exaggerated and flamboyant style to glorify the pharaoh. As one scribe put it, perhaps as long ago as 2000BC:

"The king, lord of courtiers, cannot be foolish.
At his coming forth from the womb he was wise,
And god has distinguished him before a million other men."

Thus no king of Egypt could take part in a military campaign that was anything but victorious. One of the most common royal scenes was the "smiting scene", in which the king, in a ritual pose that was scarcely altered by Egyptian artists over a period of 3,000 years, holds a weapon over the head of his defeated enemy. Stylized drawings of hordes of captives – usually carefully enumerated in their thousands – and piles of corpses are generally part of the standard display.

Sometimes, such victory monuments were to all intents and purposes fantasies, although more often they were idealized versions of something that had actually occurred. An interesting example in the mortuary temple reliefs of Ramesses III, at Medinet Habu, depicts a battle around 1186BC against the Pelesets, one of the groups of "Sea Peoples" whose aggressive migrations from the Aegean area disturbed the peace of the Mediterranean in the late second millennium BC.

According to Ramesses's official history, the battle was a very one-sided affair, fought on both sea and land. The migrants' troops were trapped "like birds in a net", and in some temples there are fine carved reliefs showing them meeting their just deserts at the hands of the mighty pharaoh. Afterwards, says the chronicle succinctly, "the Pelesets were made ashes".

However, other documents from Ramesses's reign indicate that later invaders were granted

The Birth of Hatshepsut

Hatshepsut was daughter of Thutmose I and wife to Thutmose II, at whose death the throne passed to Hatshepsut's young stepson, the future Thutmose III. But Hatshepsut assumed full powers of regency, and after two years she had herself crowned king – not queen – in her own right. This audacious move required an appropriate genealogy from the gods to make it acceptable.

Following the death of Queen Hatshepsut, who assumed the masculine regalia of kingship, her step-son and successor Thutmose III either defaced or usurped her images in a gesture of supremacy. This relief may represent Hatshepsut or Thutmose.

According to an inscription in Hatshepsut's temple at Deir el-Bahri, Amun-Re, having gathered the lesser gods around his throne, told them: "I will create a queen to rule over Egypt." Accompanied by the messenger god Thoth, Amun-Re went to the palace of King Thutmose I and, taking on the appearance of the pharaoh, appeared at the bed of his wife, Ahmose. Naturally, "she rejoiced at his virility", and as "the palace became inundated with the scent of god", he had his way with her.

According to one version, the god explained to Ahmose: "Truly, Hatshepsut will be the name of the child I have placed in you, for this was what you exclaimed!" The word translates approximately as "the noble best": thus the future she-king was named by her mother's cry of passion in the arms of Amun-Re.

Certainly, Hatshepsut was favoured by the gods during her fifteen-year rule. But later dynasties tried to remove her name and image as her rule was considered contrary to *ma'at* (natural order). And yet, more than 3,000 years after her death, she is still renowned as one of the greatest pharaohs.

The Dream of Thutmose

Between the paws of the Great Sphinx at Giza, one of the most powerful of all the monuments of Egypt, there lies a granite stele *inscribed with a strange story – an account of certain curious events during the reign of King Amenhotep II (c.1426–1400BC).*

Prince Thutmose overseeing workers who are clearing drifts of sand covering the body of the Great Sphinx of Giza.

It so happened, recounts the *stele*, that a young prince of the royal house was hunting in the desert near Giza. His name was Thutmose; and as one of the king's younger sons, he had no hopes of the succession – or so he believed.

That day the sun burned particularly fiercely, and by noon the prince was very weary. Finding himself close to the Great Sphinx – of which only the head still showed above the windblown desert sands – he sought out a cool spot in its ancient shade and promptly fell asleep.

Immediately, there came upon him an extraordinary dream in which the Sphinx itself came to life and spoke to him, saying, "I am the sun god, and your father. Listen, and hear how you shall be the ruler of all Egypt." There was one condition – Thutmose must clear away the desert sands that were engulfing the Sphinx.

When he awoke, he hurried at once to Memphis to organize a team of workmen to shift the sand from the lion-body. The Sphinx remained true to its word and Thutmose was chosen as king above his elder brothers. In due course he was crowned as Thutmose IV. His reign lasted for ten years, and throughout that time he honoured the Sphinx.

royal permission to settle on the same land where they had fought, which happened to be one of the most fertile pieces of land in the region. Such indications that the enemy did not, perhaps, come off so badly after all had no place in royal myth.

A specific discrepancy between the official version of events and reality is found in the reign of Ramesses II, a century earlier. Ramesses II – "the Great" – spent many years struggling against the Hittite kingdom in Anatolia and northern Syria, at a time when Egypt controlled most of Palestine and the southern Lebanon. Between the two powers was a kind of political buffer zone.

In *c.*1275BC, Ramesses led a powerful expedition north through Gaza all the way to the Hittite city of Qadesh (Kadesh) on the Orontes river. The advance guard of the Egyptian army, led by the king, had barely begun to make camp by Qadesh when the approaching support division was ambushed by a large force under the Hittite king Muwatallis. At least one Egyptian division was scattered; Ramesses, commanding from the camp, managed to hold off the main Hittite attack long enough for reinforcements to arrive. The battle ended in some sort of stalemate, and a few days later the Egyptian host, or what was left of it, marched home again – leaving Qadesh unscathed. From the Egyptian point of view, the battle was clearly a shambles from which they were lucky to escape without suffering total disaster.

For Ramesses, though, it was a great victory, and he made sure that all Egypt knew of it. The battle is lavishly described on the walls of five of his temple buildings, at Abydos, Luxor, Karnak, Abu Simbel and the Ramesseum. And it was told and retold on endless papyri as an exercise for schoolboys and trainee scribes. In this "official" version, Ramesses is surrounded by 2,500 Hittite chariots; yet with the aid of Amun – "Forward, I am with you/ I, your father, my hand is with you/ I prevail over a hundred thousand men" – the pharaoh sees the enemy off almost single-handed.

After his mighty victory, the Hittites beg for peace. "Look, you spent yesterday killing a hundred thousand, and today you came back and left us no heirs. Be not hard in your dealings, victorious king! Peace is better than fighting. Give us breath." Ramesses, marching briskly back to Egypt, is naturally prepared to be magnanimous.

A few years later, the Hittites were plagued by internal revolt and threatened from the east by Assyria. But the region was simply too far away for Egypt's domination to be long-lasting. In the end,

Ramesses II, "the Great", shown with the creator god Amun. Ramesses, on the left, wears the double crown of Upper and Lower Egypt, but there is little to distinguish the two figures – Ramesses was himself a god, after all.

63

This image of **Thutmose III** radiates a tranquillity that belies his record as one of Egypt's most formidable military leaders. The Syrians took many years to recover from his campaigns.

with both sides weary of the constant destructive skirmishing, a peace treaty was signed between Ramesses II and the newly enthroned king of the Hittites, Hattusilis III.

This agreement – which has survived in both Egyptian and Hittite versions, each claiming that the first, humiliating request for peace came from the other – is the oldest existing example of a peaceable international accord. (A copy is kept in the United Nations building in New York.) The treaty seems to have been successful, since there were no further Hittite wars during the remainder of Ramesses' sixty-six-year reign. As part of the settlement, in the thirty-third year of his reign, the pharaoh married a daughter of the Hittite king and, to consolidate matters still further, he married a second daughter eleven years later – events celebrated in temple and *stele* inscriptions.

A Cunning General

Even on those rare occasions when neither the pharaoh nor one of the other gods was the chief protagonist, every tale naturally redounded to the king's great credit. One of the more entertaining tales concerned the *ruse de guerre* used by Djehuty, a general of Thutmose III, to capture the city of Joppa (present-day Jaffa) in Canaan.

One account of this rebellion, written many years later, was, to a large extent, fictional. A revolt had taken place in Joppa, and not for the first time. During the course of his reign, Thutmose fought numerous campaigns in the area. Clearly, it was imperative to bring the city to heel at once. Thutmose, unable to leave Egypt, sent instead his resourceful General Djehuty, entrusting him with the royal mace as a sign of the powers that had been delegated to him.

When Djehuty reached Joppa, he was daunted by the city's towering walls. Reluctantly he ordered an all-out assault which resulted in heavy Egyptian losses, with nothing to show for them. So Djehuty decided to try cunning against his opponents. He sent a formal letter to the prince, once more demanding surrender. Attached

Sinuhe

One of Egypt's most-loved stories – it exists in many versions – celebrates the values that the pharaohs' subjects held dear. It tells the story of Sinuhe, a high court official of the Twelfth Dynasty.

Sinuhe was a trusted servant at the court of King Amenemhet. When his master died – it is thought by assassination – he was convinced that, regardless of his innocence, he might be implicated and punished by the king's successor. So he fled through the Sinai Desert, and sought refuge in Syria.

There he thrived mightily. The local prince showed him great favour, even granting him his eldest daughter in marriage. Over the years, he grew in

King Senwosret I is embraced by Ptah, creator-god of Memphis. Senwosret's father was apparently assassinated. The tale of the father's servant Sinuhe tells how he fled Egypt to escape suspicion of the murder.

wealth and stature. But all this was meaningless to Sinuhe, for there could be no real happiness for him outside his own country. At last Senwosret I, who was now king, hearing of Sinuhe's unhappiness, sent a message to the former servant: "You shall not die abroad. Think of your dead body. Come home."

At once Sinuhe gave all his goods to his eldest son, and set off for Egypt. At last he met the king. "My limbs trembled," he said, "when this god addressed me." But Senwosret I was inclined to be generous: he made him a "Companion among the Nobles" and ordered that he should be bathed, anointed and dressed as an Egyptian once more. Moreover, there was even better to come. For the king not only granted him land and a house – but, far more important to the Egyptians, he gave him a proper tomb.

---

to the official scroll, however, he added a private message: it was clear that he could not take the city, wrote the general, and he was much afraid of the consequent wrath of Thutmose. Therefore, for a handsome bribe, he would change sides. Perhaps the prince would agree to meet to discuss terms with him?

The prince, who ought to have known better, was willing to compromise. Under a flag of truce, the two men discussed matters amicably; then the prince asked if he could see the famous mace. In the privacy of Djehuty's tent, the general produced the great symbol of authority. But the prince did not have long to marvel at the mace before Djehuty knocked him unconscious, using the exquisite treasure as a weapon.

While some of his men bound the luckless ruler, Djehuty told the prince's servants that he had prepared many gifts for Joppa, to display where his new loyalties lay. The gifts were impressive and numerous: they filled 200 large baskets, each carried by two unarmed men. The people of Joppa opened their gates to allow the tribute to enter.

Once inside, however, the trap was sprung. From each basket leaped an Egyptian soldier – carrying extra weapons on behalf of his two bearers. Within minutes, the Egyptian force had seized the gates, and the rest of Djehuty's men flooded through to victory.

In due course, the city's booty and its fettered prince were brought to Egypt and the king's ingenious general was heaped with rewards.

Preparing for Eternity

Ancient Egyptians believed that preserving the corpse was crucial to its attaining the afterlife. Initially, bodies buried in shallow pits were protected by the desiccating effect of the desert. Later, the process of mummification served the same function in the tomb.

In addition to the physical body (*sah*) and its heart (*ib*, regarded as the seat of intelligence and emotion), the Egyptians believed that each individual was made up of five distinctive parts: the *ka* (life-force or soul), the *ba* (personality or spirit), the *akh* (immortal unification of the *ka* and *ba*), the *ren* (name) and the *shuwt* (shadow). Both the name and the shadow had metaphysical qualities thought to protect the individual. This fivefold division had particular significance after death, during the hazardous journey through the underworld.

When the creator god Khnum moulded every person from clay at birth, he created a spiritual replica, called the *ka*. After death the *ka* was free to dwell in the tomb, absorbing the life-giving

Two mummies at the end of the 70-day mummification process, from a fragment of a painted wall scene from the 18th-Dynasty Theban tomb of Meryma'at, priest of Ma'at (*c.*1391–*c.*1353BC, the reign of Amenhotep III). The body had to be preserved in the best form possible in readiness for the pleasures of the hereafter.

properties of the offerings (known as *kaw*) left by priests and the family. The *ba*, similar to our concept of the personality, was usually shown as a human-headed bird that dwelled in the tomb at night. Its distinctive physical qualities differentiated one individual from another. The *ba* could also represent a god's power on Earth: the Memphite Apis bull, for example, was the *ba* of Osiris. Unlike the *ka*, the *ba* was able to visit the living world or travel through the heavens with the gods. Its role in guaranteeing the deceased's immortality was crucial: it had to travel through the underworld, overcoming a series of trials, before it could be reunited with the *ka* and become an *akh*.

The *akh*, symbolized by a crested ibis, represented the final and most complete form of existence to which every Egyptian aspired, and once formed would last for eternity. In some funerary texts it is written that the *akh* dwelled in the heavens with the gods. But the formation of the *akh*, which resulted from the unification of the *ka* and *ba*, depended on the successful physical preparation of the corpse for the afterlife. The Egyptians believed that life after death could be enjoyed only if three conditions were met: the dead body had to be preserved in pristine condition; the *ka* had to be supplied with sustenance; and the deceased's name had to be commemorated by prayer.

Mummification

The first step towards meeting these conditions was to initiate a process, now known as mummification, designed to preserve the corpse. This involved evisceration (removal of the internal organs), followed by dehydration of the body with natron – a form of sodium that absorbed water.

Anubis, God of Mummification

Anubis was the protective deity of cemeteries, credited with the invention of embalming because he helped Isis to preserve her brother Osiris, whose body was the first to be mummified. Usually depicted as a reclining black jackal, or a man with a jackal head, he was thought to ward off scavengers. Osiris's blackness symbolized the rich soil of Egypt and the appearance of a mummified corpse.

The jackal-headed god Anubis attends to a dead person in his role as an embalmer. This 19th-Dynasty wall painting is from the tomb of the workman Sennedjem at Deir el-Medina in Thebes.

Mummification was a complex procedure which involved a series of detailed operations and rituals.

To begin with, the body was washed and purified, and then the perishable organs were removed. First, the brain was extracted through the nasal passage using a long metal hook, and then the left side of the body was opened up to remove the liver, lungs, stomach and intestines. The brains were discarded as worthless, but the heart, which was seen as the seat of all thought, was left in place. The removed organs were then washed and dried separately with natron (a type of sodium salt), treated with aromatic oils and resins, wrapped in linen, and then placed into the four Canopic jars – so-called because of a long-standing misconception that they were related to human-headed jars that were worshipped as manifestations of Osiris in the Delta port of Canopus.

Each jar was then entrusted to the care of one of Horus's four sons, who were believed to be present at the soul's final judgement before Osiris. The liver was protected by the human-headed Imsety, the lungs by the baboon-headed Hapy, the stomach by the jackal-headed Duamutef, and the intestines by the hawk-headed Qebehsenuef. Each creature featured on the stoppers of the jars.

After evisceration the body cavity was washed out and scented, then stuffed with temporary packing, which included natron to help dry the body's interior. Natron was also placed over the corpse for forty days. During this stage in the process, the body lost up to 75 per cent of its weight. The temporary stuffing would eventually be removed and the body cavity refilled with fresh natron and resin-soaked linen to restore its former shape, after which cosmetic decorations were made. After being coated in cedar oil and scented resins, the body was wrapped in bandages while priests read out the appropriate incantations from *The Book of the Dead.*

The corpse was then anointed with aromatic oils and resin before being wrapped in strips of linen. The oldest intact mummy found *in situ* was discovered in the Saqqara tomb of a court singer, Nefer, who died *c*.2470BC. He was expertly wrapped and preserved, with details such as eyebrows and a moustache painted onto his bandaged face.

As the embalmers acquired experience, certain techniques gained prestige and the experts codified their practices in manuals that described each step of the work. The oldest such manuals date from the first century AD, but they are undoubtedly based on earlier texts. Initially, mummification was reserved for royalty, but gradually embalming became available to all who could afford it. By the time of Herodotus, in the fifth century BC, it had become a relatively common phenomenon. The Greek historian described a scene in an embalming parlour:

"When a corpse is carried in to [the embalmers], they show the bearers wooden models of mummies, painted in exact imitation of the real thing. The best method of embalming, so they say, is that which was practised on [the god Osiris]. The second method that they demonstrate is rather inferior and costs less. The third is cheapest of all. Having indicated the differences, they ask by which method the corpse is to be prepared. And when the bearers have agreed a price and departed, the embalmers, left behind in the workshop, set to work."

Despite such commercialism, embalming continued to hold mystic significance. Regardless of cost, the minimum length of time required to complete a mummification was seventy days. This period was not determined by practicalities: experiments have shown that the procedure had no benefit beyond forty days. There is biblical evidence in *Genesis* that Jacob was embalmed, probably because his son Joseph was a high official at the Egyptian court and because Jacob's body had to be returned to Canaan for burial. "Forty days were fulfilled for him, for so are fulfilled the days of those which are embalmed; and the Egyptians mourned for him for three score and ten days." The Egyptians clearly mourned until the seventy-day period was complete. The length of time necessary to mummify the corpse may have been dictated by the period when the rising Dog Star, Sirius, was temporarily hidden by its proximity to the sun. Sirius was of particular importance because its appearance heralded the annual flood.

The head of an anonymous mummy. Many mummified bodies have been found in a remarkable state of preservation some thousands of years after death.

The Ripper-out

In the most elaborate embalming rituals, the body was subjected to complicated procedures. For example, although it was possible to remove some internal organs via bodily orifices without making an incision, it was easier to open up the abdominal cavity. This operation was performed with a flint blade by the "ripper-out" or "slitter", as the Greeks graphically called the practitioner.

Amulets were often distributed among the bandages of a mummy to protect it during its voyage through the underworld. This glazed scarab amulet of *c.*1295BC depicts the sun god in his morning form as Khepri, flanked by the sisters Isis and Nephthys.

According to Greek sources, he was then ritually chased from the corpse – an act that possibly alluded to the role of Seth in the Osiris myth (see pages 50–58).

Protecting the Dead

The Egyptians' meticulous treatment of the body after death corresponded to their concern for the spirit, which also required a great deal of preparation before embarking on its journey through the underworld. During this voyage the *ba* was expected to encounter a variety of hazards, and so the living equipped the dead with many magical devices, such as protective amulets which were placed in the bandages surrounding the corpse. One of particular importance was the so-called *djed* pillar, an upright column topped by four cross-bars. Its origin remains uncertain, but *The Book of the Dead* refers to it as the backbone of Osiris, and it was intended to give the corpse stability in the afterlife. At various sites in Egypt the ceremony of "The Raising of the Djed Pillar" was performed during royal jubilee festivals and during rituals for the dead king.

There were other types of amulet, including the heart scarab, which alludes to the heart's role as the seat of all intelligence and the centre of personality. As such, the heart would be weighed during the judgement before Osiris, and, if it was found to be heavy with sin, the deceased would be condemned. To prevent the heart from confessing its sin, the heart scarab was placed over the chest among the mummy wrappings, and inscribed with Chapter 30 of *The Book of the Dead*: "Oh my heart which I had from my mother, Oh my heart which I had upon Earth, do not rise up against me as a witness in the presence of the Lord of Things." Additional amulets could be shaped as miniature gods and goddesses or parts of the body. The former were protective, while the latter acted as substitutes if, by misfortune, the embalming process should fail. Thus arrayed, and wrapped within its outer shroud, the body was ready for the coffin.

Coffins and Tombs

Laying the corpse to rest was accompanied by rituals no less elaborate than those of mummification. Around the time of the unification of the Two Lands (3100BC), coffins were generally made of mud, basketwork or wood, with the body (not embalmed at this period) doubled-up inside. Later the mummified corpse was usually laid out flat inside one or more wooden coffins, one within the other, both covered in spells and texts to assist the deceased in the afterlife. Sometimes the coffins were fashioned in human form, and were painted to resemble the deceased occupant and inscribed with further protective texts. The wealthy could also afford an extra layer, consisting of a stone sarcophagus (from a Greek word meaning "flesh-eating") within which the wooden coffins would be carefully placed.

Tombs can be seen as larger versions of coffins. The walls were painted with scenes of daily life alongside visions of the afterlife, spells to protect the deceased, and symbols of rebirth. Also contained within the tomb walls were funerary papyri, such as *The Book of the Dead* (see box, page 14), *The Book of Gates* and *The Book of Caverns,* which were also placed in the tomb to help the *ba* overcome the many difficulties ahead.

Inside the tomb was everything that the dead person might need: furniture, clothing, food, tools, boats (for the journey) and sometimes even toilet facilities. Also among the grave goods were personal items that the deceased had used or had been fond of when alive. Another important inclusion in the tomb was a statue or image of the departed. It was believed that the *ka* could inhabit this representation in order to enjoy the items

The Opening of the Mouth

This crucial tombside ceremony was designed to revitalize the deceased by restoring his or her senses so that the body could become animated once again in readiness for the afterlife.

The ceremony appears to derive from a rite originally performed on gods' statues so that they could partake in ritual. The Old Kingdom *Pyramid Texts* refer to the mummy of the king as being involved in a re-enactment of Horus restoring the body of his father Osiris. By the New Kingdom the ceremony was performed (with many different stages) at every funeral. The coffin was placed in front of the tomb and was then purified with water and incense. Different parts of the body were restored to life with incantations and ceremonial implements, including the *peshkef* knife, an iron *netjeri* blade and an adze. Then the right foreleg of a sacrificial ox was held to the deceased's mouth, possibly to transfer the animal's symbolic power to the corpse. Occasionally, the ceremony was performed not on the body but on its tomb statue, which was believed to be inhabited by the *ka*.

As described in *The Book of the Dead*, the Opening of the Mouth ceremony was performed with ritual instruments on the mummy, which was held up by a priest wearing the mask of Anubis, guardian of the necropolis.

left for it, and such a figure could also act as a substitute for the body if the mummy was destroyed. In Old Kingdom *mastaba* tombs, such statues were often placed inside buildings which today we call *serdabs* (the ancient term was *per tuwt*, meaning "statue house"). These were small rooms with holes at eye-level through which the *ka* of the deceased could see and magically absorb the beneficial offerings and observe the commemorative rituals performed on its behalf. Sometimes a stone portrait head (now known as a "reserve head") was also placed in the tomb.

The final earthly stage on the journey to eternity was the funeral itself. In a procession accompanied by a crowd of professional mourners, who pulled at their hair and smeared their faces with dust in traditional gestures of grief, the mummified body was taken to the tomb, with family, friends and servants carrying funerary goods and the deceased's belongings. The funeral was also attended by the embalmer and the funerary priests, and when the procession arrived at the tomb it was greeted by *muu* dancers in distinctive reed headdresses. If a pharaoh was being buried, it is likely that most of Egypt's populace turned out to mark the event.

The climax of the funeral came with a ceremony called "The Opening of the Mouth", in which the deceased's *ka* was reanimated by the funerary priest (see box, opposite). Then priests and retinue departed, leaving workers to fill the tomb entrance with rubble and coat it in plaster. The plaster on a king's tomb was impressed with an image of a recumbent jackal representing Anubis, guardian of the necropolis and god of embalming.

In basing their view of the afterlife so strongly on material considerations such as the condition of the corpse, the sustenance of the *ka* and the continuation of priestly rituals, the Egyptians left their spirits open to all the dangers of mortal existence. The scavenging jackal was one of these perils (as one later Egyptologist remarked, he only needed to follow jackal trails to find a grave). But while it was comparatively easy to protect the corpse against jackals, human scavengers constituted a

Rock-cut tombs near Qena in Upper Egypt. In order to protect a body from tomb-robbers, the entrance to a rock-cut tomb was often carefully concealed.

greater threat. Throughout Egypt's history, grave-robbing was rife. Despite all precautions, most graves were ransacked. In the Valley of the Kings on the west bank of the Nile, a practice was adopted of separating the tombs from the mortuary temples where priests conducted daily ceremonies ensuring the deceased's well-being in the afterlife. In this way, funerary rituals could take place without drawing attention to the whereabouts of the body. Nevertheless, a mortuary temple indicated that a tomb was in the vicinity, and mummies and funerary treasures were still violated. Even after the separation of the tomb from the temple site, the Valley of the Kings was patrolled by guards. But the pharaohs' graves were never entirely impenetrable – any disruption in political stability gave tomb-robbers ample opportunity to forcefully enter the burial chambers and pillage the funerary goods.

71

Journey into Darkness

When the spirit left the body, it was thought to wander the pathways and corridors of the underworld in search of the Hall of Judgement where Osiris sat on his throne. Throughout the journey, the soul used spells to overcome hostile beings such as serpents and demons.

After death, the Egyptians hoped to become one with Osiris, god of resurrection and the underworld. Through him alone could immortality be achieved. He was usually shown wrapped as a mummy clutching the emblems of kingship, the crook and flail, which indicated his original role as an earthly ruler and father of Horus, with whom all pharaohs were identified. Known as the "eternally incorruptible", he additionally acquired the epithet "foremost of the Westerners", a description originally applied to his predecessor as god of the dead, the jackal god Khentimentiu. First mentioned in the Fifth Dynasty (c.2500–2350BC), Osiris was an

This painted scene from inside the tomb of King Ramesses I (c.1292–c.1290BC) shows Re, in his ram-headed form as "Flesh of Re", on his journey through the Duat in the Boat of Millions. The deceased pharaoh was believed to join Re on this voyage. Other tomb paintings of this subject show the boat filled with crowds of figures believed to be the souls of the blessed.

important figure in the mythological tradition based in the cult centre of Heliopolis where Re was principal deity. There may have been rivalry between the two gods, who were both key figures in the underworld. However, a description of the couple embracing to become "Twin Souls"

Osiris, Lord of the Underworld

Osiris's main function was to rule the underworld, but he also acted as a god of fertility and agriculture. One of the most enduring deities, he was worshipped throughout Egypt as patron of the dead, lord of the necropolis and the guarantor of rebirth.

Osiris was of prime importance in Egyptian mythology. As a god of fertility, he was seen as the life-force behind all things.

Yet, at the same time, he was lord of the underworld, and this combination of aspects led him to be identified with resurrection. Osiris was reborn after he had been killed by Seth, who dismembered his body and scattered it across Egypt (see box, page 50). His resurrection was achieved with the help of his sister Isis, who reassembled his scattered limbs in the form of the first mummy so that his spirit could inhabit his body once again.

Osiris's main cult centre was Abydos, in Upper Egypt, where his head was thought to be interred. Some priests went so far as to claim that the tomb of the First Dynasty monarch Djer, who ruled *c.*2900BC, was in fact Osiris's burial place. But the god was also described as "he who dwells in Heliopolis", which was the cult centre of Re, thereby linking him with the sun god.

This statue of Osiris from the 26th Dynasty (664–525BC) shows his crown typically flanked by ostrich feathers and adorned with the *uraeus* (cobra) which symbolized the power of kingship. He also holds in his hands the crook and flail, two further insignia of sovereignty.

would suggest that this opposition was in due course resolved.

Osiris's role in mythology was complex: strongly associated with the living earth, he was also identified with death. So important was the union between the individual soul and Osiris that in funerary inscriptions the god's name became a prefix of the deceased's own name – thus X, when alive, became Osiris-X after death. Osiris was considered an equitable god, and it was thought that all who had been virtuous in life would be granted entry by him to the afterlife. But even the most virtuous conscience had to prove itself: while the body lay in the tomb, its *ba* had to undergo a series of arduous tests before achieving its ultimate aim – spiritual bliss in the hereafter.

The Duat

The Egyptians' vision of the afterlife was modelled on the land of the living. There was a river with sandy shores – directly analogous to the Nile –

which ran through a plain surrounded on all sides by mountains. A narrow gorge at the western end, through which the sun god entered at the end of the day and humans passed at the end of their lives, was the only feature that could not be found on Earth.

As a replica of Egypt, this underworld domain was in many ways familiar to every Egyptian, but for the newly arrived *ba* it held terrifying obstacles. The topography of the Duat included natural features such as lakes, deserts and islands but it also held hazards such as lakes of fire and a mound from which a head, called the flesh of Isis, emerged as the soul approached. The *ba's* way was also hindered by demons, with names such as "Backward-facing one who comes from the abyss". They tried to ensnare the *ba* with sticks, spears, bird-traps and nets, and the soul could protect itself only if it had knowledge of the demons' secret names. Funerary texts supplied maps of the underworld, together with all the spells necessary to overcome the hazards encountered there. These texts also described the fates lying in wait for those who were judged to be the enemies of Re – beheading, dismemberment, sacrificial burning or being boiled alive in a cauldron.

Like the sun god Re on his nightly voyage, the *ba* passed through the Duat until the moment

The jackal-headed god Anubis was responsible for weighing the heart of the deceased against the feather of truth, belonging to Ma'at (top right). The Devourer of the Condemned Dead waits hungrily for those hearts that are heavy with sin. This image is commonly found in *Book of the Dead* funerary scenes.

of rebirth finally arrived. Unlike Re, however, who negotiated all twelve hours of the night, the *ba* had to go no further than the Sixth Gate to discover its destiny. Here, Osiris sat on his throne in a hall of judgement flanked by the goddesses Isis and Nephthys. Before him, the heart of the deceased was weighed on scales against the feather of Ma'at, goddess of truth, divine order and justice. The scales were then checked by Anubis and the result recorded by Thoth. At the same time, the deceased declared that he or she was innocent of specific crimes, in a ritual called the "Negative Confession". These offences included treason, boastfulness and deceit, but mostly were of a civic nature, including crimes against the laws of property. The *ba* had to stand before a tribunal of forty-two assessor gods, and address each one by name. The Negative Confession provided the *ba* with total immunity: "nothing evil shall come into being against me ... in this Hall of Justice because I know the names of these gods who are in it".

If the balance of Osiris's scales should tip towards the heart, then the soul was heavy with sin and redemption was lost; if it should tip the other way, the soul was saved. Lurking ravenously beneath the scales was the monster Ammut, "Devourer of the Condemned Dead", who had the head of a dog or a crocodile, the forelegs of a lion and the hindquarters of a hippopotamus. Into the jaws of this monster the heart of the deceased was destined to fall if it was encumbered with wrongdoing.

Magic Texts

Various texts inside the tomb proffered spells and other safeguards to protect the deceased's soul against an unfavourable judgement and malevolent spirits in the Duat. Particularly effective were those spells inscribed on heart scarab amulets, which were believed to prevent the heart from testifying against its owner (see page 69). Similar safeguards could be found in the *Coffin Texts*, which contained advice on "How not to rot and not to do work in the kingdom of the dead."

Although the funerary texts were often quite precise in their directions for attaining immortality, they also presented more than one view of the soul's destination. In some interpretations the soul rose to the sky, although the texts differed on the exact destination. The Old Kingdom *Pyramid Texts*

placed the dead pharaoh among the circumpolar stars (that is, stars that turn in a circle around the North Pole), as well as describing him joining Re's entourage in the solar barque. Ultimately, they identified the dead king with Osiris himself. During the Middle Kingdom these divergent funerary beliefs became more widespread through the *Coffin Texts*. One of these, known as *The Book of Two Ways*, complicated the picture further by allocating a place for the spirit in the night sky among the attendants of Thoth, the moon god. This source also provided a map, with two alternative paths (possibly one of fire and one of water) to assist the deceased on his or her journey to the lands of Osiris. The idea of spending an eternity with Osiris, in his role as god of resurrection,

The soul of the dead had to undergo various trials and tests in the underworld. This priest from the 21st Dynasty (1075–945BC) is threatened by three demons who are armed with knives. The bound ass above the demons represents one of their previous victims, turned into animal form.

Servants of the Dead

In the earliest times pharaonic tombs were surrounded by pits containing the bodies of servants who were expected to serve their master in death as in life. Human attendants were later replaced by models, often inscribed with hieroglyphs.

Just as the pharaoh might ask his subjects to perform various labours, so might the gods ask the spirit of the deceased to work on their behalf. To avoid an afterlife of eternal servitude, Egyptians were buried with models representing attendants who would do work for them. Called *shabti*s, perhaps after the Egyptian word *wesheb* meaning "answer", these little figurines were expected to answer whatever demands were made on the soul with an eager "Here I am! I shall do it!"

Up to 401 *shabti*s could be buried in a tomb. This number included a servant for every day of the year, and thirty-six foremen to organize each group of ten workers. The *shabti*s were generally inscribed with the name of their owner and the sixth chapter of *The Book of the Dead,* which enabled the figures to accomplish their tasks. One surviving text refers to a noblewoman who actually paid the *shabti*s in advance. This action bound the *shabti*s contractually to her, and ensured that she herself would not have to work for the gods in the afterlife.

The use of these figurines began during the Middle Kingdom, and developed from the earlier use of funerary statues in the Old Kingdom. It was not until the Ptolemaic period that *shabti*s ceased to be popular.

This *shabti* and its model sarcophagus represented Huy, a royal steward and scribe of Amenhotep III. Only 6in high, he is shown holding amulets symbolizing *sa* (protection) and *djed* (stability).

became increasingly popular, and developed into the New Kingdom texts that we now call *The Book of the Dead*.

In the earliest of the *Pyramid Texts*, the deceased pharaoh was described as crossing to the eastern part of the sky to join the sun god: "The sky's reed floats are launched for Unas [the particular pharaoh to whom this text refers], that he may cross on them to light-land, to Re." To make this crossing, the deceased pharaoh had to summon the ferryman, called "Backwards Looker" because of the direction he faced during the passage: "Awake in peace, Backwards Looker ... Unas has come to you that you might ferry him in this boat in which you ferry the gods." However, the ferryman would only accept his royal passenger on the two conditions that he could show himself to be free of sin, and that he could say the ferryman's name and the names of each part of his boat.

On the far shore of what seems to have been envisaged as a vast celestial lake, heralds greeted the pharaoh and announced his arrival to the other gods. In a gesture of welcome and goodwill, accepting him as one of their own, the gods "cast off their white sandals to earth ... They throw off their garments. 'Our heart was not glad until thy coming,' they say."

Although some texts described the pharaoh in the afterlife as ruling a court, as he had done on Earth, or else sailing in Re's heavenly barque, he was sometimes imagined as merely taking on the

Beliefs as to the destiny of virtuous souls varied. This coffin from Thebes (*c.*650BC) shows the deceased seated opposite a priest. Between the two figures are some loaves shaped to allude to the Field of Reeds, where the dead enjoyed the afterlife in a land of fecundity.

role of Re's secretary, sealing his documents and dispatching his edicts. This view of the pharaoh's afterlife portrays him as greatly reduced in status from his omnipotent position as an earthly ruler. So it was at the time of Unas, as the text puts it bluntly: "King Unas does what Re tells King Unas."

The Field of Reeds

In one portrayal of the afterlife, the deceased inhabited an underworld that corresponded to Egypt. Known in some texts as the Field of Reeds, this region lay below the western horizon, and was presided over by Osiris. Here the dead could enjoy a world of astonishing fertility, and resume human activities such as eating and lovemaking, as promised in the *Coffin Texts*. However, as on Earth, these recreations could not be savoured until after the crops had been harvested and construction work completed. To release them from these chores, the dead were equipped with spells and diminutive model servants who would answer any call made on them (see box, opposite).

At the same time there was a more spiritual view of the afterlife, involving Osiris as a god of fertility. In this version, the soul was integrated with all living things to become the essence of life itself. "I am the plant of life," ran one spell in the *Coffin Texts*, "which allows the people to live, which makes the gods divine ... I live as corn, the life of the living ... the love of me is in the sky, on earth, on the water and in the fields."

77

Just as the crops appeared from the soil every year, so the souls of the dead were expected to rise again from the underworld kingdom, reabsorbed into nature. The imagery of growth was everywhere to be seen. Osiris himself was sometimes depicted with black or green skin, representing the fertile Egyptian soil and flourishing crops. Moreover, seed-beds shaped as Osiris were sometimes placed in tombs: filled with Nile earth and sown with barley, they were wrapped as mummies and placed beside the corpse. These symbolized the rebirth of the soul and Osiris's ultimate victory in defying death.

Offsetting this harmonious vision of natural recycling was a bleak alternative view of a gloomy underworld where the soul was trapped forever. Some texts described rows of mummified corpses sleeping in complete darkness, awakening only briefly each time the sun god passed overhead on his nightly journey.

Living with the Dead

Having reached the afterlife, the spirit did not necessarily forsake the earthly domain. An *akh* (see page 66) could be called upon to help humans in their day-to-day activities. State officials, who had held important positions while alive, were considered equally influential in the spirit world: people seeking favours laid offerings at their tombs and before their statues. The spirits of lesser mortals received letters from relatives begging for help with domestic problems.

Unfortunately, not all spirits were benign, and sometimes it was feared that they would return to Earth to torment the living. During the seventy-day period of mummification, the spirit's whereabouts was a cause for particular concern. Priests believed – not unscientifically – that corpses exuded an unhealthy discharge which could potentially endanger the living. They enlisted the help of post-mortem spells, such as the one for "making an *akh*" that was intended to hasten the dead on their journey to the afterlife. This ensured that the deceased's *ba* and *ka* were successfully united after a favourable judgement before the throne of

Osiris so that they became an *akh*. Thus the individual's soul could enjoy a state of eternal bliss from which his or her family were also likely to benefit. Other spells were designed to counter a truly dreadful possibility: that the spirit was determined to return to trouble the living.

The Mummy's Curse

To protect the mummy and tomb against potential violators, curses were included among funerary texts. These drew on the negative alternative to the *akh*, a damned soul that either refused or was unable to enter the afterlife. Known as the *mut*, its powers were formidable and caused nightmares, illness and even death. Spells were cast to counter its malign presence, and exorcism ceremonies were performed on any living persons believed to be possessed. During these, it was often discovered that the *mut* was restless because its tomb had fallen into disrepair or because it no longer received offerings.

The Egyptians sometimes called upon the *mut*'s powers to satisfy their own earthly purposes. Spells, typically involving two highly potent ingredients, grave dirt and the hair of a corpse, were used to deliver enemies into the domain of the malign spirits. Curses were buried in the tombs of people who had died a violent death in the hope that the *mut* would return to enforce them. The spirit's destructive capabilities were also enlisted to prevent tomb-robbing. Inscriptions warned that " ... all people ... who shall make a disturbance in this tomb ... will fall under the anger of Thoth". While this seems to have done little to deter thieves, it became a modern legend after the opening of the tomb of Tutankhamun. A number of people connected in some way with the dig died in tragic circumstances and the press hailed the deaths as being a result of the curse. But, a decade later, of the twenty-two who had actually witnessed the opening of the sarcophagus, only two had died, neither of whom had watched the mummy being unwrapped. If Tutankhamun's spirit had returned in anger, it was peculiarly selective.

Setne Khamwas and the Book of Magic

The dangers of interfering with the dead are highlighted by the story of Setne Khamwas. Based on the historical figure of Khamwas, a high priest of Ptah and the fourth son of Ramesses II, the tale was discovered on papyri dating from the third century BC.

The scholar Setne Khamwas plays draughts to win Thoth's book of magic.

Setne Khamwas, a learned scholar, was intrigued to hear about a book of magic that had been written by the god Thoth. He was assured that it was hidden in Prince Neferkaptah's tomb in the vast necropolis to the west of Memphis. Setne Khamwas determined at once that the book should be his.

He found the tomb and, with the help of his brother Inaros, forced it open. There, shining brightly, was the magic book, but when Setne Khamwas went to take it, he was confronted by the spirits of the dead Prince Neferkaptah, his wife Ihwey,

and their son Merib. Setne Khamwas tried to snatch the book from Neferkaptah, who stopped him. "If you want the book," he said, "you will have to play draughts for it." So they took out a board and began to play.

Setne Khamwas lost three games. After each victory, Neferkaptah hit his opponent over the head and drove him into the ground until, finally, only his head was above the soil. At this point Setne Khamwas sent his

brother to fetch his magic amulets and, by their power, he was able to break free and grab the book.

On his return to the outside world, he began to read avidly, ignoring all advice to return the book. Shortly afterwards, however, he saw a beautiful woman walking past his window and was smitten with desire. He begged her to make love to him. She said she would, but only on condition that he hand all his property over to her and kill his own children. Setne agreed, little knowing that the woman was a spirit called Tabubu and that he was under her spell.

Setne Khamwas had hardly had time to remove his clothes when Tabubu vanished, and the pharaoh entered the room. His embarrassment was relieved only by the news that it had all been a bad dream and his children were still alive. He determined to return the book to Neferkaptah's grave and relinquish ownership of it.

The dead prince greeted him with amusement but demanded a favour to atone for the theft. His request was that Setne Khamwas find the bodies of his wife and son and bring them to him. Setne Khamwas unearthed the bodies and returned them to Neferkaptah's tomb, which he then sealed, consigning the dangerous book to eternity.

THE TOMB OF TUTANKHAMUN

The discovery of Tutankhamun's tomb in the Valley of the Kings (opposite Thebes), by Howard Carter in 1922, represents the zenith of archaeological work by Egyptologists. News of the finding of the first-ever intact royal burial chamber caused an international sensation as the press reported tales of incomparable and mysterious riches from the tomb of the little-known boy-king, whose reign (*c*.1333–*c*.1323BC) lasted only ten years. Brimming with funerary equipment made from the finest materials, the small chamber was also decorated with depictions of the afterlife.

Above: Queen Ankhesenamun assists the young king during a royal bird hunt. From a panel on the right-hand side of a small gilded shrine, this tender scene evokes aspects of the couple's life together.

Left: Lions were revered by the Egyptians and deified as Bastet and Re (see pages 21 and 46–47). This protective lioness-head, made of gilded wood with eye markings of blue glass, is part of a funerary couch – one of three ritual couches found in the antechamber of Tutankhamun's tomb.

Above: The lavishly decorated golden mask of Tutankhamun is generally recognized as the greatest of Egypt's ancient treasures. It covered the head of the mummified pharaoh. Spell 151b from *The Book of the Dead*, engraved on the back of the mask, gave it an important protective function.

Right: The scarab beetle represented the sun god Re. This exquisite pectoral ornament, found in a jewel box in the tomb, bears signs that include the king's throne name.

Below left: The feet of Tutankhamun's throne take the form of lion claws and lion heads surmount its front legs to symbolize power. The backrest displays a royal scene beneath the sun disc.

Below right: This beautiful six-feet-high Canopic chest was carved from a single block of calcite (quartz). The goddesses Isis, Nephthys, Selkis and Neith embrace the four corners of the shrine. Beneath its lid are funerary jars.

ANCIENT MESOPOTAMIA

In 1616 an Italian called Pietro della Valle, a traveller through the old fertile river valleys of the Tigris and the Euphrates (Mesopotamia, meaning "between the rivers"), dug out a few mud bricks from a spoil-heap the local Arabs called Tell al Muqayyar ("the mound of pitch"). The bricks were marked with writing "in unknown characters" and the puzzle that they presented was revealed only slowly, after generations of scholarly work. It transpired that beneath the neglected mounds lay nothing less than evidence of the origins of civilization – once great cities, such as Babylon, Ur, Nineveh and Ashur, which are referred to in the Bible. By c.3300BC some of these cities were thriving and each was home to thousands of people: Sumerians, Akkadians, Assyrians, Hittites, Canaanites and others. Their tales had merely been hidden, waiting to be remembered again.

We now know that the Mesopotamian gods originated either as the personification of towns and cities or as elemental forces, and they were portrayed with a full range of human emotions and individual characteristics. The society of the gods was no different from that of humans, and many myths give a divine justification for those institutions crucial to the organization of Mesopotamian culture, such as the temple.

The senior Sumerian gods were headed by An, or Anu in Akkadian, a remote authority figure in control of kingship and the cosmic laws that determined individual destinies. A more complex god was Enlil (Ellil), a powerful and aggressive warrior who manifested himself in violent storms, but also fostered crop growth. Ninhursaga, the primary goddess, represented motherhood and was known by many other names according to her different functions. She often worked in partnership or rivalry with Enki (Ea), the divine craftsman of the gods, who solved problems not with force like a warrior, but with cleverness and cunning. Enki used his intelligence to bring the clay in Ninhursaga's hands to life, just as he aided the land by filling the irrigation canals with water (the Sumerian word for water also meant semen).

The kings of Mesopotamia's city states acted as agents of the gods. In the stories the deities have mortal qualities, in part because the life-force in humans was thought to be derived from the blood of a deity. Humankind was created to perform the drudgery of heavy labour on behalf of the gods, who regarded humans as their progeny, protecting and punishing them by turns.

Above: **A heraldic figure, associated with Enkidu, the companion of Gilgamesh, decorates this gold plaque made in Persia c.350BC.**

Opposite: **The hero in the centre of this Hittite carving has been identified as Gilgamesh. He is shown sheltering under a sacred symbol composed of a winged disc supported by a pair of bull-men.**

Divine Creators

The most complete and best known Mesopotamian creation myth is the Akkadian story named after its opening words, *Enuma elish*, "When on high ... ". Predominantly a work of propaganda promoting the god Marduk and his city of Babylon, the myth charts the development of the cosmos as if it were a political organization.

This statue of Marduk, great god of Babylon, dates from the second millennium BC. He was mighty in every way: he had exceptional powers of hearing and sight, and he breathed fire.

The *Enuma elish* may date from as early as 1900BC, but was probably composed in its present form in about 1100BC to celebrate the triumphal return of the statue of Marduk to Babylon after its humiliating capture by the Assyrians, who had held it for a century. The poem was recited each spring on the evening of the fourth day of the Akitu ceremony during the New Year festival.

According to the *Enuma elish,* when the skies above and the Earth below were unformed, only the primordial fresh waters – the god Apsu – and the salt waters – the goddess Tiamat – existed. These two waters came together and Tiamat gave birth to Lahmu and Lahamu. The world gradually took shape: Lahmu and Lahamu also coupled and produced Anshar and Kishar, the rims of the sky and the Earth which meet at the horizon. Anshar begat Anu, the heavens (An or "sky" in Sumerian), and Anu begat Ea (known in Sumerian as Enki), the cunning god who would later usurp Apsu and become the god of fresh water.

As the world became more complicated, these beings became progressively less passive and more active. Eventually tension and conflict arose between the inert ancient gods and the restless, striving younger gods, who were endowed with human qualities.

The young gods started to play and shout and disturb the tranquillity of Apsu and Tiamat, so Apsu proposed to exterminate them in order to re-establish silence. Tiamat responded angrily and shouted at her consort, "How could we allow what we ourselves created to perish?" Disregarding her protest, Apsu secretly plotted to kill the younger gods. But Ea, already displaying his nature as the cleverest of the deities, foiled his father: while his siblings panicked he recited a spell which sent Apsu into a deep sleep. Then he seized Apsu's crown and cloak of fiery rays and killed his father.

Having vanquished Apsu, Ea gained control of the deep underground ocean of fresh water which was likewise called the *apsu*. On top of this he established his own temple and dwelled there

The Mesopotamian Cosmos

In the Sumerian imagination the universe consisted of an (heaven) and ki (Earth), the latter envisaged as a rectangular field with four corners. Originally these were fused and inhabited by the gods alone, but at some stage they were separated, possibly to accommodate humankind. All around this universe, both above and below, was a boundless saltwater ocean.

Throughout ancient Mesopotamia, heaven and Earth were thought to have been formed by means of a cataclysm which churned up the primordial ocean. According to the Babylonian poem, *Enuma elish*, it was Marduk who accomplished this by splitting open the body of the sea goddess Tiamat (see pages 86–88). In another Sumerian tradition the goddess of the primordial ocean, called Nammu, spontaneously engendered a male sky and a female Earth. At first these two were inseparably joined, until they were parted by their own son Enlil, who then created animals, plants and humans.

But the *Enuma elish* also reveals elements of another widespread view that the cosmos contained several layers: the realm of Anu constituted an upper heaven, the realm of Enlil formed a lower heaven with the Earth beneath, and finally, below that, was the abyss or fresh-water ocean called *apsu*. Other versions of a layered cosmos put the realm of Anu on top, the realm of the Igigi gods (the Sumerian sky gods) below that, and the realm of the stars beneath, closest to Earth.

In addition, there was often said to be an underworld where the dead were thought to dwell, albeit in inferior conditions. This realm was reached by two flights of steps at the eastern and western horizons. It was thought that the sun passed through gates guarding the underworld each day as it rose and set, even though it was described as residing in the "interior" of heaven overnight. The gates to the underworld were securely barred; and, once inside, there was normally no return (see pages 100–105). The underworld was also said to be reached across a river sometimes referred to by the names of actual rivers beyond the furthest boundaries of Sumer. Thus the realm of the dead may have been conceived as some remote place on Earth.

A 7th-century BC clay tablet from Sippar shows a map of the world and the ocean surrounding it.

with his consort Damkina. Here they engendered the handsome and mighty Marduk, who was more splendid than any of his predecessors; he had four eyes and four ears which endowed him with exceptional powers of sight and hearing.

Marduk's grandfather Anu made the four winds as toys for the young god to play with. But their games raised storms on the surface of Tiamat, the sea, and disturbed the peace of the other gods. In their annoyance they began to taunt Tiamat for failing to avenge the death of her husband Apsu. Stung by their criticism, the goddess agreed to destroy the young Marduk. She created eleven dragons and other fearsome monsters and put them under the command of the god Qingu to whom she gave the Tablet of Destinies, which bestowed supreme power on its holder.

The First King

At the news of Tiamat's preparations, the gods panicked once again. As before, Ea made the first attempt to subdue Tiamat, but retired defeated. Then Anu tried, but retreated at the mere sight of the raging goddess, who was much more fearsome than Apsu had ever been. Finally the gods begged Ea's mighty son Marduk to save them.

Marduk agreed to fight Tiamat, but on condition that he was given absolute authority over his fellow gods. The younger gods gathered at a celebratory feast and, relaxed by drinking beer, readily agreed to Marduk's conditions. Thus the institution of kingship was established at a moment of emergency for the sake of collective security. Marduk was invested with the king's magical power of command: as the other gods told him, "From this day onward no one will go against your orders."

Decorated with the insignia of kingship and possessed of a fearsome arsenal of weapons, Marduk advanced to fight the enraged Tiamat. He commanded the four winds, which had provoked Tiamat in the first place, to stir her up even further. While Qingu and Tiamat's other helpers became distracted and confused, Marduk forced the winds in through Tiamat's open mouth, inflating her

The first ever king, Marduk, was a great warrior like the Babylonian king in this limestone relief (c.1100BC). To win the insignia of kingship, he battled with Tiamat, the ocean goddess.

belly. Then he shot an arrow into her distended body and split it open down the middle. Standing on her corpse, he bound her army with his net and seized the Tablet of Destinies from Qingu. This he fastened to his own breast.

With the defeat of Tiamat and the capture of the Tablet of Destinies, Marduk's takeover of the insignia and powers of kingship had reached completion. Now, having gained the status of both a god and a king, he embarked on an organized programme of action. According to Babylonian writers, the heroic struggle with the ocean goddess Tiamat was the first, essential step in the stages of establishing social order.

The Gods of Dunnu

In order to create and dominate the world, the gods resorted to incest and patricide, according to the Enuma elish. *These motifs recur in other Mesopotamian creation myths, as well as the mythologies of many other parts of the world, and they appear regularly in a Mesopotamian myth that explains the origin of the gods. A minor city called Dunnu provides a backdrop to this dramatic story.*

In the beginning, there was the Plough and the Earth; from their union they created the Sea. Soon after, the Cattle God and the eternal city of Dunnu came into being. The Cattle God then made love to his mother the Earth, killed his father the Plough and married his sister the Sea. The same pattern was repeated in the following generation: the Cattle God's son, the God of Flocks, likewise killed his father and married his mother the Sea. For generation after generation a series of male gods, some of them named after the flocks and herds which roamed the land, killed their fathers and married their sisters or mothers, who often represented features of the landscape such as a river, tree or meadow.

Although many details remain obscure, the story can be interpreted as representing the changes of the seasons during the year, each one "killing" or replacing the previous one. Eventually, however, the pattern altered dramatically: one of the gods, instead of killing his father so that he could take over his dominion and marry his

mother, merely imprisoned him. This happened at New Year, celebrated by the Babylonians during April, which might suggest that this song was recited at the New Year festival. But because the rest of the text is missing, the significance of this interruption in the cycle of patricides has been obscured.

This myth reinforces the general impression given by the *Enuma elish* that creation stories were often highly politicized and they served to glorify a particular city by giving it a pivotal role in

the story. In this version of creation, as each god is killed he is laid to rest in Dunnu, a city that was dearly loved by each dead god. As in the *Enuma elish*, the birth of the world is closely linked to the establishment of the most important social and political institution of all – the city.

The Cattle God kills his father, personified as a plough, so that he can couple with his mother. Later, he married his sister, the Sea.

A detail of a glazed mural, which decorated the gates surrounding the inner city of Babylon (*c*.604–561BC), depicts a hybrid creature or monster. Marduk transformed Tiamat's eleven monsters, created to do battle against him, into statues that decorated the temple over the primordial ocean.

Marduk contemplated Tiamat's body to see what he could make from it. He split her into two halves "like a dried fish", and made one half into the sky, and the other into the Earth. To emphasize his legitimacy as successor to Ea, Marduk built his own home, Esharra, in the heavens directly above his father Ea's dwelling on top of the *apsu*.

Turning his attention to the heavens, Marduk then established the constellations, instructed the moon in its monthly cycle, and made rainclouds from Tiamat's spittle. Next, he formed the Earth from the lower half of Tiamat's body. Then he made the rivers Tigris and Euphrates flow from her eyes and turned her breasts into mountains from which freshwater springs cascaded. As a memorial to his battle with her, he created statues from the corpses of Tiamat's eleven monsters and placed them at the entrance of Ea's temple.

The gods were delighted with Marduk's changes and willingly reaffirmed his title as king. Whereas they had originally conferred this title in an emergency, now they acknowledged his ability to bestow the benefits of stable government. Marduk commanded the gods to build a city which would be both a palace and a temple. This city was to be named Babylon. He also decided to make a new creature. "Let me put blood together, and make bones too," he declared. "Let me make a primeval savage, and call him Lullu, 'Man'. Let him bear the drudgery of the gods, so that they can relax at their leisure." So Marduk asked the assembled gods to name the one who had led Tiamat's revolt. They singled out the prisoner Qingu and he was punished by having his veins slit open. From Qingu's blood, following Marduk's ingenious instructions which were said to be beyond earthly understanding, Ea created humankind.

The creative phase of the story ends there, but the poem continues at length to praise Marduk and to strengthen his link with the city of Babylon and its institutions. Despite having created man to dig irrigation ditches, the gods finished the task of building the palace and temple of Babylon with their own hands. At the great feast which followed, they heaped praise upon the weapons with which Marduk had vanquished Tiamat and recited his fifty names, each of which described some aspect of Marduk's character, exploits or cult.

Enki, Creator of the World Order

*The **Enuma elish** explains how natural phenomena and social institutions on Earth came to be created and regulated. In an earlier Sumerian source, however, the story is different – everything is established by the god Enki, the clever craftsman who presided over life-giving fresh water. The god's praise is sung both by the author of the poem and in the voice of Enki himself as he celebrates his own might. The goddess Inana also makes a bid for power in the poem (see pages 96–98).*

Enki blessed the cities of Nippur, "the place where the gods are born", Ur, Meluhha (in the Indus Valley) and Dilmun (probably Bahrain, see page 90) with abundant crops, flocks, precious metals and success in war. Then he organized the sea, rivers, clouds and rain, turning the barren hills into fields and creating the rivers Tigris and Euphrates by filling their beds with a stream of his own semen. He made the sheep, cattle and crops multiply, and established the skills of building and weaving.

As Enki created each domain, he appointed a god to supervise it. But when he had finished, Inana came to him complaining that he had failed to give her a domain. She described the realms of Nintu the womb-goddess, Nidaba the goddess of surveying, and Nanshe the goddess of the fisheries, and asked plaintively, "As for me, the holy Inana, what is my domain?"

Enki responded by listing the numerous powers and dominions which Inana did indeed have, adding each time, "Young Inana, what more could we add for you?" Unfortunately these lines are fragmented and very hard to interpret, but it has been suggested that he reminded her of her dominion not only of the shepherd's crook and staff, but of the bloody business of battle, and certain kinds of cloth and musical instruments that were linked to war, death and funeral rites as well. Enki concluded that Inana's domain was substantial and extremely powerful, and he finally told her, "Inana, you have the power to destroy what cannot be destroyed, and to set up what cannot be set up."

Enki arranges all the waters of the Earth and turns the barren hills into fields, before creating rivers and cattle.

Enki and the Island of Dilmun

Enki's ability to nurture living creatures and plants with life-giving fresh water (associated with his semen) was a gift that made him a useful ally for other gods and humans alike. His virility is central to a myth set on the once barren island of Dilmun, which some scholars identify as what is now Bahrain.

Enki slept with the patron goddess of Dilmun, an island described as lacking almost everything – people, animals and fresh water were all absent. So Enki formed a plan: he asked the sun god Utu to make footprints on the ground, so that he could fill them with fresh water transported underground all the way from Ur. The water made agriculture possible and Dilmun became a great centre of foreign trade in luxury goods such as precious stones, rare woods and copper gongs.

In a series of incestuous unions, Enki fathered a number of gods and goddesses. In the first stage of his creation he begged the goddess Ninhursaga to let him sleep with her. She agreed to his request and he poured his semen into her womb so that she conceived. Within nine days of this union she had given birth to the goddess Ninsar.

Enki (centre, right), the cunning god who provided the Earth with fresh water, participates in a New Year ritual. From an Akkadian cylinder seal impression, c.2400–2200BC.

Ninsar grew up and, as her mother had done, visited the riverbank. Enki looked up at her from his domain in the water and desired to possess her. He asked his minister Isimu, who was always at his side, "Shall I not kiss this beautiful young girl called Ninsar?" With the encouragement of Isimu, Enki kissed Ninsar and poured his semen into her womb. Once again after only nine days, Ninsar gave birth to a daughter, this time called Ninkurra, Mistress of the Mountains. In the same way, when she came of age, Enki impregnated Ninkurra. After her came another daughter Ninimma, Lady Vulva. She too had intercourse with Enki.

Ninimma in her turn gave birth to Uttu, considered even more beautiful than any woman from the previous generations. Uttu's great-grandmother Ninhursaga warned her not to yield to Enki's advances unless he brought her the fruits of irrigated gardening such as cucumbers, apples and grapes. When Uttu did as she was told and resisted Enki, the god hastened to a gardener whose work had been frustrated by drought. Enki filled up the nearby irrigation canals and in gratitude the gardener gave him the fruits he needed.

When Enki presented the gifts to Uttu she let him make love to her. As he poured his semen on to her body, she cried out, and, in a passage which is hard to decipher, it seems that Ninhursaga heard the cry and rushed to her great-granddaughter's aid. She quickly wiped Enki's semen from Uttu's body and planted it in the ground nearby.

This time, instead of creating a daughter, Enki's semen sprouted into eight different kinds of plant. Now when Enki looked up from the river he saw not a beautiful girl, but these unusual new crops. Since he did not realize that they were his own offspring, and fuelled by his curiosity, Enki asked his minister Isimu to harvest these oddities for him so that he could discover their nature. Isimu did as he was told, and gave the plants to his master, who decided to eat them.

Enki grew sick and, for reasons which the text does not make clear, Ninhursaga swore that she would no longer be associated with him. The other gods sat down in the dust in despair, until a clever fox, carefully dressed for the occasion, managed to persuade the goddess to return. She had sex with Enki whose illness had spread to specific parts of his body. Ninhursaga was able to cure him by giving birth to eight deities whose names corresponded to his afflicted body parts. Among the eight deities were the lords of Dilmun and Magan (now Oman in Arabia).

Thus the myth resolves the horror of repeated incestuous rape and the constant threat of Enki's unbridled desire and sexuality. However, with the assistance of the benign mother Ninhursaga, Enki is saved from severe illness and eight deities are born who are favourable to humankind.

Vital Water

Enki's domain was the apsu, an ocean of fresh water which was believed to lie deep beneath the ground. It was vital to existence on Earth.

Civilization in Mesopotamia depended on an elaborate and extensive systems of canals, created to irrigate the land between the Tigris and the Euphrates rivers. Regular spring floods washed away the boundaries of fields and necessitated the development of a more sophisticated system of surveying. To dig and maintain these canals required a centralized authority to organize and control mass labour.

The development of kingship, law and writing was thus closely linked to the regulation of the water supply, which was policed by a special canal inspectorate. It was said that whoever controlled the canals controlled the land, and cities often went to war over access to water.

Verdure cloaks the Island of Ana in the river Euphrates, a source of water for Mesopotamian civilizations.

The Suffering of Humanity

A number of imperfections were introduced to the world as a result of a creature-making contest involving Enki, the divine craftsman, and Ninmah (another name for the mother goddess Ninhursaga), whose skills were inadequate for the challenge – leaving humanity to suffer the consequences. The original text commends Enki, who found roles for the handicapped people, and concludes with the words, "O Father Enki, your praise is sweet!"

Creation was seen, above all, as an act of skilled craftsmanship, the master of which was Enki. In the old days, the gods were forced to work hard excavating irrigation canals – the senior gods did the digging while the younger gods carried away baskets of earth. They all complained bitterly about their circumstances. But the only god able to alter their fate was the wise and resourceful Enki, and he was deep in sleep in his watery domain. So Nammu, the mother of all the gods, went in search

of him and roused him so that he might fashion a substitute to undertake the arduous task. Enki, "the creator of forms", was deep in thought for a while and then said to Nammu, "Mother, you yourself can knead such a thing from the clay which lies above the *apsu*. Let the goddess Ninmah assist you." And so it came about, while Nammu decreed the fate of each human being, Ninmah's task was simply to command the individual, after creation, to carry baskets of earth.

After the task had been completed, Enki held a feast to celebrate the new-found leisure of the gods, who praised him for his accomplishment, saying, "Oh lord of wide understanding, who is wise like you? Who can equal your actions?" As the feast progressed, Enki and Ninmah overindulged and drank too much beer so that they became intoxicated. Belligerently, Ninmah said to Enki, "I could make humans by myself and give them a good or bad fate, as I please." Enki replied, "Whatever kind of human you create, I can turn to advantage the fate you bestow on it."

Ninmah set about making her first human. Perhaps deliberately to challenge Enki, perhaps because she had only been Nammu's assistant and had limited skill, she produced creatures with physical handicaps. Yet despite their problems, Enki was able to find a useful role for each of them. When Ninmah made a man unable to stretch out his hands and grasp things, Enki made him a servant of the king because he would not be able to steal. The second man she made was blind, but Enki gave him the gift of musicianship so that he too could serve the king. Translators have not

The figures incised on this Uruk Period (*c*.4000–3000BC) alabaster vase, found in modern-day Iraq, present offerings to the gods who created the world.

A detail from the Standard of Ur (*c.*2600–2400BC), which once decorated a royal cemetery, depicts court servants and musicians. The handicapped people made by Ninmah were given such roles by Enki.

been able to decipher the nature of Ninmah's third creature, but her fourth was a man who could not hold his semen. Enki was able to cure him by giving him a purifying bath. Ninmah's fifth creature was a barren woman, but Enki turned this to her advantage by placing her in a harem. The sixth and final creature, a sexless being, was also appointed as an attendant to the king. Enki concluded "I have found a role and given bread to every misformed creature of yours."

Having outdone Ninmah, Enki had to challenge her in turn, and it seems that he deliberately procured unfortunate beings in order to test her abilities. His first creature was a woman who was having difficulty in giving birth. Ninmah's powers

proved insufficient to reverse her fate. His second being was an *umul*, or very old man whose heart, bowels and lungs were so afflicted that he could not answer Ninmah's questions. Frustrated, Ninmah complained that he was neither alive nor dead – she could do nothing to improve his deteriorating condition.

While Enki had managed to provide Ninmah's malformed creations with positive roles that were recognized within the community, Ninmah proved unable to do the same for Enki's creations, so their disabilities remained a problem for Mesopotamian society. The vagaries of creation had come into being as a result of Enki's drunken gambling with the ambitious Ninmah.

93

How the Moon was Saved

In one myth Enlil, as the god of spring rainstorms, married the goddess of the young corn, Ninlil ("Lady of the Wind"), and they produced a son Suen (Sin or Nanna-Suen), the moon, known as "the Bright Lone Divine Traveller". Unfortunately, once born, the moon was destined to stay in the underworld forever – unless his parents could appease its gods. Enlil devised a cunning solution that allowed his son to travel through the sky at night.

The first encounter between Enlil and Ninlil is reminiscent of the story of Enki and Uttu (see page 91). Ninlil's mother warned her young daughter not to bathe in the Nunbirdu canal because Enlil might seduce her and make her pregnant. But Ninlil disobeyed, and Enlil, delighted by the sight of her naked body, did indeed proposition her from the opposite bank. For a while Ninlil

refused him, saying that she was too young, her lips were unused to kissing and that her parents would be angry. She also argued that she would find it difficult to keep the romance secret from her girlfriend.

Unwilling to accept her rejection, Enlil ordered his servant to make him a boat so that he could cross the river and join her. By the time he reached the opposite bank, Ninlil had already changed her mind and agreed willingly to his advances. The couple made love and she became pregnant with the moon god Suen. But when Enlil returned to the city of Nippur – where he was considered a chief of the gods – he was falsely accused of raping Ninlil and arrested. Branded a sex offender by the fifty great gods and the seven decision-makers, he was banished from the city. To fulfil his sentence, Enlil had to go on a long journey which took him as far as the river leading into the underworld. So Ninlil, who did not want to be separated from her beloved, set out in pursuit. As he passed out through the city gate, Enlil said to the keeper of the gate, "Ninlil is following close behind me. If she asks you where I have gone, do not tell her."

A boundary stone, or *kudurru*, typical of the Babylonian Kassite Period (*c.*1415–1154BC). It depicts, in bas-relief, King Melishipak II presenting his daughter to the moon god Suen, son of Enlil.

In Praise of Enlil

In eulogies to Enlil his great powers in the realms of agriculture, fertility and civil organization were praised.

Enlil encouraged humans, cattle, fish and crops to multiply. The text which recounts the story of his relationship with Ninlil ends: "You are the lord! You are a great lord, a lord of the granary! You are the lord who makes the barley sprout! You are the lord who makes the vines sprout!"

Enlil's managerial role extended to the sanctioning of social institutions. Another hymn to him proclaims: "Without

Enlil's warrant, no city could be built and settled, no cattle-pen or sheepfold could be constructed, no king or lord appointed, no high priest or priestess picked out by a divine sign."

As the god of fresh water, Enlil's favour had to be won by all farmers to ensure a good harvest. This farmer, depicted on an Akkadian cylinder seal (*c*.2200BC), uses a plough drawn by an ox.

Substitutes for the Moon

When Ninlil reached the gate and asked the gatekeeper about Enlil's whereabouts, the gatekeeper replied, "I have never had the privilege of chatting with Enlil." Ninlil proudly told him that Enlil had made her pregnant and that she was carrying the precious moon in her womb.

Somehow, the gatekeeper knew that the unborn moon had to be saved from an eternity stuck in the underworld and offered to impregnate the goddess with another child, saying, "May the sperm which will become the moon go heavenwards, and may my own progeny go to the underworld as his substitute."

Ninlil agreed and lay with the man in the gatekeeper's chamber. Little did she know that Enlil had disguised himself and exchanged places with the gatekeeper. In this way, she conceived a second son by Enlil called Nergal, who was indeed destined to remain in the underworld forever and reign there as king (see pages 104–105).

Enlil continued on his journey, and again Ninlil followed close behind. Eventually, Enlil reached the mountain river that led down into the underworld. As before, he told the guardian of the river not to reveal to Ninlil where he had gone. Not long afterwards, Ninlil arrived at the river. She asked its guardian where Enlil was and received the same negative reply as before at the city gate. Again, she announced that she was bearing the moon in her womb and the guardian offered to impregnate her with a second substitute, who would also remain down in the underworld.

Again, the man she lay with was Enlil in disguise, and she conceived the underworld god called Ninazu. At the third and final stopping point in the journey, Enlil disguised himself again. Ninlil, thinking that she was coupling with the ferryman of the underworld, conceived Enbilulu, who became a god of the underworld river. In this way the moon was saved for the upper world by the creation of three substitutes.

95

Lady of Heaven

Inana is the most complex of all the Mesopotamian goddesses. Her name is Sumerian and probably means "Lady of Heaven", while her name in Akkadian, Ishtar, is related to that of the Syrian goddess Astarte. Inana was variously said to be the daughter of An, Enlil or even Enki. In the myths of the death of her lover Dumuzi (see page 103), Inana is the daughter of the moon god Suen and sister of the sun god Utu. Her elder sister is Ereshkigal, queen of the underworld, and an intense jealousy rages between the two of them.

Inana's principal shrine was in the great city of Uruk, although it is likely that local goddesses in other places were also assimilated into her cult over time. This may explain why Inana combines several different roles which seem incompatible.

As Lady of Heaven, Inana was identified with the planet Venus, whose disappearance and reappearance in the night sky may be reflected in the myth of the goddess's descent to and return from the underworld (see pages 100–103).

Inana is also sometimes portrayed as keeper of the cosmic laws, or *me*, which, in one myth, she obtained from her father Enki (see box, opposite). Her constant quest for greater powers led her to try to take control of her sister's realm of the dead. This lust for power may have complemented her role as a goddess of war, in which she is described as enjoying battle as if it were a game or a dance. She is portrayed in Mesopotamian art as a heavily armed warrior.

A relief from Tell Asmar shows Ishtar (Inana), standing on her sacred lion. This 8th-century BC Babylonian artefact depicts the goddess as a powerful warrior.

Yet Inana is perhaps best known as the goddess of amorous liaisons and sexual love. In the Gilgamesh epic (see pages 116–133), Inana is reproached for her maltreatment of a series of lovers, and the hero himself turns her down. More tragically, her passionate affair with the shepherd god Dumuzi ends with his death and the goddess's grief.

Inana was also the protectress of prostitutes. In this aspect, one of her most important jobs was to couple once a year with the real-life king. This union may have been performed ritually by the living king with a temple prostitute, who stood in for the goddess.

The combination of all these aspects creates a fully rounded character who is headstrong, ruthless and dangerously seductive to men. Whether she appears as a virgin or as sexually promiscuous, Inana is always portrayed as a young woman free of the usual responsibilities of a wife and a mother.

The Importance of the *Me*

The me *(pronounced "may") were the unwritten fundamental laws of the universe. They formed the basis of society and ensured that the cosmos could function.*

The most comprehensive surviving list of *me* gives around 100 powers, not all of which are easily translated. These constituted offices and roles, such as kingship, priestship, godship, eldership, and occupations, including scribe, shepherd, blacksmith and leatherworker. Others included important human actions, qualities of character, moral values and emotions. Law, music and art feature, as do enmity, judgement, wisdom, truth, falsehood, sexual intercourse, prostitution, the destruction of cities, lamentation and rejoicing.

These properties were considered to be the basic components of action and consciousness that dictate human existence. Some were thought to reside in material objects, such as drums which contained rhythm, or thrones, which embodied kingship.

To possess the *me* was immensely empowering but also entailed great responsibility. Generally, they were said to be conferred by the senior male gods An or Enlil, but in one tradition they were handed to Enki for safekeeping in his temple at Eridu. They could also be transferred from one god to another if a task had to be delegated. Like the Tablet of Destinies (see pages 86 and 107) they could be stolen.

Inana, who on one occasion complained that she did not have enough power (see box, page 89), contrived to take the *me* from her father Enki, who resided at Eridu, to her own patron city, Uruk. Inana visited

Enki, who received her with hospitality and generous amounts of beer. As they sat together drinking, Enki became more and more intoxicated and offered the *me* to Inana, instructing his minister to hand them over to her one by one. When she had gathered them all, Inana loaded them onto her barge and cast off for Uruk.

The effect of the beer wore off and Enki realized that the *me* were missing. He questioned his minister, who told him that he himself had just given them all away. In consternation, Enki sent his official in pursuit of Inana to demand their return.

Six times his minister caught up with the goddess at halting points on her route home, and each time various creatures from Enki's subaquatic realm challenged her and tried to regain the *me*. First, a little frog was dispatched, then other animals followed in its wake. Unperturbed, Inana pointed out that Enki had given her the powers under oath.

Finally, having kept her cargo intact, the goddess reached her own city of Uruk in triumph and unloaded the *me*.

The title of scribe is one of many offices incorporated in the Sumerian *me*. On this neo-Hittite stele, the scribe Tahunpigas is represented as a child on his mother's knee.

The Vengeance of Inana

In one myth, Inana is presented in her role as custodian of the *me*, or cosmic laws, when she is raped by Shu-kale-tuda, a mere gardener's boy. The story suggests that in daring to violate the goddess, Shu-kale-tuda also failed to respect the *me* and put his whole nation under threat. Her wrath was not to be taken lightly, as the killers of Dumuzi also discovered.

One day Inana ascended the mountains so that she could view the land of Sumer, to search out falsehood and injustice and distinguish criminals from righteous people. This process is described as "allowing the *me* to display their perfection".

Eventually, wearied by her inspection of heaven and Earth, the goddess lay down to rest in the deep shade of a poplar tree. She carried the *me* in the form of seven holy tablets, which she had tied tightly across her lap. Catching sight of her from his vegetable garden nearby, Shu-kale-tuda approached Inana and lay down beside her.

He then removed the tablets and raped her while she was asleep. Before dawn, he returned with the tablets to the garden.

Inana awoke, realized what had happened and determined to find the culprit wherever he might be hiding. But, in her anger, she also punished the land of Sumer three times over. First, she turned the water in all the wells into blood and the people could find nothing that they could drink. Shu-kale-tuda understood from this sign that he was in trouble and confessed his crime to his father, who advised him to join his brothers in the city, where he would escape detection among the crowd. Although Inana searched for him high and low, she failed to find him, so she punished Sumer once more, this time with floods and dust storms. Shu-kale-tuda continued to avoid detection by hiding in the city. Her anger mounting, Inana punished the land for a third time, in a way which cannot be deciphered in the text, but once again, the guilty Shu-kale-tuda evaded her.

Finally, Inana turned for help to her father Enki at Eridu. Somehow, Enki was able to help her isolate Shu-kale-tuda from the crowd, rendering him small and helpless. Cornered at last, the malefactor confessed his guilt and Inana pronounced judgement on him. "You must die," she said, "but, nevertheless, your name will live on in a song which will be sung throughout the land, from the king's glorious palace to the remotest and humblest shepherd's camp."

The goddess Inana sleeps with the holy tablets of the *me*, or cosmic laws, strapped across her lap. But they will not protect her from the sexual predations of Shu-kale-tuda.

The Goddess and the Bandit Woman

Retribution is also to the fore in several versions of the myth of the death of Inana's lover, the shepherd Dumuzi (see page 103). In one story, rather than handing him over to his would-be murderers, Inana takes vengeance on the old bandit woman Bilulu and her son, who had killed him in order to steal his herd. Like many poems about Dumuzi, the story opens with a lamentation for his demise.

When Inana was told that Dumuzi was dead she burst out weeping at the loss of her lover. "Dumuzi, with your fair mouth and kind eyes! Oh, my boy, my husband, my provider, sweet as the date!"

Summoning up sufficient courage, she asked her mother's permission to go to the sheepfold where he had been horribly killed. As she approached the fateful spot, she remembered the terrible details of how Dumuzi had been found with his head badly beaten. She was even further incensed at the thought of his sheep and cattle being herded away by the bandits who had stolen them.

Again, Inana sang a lament, praising Dumuzi's tireless work. As she sang, she felt her heart swell with a great desire to avenge her lover. And so, while the old bandit woman Bilulu and her gang were counting their ill-gotten gains, Inana determined to kill them so that her beloved could rest in peace.

She discovered them in a beer-house, stole up to them and ruthlessly killed them. To make the punishment fit the crime, she also cursed Bilulu and transformed her into a waterskin so that shepherds like Dumuzi could use her to quench their thirst in the desert heat. "Let the old woman gladden his heart!" she declared grimly. She also transformed Bilulu's son into a desert spirit whose job would be to call Dumuzi to receive libations of water and flour whenever humans placed and poured these offerings upon the ground. In this way Dumuzi's spirit was returned to the desert, "the place from which he had vanished".

Unlike some other versions of the death of Dumuzi, there is no mention in this story of his subsequent resurrection each year as part of the seasonal cycle, although his presence in the desert to receive offerings could be interpreted as such.

This version concludes with Inana joining Dumuzi's sister Geshtin-ana (who, in the account of Dumuzi's prophecy of death, interprets the disturbing dream he has had and does everything possible to hide his whereabouts from the *gallas* – see box, page 102). Together the young women lamented the death of the young man that they had both loved.

Above: A ritual bowl (*c.*300BC) from Uruk is decorated with domesticated herd animals. Inana's lover, Dumuzi, was the deity of shepherds and the account of his death at the hands of bandits is suggestive both of the threat of criminal marauders and of occasional social tensions between nomadic herders, represented by Dumuzi, and settled farmers. Also, while crops depended on water and irrigation, herding relied on successful mating and helps to explain the sexual ritual of Dumuzi's cult.

A Descent into the Underworld

Inana's impulsive and assertive character is depicted to the full in an early Sumerian version of a myth in which she ventures to the underworld only to be unexpectedly humbled by her elder sister Ereshkigal. Like the story of the descent of Nergal to the underworld (see pages 104–105), which has survived in two versions (both written in Akkadian), this tale confirms that no one can return from the netherworld without cost.

One day, the goddess Inana decided to descend to the underworld. She dressed confidently in all her finery and took with her the seven tablets of the *me*. But as a precaution she left instructions with her maidservant Ninshubur: "If I do not return within three days, you are to beat the funeral drum and cry a lament for my death. Go to Enlil for help. If Enlil will not help, go to Nanna. If Nanna will not help, go to Enki, the one who knows the herbs and water that bring the dead back to life."

Having left these instructions, Inana set out and was soon hammering at the gates of the underworld to be given entry. When Ereshkigal's minister Namtar enquired of her business, she made the excuse that she had come for the funeral of her sister's husband Gugal-ana. Namtar passed her message on to Ereshkigal, who was greatly disturbed. Biting her lip, she told him, "Let her in, but mind you bolt each of the seven gates tightly as she passes along the road of no return."

As Inana proceeded through each of the first six gates, she was gradually stripped of her items of jewellery from the upper world. She was shocked by this, but Namtar told her that this was in accordance with the *me* of the underworld, which were different to those of Earth. At the seventh and last gate, her dress was removed and Inana stood naked before Ereshkigal.

Inana was forced gradually to remove all her ornaments
as she passed through the seven gates of the
underworld. This beautiful necklace from Sumer
dates from *c.*2600–2400BC.

The demon Pazuzu was commonly depicted with a canine face and scaled body. Although he was regarded as an underworld monster, women wore representations of him on chains around their necks to protect their children from death.

Ereshkigal descended from her throne and Inana rushed forwards and sat there in her place. Her impetuous attempt at seizing power, however, was short-lived. The seven judges of the underworld looked upon her with the perishing stare of death and she was turned into a corpse and hung on a hook.

Meanwhile, in the upper world, Inana's servant Ninshubur prepared to carry out her instructions. She journeyed to Enlil's temple in Nippur to plead with him to rescue her mistress, but the great god flew into a rage, shouting, "Inana was not satisfied with dominion in the upper world but craved power in the lower world too! Having accepted the *me* of the underworld, she must remain there!"

Unperturbed, Ninshubur then went to the temple of Nanna in Ur, but here also she was denied help. Finally, she made her way to Enki's temple in Eridu. Enki complained that he was tired of Inana's foolish escapades, but nevertheless agreed to rescue her. He scraped some dirt from his fingernails and created two sexless creatures who were able to enter the underworld and return with impunity. Enki gave them the life-giving plant and restorative water, and specific instructions for their journey: "Steal into the underworld, passing like flies through the gaps by the hinges of the gates. There you will find Ereshkigal in labour. As she cries out in pain you must echo her cries. She will appreciate your sympathy and will offer you anything you wish as a reward. But even if she offers you a whole river to drink and a field of corn to eat, you must not accept them. Ask only for the corpse of Inana."

The sexless creatures carried out their instructions with precision and everything happened as Enki had predicted: Inana's corpse was revived with the life-giving plant and water, and the three of them set off back to the upper world. It seemed that Enki's plan was succeeding, but just before the refugees reached safety, the seven judges of the underworld caught up with Inana and seized her, saying, "Who has ever risen from the underworld alive?" They insisted that if she was to escape, she must provide a substitute to take her place in the realm of death. To ensure that she did so, they sent an escort of demon guards (*galla*) to accompany her to the land of the living.

The first person that they met on Earth was Ninshubur herself, clothed in rags of mourning and thrashing in the dust. Inana could not bring herself to condemn her faithful servant to a life in the underworld, and so they went on to seek another substitute. They met Shara, the god of the city of Umma, who was also in mourning. Inana was unwilling to consign him to death, as he was her singer, hairdresser and manicurist. Then, under

101

Demons of Death

Some Mesopotamian demons were created by the gods as weapons of war, but the gallas of the underworld (humorously named after real-life officers of the law similar to modern-day constables) were sent to arrest those destined to die.

The pitiless nature of the *galla*s is emphasized by their lack of normal human needs and emotions. They did not enjoy food or drink, nor did they indulge in the pleasure of sexual intercourse, and they never experienced the joy of playing with children. Instead, they snatched children from their parents' knees, and stole young brides from their marriage chambers.

In an account of the shepherd

Dumuzi's death, he has a terrifying dream that foretells his own demise whereupon he is ruthlessly tracked down like quarry by the *galla*s, despite his sister's best efforts to protect him.

Given their resemblance to hunters, it may be significant that

Dumuzi tries to elude the *galla*s by having Utu transform him into a gazelle. But at the climax, the way in which they destroy his sheepfold suggests that the *galla*s were also modelled on the bandits who presented a real threat to Mesopotamian society.

Some demons had beneficial powers: the winged monster in this 9th-century BC Assyrian relief is gripping a symbol of purification.

the great apple tree in the plain of Kulaba, they came upon Inana's lover, the shepherd god Dumuzi. But far from mourning for Inana, Dumuzi was sitting on a magnificent throne, clothed in glorious raiment. Inana was incensed and agreed to his capture. As the demons seized him and spilled the milk from his churns on to the ground, Inana looked upon him with the very same look of death to which she had been subjected by the seven judges of the underworld.

Dumuzi turned pale and appealed to Inana's brother, the sun god Utu, to transform him into a snake so that he could wriggle out of the demons' grasp. It seems that Utu answered Dumuzi's prayer. The metamorphosis, however, lasted only half the year. It also seems that Inana regretted handing Dumuzi over to the demons, and agreed that his sister Geshtin-ana should remain in the underworld for half the year, as his substitute.

Ishtar and her Sister

In the shorter, Akkadian, version of this story, Inana is called Ishtar. As in the earlier Sumerian version, her motive for descending to the underworld seems to have been a wilful desire to take over her sister's realm. Her behaviour at the gate was similarly aggressive, and she added a chilling threat: "If you do not open the gate I shall smash it down and release the dead into the upper world, so that they outnumber the living!" This version describes Ereshkigal's fear of her younger sister: "Her face grew livid as cut tamarisk, her lips grew dark as the rim of a black-lipped cooking vessel." The text also makes it clear that Ereshkigal was tricked against her will into handing over her sister to the rescuers from the upper world.

As in the Sumerian version, Ishtar passed through each of the seven gates and was progressively stripped, until finally at the seventh gate her dress itself was removed. Once again, she was told by the gatekeeper that this was the custom of the underworld. Ereshkigal then sent sixty diseases to attack her sister's naked body and hung her on a hook, not as a corpse, but as a waterskin.

Meanwhile back on Earth, preparations were being made to orchestrate Ishtar's rescue. In this version the gods were forced to act by a curse of sterility that fell upon the world of the living. Without Ishtar's presence, procreation ceased among both animals and humans. In this version, too, it is Ea (Enki) who contrived her rescue: he created a pretty young man and sent him down to Ereshkigal's realm to lighten her mood. He succeeded and when the time came to name his reward, he asked for the waterskin which represented the remains of Ishtar. When she heard this, Ereshkigal said, "You have asked me for something that you should not have!" She cursed the young man to a life of poverty and squalor, but nonetheless was forced to release Ishtar who returned through each of the seven gates, with her belongings restored to her.

There is no mention in this story of the seven judges and their guards, nor of Dumuzi's transformation into a snake. Instead, the role of Dumuzi as a substitute is not debated, and instructions are given for his funeral rites. It is possible that these instructions related to a ritual held annually at Nineveh in the month named after Dumuzi, part July and part August, during which a statue of the shepherd was laid out for burial. Dumuzi's sister Belili (equivalent to Geshtin-ana) lamented his death, and declared that Dumuzi's return from his half-yearly stay in the underworld would be the occasion for a burial rite.

During her passage through the seven gates of the underworld, Ishtar was requested to remove her jewellery and clothing. This Akkadian figurine from the Agade Period (c.2400BC) shows her with a minimum of clothing.

103

The Marriage of Nergal and Ereshkigal

How Nergal came to rule with Ereshkigal is told in two myths that are filled with violence and eroticism. In the earlier version, from the fifteenth or fourteenth century BC, Nergal visits the underworld, seizes Ereshkigal's throne and remains there as king. In the seventh-century BC version, Nergal escapes to the upper world but cannot exist without his queen.

The gods in heaven were feasting, but their sister Ereshkigal could not come up from the underworld to join them, so they invited her to send her minister Namtar (whose name in Sumerian means "Fate") to collect some delicacies from the table. When Namtar arrived, all the gods knelt before him out of respect for the goddess of death – with the exception of Nergal. Namtar returned and reported the news to Ereshkigal, who was furious. "Bring Nergal to me," she said, "and he shall die!"

Namtar approached the gods with Ereshkigal's demand, and they agreed that Nergal should be taken captive because of his irreverence. But Nergal hid among the other gods and, although he tried, Namtar was unable to find him. So the minister returned alone to Ereshkigal, who sent him again to find the offender. No longer able to hide, Nergal appealed to his father Ea, who responded by giving him seven pairs of demons to assist him in the underworld.

No sooner had Namtar admitted him through the outer gate of the underworld, than Nergal's fourteen demons pushed through and stationed themselves in pairs at each of the seven gates leading into Erishkigal's domain. This allowed Nergal to rush through the gates unhindered into the goddess's palace. There he seized her by the hair and pulled her from her throne, intending to cut off her head. But Ereshkigal begged

Nergal met the goddess of death, Ereshkigal, with the help of fourteen demons. This 7th-century BC Assyrian statuette depicts Pazuzu, a wind demon.

Ea suggested that Nergal should take an imitation throne with him to the underworld.
It might have resembled the chair in this banquet scene from the walls of the
Southwest Palace at Nineveh (c.630–620BC).

him to be her husband: "You will be master and I shall be mistress!" At these words, Nergal wept, then brushed away his tears and kissed her.

In the later version, Nergal sleeps with Ereshkigal on his first visit and then escapes, but cannot resist returning. In this version, Nergal made the journey to the underworld because death, personified as Ereshkigal, fascinated him. But since he wished to return to the upper world again, his father Ea made him build a wooden chair to take with him. This chair was an imitation throne, painted and set with colored pastes to simulate silver, gold and lapis lazuli. This may refer to part of a Babylonian funeral rite in which a chair was left out for ghosts to sit on, to distract them and prevent them from seizing a living person.

Ea instructed Nergal not to sit in any other chair while in the underworld, nor to accept any food, or sexual relations with Ereshkigal, as all these would make it impossible for him to return.

But Nergal caught a glimpse of Ereshkigal naked after bathing. Initially he resisted the temptation to seduce her, but eventually he gave in and they embraced passionately. After they had made love for seven days, Nergal escaped, and Ereshkigal fell into a fit of grief. She sent Namtar back to the gods to beg them to return her lover to her.

As in the earlier version, Namtar was unable to locate Nergal – Ea had disguised him as an idiot. But then Nergal apparently decided to return to the underworld of his own accord. On his arrival, Namtar gave him some advice. "Beware of the keepers of the seven gates who will try to catch you as you pass through." Nergal knocked down each of the gatekeepers before they could catch him, and rushed to join Ereshkigal. With a laugh he seized her by the hair and pulled her from her throne. They embraced and then made love again for another seven days, and it was decreed that Nergal should stay with Ereshkigal forever.

The Warrior King

Enki's son Ninurta was the god of the thunderstorm, the flood and the plough, and was respected as an impressive warrior. The most important myth about him comes from *Lugale*, a poem which has these opening words: "Oh Warrior King!" It tells how Ninurta fought a mighty monster in the eastern mountains and conquered its family of rocks that had rolled on to the plains to attack civilization.

As Ninurta was feasting with the other gods, he received some bad news from Sharur – his loyal weapon, the mace whose name meant "Smasher of Thousands". It was able to move around independently and communicate with the gods. High up in the mountains, the rocks and plants had risen in revolt against the plains, Sharur told Ninurta. As their leader they had chosen a fierce warrior called the Azag. The Azag did not have human qualities: it was a kind of stone, resistant to the blows of the spear and the axe. To spread its progeny far around the land, the Azag had intercourse with the mountains. Incited by the Azag, rocks were constantly rolling down the mountains to crush cities on the plain. Sharur warned Ninurta that the Azag was taking control of the eastern border districts and was plotting to snatch away his kingship.

This report spoiled the atmosphere of the feast and sent the gods into a panic. So Ninurta dressed and prepared for war. Then he set out in all his glory, heralded by tempests of wind and fire, to confront his enemy. The Azag had flattened hills and destroyed all the forests in his path, pinioned birds to the ground, boiled the fish in the rivers and crushed the population of the rebel region as if they were butterflies.

Sharur, having gone ahead to reconnoitre, came back with a warning. Despite the great monsters that Ninurta had conquered in the past, he would be no match for the Azag, who was unlike any other opponent. But Ninurta took no notice of Sharur's advice and pursued his attack.

In the mighty battle that ensued, the Azag attacked Ninurta with massive landslides. It flung a wall of rock against him, tore up tamarisk trees by the roots and gouged gashes in the Earth. Ninurta began to retreat. An, Enlil and the other gods were dismayed, but the mace Sharur flew off to Ninurta's father Enki for advice, and returned with a message. "Your father says you should keep attacking the Azag with your rainstorm and eventually you will be able to thrust your spear into it." With this encouragement, Ninurta finally overcame the Azag. He also cunningly destroyed its power to reproduce itself, thus ensuring a complete end to its tyranny.

A detail from a 3rd-millennium BC mosaic shows a warrior guarding a prisoner. The motif of battle and civil unrest is woven into the myth of the Azag monster to explain the occurrence of natural phenomena such as landslides.

Ninurta and the Turtle

A fragment of a text in Sumerian contains an amusing episode from a longer story about the theft of the Tablet of Destinies by the formidable Anzu bird. In this version the custodian of the Tablet of Destinies is the god of fresh water, Enki. The story pokes fun at Ninurta, taught a lesson in humility by Enki who enlists the help of a turtle.

After Anzu had stolen the Tablet of Destinies and flown off with it, Ninurta attacked the bird and made him drop the tablet back into the *apsu*, Enki's watery domain. Enki was delighted and praised Ninurta as the great conqueror of Anzu, saying that his name would be honoured for ever.

But Ninurta was not satisfied with this blessing. His face went dark and pale in turns, and he started to plot against Enki. He decided that he wanted to take over the whole universe, and the key to this plan lay with the Tablet of Destinies. But Enki, being clever, guessed what was in Ninurta's heart. As a warning, he stirred up the waves of his *apsu* and sent his minister Isimu to see his son. But Ninurta's arrogance was so great that he even dared to raise his hand against Isimu.

After his conflict with Enki, Ninurta finds himself trapped in the nest of a giant turtle that was created by his own father, Enki, in order to torment him.

This was too much for Enki. In exasperation, he moulded some clay from the *apsu* to form a turtle. Giving it life, he set it to work scraping out a deep pit with its strong claws. When Ninurta continued to threaten him, Enki retreated gradually towards the trap. Suddenly, the turtle came out from behind him and seized Ninurta, while Enki gave him a shove into the pit.

Ninurta was unable to climb out of the hole. Enki stood on the edge of the pit and looked down at Ninurta far below, where he was still being clawed by the turtle. "You were planning to kill me," he mocked loudly, "you with your big ideas! You have tamed mountains and now you can't even climb out of a pit dug by a turtle! What kind of a hero are you?"

Fortunately for Ninurta, his mother Ninhursaga came along and saw her husband tormenting their son. She stopped to reprimand Enki and reminded him of the time she saved his life when he had eaten the eight plants (see pages 90–91). "What about you, you plant-eater?", she demanded, "I saved you, so now save your son!"

107

Ninurta Civilizes the Rocks

Ninurta's victory over the leader of the mountain army thus assured, he began to adapt the wild mountain rocks for use by humankind. The myth recounts that in those days the mountain streams did not flow down into the plain; instead their waters ran uncontrolled and were wasted. The art of digging and dredging ditches was at that time unknown to human society, so Ninurta decided to improve the situation by using the rocks which he had conquered. He piled them up to create embankments for watercourses and to channel the flow into a river so that the mountain waters could be used to sustain the barley in the fields and the fruits and vegetables of the orchards and gardens. This long and hard campaign kept Ninurta away from his home. His mother Ninmah had been missing him and complained that he had neglected her during his conflict with the fierce Azag. So Ninurta proved his affection for her by giving her a brand new name in honour of his organization of the rocks into channels that guided the waters down the mountains to the plains. He called her Ninhursaga, "Mistress of the Rocky Foothills".

Ninurta embarked next on the second stage of his plan to use the rocks advantageously. He analyzed each kind of rock and decided on a function for it. This section of the story gives an explanation for the technological use of a wide range of important minerals imported from the mountains into Mesopotamian cities. Each use is presented as either honourable or humiliating, according to Ninurta's decision either to reward or to punish that particular type of rock for its conduct in the mountain revolt.

Not all of the rocks referred to in this myth can be identified, and some of the processes associated with them are hard to envisage. Some rocks he punished by making them vulnerable to erosion; others were forced to become grinding powders used to break down the other rocks; others were carved, pierced and polished in various ways. He punished lava and basalt, which had formed ramparts against him, by making them into moulds for goldsmiths. Limestone, which had plotted to seize Ninurta's office, was designated for use in foundations on muddy ground; it was also destined to crumble rapidly in water. Flint was punished by having to flake at the touch of an animal's horn.

However, those rocks that had changed their allegiances during the battle and refrained from assaulting Ninurta, the storm god decided to reward. For example, Ninurta chose to turn dolerite into an enormous statue in the E-ninnu temple in Girsu. It was decreed that lapis lazuli and other precious stones that had not committed offences should also be honoured.

Having conquered the rebellious rocks, Ninurta gave them functions – such as providing material for artists. This statuette of Ebih-II, an official at the Temple of Ishtar, in Mari (c.2400BC), is sculpted alabaster.

The Creation of Humankind

The creation of the world is presented in the *Enuma elish* as a primal, elemental process which heralded the social charter of kingship established by the god Marduk (see pages 84–86 and page 88). A human figure rather than a god emerges as the central character in the story of Atra-hasis, which is concerned primarily with the creation of humanity and its early history. Atra-hasis, whose name means "Extremely Wise" in Akkadian, also appears in the Gilgamesh epic, where he is called Ut-napishti, "He Who Found Life".

Atra-hasis is described as monarch of the city of Shuruppag on a version of the Sumerian King List. This clay tablet list is divided into those who ruled before and those who ruled after the Flood (antediluvian and postdiluvian), a cataclysmic downpour perceived as a historical event by the ancient Mesopotamians. Atra-hasis is clearly a precursor of the biblical Noah. Like Noah, he was chosen to survive a deluge intended to destroy humanity and was warned to build a ship and fill it with pairs of animals. But in contrast to Noah, who was under orders from the one God of the Hebrews, Atra-hasis was at the whim of a quarrelling pantheon.

Before the creation of human beings, when the gods did all the work, dominion over the cosmos was divided by lot. The realm of the sky was allocated to An, the Earth to Enlil and the ocean to Enki. These senior gods, called the Anunnakku, forced the junior gods, the Igigi, to dig the Tigris, the Euphrates and numerous irrigation canals.

For 3,600 years the Igigi tolerated this imposition. But eventually they rebelled, burning their tools in a demonstration staged outside the house of Enlil, god of the Earth on which they toiled.

Enlil was frightened at the anger of his own descendants and his face turned as sallow as tamarisk wood. He summoned his fellow rulers An and Enki for a conference and asked the strikers for the name of their leader. But the Igigi replied, "Together we have declared war on you! Our work is too hard, it is killing us!" Enlil continued to try to single out the strikers' ringleader, but An and Enki pointed out that the demonstrators were not

The once marshy banks of the river Euphrates have been transformed into pasture land by irrigation. Before the creation of humankind, it was the task of the junior Mesopotamian gods to dig the canals for drainage.

altogether wrong: "Why are we complaining? Their work really has been too hard."

An and Enki suggested that a substitute should be created to relieve the junior gods. They asked the womb-goddess Mami (also known as Nintu and Belet-ili) to make a new kind of creature. Enki, the clever craftsman, explained what to do. "Select one of the junior gods and kill him. Then let Nintu mix clay with his blood and his intelligence. God and man will be mixed together

109

As humans were created from the blood of a sacrificed god, ancient worshippers paid homage
to their creators through sacrificial offerings. An 18th-century BC mural from Mari,
in northern Mesopotamia, shows a priest leading a bull to its death as a sacrificial offering.

in the clay and we shall hear the drumbeat forever." The beat of the drum may have represented the sound of the temple drum when it was played by humans worshipping the gods, or possibly the sound of the human heartbeat.

Mami and Enki went into a secret place where they moulded humans, seven female and seven male, out of fourteen pieces of clay, in a process which was clearly based on the technique for brick-making. A rebel Igigi god was selected for sacrifice, so although human life contained a divine portion, it was also inherently flawed because it came from a recalcitrant god.

Humanity Proliferates

The gods' act of creation gave rise to trouble. Six hundred years later humans had become a pest on the surface of the Earth; they were "as noisy as a bellowing bull". Angered, Enlil declared, "I can't sleep for the din. Order an outbreak of plague."

Just as in the *Enuma elish* Apsu had tried to kill the noisy younger gods, so Enlil now decided to take action. He first made three attempts at long intervals to reduce the human population, and it was only when these did not work that he finally decided to send a devastating flood which would wipe them out altogether. At each of these attempts, Enlil's plans were frustrated by the special protective relationship which the god Enki had formed with a loyal human called Atra-hasis.

In his first attempt, Enlil told the plague god Namtara to kill large numbers of humans. But sympathetic Enki taught Atra-hasis and his people to ignore the other gods and to sacrifice only to the god Namtara, as

the source of their distress. The god was flattered by their unaccustomed attention and decided at once to bring the plague to an end.

However, after another 600 years, humanity had once again become too numerous and noisy. So Enlil instructed the rain god Adad to withhold his rain and cause a drought on Earth. But again Enki taught humans to sacrifice directly to Adad, who, feeling flattered, secretly moistened the Earth with dew at night and mist in the morning, so that the harvests could survive.

Some time later, Enlil mounted his next attack on humanity. This time he arranged for heaven, Earth and water to conspire so that every means of nourishment was withheld from the people. For six years the rivers failed to rise, salt crystals appeared on the surface of the parched fields and women's wombs became constricted so they were unable to give birth. Year after year, the people grew more desperate until by the fifth year they were selling their own children, and by the sixth year they were killing and eating them.

At this point the text fragments and it is not clear how total extinction was averted. But once again it was the initiative of Enki that returned water to the Earth.

Enlil was furious and summoned an assembly of the gods. He berated them for sabotaging his plan and persuaded them to collaborate in another scheme that would finally rid the Earth of human life. He intended to send a flood that would wipe out everything in existence.

Suspecting that Enki, loyal as ever, would warn humanity to save itself, Enlil forbade him to

The exultant rain and weather god, Adad, stands astride a steer on this 800BC basalt stele from Assyria. He caused a drought that almost wiped out humankind.

111

communicate with the people on Earth at any time. But Enki found a way to circumvent Enlil's prohibition: he addressed his warning to a reed hut's wall, knowing that Atra-hasis was lying awake behind it, trying to decipher a recent dream. Time was short and Enki spoke tersely. "Listen very carefully," he said. "Destroy a house and build a boat. Abandon your property and save life. Roof the boat all over and seal it with strong pitch."

Atra-hasis understood the message and set his people to work building a boat. He was so nervous that "his heart was breaking and he was vomiting bile", but he continued to gather up pairs of every kind of creature, from wild animals to birds. He only just managed to seal the door and cut the mooring rope when the rain god Adad began to bellow from the gathering stormclouds. The ensuing tempest drowned the remainder of humanity "like dragonflies". The womb goddess Mami, who had created the human race, watched the raging waves and heard her offspring

A detail of a victory feast from the exquisitely crafted Standard of Ur (c.2600–2400BC). The gods in heaven were envisaged as a glittering celestial court, who gathered to feast on the offerings presented by humans on Earth below.

screaming for help. She wept to think how she had complied with Enlil's wicked plan.

The flood lasted for seven days, and as it continued the gods began to suffer terrible hunger cramps caused by the lack of sacrificial offerings from humankind. When Atra-hasis's boat finally ran aground, his first action was to make a sacrifice to the gods, who gathered around the delicious aroma like flies.

The only exception was Enlil, who surveyed the failure of his grandest plan and asked angrily, "How did any man escape this catastrophe?" Enki confessed that he had secretly prepared Atra-hasis

for the deluge by suggesting that he build a boat. But he agreed to work with the womb goddess Mami in devising other ways of controlling the human population.

To this end Enki and Mami created three kinds of being who would help reduce the birthrate. The first was a class of infertile women, the second a demon who would steal and kill young children, while the third consisted of several kinds of religious devotee for whom it was prohibited to bear children. In this way the myth presents a lack of fertility in some humans as a compensation for excessive fertility in others.

KINGS AND PRINCES

The king's duties throughout the ancient Middle East included religious observances as well as affairs of state. Indeed, the Sumerians believed the king was chosen by the gods to be responsible for the people's welfare. For centuries the temple controlled the administrative business of the state, but gradually temporal power shifted to the palace. Although the kings were agents of the gods and had to perform various ceremonies, they were rarely, during the two and a half millennia of Mesopotamian hegemony, regarded as divine themselves.

Left: **Ginak was Prince of E-edin, presumed to be a border town in northern Mesopotamia. He wears a sheepskin skirt, a symbol of status that was reserved for ceremony.**

Above: **This sculpture of King Idrimi II of Alalah (c.1500BC) bears an inscription that tells how he fled to Aleppo, lived for a time in Canaan and came to be king of Alalah – a city north of Ugarit – as a vassal of the Hurrians.**

Left: **This granite portrait of King Gudea, ruler of Lagash, was carved c.2100BC. Lagash was a city state in the south of Mesopotamia that became independent after the collapse of the Akkadian empire.**

Above: Shalmaneser III (858–824BC), the Assyrian king, extended his empire as far west as Phoenicia, the home of these tribute bearers carved on a black obelisk.

Far left: This limestone statue shows Ashurnasirpal II (883–859BC) in a priestly role. The prefix Ashur- in several Assyrian kings' names refers to their chief god.

Left: A stele commemorating the victories of Naram-Sin (2254–2218BC). The ruler of an empire that stretched from the Mediterranean to east of the Gulf, Naram-Sin declared himself to be a god.

The Quest of a Superhero

The mightiest of Mesopotamia's heroes is Gilgamesh – "one-third human, two-thirds divine". Based on a real-life king, he is portrayed in sculptures and reliefs from every period of the region's civilization as a robust, bearded warrior, who struggles with lions, bulls and assorted monsters. He owes his immortality to the great epic poem that came to be written about him – the very first such literature known to humankind.

Gilgamesh is believed to have been a king of the Sumerian city of Unug (better known as Uruk in Akkadian) early on in the history of Mesopotamia. It was said that he built the city with his own hands. However, some centuries later, he was being worshipped as a god at several sites.

The extant tales about Gilgamesh start to appear *c.*2100BC, although the copies that have survived are mostly of a later date. The earliest stories, written in Sumerian, are all distinct episodes that the court poets of Ur would probably have based on versions which had been circulated orally for centuries before their time. They are not very different from those legends describing the exploits of other Sumerian heroes – far-fetched adventures with a great deal of action and frequent signs of godly favouritism.

However, the Gilgamesh epic itself is the Old Babylonian period's crowning literary achievement and in its themes of great friendship and loss it is a work comparable to the Greek *Iliad*. It was written in Akkadian *c.*1600BC (although the Sumerian form An has been used here for the sky god's name rather than Anu). The principal version that has survived was recorded on twelve clay tablets by the Babylonian scholar Sin-lege-unninni *c.*1100BC. How much he invented, and how much he collated from older material, we shall never know.

The imposing figure of the hero Gilgamesh is depicted gripping a lion cub in this Assyrian stone relief from the Palace of Sargon at Khorsabad in modern-day Iraq (*c.*800BC).

The Historical Gilgamesh

Gilgamesh was no literary invention. The hero of the epic was based on a real king who ruled Uruk c.2600BC, and whose prowess was the subject of tales circulating centuries before the poem was written. The Sumerian King List records him as the fifth ruler in Uruk's First Dynasty and provides him with the customary divine antecedents: his mother, it is said, was the goddess Ninsun.

Such divine ancestry was obligatory, for kingship in ancient Sumer was a blend of secular politics and religion. As ruler, Gilgamesh was *en* of the city. The word meant "lord", but had priestly associations too. The *en* was the conduit through which the city's gods spoke to their people. It was an intimate relationship: each year, the *en* went through a ritual marriage with the goddess Inana, who made Uruk her special charge.

The ceremony was also a way of ensuring the fertility of both the city's fields and its female inhabitants. A successful *en,* one who presided over abundant harvests and a contented population, could expect not only the citizens' loyalty while he lived, but even greater esteem after he died, when he would become a godlike figure to whom prayers and sacrifices might be offered.

Gilgamesh's role was not solely religious. He was also the military leader of a city state that was one among many jostling for supremacy. The political situation resembled that of classical Greece: no one city was strong enough to impose its will on all the others, but many were keen to try. To have thrived in such circumstances, Gilgamesh must have been skilled in battle and diplomacy.

Surviving historical records are non-existent, but the veneration accorded to Gilgamesh in Sumerian tradition suggests that he was successful in both roles. Long before the epic was written, religious writings testify to his deification, and he regularly features in tales of Uruk's military might.

The kings of Ur's Third Dynasty, *c.*2100BC, liked to boast of their supposed descent from Gilgamesh, and by *c.*1800BC he was credited with having built the city's walls – which in fact predate his lifetime by at least 1,000 years.

Gilgamesh demonstrates his legendary strength by raising a lion above his head, on this impression of an Assyrian cylinder seal from *c.*1350–1000BC.

Further episodes have been assembled from a variety of archaeological sources, most of them fragmentary. Some are "official" copies of the epic from city archives, especially the great library of Ashurbanipal at Nineveh. Others may be the remains of assignments at Mesopotamia's many scribal schools: some tablets are clearly the work of student copyists, and there are variant readings. But we have reason to be grateful to these sometimes clumsy trainee scribes. The enormous quantity of cuneiform writing left behind means that although many tablets are badly damaged, they are seldom damaged in the same way, so it has been possible to reconstitute most of the text.

There are irritating gaps here and there, and the surviving sections of the story do not connect in the way that their original authors perhaps intended. But the tale can be read in much the same form as the old Mesopotamians had it, and for the same reasons: for philosophical instruction in the ways of men and gods, of course, but also for sheer entertainment.

Heroes in Partnership

Far from being a mere relic, the Gilgamesh epic is one of the most dramatic stories ever told. Even today, 3,500 years after its composition, its themes of friendship, loss and the fear of death have profound resonance. In Sumerian times, the epic must have enthralled its readers or, more often, its listeners – for in a society where only a small number were literate this poem was surely written to be read aloud.

The work begins with a bill of fare to whet the appetite of an eager audience. We are about to hear the adventures of someone special "who brought back a tale of times before the flood".

As Gilgamesh the hero quests for eternal life, he encounters episodes of sex and violence, love and death, friendship and parting. Naturally, like all great quests, this one ends in seeming failure. But in failing, the hero finds self-knowledge and comes of age.

This is a story – as the narrator is at pains to establish – rooted in the historical experience of the people of Mesopotamia. Indeed, the opening verses stress the immediacy of what is to follow: "Go up on to the wall of Uruk and walk around! Inspect the foundations, study the brickwork. Testify that its bricks are baked bricks."

Gilgamesh is first mentioned as a historical ruler of the city of Uruk in Sumerian legend. He is recorded in the King List as the fifth king of the First Dynasty, son of the semi-divine Lugalbanda and the goddess Ninsun, making him "two-thirds divine, and one-third mortal".

Most of the poem's first section is a hymn to the virtues of the god-prince, superlative in his strength and as a warrior of great stature. In his city,

The goddess Ninsun, mother of Gilgamesh and wife of Lugalbanda, is shown sitting in a serene state on this Sumerian stone relief of the 3rd millennium BC.

So she took a lump of clay and made a double for Uruk's wayward ruler. She shaped Enkidu, a shaggy giant of a man, in the hope that he would combat Gilgamesh. In every way he was the opposite of the urban, sophisticated hero: "He knew neither people nor country; he was dressed as cattle are." Enkidu lived among the animals and knew their ways: he was, in fact, more animal than human, bonding with the creatures of the wilderness and sometimes saving them from the harsh snares of Uruk's hunters.

One such hunter, distressed by the sabotaging of his animal traps and pits – and even more alarmed by the sight of Enkidu himself – went before Gilgamesh to seek assistance. "I am too frightened to approach him," he explained. "But he will not allow me to do my work."

Gilgamesh decided to use a subtle weapon against Enkidu: from his own experience, he knew of one likely weakness in the strongest of men. "Go," he told the hunter, "and lead forth the harlot Shamhat. She must take off her clothes and reveal her attractions." Gilgamesh predicted that once Enkidu had fallen for the prostitute's charms, he would lose his powers over the animals and they would become alien to him.

So it came to pass: the hunter took Shamhat out into the countryside, where the two lay in wait by a watering hole. After three days, Enkidu appeared as they anticipated. Shamhat, looking seductive with her breasts bared and undergarments carefully loosened, stepped boldly from her hiding place and everything happened as Gilgamesh foretold. "She did for him, the primitive man, as women do." For six days and seven nights, their lovemaking shook the Earth.

Afterwards, Enkidu discovered the price he had to pay for his passionate affair: the wild beasts who had been his friends fled from him, and when he tried to run after them he found his limbs had lost their former strength.

The shaggy features of the wild man Enkidu (left) peer out from among his friends – the wild animals – on this Mesopotamian stone vase dating from c.3000BC.

"Uruk the sheepfold", he walked tall, a full sixteen feet in height, according to a Hittite version of the epic. But for all his perfection, Gilgamesh had one debilitating flaw: a weakness for women. Although he was expected to be the shepherd of the city, he spent more time as a "rampant wild bull". The tablet states the problem bluntly: "Gilgamesh would not leave alone young girls, the daughters of warriors, the brides of young men."

Not surprisingly, the heavens rang with the complaints of the harassed women. Their noisy grievances did not go unheard. "Create a rival for him," the people prayed fervently to the mother goddess Araru, "someone to absorb his energies, and let Uruk be allowed peace!" The goddess listened and agreed to help.

The Birth of Epic Poetry

When in the eleventh century BC the scribe Sin-lege-unninni, working in the libraries of Nineveh, wrote down on twelve clay tablets the Gilgamesh cycle in its final, polished form, he created the world's very first recorded epic – and the conventions that he observed have been followed by his successors and continue to be so to this day.

The distinctive stamp of the epic genre is the way in which the hero almost always occupies the centre of the story, and Gilgamesh conforms with this. The poem is not ultimately about the fate of cities, kingdoms or civilizations, but about the destiny of just one man. The narrative may digress on occasions – to describe the creation of Enkidu, for example, or the Great Flood – but it always returns to the actions of its hero, as he matures from a relatively uncomplicated "death or glory" warrior to the pensive seeker after immortality we see in the epic's later sections.

Dreams play a major part in the plot, as is to be expected from a society that saw them as messages from the gods. The dream material is often presented in a terse style that cranks up the dramatic tension of the story. By contrast, the speeches of gods and men alike are given at some length in a declamatory style marked by frequent repetition. Ultimately, the writers are conscious of their duty to tell a good story: whatever the moral message they are trying to get across, however grand their theme, their role is to entertain.

In later times, Greek, Indian, Roman and northern European poets were to adopt similar techniques in works such as the *Odyssey*, the *Bhagavad Gita*, the *Aeneid* and *Beowulf*.

The Babylonian account of the Flood was recorded on the 11th tablet of the Gilgamesh epic. The story dates back to the 11th century BC and was possibly the source of the biblical version in *Genesis*.

This was a near-catastrophic loss of innocence for Enkidu. But there were compensations. Not only had he learned the pleasures of adult life, but he had acquired the rudiments of judgement – he had grown up. And if Shamhat had destroyed his youthful naivety, at least she offered him some compensatory enticements. First she flattered his manhood, and then she told him of the joys of city life. She explained that in Uruk the girls would show off their bodies to him, and a life of happiness awaited. Besides, in Uruk he would find Gilgamesh, "perfect in strength, like a wild bull", with whom he could find real friendship. Enkidu, seduced once more, agreed to go with Shamhat to the city. But he added that, if Gilgamesh really was like a wild bull, he would have to challenge him.

Thought to represent the hero Gilgamesh, this Assyrian terracotta statue of the 7th century BC was probably buried in the foundations of a house to protect it against evil spirits.

So Shamhat dressed Enkidu in some of her own clothes and led him towards Uruk, where Gilgamesh was already having baffling dream premonitions that presaged the wild man's arrival. In the first dream, a thunderbolt fell to the ground and Gilgamesh could not lift it. In the second, a copper axe was thrown into an Uruk street, and the dream-figure of Gilgamesh presented it as an offering to his mother, the goddess Ninsun. She interpreted the visions for Gilgamesh: thunderbolt and axe alike represented a man, great in strength, whom Gilgamesh would learn to love.

Meanwhile, en route for Uruk, Enkidu and his harlot stopped for a few days at a shepherds' camp, where the delighted giant discovered bread and beer: another stage in the civilizing process was completed. This indulgent interlude in the story comes to an end when a young man rushes past. "What's the hurry?" asks Enkidu. "A wedding is about to take place in the city," the young man explained, "and Gilgamesh is expected to exercise his *droit de seigneur* over the bride."

Incensed by this information, Enkidu set off directly for Uruk and the wedding-house. When he reached the city, he caused a sensation among the local people. "He is just like Gilgamesh," they cried. "Mountains gave birth to him!" They rejoiced that the gods had found a perfect match for their ruler. When Gilgamesh approached the house, Enkidu barred his entry, and the two engaged in a furious battle before an awestruck crowd of citizens: "As wrestlers they grappled and crouched. They demolished the doorframe. The wall shook."

To Gilgamesh's dismay, he could not prevail over a man built so strongly that he resembled the battlements of the city, and Enkidu won the contest. But in his victory, the wild man yielded magnanimously to the loser. "Your mother bore you to be unique," Enkidu told Gilgamesh. "Enlil decreed that you should be king." And he raised Gilgamesh from the dusty ground, and they kissed each other and became friends.

A Companion for Gilgamesh

For the inhabitants of Uruk, this reconciliation was a huge relief. Gilgamesh was now much less interested in the women of the city. It was just as his dream prophesied: at last he had found a mighty partner, a man whose companionship he would come to cherish almost as much as marriage.

After a while, however, Enkidu began to pine. The comforts of city living, prostitutes included, did not seem to agree with him. He was reduced to tears of rage and frustration, and, even worse, his strength began to fade away.

But Gilgamesh knew the answer to his friend's problem: they needed an adventure, and he had one in mind. Far away to the west, deep in the mighty forests, lived a monstrous being called Huwawa. Gilgamesh proposed to Enkidu that they should search for him and end his life.

121

Hunting the Forest Monster

Gilgamesh's proposed adventure did not immediately appeal to Enkidu. Unlike his friend, to whom Huwawa was simply a name, Enkidu had actually seen the monster, back in the days when he had run wild in the woods. He knew what they were letting themselves in for. "His utterance is fire. His breath is death. Why do you want to do this?" he asked. Besides, it was the great god Enlil who had appointed Huwawa as guardian of the forest. "It is an impossible challenge," Enkidu declared.

Gilgamesh was determined to pursue the monster, despite his companion's doubt. In heroic style he declared: "If I should fall, I shall have won fame. People will say, 'Gilgamesh grappled with ferocious Huwawa. He was nobly born.'" He then reproached Enkidu for his lack of fighting spirit.

At the same time he had an incentive to offer: the smiths of Uruk would forge for the friends mighty weapons, the greatest swords and axes ever seen. Stung by Gilgamesh's jibes and impressed by the promise of fine new weaponry, Enkidu agreed to take part in the expedition westwards. Before they left, the two were feted by the councillors of Uruk, who offered some sterling advice: "Do not rely, Gilgamesh, on your own strength. Keep your eyes sharp and guard yourself! Let Enkidu walk ahead of you ... " Enkidu was renowned for his familiarity with the forest paths and the tricks of Huwawa. It was he who would be able to guide Gilgamesh in the hostile forest.

The journey to the west was arduous and long – "the new moon to the full moon, then three days more" – and during the course of the expedition Gilgamesh was troubled by several ominous dreams. In one, he saw the adventurers fallen "like flies" at the foot of a mountain; in another, heaven cried out and the Earth groaned. But Enkidu found a favourable interpretation. He explained the meaning of the dream to his friend: Huwawa, he prophesied, would lie dead at their feet. They

This grisly terracotta image of Huwawa dates from c.2000BC. The forest monster was feared even by Enkidu, who was familiar with the ways of the wilderness.

The Humiliation of Akka

One of the oldest legends about Gilgamesh – long predating the epic that bears his name – tells how he defeated the neighbouring city of Kish. The story is probably based on one of the many historical wars between the city states of Sumer.

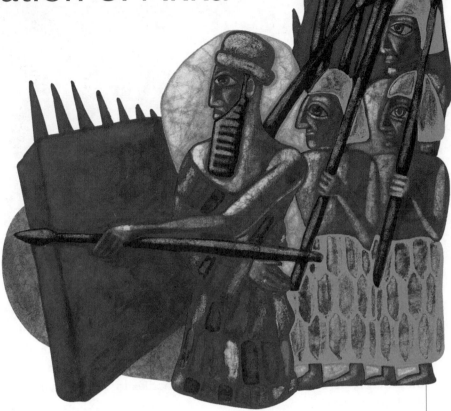

War began when Akka, king of Kish, sent envoys to Uruk demanding submission. Gilgamesh called the city elders together to discuss their response. He, of course, favoured resistance, but the elders, nervous of Kish's power, advocated surrender. An assembly of the city's fighting men agreed with Gilgamesh, however, and ordered Uruk's defences to be made ready.

Soon afterwards, Akka arrived at Uruk and besieged the city with an army large enough to dismay the defenders. But Gilgamesh was not intimidated. He told Enkidu, who again appears in this tale as his right hand man, to gather weapons for a show of strength that would so startle Akka "that his wits would become confused".

Gilgamesh also sent his bodyguard Birhurture to the camp of the enemy king. As soon as he stepped outside Uruk's gates, Birhurture was seized by the Kish soldiery and brought before Akka. At that point, the cupbearer of Gilgamesh peered out over the battlements of Uruk. "Is that man your king?" Akka asked Birhurture. Scornfully, the bodyguard replied, "Were that man my king, would not all foreign troops be overwhelmed, would not the mouths of the land be filled with dust, and would not Akka be captured in the midst of his troops?"

For his insolence, Birhurture received a beating. But now Gilgamesh himself "in terrifying splendour" mounted the walls of Uruk. The gates were thrown open and the city's soldiers, led by Enkidu, emerged in full battle order. Alarmed, Akka pointed to the battlements and cried to

Gilgamesh musters an army of warriors to defend their mighty city of Uruk and to do battle against King Akka of Kish.

Enkidu: "Is that man your king?" Enkidu replied, "That man is indeed my king." And so, after a brisk fight, Akka the king of Kish was taken captive, fulfilling Birhurture's prediction. Generously, Gilgamesh spared Akka's life and confirmed him in his titles.

For many years, the kings of Babylonia took the title "King of Kish" after the legendary days of Kish's independence.

An impression from a Mesopotamian cylinder seal of *c.*2300BC depicting Gilgamesh and Enkidu killing the Bull of Heaven, among other monsters.

continued to Huwawa's forest, where the monster greeted them scornfully: "The fool Gilgamesh and the brutish man ought to ask themselves why they have come to see me." He intended to bite through their necks, he declared, and leave their bodies to the birds of prey.

Gilgamesh's nerve almost failed him, but once more he was encouraged by Enkidu: "Don't turn back! Make your blows fall harder!" The combat was fast and furious, accompanied by terrible storms, while the land itself was split apart by their wrestling. In the end, Huwawa lay prostrate at Gilgamesh's feet, pleading for mercy.

The Monster Meets a Violent End

Gilgamesh was inclined to grant a reprieve for Huwawa. But Enkidu, his early reservations forgotten, disagreed with his companion: "My friend, catch a bird and where do its fledglings go?" he said cryptically. "Finish him off, slay him, grind him up." So Gilgamesh stabbed Huwawa and Enkidu struck off his head.

It was a deed they would both have cause to regret – they had forgotten that Huwawa was the appointed forester of Enlil; the god was bound to avenge his servant. But for the moment, all was triumph. Gilgamesh and Enkidu returned to Uruk elated by their glorious conquest.

Back in his own city, Gilgamesh washed his filthy hair and cleaned his gear. He put on his best clothes and his crown, cutting quite a dash for the women of Uruk, although mortal females were not the only ones to fall under his spell. The goddess Ishtar (Inana in Sumerian), protector of Uruk, was also greatly impressed, and she was nothing if not direct: "Come to me, Gilgamesh, and be my lover! Bestow on me the gift of your fruit." The goddess went on to recite a long list of advantages that she would bring as a wife – a chariot of gold and lapis lazuli for a start. And best of all, "Kings, nobles, princes will bow down beneath you!"

Clearly, Gilgamesh was on difficult ground. He had already offended Enlil; so he had to handle Ishtar with some tact. But fresh from his triumph over Huwawa, the young prince was in no mood for diplomacy, not even with a goddess. He haughtily rejected her proffered favours.

What is Ishtar, he asked himself? "A draughty door that can't keep out winds and gusts. A palace that rejects its own warriors." He went on to compare her to a leaky waterskin, a battering-ram that destroys its own city wall, and an ill-fitting shoe. Worse still, he referred to the goddess's chequered past. "Come", he said cruelly, "let me describe your lovers to you." One by one, he enumerated the evil fates that had befallen those who had succumbed to Ishtar's charms.

Such a litany would have outraged the most patient of people, and Ishtar was predictably furious. She went at once to her father, the sky god An, crying out, "Father, Gilgamesh has spelled out my dishonour." An mildly pointed out that if she was so angry, she should have dealt with Gilgamesh herself. But Ishtar wanted something special by way of revenge: the Bull of Heaven. She threatened that if An would not let her have it, then she would raise up the dead, so that they could eat the living and outnumber them.

An warned his daughter that the Bull of Heaven would bring seven years of famine to Uruk. But when Ishtar claimed to have put aside a store of grain to overcome hardship, An had to grant her request.

At first, the animal lived up to its reputation. When it snorted near the river of Uruk, a chasm opened, swallowing 100 young men. It snorted again, and 200–300 young men fell into it. When its next snort created a third chasm, Enkidu himself fell into it.

But Enkidu understood cattle, however fierce. He leaped from the chasm and seized the bull by the horns, so that it could only blow spittle into his face. Enkidu shouted to Gilgamesh to plunge his sword between its horns and neck tendons. Enkidu distracted the bull by seizing its tail, Gilgamesh took a mighty swing at the great beast and it fell to the ground.

Ishtar was beside herself with rage: "That man Gilgamesh who reviled me has killed the Bull of Heaven." But Enkidu was not at all impressed. Ripping off a limb from the dead animal, he threw it into Ishtar's face, threatening to do the same to her. To add insult to injury, Gilgamesh called to the craftsmen of Uruk to admire the colossal horns of the beast and to prepare them for gilding. They were to hang, he said, as a trophy above his bed.

The two heroes washed themselves in the Euphrates, then rode in triumph through the city. It was their finest moment. "Who is proudest among the men?" Gilgamesh asked his retainers. And then he celebrated in his palace.

But while his admirers were sleeping off their carousing, Enkidu had a dream, the most ominous so far. In it, the gods were consulting together and, on awaking, Enkidu suspected he knew why.

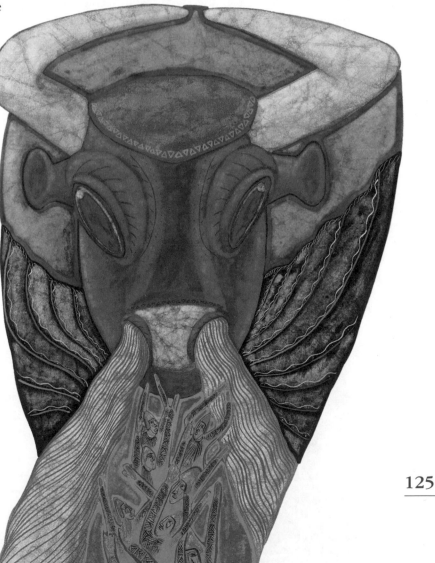

When the fearsome Bull of Heaven snorted, a chasm large enough to swallow hundreds of men opened up. So to exact her revenge, Ishtar borrowed the bull from the gods.

Enkidu Pays the Price

The killing of Huwawa, the humiliation of Ishtar and the slaughter of the Bull of Heaven were insults that the gods were unlikely to pass over lightly. And so it was that Enkidu's dream turned out to be a true prophecy of coming events.

In the dream, the gods discussed the overweening pride of the two heroes and planned an appropriate punishment. The sky god An, smarting at the loss of his mighty bull, insisted that one of them die. "Let it be Enkidu," said Enlil, remembering his slaughtered steward. After waking up, Enkidu was distraught, not only at the prospect of his own death, but because he would have to part from Gilgamesh. "O my brother," Enkidu wailed, "they are taking me away from you." "They have left a legacy of grief for the next year," Gilgamesh replied. He prayed to heaven for help, but in vain.

There was to be no heroic deathblow for his friend: Enkidu's end crept nearer in the form of a debilitating sickness while he railed against his fate. Remembering the happy innocence of his wild days in the woods, he cursed the hunter who first saw him, the harlot Shamhat who seduced him and the walls of Uruk themselves.

Then the sun god Shamash (Utu) intervened. Enkidu had no right to curse the harlot:

"Who fed you on food fit for gods,
Gave you ale to drink, fit for kings,
Clothed you with a great robe,
Then provided you with Gilgamesh?"

Enkidu was ashamed: these were indeed great gifts. As he weakened, he retracted his curse on Shamhat and replaced it with a blessing.

But for Enkidu, the outcome was inevitable. Slowly he wasted away, and on the twelfth night he died. The following dawn, Gilgamesh could not believe that his friend was gone. "Now what is this sleep that has taken hold of you? Turn to me, you! You aren't listening to me!" For six days and seven nights he wept over his friend, refusing even to permit the rites of burial until, horribly, "a worm fell out of his nose".

A great change now came over Gilgamesh. Once he had believed it was enough for a man to leave a good name behind him: had he not told Enkidu, on the eve of their journey to meet the Huwawa, "If I should fall, I shall have won fame"? Back then, he had also said, "Humankind can

This horned cap is thought to symbolize the sky god An, or Anu, and the omnipotent Enlil, or Ellil, who decreed Enkidu's end. It was found in Babylon and dates from c.1120BC.

The Sacred Marriage

According to the Mesopotamian world-view, the sole purpose of man's existence was to serve the gods. And the best way to do this and to ensure divine favour was through the scrupulously accurate performance of prescribed rituals.

One of the most important ceremonies was the traditional sacred marriage between earthly kings and the goddess Inana (Ishtar in Akkadian). Uruk's three greatest heroes – a priest-king Enmerkar, Lugalbanda and Gilgamesh – were all described as "bridegrooms of Inana", and their union with the goddess played a decisive part in their stories. Indeed, when Gilgamesh was foolish enough to reject her advances (see page 124), he precipitated both the death of his closest friend and his own obsessive quest for immortality.

Although the three heroes all claimed a privileged relationship with Inana, the status of divine bridegroom was something they shared with the king of every Sumerian city state. Each New Year's Day, a ritual marriage between ruler and goddess confirmed the structure of temporal power and ensured the goddess's favour in the months to come. Naturally, it was also the occasion for great public celebration and feasting.

Surviving texts of these rituals have both charm and a steamy intimacy. Thus at one ritual wedding Inana welcomed her suitor in these forthright terms: "My parts are well-watered lowlands ... Who will put plough oxen to them?"

In fact, the ceremony may have involved actual sexual congress. For ritual purposes, the king temporarily assumed divine status, and the symbolic marriage was celebrated in poems in which the king took on the role of Inana's husband.

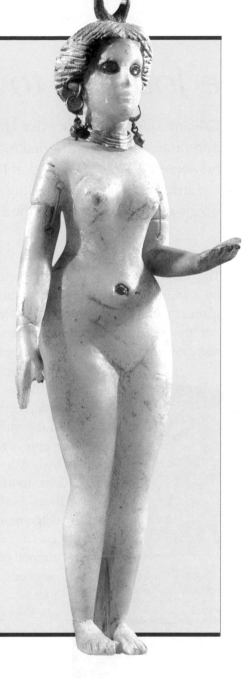

The seductive goddess of love was a favourite subject for Babylonian craftsmen. This statuette dates from the 3rd century BC.

---

number its days. Whatever may be achieved, it is only wind." Now, faced with the terrible reality of a death, he began to understand that such heroic attitudes are meaningless. It dawned on him that he too was mortal. He roamed the countryside around Uruk, sick with apprehension at the thought of his own extinction. "Shall I die too? Am I not like Enkidu? Grief has entered my innermost being. I am afraid of death."

The Gilgamesh epic might have ended at this point. Instead, the story sets off in a new and rather different direction. Perhaps, Gilgamesh thought, a way may be found to defeat death. Searching his memory, he recalled the story of Ut-napishti (see page 109), one of his own distant ancestors. This man had stood before the gods' assembly and sought eternal life. Might it be possible to discover immortality as he had done?

For Gilgamesh, it was no longer a matter of merely seeking adventure. No longer was he to battle with men and monsters for the sake of fame: now he waged war with death itself, and eternal life was the prize. A journey to find Ut-napishti had to be the first step.

The Journey towards Immortality

Gilgamesh's distant ancestor Ut-napishti was the only human being ever to become immortal. After Enkidu's death, Gilgamesh determined to track him down and find out his secret. Ut-napishti lived at the end of the Earth, so Gilgamesh's journey was extremely hazardous. He set off, heading west across the mountains towards the mighty portal that opens each night to admit the sun.

The main portal to the underworld was guarded by a frightful scorpion-man and his wife, "whose glances were death". Gilgamesh was rightly afraid, but nevertheless greeted them courteously. The scorpion-man, recognizing something unusual about the traveller, declared, "His body is flesh of the gods."

His wife, echoing a phrase from the very beginning of the epic, described him as "two-thirds divine, one-third mortal". But when they both heard that Gilgamesh intended to go through the night tunnel of the sun they advised against it. The journey, through utter darkness, was quite impossible, they said.

Nonetheless, they allowed Gilgamesh to proceed. After long hours in impenetrable darkness, he burst into the bright sunlight of a magical valley that was delightful to his eyes.

A frieze of gods and animals provides symbolic protection to the grant of land described on this Babylonian boundary stone of c.1100BC.

He walked through jewelled bushes and thorns down to the shore of a great sea. There he encountered Siduri the ale-wife, surrounded by her brewing vats and other objects of her trade.

The sight of Gilgamesh – lean, weathered and wearing only a lionskin – alarmed her; and at first, fearing that he might be an assassin, she locked him out. But she became more sympathetic when he told her about Enkidu's death, his overwhelming grief and the mission he had set himself.

He told her that since Enkidu's death he had set out in search of eternal life: "I keep wandering like a bandit in the open country. Now that I have found you, ale-wife, may I not find the death I dread." However, when Gilgamesh asked her to tell him the way to Ut-napishti's dwelling, she tried to dissuade him. Ut-napishti, she explained, lived across the sea, but the waters were lethal to the touch and there was no ferry; only the sun god could cross over. She also offered him some sound advice: "You will not find the eternal life that you seek. When the gods created humankind, they appointed death to the race."

But in the face of Gilgamesh's urgent pleading, she relented. "There *is* a boatman," she told him, "a servant of Ut-napishti himself. This man, named Ur-shanabi, may be able to help. Go and let him see your face. If it is possible, cross with him. If it is impossible, retreat!" Gilgamesh would recognize the man, she explained, because of the curious "things of stone" he had with him.

Ur-shanabi was working in the forest when Gilgamesh located him. The encounter began awkwardly when Gilgamesh, mad with impatience, seized the boatman and broke the stone objects during the struggle. But then calm prevailed, and Ur-shanabi settled down to listen to his story.

Gilgamesh began immediately to tell of his fear "My friend whom I love has turned to clay. Am I not like him? Must I lie down too, never to rise, ever again?" Sympathizing with the hero's quest for immortality, Ur-shanabi told him how they might cross the treacherous sea in order to reach the safety of shore. The "things of stone" which Gilgamesh had damaged were punting poles used to pass over the water without touching it. So the hero had to cut 300 replacements from the forest – for since they were of wood, not stone, each one could be used

A Babylonian artefact from the 11th century BC bears the image of a scorpion, a protective symbol – hence the significance of scorpion-man defending the portal to the underworld.

only once and then had to be discarded. With careful punting, they would be able to traverse the most dangerous stretch of the waters.

The plan succeeded – but only just, with every pole having to be used. Gilgamesh's mission appeared to be close to completion. On the far shore, Ut-napishti was waiting for him, alive and well despite his immense age. He looked out in surprise and perplexity at the strange sight of a visitor. At last, the coveted secret of eternal life seemed to be within Gilgamesh's reach.

God-given Dreams

Dreams were taken seriously in Mesopotamia. They were almost always regarded as prefiguring the future, and sometimes even as a personal communication from a god. At best, they gave a warning that a wise man could act upon; at worst, they at least granted the dreamer time to reconcile himself to an impending and irrevocable doom.

In the Gilgamesh epic, as in many of Mesopotamia's heroic tales, dreams play a decisive role in the plot. Most of the key incidents of the epic – the successful fight with the monster Huwawa, for example, and the death of Enkidu, which sends Gilgamesh reeling off on his quest for immortality – are foreshadowed in dreams. In the the original text, these are often described at greater length than the actions that ensue.

The dream sequences also give a powerful impulse to the poem's narrative flow: how, the reader wants to know, will these cryptic prophecies be fulfilled?

Dreams were one of the few experiences that ordinary Mesopotamians could share with the great and the legendary. But even though almost anyone could take a dream-glimpse into the future, it was a specialist's job to elucidate their true meaning. The practice of interpreting dreams was the vocation of a specially trained class of priests, who were able to explain their significance to the unenlightened and offer suitable advice after the analysis.

Kings, of course, could ask the gods directly. Thus when Gudea, ruler of Lagash in c.2140BC, was told in a dream to rebuild the ruined temple of his city, he checked his interpretation of the vision with the goddess Nanshe herself. Only when she gave her approval did he launch into a full-scale reconstruction programme. Little of Gudea's ancient temple now survives – except for the very inscriptions that explain to posterity just what made the king undertake the task.

Gilgamesh and the Flood

After a dreadful journey in which his wits had been tested and proven, Gilgamesh's hopes of gaining immortality were high. But they were almost immediately dashed. Pityingly, Ut-napishti told him that his long search has been in vain.

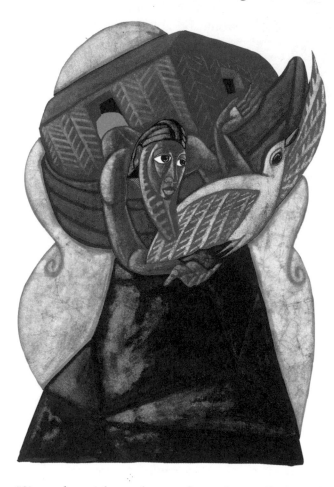

Ut-napishti's ark, which saved humankind from extinction, was unusual in size and shape and filled with every type of animal so that the world could be repopulated after the flood.

"Since the gods made you from divine flesh and the flesh of humankind, death is inevitable at some time, both for Gilgamesh and for a fool," Ut-napishti warned his visitor. But death was clearly not a threat to Ut-napishti, who, despite his great age, was still in perfect shape. "I look at you," Gilgamesh said to the sole human immortal, "and you are just like me." "Let me reveal to you a closely guarded matter," and Ut-napishti told Gilgamesh the story of the Flood. It is remarkably similar to the account of Noah in the *Book of Genesis*, so close that both versions are likely to have sprung from the same original source.

Long before, when Ut-napishti lived in the ancient city of Shuruppag, the gods, after repeated efforts to reduce the human population, decided to finish it off for good by flooding the Earth. As already seen in the variant version of this myth featuring Atra-hasis (see pages 109–113), the god Enki was expressly forbidden to reveal the plan to the human race, but did so indirectly by addressing a reed hut. "Reed hut, brick wall, listen, reed hut, and pay attention, brick wall."

Just like Atra-hasis in the other version of the story, Ut-napishti was sitting on the other side of the wall. He listened carefully while Enki gave a list of detailed instructions. "Dismantle your house, and build a boat with harmonious dimensions. Leave your possessions behind, and fill the boat with the seed of all living things."

And so it was done. Ut-napishti's ark was vast in circumference, cube shaped with six decks. In due course the vessel, loaded with the seed of all living things as well as Ut-napishti's kin, was completed, and only just in time. For six days and seven nights, a tempest raged over the Earth. On the seventh day, Ut-napishti looked from his ark and saw that "all humankind had returned to clay. The flood plain was flat as a roof."

After a while the ark came to rest on the top of a mountain, and Ut-napishti released a dove. But the bird came back, for it had found nowhere to perch. Next, he released a swallow, with the same result. But on the third day, he sent off a raven, and the bird did not return: it seemed as though the floodwaters were receding.

Symbols of Untamed Power

The domestication of wild cattle was a huge advance for civilization. And in the days when the first cities and communities were developing on the fertile soils between the rivers, it was not so far in the past that people took it for granted. Although the beasts had been mastered, they were capable at any time of escaping all constraint. The bull, with its aggressive masculinity, was much celebrated in Mesopotamian art as a symbol of power.

In mythology the bull was usually linked closely with the storm god Ishkur (Adad); thunderclouds were often described as "bull calves". The Bull of Heaven that features in the Gilgamesh epic was one of the most dangerous weapons of the gods, not to be unleashed without good reason. At the same time, An himself, sky god and chief among the creators, was sometimes referred to as the "fecund breed-bull". And statues of a man-headed bull, sometimes equipped with wings, are found all over Mesopotamia, often serving as gatekeepers.

Right from the Early Dynastic period – that is, well before the historical Gilgamesh was ruling Uruk – the mysterious figure of a bull-man, human above the waist and taurine below, appears frequently in seals and clay reliefs. The creature was known as *kusarikku*, according to some scholars the word also used for the Mesopotamian bison, which became extinct some time before the first flourishing of Sumerian culture.

Perhaps this association with a great beast now vanished from the Earth brought special powers; at any rate, the bull-man endured long into the Assyrian era, by which time he had evolved into a friendly demon whose protective powers could shield buildings and their occupants from evil.

This alabaster statue of a human-headed bull dates from the 3rd millennium BC and represents a magically protective demon.

"No one should have lived through the destruction!" shouted the furious Enlil. But Enki calmed him down. Sinners and criminals should certainly be punished, he conceded, but wiping out every living thing on the Earth was excessive. Enlil allowed himself to be convinced, and the entire council of the gods eventually came to appreciate just how much was owed to Ut-napishti. Such bravery deserved a reward. So Enlil brought Ut-napishti and his wife before the assembled gods and blessed them with immortality.

Defeated by Sleep

But this extraordinary tale contained no shred of hope for Gilgamesh, as Ut-napishti was quick to point out. "Who can persuade the gods on your behalf?" he asked. Indeed, he planned to teach Gilgamesh a lesson. If the hero wanted to conquer death, then let him first try to conquer sleep, surely a much easier task. Ut-napishti challenged him to stay awake for six days and seven nights.

But Gilgamesh failed. Ut-napishti declared scornfully to his wife, "Look at the young man who wants eternal life! Sleep breathes over him like a fog." When Gilgamesh woke up, he was dis-tressed: not only his struggle against sleep but his entire quest had ended in failure. "Wherever I set my foot, death is there too," he complained.

This was no more than Ut-napishti had told him already. But the immortal eventually took pity on Gilgamesh. The young man was in terrible physical condition, with filthy, matted hair. Ut-napishti ordered the boatman Ur-shanabi to wash him well, and for his return journey provide him with a set of magical clothes: they would stay clean "until he returns to his city".

A disconsolate Gilgamesh once more boarded the boat to recross the fatal sea. He was almost out of sight when Ut-napishti's wife chided her husband for his lack of generosity. "Gilgamesh came weary, striving. What will you give him to take back to his country?" Hearing this, Gilgamesh rapidly returned to the shore. Relenting, Ut-napishti told of a plant whose root resembled a camel-thorn. It grew deep underground in the *apsu* – the freshwater ocean under the Earth. "If you can win that plant, you will be rejuvenated."

Gilgamesh at once opened the gateway to the *apsu*, tied heavy stones around his feet and plunged in. He found the plant and returned to the surface in high spirits. At last he had something to

The Death of Gilgamesh

An alternative conclusion to the story of Gilgamesh has survived. This earlier, Sumerian account of the hero's end may enshrine the memory of a mass human sacrifice.

All that survives of the other death story are two fragments of a much longer poem. In the first fragment, Enlil warns the hero that he is not destined for immortality. In compensation, however, he has been granted supremacy over mankind during the rest of his lifetime, as well as invincible military skill. But die Gilgamesh must; and eventually, after many years of triumph, "He lies, he rises not."

In the next, apparently final section, Gilgamesh is already in the underworld, amid the gods who live there and the shades of the illustrious dead who have

A 13th-century BC Assyrian relief depicts wooden boats, perhaps similar to the one in which Gilgamesh travelled to the underworld.

make his long ordeal worthwhile. As he told the boatman, "This is a plant to cure a crisis!" With uncharacteristic caution, however, he decided to take it back to Uruk with him. "I shall give it to an elder to eat, and so try out the plant," he said.

But it was not to be. On the way home, he and Ur-shanabi stopped for the night by a pool of cool water. Gilgamesh, hot and weary, decided to bathe. But while he was relaxing in the pool, a snake smelled the fragrance of the magical plant, came up silently and stole it away, simultaneously shedding its scaly skin. Seeing the useless pelt before him and realizing his loss, Gilgamesh

broke down and wept. "For what purpose have my arms grown weary?" he asked the boatman. "I have gained nothing for myself, only for the serpent." And with that he gave up his quest. There was to be no eternal life for Gilgamesh, or any other man. Yet in his failure, he overcame the fear that had haunted him since the death of Enkidu, he became resigned to his own mortality.

Gilgamesh's journey ended where it had started, beneath the imposing walls of Uruk, where it is said he spent his last years beautifying the city. Even if he never achieved immortality, he was determined to live on in human memory.

preceded him. But he has not made his final journey alone, for we are given a long list of his companions, including his wives, his concubines, his musicians and entertainers, and even his valet. The text goes on to describe how Gilgamesh makes offerings to the gods of the underworld to persuade them to accept the new arrivals.

Uruk, occupied for 5,000 years, was surrounded by a 6-mile wall. It is said that Gilgamesh took great comfort in its construction.

In this list of names and rituals, we are probably reading an authentic description of a mass human sacrifice. The retinue that followed Gilgamesh on his final journey may well have been slaughtered to order.

Archaeology supports this grim interpretation. When Sir Leonard Woolley excavated the royal tombs of Ur, he found not only the bodies of Ur's rulers, but around them scores of retainers who had been killed so that they could serve their masters beyond the grave.

133

THE GLORIES OF GREECE AND ROME

The Greek mythological heritage has exercised a very powerful influence on Western culture and the continued presence of the Olympian gods – in literature and scientific terminology – is a tribute to the power of the classical imagination. Initially, the myths travelled with the Greeks around the Mediterranean and, later, with the Romans to regions further afield. Neither culture had one authoritative version of the story of creation – instead, countless, often contradictory, stories existed to explain the origin of their world, of the gods they worshipped, and their own beginnings as peoples. Storytellers and writers added to the profusion of ancient mythological tales by producing their own versions over the centuries. Many of these have been lost, and the earliest extant accounts are in the works attributed to the Greek poets Hesiod and Homer.

The tumultuous history of civilization in the Mediterranean and the preponderance of city states help to explain the abundance of myths. The Greek and Roman cultures both evolved out of many different traditions – the rich body of classical myth was the product of the belief systems and traditions of successive waves of invaders, combined with the mythological tales of the native civilizations that they overran and conquered.

One thing that all the classical stories had in common was that they told of a long, eventful history. The ancient Greeks believed that both they themselves and the gods they worshipped were the products of generations of change and sometimes of violent revolution. Their sovereign deities, the Olympians, were not those who made the world, but rather, they represented the third generation of ruling divinities. Similarly, the race of humans of the classical period was – according to different sources – either the fourth or the fifth to live and breathe upon the Earth.

That this rich body of stories has survived until the present can, perhaps, be attributed to the fact that they have never lost their relevance: they recount universal truths, in the context of themes ranging from love to war, with which we can still identify millennia later.

Opposite: **Hecate, goddess of witchcraft (centre), battles against a giant in this sculpture dating from 180BC, which once decorated an altar in honour of Zeus.**

Above: **In this detail from a 6th-century BC vase, a mischievous centaur, half man and half horse, has armed himself with a rock and a tree. Centaurs and other magical creatures, both good and bad, were generated in the early phases of creation.**

135

Chaos and its Offspring

The great mysteries of creation were explained by the Greeks and Romans in a number of different myths. The *Theogony*, written by Hesiod in the eighth century BC, provided the earliest coherent account of how the cosmos, the gods and mortals came into being. The poet also drew up a complete genealogy that traced the heritage of the Olympians, humanity's sovereign deities, back to the divine forces involved in the first acts of creation.

Gaia, Mother Earth, is seated on her throne holding a newborn infant, a symbol of fertility, in this 5th-century BC statue from Thebes.

Hesiod was working from an oral tradition – a series of stories and songs that no longer exist. Other poets contemporary with him also composed accounts of the creation and genealogies of the gods. It is possible that the reason his version is the only one to have survived in its complete form is that it was the most comprehensive.

In Hesiod's account, the world evolved out of an enormous, shapeless darkness he called Chaos (meaning in Greek "a yawning void"). It was an abstract principle, the ultimate source of creation, and was not personified in any way as a primal god. Hesiod left open the question of how Chaos itself arose, because his aim was to provide a history of the gods, not of the universe: cosmogony was discussed only in terms of its effects on the intricate family tree he was creating. Nor did Hesiod explain how Chaos produced the five original elements: Gaia, the Earth; Tartarus, the underworld located in the depths of the Earth; Erebus, the gloom of Tartarus; Eros, the force of love; and Nyx (Night), the power of darkness.

Throughout the ancient world, the night was acknowledged as an elemental force, since its mysterious darkness could conceal unknown evil and enemies. Its personification in myth as a goddess gave it a character and therefore made it a little less mysterious. Nevertheless, in Greek and Roman mythology, the goddess

Nyx was feared and respected even by her peers – Homer's *Iliad* describes her as having power over gods and men. She played a crucial role in most classical creation myths, and Hesiod's was no exception. In the *Theogony*, she was the first of the children of Chaos to give birth to other elements of the universe. Mating with Erebus, she bore Day and Aether, the pure upper atmosphere. Later she gave birth to many of the evils that cloud the lives

of gods and humans, including Doom, Death, Misery, Resentment, Deceit and Strife; Strife herself went on to give birth to further afflictions, such as Murder, Carnage, Battle and Lawlessness.

Gaia, the Earth, was next to produce offspring and she did so on her own. Without any sexual congress, she produced Uranus, the starry heavens, to cover her and to be a home for the gods who were to be created later. She also generated the

First Causes of Creation

Hesiod's story was only one version of the creation of the world. Many other influential myths of creation were also current.

Homer's account of creation respected the traditions of the seafaring folk for whom he originally composed his great epics. In the *Iliad* he told how all the gods and all living creatures began in Oceanus, the great sea that girdles the world.

Another early story described how a goddess was born spontaneously from Chaos. Finding nothing for her feet to rest on, she created the ocean and danced on its waves. The wind caused by her movements became the material from which she created a partner, a giant serpent. Taking the form of a dove, she laid a huge egg, which was fertilized by the serpent. Everything in the universe hatched from this primal egg.

In the creation myth of the Orphic cult, a major mystery religion, Chronos, the personification of time, constructed an egg from which was born Phanes, the firstborn of

The cosmic egg is a source of creation in several different myths from ancient Greece and Rome, and in other parts of the world.

the gods and the universal creator. Phanes took many forms, including Eros, the power of love. Eros was double-sexed, golden-winged and four-headed. Night, his daughter, was also his consort and ultimately his successor. Everything on Earth and in the heavens resulted from their union.

While creation myths provided many people with sufficient answers to their questions about the origins of the universe, philosophers and scientists began their own investigations around the sixth century BC. At first, scientific explanations reflected myth, as thinkers concentrated on defining the principle that first organized Chaos, a mystery that Hesiod and many other recorders of myth had left unsolved. For centuries, the organizing principle, whether conceived as one of the elements or as an intangible force, was thought to be divine. It was not until the late fifth century BC that a scientist, Democritus, proposed a purely materialistic explanation of the existence of the world – one without a divine cause.

towering Mountains (who had a divine nature) and Pontus, the mythological personification of the sea, thereby bringing into existence the basic structure of the physical world.

Hesiod described Gaia as "broad-breasted, the secure foundation of all forever". Other classical poets called her the ultimate mother and nourisher, the source of all fertility in nature. Thus, she was not only the physical body of the Earth but also its essence and power (just as her first chil-dren were at the same time divinities and elements of the cosmos). Belief in Gaia may predate that of the Olympian gods: archaeological evidence suggests that a female Earth divinity was worshipped in the Mediterranean from the earliest times. In some parts of Greece, as well as in Rome, where she was known as Tellus, she continued to be revered after the establishment of a pantheon of newer gods. The Romans, for example, worshipped her as the source of all babies, and for this reason they always placed their newborn infants momentarily on the ground just after birth to acknowledge the power of Tellus and draw strength from her.

Hesiod's myth of the formation of the physical world reflected the early Greek concept of the shape of the Earth. They believed that it was a flat disc rather than a sphere, and that their territory lay in the middle of that disc. Some identified its absolute centre as Mount Olympus, the highest mountain of mainland Greece (see pages 154–155); others said it was the sacred oracular shrine of Delphi, the "navel of the world" (see box, page 185). The land mass was completely encircled by a saltwater sea, known as Oceanus (see box, page 137).

In myth, Oceanus, the child of Gaia and Uranus, was portrayed as a stream that always flowed smoothly, unaffected by storms or wind, and as the source of all other rivers. The idea that the Earth was a sphere first arose in the fourth century BC, but even then the belief in an all-encircling Oceanus persisted, neither proved nor disproved by early seafaring explorers who attempted to circumnavigate the disc.

On this 6th- or 5th-century BC Greek vase, Gaia (centre) is shown emerging from the Earth and presenting an infant to Athene, as Zeus (left) looks on. Among the Greeks and the Romans, Gaia was revered as the source of newborn babies.

Children of the Earth and the Heavens

Although Uranus was born from Gaia, and so in one sense was her "son", he was not her dependent, being seen as her equal partner, consort and husband. The union between Gaia and Uranus was a sacred marriage that brought together Earth and heavens, joining a fertility goddess with a sky god.

The union between Gaia and Uranus was not viewed as improper in any way, despite the fact that Gaia was Uranus's mother. Two of their children would also marry each other, as would two of their grandchildren. With these marriages began a tradition that gods could break the taboo of incest, which for humans was inviolable.

Gaia and Uranus had numerous children, of whom many were monstrous in form and character. Their firstborn were the three Hecatonchires (the Hundred-handed) – male monsters with a semi-human form, but with 100 arms and fifty heads each. Next came three more children, the one-eyed Cyclopes, named Arges (Bright), Brontes (Thunder) and Steropes (Lightning). They were strong and wild like their multi-handed brothers. But they were also skilful stone-workers, believed to be the builders of the ancient, massive walls of Mycenae and the nearby fortress of Tiryns on the Peloponnese. Later Gaia, on her own or by various lovers, bore many other children. Most of these were also monsters, but not all: for example, one of her daughters was the lovely virgin nymph Daphne, whom Apollo lusted after without success.

The most famous children of Uranus and Gaia were the twelve Titans, six sons and six daughters, who became the first gods: Oceanus, god of the seas (distinct from the geographical Oceanus), and his sister and mate, Tethys; Hyperion, a sun god, and his sister and mate Theia; Themis and Rhea, both Earth goddesses; Mnemosyne, the goddess of memory; Iapetus, Coeus, Crius and Phoebe, whose specific functions are no longer known; and

Tellus, the Roman version of Gaia, is shown surrounded by her children on this relief panel from the Altar of Peace, commissioned by the emperor Augustus in 13BC.

Cronus, the youngest, boldest and craftiest of the family, who hated his father and was to replace him as supreme god.

The Titans appeared early in the development of mythology in the eastern Mediterranean and in parts of Asia Minor. Most personified natural forces; Mnemosyne was an exception in being a personification of a human attribute – memory – and was a late addition to the pantheon. Although the generation of gods the Titans produced, the Olympians, was to become more influential than them in Greek and Roman religion, the stories of the Titans had a great significance. Many common themes of classical mythology derive from the tales that were told: notably the idea of a family of gods; of divine intermarriage, often within the same kinship group; and of power-sharing co-existing with competition for power.

The characters of the Titans, their children and the other monsters and divinities from this stage of creation are not as carefully delineated as those of the Olympians and other later gods. The few tales involving them usually serve to explain the nature of the physical world or the origins of the dominant generation of gods. This is true, for example, of Atlas, whose myths explain important aspects of geography and cosmology. Son of the Titan Iapetus and of Asia, a daughter of Oceanus, Atlas was condemned in perpetuity to hold up the sky and prevent it from falling to the Earth. This was his punishment for taking the Titans' side in a war between them and the Olympians (see page 148). According to one account, the range of mountains in northwest Africa that carries his name was created when he was turned to stone so that he would be strong enough to bear this oppressive burden. But despite his crucial respon-sibility for maintaining the position of the Earth, Atlas remains a one-dimensional figure in Greek myth, lacking any detailed characterization.

Mountains and Volcanoes

Behind the narrow strip of fertile land bordering the Greek coastline rise the mountains of the mainland interior. To people living near the coast, who were dependent on the sea, these mountain ranges must have seemed an alien territory, the domain of gods and strange creatures.

For the ancient Greeks, mountains were powerful, magical places. They were riddled with mysterious caves, fissures, sudden springs and river sources, and their summits were often concealed by clouds, mists and snow. In myth, they were the homes of gods, heroes and monsters. Some myths explained the origins of specific peaks, including Atlas, Olympus and Parnassus.

The volcanoes of the Mediterranean were an even greater source of wonder and apprehension. In addition to Etna and Vesuvius, which have erupted in modern times, many others, now quiescent, were still active in the classical period. The eruption of Thera (Santorini) *c.*1400BC, for example, devastated a thriving culture on that island. There were many stories that explained the violent behaviour of active volcanoes. Etna was said to be the prison of a destructive monster, Typhon (see box, page 149), or the noisy workshop of Hephaistos, the divine smith, and Vesuvius was the explosive battleground of the ancient gods.

A fiery lava flow from Mount Vesuvius cuts a destructive path through nearby vineyards, orchards and settlements.

The Castration of Uranus

The marriage of Gaia and Uranus was riven by conflict. Gaia loved her children deeply, but their father felt only a jealous contempt for them, fearing that one of his sons would eventually depose him.

Uranus buried his children deep within the Earth, locking them up again inside their mother's body as soon as they were born. Gaia had to endure double pain: the heartbreak of losing her children and the physical pain of their confinement within her own form. The monstrous Hundred-handed were held in Tartarus, a place so deep in the Earth that it would take an anvil thrown from heaven nine days to land there. The Cyclopes were condemned to live inside the volcanic core of Mount Etna, where their savage roaring was said to cause its frequently thunderous eruptions.

Eventually, Gaia was no longer able to bear either her own pain or the insult to her and her children. She appealed to her Titan sons to liberate them all from their father's tyranny, but they were frightened of Uranus and one by one they turned down the challenge. Only Cronus, the youngest, dared to take up his mother's cause.

Gaia made a sickle for Cronus out of a material so hard that only the gods could make weapons from it. She plotted with her son how to catch Uranus off-guard, and showed him where to lie in wait within her body. As night fell, Uranus spread himself over the Earth and lowered himself towards his wife to make love to her. Cronus lashed out with his sickle and castrated his father, then flung away his genitals.

Many important mythical characters were born from the splashes of Uranus's blood, including the Giants, who were to become bitter enemies of a later generation of gods (see pages 148–149), the Erinyes, the vengeful goddesses who punished parricides and other wrongdoers (see pages 160–161), and the Meliae, nymphs of ash trees. Uranus's severed genitals landed in the sea, where the mingling of the waves with the sperm that was released created the foam that gave birth to Aphrodite, who was later to become the Olympian goddess of love (see pages 166–171).

Shorn of generative power by his own son, Uranus was utterly humiliated and took little part in subsequent tales. Cronus took his place as an all-powerful sky god and soon set about establishing his own dynasty. Gaia, however, did not fade into the background in the same way that Uranus did. Although some of her roles and functions were adopted by future consorts of the principal god, she herself continued to be worshipped, particularly in Greece where she was a giver of oracles, and she appears infrequently but importantly in many later stories, often as an adviser to the gods or as a surrogate mother to them.

Cronus wielded a sickle as a weapon, but a more typical use of such a blade was to harvest grain and corn.

A 3rd-century Roman statuette of Saturn, found in a settlement in Tunisia. Saturn was the Roman equivalent of the god Cronus, who castrated his own father Uranus.

Helios and Phaethon

The Titans and their offspring played a role in establishing the natural order on Earth. Helios, the son of the Titan sun god Hyperion and his partner Theia, drove the chariot of the sun across the sky.

Helios steers the solar chariot from east to west in a 5th-century BC Greek vase painting. The young boys leaping before him represent the stars fading in the light of day.

Although Helios tried desperately to dissuade him, Phaethon was insistent, and Helios was bound by the promise he had made. He coated his son's face in an oil to protect his skin against the heat of the solar rays and tried to teach him the correct way to drive the chariot, but Phaethon was too impatient to listen.

The boy set out boldly, but as the horses rose into the sky they sensed their driver's inexperience and bolted downwards. The terrified boy could not control the chariot and the horses drew the vehicle ever lower, searing much of the Earth with the sun's heat. The Nubian desert, once a fertile land, never recovered from this event, and the peoples of the south were so badly scorched that their skins turned black.

Seeing that the Earth risked total destruction, the gods blasted Phaethon, whose body crashed to Earth in flames. To save other lands from devastation, the gods cooled the heat of the solar chariot with a drenching cloudburst.

Phaethon was the son of Helios. His friends often teased him, saying that he could not be the son of a god, and even though his mother swore that it was true, the boy was not reassured. His mother finally advised him to visit his father Helios and ask him directly.

Phaethon travelled to Helios's magnificent palace to find out the truth. At first the boy could not approach his father because he was dazzled by the solar rays the god wore on his head. Putting the rays aside, Helios greeted his son with great affection and rashly promised to give the boy anything he wanted. Phaethon immediately asked to drive the chariot of the sun for one day.

The Birth of Zeus

After defeating Uranus, Cronus became supreme ruler of the Titans. However, like his father, he feared being overthrown by a younger generation. Although he did his best to prevent this from happening, his children proved to be too clever for him.

The Greeks and Romans had different conceptions of Cronus. To the Greeks, the Titans were savage and uncouth in comparison with the later generation of Olympian gods. Nonetheless, Cronus was believed by some to have ruled over a golden age for humans (see page 150), and when he ceased to reign as supreme god, he retired to the Islands of the Blessed, a paradise somewhere in the far reaches of Oceanus, the great sea.

The Romans associated Cronus with Saturn, a god of agriculture, who possibly had native Italian roots or might have been an early import from the eastern Mediterranean. Like Cronus, Saturn was believed to have presided over a golden age in which humankind lived safely and peacefully. Always anxious to trace their own ancestry back to the gods, the Romans also devised a story that he was the first king of Latium and, through his son Picus, an ancestor of the Roman kings.

Both the Greeks and Romans agreed that Cronus was proud and confident. After the defeat of Uranus, he refused to bow to Gaia's wishes and release either the Hundred-handed or the Cyclopes from their prisons deep within the Earth – the injustice that had led her to promote Cronus over and above her husband in the first place. According to a slightly different version of the myth, he allowed Gaia to release them, but almost immediately reimprisoned them.

Cronus then married his sister Rhea, repeating the pattern of a male sky god marrying a mother goddess who represented the Earth and fertility. The other Titans also married each other, and six divine couples ruled the world together.

Cronus and Rhea had six children: Demeter, Hera, Hades, Poseidon, Hestia and Zeus. However, Cronus had been warned by Gaia and the

Rhea hands Cronus a stone wrapped in swaddling blankets in place of the infant Zeus, thereby saving the baby's life (see page 144), in a Roman marble relief dating from the 1st century BC.

wounded Uranus that he was fated to be supplanted by his son, just as he had deposed his father. Heeding this warning and hoping to cheat destiny, he ate all of his children at birth. In another version of the myth, his brothers allowed him to marry Rhea and act as supreme ruler on condition that he should not have any sons who could threaten his power and thus the security of the other Titans.

143

It was sometimes said that Zeus had been raised on Mount Dicte, Crete. The island's mountainous interior was sparsely populated in classical times and people regarded it as a place of mystery.

Rhea, like her mother Gaia before her, was anguished by this destruction of her children, and she and Gaia conspired to protect her last baby. As soon as her son Zeus was born, Gaia carried him away to safety, while Rhea wrapped a stone in swaddling blankets and took it to Cronus, who swallowed the stone in place of the baby.

Gaia hid the infant god in a cave, usually believed to be at Mount Dicte on Crete, although Attica also claimed this honour. In this place of safety he was nursed by Amaltheia, who was both a goat and a nymph, and he was fed on her milk and on honey. Zeus later rewarded her faithful service by installing her in the heavens as the constellation Capricorn, the goat.

According to one myth, Rhea was concerned that her husband would find out about the child if he were to cry, and ordered a group of men to dance constantly around the cave entrance, singing loudly and clashing their spears and shields together to drown any sound the baby might make. These were the Curetes – mysterious, semi-divine young men noted for their noisy dances, who were mentioned frequently in Greek poetry. Scholars believe that they were mythical

counterparts to the young Cretans who performed armed dances in rituals that honoured their local version of Zeus.

Little is known about Zeus's education and upbringing on Crete. Some stories said that he was taught by Pan, half-man, half-goat and the god of the woodlands; others that he grew up with the shepherds of Mount Ida. However, by the time Zeus came of age, he had learned of his mother's suffering, the destruction of his brothers and sisters, and Cronus's attempt to destroy him. He vowed that he would take his revenge.

Zeus's first wife was Metis, a sea-nymph famous for her wisdom and cunning, who was later to become the mother of Athene (see page 174). Zeus persuaded her to administer an emetic to Cronus, which made him regurgitate Rhea's stone, followed by all the children he had swallowed earlier. The stone he had mistaken for Zeus was sometimes said to have been preserved at the oracular sanctuary at Delphi (see box, page 185). His brothers and sisters, grateful for their new-found liberty, immediately joined Zeus in an attempt to overthrow their father, and with him the entire race of the Titans.

Cybele, the Mother Goddess

Cybele was an Eastern fertility goddess whose cult was incorporated into Greek and Roman religion. She was often identified with Rhea, the Titaness and mother of Zeus.

According to the mythology, Cybele had once fallen passionately in love with a beautiful young man called Attis. She appointed him a priest of her temple at Pessinus in Phrygia (Anatolia). As priest, he was bound by an oath of chastity, but he broke this promise for love of the nymph Sagaris, whom he planned to marry. In her anger and jealousy, Cybele drove him insane so that he castrated himself and died.

A religious ritual developed around this narrative. The priests of Cybele were voluntary eunuchs known as *galli*. At the goddess's festivals they performed ritual dances in which they pretended to be mad – howling, shrieking, moaning, banging drums and brandishing spears and shields. Because Cybele was often associated with Rhea, Zeus's mother, there appears to have been a connection between this curious ritual and the mythological dances of the Curetes who had protected Rhea's baby, the infant Zeus.

Cybele was more central to the Romans than she was to the Greeks. Inspired by the Sybilline Books, the Roman sacred prophetic literature, envoys brought the statue of Cybele from the temple at Pessinus to Rome in AD204–5. The goddess's public standing was enhanced by a legend about the statue's arrival. The ship carrying it became stuck on a mud shoal in the Tiber River, and no amount of effort could refloat it. At the same time, a Vestal Virgin named Claudia was defending herself against claims that she had broken her sacred vow of chastity (an oath taken in honour of Vesta, goddess of the hearth, whose temple these chosen girls of the nobility tended). Claudia offered a test of her virtue: if she were still a virgin, Cybele would enable her to free the ship. She took her girdle, placed it around the prow and effortlessly pulled the ship off the mud.

Cybele was usually represented as an imposing woman with a towering crown, riding in a chariot drawn by lions. Sometimes she was depicted with many breasts, or with two lion cubs held under her arms. Attis was often shown standing by her side, or following behind her.

A 4th-century BC Greek carving shows Cybele, seated with a lion cub by her side, with Persephone, the daughter of Demeter.

The Battles of the Gods

Victory over his father did not come as easily to Zeus as it had to Cronus. Having rejected his son's claim to supremacy, Cronus called the other Titans and their children to his aid. Thus began the Titanomachy, a terrible war that would last for ten years. To the ancient Greeks, Hesiod's description of the battle would have seemed very real because of his reference to actual geographical features. Zeus and his siblings based themselves on Mount Olympus, in northern Greece, and his father and his allies established themselves to the south on Mount Othrys.

In his fight to defeat his son, Cronus could rely on most of his brothers and sisters, who were reluctant to lose what power they had under his leadership. Many of them had also produced powerful children, who were prepared to come to the aid of their uncle. Zeus and his siblings found themselves severely outnumbered.

Zeus then made a bold decision: he set free the Cyclopes, who had been imprisoned by Uranus, on the condition that they would make weapons for the Olympians. They accepted the offer, and made a helmet of darkness (or invisibility) for Hades, the great trident (a three-pronged fork) for Poseidon, and finally the thunderbolts that became both the instruments and symbol of Zeus's power. Following that, he released the Hundred-handed from Tartarus. They would prove to be powerful allies, because their multiple hands could hurl massive stones with great accuracy. These two moves also gained for Zeus the allegiance of Gaia, who had long been desperate to free her children.

Gaia urged the Titans to accept the rule of Zeus and depose Cronus peacefully. The wisest of her children agreed to do so, but most of them continued to support their brother. The Titans appointed Atlas, a son of Iapetus, as their military commander, and under his leadership a full-scale

The violence of the divine wars is captured in this altar to Zeus from a temple in Pergamon, c.180BC. It shows a hound in Zeus's service killing a Giant.

Benevolent Monsters

In addition to the Titans and the Giants, the early period of creation produced many semi-human figures, not all of whom were vicious – some were even forces for good.

Pan, a god of the forests who introduced music to the world, was part goat and part human (see box, page 189). In most stories, he is considered the son of either Apollo or Hermes and a female nature spirit or nymph. The satyrs who accompanied Pan were endowed with similar animal features. They sometimes ran wild but at the same time they presented a joyous image of the creative life-force in their ecstatic dancing and pipe-playing.

Pegasus, the entrancing winged horse, had monstrous origins – born from the neck of the snake-haired Gorgon, Medusa, when the hero Perseus cut her head off. His father was Poseidon, who had slept with Medusa before she was transformed into a Gorgon by Athene, for thoughtlessly defiling her sanctuary. Pegasus at first lived wild on Mount Helicon with the Muses, the nine immortal nymphs who represented the range of the classical arts. He was later tamed by Bellerophon, who rode the winged steed during his adventures. When the hero became arrogant enough to believe that he, a mortal, could reach Mount Olympus, Zeus caused Pegasus to rear up, throwing Bellerophon back down to Earth. The winged stallion then became the bearer of Zeus's thunderbolts. For his faithful service, Zeus honoured Pegasus with a constellation.

The most famous benevolent monster was Chiron, a child of Cronus and the nymph Philyra, who was born a centaur, with the head and torso of a man and the body and legs of a horse. Although most centaurs were wild and cruel, Chiron grew up to be the wisest teacher in the world, and many of the heroes and the younger gods, including Asclepius, the son of Apollo and a renowned healer (see box, page 187), were sent to him for their education in music, medicine and the arts. When Herakles wounded him accidentally, he suffered such agonies that he begged the gods to relieve him of his immortality and let him die peacefully. Although the request was unprecedented, Zeus agreed. After his death, Chiron was honoured with a place in the heavens, in the constellation Sagittarius.

Centaurs cavort in this idyllic scene from a late Roman mosaic.

war broke out. At first the immense power of the thunderbolts seemed to give the Olympians an advantage, but Atlas rallied the Titans and their allies into a long resistance.

Eventually, Zeus's side began to regain the upper hand, and the Titans were besieged on Mount Othrys. The three brothers, Zeus, Hades and Poseidon, held a war council, and a plot was laid. First, Hades crept unseen into Cronus's presence and stole his weapons. Then Poseidon began to threaten Cronus with the trident, while Zeus blasted him with his thunderbolts. Immediately after that the Hundred-handed started to rain rocks upon the remaining Titans.

This sudden combined attack led to total victory for Zeus's forces. Most of the Titans were hurled down into Tartarus, where they were guarded in perpetuity by the Hundred-handed. Atlas, as their military leader, was allotted a harsher punishment: he had to support the heavens on his shoulders for eternity (see page 140). Accounts differ as to whether Cronus was sent to be imprisoned in Tartarus or allowed to take up a dignified exile in the Islands of the Blessed. Some tales maintain that once Zeus had established his supremacy, he relented and pardoned all the Titans, leaving Atlas alone to bear his punishment.

The story of the Titanomachy reflects contemporary attitudes towards warfare. The ancient Greeks were themselves continually engaged in wars, between one city state and another or against foreign enemies such as the Persians, and they valued courage and military skill highly. At the same time, they were suspicious of bloodlust and a mindless enthusiasm for destruction. Their mythical heroes were often those who used guile or knowledge, rather than sheer physical strength, to achieve their ends. This theme emerges clearly in the tale of the battle of the Olympians against the Titans. Success for the young gods depended on co-operation and careful planning, while the cruder Titans were defeated, despite their greater strength.

Zeus had two more contests to face before he could confidently assert his authority over the world. The first was the Gigantomachy, the war against the Giants, which was one of the most popular myths in ancient Greece.

A centaur battles against a Lapith, a mythical inhabitant of Thessaly, on one of the metopes (carved panels) from the Parthenon, c.440BC.

Monstrous and Terrifying Spirits

During the violent wars of the gods in these earliest times, many dark forces were created. Some of them survived the conflicts and continued to haunt and endanger humanity.

The Gorgons, three sisters with hideous round faces and snakes instead of hair, had the ability to turn any man who looked upon them into stone. The sisters of the Gorgons were the Graeae, who symbolized old age. At first they were conceived of as women who were born old and white-haired. In later tradition, they became hideous hags, grey-haired from birth, who shared only one tooth and one eye.

Echidna, described by Hesiod as an "impossible monster", was a beautiful woman from the waist up, and below a hideous serpent. She gave birth to a

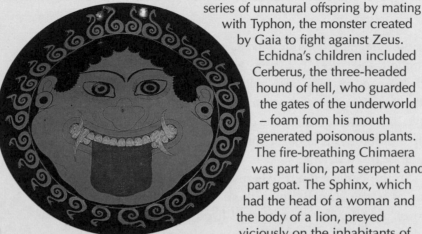

A detail from a 5th-century BC Greek vase showing the head of a Gorgon, with snakes in place of hair.

series of unnatural offspring by mating with Typhon, the monster created by Gaia to fight against Zeus. Echidna's children included Cerberus, the three-headed hound of hell, who guarded the gates of the underworld – foam from his mouth generated poisonous plants. The fire-breathing Chimaera was part lion, part serpent and part goat. The Sphinx, which had the head of a woman and the body of a lion, preyed viciously on the inhabitants of Thebes; similarly the Nemean Lion was reputed to harass and attack the hapless people of the town of Nemea.

Although Gaia had sided with Zeus, her grandson, against her own children, she became infuriated by his high-handed ways and turned to the Giants to help her defeat him. There are two accounts of their origins: some claimed that the Giants already existed, conceived from the blood of Uranus's castration (see page 141); other versions said that Gaia only generated these offspring after the defeat of the Titans.

Encouraged by Gaia, the Giants hurled huge rocks and burning oak trees at the heavens. Fighting against them, Zeus, Poseidon and Hades were now assisted by their children, and Ares, Hermes, Apollo, Artemis and Athene all played crucial parts in the war. The gods learned through an oracle that, although they would be able to injure the Giants, it would take a mortal to issue the death-blow. Athene, with Zeus's permission, enlisted Herakles, a half-human half-god known

for his strength, to the gods' side. With his help, the Olympians were finally able to kill the Giants.

However, Gaia's anger did not abate after Zeus and the Olympians had defeated her champions. She immediately generated an even more formidable monster, Typhon, who had 100 dragon heads, coiling serpents for legs and hundreds of hands. Zeus took on this terrifying adversary in one-to-one combat. At one point Typhon managed to slice out Zeus's sinews from his hands and feet and hide them, but they were found by Hermes who refitted them. Restored to strength, Zeus returned to the fray. Gradually he was able to drive Typhon out of Greece, finally crushing it under volcanic Mount Etna.

This proved to be Gaia's final effort against Zeus. She now acknowledged his supremacy, and he and his clan at last returned victorious to their home on Olympus.

The Ages of Humankind

Just as there are a variety of myths explaining the beginning of the world and the origins of the gods, so there are a number of different traditions about the creation of humanity. The myths even differed as to which god, Cronus or Zeus, was responsible.

Hesiod, the eighth-century BC Greek poet who compiled the most coherent genealogy of the gods (see page 136), also told the story of the birth of humanity in a poem called *Works and Days*. In this he described the creation by the gods of five different races of human beings who lived one after the other.

In the earliest times, when Cronus, father of Zeus, was the supreme god, there was a golden race of mortals. The men of gold lived free from all cares and worries, eternally young. Hesiod was not clear about what happened to this blessed race, saying only that the Earth covered it over, burying it, and that the souls of the golden ones survived as guardian spirits. Other writers suggested that the terrible wars of the gods led to their destruction. A later Roman version of this myth maintained that the people of the golden age lived in Italy where they were ruled over by Saturn, the god whom the Romans associated with Cronus. This version was written for patriotic motives to glorify Saturn, from whom the Romans traced their ancestry.

Hesiod claimed that after the golden race vanished from the Earth, Zeus created a race of silver. These mortals were inferior to those created by his father, and their lives were less idyllic. The seasons divided the year up, and the cold and rain of winter obliged people to live in caves. The Earth no longer provided them with food spontaneously. This race turned out to be childish and irresponsible. They refused to offer sacrifices and treated the gods who came among them with contempt. In the end they so infuriated the Olympians that they were all destroyed.

Zeus then decided to experiment with a race of bronze, made from ash trees and endowed with

In this early Roman relief, Saturn is shown holding a knife and standing before an animal that is about to be sacrificed. Originally an Italian god of agriculture, Saturn came to be identified with the Greek deity Cronus and was said to have ruled over a golden race of mortals.

hearts of stone. They were highly skilled in bronze-work, arming themselves and building their houses out of the metal. However, the men of this race were terrifying and warlike – they were so addicted to fighting and combat that they soon annihilated each other and dwelled thereafter in the underworld.

The heroic age followed this disastrous experiment. While the inclusion of a heroic age

Prometheus, Friend of Humankind

Not all the classical creation myths identified Zeus as the creator of humankind. One tradition maintained that Prometheus, a Titan, created the human race and then remained its advocate in the face of the supreme god's hostility.

During the war between the Titans and Olympians, some of the Titans' children sided with Zeus and his brothers. One of these was Prometheus, whose name in Greek means "forethought" and who was able to foresee that Zeus would be victorious. To reward him for his faithful service, Zeus gave him the task of creating life for the Earth. After he had made the animals with Zeus's approval, Prometheus sculpted clay figures, modelled on the gods, which could stand upright. Pleased with his work, he gave these figures life, but this time without seeking Zeus's permission.

Because of this insult, Zeus never cared for humans. Only Prometheus's intervention eased their lives. For example, it was his guile that won for them the better portion of the meat from sacrificial animals. He hid the choice cuts of meat under an animal's stomach, then wrapped the bones and entrails in delicious-looking fat, before inviting Zeus to choose the gods' portion. Zeus was deceived, and the people had meat to eat. Ever afterwards, human celebrants at sacrifices received the tastiest parts of the animal (see box, page 155).

Then Prometheus stole fire from heaven and gave it to his human creations. Zeus was outraged by this act and ordered that the thief should be tied to a rock for eternity. Each day an eagle came and ate out his liver, which grew again the following night.

To punish humankind for Prometheus's gifts, Zeus had Hephaistos, the heavenly craftsman and god of metalwork, fashion a beautiful but wicked novelty – a woman, Pandora, who was as foolish as she was alluring. Zeus sent her to Earth carrying a pot ("Pandora's box") that she was ordered never to open. The men, enchanted by her charm, welcomed her among them. But soon, stupidly, she opened the secret vessel, as Zeus knew she would, and out of it flew the miseries that afflict humanity, such as war, famine, sickness, evil and sin. Only hope, ever deceptive, remained in the pot, a slight comfort.

Prometheus himself was released from his daily torture after 30,000 years. It was said that he possessed a secret of such importance that Zeus gave him his freedom in exchange for the knowledge. This information was that Zeus could only be overthrown by a child he fathered by the nymph Thetis, and with this warning Zeus was able to avoid the fate that had befallen his father and his grandfather.

Deucalion and Pyrrha

The story of a destructive flood that leaves the Earth ready for repopulation is one of the most common myths in cultures all around the globe.

The idea of widespread human evil being punished by a global catastrophe is shared by many mythological traditions, including those of India, Native America and Aboriginal Australia. Usually, a few righteous people are saved from the devastation, and they repopulate the world, passing on their knowledge, skills and high moral standards. The biblical account of Noah and the ark is perhaps the best-known example of such a story. It may derive from a Mesopotamian account of a catastrophic deluge (see page 130), which also may have influenced the Greek tale of Deucalion and Pyrrha.

In this story, Zeus, disgusted by the wickedness of the people of the iron age, determined to destroy the human race. He decided to do so by means of a deluge that would inundate the Earth, drowning all the people. While he unleashed torrential rain, Poseidon stirred up the rivers and the seas and caused earthquakes. Nearly all the people on Earth died, either by drowning or from starvation.

Only two good and reverent individuals were saved: Deucalion, son of Prometheus and king of Pthia, and his wife Pyrrha. Warned of the flood by Prometheus, they had time to seek safety in a boat that was well provided with food. After nine days, the boat came to land on the peak of Mount Parnassus. Zeus, recognizing their virtue, let them live. The rains stopped, and the waters gradually fell. At length, the couple were able to descend the mountain to the sacred cave of Delphi.

Deucalion and Pyrrha were safe but sad, lonely and purposeless in the empty world. They offered up prayers. From the cave the oracle spoke to them: "Throw your mother's bones over your shoulders."

This instruction at first dismayed the couple, because disrespect for the bones of an ancestor was among the worst of sacrileges. But suddenly Deucalion understood the oracle's puzzling command. The Earth was their mother, and the rocks around them were her bones. Picking up stones, he threw them over his shoulder, and Pyrrha followed suit. Each stone that Deucalion threw hit the ground and became a man, and each of Pyrrha's stones became a woman, until the world was peopled again.

disrupted the pattern of ages of metal, it allowed Hesiod to accommodate the epic tradition of the legendary heroes, considered his immediate predecessors. Hence the heroic age was a race of demi-gods, also created by Zeus – the men who were celebrated in the great heroic myths. When they died, many of these heroes were either placed in the heavens as constellations, became companions to the gods, or were granted a blissful existence in the Islands of the Blessed.

Finally, Zeus created the present age of human beings, the age of iron. This race was born to toil and was afflicted with all kinds of troubles by the gods. Hesiod believed that the race of iron was fated for destruction: it would be wiped out either by an act of Zeus or by warfare. The end would be near when babies began to be born white-haired and prematurely senile.

When, 800 years later, the Roman poet Ovid came to rewrite these myths in his great work, the *Metamorphoses*, he omitted the heroic age from his account. The tradition of the heroes was no longer as influential in his time as it had been in Hesiod's, and thus he wrote only of four ages of mankind rather than five. Although the heroic age was not a significant strand in mythology, the continued importance of heroes was shown by the widespread religious practice of hero sacrifice. This had less in common with sacrifices to the Olympian gods than with those made to the chthonic deities – the local "earth spirits" linked to an earlier cult of the dead – in that these were evening rites and involved the offering of a black animal. These sacrifices sought the goodwill of a person whose greatness while alive had gained him or her continued power after death. Sacrifices were offered to dead ancestors, but also to kings, soldiers and even valiant enemies, because a bold enemy was respected as a hero. Roman emperors based their claim to divinity in part on this tradition: the idea that men could be demi-gods, eternally powerful, gave the emperors a way in which to promote themselves from powerful mortals to incarnate gods during their own lifetimes.

Achilles, one of the mythical Greek heroes of the Trojan War (see pages 206–225), dies in the arms of his comrades. His story is memorably told in Homer's *Iliad*. The myths of the heroes were so influential in ancient Greece that Hesiod included a race of heroes in his account of the origins of mankind.

Olympus: Dwelling of the Gods

Once victorious, the children of Cronus and Rhea were free to establish their kingdom. They made their home on the highest mountain in northern Greece, an isolated peak surrounded by beautiful countryside and known as Mount Olympus. Although the actual mountain is craggy and forbidding, life on the mythical peak was idyllic.

To the early Greek city states, Mount Olympus had great strategic importance because it formed a key part of the natural defence against invaders from the north. The need for such a defence against a common enemy was an important source of solidarity between the city states. They also shared a language and a belief in the same pantheon of gods, although they were governed independently and remained geographically separate. By establishing Mount Olympus as the home of these gods, the Greeks acknowledged its strategic and psychological significance. In addition, by giving the Olympians a common residence, they reinforced the concept of a family of divinities.

In their legends and their worship, the Greeks behaved as though the gods actually lived on Mount Olympus. At the same time, they were aware that this was not reality, and that the home of the gods was a remote place above the heavens. None the less, it is in real locations that most of the episodes of classical myth unfold.

On the Olympus of the imagination, as on Earth, the sun would rise in the morning and set in the evening, but the weather was always clear and calm. The grand entrance made of clouds was guarded not by armed warriors or threatening animals, but by the Horae – three beautiful goddesses, also called the Seasons (the classical people of the Mediterranean recognized only spring, winter and summer). The Horae kept track of which gods were abroad in the world, and welcomed them on their return.

Inside the realm of Olympus, each of the gods had a home of his or her own, designed in solid brass by Hephaistos, the divine smith and husband of Aphrodite. But the centre of Olympian

At its highest point, Mount Olympus reaches 9,840 feet. Its summit is known as "The Throne of Zeus". In mythology, the mountain was home to the Olympian gods; historically it played an important strategic role for the ancient Greeks, helping to protect their territory against invaders from the north.

life was the palace of Zeus. All the gods would come to its great hall when summoned, and they feasted there nightly on ambrosia and nectar, their divine food and drink.

154

Life on Olympus was marked by beauty, ingenuity and creativity. Hephaistos, with divine artistry, designed every sort of comfort for his fellow gods – the solid gold tables and chairs could even move themselves in and out of the great hall as occasion demanded. The gods' clothes were woven by Athene (see pages 176–177) and the Graces (see page 166).

Mortals were never permitted to enter the home of the gods, even in times of desperate need. Virtuous Greeks or Romans did not expect to go to Olympus when they died – they would go to the Elysian Fields (see pages 192–194), deep in the underworld, or to the Islands of the Blessed, situated at the far edge of the Earth, in Oceanus, the mythical sea.

The Importance of Sacrifice

In addition to a common home, the Olympians shared one form of worship. The sacrifice of animals was a central part of religious observance honouring all the gods. The Greeks and Romans believed keenly in the principle of reciprocity: offerings to the gods were made to thank them for their favour and at the same time to bind them by honour to continue to extend their goodwill.

Some myths contain mentions of human sacrifice, mainly associated with the goddess Artemis (see box, page 182). However, it is not clear whether these reflect historical reality or are purely fictitious. By the time of Homer, it is clear that only animals were offered in sacrifice. Each god had a characteristic sacrificial animal. For example, bulls were sacred to Zeus, horses to Poseidon and cows to Hera. It was essential that the sacrificial animal was in perfect condition – sacrificing a blemished or diseased animal was considered an insult to the god. The Romans most commonly sacrificed pigs, although sheep and oxen were also offered on important occasions. But only parts of the animal were presented to the god. In Greece the god received a burnt portion sometimes consisting just of the bones and the tail, while in Rome the god's lot was the heart, liver or kidneys. The rest of the meat was eaten by the priests and the participants in the sacrificial rite.

Each sacrifice was accompanied by prayers and other practices, such as ritual washing and the offering of grain and hair. Sacrifices to the Olympian gods took place at dawn and to the chthonic deities (see page 153), such as Hades, at sunset. They were an essential part of festivals and competitions honouring the gods, but sacrifices could also be made at other times, often preceding, for example, important state occasions, battles or the signing of treaties.

In Rome, sacrifice took on additional significance because of the belief in augury – seeking out omens and signs of the future. While those Greeks seeking to learn their future often consulted oracles, the Romans preferred an elaborate system of examining the entrails of sacrificed animals before making any major political or personal decisions.

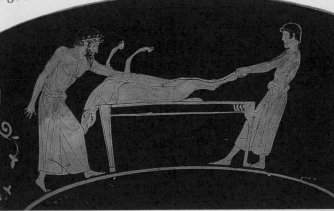

This detail from a red-figure vase, dating from the end of the 5th century BC, shows the ritual slaughter of a deer in honour of the gods.

155

The First Couple, Zeus and Hera

After Cronus's sons defeated their father and his generation of gods, they divided up the universe among themselves. Zeus, formerly the leader of the rebellion against the older generation, took the heavens for his share and now assumed supremacy over gods and humankind. His consort, Hera, had an equally exalted position.

Zeus was the supreme god, the father figure of Mount Olympus who maintained order among the often quarrelsome Olympian gods. On Earth, Zeus was worshipped as the ultimate protector of state and family, and as the source of the most esteemed qualities, such as justice, hospitality, fair government and the honouring of oaths. In sacrifices, he was offered the blood of goats, sheep and especially white bulls – because bulls were the fiercest and most powerful animals known to the early Greeks, they were particularly sacred to Zeus, the mightiest of the gods. Oak trees were also sacred to him. The Olympic Games, the athletic contest founded in 776BC and held regularly in Zeus's honour, was among the most important festivals in ancient Greece, and they continued to be staged throughout the Roman period. The four-year interval between each games' festival became a chronological reference point, much in the same way as decades are today.

In art, Zeus was often represented in great majesty, sitting on a gold or ivory throne, with his thunderbolts ready in one hand and a sceptre in the other, accompanied by a sacred eagle with its wings spread. One of the seven wonders of the ancient world was the forty-two-feet-high statue of Zeus that stood in his temple at Olympia, in the Peloponnese. Crafted by Phidias, the foremost Athenian sculptor, and completed *c*.430BC, it was covered with gold, ivory and precious metals.

Although he had the highest status among the gods, many of the stories told about Zeus present a less than admirable side to his nature. He was frequently angry, temperamental and unreasonable, hurling his thunderbolts impetuously, tricking his friends and deceiving Hera. Above all, Zeus was highly amorous, and in his efforts to seduce, he knew no boundaries. In many tales, he assumed false shapes in order to beguile the women on whom he had set his eye. This was partly because mortals would die instantly upon seeing him in his full splendour; but Zeus also relied on deception to achieve his ends. For

156

Zeus stands ready for battle, holding his thunderbolt high, in a bronze statue dating from the 6th century BC.

example, he disguised himself as Artemis in order to corrupt Callisto, one of the virgin nymphs who accompanied that chaste goddess; he came to Danae as a shower of gold, and to Aegina as a flame of fire. And, perhaps most famously of all, as a great white swan he raped Leda, wife of Tyndarus, king of Sparta, even though he knew she was pregnant.

As a great god, Zeus was extremely potent – he had such an enormous number of children, including gods, immortals and humans, that it is impossible to give a full list of his offspring. Apart from the second generation of the Olympians, all of whom were his progeny, he was the father of many of the minor gods, including Hermes, the Fates, the Muses, the Seasons and the Graces, and also of several key characters in the great stories of classical mythology, such as Persephone, whose mother Demeter was his sister. In addition, he was the father of a number of the heroes, including Herakles.

Zeus's promiscuity played a key role in the development of a unified mythology. The common religion of the Greek world was an amalgam of local traditions that combined over the centuries with belief systems introduced by invading tribes and other foreign influences. One of the easiest ways for early mythographers to incorporate a new tradition within the core body of myth was to identify imported deities with the Olympian gods. Sometimes, the Olympian would take on the attributes of the new god. For example, Zeus possesses traits of a sky god who was held sacred by the earliest Greek-speaking people in the second millennium BC, as well as those of a Cretan sky god, confirming his close ties with the island. In other cases, the local god or goddess became a sexual conquest of one of the Olympian gods, most often Zeus.

Given the fact that he had overthrown his own father, Cronus, to become ruler of the world (just as Cronus had usurped Uranus), Zeus was understandably wary that he too was fated to be supplanted by his children. However, he was able to break the pattern because he was not only

This temple to Hera, the wife of Zeus, was built in the Greek colony of Poseidonia, known to the Romans as Paestum, in southern Italy in the mid-6th century BC. Its mighty columns have withstood the test of time. It stands next to an equally impressive temple to Poseidon that was built a century later.

warned of the danger of overthrow (see box, page 151) but also took steps to avoid it. He restrained his lust for the Nereid, or sea-nymph, Thetis, because she was fated to bear a son who would be mightier than his father. He also swallowed Metis, the Titan goddess of wisdom, after he made her pregnant, because it was prophesied that their offspring too would be powerful. He gave birth to their child, Athene, on his own, thus neutralizing the prophecy (see page 174).

Disloyal and even cruel to his wife and mistresses, he nonetheless honoured his family. In this respect, he reflected classical society. Both Greek and Roman men esteemed family honour, but the Greek male social elite had no problem reconciling this with extramarital sex involving both women and younger men. And although in the early days of the Roman republic sexual morality was somewhat stricter, the emperors were notoriously less inhibited in their behaviour – as though, once they started to think of themselves as representatives of Jupiter (the Roman Zeus), they felt free to emulate his sexual habits.

157

Nothing so clearly shows the division between the public and the private roles of Zeus as the relationship with his wife Hera. The couple were brother and sister, joined in a sacred marriage between a sky god and an earth goddess, just as Gaia and Uranus and Rhea and Cronus had been before them. They were brought together as a result of Zeus's sexual trickery. Charmed by his sister, Zeus disguised himself as a cuckoo and, feigning cold, snuggled himself to her breast, where she received him tenderly, becoming yet another victim of his amorous deceptions.

As Zeus's wife, Hera was queen of all the gods. Her worship was as widespread as his, and a ewe lamb and a sow were usually sacrificed to her on the first day of every month. She was the patroness of marriage and married women, punishing adultery severely and rewarding chastity and devotion. Like some of the other female Olympians, she had a role as a protector of childbirth: the Milky Way is so called because it was created from milk that had spilled from her breasts when she was nursing the hero Herakles. Her milk could confer immortality. In Rome, where home and household were extremely important, her authority was even greater. In her Roman form of Juno, she was goddess of cleanliness and good order, as well as of power, empire and riches. She could give or withhold prosperity and worldly success, and all the consuls were required to make a special sacrifice to her before they could take up office. Her representation in art reflects this high esteem. She is usually shown seated on a throne or driving a chariot drawn by peacocks, attended by Iris, goddess of the rainbow.

Despite her high status, her married life was chaotic. She was almost insanely jealous of her husband's mistresses, persecuting them unmercifully and punishing their offspring. Zeus retaliated with abuse and violence, once hanging her up in the great hall of Olympus for the other gods to laugh at. At one time she left him and went to live on Euboea, an island close to the east coast of mainland Greece. Zeus desperately wanted her back and finally effected a reconciliation, but their reunion did not last. Despite this endless cycle of infidelity and jealousy, however, the long-lasting bond of Zeus and Hera symbolized the significance and the strength of marriage in Greek and Roman culture.

This pattern of public dignity and private licence, of immense divine power and squabbling pettiness, distinguishes the characters of all the gods of Greece and Rome. In terms of personality, their supreme deities are remarkably human – none of the gods is either totally good or totally bad, but like humankind, they combine both positive and negative traits. Zeus and Hera, the first couple of Olympus, were subject to the same emotional complexity as mortals.

In this 5th-century BC terracotta, Zeus is accompanied by Ganymede, a mortal youth of whom he was enamoured. The statue was found in Zeus's sanctuary at Olympia.

Europa and the Bull

Zeus was famous for his sexual adventures, and many of the stories of classical mythology start with his seduction of a mortal woman. For example, the city of Thebes was said to have been founded as a result of Zeus's desire for Europa, daughter of the king of Phoenicia.

One day Princess Europa went with her friends to gather flowers in a meadow beside the ocean. The group of laughing girls in the hot sunshine was a charming sight, and most delightful of all was Europa herself. She was so appealing that Zeus could not resist her. But knowing everything, he was aware that she was as pure as she was beautiful, and that he would be able to seduce her only through subterfuge.

In the meadows where the girls played, a herd of handsome cows was grazing peacefully. They were the prize cattle of Europa's father, and the girls paid little attention to them. Then one of them noticed a new bull in the herd. They were curious, as young girls are, because the bull was more beautiful, stronger and larger than any they had ever seen. The princess went up to the animal and, despite its strength and size, it turned out to be gentle and playful. Her companions told their parents later that they had plaited flower garlands for the bull and it had let them dress it up and pet it. "It was a game," they said, "just a game. It knelt down and she climbed on its back."

Hardly had Europa settled on the bull's broad shoulders than it charged down towards the shore with the girl clinging desperately to its horns. It galloped into the waves, and by the time Europa realized that this was no game, the bull was swimming; she was out of her depth and there was no alternative but to cling on tightly.

Only when they came ashore on the island of Crete did Zeus reveal to her his true identity. Europa was unable to resist him and eventually bore him three sons, Minos, Rhadamanthus and Sarpedon (see page 194).

This 1st-century AD wall painting from Pompeii shows Europa, accompanied by her friends, sitting on the back of a magnificent bull, which was actually Zeus in disguise.

Back in Phoenicia her family continued to mourn their loss. Finally, Europa's brother Cadmus, feeling compelled to take action, set out and wandered over all the world seeking his lovely sister. But he never discovered where Zeus had hidden her. Unable to return home and face his father's profound grief, he built a new city in Greece: Thebes.

Hades, God of the Underworld

With Zeus receiving the heavens and Poseidon the oceans, the third of the victorious sons of Cronus and Rhea, Hades, was given the underworld when his father's kingdom was divided. Hades presided over not only the lands where the dead dwelled (see pages 192–194) but also everything that lay beneath the Earth's surface – the king of death therefore controlled wealth itself in the form of the Earth's agricultural riches and minerals. For this reason, he was known to the Romans as Pluto or Dis, both of which mean "wealth".

The Greeks and Romans were lovers of life and showed little interest in the rewards offered to the virtuous after death. For the Greeks in particular, the heroic ideal held that it was important to achieve glory during one's time on Earth. Occasionally, a mortal beloved by the gods was given a form of immortality as a star, a constellation or a plant, but for the most part death was unnervingly permanent and the afterlife could not be relied on to bring any reward for goodness in life. At the same time, the Greeks, and the Romans to an even more marked degree, were deeply moralistic and believed that the wicked would be punished.

Perhaps because of this combination of concepts, Hades was seen as a dark and unattractive god, hard-hearted and merciless. He was generally unaware of what was happening among mortals or on Olympus – he remained instead in his realm under the Earth. His reluctance to ascend from the underworld emphasized the permanence of death. He was also the supreme god of the chthonic or earth deities (see page 153), and was sometimes referred to as Chthonian Zeus.

In this 5th-century BC vase painting, Hades banquets with his wife, Persephone. Hades was as rare a subject for vase paintings as he was for mythological tales. This example is particularly unusual in its depiction of the god of the underworld as a loving husband in a domestic scene – mostly, he is shown on his throne.

Hades had the ability to remain unseen, because during the war against the Titans the Cyclopes gave him a helmet that rendered its wearer invisible, so that one could never see death approaching. When Hades *was* seen, he was often carrying keys – an indication that there was no way out of his kingdom.

His personal appearance was so grim and his residence was so dismal that he was unable to persuade any of the goddesses to marry him willingly, despite his power and his riches. Unlike his brothers he was seldom associated with seduction or sex and consequently produced few if any offspring. His frustration at being unable to win either a wife or a lover led him to abduct Persephone from her mother, Demeter, and to attempt to install her as queen of the underworld (see pages 162–165) in what was one of the most dramatic episodes of classical myth.

Hades was surrounded by a strange court. The three Erinyes – the Romans called them Furies – were regarded by some of the poets as his daughters, and by others as the offspring of Gaia (see page 141). The Furies – Tisiphone, Alecto and Megaera – were of fearsome appearance, often garbed in black cloaks soaked in blood, wielding whips of scorpions, and with snakes instead of hair. They relentlessly enacted the vengeance of the gods, above all on those who murdered their own kin. When the Greeks dared to address them directly, they often called them the Eumenides, the benevolent ones. In myth, they were said to have earned this name by ending their persecution of a young man, Orestes, who killed his mother to avenge her murder of his father. However, it was also a superstition to refer to dark forces with flattering names, in order to ward off their evil power. Another companion of Hades was Hecate, a goddess associated with ghosts, black magic and crossroads (see page 181).

With the exception of his role in the tale of Persephone, Hades rarely features in classical mythology. In the stories of punishment after death, or of the living humans who visited his dark country, he is seldom involved personally. When he is, a softer, almost pitiful aspect to his character is shown. Even in the abduction of Persephone, his loneliness makes him a sad figure. In the account of Orpheus's journey to the underworld to reclaim his young wife (see box, page 193), Hades is said to have wept when he heard Orpheus's music and was so moved that he allowed Orpheus to try to take his wife back to the land of the living.

Nonetheless, Hades does not have a fully rounded, almost human character like the other Olympian gods. This is partly a result of his chastity. With the exception of his abduction of Persephone, he did not become involved in the passions, intrigues and jealousies that make up so much of the narrative of classical mythology. It is as if the classical authors felt uneasy telling stories about so dark a power.

Little religious ritual built up around Hades. Although he was acknowledged as part of the Olympian pantheon, no temples were built to him. Only black animals, usually black bulls, were sacrificed to him, and after the bull's throat was cut, the blood was not collected in vessels or sprinkled on an altar as it was at other sacrifices, but was left to drain down into the earth. Cypress trees, narcissi and the maidenhair fern were all sacred to Hades, as was the number two, which was always regarded as inauspicious.

An ornate vase, dating from _c._325BC and made in a Greek colony in Italy, bears an image of Hades greeting a mythological hero upon his arrival in the underworld.

161

Demeter's Tale of Death and Rebirth

The goddess of corn and harvest, of agriculture and country life, was Demeter. This figure of fertility was always ready to nourish the Earth and make it fruitful, and she was central to one of the most powerful classical myths explaining the cycle of the seasons.

Despite gradual commercial and cultural development, in antiquity the central and western Mediterranean remained an agricultural region dependent on successful harvests and domesticated animals. Foreign trade was not sufficiently developed to supply the daily needs of a growing populace. Demeter, as the goddess of agricultural fertility, represented an essential life-force. Her roots probably lay in the most ancient culture of the region and she was often associated with the previous generations of the gods as much as with the Olympians. For the Greeks, Demeter was sometimes identical to Rhea, or even Gaia, the Earth herself. Later, when the Greeks and Romans incorporated aspects of legends from Egypt into their mythology, Demeter was identified with Isis, who was also a goddess of rebirth and fertility (see pages 42–43).

Although she rarely appears in the adventures of the deities and heroes, Demeter was popular among the gods and humankind alike. She was always welcome on Olympus, but she preferred to stay on the Earth, where she wandered freely, looking after the cornfields. Sicily and the countryside of Attica were regarded as her particular homes. She was typically represented wearing a crown made of ears of corn, but there were other, stranger images of her. In Sicily she was often shown veiled in black and with the head of a horse: this depiction is probably connected with the story that Poseidon, the sea god, coupled with Demeter when they had both disguised themselves as horses. Because of this story, she is sometimes shown carrying a dolphin, the fish companion of Poseidon.

In the spring, a pregnant pig was sacrificed to Demeter, no doubt partly because pigs were regarded as highly fertile, and partly because pregnant sows are notorious for the damage they can do to new crops.

Demeter features in one of the most important and unusually consistent classical myths, which explains the

In this 2nd-century BC Greek sculpture, Demeter assumes a typical pose, holding a horn of plenty in one hand and a bouquet of corn and poppies in the other, symbolizing nature's fertility.

162

Nature Spirits

The Greeks and Romans saw nature as full of divinity. They believed that some spirits inhabited rivers and forests and others personified natural forces. These beings were popular subjects for Greek and Roman art.

Nature spirits feature in the earliest surviving classical myths. And even in later, more sophisticated times, the Greeks and Romans felt a strong connection to the natural world.

Many of these spirits belonged to a specific place. For example, almost all rivers, springs and fountains had their own individual guardian spirits or gods. Other figures were more generic. The Nereids, children of Pontus and Gaia, and the Oceanids, children of two Titans, were sea-nymphs; the Dryads and Hamadryads presided over woodlands; while the Oreads were responsible for hills and mountains. There were also minor nature gods with more specific duties. Triton, for

This sleeping woodland spirit was carved in Greece in the 3rd century BC.

example, was responsible for calming storms; Priapus was the god of gardens and sexual organs; and Aurora was goddess of the dawn.

The chief of these diverse spirits was Pan, god of the countryside and of goatherds and shepherds. He lived in wild places accompanied by satyrs, male nature spirits who were half-man and half-goat. With his horns and hairy goat's legs, he was so ugly that no nymph would have him as a mate, but he made beautiful music on his pipes.

annual cycle of the seasons, the rhythms of sowing and harvesting, and the contrast between summer and winter. Zeus remained close to his sister Demeter after he had married Hera – he was even the father of Persephone, Demeter's daughter. Although Hera was ordinarily jealous of Zeus's relationships with other women, there was no resentment towards Demeter, it being acceptable for Olympian gods to have incestuous unions.

Demeter was a devoted mother and she doted on her beautiful Persephone, who was brought up in Sicily and educated and accompanied by a troupe of nymphs (young female nature spirits). However, Hades was attracted to Persephone and with the tacit approval of her father Zeus, his own brother, he decided to abduct her. In one version of this story, Aphrodite, the goddess of love, deliberately caused Hades to fall in love with Persephone, because she was reluctant to see too many attractive young women remaining chaste. Hades found Persephone gathering flowers near Mount Etna. He swept her up into his chariot and carried her away. On the shores of Lake Cyane in Sicily he struck the ground and it opened up so that he could carry his prize down into his realm.

Demeter searched Sicily for Persephone, but without success. Thereafter she wandered, half mad, across the world looking for her lost daughter and refusing to perform any of her normal

163

The Eleusinian Mysteries

Every year, for more than 2,000 years, the Greeks celebrated a strange and solemn festival in thanks for Demeter's gift of agriculture to humanity. The Eleusinian Mysteries, as they were known, were so highly regarded that some people esteemed them above even the Olympic Games.

The cult, with its main sanctuary at Eleusis, only fifteen miles from Athens, was essentially egalitarian. Men and women of all ages could be initiated on equal terms, and the celebrations were designed so that there was no distinction between rich and poor. To ensure this, anyone arriving in Eleusis in a chariot was very heavily fined. The only people barred from admission were serious criminals, practitioners of witchcraft, and anyone who had, even accidentally, taken another's life.

Initiation into the Mysteries earned a person a special relationship with all the gods, securing happiness and success, and guaranteeing privileges in the underworld. Members of the cult were bound to secrecy, and to reveal the rituals was to risk severe punishment, even death. Because of this, scholars know little about what happened during the ceremonies. What is known, thanks to comments by several writers including Pindar and Sophocles, is that the participants in the rites at Eleusis found the festival emotionally satisfying.

A year before attending the great Mysteries, candidates had to go through a lesser ritual that began with an extensive purification rite. The actual moment of initiation was terrifying: hallucinatory visions and spectres appeared, the temple shook, hideous noises sounded, lightning flashed, and there was a background of either intense dark or leaping flames. After initiation the new cult members could join a nine-day festival, the Greater Mysteries, which included processions, ritual baths, games, sacrifices, libations and chanting.

Demeter was known to the Romans as Ceres and there was a festival held in her honour each April. A Roman mosaic from the 1st century AD, found in Valpolicella, depicts a priest with an initiate into the Eleusinian Mysteries. Because initiates were sworn to secrecy, such imagery offers valuable insights into these esoteric religious practices.

duties. As a result crops failed, farm animals became infertile and the world suffered from desperate famine. After some months of this, Demeter gave in to despair, and she sat on a rock in Attica and wept for nine days. By tradition, this rock was the foundation stone of Eleusis, site of Demeter's greatest sanctuary (see box, opposite). Demeter was rescued from her misery by Celeus, king of Attica, and his wife Metaneira, who kindly took her in, even though they believed she was just a mad woman. In gratitude she blessed their two sons, Demophon and Triptolemus, and instructed the latter in the art of agriculture.

After this interlude Demeter resumed her search. Accounts vary as to who told her the truth about her daughter's disappearance: some versions say that it was Arethusa, a river nymph; another that it was a shepherd who heard the tale from a colleague who had witnessed the abduction first-hand. As soon as she received this crucial information, Demeter rushed to Olympus to demand that Zeus exercise his powers and restore their daughter to her. Zeus tried to persuade her that Hades was a suitable husband for Persephone, but Demeter remained resolute in her desire to have her daughter back. Her mourning, and thus the famine, continued.

Finally Zeus relented. He agreed that Hades should be made to give up his bride provided that she had not eaten anything in the underworld: it was impossible to return to Earth after eating the food of the dead. Unfortunately, Persephone had swallowed seven pomegranate seeds. Even Hades did not know this, but she was betrayed by Ascalaphus, one of Hades's gardeners. Demeter turned him into an owl in her anger, which is why the bird is a symbol of ill omen.

A compromise was eventually reached whereby Persephone would remain Hades's bride and would live with him for six months each year, but for the other six months she was allowed to return to her mother. When Persephone was on the Earth, a happy Demeter made the world fruitful, but during the time her daughter spent with Hades, Demeter mourned and nothing grew.

A 5th-century BC Greek vase painting of a woman bringing an offering to an altar. Like the other Greek gods, Demeter was propitiated with sacrifices, typically of pigs and sheep.

This myth appealed on many levels, but most particularly by exploring the natural cycle of seasonal death and rebirth. In doing so, it addresses one of humankind's essential fears – that the barren winter months might never end. The involvement of the Olympian gods, and Demeter's desire to see her daughter again after a long, lonely winter, made it inevitable, in very human terms, that spring would reappear each year.

165

Aphrodite, Goddess of Love

Aphrodite, the goddess of love, marriage and beauty, personified not only romantic love but also sexual passion, and her unearthly charm attracted both gods and mortals. Throughout the centuries artists rivalled one another in their attempts to capture her beauty, helping to make her perhaps the best known of the classical gods.

There are two main mythic traditions associated with the origins of Aphrodite, which are reflected in the epithets that were commonly attached to her name. Some accounts describe her as the daughter of Zeus and a nymph called Dione: as the fruit of Zeus's philandering, she was the personification of sexual attraction and physical love. This was Aphrodite Pandemos, or Aphrodite of the people.

Another version of Aphrodite's birth makes her the most senior and venerable of all the Olympian deities. This portrays her as Aphrodite Urania, the offspring of Uranus, the first sky god, and therefore a survivor from the earliest times

The new-born Aphrodite is lifted from the sea by two of the Graces, her handmaidens. Dating from the 5th century BC, this carving once adorned the back of a chair.

(see page 141). In this tradition, she represents sacred love. When Cronus castrated his father, Uranus, he flung his genitals into the ocean and there his semen mixed with the sea foam. From that union, untainted by sexual contact, Aphrodite was conceived. The tides and winds of the sea carried her gently, first to the island of Cythera and then to Cyprus where she was brought up by the Graces. When the Olympians defeated Cronus, she was taken to Olympus, where the gods, moved by her beauty, welcomed her.

Aphrodite therefore represented both sacred and profane love. She was goddess of harlotry and prostitution, but also of marriage. She led women into adultery, but also encouraged them to be faithful and chaste. She punished viciously, but rewarded generously. These mixed messages are consistent with the conflicting versions of her beginnings. She existed before the Olympians came into being, but she was younger and lovelier than any of the other goddesses. She was patroness of sex and therefore of procreation and the future of civilization, but at the same time she delighted in bawdy comedy.

The different ways in which Aphrodite has been represented in art illustrate the two sides to her nature. Sometimes she is depicted as a fertility goddess, with exaggerated sexual attributes. More often, however, she is portrayed as an idealized version of femininity, as typified by the renowned statue, the Venus de Milo, from *c.*100BC. In these artistic images she is often depicted wearing her famous girdle. Any woman who wore this magical belt became instantly beautiful and desirable in the eyes of whoever saw her. Even Hera, who seldom associated with Aphrodite, was known to have borrowed the girdle to rekindle Zeus's desire for her. It was so powerful that when Aphrodite herself wore it, even her infuriated and cuckolded husband, Hephaistos (see boxes, page 151 and page 154), was happy to forgive her all her infidelities.

This ambiguity inherent in Aphrodite's imagery is shown in a story about the Greek sculptor Praxiteles, who worked in the second half of the third century BC and was noted for his carvings in Parian marble, the shining white stone particu-

A detail from a 1st-century AD fresco in Pompeii shows two of the three Graces, companions of Aphrodite. As the goddess of beauty, she drew to her the most attractive of the divine beings.

larly prized by Greek sculptors. Praxiteles was invited to make a statue of Aphrodite for a temple on the island of Cos. He was not sure which image of the goddess the purchasers wanted, so he made two, one presenting the sexual side of Aphrodite and the other showing her veiled. Even though the naked Aphrodite was superior in workmanship, the people of Cos preferred the veiled statue because the priests wished to encourage modesty and decorum – given that it was the fashion for the women of Cos to wear white garments of cloth so fine that it was transparent, perhaps this priestly ambition was wise. The people of Cnidos, however, bought the naked statue for their temple. It was said to be so beautiful that one young man broke into the temple at night to try to gratify his desire for the goddess.

All the male gods were fascinated by Aphrodite's beauty. This made her unpopular with the other goddesses, especially Hera, whose annoyance increased when Zeus attempted to seduce Aphrodite, despite the fact that she refused to submit to him even when he threatened her with violence. Because she was the goddess of sexual passion, she had absolute control over lust and even Zeus was not able to rape her; instead, to punish her for her refusal, he forced her to marry Hephaistos, the least attractive of the Olympian gods.

Her marriage did not prevent Aphrodite from indulging in a long stream of relationships with both gods and mortals, and she had several children whose myths explore the kinds of love that came to humankind – mutual tenderness, mad passion, the love between humans and gods, and sexual desire between men and women and men and men. Aphrodite had two children with

167

Hermes (see page 191), the messenger of the gods. The most famous of them was Eros, known to the Romans as Cupid (see box, page 171), the winged god of passion, whose arrows caused his victims to fall in love instantly and totally, making them desperate with often unreciprocated desire. He frequently accompanied Aphrodite in her adventures or ran errands for her, typically causing those who had offended her to fall in love with inappropriate or unsympathetic people. Her second child by Hermes was Hermaphroditus, who fused with a sea-nymph – their bodies were joined into one being, half-man and half-woman. With Dionysus, Aphrodite conceived Priapus, a fertility god who is always depicted with a huge, erect phallus.

Her most famous lover was Ares, the god of war. Their lengthy relationship scandalized even the free-living Olympians. With Ares, Aphrodite had two children. Anteros was the god of orderly, lawful love, and especially of shared tenderness. Although few stories were told about him, he was often depicted in paintings and vase decoration, usually wrestling with Eros. In Greek schools there was sometimes a wall paining of Anteros to remind students that it was their duty to love and respect their teachers.

Harmony was Aphrodite's second child by Ares. Her gentle nature demonstrated the way in which love can moderate the anger of conflict. She was given in marriage to Cadmus, the founder of Thebes. All the Olympian gods attended this wedding and showered the couple with gifts, including a famous necklace made for her by Hephaistos. But because Harmony was Aphrodite's child, she had unwittingly attracted the hatred of Hera; worse still, Cadmus was the brother of Europa (see box, page 159), another of Zeus's conquests, whom the divine consort disliked even more. So although the couple was virtuous, Hera ensured tragedy befell the family.

Aphrodite was one of the most widely worshipped of all the Olympian goddesses because it was understood that without love and sex, there would be no life or future for humanity. As well as being the goddess of love, she was regarded as the patroness of beauty, elegance, pleasure, the graces and social amenities. She was also the goddess of laughter, so comedy came under her influence. Roses, myrtles and apples were sacred to Aphrodite, as were doves, swans and spar-

The Aphrodite of Cnidos, carved in Parian marble by the renowned sculptor Praxiteles in 340BC. It was offered first to the people of Cos, who were concerned it would discourage modesty.

rows, and these birds shared the honour of drawing her chariot. In her temples, ritual prostitution or sex with fellow worshippers was sometimes practised in addition to the offering of blood sacrifices, and there were frequent complaints about the excesses that occurred at some of her rites.

Aphrodite played a key role in the Trojan War (see pages 206–225), recorded in the great epics of Homer and Virgil. According to myth, the conflict started because the gods found a golden apple that was said to belong to the most beautiful goddess of all. Aphrodite, Hera and Athene all claimed their right to the prize and, too nervous to make a decision himself, Zeus appointed Paris, prince of Troy, to judge between them. Each of the three bribed Paris with some kind of honour, and Paris chose Aphrodite after she offered him the most beautiful woman in the world as his bride. Her rash promise led to the abduction of the wife of Menelaus, Helen, who was noted as the loveliest of mortals. Menelaus led an army of Greeks to Troy to reclaim her, initiating the

Eos and Tithonus

Although far from faithful herself, Aphrodite was vindictive towards her rivals. Following the usual practice of Olympian goddesses, it was the woman, rather than the man, whom she blamed, and her punishments were always ferocious.

Although he enjoyed the sexual favours of Aphrodite, Ares continued to seek his satisfaction wherever he desired, and he embarked on an affair with Eos, the goddess of the dawn.

One day Aphrodite caught the two together, and her jealousy was aroused. She pronounced a terrible curse on Eos. Never would she love a god again – she would desire only mortal men. And so it happened that Eos, a goddess, fell in love with Tithonus, a handsome prince of Troy. They were so happy together that he begged her to grant him the gift of everlasting life, and she foolishly agreed.

At first all seemed well. But they had forgotten to arrange for him to remain youthful and in good health. He grew older, more frail and decrepit, until his life became unbearable and he begged his lover to let him die peacefully.

She sought the help of Zeus, but even he could not take away the gift of another god. In the end, since Tithonus could neither live nor die, he was changed into a grasshopper, which ever since has greeted its former lover by chirping at the first light of dawn.

Aphrodite, a vengeful goddess when betrayed, is shown with her lover, Ares, in this 5th-century BC votive relief.

Aphrodite rests in a giant shell, attended by Cupid, in this 1st-century Roman wall painting from Pompeii.

ten-year war. Paris, in choosing Aphrodite, allied her with the Trojan side against the Greeks, who were favoured by Hera and Athene.

Meanwhile, Aphrodite had taken a human lover, Anchises, a Trojan nobleman, by whom she had a son, Aeneas. When the Greeks finally won the war and set the city of Troy on fire, Aphrodite intervened to assist her mortal child to escape, carrying his now aged father on his back. Although she was unable to protect him from the wrath of the other Olympians, she helped and guided him throughout ten years of travel and exile, as recorded in Virgil's *Aeneid*.

The Romans regarded Aeneas as the father of Rome because he founded the royal line that was later to build the city on the seven hills. In their

desire to be perceived as a noble nation associated with the heroic stories of Greece and the eastern Mediterranean, the Romans found that Aeneas's parentage, with Aphrodite as his mother, provided them with the legitimacy they sought. Later, the emperors claimed to be descended, through Aeneas, directly from the Olympian gods. Under the Romans, Aphrodite – named Venus – became a gentle, more dignified goddess of beauty and love, the queen of laughter and patron of social life and sensual pleasures, all of which the Romans enjoyed so much (see also pages 238–243).

The Power of Cupid's Arrow

Eros, the quintessence of love, was originally a mysterious, primeval force. But with time he was gradually transformed into the familiar, winged Roman figure of Cupid – the mischievous, cherubic infant equipped with the bow and arrows of desire.

As with Aphrodite, there are two traditions explaining Eros's or Cupid's birth. One associates him with the pre-Olympian world. The poet Hesiod told how Eros came into existence as the power of love at the very beginning of the world, along with Gaia (the Earth) and Tartarus (the underworld). Other accounts say that the world came into being with the mating of Eros and Chaos, so that even the gods owe their existence to him.

Gradually, however, as the various myths and mythic themes consolidated around the individual gods, Aphrodite became the divine personification of love. But because his worship was so well established, Eros was assimilated into this new tradition as the son of Aphrodite. As the offspring of the goddess, Eros came to represent the masculine ideal of love, in the same way that Aphrodite represented the feminine ideal, and he was always depicted as being as young and beautiful as she was.

As the mythic tradition developed over the centuries and Zeus became more powerful, so, increasingly, Aphrodite was seen as his daughter, and therefore under his power like the other Olympians, rather than as a goddess born to Uranus, who

A 4th-century AD Roman mosaic shows several Cupids fishing. In this typical late depiction of the god, he is chubby and playful. The Romans often used images of Cupid as a decorative element in mosaics, frescoes and carvings.

belonged to an earlier divine generation. Her loss of status affected her son. His appearance became less impressive: his wings and arrows were introduced, as were tales of his mischievous nature and his light-heartedness about passion.

When the Romans established their control over the body of myth, Cupid, as they called Eros,

became less mysterious still. He was depicted both in stories and in art as a chubby child, often naughty, but always charming. He appeared in art as decoration, portrayed as a whimsical cherub, frequently playing with a hoop or a butterfly – in contrast to the mighty god he had originally been among the Greeks.

THE CITY ON THE HILL

To the millions of tourists who visit it each year, the Acropolis (literally, "high city") in the Greek capital of Athens is an architectural showplace. But for the ancient Greeks, the site had a more profound significance. Part walled citadel and part civic centre, the 1,000-feet-long complex was also a sacred precinct dedicated to the Olympian gods. Pride of place went to the city's patron, Athene. A thirty-nine-feet-high sculpture of the goddess stood in her great temple, the Parthenon, and all twelve Olympian deities were celebrated on the building's eastern frieze. A much-used theatre on the southern slope of the hill was dedicated to Dionysus.

Above: Built in the 5th century BC, Athene's magnificent temple, the Parthenon, was the Acropolis's ceremonial centrepiece. Sculptures on the building depicted scenes from her life and the nature of her worship.

Above: Despite the ravages of time, the Acropolis dominates the Athenian skyline today just as it did in classical times. Many of the gods had sanctuaries on the sacred hilltop.

Right: The Theatre of Herodes Atticus was built on the Acropolis in the 2nd century AD. Similar theatres were built throughout the Greek world. Ancient Greek plays are once more staged in the amphitheatre today.

Left: Statues dating from the late 5th century BC support the roof of the Porch of the Caryatids in the Erechtheion. This temple contained altars to Athene, Poseidon and Hephaistos.

Below: This section from the sculpted frieze that once decorated the Parthenon shows horses carrying their riders bareback as part of the great procession that introduced the annual Panathenaea, the festival held in Athene's honour.

Athene, Goddess of Good Counsel

Of all his children, Zeus was fondest of his daughter Athene, the virgin goddess of wisdom, who presided over crafts and skills, including those associated with both war and peace. She was the patron of Athens, and her prestige increased with the city's fortunes, so that as it became the pre-eminent Greek city her status among the Olympians grew.

The story of the birth of Athene, who was to become Zeus's closest and best-loved companion, contains the same elements as other myths about the birth of gods. Just as Uranus and Cronus feared (rightly so) that their children would supplant them, Zeus knew he also might be supplanted by one of his offspring.

In the older accounts of the story, typified by Hesiod's *Theogony*, Metis, the Titan goddess of prudence and sagacity, became pregnant by Zeus. Fearful that the child might prove to be more wise and powerful than he was, and encouraged by Gaia and Uranus, Zeus swallowed Metis, hoping to kill the unborn child but at the same time keeping

the Titaness's wisdom for himself. Some months later he developed an agonizing headache. Such was the pain that he commanded Hephaistos to cut his head open with an axe. Athene sprang, adult and fully armed, from the gash.

In many myths Athene opposes or counterpoints Aphrodite: reason against passion, wisdom against beauty. As patron of Athens, the first city of Greece, Athene came to stand for everything Greek culture most valued. In many of the stories about her, she represents the power of intelligence and self-possession, of knowledge and sagacity. She is committed to chastity and remains unswayed by the irrationality of love or passion.

The moment of Athene's birth is depicted on this Athenian cup dating from *c.*550BC. Hephaistos, the divine smith, has split Zeus's head with an axe, and Athene emerges from the wound, fully grown and armed with a shield. Because of this unique birth, father and daughter always shared a special bond.

The Contest over Athens

Athene was the patron goddess of Athens, and her great temple, the Parthenon, dominated the city from its high rock (see pages 172–173). She had won the accolade as a prize in recognition of her wisdom and her generosity to humankind.

Cecrops, king of Attica in Greece, encouraged the tribes of the region to join together in order to create a city state. The gods watched Cecrops from Olympus, and knew that the city he was building would become one of the greatest in the world. Not surprisingly, many of the gods wanted to be the settlement's patron, leading to a heated debate about who deserved this privilege. Eventually, it was recognized that two deities had the best claims to this honour: Poseidon, because the city was close to the sea, his domain; and Athene because the arts of civilized life were bound to flourish there.

However, neither would give way to the other, and even Zeus was alarmed at the consequences of a quarrel between two such powerful Olympians. So he proposed a competition, to be judged by the other gods. Each contestant was challenged to produce a novelty for humanity, something both useful and beautiful, and whoever came up with the finest invention would be given the new city as a prize.

Poseidon immediately struck the ground with his trident and a huge black animal appeared, tossing its mane and pawing the ground. It was strong, fast and beautiful, yet amenable – it was, in fact, the first horse. The gods were highly impressed and imagined that the matter was settled, but Athene, smiling gently, instantly produced out of the rocky soil a tree with grey leaves and small oval green fruits – the olive.

The olive, she pointed out, would provide both food for human beings and oil for sacrifices to the gods. The tree would be hardy and enduring, bearing fruit even in the roughest, driest ground. But what is more important, she said, is that the olive tree represents peace, while the horse represents war. Surely peace was more useful to mortals and more beautiful than war?

Although none of the gods wanted to offend Poseidon and they all admired his magnificent invention, they were forced to acknowledge that Athene was the winner. Her olive tree was one of the most precious gifts the gods ever gave the people of Greece. Amid the cheers of the Olympians, the nascent city received both a name and a powerful patron at the same time.

Nonetheless, she did have a child. Hephaistos wanted to marry her, and when she refused he attempted to rape her. She resisted him successfully, but afterwards she had to wipe his semen off her body with a tuft of wool that she then threw down on to the Earth. From this botched coupling, Erichthonius, a strange monster with a man's body but a serpent's tail instead of legs, was born.

Despite the circumstances of his conception, and the fact that she had never carried him in her womb, Athene took responsibility for him, arranged his upbringing and education, and eventually made him king of Athens. After he died she transformed him into a star in the constellation Auriga, the charioteer.

Guardian of Heroes

Apart from the episode with Hephaistos, there are no stories about Athene having romantic or sexual involvements. Instead she became known as a protector of heroes: Jason who led the Argonauts in search of the Golden Fleece; Orestes, who murdered his adulterous mother, Clytemnestra; Theseus, who slew the Minotaur and became king of Athens; Herakles (Hercules to the Romans; see pages 196–205); and Odysseus (Ulysses to the Romans), whose ten-year journey back to his Ithaca home after the Trojan War was recounted in Homer's *Odyssey* (see pages 228–237).

Among her favourites was Perseus, a son of Zeus by one of his mistresses, and therefore a victim of Hera's jealousy, whom Athene protected and advised through his adventures. To help him slay Medusa, the monstrous Gorgon with a headful of writhing snakes, she lent him her magical shield. Perseus then used this as a mirror to approach the Gorgon obliquely, since any direct glance into her hideous face immediately turned a man to stone. After Perseus came back triumphant from this adventure, he returned the shield to Athene, and also presented to her Medusa's head. In art, the image of this head is emblazoned in the centre of Athene's shield or on her breastplate or helmet.

Patron of Many Talents

Athene was involved in both the public and the personal lives of almost every member of society. As the goddess of useful skills and crafts, she watched over military competence, but unlike Poseidon and Ares she was never seen as a bloodthirsty warrior. She was equally interested in the creative arts of spinning and weaving, and is

This sculpture of Athene, carved between 525 and 520BC, adorned one of the temples on the Acropolis (see pages 172–173), the main religious complex of Athens, set on a hill overlooking the city. It was there that the citizens of Athens constructed the Parthenon, the magnificent temple dedicated to Athene, in the 5th century BC.

sometimes shown seated in full armour, but with a distaff for spinning wool or flax in her right hand instead of a spear. Athenians looked to her as patron of their children's education and of the building of houses and temples. She also had a special relationship with sailors, since she was believed to have invented the first ship and taught humanity how to sail it. Above all, she alone among the gods could assuage the anger of Zeus, and even persuade him to change his mind.

Like the other Olympians, Athene could be jealous or spiteful. For example, she gave her unqualified support to the Greeks throughout the Trojan War, because Paris, the prince of Troy, had judged her less beautiful than Aphrodite, even though she had offered him immortal fame as a hero to award the prize to her. Equally severe was her treatment of Arachne, a presumptuous young woman who was a noted weaver and embroi-

derer. Despite warnings, she challenged Athene to a contest of skill, which Athene accepted. In the Roman poet Ovid's retelling of this story, Athene wove a picture showing the triumphs of the gods while Arachne created a series of pictures showing their vices, particularly the lusts of Zeus. Athene not only won the competition, but she turned her competitor into a spider as punishment for having dared to issue the challenge.

The worship of Athene, particularly in Athens, took place in impressive settings and involved intricate rituals. Her temple, the Parthenon, named after her title of Parthenos, "the Virgin", dominated the city. One of the rituals in her worship involved young boys, wearing full armour, performing a dance in imitation of the great victory ritual that Athene was said to have staged for the Olympian gods to celebrate the defeat of the Titans.

The Numerous Names of Athene

Like all the other Olympian divinities, Athene had a number of different names, or epithets. Some of these were regional variations, others referred to part of her function or her nature, and others again described aspects of her worship.

Athene, armed with a shield and a spear, on the reverse of a silver tetradrachma, a Greek coin, dating from c.324BC.

Athene is most frequently known as Pallas Athene. The name derives from an episode during the war against the Titans (see pages 146–149) when she personally fought and killed Pallas, a son of Uranus and Gaia. After her victory, she dressed herself in his skin and so took on his powers, his masculine strength adding to her womanly wisdom.

She was also called "Parthenos", from the Greek word for a virgin, in honour of her unwavering chastity; "Glaukopis", after her clear, bluish-grey eyes; "Hippia",

"horsewoman", because she taught mortals how to tame horses; "Coryphagenes", or "born from the head", to describe her birth from Zeus's head; and "Athene Sais", because she was worshipped particularly in that Egyptian city. Each of these names was associated with a specific emblem. As Pallas Athene she was accompanied by an owl, the symbol of wisdom, whereas the imagery of Sais crowned her helmet with a cockerel. And as Athene Parthenos she sat on a throne, fully armed with shield and spear.

Artemis, Virgin Huntress

Artemis was the virgin goddess of the hunt, of uncultivated land and wild animals, as well as of the moon. She preferred the wilderness and the woodlands to cities, had few dealings with men and seldom visited Olympus.

Artemis was born from Zeus's passion for Leto, daughter of two Titans and famous for her beauty. Hera discovered his infidelity and persecuted Leto with an ingenious range of cruelties. First she sent a terrible serpent, the Python, to torture the pregnant woman. To protect Leto and her unborn child, Zeus turned her into a quail so that she could fly away, but even this did not end his wife's persecution of the lovely young woman. Hera, unrelenting, refused to allow Leto to return to the ground to give birth.

As Leto flew desperately out over the sea, the island of Delos took pity on her and allowed her access on condition that it would be established as the cult centre of the god to whom she was about to give birth. Once she was safe on the island, Zeus transformed her into a woman again and she went into labour leaning against a palm tree.

First she gave birth to Artemis, but she remained in labour. The newly born goddess had to watch her mother's struggles continue, and assisted her to give birth to her twin brother, Apollo. So shocked was Artemis by this experience of childbirth that she told her father, Zeus, that she wanted to be allowed to remain a virgin always, and also to be given the power to assist all women in childbirth. She shared her role as protector of childbirth with Hera herself and with Eileithyia, who was a daughter of Zeus and Hera but was not one of the Olympian gods.

Artemis's most important role was as the goddess of women and of female secrets. She was also closely associated with the moon, whose four-week cycle of waxing and waning relates to the female 28-day fertility cycle. As the protectress of women, Artemis had special concern for adolescent girls and for women who wished to remain virgins, as well as for women in labour.

Preferring the company of women and shunning the presence of men as far as possible, Artemis lived as a huntress, roaming the wildest parts of the countryside. She was served by sixty of the Oceanids, and accompanied by other nymphs and mortals who were all virgins. Artemis was also associated with the Amazons, a tribe of women warriors who were said to live in the eastern hinterland of what is now

Because of her role as a fertility goddess, Artemis was sometimes depicted as having many breasts, as in this marble statue of the 2nd century AD from Ephesus, in present-day Turkey.

Right: **Diana, the Roman equivalent to Artemis, was most commonly associated with hunting, as shown in this 1st-century AD Roman fresco from Stabia, near Naples, Italy. The town was destroyed in the eruption of Mount Vesuvius in AD79.**

The Islands of Greece

The eastern Mediterranean is scattered with islands: besides Crete, Cyprus and the major Aegean archipelagoes of the Cyclades and the Dodecanese, many small islands fringe mainland Greece and Asia Minor. Several religious cults and myths have their origins here.

The gods were often said to have been born or brought up on islands. For example, Artemis and Apollo started life on Delos, near Mykonos in the middle of the Cyclades. Aphrodite came ashore and grew up on Cythera or, in some versions, Cyprus. When Hephaistos was thrown down from Olympus, he landed on Lemnos, where he set up his forges and where he always worked. Zeus was secretly brought up in Crete; and Hera, when she could no longer tolerate living with Zeus, found refuge on Euboea. Demeter's favoured home was the island of Sicily, and it was from here that her daughter was abducted; in her mad, wandering search for Persephone, she visited most of the islands of the Aegean, as did Dionysus on his journey from the east.

Every island seems to have contributed a god, a myth or an immortal. The genius of the Greek imagination lay in synthesizing these tales into manageable, interconnected narratives. Common themes found throughout them, such as the constant travels of the gods, allowed story-tellers to incorporate different island traditions into one coherent body of myth. The atmosphere of multiplicity and variety, and the notion of metamorphosis (magical change and fluidity), were also creative responses to the challenge presented by the fragmented geography of the Mediterranean region.

There are hundreds of islands in the eastern Mediterranean, and many were sacred to the gods.

Turkey. They mated with men only once a year and they immediately destroyed any male children who were born to them.

Although fiercely protective of these women, Artemis dealt ruthlessly with those who broke their vows of chastity. One of her attendants was a lovely young princess named Callisto, who was seduced by Zeus disguised as Artemis herself. Later, when she was bathing with Artemis, the goddess noticed that Callisto was pregnant. Furious, she refused to accept even Zeus's explanation of his deception as an excuse. She turned Callisto into a bear, to be hunted. Zeus, anxious to save her, snatched Callisto away and placed her, with her son, in the heavens as twin constellations, the Great and the Lesser Bear. On another occasion Actaeon of Thebes, a follower of Artemis and himself sworn to chastity, accidentally caught sight of the goddess bathing naked while he was hunting in the forest. He was instantly turned into a stag and pursued to the death by his own hounds (see illustration, opposite).

Artemis's concept of chastity was completely different from that of Athene, whose refusal to marry did not in any way alienate her from male company – on the contrary, she seems to have sought it out, taking young heroes under her patronage and freely involving herself in all the public, and therefore masculine, affairs of mortals, particularly in wars and politics. Artemis, on the other hand, actively repudiated male company, and showed no interest in boy children. Nonetheless, there are stories that suggest that she lapsed occasionally from her austere purity. Some myths maintain that she succumbed to Pan when the woodland god came to her disguised as a white goat. Also, different reasons are given to explain her shooting of the beautiful giant hunter Orion: some poets claim she did so because she was jealous that he preferred Aurora, goddess of the dawn, although most say it was because he assaulted one of her nymphs or even Artemis herself. He was later transformed into a constellation (see box, page 182).

Moon Goddess

It is significant that some myths imply that Artemis had a sexual side to her nature. These stories, as well as Artemis's role as protectress of childbirth, associate her with fertility, in contrast to her main identity as a virgin goddess. Her role as moon goddess also reinforces this connection. Artemis originally had no lunar associations, but as the mythic tradition developed and centred around the Olympian gods, she came to subsume the identity of Selene, a daughter of the Titans, who was the original goddess of the moon. (Similarly, the identity of Helios, the sun god, merged with Apollo, Artemis's twin brother; see page 184.) In addition Artemis partially absorbed the attributes of Hecate, another goddess of the moon and also of ghosts and witchcraft, who resided under the Earth in the realm of Hades. Among Hecate's powers was a measure of control over the fertility of the Earth. This association with a feared sorceress gave a menacing aspect to Artemis's character.

The three moon goddesses were often depicted as one, and some statues of Artemis showed her with three heads, combining all three aspects of her character. Ovid, the Roman poet, explained that the goddess was called Luna (the moon) in the heavens, Artemis on the Earth and

This Greek stone relief, dated *c.*470BC, once adorned a temple in Asia Minor. Actaeon, prince of Thebes, is being attacked by his own hunting dogs, after provoking the wrath of Artemis.

Hecate in the underworld. The linked goddesses also symbolized the three phases of the lunar cycle, with Artemis representing the crescent-shaped moon, Selene the full moon and Hecate the new moon.

Artemis, or Diana to the Romans, was always more popular in the eastern areas of the Mediterranean and in the Aegean islands than in mainland Greece or Italy. Her main temple, at Ephesus in Asia Minor, was considered one of the seven wonders of the ancient world. It remained an important religious site for centuries: in the first century AD Paul of Tarsus caused a riot in Ephesus by trying to preach the Christian faith there. The statue of her in this temple (see page 178) showed her with many breasts and with other symbols

The Gods and the Heavens

Orion, the victim of Artemis's wrath, was just one among many Greek mythological characters to have given their names to the stars, constellations and planets.

The Greeks were magnificent astronomers, combining the accumulated wisdom of Mesopotamian, Persian and Egyptian science with their own keen observations and geometrical calculations, and their work formed the basis for much of the later Western investigations of the heavens. By the second century AD, the renowned Greek astronomer Ptolemy had catalogued more than 1,000 stars, divided into forty-eight constellations.

All the prominent constellations of the northern hemisphere were named by the Greeks, who were sometimes influenced by the symbolism perceived by earlier traditions. Most of the constellations were named after mythological characters or stories: for example, Orion is named for the giant hunter who fell victim to one of Artemis's arrows.

The classical astronomers knew of only five planets, other than our own, which were distinguished from the stars because their relative positions in the heavens were not fixed. The innermost of these, Mercury, moves the fastest, and was therefore named after the fleet-footed messenger of the gods. Venus was the most beautiful Olympian, and her planet is the brightest object (after the sun and the moon) in the heavens, glowing pale and serene at dawn and dusk. Mars is red, the color of war. Jupiter, as the largest, was named after the greatest of the gods. Saturn, the most distant planet visible to the ancients, was identified by the Romans with the Titan Cronus, and was named for the popular agricultural god Saturn, his Roman equivalent. His festival, the Saturnalia, was celebrated when the sun entered Capricorn, the zodiacal sign governed by Saturn.

The astronomers who named the first three planets discovered since then respected this tradition. Uranus is more distant than Saturn, meaning that the three generations of sky god – Jupiter (Zeus), Saturn (Cronus) and Uranus – stretch out into the heavens in generational order. Astronomers agreed to name the eighth planet, discovered in the nineteenth century, after Neptune (Poseidon), Jupiter's brother and one of the most illustrious of the Olympian gods. The final planet, discovered in 1930, was named Pluto (Hades) after the third of the brothers who defeated the Titans.

According to Greek myth, the hunter Orion was turned into a constellation after he was killed by Artemis for having offended her.

connected with fertility goddesses. More usually, however, she was represented as young and tall, wearing a short, practical tunic, carrying a bow and arrow and accompanied by her hounds. Occasionally she drove a chariot drawn by two heifers or horses, each a different color. In rural areas, her statue was sometimes set up at cross-roads: this acknowledged her connection with

the Black Sea were said to sacrifice to Artemis anyone who was shipwrecked on their coast, and legend had it that the Spartans only gave up their annual human sacrifice to her in the reforms of the lawgiver Lycurgus in the ninth century BC, replacing this ceremony with a ritual of self-flagellation.

The Romans seem to have found Diana, their equivalent to Artemis, less attractive than the rest

Hecate, because in popular superstition cross-roads were often considered to be haunted. As a result of this she came to be known during the Roman period as Diana Trivia – *trivia* being the Latin word for crossroads.

Artemis was associated with human sacrifice for longer than the other Olympian gods, and this connection may in part account for the element of fear and loathing that was sometimes attached to her name. The people of the Tauric Chersonese on

On this 7th-century BC set of gold pectoral plaques, Artemis is depicted in her guise as Mistress of Animals. She was the goddess of the woods and wild places.

of their imported pantheon, despite the fact that she was sister to Apollo, one of their most important gods. Juno, the Roman form of Hera, took over many of her responsibilities towards women and children, and religious devotion to her consequently declined.

183

Apollo, God of Light

The twin brother of Artemis, Apollo was the god of light, and of the sun itself, but he was also the patron of music, poetry and all the fine arts, and of healing and prophesy. Although he was a figure of great beauty, and therefore a favoured subject of artists and sculptors, he was often unhappy in love.

Apollo, the younger twin born to Zeus and Leto, attracted none of the jealous punishment that Hera usually wreaked on her husband's illegitimate offspring. He was always an imposing figure on Olympus, and Zeus entrusted him with the power of knowing the future.

Just as Artemis took on the attributes of Selene, the moon goddess, so Apollo came to appropriate the qualities of Helios, god of the sun (see box, page 142). He was commonly called Phoebus Apollo – *phoibos*, meaning bright, was the epithet originally applied to Helios. This synthesis of two myths led to some confusion. The sun was seen in mythology as a fiery chariot pulled by two flying horses, which the sun god drove daily across the sky. But although he was regarded as the sun god, Apollo was never thought to perform this task. Instead it continued to be carried out by Helios, who maintained a separate identity from Apollo. This stands as an example of how the Greeks, in particular, could happily accept contradictions within their mythology.

Stories of Apollo's childhood and upbringing are rare. It is told that, as an infant (see page 149), Apollo joined his sister in coming to the aid of their father and uncles in the struggle known as the Gigantomachy. He was also said to have shot the serpent-monster Python, which had been torturing his mother at the behest of Hera. By killing it he gained possession of the oracular site at Delphi, where the monster had dwelled.

Apollo lived on Olympus and was usually highly honoured by Zeus, although they quarrelled

Apollo and his twin sister Diana (Artemis) are shown decorating a sacred pillar, in this terracotta plaque from the Temple of Apollo on the Palatine hill in Rome.

The Sacred Oracle at Delphi

From as early as the third millennium BC, Delphi was an important sacred site. The Greeks dedicated the complex to Apollo, and it was believed that the god himself spoke there through the mouth of his priestess, the Pythia.

The importance of this oracle can hardly be exaggerated. It was a major centre of the Greek world, unifying the city states. In addition, it drew visitors, many of them rulers, from all over the Mediterranean and the Middle East. Delphi came to be regarded as the geographical centre of the universe and was often called "the navel of the world", after a sacred stone known as the *omphalos* (navel) that was located there. This stone was said to have been the one given by Rhea to Cronus to swallow in place of the infant Zeus (see page 144).

A complex ritual developed at Delphi. Anyone who wanted to know their destiny made offerings of a sacred cake and a goat or a sheep, before consulting the Pythia, the priestess of the shrine.

After careful purification she sat on a tripod, a bowl on three legs, and fell into a trance-like state in which she received answers from Apollo. When she spoke, her words were copied down by a group of priests who then interpreted them and delivered the results to the supplicant. When the message of the god was negative, the Pythia refused to speak at all. Sometimes the prophecies at Delphi were ambiguous. Croesus, emperor of Lydia, consulted the oracle when considering a campaign against Persia and was told that he would destroy a great empire – he did, but unfortunately it was his own. More often they were extremely obscure, or open to almost any meaning.

Despite difficulties of interpretation, the oracle at Delphi was regarded as authoritative. It was consulted by anyone seeking guidance on major affairs of state, military expeditions, or religious or moral issues. Around the cave a large complex of temples, treasuries and hostels developed, with a great arena for the important Pythian Games, which were founded in 582BC. Colonnaded walks displayed statues of gods and heroes that had been donated in Apollo's honour.

Delphi's importance both as an oracle and as a social focus began to wane in the third century BC, as the Greek world expanded. In Roman times, its popularity was overtaken by other forms of augury, such as the skilled interpretation of dreams, weather patterns or the flight of birds.

The oracle at Delphi was built on the slope of Mount Parnassus. Homer stated that Apollo made his sanctuary there after ridding it of the Python.

bitterly when Apollo killed the Python, which was sacred to Gaia. Because of this, Apollo was exiled from Olympus and was forced to live for nine years on Earth. There he became a shepherd to Admetus, king of Thessaly, whom he later rewarded with immortality because he had proved such a generous employer. Apollo was known as the god of shepherds, and for this reason a wolf, the scourge of shepherds, was often sacrificed to him.

Apollo was commonly known as the god of music. There are many representations that show him with the lyre, the hand-held, seven-stringed musical instrument popular with the Greeks, and particularly important because it was used to accompany performances of poetry. Apollo had obtained the lyre from Hermes (see page 189), who invented it, and became immensely skilled at playing the instrument; he also instructed mortals in its use.

He was proud of his musical ability. Marsyas, a satyr, once challenged him to a competition, claiming that the music of his flute was sweeter than Apollo's lyre. After the Muses, who were the judges in the contest, had declared Apollo the winner, he had Marsyas flayed alive for his impertinence. On another occasion, he inflicted donkey's ears on King Midas for daring to prefer Pan's pipes to his lyre. But he could also use his musical gifts on behalf of humanity. For example, he assisted Poseidon in the founding of Troy, playing his lyre so sweetly that city walls seemed to grow to the sound of his music.

Like the other Olympians, Apollo was frequently involved in love affairs, many of which ended unhappily. He was unfaithful to the nymph Clytia, who pined to death and was reborn as the sunflower, always turning her face towards the sun, her lost lover. Daphne was so desperate to escape his amorous advances that she had her

This Etruscan terracotta figure of Apollo, known as the Apollo of Veii, was crafted in the 5th century BC. It is one of the oldest Italian representations of the Greek gods. With its fixed eyes and blank smile, the statue was fashioned in a style reminiscent of very early Greek figures.

mother Gaia turn her into a laurel tree, which is why Apollo was associated with it and awarded a crown made from its branches to deserving musicians and poets. In an attempt to seduce Cassandra, princess of Troy, Apollo rashly gave her the gift of prophesy. Although she still rejected him, he could not take back the gift, so he punished her by ordaining that nobody would ever believe her truthful prophesies. When she foretold the fall of Troy, her own people assumed she was mad and refused to heed her warnings.

Apollo's authority was tremendous and stemmed in part from his role as the god of divination. His temple and shrine at Delphi were the most famous in the Mediterranean world, but he had numerous other oracles. His two mottoes, "Know yourself" and "Nothing in excess", which were carved on a gateway there, reflected the Greek philosophy of life. His male beauty also epitomized a Greek ideal.

Apollo was the only Olympian god whose name was not changed when he was adopted into the Roman pantheon. Rather than being gradually merged with local Italian gods, he was introduced suddenly, in response to an oracle following an epidemic. He was important to the Romans for his role as a healer but was never as prominent among them as he was among the Greeks.

Asclepius, the Healer

Apollo's gift of healing was inherited by one of his sons, Asclepius, who was so skilled a doctor that after his death he was transformed into the god of medicine.

Apollo's lover, Coronis, was unfaithful to him, even though she was pregnant. For this, he exacted fierce revenge: he burned her to death with lightning but rescued the child from her womb and sent him to be educated by Chiron, the wise centaur.

Apollo's son by Coronis, Asclepius, became a healer, and was regarded as the inventor of medicine itself; he was physician to the Argonauts on their great journey to Colchis. So great were his skills that he began to restore the dead to life. An offended Hades complained to Zeus, who punished such

Asclepius is shown exercising his legendary healing powers on a Greek man who is identified as Archinus on this 4th-century BC relief.

presumption by killing Asclepius with a thunderbolt while Apollo was exiled from Olympus. When Apollo returned, he gave Asclepius divine status as god of medicine.

His principal temple was at Epidaurus, but he also had many others throughout the classical world. The Romans built him a major shrine after their city was delivered from a plague. His temples were equipped with gymnasia and baths, and while many of the recorded cures were miraculous, others were probably due to the priests' knowledge of herbal remedies and sound therapeutic regimens.

Hermes, Fleet of Foot

A special place in popular affections was held by those Olympians whom ordinary people could more readily identify with, such as Hermes, the god of flocks, travellers and boundaries, traders and thieves – people who lived on their wits. He was also a divine messenger, a trickster and the Psychopomp, who conducted dead souls to the underworld.

Hermes was said to have been born on Mount Kyllene, the highest point in the northern Peloponnese in Greece. His father was Zeus and his mother the goddess Maia, daughter of Atlas who held up the world.

The god was precocious as a baby. On the morning of his birth, he crawled out of the cave where his mother was sheltering and came upon a tortoise. Looking at it, he had the idea of using the shell as the sounding-board of a musical instrument. After killing the creature he added two arms, a cross-piece and strings to its shell, and so invented the first lyre.

He wandered on until he came to Pieria in northern Greece. Seeing a herd of well-fed cattle grazing in a meadow, he decided to steal fifty of the beasts. Born cunning, he plotted to conceal the deed: he led the cattle away backwards, and made large sandals out of bark for himself to disguise his own footprints. Then he hurried them home, stopping only to kill and eat a couple of the cows, piously sacrificing some of the meat.

The cattle were the prized possessions of Apollo, and the sun god was furious to learn of his loss. He travelled all over Greece looking for the missing beasts and eventually offered a reward for information. Some versions of the myth say it was Silenus and his satyrs who led Apollo to Maia's cave, others that it was the flight of a divinatory bird. Either way, arriving at the cave and finding some familiar cowhides stretched nearby, Apollo at once accused the innocent-looking infant of the

In this early Greek relief, Hermes is shown carrying a ram, symbolizing his role as a pastoral god. He was also frequently depicted holding a shepherd's staff.

theft. At first his mother Maia did not believe him, but Apollo persisted in his accusations. Eventually, Zeus was forced to intervene, and Hermes had to confess and return the cattle.

To soothe Apollo's anger, the baby started playing tunes on the lyre he had invented. Apollo was so entranced by the beauty of the sound that when the infant offered to give him the instrument as compensation, he forgave him, and the two became firm friends. In return for the lyre, Apollo offered Hermes the shepherd's staff that was to become his symbol. Known as the *caduceus*, it was represented in later years with two snakes entwined around it.

That was the mythical account of the baby-hood of Hermes. His name actually had a more mundane origin. It derives from the word *herma*, a rock-pile or cairn used to mark roads and frontiers, an apt name for the god of travellers and boundaries. In paintings and sculptures he was often shown as an adult wearing the short cape, broad-brimmed hat and sandals favoured by voyaging Greeks. In his case, however, the hat and sandals had wings, given by Zeus to speed him on his way.

Among the Olympians, the role of Hermes was to act as messenger of the gods, helping to put their plans into action. For example, in the

Divine Music

Music in Greek myth was associated with the pastoral gods, Hermes, Apollo and Pan. Hermes invented the lyre, and Apollo became its greatest exponent. Pan, the woodland god, created a musical instrument of his own.

Like all the satyrs, who were half man and half goat as he was, the god Pan adored music, dancing and beautiful women. He fell passionately in love with a nymph named Syrinx, but his appearance terrified her and she fled from him. The god was about to catch up with her when the desperate nymph sent a prayer to Gaia, Mother Earth. To Pan's dismay, Gaia rescued her by instantly transforming her into a clump of reeds.

Distraught, the frustrated lover threw himself down among the plants, sighing deeply. The reeds caught his breath and amplified it plaintively. Intrigued, Pan picked seven reeds of differing lengths and bound them together. So was born the instrument the Greeks called *syrinx* but which is now known as the Pan pipes.

Although the Greeks delighted in music, it often had tragic associations in their myths. The satyr Marsyas, who challenged the god Apollo to a musical contest and lost, was flayed alive for his arrogance (see page 186). And King Midas, who had the bad taste to prefer the music of Pan to that of the sun god in a similar competition, was punished by Apollo with a pair of ass's ears.

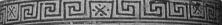

A Greek vase from c.440BC, decorated with one of the Muses playing a lyre.

The Wanderings of Io

In the story of Zeus's affair with Io, Hermes plays a typical role, stepping in to help the god out of a difficult situation. The story may reflect myths of Hathor, the cow-headed goddess of the ancient Egyptians, which were brought back to Greece by early travellers to the kingdom.

Io, a priestess of Hera, had been seduced by Zeus, like many beautiful mortals. Hera herself came upon the couple one day as they dallied in a meadow. Desperate to hide his infidelity, Zeus turned his lover into a heifer, hoping that the harmless-looking beast would escape his wife's jealous attention. But Hera at once suspected trickery, and insisted on taking the animal for herself. She entrusted it for safe-keeping to her monstrous servant, the 100-eyed Argus, who was said never to close all his eyes at once.

Io watches Hermes kill the 100-eyed Argus: a Greek vase decoration.

To recover his mistress, Zeus turned to Hermes for help. The younger god disguised himself as a goatherd and approached Argus, playing such sweet music on his flute that the monster dozed off. Seizing the chance, Hermes snatched up a boulder and killed him with a blow to the head. As a memorial to him, Hera later placed Argus's eyes in the peacock's tail.

Hera had been watching Hermes. Furious, she sent a gadfly to torment the cow, which ran off in a wild flight to escape the insect. Finally it reached the sea later known as the Ionian. Leaping in, the beast swam all the way to Egypt.

There Io's fortunes improved. She was turned back into human shape by Zeus, and in due course bore him a son, Epaphus.

Judgement of Paris (see pages 169 and 206), it was Hermes who led Paris to the divine beauty contest, after he had been elected as arbiter.

Zeus in particular made use of Hermes's services, seeking his aid in compromising situations. When the nymph Callisto bore him a child, he entrusted the baby to Hermes for safe-keeping from Hera's wrath. He asked Hermes to rescue Io from Argus, the monstrous guardian that Hera had set over her (see box, above).

Hermes also helped the other gods. When Ares was overwhelmed by two giants, Otus and Ephialtes, who managed to imprison him in a great bronze jar, it was Hermes who sneaked in to secure his release. When the pregnant Semele, bearing Dionysus, god of wine, was consumed by flames after she requested to see Zeus in all his glory, Hermes saved the life of the infant god by rescuing him from the fire. He also put the newly born Herakles to Hera's breast, whose milk could confer immortality on the human. In this instance, though, his efforts went unrewarded. The baby bit the breast, earning the goddess's hatred and causing her milk to spurt across the heavens, where it created the galaxy known as the Milky Way.

In such myths, Hermes's role was ancillary. Yet in ancient Greek ritual and religion, there are indications that Hermes had a more significant role to play. Initially he was a pastoral god. Literary references also suggest that originally he might have been a Master of Animals, with dominion over wild beasts. His cult was centred around the place of his birth – Arcadia, a mountainous region in the northern Peloponnese, where archaeological evidence suggests that he was honoured as early as the second millennium BC.

His worship may have predated that of Apollo, another pastoral deity, whose cult came to Greece with invaders from the north, probably in the last centuries of the second millennium. The story of the theft of Apollo's cattle and the gods' reconciliation may reflect a rivalry between the two cults, and their eventual accommodation. A third pastoral divinity was also associated with them: Pan, half-man and half-goat, whom some myths made out to be Hermes's own son.

Both Pan and Hermes are portrayed in myths as highly sexed. Some myths claim that Hermes was the lover of Aphrodite. One of the results of their liaison was Hermaphroditus, a youth so beautiful that the nymph Salmacis was overwhelmed by desire for him when she saw him bathing naked. The two made love so passionately that their bodies fused. Thereafter, Hermaphroditus was represented with a woman's body and a man's genitals – the original hermaphrodite.

Hermes was also associated with fertility cults. The cairns from which he originally took his name were simply standing pillars surrounded by piles of loose stones, used as waymarkers. But over the centuries, the pillar's own phallic qualities were elaborated upon, and it evolved into a column topped by a bearded head and with a horizontal projection representing the male member. These "herms" were set in public places throughout Greece, being thought to bring good luck. A distant memory of them may explain the Romans' fondness for using small statues of Mercury (their equivalent to Hermes) as outdoor ornaments.

Hermes's opportunism combined with his reputation for cunning to earn him a reputation as a divine trickster. He was credited with the invention of dice, and gamblers invoked his name when betting. He was also the patron of thieves. An unexpected piece of good luck was referred to as "a gift from Hermes", just as a sudden silence would be explained with the remark that "Hermes must have entered the room". Perhaps because "herms" were often set up in market-places, Hermes became a god of trade, and the Romans identified him with their deity of commerce, Mercury. For luck, merchants would sprinkle water from a spring sacred to him on their wares.

This popular god's other role was as Hermes Psychopompus, literally "the conductor of souls" who led spirits to the underworld after death. The responsibility perhaps reflected his original incarnation as a god of roads, because in early times graves were commonly dug by the wayside; in addition, as the god of boundaries, he was naturally able to cross what was for humans the biggest boundary of them all. This role also combined well with his duties as a divine messenger to whom, alone of the Olympians, Zeus had accorded free access to all three worlds – Olympus, Earth and the underworld.

The Greek master sculptor Praxiteles crafted this marble statue of Hermes holding the infant Dionysus c.400BC. Hermes saved the baby from Semele's body after she had been burnt to ashes by the sight of Zeus in all his glory.

191

The Realm of the Shades

The Greeks and Romans were in agreement that after death souls went to the underworld, somewhere far beneath the Earth. There, where the sun never shone, the dreaded god Hades ruled a kingdom that few were anxious to visit.

The earliest written accounts of the underworld are found in the Homeric epics, and the picture they paint of life after death is not a pleasant one. Homer's dead are restless shades without strength or will, bearing the marks of the disease or injury that killed them. For example, in the *Odyssey*, the once great Achilles bemoans his fate as one of the ghosts, claiming that he would rather be a poor man's slave on Earth than a ruler of the dead.

There were, however, other prospects for the souls of the deceased. A few favourites of the gods were carried off to the Elysian Fields, lying somewhere at the ends of the Earth, where they spent their days in a sunny paradise. In contrast, wicked individuals who directly offended Zeus were

imprisoned for eternity in Tartarus in the depths of the Earth to suffer the torments of the damned.

For a millennium or more, the Greeks and Romans continued to accept this broad threefold division of the underworld. But the rules that operated in Hades's domain gradually changed. As the Greeks' moral consciousness altered, reward and punishment after death became less a matter of divine whim and more a question of what individuals had deserved during their lives.

Much of the change came about as a result of the activities of the Greek mystery religions. The cult of Eleusis (see box, page 164) taught that its initiates could earn a place in Elysium. The Orphics added a belief in reincarnation. In their

In this Etruscan funerary relief from the 5th century BC, the deceased is carried to the underworld on horseback as servants of Hades look on.

Orpheus and Eurydice

Nowhere in world myth are the themes of love, death and creativity interwoven as poignantly as in the story of Orpheus and Eurydice.

The son of a king of Thrace and the muse Calliope, Orpheus was a great poet and musician. The music he made was so sweet that wild beasts and even rocks and trees would follow him when he was playing.

Orpheus's young bride was the beautiful Eurydice. However, they had not been long married when she stepped on a snake, whose venom killed her.

Distraught at the loss of the woman he loved, Orpheus determined to have her brought back to life. Carrying only his lyre, he went to the underworld to plead with its ruler, Hades, for Eurydice's release. He sang of love as a force that even Hades could not resist, and explained that he was determined not to leave the shades of the dead without his wife.

When even the damned wept at his song, Hades agreed that Eurydice could return with Orpheus on one condition: that he should not look at her until both had left the underworld. Orpheus guided his wife by striking notes on his lyre as they toiled up the dark path. But at the last moment, his longing to see Eurydice overcame him. He turned to embrace her, only to see her slip back into the

shadows with a piteous cry.

Overwhelmed by this second bereavement, Orpheus returned to Thrace, where he hardened his heart against women. This, and his attachment to Apollo, aroused the anger of the wild Maenads, female followers of the rival god Dionysus. In one of their crazed orgies, they fell upon the poet and tore him limb from limb, then threw his head into the river Hebrus.

Orpheus and Eurydice gaze sadly at each other, as Hermes waits to guide her dead soul to the underworld, in this 5th-century BC carving.

Even then, Orpheus was not to be silenced. The head floated, still singing, down to the sea, where it was carried by currents to the island of Lesbos. There it was finally laid to rest in a cave, where it served as an oracle for all who came to consult it.

view, each soul was born ten times, and each life-cycle totalled 1,000 years, most of them spent in the underworld. Before returning to Earth for the next cycle, each soul had to drink the waters of Lethe, the river of forgetfulness, to ensure that all knowledge of the afterlife was left behind.

While the cultists added new dimensions to ideas of the afterlife, the poets were refining people's views of its layout and features. By the third century BC the realm of Hades had been well mapped, and most citizens had a clear idea of what to expect after death.

The first essential step was burial, since the unburied were condemned to roam the upper world as ghosts. Once the formality of interment was completed, the soul set off on the first leg of its journey, guided by the god Hermes in his role as the Psychopomp, or conductor of the dead (see page 191).

Hermes led souls to the underground river, sometimes identified as the Acheron, more often as the Styx, that marked the boundary of Hades's realm. The only way to cross the stream was by ferry. The ferryman Charon, a dishevelled figure, arbitrarily selected those spirits he would carry across and those who had to wait. The fare was an *obol*, a small coin; relatives were careful to ensure that one was placed in a dead person's mouth before burial, because those who arrived penniless were condemned to wander along the riverbank.

The gates of Hades's realm across the stream were guarded by a fierce watchdog, three-headed

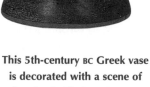

This 5th-century BC Greek vase is decorated with a scene of feasting in Elysium. Among the guests is Eros, bottom right with wings.

Cerberus. Before the palace of Hades lay two springs. One contained the waters of Lethe, or Waters of Forgetfulness, and the other the Waters of Remembrance, which gave access to the ranks of the blessed. One of the rewards of following a mystery religion was that initiates were advised which spring to drink from.

Eventually the spirit reached a place where three roads met. This was the seat of judgement, where the underworld's three arbiters waited to decide the fate of each soul. Two of them, Minos and Rhadamanthus, were sons of Europa after her abduction by Zeus (see box, page 159). Both had been legendary kings of Crete, where Minos had given his name to the monster, half-man and half-bull, called the Minotaur. The third judge was Aiacus, another son of Zeus by a river nymph; he had earned a reputation for justice as ruler of the island of Aegina.

When the judges passed a verdict, the soul was dispatched down one of the three roads, which led respectively to Elysium (now located in Hades's domain), the Asphodel Fields – the Greek equivalent of Purgatory – and Tartarus. Ideas about the first two destinations had changed little since Homer's day. The real terror that assailed the dying was the thought of being condemned to take the road to Tartarus, increasingly thought of as the destination of sinners.

Tartarus was a pit so deep that it was said that an anvil dropped from Earth would take nine or ten days to reach the bottom. Much of it was in total darkness. Within its bounds, wrong-doers faced eternity under the worst torments. One was Ixion, who had killed his future father-in-law, then tried to carry off Zeus's own wife; his fate was to be stretched forever on a wheel of fire. Others suffered the misery of striving endlessly to perform tasks that could never be completed. Sisyphus, who had seized his brother's throne and betrayed Zeus's secrets, had to keep pushing a huge boulder up a steep hill, only to see it roll down each time he neared the top.

Tantalus stood accused of a peculiarly horrible crime. As a test of the gods' omniscience, he had served up the flesh of his own son at a banquet to see whether they could tell it from ordinary meat. His penalty was to stand, tormented by thirst, in a pool of water that receded when he stooped to drink; meanwhile fruit that would have satisfied his hunger hung from a bough that remained eternally just out of reach.

Tartarus's horrors endured in a long lineage of colorful accounts. They were described by the Roman poet Virgil in the first century BC. Thirteen hundred years later, Virgil's poetic vision was in Dante's mind when he wrote his *Inferno*, although by then Tartarus had been subsumed into Christian notions of hell. Few concepts were so little altered by the triumph of Christianity as that of the eternal punishment of the damned.

The Cave of Sleep and Death

The Greek god of sleep, Hypnos, was pictured sharing a gloomy cavern near the River Styx with his brother, Thanatos, the god of death. Although these sibling deities were minor divinities they particularly appealed to the classical poets.

The two gods the Greeks called Hypnos and Thanatos are more familiar today by their Roman names, Somnus and Mors. Ovid described their home as lying beyond the reach of the sun's rays in a remote and quiet valley. Its mouth was clogged by poppies whose drowsy scent suffused the heavy air inside its shadowy depths.

In this tranquil-sounding place, Somnus, a handsome youth with a crown of poppies around his brow, dreamed away the days on an ebony couch hemmed in by black drapes. His principal assistant, Morpheus, gave form to these airy nothings and above his head flitted dreams, waiting to be carried by Mercury, the gods' messenger, to sleeping humans.

Meanwhile, in a remote corner of the cave, sat a very different figure – Mors, or Death, dressed in a black cloak over impenetrable armour and with the face of a corpse. His eyes were fixed on an hourglass to note when the sands of life were running out for someone – when they stopped he would venture forth to cut down another mortal victim.

Hypnos (Sleep) and Thanatos (Death) carrying a dead man to the underworld, depicted on a 5th-century BC Greek vase.

The Labours of Herakles

Of all the classical myths, perhaps those most familiar to us today concern the actions of the great heroes. Among these larger-than-life figures, the Greek hero Herakles – known to the Romans as Hercules – was unmatched for strength or courage. Yet unrelenting animosity from the goddess Hera ensured that his life was dogged by trials, and other people benefited from his deeds more than he did.

Herakles was the son of Zeus and Alcmene, a mortal woman and granddaughter of Perseus. Overcome with desire, Zeus assumed the form of her intended, Amphitryon, in order to make love to her. The betrothed couple only learned the truth when the prophet Tiresias revealed Zeus's trick.

Nine months after the visit, Alcmene gave birth to twins, Herakles and Iphikles. Zeus, who was determined that the first-born should not just be the mightiest of men but also eventually a god, tricked the goddess Hera into breast-feeding the new-born baby, thereby suckling him on the milk of immortality. But the lusty infant drew so forcefully on Hera's nipple that she pulled away in pain (see also page 190). When she learned that the infant who had caused her such pain was also Zeus's illegitimate son, her anger escalated and she became the future hero's lifelong enemy.

Herakles was still asleep in his cradle when Hera first tried to get revenge. She sent two serpents into the twins' bedroom, but the young hero's strength was already phenomenal, and when his parents rushed in to find the cause of the commotion, they found the infant proudly holding up the dead snakes. Thereafter Hera never again tried directly to kill Herakles; instead she used more subtle means to bring about his destruction.

Herakles's childhood was happy and for the most part uneventful. He grew up more skilled in archery, swordplay, boxing and wrestling than

Herakles's great physical presence is emphasized in this Greek statue of the 1st century BC. Yet his qualities of strength and endurance were undermined by vices – several times he was undone by his violent temper and his lust for women.

Tiresias the Prophet

Tiresias was no ordinary mortal. He lived for seven lifespans, in the course of which he spent time as a woman as well as a man. Even after death, he alone of the shades in Hades's realm was allowed to retain the gifts of speech and understanding, enabling him to continue his role as a prophet.

Tiresias's first transformation took place one day on Mount Kyllene, where he saw two snakes coupling. He struck them with his staff, killing the female. Instantly he found himself transformed into a woman. Seven years later, he saw another pair of snakes similarly occupied. This time he dispatched the male, and was turned back into a man.

Some time later, Zeus and Hera were arguing over which partner gets the most pleasure from the sexual act, and to settle the dispute they decided to consult the one person on Earth to have had experience of both conditions. Tiresias replied that, judged out of ten, the female gets nine parts of the enjoyment and the man only one – an answer that so infuriated Hera that she struck him blind on the spot. In consolation, Zeus bestowed upon him the gifts of long life and of prophecy.

Subsequently, Tiresias became famous for his ability to foresee the future. Among many episodes in which he was involved, he was consulted by Amphitryon and Alcmene, Herakles's parents, over the deception involved in her pregnancy, and he gave crucial advice to the rulers of Thebes during two successive sieges. His powers even continued after his death: in the *Odyssey*, Homer describes how Odysseus consulted him in the land of the dead to learn the outcome of his journey home.

Debates between Zeus and Hera, as depicted in this 5th-century BC carving, kept the gods amused. Tiresias was consulted to settle one such dispute.

any other mortal; and he also learned the arts of singing and music. Yet his fierce temper and great strength soon got him into trouble. Scolded by a music teacher, he retaliated so violently that the man died. Although he was pardoned, Herakles was sent away from his parents' home to tend herds on Mount Cithaeron. He then faced his first real challenge when he tracked down a fierce lion that had been savaging cattle. He killed it with an olivewood cudgel and removed its pelt. In time the club and the lionskin worn over his shoulder would become his trademarks.

As he was returning to his home in Thebes, Herakles fell in with heralds from the nearby city of Orchomenus and asked them the reason for their journey. They had come, they explained, to claim the annual tribute that the Thebans paid to their ruler, the king of the Minyan people. The tribute, the heralds said, reflected the Thebans' gratitude to the Minyan king for refraining from slicing off their hands, ears and noses. Herakles was outraged and he treated the heralds in just the way they had described, sending them back to their master horribly mutilated. Inevitably, war ensued between the two peoples. Herakles led the Thebans and almost single-handedly vanquished the Minyans, killing their arrogant monarch. He returned to Thebes a hero, and the Theban king rewarded him with the hand of his own daughter, the princess Megara.

So began the happiest period of Herakles's life. He and his wife had three sons, and he led a quiet existence with his family, expecting to inherit the throne of Thebes when the old king died. But Hera had not forgotten her grudge. Now she struck, making Herakles insane so that he mistook his own sons for enemies and killed them. On hearing the news, Megara died of a broken heart.

When he came to his senses again and realized what he had done, Herakles at first lost the will to live. Then he determined to go to Delphi to ask Apollo's priestess if there was any way in which he could atone for the crime he had committed. The prophetess gave him clear instructions: he was to leave for Tiryns, in the territory of his cousin Eurystheus, king of Mycenae, whose service he must enter; and he must remain there for an unspecified length of time, performing whatever labours the ruler demanded of him. If he did so, he would be rewarded with immortality. Eager to make amends, the hero accepted his abasement.

Herakles's Penance Begins

Eurystheus was far from pleased to see Herakles, for the newcomer had royal blood in his veins; his earthly father Amphitryon had been king of Mycenae before being deposed after he accidentally killed a relative. Eurystheus sensed the presence of a rival. But he saw in the labours that Herakles had sworn to perform a heaven-sent

A Greek carving of Herakles overpowering the fearsome Nemean lion, which he then put in the night sky as the constellation Leo.

chance to rid himself of the upstart. The fearful ruler racked his brains for a challenge likely to prove fatal, and came up with an idea: the Nemean lion. Invulnerable to weapons, this beast was terrorizing a district just to the north of Mycenae. When Herakles had tracked the lion down, he first tried firing arrows at it, but found that they rebounded. Then he battered it with his club, which only drove it back into its cave. Realizing that he would have to use his bare hands, Herakles entered the lair and wrestled with the lion, eventually throttling it. He tried to skin it, but his sword would not penetrate its flesh. Finally he used the beast's own claws to remove the pelt, which he wore in place of his old lionskin. Eurystheus was less than pleased to see Herakles return safely. In terror, he realized that any man who could kill such a beast would have very little trouble disposing of him, so he had an enormous brass jar made in which he could shelter while Herakles was in his palace. Henceforward, all his instructions to the hero were delivered by his herald.

Eurystheus had great hopes that the next task he had in mind would finish

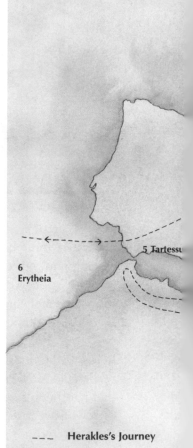

5 Tartessu

6 Erytheia

--- Herakles's Journey

Herakles off. This time he instructed the hero to go to Lerna, at the head of the Gulf of Argos southwest of Mycenae. There he had to kill the Hydra, a venomous nine-headed water snake.

Taking Iphikles's son Iolaus with him as a helper, Herakles made his way carefully through the marshes where the creature lived. On the advice of Athene, he forced it into the open by firing burning arrows into its lair, then set about it with his club. But every time he crushed one of the writhing heads, two more instantly grew in its place. And to make matters worse, the commotion attracted the attention of an enormous crab, which emerged from the slime and seized the hero's foot.

A powerful cudgel-blow soon dealt with that problem, but the Hydra itself proved harder to handle. Then Herakles had an idea. Shouting to Iolaus to pass him a lighted torch, he used the brand to sear the flesh each time he crushed one

of the heads so that no new growth could force its way through. The ruse worked, and before long only the central head remained. Athene had warned him that this one was immortal, so he lopped it off with his sword and then buried it under a great boulder. Before leaving the spot, Herakles dipped his arrowheads in the dead monster's poison-glands. Now they were doubly lethal, for there was no known antidote for the venom.

Eurystheus was dismissive of this exploit, claiming Herakles had cheated by calling on Iolaus for help. He next sent him off to capture the Ceryneian Hind, a deer of extraordinary beauty with golden antlers and bronze hooves. This

Over the centuries, scholars have plotted various different routes for Herakles. Apollodorus (c.3rd century BC) compiled this set of tasks and mapped the route, which – unusually – puts the Gardens of the Hesperides in the north instead of the west.

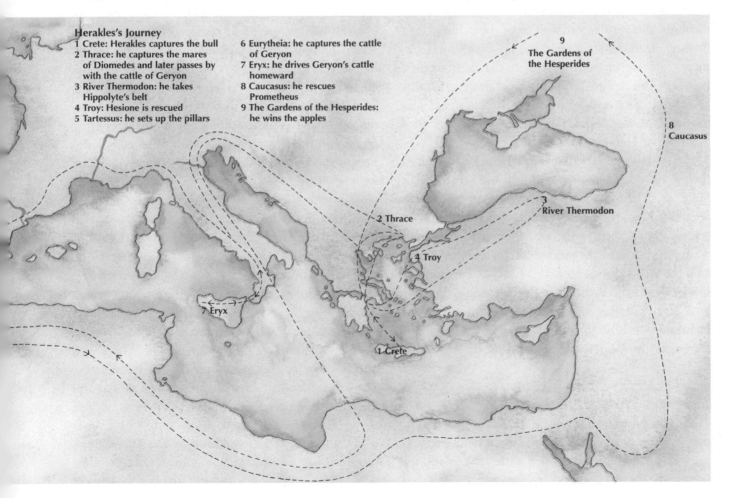

Herakles's Journey
1 Crete: Herakles captures the bull
2 Thrace: he captures the mares of Diomedes and later passes by with the cattle of Geryon
3 River Thermodon: he takes Hippolyte's belt
4 Troy: Hesione is rescued
5 Tartessus: he sets up the pillars
6 Eurytheia: he captures the cattle of Geryon
7 Eryx: he drives Geryon's cattle homeward
8 Caucasus: he rescues Prometheus
9 The Gardens of the Hesperides: he wins the apples

9 The Gardens of the Hesperides

8 Caucasus

3 River Thermodon

2 Thrace

4 Troy

7 Eryx

1 Crete

labour tested Herakles's fleetness of foot; the hero chased it for a whole year before finally catching it and bringing it back unharmed to Mycenae.

For his fourth task, Herakles had to bring another beast back alive. This one was an enormous boar that lived on the slopes of Mount Erymanthus. The hero chased his prey into a snowdrift, where it became trapped, then carried it in fetters back to Eurystheus.

The fifth labour took Herakles beyond Mount Erymanthus to Elis, near the western coast of the Peloponnese. The ruler of the city, King Augeas, was famous for his huge herd of cattle, but the byres in which the beasts were kept had never been cleaned. Herakles's orders were to clear out many years' accumulation of dung in a single day.

Before undertaking the task, the hero asked Augeas for a tenth of his herd in return for the deed. The king agreed, whereupon Herakles dug trenches to divert the course of two nearby rivers through the cattle yards. Once they had been flushed clean, he staunched the flow with embankments and returned the streams to their normal courses. But when he went to the king for his reward, Augeas refused payment, saying that it was the rivers that had really done the work. This was a snub that Herakles was not to forget.

The next labour that Eurystheus had planned for the hero lay closer to hand. In the Stymphalian Marshes to the northwest of Mycenae dwelled a fearsome flock of birds. The creatures had brazen wings, claws and beaks, and they fed on human flesh. Eurystheus demanded that Herakles eradicate them. To do so, Herakles used a bronze rattle made by Hephaistos himself. The noise it made was so awful that the birds rose in droves, and Herakles was able to use his legendary marksmanship with the bow to shoot them on the wing.

Herakles Travels Further Afield

These six labours had all been performed within the Peloponnese, but for the seventh Eurystheus looked further afield. At the time, the island of Crete was being plagued by the white bull from the sea that had fathered the Minotaur (see page 194). Herakles's task was to rid the island of the scourge and bring the bull back alive. He managed the feat without difficulty and carried the animal back to Eurystheus, who only just had time to jump into his jar as it ran through the palace. He quickly instructed Herakles to set it free.

By now Eurystheus was hard put to find suitable challenges anywhere in the Greek heartland, so for the next task he dispatched the hero to faraway Thrace on the northern shores of the Aegean Sea. Word had reached Mycenae of a ruler called Diomedes who had four mares that fed on human flesh. Herakles's task was to fetch and tame these terrible creatures. To aid him in his quest, Herakles called for a band of volunteers. Landing on the Thracian coast, the group hurried to the royal stables and overpowered the grooms. But the alarm had been raised, and as the mares were being driven back to the ships, the king himself rode out behind them at the head of the palace guard.

Thinking quickly, Herakles drove the horses to the top of a small knoll, leaving them in the charge of Abderus. Then, with the rest of his men, he rushed to a sea dyke and tore a channel through it, so water poured on to the low-lying plain. Diomedes's men fled, with Herakles charging through the flood in pursuit. He captured the king and carried him to the knoll where the horses were waiting. There he found a terrible sight. In their panic as the waters rose, the mares had knocked Abderus down and eaten him. In his anger and grief, Herakles tossed the king to the still-hungry beasts, and he too was devoured.

With their appetites sated, the mares became tractable, and it proved easy to herd them onto the ship. Herakles and his men sailed back to Mycenae with their quarry, and by the time they reached Eurystheus's court the animals were quite tame. The king mated them with his own stallions, and the foals they bore were said to be Greece's finest.

Herakles's next task took him still further away, through the Bosphorus to the Black Sea's southern shores, home of the fabled Amazons (see box, page 205). Eurystheus's daughter Admete coveted a famous girdle given to the Amazons' queen, Hippolyte, by the war god Ares. Herakles's job was to bring the belt back for her.

Once more Herakles sailed with a band of comrades – among them Theseus and Peleus, the future father of Achilles. When they reached the Amazonian shore, Queen Hippolyte was so taken with Herakles that she offered him her belt as a love-gift. But the hero's old enemy Hera set to work, spreading a rumour among the queen's subjects that the strangers had come to abduct her. Incensed, the Amazons took to arms and a fierce battle ensued. The women fought bravely, and the Greeks were hard pressed. But in the thick of battle, Herakles seized Hippolyte's sister, Melanippe, and threatened to kill her unless his men were free to depart unharmed. The Amazons fell back, and the raiders regained their ship and slipped away, carrying Hippolyte's precious girdle with them.

Sailing back through the Dardanelles into the Aegean Sea, Herakles came across a remarkable sight: a naked maiden chained to a rock and crying piteously. Putting ashore to free her, Herakles learned that she was Hesione, daughter of King Laomedon of Troy, and that she had been left there as a sacrifice to a fearful sea monster sent by Poseidon to ravage the district.

Returning Hesione to her father, Herakles offered to rid the region of the scourge. In return, he asked for the pair of immortal, snow-white horses that were said to have been given to Laomedon by Zeus himself. The king readily agreed, and the hero prepared for battle.

A 6th-century BC Greek vase decorated with elements of the story about Herakles's labours: Eurystheus cowers in the brass jar he used as a hiding place; Herakles hoists the sturdy Erymanthian boar over his shoulder; and Athene watches (right).

Single Combat Against Death

A chance visit to the palace of an old friend, King Admetus of Pherae, while on the way to bring Diomedes's mares from Thrace presented Herakles with one of his most daunting challenges. Determined to save the virtuous wife of the mortally ill king, Herakles had to confront nothing less than Death himself.

When Herakles visited his friend King Admetus, he was saddened to learn that his wife Alcestis was close to death. He was even more disturbed when he learned that she had wished her demise upon herself, hoping by it to save the life of her husband, who was dying. The god Apollo had promised to revive the king if someone else would die in his place. Alcestis was the only person who had proved willing to make the sacrifice.

Hearing this, Herakles determined to save her. He stood by Alcestis's side waiting for Death to arrive, and when the dreaded god came Herakles challenged him to a wrestling match. Death accepted willingly enough, for he had never before been bested, but not even he could match Herakles's strength. After a long struggle, he was forced to submit and leave without his victim. So Alcestis was saved, and the hero went on his way with the gratitude of the king ringing in his ears.

The sea monster proved a formidable adversary, and Herakles was eventually only able to dispatch it by climbing into its gaping jaws and hewing at its intestines from inside. When he emerged, Laomedon presented him with the horses. But one glance was enough to persuade Herakles that these were mortal beasts, not the divine ones he had been promised. He swore that he would gain revenge against Troy's deceitful ruler.

The last three labours had taken Herakles far to the north, south and east, but now Eurystheus determined to send him to the mystic west, the least-charted destination of all. For the Greeks, what lay to the west – beyond the Mediterranean – was uncertain, though some claimed that the Islands of the Blessed, where fortunate people went after death, were there. For his tenth labour, Herakles was sent to steal the cattle of Geryon, an ogre with three heads who lived on the island of Eurytheia somewhere in the uncharted Atlantic Ocean. His route took him to the mouth of the Mediterranean, which he marked by building two vast piles of stone on the north and south shores – still known to this day as the Pillars of Hercules, using the Romanized version of the hero's name.

While Herakles was working, Helios the sun god shone down on him so fiercely that the sweating hero eventually loosed an arrow at him. When the god reprimanded him, Herakles apologized and unstrung his bow. In return, Helios lent him his golden goblet, and in this vessel the hero was able to sail magically to his destination. There, he obtained the cattle after killing Geryon.

Herakles Herds the Cattle to Greece

After returning Helios's goblet, Herakles began a long and weary journey overland back to Greece, driving the cattle before him. When he finally arrived, it was only to find that he was expected to set off westwards once more. He had to locate

A vase of *c*.500 BC shows Herakles grappling with the sea monster that threatened Troy. Poseidon had sent it because King Laomedon had tried to avoid paying the sea god for Troy's walls.

the Garden of the Hesperides, Mother Earth's wedding gift to Hera, and bring from it some golden apples. It was a labour in itself to find where the garden lay, for no mortal knew. Eventually Herakles learned from Nereus, the Old Man of the Sea, that he could only hope to obtain the fruit by seeking the help of Atlas. The Titan proved a willing helper, for the three Hesperides whom Hera had appointed to guard the garden were his daughters. He offered to fetch the apples himself if only Herakles would take over his burden.

The hero put his shoulders to the sky to hold it up while Atlas went off to get the apples. But Atlas was so relieved to be free of his backbreaking burden that, when he finally returned, he proved unwilling to swap places again. Herakles employed a ruse, asking him to bear its weight momentarily while he adjusted his position. Atlas agreed, and Herakles beat a hasty retreat, leaving the giant to rue for all eternity his act of kindness.

Voyage to the Underworld

For Herakles's twelfth and last labour, Eurystheus set a challenge that recalled the promise of immortality made to the hero as a reward for completing his long servitude. This time he must go into the underworld realm of Hades and bring back the triple-headed guard dog Cerberus.

After participating in the Eleusinian Mysteries, which prepared men for the

experience of Hades's domain, Herakles called on Athene and Hermes to guide him. When encountered, Hades grimly consented to let Herakles borrow Cerberus if he could master the beast without recourse to weapons. The sight of the monstrous creature, its three heads maned with serpents, would have deterred a lesser man, but Herakles gripped it in an armlock, relying on his impenetrable lionskin to protect him from its teeth.

When the animal finally yielded, Herakles bound it and dragged it to the upper world, where the foam that slavered from its mouth congealed to form the plant known as deadly nightshade. The sight of this hound from hell terrified Eurystheus more than anything he had yet seen, and he was very glad to release Herakles formally from his servitude and bid him be gone for ever.

Having returned Cerberus as promised to the Styx's shore, Herakles strode joyfully out into the sunshine, a free man at last. Yet, although his lengthy trial was over, there was still unfinished business remaining from the labours. In the years that followed, Herakles would return to Troy to punish the deceitful King Laomedon, and to Elis, where he would depose Augeas and sack the city.

Slavery and Death

Before Herakles could embark on these missions of revenge, he was sentenced to three years of servitude as punishment for killing a son of Eurytus, the ruler of Euboea island off Greece's eastern coast. Eurytus had insulted Herakles when the hero sought unsuccessfully to wed the king's daughter Iole, and Herakles had struck down the ruler's son Iphitus.

Herakles was purchased by Queen Omphale of Lydia on the Aegean's eastern coast. She was a beautiful woman, and the hero was soon as much in her thrall emotionally as he was legally. However, when this bondage came to an end, Herakles left Lydia still intent on finding himself a new wife. At the court of King Oeneus of Calydon near the mouth of the Gulf of Corinth, he fell in love with Princess Deianira. He won her hand, but it was to be through her that Herakles eventually met his death, with the villain of the piece a centaur named Nessus. The couple were on their way to visit a friend when the centaur offered to carry Deianira over a river, only to run off with her. Herakles shot him down with one of his venom-tipped arrows (see page 199).

But the dying centaur, who realized his blood was poisoned, asked Deianira to dip a cloth in it, telling her falsely that it had infallible properties as a love potion; if ever she suspected that she was losing her husband's affections, she must sprinkle some over his clothing and he would never leave. When the couple reached their destination Deianira surreptitiously wrung Nessus's blood from the still-damp cloth into a small phial.

Years passed in which Deianira had no need of Nessus's lethal gift, for her husband was busy fighting battles, sacking cities and challenging champions. Eventually, however, Herakles captured Princess Iole. Seeing this rival for her husband's affections in her own home, Deianira took the supposed love potion and rubbed it into one of her husband's garments. As the potion began to act, Herakles collapsed in agony. Realizing that he was close to death, he instructed that he should be taken to a nearby peak. It was there, according to a prophecy, that the hero was destined to die.

On the mountain summit, his companions informed him that Deianira had taken her own life when she discovered the trick that the centaur had played on her. The hero ordered them to prepare a pyre. When all was ready, he climbed up on to the stack of tinder and gave a command for the fire to be lit. None of his friends dared obey and it was a passing shepherd who ordered his son Philoctetes to set the pyre alight. In gratitude, Herakles gave the boy his quiver, bow and arrows.

As the flames rose, a serene Herakles had his eyes raised to the heavens. Then a rain of thunderbolts temporarily blinded the onlookers — when they reopened their eyes both Herakles and the pyre had gone. The hero's sufferings were over; his father Zeus had claimed him and taken him to Mount Olympus to become an immortal.

The Warrior Society of the Amazons

Amazon women – who worshipped the war god, Ares, and the goddess of virginity, Artemis – flouted the Greek natural order. They excelled at the traditional male pursuits of hunting and fighting, and according to some accounts they lopped off their right breasts to make it easier to draw a bow.

Ruled by a queen, the Amazons lived in an all-female society. To prevent the race from dying out, they called on the services of a neighbouring people's menfolk once a year, solely for purposes of procreation. Boy children resulting from these brief encounters were killed or, in some accounts, sent back to the neighbours, but girls were kept and brought up in the Amazon lands, where they were trained in all the arts of war, learning to fight on horseback armed with battleaxes and bows.

Their homeland was said to be somewhere in Asia Minor, where in historical reality women of the Carian and Phrygian peoples did sometimes bear arms. According to legend, the Amazons founded many cities, including the Aegean ports of Smyrna and Ephesus, though their realm was usually described as lying on the southern shores of the Black Sea, near modern-day Trabzon. A separate tribe of Libyan Amazons was said to reside on the western borders of Egypt.

A Trojan Tragedy: Gathering the Host

It was an intrigue on Mount Olympus that began a chain of events that culminated in the destruction of Troy, or Ilium. In the unfolding tragedy, humans were mere playthings of the gods. Homer's account in the *Iliad* led to the development of a massive Trojan Cycle, devoted to recalling what was commonly considered to be a glorious age of heroes.

Among the beauties who stirred Zeus's fancy was the sea-nymph Thetis. He would no doubt have forced his attentions on her but for a prophecy that Thetis's son would grow up greater than his father (see box, page 151 and page 157). So the chief of the gods abandoned the idea of such a liaison and decided to find Thetis a safe husband. He selected Peleus, a human hero and a comrade of Herakles (see page 201).

Thetis was less than pleased to become the bride of a mortal. Only when Zeus guaranteed her a grand wedding with all Olympus in attendance did she consent to become betrothed. Zeus lived up to his word, and the day was everything Thetis could have wished for. But among the company, there was one uninvited guest – Eris ("Strife"), and she had turned up intent on revenge for the slight.

Bursting into the feast, she tossed an apple bearing the inscription "For the Fairest" on to the table where the principal goddesses sat. Three deities at once claimed the fruit: Zeus's consort Hera; his daughter Athene, goddess of wisdom;

and Aphrodite, the radiant divinity of beauty and love. The trio appealed to Zeus to settle the dispute. But he, realizing the jealousies any judgement would stir up, decided to delegate the task.

The judge he chose was Paris, a mortal who was then earning his living as a cowherd on Mount Ida. He had attracted the attention of the gods first by boasting that his herd included the finest bull in the region; and then, when the god Ares jestingly took on a bull's form to contest the claim, by unhesitatingly admitting the challenger's supremacy. This act won him a reputation for fairness.

When Zeus's messenger Hermes brought Paris to make the judgement, each contender did her best to influence his choice. Hera offered him power over men and nations; Athene promised the gift of wisdom and good counsel. But Paris had eyes only for Aphrodite who, as goddess of love, promised him the most beautiful woman in the world. As Paris gave her the apple, she curled her lip in triumph; but her two defeated rivals made no attempt to conceal their bitterness.

Their hatred was to have momentous consequences, for Paris, as it happened, was no ordinary cowherd. He had been born a son of Priam, king of Troy, but at his birth a prophet had foretold that he would cause the ruin of the city, so his father had decided that the baby must be left to die on the flanks of Mount Ida. But little Paris was saved first by a she-bear who suckled him, and then by

Above: **The wedding procession of the nymph Thetis and the human hero Peleus was as magnificent as it appears on this Etruscan tomb painting from *c.*570BC. All Olympus was there. But at the feast, the first move was made in the terrible game of the gods that was to climax with the sack of Troy.**

a servant of Priam who took the infant into his own household and brought him up to herd cattle.

Paris grew to be a youth of great strength and beauty. Not long after his trip to Olympus, messengers from King Priam came to Ida seeking a bull to sacrifice at games that were to take place in the city. Paris decided to compete, and returned to Troy with the envoys. He won all the contests he entered, drawing so much attention to himself that the retainer who had sheltered him came forward to reveal that the young man was Priam's son. The king was so impressed by Paris's feats that, dismissing earlier fears, he restored his son to the palace.

And so it was as a prince of Troy that Paris claimed his prize from Aphrodite; and the goddess revealed to him that it took the glorious shape of Helen, queen of Sparta, and daughter of Zeus. Unfortunately, she was also the wife of King Menelaus. Helen was the result of Zeus's liaison with Leda, wife of the Spartan king Tyndareus. As Helen grew up, the fame of her loveliness spread throughout Greece, and when she had reached a marriageable age she was courted by most of the leading figures in the Greek world. Indeed, she had so many influential suitors that her stepfather Tyndareus became worried that those she rejected might turn sour. So, on the advice of the cunning Odysseus, he got all the contenders to swear to come to the aid of her future husband if anyone should challenge his

Menelaus, Helen's husband, inherited the kingdom of Sparta on the Peloponnese from his wife's stepfather, King Tyndareus. Menelaus's brother, Agamemnon, the king of neighbouring Mycenae, was married to Helen's sister, Clytemnestra. Together, Sparta and Mycenae were the leading powers on mainland Greece. This sculpture shows Menelaus ready for battle.

position. Eventually, Helen chose the handsome and aristocratic Menelaus as her husband and Tyndareus made him king of Sparta.

The Abduction of Helen

When Paris arrived at Sparta with a fleet from Troy, Menelaus received the Trojan prince as an honoured guest. Paris repaid this hospitality by seducing Menelaus's wife, a task he soon accomplished with Aphrodite's aid. So when Menelaus was called away to Crete, Paris had little trouble in persuading Helen to flee with him to Troy.

When the Spartan king came home to find his wife gone, he turned first to his brother, Greece's most powerful king, Agamemnon of Mycenae. Then he called on all Helen's old suitors. Agamemnon sent envoys to King Priam in Troy to demand restitution; but when they returned empty-handed, the Mycenaean ruler sent out a general call to arms.

Some of Helen's former suitors proved less than eager to respond. Odysseus, who was by then happily married, pretended to be mad. Envoys found him dressed in peasant's clothing ploughing the beach, throwing salt over his shoulder as he went as if it were seed. When he pretended not to recognize his distinguished guests, a wily nobleman named Palamedes seized Odysseus's infant son and threw him in the path of the plough. At once the supposed madman rushed to the boy's rescue. Unmasked, Odysseus sheepishly agreed to join Agamemnon's army; but he harboured a lasting grudge against Palamedes.

Eventually, all the forces gathered at the port of Aulis on Greece's Aegean coast, where they were bolstered by a sizeable contingent from

Early listeners to Homer's epic of Troy would have imagined the heroes wearing armour such as this 6th-century BC bronze helmet.

Crete under Idomeneus, the island's king. Among the others who answered the call was the brave warrior Diomedes, who had been deeply in love with Helen, and wise old Nestor, the king of Pylus, whose counsel was prized above all others'. There was Ajax, a giant of a man and a feared fighter, and Calchas, a renegade from Troy whose gift of prophecy had suggested to him that he might be better off supporting Greece than Troy. But no warrior was more eagerly welcomed than the mighty Achilles, who arrived in the company of his cousin and closest friend, Patroclus.

Before the fleet set sail, a strange event took place that was considered a portent. As Agamemnon was sacrificing to Zeus, a snake darted from beneath the altar and up a tree. There it devoured eight fledgling sparrows in a nest, finally swallowing the mother bird. Immediately it froze into immobility and turned to stone. Calchas at once recognized a sign from Zeus: the coming war would continue through eight years, but in the ninth would reach a successful conclusion. Cheered by the omen, the army set sail.

But they had no pilot to guide them, and they struck the Asian coast not on Trojan soil but at neighbouring Mysia. Seeing his realm invaded, its king Telephus led his troops out to do battle. The fight that followed was short but sharp; the Greeks suffered their first casualties, and Telephus himself was wounded by Achilles, who speared him in the thigh. Then, realizing their mistake, Agamemnon's men returned to their ships and sailed back to the Greek mainland.

Telephus's wound festered and refused to mend. He sent envoys to the oracle at Delphi in search of a cure, and they came back with the pronouncement that only the giver of the wound could heal it. So Telephus took a ship across the Aegean and, disguising himself as a beggar, made his way into the Greek camp. There he seized Agamemnon's infant son, Orestes, and threatened to kill the baby unless Achilles cured him. But Odysseus, on hearing the oracle, suggested that the words might apply to the weapon rather than the man. Sure enough, a scraping of rust from Achilles's spear did the trick when applied to Telephus's thigh; and in return, the Mysian king agreed to give the fleet directions to Troy.

The Goddess Demands a Sacrifice

So the great host gathered once more at Aulis for the expedition to begin. But they were thwarted again, for this time no wind sprang up to carry them eastwards across the Aegean. As days of forced inactivity turned to weeks, the Greek leaders turned to Calchas for an explanation. Agamemnon had angered Artemis, the seer proclaimed, by boasting that he was more skilled in the hunt than she was. She would only send a favourable wind if the king propitiated her by offering up Iphigenia, the most beautiful of his daughters, as a sacrifice to the goddess. When Agamemnon first heard Calchas's suggestion, he indignantly refused to consider the idea. But as time passed and his forces became increasingly restless, he had second thoughts. Finally, he sent messengers to Sparta to seek the young girl; and to calm his wife Clytemnestra's fears, he instructed them to spread the word that he intended Iphigenia to be the bride of Achilles.

Delighted by the news, the happy mother accompanied her daughter to the camp, but on meeting Achilles she learned of her husband's deception. Frantically she begged him to spare the girl, but Agamemnon's mind was made up. And so Iphigenia had to give up her life for her father's cause; though some say that at the last moment Artemis herself relented (see box, page 211).

Soon the winds set fair for Troy, and the fleet set off once more. Landing on Tenedos, within sight of their destination, they quickly took control

Greek soldiers had little protection aside from their elaborate plumed helmets and light, round shields. Horses would have been a luxury available only to the wealthy.

209

hesitant to leave the boats, for they had heard a prophecy that the first man to do so would be the first to die. So Protesilaus, an uncle of Philoctetes, leaped into the surf and, shouting a war cry, charged the Trojan forces drawn up on the beach. He killed several men before he was cut down by Hector; but by that time the rest of Agamemnon's army had followed his example, and they soon drove the foe back to the walls of their city a few miles away across the coastal plain.

Having established a beach-head, the Greeks drew their ships up behind a stockade and settled down for a lengthy campaign. Even though their fleet numbered 1,000 vessels, they had neither the men nor the resources to invest the town, so throughout the long years of war the Trojans were able to replenish their stocks of food and to receive reinforcements freely. Agamemnon's strategy was to pursue a war of attrition. The Greeks concentrated on attacking and sacking the smaller towns of the Troad, ravaging the surrounding countryside, and staging raids on Troy's many allies along the coast and on nearby islands.

Odysseus's Revenge

Few details survive of the first years of the war, but one story tells of the unsavoury revenge of Odysseus on Palamedes, who had exposed his feigned madness. The Ithacan ruler forced a prisoner to forge a letter, purportedly from King Priam, promising Palamedes payment in return for betraying the Greek camp. When his tent was subsequently searched, gold was indeed found buried beneath it – where it had been placed shortly before on Odysseus's orders. This act of underhand cunning proved lethally effective. Palamedes vehemently protested his innocence, but he was put on trial for treason, found guilty and stoned to death. This incident illustrates one of the Troy saga's distinctive features: its harsh moral realism.

of the island, killing its ruler in the fray. In the course of the celebration that followed, a snake bit the famous archer Philoctetes (see page 204) in the foot. The wound turned septic, causing him agonizing pain, and his constant groans so disturbed his comrades that Agamemnon's patience snapped. He ordered Odysseus to take the archer to the nearby island of Lemnos and maroon him. The castaway was to survive there for many years, living on what he could forage in the wild; and in time his comrades would have need of him again.

A strait only six miles wide separated the Greek army at Tenedos from the Troad, as the region around Troy was known. But before launching their attack, the invaders made a final attempt to reclaim Helen peacefully. Menelaus, Odysseus and Palamedes went to the city to demand the return of Helen. But by this time the Trojans had made up their minds, and they sent the envoys back empty-handed. Some even wished to kill them; but Antenor, a leading citizen in whose house they were staying, insisted that no harm should be done to his guests.

The Greeks then lost no more time before making their move. Yet their warriors were initially

Iphigenia's Escape

The sacrifice of Iphigenia to Artemis to secure favourable winds for Agamemnon's fleet shocked the Greeks. So poets put forward an alternative version with a happy ending, in which the goddess herself intervened to save the young princess.

According to the uplifting version, Artemis appeared in person just as the young girl was stretched out beneath the sacrificial knife. The goddess snatched her away to safety, leaving a hind to be killed in her place. Artemis carried Iphigenia to the land of the Tauroi, who lived far away across the Black Sea in what is now the Crimea. There the Greek princess became a priestess in a temple that contained a celebrated image of the goddess.

It was the custom of this barbarous land to sacrifice to Artemis all the strangers who visited the country, and for many years Iphigenia was forced to preside over these bloody rites. Then one day her own brother Orestes came to Taurian shores and was handed over to her in order to be killed.

Recognizing one another, the long-separated pair suppressed their joy at the unexpected reunion only long enough to plan their escape. And when they did succeed in slipping away, they took the statue of Artemis with them because they wished to find a more suitable home for it in Greece. In later years, many cities claimed to be the statue's final resting place. Once back at home, Iphigenia became a priestess to Artemis again.

The Wrath of Achilles

The segment of the Troy saga described in Homer's *Iliad* covers only a brief period in the ninth and final year of the war. But it is a decisive moment when the military stand-off comes to an end, and the opposing forces meet in open battle, face to face.

Homer himself accurately described the subject of his epic in its opening lines, when he calls on the Muse to sing "the wrath of Achilles". The 15,692 lines that follow recount the hero's quarrel with Agamemnon, the supreme commander of the Greek forces, and its dire consequences for all concerned. The action plays out on two levels: in the human sphere, where men fight and die horribly in hand-to-hand combat on the battlefield; and among the Immortals, who loftily and unconcernedly manipulate the fate of the human players in an unending struggle for status.

Just as the entire war was fought over the lovely Helen, so Agamemnon and Achilles fell out over a woman. Her name was Briseis, and she had been seized as booty in the course of one of the many minor actions that took up the first eight years of the siege. She was assigned as a concubine to Achilles, who cherished her for her beauty.

Meanwhile Agamemnon had acquired a mistress of his own in similar fashion. Called Chryseis, she was the daughter of a priest of Apollo in one of the cities of the Troad that the Greeks had stormed. When her father tried to ransom her, the Mycenaean ruler scornfully rejected his offer. The priest then prayed to Apollo, who heard his prayer. To punish Agamemnon's arrogance, he sent a plague to afflict the Greek ranks. Soon the camp was loud with the cries of the sick and dying.

A Bitter Dispute

The seer Calchas revealed that Apollo must be appeased if the scourge was to be lifted, and Agamemnon angrily agreed to send Chryseis back. But he demanded compensation for his sacrifice — and he chose to take it in the form of Briseis.

This Etruscan fresco depicts the mounted warrior Achilles waiting outside the walls of Troy. In the ancient world, Achilles was considered the epitome of manly courage.

When Achilles was informed that he was to lose the girl, he flew into a rage. As commander-in-chief of the expedition, Agamemnon apportioned all booty, human or otherwise, that was seized in the course of the campaigns, and he was technically within his rights in demanding Briseis.

Achilles was forced to swallow his pride and consent to his commander's bidding. However, to show his bitter resentment, he retreated to his tent and swore loudly that he and the force he commanded, the much-feared Myrmidons of Thessaly, would play no further part in the war. In his anger,

The Childhood of Achilles

Fearing what the future might have in store for her warrior son, the sea-nymph Thetis did all she could to shield Achilles from danger. But destiny decreed that all her efforts were to be in vain.

Forced by Zeus to marry a mortal (see page 184), Thetis vowed that no child of hers should bear her husband's taint. So she cast her first six offspring into fire, hoping to burn out of them all that was not divine. None survived. But when a seventh baby was born, her husband Peleus stopped her and saved the infant's life.

The boy grew up strong and handsome, and Thetis soon became reconciled to him, naming him Achilles. Yet, still fearing his human weakness, she made one more attempt to protect him. Taking him to the Styx, the underworld river whose waters were believed to convey immortality, she dipped him in. His whole body was submerged but for the heel by which she held him – and that small area was to remain fatally vulnerable.

For his education, Achilles was sent to an unlikely tutor. Chiron was a centaur who lived on remote Mount Pelion; but he was renowned for his wisdom. Under his tutelage the young man grew up unmatched in the arts of peace and war.

So when news came that all the greatest warriors of Greece were gathering to attack Troy, Thetis at once feared that her son would be summoned. To protect him, she disguised him as a girl and sent him to the island of Skyros. The king's daughter Deidameia was only too happy to learn the truth of the imposture; in time she bore the newcomer a son.

Yet, as Thetis had feared, envoys eventually tracked Achilles down. They had trouble recognizing him, for his real identity was well hidden. But then Odysseus employed a ruse. He sent a selection of gifts into the women's quarters that included, alongside jewellery and personal adornments, some armour and a sword. When one of the "maidens" was seen practising swordplay, the envoys at once identified their target, Achilles. At their demand he consented to set off to the war, thereby realizing all his doting mother's worst fears.

A Roman fresco at Skyros shows Achilles (centre) with Odysseus (right).

Achilles turned for help to his mother Thetis. She took his case to Zeus, who agreed to give the Trojans the upper hand in the struggle until the slight had been avenged. To that end, the god sent a deceitful dream to Agamemnon, seeming to promise the Greek king victory if he led out his forces for a pitched battle.

When the opposing armies confronted each other, the Trojan leader Hector strode forward with a proposition. Since it was the quarrel of Paris and Menelaus over Helen that had caused the war, he suggested, let the two men settle their difference in single combat. Both armies welcomed the suggestion, and a truce was hastily arranged to allow the fight to take place.

Heroes in Single Combat

The two champions, Paris and Menelaus, confronted one another in the no man's land between the Greek and Trojan armies. Menelaus had the better of the fight and was on the point of killing Paris, a deed that might have allowed him to reclaim Helen and bring the long war to an end. But divine intervention quickly scuppered that possibility. First Aphrodite, seeing her beloved Paris close to death, chose to wrap him in a mist and waft him away from the battle to the safety of the bedchamber that he shared with Helen. Then Athene, bent on Troy's destruction, induced a Trojan, Pandarus, to loose an arrow at Menelaus, wounding him slightly in the thigh. This sudden and treacherous attack at once broke the truce, and all chance of a peaceful conclusion to the struggle was definitely at an end.

The Greeks fought bravely in the ensuing fray, fired up by anger at the Trojan's perfidy. Diomedes in particular raged through the enemy ranks, first wounding Aeneas and then nicking Aphrodite herself in the wrist when she rushed to carry the young prince to safety. Even Ares, god of war, was not immune; when he came down to rally the Trojan ranks, a Greek warrior speared him in the loins, sending him post-haste back to his home on Mount Olympus. Even so, the battle

remained indecisive, and the Greeks had eventually to withdraw to their camp and to strengthen its fortifications against a possible Trojan attack.

The warlords met in conclave, and Agamemnon allowed himself to be persuaded that they could not hope to win the war without Achilles's assistance. He sent heralds and emissaries – led by Odysseus – to the sulking warrior, offering lavish amends for the affront earlier offered him. Agamemnon promised not only to return the beautiful Briseis untouched, along with lavish gifts of horses, gold and slaves; he also offered Achilles the choice of his own royal daughters for a wife when the expedition eventually returned to Greece, along with a dowry of seven cities.

The proposition was a generous one, and the envoys were startled when Achilles turned it down, saying that he planned to set sail for home on the following morning and reiterating that he would only consent to fight when his own ships were threatened. This was a major setback to the Greek cause and Agamemnon, disheartened, began to plan a withdrawal.

A Stealthy Night Attack

At this time of crisis, Odysseus showed greater fortitude. He decided to take advantage of the fact that the Trojan army was bivouacked outside the walls of the city and stage a guerrilla raid. Taking Diomedes as a companion, he infiltrated the Trojan lines by moonlight.

The two Greeks killed a patrolling guard after forcing him to reveal details of the layout of the Trojan encampment. Then, using this information, they found their way to the tent of King Rhesus, who had arrived that very day with reinforcements from Thrace. They killed the slumbering ruler and his twelve companions, then drove his magnificent white horses back to the Greek lines – an important prize, for it had been prophesied that Troy would never fall if these beasts drank from the nearby River Scamander.

Despite this small victory, the next day went badly for Agamemnon's men. Hector led the

Trojan forces like a man possessed, and one by one all the Greek champions – Odysseus, Diomedes, even the king – were worsted and wounded in the fighting. For a while, Poseidon lent his aid to the Greeks and helped to keep the Trojans at bay. During this stage of the fighting, Ajax almost succeeded in crushing Hector with a heavy rock. But Zeus ordered the sea god from the battlefield, restored Hector's strength and fired up the Trojans' valour. The attackers swept forwards once more. Then the line of defences protecting the Greek ships was breached. One of the vessels was set alight and the flames blazed in the sky.

The Two Armies

Both sides in the Trojan conflict had their share of heroes. Below are the most famous.

THE GREEKS
Achilles the Greeks' greatest warrior
Agamemnon king of Mycenae and leader of the Greek forces
Ajax the best fighter after Achilles
The lesser Ajax a warrior who was to anger the gods by raping Priam's daughter Cassandra
Calchas Trojan seer who defected to the Greek camp and forecast Achilles's role in Troy's fall
Diomedes A fine warrior and Odysseus's trusted companion on several forays
Menelaus king of Sparta, husband of Helen and brother of Agamemnon
Nestor king of Pylos, respected for his wisdom
Odysseus a cunning and wily fighter
Patroclus Achilles's cousin and best friend

THE TROJANS AND THEIR ALLIES
Aeneas a son of Aphrodite who would go on to have his own legend
Glaucus Troy's Lycian ally
Hector King Priam's eldest son and the Trojans' finest warrior
Paris another of Priam's sons, Helen's seducer and so provoker of the Trojan War
Priam king of Troy
Penthesilea queen of the Amazons
Memnon king of Ethiopia and the most handsome man alive
Rhesus king of Thrace and owner of a magnificent team of horses

Patroclus Pleads with his Cousin

In this desperate situation, Achilles's beloved cousin Patroclus appealed once more to the Greek champion to forget his grievance and join the battle against the Trojans. Achilles again would not agree to fight in person, but this time relented sufficiently to allow Patroclus to lead out the Myrmidons in his place. In addition, Achilles lent his cousin his own magnificent armour, knowing that merely the sight of it would spread terror through the Trojan ranks, like flames through dry wood. However, he also gave Patroclus strict instructions only to drive the Trojans back from the Greek ships and not to follow the enemy as they retreated back to the walls of Troy itself.

The ruse worked. At the sight of Achilles's armour the Greeks took heart and the Trojans fell back. Buoyed by his reflected glory, Patroclus fought as he had never before, slaying Sarpedon, a son of Zeus and commander of the Lycian contingent, and driving the enemy back towards Troy. In the heat of battle he forgot Achilles's warning and pursued the foe to the walls of the city. There the god Apollo, hidden in a cloud of mist, struck him down, knocking his shield and weapons away and rendering him powerless; and Hector, seizing the opportunity, delivered the coup de grace. Then, in his triumph, he stripped off Achilles's armour as a battle trophy; and it was with great difficulty that the Greeks managed to rescue Patroclus's body from Trojan hands.

When Achilles heard the news of his friend's death, he was seized by a paroxysm of grief, tearing his hair and strewing dust clawed from the ground over his face. Then, furious for revenge, he rushed unarmed to the ramparts and let out a terrible battle-cry. The sight of the hero Achilles and the blood-curdling howl he emitted were so fearsome that the Trojans stopped in their tracks.

215

The Greeks took advantage of this respite to drag Patroclus's battered, lifeless body back behind the safety of their own lines.

The Vengeance of Achilles

Equipped with brand new armour made for him by the god Hephaistos (see box, page 218), Achilles rose the next day with only one thought in his head: revenge on Hector for the killing of his friend. Even a warning from his mother Thetis that his own death would soon follow that of the Trojan champion could not restrain Achilles. Before setting out to seek his adversary, however, he first made his peace with Agamemnon, accepting the offer the envoys had brought him a couple of days earlier and taking Briseis back again.

Then Achilles went to war. No Trojan dared face the Greek hero in his battle fury, and the enemy army broke and fled before him towards the River Scamander. The river god himself rose against the Greek, only to be beaten back – in some accounts, Hephaistos directed a blaze of flame at the river, drying it up in an instant. As for Achilles's human foes, those who survived the onslaught fled back to the safety of the city like a pack of frightened animals.

Only Hector was brave enough to face Achilles. He waited alone outside the gates of Troy to meet the Greek. But even the most gallant of the Trojans was unnerved by the sight of the fearsome warrior with the light flashing off his bronze armour like the sun itself, and for all his good intentions Hector took to his heels. Some sources say he hoped to tire the Greek, knowing that Achilles had been inactive for some time and was therefore not as fit as usual.

Three times Achilles chased him round the walls of Troy while Hector's fellow citizens looked on in horror from the ramparts. Each time he tried to take shelter at one of the gates, Achilles drove him back into the open. Then the goddess Athene granted the Trojan a fresh access of courage, and he turned on his pursuer for what he knew would be a last stand. He fought bravely but his fears were soon realized, for Achilles quickly killed him with a spear thrust through the throat.

With his dying breath, Hector beseeched Achilles to treat his body with respect, reminding him of his own impending doom. But the Greek champion's anger was still undimmed. Stripping the corpse of the defeated Hector, he tied it to his chariot and dragged it unceremoniously away feet-first. Hector's long black hair spread out behind him as his head bumped across the hard ground. A great cloud of dust rose up behind Achilles as he

Troy's Tragic Champion

To modern eyes, the Iliad's supreme military champion Achilles seems a self-absorbed killing machine, as obsessed with his own image as any of the Olympians. The Trojan Hector now appears the more attractive figure, showing genuine concern over the fate of his family and his country.

As Priam's eldest son and heir, Hector was the leader of the Trojan forces and a born warrior. Yet as Homer presents the story, military honour was not his only concern. Because of his awareness of the damage war could do, it was he who proposed that Menelaus and Paris should settle their quarrel in single combat, so obviating the need for further bloodshed.

When his peacemaking efforts came to nothing, Hector resigned himself to seeing through a contest that he sensed could only lead to disaster. He led the Trojan forces bravely, driving the Greek invaders back to their ships and taking on Achilles's friend Patroclus hand-to-hand. By killing Patroclus he became the target of Achilles's murderous wrath, eventually meeting at the Greek hero's hands the death fated on him by the implacable hatred of the goddess Athene, the deadly foe of Troy.

Two scenes in the *Iliad* add a note of pathos to his death. One is his leave-taking of his wife Andromache and their young son. When the warrior tries to kiss the boy farewell, the child instinctively shies back, terrified by his father's bronze helmet with its crest of horsehair bristles. Laughing, the proud father lifts it off to show his face and then clasps his son in a final embrace.

The other is the hero's one recorded moment of weakness. When Achilles confronts him in his battle-frenzy, the champion's nerve suddenly cracks and he flees from his adversary, who chases him three times round the walls of Troy. Then Hector finds fresh courage to confront his pursuer, going with dignity to the death he knows must follow. Such moments of fallibility, unknown to his mighty adversary, may not have enhanced his military reputation, but they give him a human dimension that his more single-minded opponent signally lacks.

dragged his terrible booty back to the Greek camp. Once he had returned, his thoughts turned again to Patroclus, and to the need to give his friend a fitting burial. On his cousin's pyre, built of wood from Mount Ida, Achilles sacrificed not just horses and two of his friend's loyal hounds but also a dozen nobly born Trojan prisoners-of-war, some of them sons of King Priam himself.

Overcome once again with emotion, he was about to hurl Hector's corpse to the surviving hounds of Patroclus's pack, when the goddess

Aphrodite intervened and persuaded him to refrain from this brutal act. After the immolation, Achilles set about organizing funeral games in which all the Greek commanders took part; Diomedes won the chariot race, while Odysseus and Ajax were jointly awarded the crown for wrestling.

Meanwhile, Achilles continued to treat the Trojan's body with hatred and contempt, attaching it to his chariot again each morning to drag it round Patroclus's pyre. Eventually the gods, who had miraculously preserved the corpse from

The Armour of Achilles

Courage, strength and fighting spirit were the key qualities of the Homeric hero. But the Iliad also pays due regard to the armaments the warriors bore – and none had a panoply to match the one Hephaistos, god of metal-working, made for Achilles.

When Hector killed Patroclus, he stripped the armour Achilles had lent the dead warrior off the body. Mad for revenge, the Greek champion had to delay his retaliation until his mother, the sea-nymph Thetis, could get him new equipment from the divine smith Hephaistos.

The *Iliad* describes in loving detail the armour that the god made. First there was a breastplate, glowing brighter than fire, then flexible tin greaves to guard the legs against sword cuts. A gold-crested helmet sheathed the head and face. But Homer reserves most of his eloquence for the shield, on which Hephaistos engraved images of a microcosm of the entire Greek world – scenes of agriculture, husbandry, warfare, celebration

and counsel, all rimmed by the mighty waters of Oceanus then thought to encircle the Earth.

In highlighting the armour, Homer was only reflecting historical Bronze Age realities. At the time, metal was an expensive luxury only available to an elite of warrior-aristocrats. The competitive edge their arms gave them on the battlefield ensured their superiority over other combatants, thus providing the technological underpinning upon which the Age of Heroes, as Hesiod called it, was based.

The god Hephaistos, Aphrodite's oft-cuckolded husband, was the Olympian blacksmith, so the armour he made for Achilles was the best in the world. The Romans identified Hephaistos with their fire god, Vulcan, shown here in a leather smith's hat.

mutilation and decay, decided that enough was enough: Achilles's vengeance was complete. At a divine council on Mount Olympus, they determined that the remains should be returned to Troy, so that Hector could be properly laid to rest. Thetis was dispatched to inform Achilles, while the goddess Iris sped to Priam's palace to tell him to prepare a suitable ransom for the dead hero.

On Zeus's orders, Hermes accompanied the Trojan king to his sad tryst, ensuring him safe conduct to the tent of Achilles. The Trojan queen, Hecuba, had warned her husband to expect no mercy from the man who had killed so many of their sons, but the old warrior's grief struck a chord with Achilles, reminding him of his feelings for his own father, Peleus.

With sorrow but no hint of bitterness, the old king pleaded for the return of Hector's body. His directness touched Achilles, who now for the first time since the death of Hector showed stirrings of pity. The two enemies mourned their dead together, and Achilles promised to arrange a twelve-day truce to allow King Priam time to organize a suitable funeral.

Hermes saw the king safely back to Troy with his bloodstained burden. And there, in Troy, Hector's body was finally burned atop a mighty funeral pyre, and the charred bones set in a golden chest buried beneath a mound of stones. The *Iliad* comes to an end with the words: "And so the Trojans buried Hector, breaker of horses."

Old King Priam falls on bended knee to beg the hot-headed young warrior Achilles for the body of his son on this silver-gilt Roman drinking vessel. Achilles had shown little respect for Hector's corpse previously, so Priam has no reason to hope for mercy, but as the king's age and bearing remind Achilles of his own much-loved father, he begins to soften.

The Fall of Troy

With the death of Hector, the Trojans had lost their greatest champion. Yet their Greek assailants still had to overcome many other hurdles before they could finally attain their goal; and even then the long-sought-for victory brought them little happiness.

After almost ten years of war, the defenders of Troy could feel the Greek noose tightening around them. The countryside around the city had been devastated, and most of the lesser towns of the Troad sacked. Yet allies still rallied to their defence, among them the female Amazon warriors of Queen Penthesilea (see box, page 205).

Another exotic force that came to help their cause were the Ethiopians of King Memnon. He was the son of the dawn goddess Eos, a fine fighter and reputedly the most handsome man alive. Taking the field against the Greeks, he killed many warriors including Nestor's son Antilochus, who was struck down trying to protect his father. He eventually agreed to meet Ajax in single combat; but Achilles, learning of Antilochus's death, insisted on taking on the African champion himself and duly killed him, throwing his head and armour on to the young Greek's funeral pyre.

The Death of Achilles

Yet Achilles's own end was now near. As he pursued the fleeing Trojans back to the city, Paris loosed an arrow at him. The god Apollo himself guided the shaft, and the poisoned tip struck the Greek in the heel, the only part of his body where he was vulnerable. With a terrible cry, Achilles died; and for a few moments the fighting came to a halt as news of the champion's death spread through the ranks. Then the Trojans rushed to seize his corpse, and for hours battle raged around it. Finally, Ajax succeeded in carrying it back to the Greek camp, where it was burned with honour.

The Greeks held funeral games for Achilles just as he himself had done for Patroclus, and in their course Agamemnon, at Thetis's suggestion,

made the rash promise that the dead man's wonderful armour should be given to the warrior who most deserved it. Odysseus and Ajax both claimed the honour, and for long the Greek leaders argued in council over which of the two had the better claim. In the end, they decided to settle the matter by sending spies to listen under the walls of Troy. The prize would go to whichever of the two their enemies most feared.

When the answer came back in Odysseus's favour, Ajax went mad with rage and grief. He stormed out of his tent that night intending to kill the Greek chiefs who had insulted him; but the goddess Athene was watching, and she led him astray into the animal enclosures, where he only killed sheep and cattle. Coming to his senses again the following morning, he was so ashamed of his actions that he went to a secluded spot outside the camp and fell on his sword, killing himself.

Stunned by the loss of two of their champions in so short a time, the Greeks sought reasons for their misfortunes. They had been promised that Troy would fall after nine years of fighting, but they were now well into the ninth and still seemed to be making little headway. In their bewilderment, they turned once more to Calchas, who said Troy could only be taken with the aid of Herakles's bow and arrows, which alone could kill Paris. But these were in the possession of Philoctetes, abandoned so long ago on the isle of Lemnos.

Odysseus was dispatched with Diomedes to track down the castaway. Amazingly, they found him alive, a filthy and bedraggled figure with his wound still festering. Odysseus realized that this living scarecrow had no reason to do the Greeks any favours, and so resorted to his usual cunning to trick him out of the weapons.

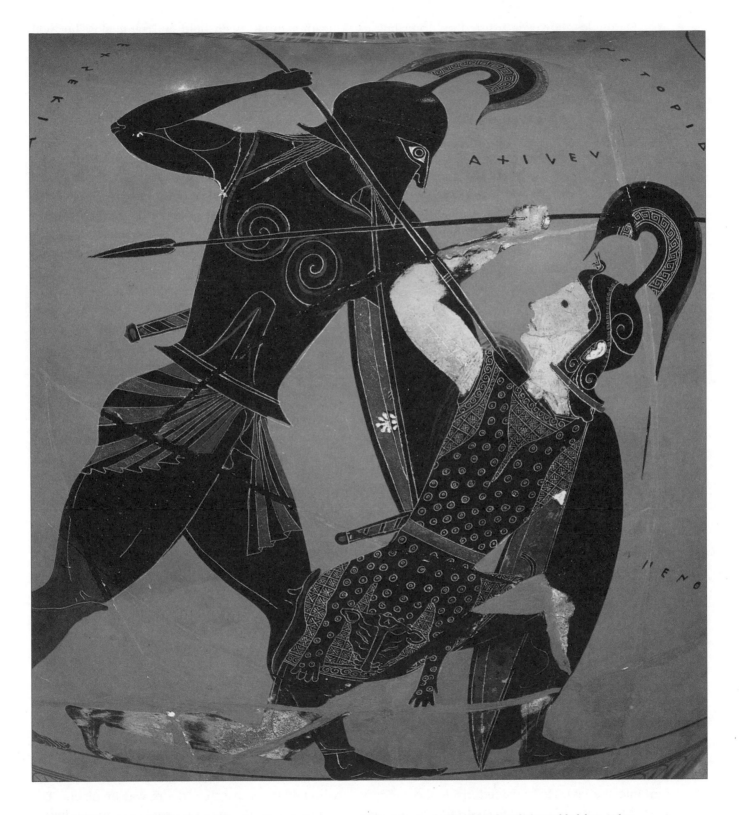

Achilles kills Queen Penthesilea by stabbing her through the heart with his spear in this scene on a red-figure vase, *c.*540BC. As the body of the dying Amazon queen fell to the ground, her helmet dropped off and her long hair tumbled free. When Achilles saw how beautiful she was, he fell in love with her and protected her body from being desecrated by the Greeks.

221

Diomedes, however, insisted on appealing to his better nature, asking him to come to the Greek camp of his own free will. Philoctetes might well have demurred had not Herakles himself – now a god – appeared to him, telling him to go and informing him too of another precondition for the fall of Troy: that Achilles's son, Neoptolemus, should join the Greek forces. So the three men travelled on to Skyros, where Odysseus persuaded the young warrior to go to the war despite the pleas of his despairing mother Deidameia.

Back in the Greek camp, Philoctetes finally had his wound cured by the surgeon Machaon. Then, taking up Herakles's bow, he ventured forth to challenge Paris. His first arrow went wide, but the second and third found their mark, fatally wounding the Trojan.

Helenus's Revenge

The Greeks were further encouraged by a tip from a captive Trojan. This warrior, Helenus, had hoped to marry Helen after Paris's death. When she was given to his brother Deiphobus instead, he got his own back by revealing a secret vital to Troy's survival: his countrymen fought in the certainty that their city could never fall so long as it was under the protection of the Palladium, or Luck of Troy – an image of Pallas Athene said to have been cast down from heaven by the goddess herself.

The Greeks decided then and there that the statue would have to be stolen, and once more Odysseus volunteered. As a preliminary, he decided to go on a reconnaissance mission to find out how the image could best be removed. To gain admittance to Troy, he disguised himself as a beggar and had himself beaten by his comrades until blood ran. He presented himself at the city's gates, claiming to come as a fugitive from the Greeks.

The guards, thinking that he might be able to provide information on the Greek camp, allowed him into the city. He remained inside the enemy's walls for some hours, undetected save by one person: Helen herself. She drew him aside surreptitiously to let him know that ever since Paris's

death she had been held in Troy against her will, and to promise the Greeks all assistance she could give them in taking the city.

Odysseus later slipped back to the Greek lines, where he laid plans to return with Diomedes under cover of darkness to snatch the Palladium. The two gained admittance to the city through a drain that Odysseus had located on his earlier visit, and between them they managed to remove the statue from its temple home. Carrying it stealthily through the sleeping streets, they exited as they had entered and regained their camp. Fearing to arouse the goddess's anger by displaying their trophy, they hid it on Mount Ida.

The success of this venture set Odysseus's mind working for other ways to smuggle soldiers into Troy. The drain could not be used again, for the Trojans would have traced his footsteps to it. But he felt sure that there must be some other stratagem that could be used to penetrate the city's formidable defences. And before long he had it.

At his suggestion, carpenters used timber from Mount Ida to make a gigantic wooden horse. It was set on wheels so that it could be easily moved, and inside it was left hollow. In the belly of the beast a door that could only be opened by an internal catch was cunningly concealed. Within the horse's flanks there was room for thirty fully armed warriors to lie concealed in darkness.

The next problem was to get the horse into Troy, and to this end Odysseus employed all his celebrated wits. He persuaded Agamemnon to break camp overnight and withdraw with all his ships, so that the Trojans would think the Greeks had finally abandoned the siege. In fact, the fleet only sailed as far as the offshore island of Tenedos, taking shelter on its lee side only a few miles from the point of departure.

Troy's citizens carried on unaware of the terrible fate which was soon to befall them. They did not heed the warnings of the princess Cassandra, who told them that their doom was imminent. The princess had the gift of prophecy, going into a trance before she spoke. But the people of the city believed she was mad.

Prophetess of Doom

The most tragic of King Priam's twelve daughters was the beautiful Cassandra, who, like her mother Hecuba and the other Trojans Calchas and Laocoon, had the gift of prophecy. But for Cassandra the gift was a curse, for she was doomed never to be believed.

When Cassandra was visiting Apollo's sanctuary one day, the god himself was struck by her beauty. As a mark of favour, he promised her the gift of prophecy. But when in return he sought to have his way with her, the young princess rebuffed his advances.

Apollo sought revenge. He could not take back his gift, for no divine edict could be undone; so instead he added a cruel rider to his bequest – that no one should ever believe her predictions.

From that time on, Cassandra could see only too clearly the tragedies that lay in store for her people. But whenever she sought to help them – by warning that Paris would bring calamity on Troy, for example, or that the wooden horse was a Greek ruse – she was greeted only with incredulity. Her name lives on to this day as a generic title for all those unfortunate enough to be able to foresee imminent disaster without being able to avert it.

When the Trojans got up the next morning, they saw an astonishing sight from the ramparts of the city: only debris where the Greek camp had been, and in its place the gigantic wooden horse towering above the plain. Scouts sent out to examine this strange beast reported that it bore an inscription offering thanks from the Greeks to Athene in return for the promise of a safe journey home. Soon people were flocking out of the city to inspect the wonder. Most were suspicious of the horse, seeing a trap in it; and none more so than Laocoon, a priest of Apollo, who argued vehemently that this unwanted gift boded ill for Troy and must be destroyed at once.

But Odysseus had one more trick up his sleeve. He had left behind one of his followers, Sinon, dressed in rags and caked in mud. This man now made his appearance and was dragged before King Priam. Sinon had a story to tell. He pretended that he had learned the truth about Palamedes's death, and that Odysseus had sought to have him killed to stop him from spreading it. He had managed to escape from his would-be assassins, but the Greek ships had meanwhile set sail without him. If he made his own way home, only death would await him there. So he begged to be allowed to remain in Troy, and promised as an earnest of his good intentions to reveal the Greeks' final secret: that the wooden horse they had left behind was under the protection of Athene, and any city that received it within its walls could never be taken. That, he claimed, was why the Greeks had made it so large – to ensure that the Trojans could not pull it through any of their gates.

While the Trojans were weighing Sinon's words, an unforeseen event occurred that swung the balance of opinion in his favour. A pair of sea serpents, sent by Poseidon, slithered up from the shore and seized the two sons of the arch-sceptic Laocoon. The priest tried to rescue them, but all three were devoured. The onlookers at once deduced that these deaths were an omen. The gods had struck Laocoon down for his insolence towards Athene; and without more ado King Priam gave instructions for a section of the walls of Troy to be dismantled so the giant horse could enter the city.

It was a fatal error. That night, under cover of darkness, the Greek fleet left its hiding place behind Tenedos and sailed back to the Trojan shore. At the same time the warriors inside the horse slipped the catch and fanned out through

A warrior flings Hector's son Astyanax to his death while King Priam lies dying on the ground and Aphrodite protects Helen from the wrath of Menelaus in this depiction of the sack of Troy on a vase made in the 3rd century BC.

the streets of the sleeping city. Hurrying to its entrances, they slit the throats of the sentinels standing guard there and flung open the gates. By the time the Trojans realized what was happening, the streets were full of armed men. Soon the first fires were started.

What followed was butchery. Driven on by stories of the fabled wealth of Troy, the Greek soldiers embarked upon an orgy of rape and destruction. On soldiers and civilians alike, they took out all the frustrations built up in the course of nine years of war. Caught unawares, the Trojans were unable to put up any resistance. Before long the corpses of men, women and children littered the cobbles, and the gutters ran with blood.

Few of the Trojan leaders survived that terrible night. King Priam saw his son Polites cut down by Neoptolemus in the courtyard of his palace, and was then himself slain. Deiphobus, Helen's new husband, fell to the sword of his rival Menelaus. Hector's infant son Astyanax was captured alive, but the Greeks decided it would be too dangerous to let him remain so, and he was hurled to his death from the city walls. Among those who did escape were Antenor, protected by Odysseus in return for his honourable behaviour at the start of the siege, and Aeneas, whose subsequent adventures were themselves to become the stuff of legend (see pages 238–243).

Meanwhile the women of the court were assigned as slaves to the Greek victors. Hector's widow Andromache fell to Neoptolemus, while Queen Hecuba was given to Odysseus. The unhappy Cassandra was raped by the younger Ajax before Agamemnon's men seized her and took her to the king; but her violator did not go unpunished for the deed, for he was shipwrecked on the way home from Troy, and when he scrambled onto rocks to seek safety, Poseidon split them with his trident so that he drowned.

The fate of Cassandra's sister Polyxena was equally unhappy. She had taken Achilles's fancy many months before when he saw her on the walls of the city, and now the prophet Calchas declared that she must be sacrificed in tribute to

Despite her adultery, Helen's undiminished beauty inspired Menelaus's forgiveness when he found her. They sailed back to Greece and lived happily for many years. Their meeting is shown on the back of this 4th-century BC Etruscan bronze mirror.

the warrior's shade if the fleet was to have favourable winds for the journey back across the Aegean. Despite the prayers of her grieving mother Hecuba, she was dispatched at his tomb as the Greek army looked on.

As for Helen, Menelaus had intended to slay her for her infidelity, and there were many in the Greek army who wished him to do so. But one sight of her beauty was enough to change his mind, and he led her away in safety to the ships.

So the Greeks made ready for the voyage home. They took substantial amounts of booty, for though Troy's treasury had been depleted by the war it was still richly endowed. Yet few found pleasure in their arduously acquired wealth, for they had been away too long and they travelled back to a world that had changed in their absence.

225

The Heroes Come Home

The Greek heroes preparing to sail from Troy after achieving their great task were looking forward to returning home after their long exile. Some launched their ships and others made the journey over land, but the fate of all remained in the hands of the fickle gods.

As the Greeks massed on the beach before Troy, a quarrel sprang up between Menelaus – who wanted to set sail for home straight away – and his brother Agamemnon, who was determined to stay awhile in order to make sacrifices to Athene. The goddess was furious at the Greek violation of her sanctuary at Troy during the battle.

Aware of Athene's anger, some Greeks set out on foot to avoid disaster at sea. Diomedes and Nestor agreed to leave with Menelaus. They set sail together, and the first two arrived home quickly – but Athene punished Menelaus by sending a storm which destroyed most of his fleet (see box, opposite). When Agamemnon finally set sail he took the Trojan princess, Cassandra, with him.

Agamemnon's wife Clytemnestra heard that he was returning with Cassandra and she plotted with her lover Aegisthus to kill him. There are different versions of how Agamemnon met his death. In the *Odyssey*, Aegisthus invited the returning king to a great feast. After they had eaten, Aegisthus and his men slaughtered Agamemnon and his followers. None were left alive.

In the version told by the Greek playwright Aeschylus in the fifth century BC, Clytemnestra welcomed Agamemnon and led him to the bathhouse, where he washed the grime from his weary body. As the king came out of the bath she threw a net over him. Aegisthus stepped forward and killed him with a double-edged sword; Clytemnestra then hacked off Agamemnon's head and murdered Cassandra with the same bloody weapon.

When the 19th-century German archaeologist Heinrich Schliemann found this gold funeral mask at the site of Mycenae, he exclaimed: "I have gazed upon the face of Agamemnon." In fact the mask predates the Trojan Wars by at least 300 years.

226

Menelaus Waits for Fair Winds

Menelaus set sail from Troy for his kingdom of Sparta with his wife Helen, whose elopement with a Trojan lover had precipitated the long and bloody war. His stubborn refusal to make sacrifices to the goddess Athene before leaving plunged him, Helen and their companions into trouble at once.

Leaving Troy with Diomedes and Nestor, Menelaus was separated from them in a great storm and his fleet was devastated. The five ships that survived were blown to Egypt, where they were becalmed for eight years.

On the island of Pharos, Menelaus met the sea-nymph Eidoethea. She told him that he must capture her father Proteus, the shepherd of fish and other sea animals, who knew all things, past, present and future. He would tell Menelaus how to raise a wind to sail home.

Menelaus and three followers disguised themselves as seals on a beach and when Proteus came out of the waves and lay down to sleep they leaped upon him. The god tried to escape by changing form, becoming a lion, a snake and even a stream, but Menelaus would not let go. Finally, Proteus told Menelaus of Agamemnon's murder (see main text) and that Odysseus was being held against his will by the sea-nymph Calypso (see page 233). He instructed Menelaus to return to Egypt and make a sacrifice to the gods. When he did this, a wind came up that carried him home.

Menelaus and Helen came to Mycenae, where they found that in an act of revenge Agamemnon's son Orestes had killed his father's murderers, Clytemnestra and Aegisthus, and was now facing trial and possible death. Orestes appealed for help but Menelaus refused. Orestes and his sister Electra then seized Helen and tried to kill her, but she was rescued by Aphrodite. Helen and Menelaus travelled on to Sparta, where they settled. When Telemachus came there seeking news of his father Odysseus (see box, page 235), he found them living happily together. On his death Menelaus was made immortal by the gods and was allowed to go to the Elysian Fields, the realm of the blessed, with Helen.

Odysseus, the Wandering Hero

The warrior Odysseus was famed above all for his quick wits. It had been his ingenious plan that finally brought the long siege of Troy to an end (see page 222). The battle done, he set out from the sacked city for Ithaca and his beloved wife, Penelope, but many perils lay ahead. He needed all his intelligence and resourcefulness to survive them.

Odysseus was impatient to be home in Ithaca, but soon after he set sail from Troy storms blew his fleet off course and he came to land in Thrace. With his followers, he attacked and burned the city of the Cicones, putting the men who defended it to the sword, but he spared Maro, a priest of Apollo, who gave the hero several skins of sweet wine. As Odysseus and his followers rested on the beach, Ciconians from further inland launched a savage reprisal raid, killing many Greeks and forcing the others to flee by sea.

Winds drove the fleet to the land of the Lotus-Eaters, in Libya. When three sailors went ashore to look for a supply of fresh water, the locals gave them pieces of their delicate fruit. Its heady taste made the travellers forget about their home and yearn to stay exactly where they were for ever. But eventually Odysseus and some followers went looking for the missing men. They, too, were tempted to stay and taste the fruit, but they managed to restrain themselves. Grabbing their shipmates, they dragged them back to the vessel.

They next came to the land of the Cyclopes, a breed of terrifying giants each with a single, vast eye in the centre of his forehead. Odysseus and

Poseidon, god of the sea – and enemy of Odysseus – features in this 2nd-century mosaic from Tunisia.

some of his men went ashore and came upon an inviting cave where they found young goats in a corner and cheeses hung from the walls. They lit a fire, killed some of the goats and settled down to feast, little realizing that the animals belonged to a Cyclops named Polyphemus – son of the sea god Poseidon. A shepherd by trade, Polyphemus loved the taste of human flesh.

Polyphemus returned with his flock and rolled a great stone across the entrance. Seeing his uninvited guests, he demanded brusquely who they were. Odysseus asked for hospitality, reminding the giant that it was a matter of honour before the gods to greet strangers kindly, but Polyphemus only grunted, grabbed two of the sailors and smashed their heads on their floor before devouring them with a crunching of bones.

A Deed Done by "Nobody"

The following morning the Cyclops breakfasted on two more men before driving off his herd and closing the cave again with the stone. Odysseus, ever cunning, devised a plan. While Polyphemus was away the hero found a long stake, sharpened it and hid it beneath some animal dung in the corner of the cave. In the evening the Cyclops returned and devoured two more unlucky sailors, but then Odysseus stepped forward, offering the monster a bowl of the wine that Maro had given the Greeks in Cicones. Polyphemus poured it down his great throat and growled with pleasure. Three times he asked the stranger to refill the bowl – then, becoming drunk, asked his name. The hero replied that it was "Nobody". Polyphemus promised that he would eat "Nobody" last, then he crashed to the floor in a drunken stupor and vomited a stream of wine and human flesh.

Odysseus and his men seized their chance. They heated the stake in the fire and rammed it into the monster's single eye, twisting it with all their strength. Polyphemus's eyeball boiled and hissed, and he gave a frightful shriek. A band of Cyclopes gathered at the entrance of the cave, asking what was the matter. Polyphemus roared "Nobody is hurting me", so they went away. When the blinded Cyclops rolled back the stone to let his flock out, Odysseus and his men escaped by tying themselves under the bellies of the sheep, hiding in their shaggy wool. The monster ran his hands over the animals' backs, but he did not notice the Greeks clinging on underneath.

They reached the safety of the ships, and Odysseus triumphantly shouted out his true name. Then the Cyclops hurled a vast rock at the hero's ship, creating a wave that almost washed it ashore once more, and he prayed to his father Poseidon to bring grief and trouble to Odysseus.

The fleet sailed on and visited Aeolus, the keeper of the winds. He gave Odysseus a bag of winds, and sent up a westerly breeze that blew the Greeks all the way home. The ships were so close to Ithaca that smoke could be seen from the palace chimneys when Odysseus, exhausted, fell asleep. In that fatal moment some of the Greek sailors, thinking that the bag contained gold, untied it. A great tempest was unleashed that blew them far out to sea again.

Then they were driven to the land of the Laestrygonian giants. Most of the ships anchored

Scholars disagree about exactly where Odysseus had his adventures and about which locations are entirely mythical. This map shows one possible reconstruction of his route and of his son Telemachus's journey around the Peloponnese.

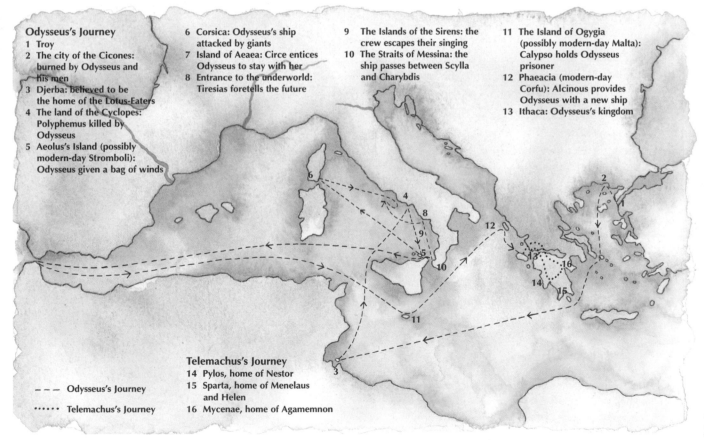

Odysseus's Journey
1 Troy
2 The city of the Cicones: burned by Odysseus and his men
3 Djerba: believed to be the home of the Lotus-Eaters
4 The land of the Cyclopes: Polyphemus killed by Odysseus
5 Aeolus's Island (possibly modern-day Stromboli): Odysseus given a bag of winds
6 Corsica: Odysseus's ship attacked by giants
7 Island of Aeaea: Circe entices Odysseus to stay with her
8 Entrance to the underworld: Tiresias foretells the future
9 The Islands of the Sirens: the crew escapes their singing
10 The Straits of Messina: the ship passes between Scylla and Charybdis
11 The Island of Ogygia (possibly modern-day Malta): Calypso holds Odysseus prisoner
12 Phaeacia (modern-day Corfu): Alcinous provides Odysseus with a new ship
13 Ithaca: Odysseus's kingdom

– – – Odysseus's Journey

‥‥‥ Telemachus's Journey

Telemachus's Journey
14 Pylos, home of Nestor
15 Sparta, home of Menelaus and Helen
16 Mycenae, home of Agamemnon

in a harbour, but Odysseus stayed further out. Three of the sailors went ashore, where they were immediately attacked. Then the giants pelted the ships in the harbour with boulders – and harpooned the men for their supper.

Odysseus's ship was the only one to escape this massacre. He sailed on to Aeaea, where some of the sailors went inland, and found the witch Circe in her palace. She invited them in to eat, and they all agreed except one, Eurylochus, who was afraid it might be a trap. He watched his friends tuck into a drugged meal; Circe then used a magic wand to transform the sailors into pigs. Eurylochus raced back to the ship and told Odysseus, who grabbed his sword and set out to seek revenge. Protected by an enchanted flower given to him by Hermes, the gods' messenger, Odysseus was immune to Circe's spells. He made her promise not to use any spells against him and to return the sailors to human form. But then she enticed him to stay; he became her lover, and the sailors stayed on the island for a whole year.

Odysseus Raises the Dead

Finally, Ithaca beckoned, and Circe – accepting that Odysseus was determined to leave – told him to seek out the blind prophet Tiresias, who would tell him how to return home. She instructed him to sail to the edge of the world, dig a trench and fill it with offerings. Then he should sacrifice a ram and a black ewe in honour of Hades and Persephone, the king and queen of the underworld, to summon the prophet.

Odysseus sailed to the land of perpetual darkness and carried out Circe's instructions. As Odysseus poured blood into the trench, the souls of the dead – girls, young men, old men and

warriors with their wounds still gaping – came swarming up from below with a gibbering sound. Terrified, Odysseus fended them off with his sword until Tiresias advanced.

A Stern Prophecy, a Grim Encounter

Tiresias foretold that the sailors would land on the island of Thrinacia, where Helios the sun god kept cattle, which must on no account be eaten. He said that Odysseus would reach Ithaca but would find

The beautiful sorceress Circe, complete with wand and potion, strides across a Greek ochre-figure vase from the 5th century BC. She had the power to change men into wolves, lions, pigs and other animals.

ODYSSEUS, THE WANDERING HERO

A Race of Beastly Shepherds

The Cyclopes, fearsome one-eyed giants, occur in the Odyssey and in early Greek myths of the creation of the world.

In the *Theogeny*, an account of the origins of the gods written by the Greek poet Hesiod in the eighth century BC, the original Cyclopes were three sons of Uranus (sky or heaven) and Gaia (Earth). Uranus threw them down into the abyss of Tartarus, and in revenge Gaia persuaded her other sons, the Titans, to castrate him.

A widespread tradition placed the Cyclopes in Sicily, where Polyphemus was said to have fallen in love with the nymph Galatea. Just as he was stupid and cruel in his dealings with Odysseus (see pages 228–229), so he was uncouth and boorish with Galatea – and she did not return his love. In one version, Polyphemus crushed his rival Acis to death with a stone. This was the version followed in the opera *Acis and Galatea* by the eighteenth-century composer Georg Friedrich Handel.

Cyclopes were also said to have built the walls of Mycenae and Tiryns, whose stone blocks were thought too large to have been set there by human hands. The term "Cyclopean" is still used to describe massive stone structures.

A prosperous Roman of the 4th century AD installed in his villa this mosaic of Polyphemus greedily accepting a bowl of Thracian wine from Odysseus. Perhaps he intended it as a wry caution against drinking too much.

great trouble there – and that his travels would not be over. He would have to set out once more, inland, carrying an oar on his shoulders until he met men who were so unfamiliar with the sea that they did not recognize it as an oar. But he would have a peaceful death in old age. In some versions of the myth Tiresias also prophesied that Odysseus's death would come from the sea.

Among the spirits that swarmed around him, Odysseus was shocked to see the pale ghost of his mother, Anticlea, because he did not know that she was dead. As soon as she drank the dark blood from the trench she recognized her son's features, and told him that she had died of grief at his long absence from Ithaca. Odysseus tried three times to embrace her but his arms passed through her shadowy body. He also spoke with many former comrades from the wars at Troy, including the great warrior Achilles, who mournfully said that he would far rather be a peasant working the land beneath the sun than live among the dead, even with great power. He met Agamemnon, who – recalling his own violent and terrible homecoming (see page 226) – warned Odysseus to return to

231

Ithaca in disguise. But finally the clamour of the dead swarming around them became so great that the sailors fled back to the ship.

They returned to Aeaea, where Circe gave them a warm welcome and advised Odysseus how to pass safely through the perils that still lay ahead. Once the Greeks set sail from her island their first trial was to pass the Sirens, whose unbearably lovely singing lured men to their deaths. Following Circe's advice, Odysseus filled his sailors' ears with beeswax so that they could not hear the songs; he planned to keep his own ears open, and ordered the men to tie him as tightly as they could to the mast – warning them that on no account should they release him. When they sailed past the Sirens, Odysseus was desperate to be free and gestured frantically to the men to untie him – but they only pulled the knots tighter. The ship sailed on and the Sirens, maddened by their failure, hurled themselves into the water, where they drowned.

Next the sailors had to pass between Scylla and Charybdis. Scylla was a monster with six heads on long necks, who squatted on a cliff and snatched sailors as they passed. Charybdis sucked in a vast amount of water three times each day, creating a whirlpool capable of swallowing ships that sailed too close. In his concern to avoid Charybdis, Odysseus sailed a little too near to Scylla and the monster bent down and snatched six of his finest sailors – one in each mouth. The men howled and begged to be rescued but Odysseus, powerless to help them, sailed on.

The male nude was an important theme in Roman art. The well-known story of Odysseus offered sculptors – such as the creator of this powerful figure from the 1st century AD – plenty of opportunities to demonstrate their skill.

The sailors then came to the island of Thrinacia, home of Helios, the sun god. Odysseus reminded his men that Tiresias had warned of terrible danger if they ate the god's cattle, and said that they should sail on, but the crew insisted on putting in. During the night, the wind changed and the sailors were trapped there for a whole month. Food ran low and the men were starving, and while Odysseus was asleep Eurylochus and the others slaughtered and roasted some of the beasts. When Odysseus awoke he was furious with his men, but they feasted for six days and then, in calm weather, set sail once more.

Helios was livid and complained to Zeus, who promised to destroy the sailors. He attacked the ship with a terrible storm and all on board were drowned – except Odysseus, who made a raft from the floating timbers. After escaping the whirlpool of Charybdis again, the hero drifted for nine days, coming to land finally on the island of Ogygia, home to the beautiful sea-nymph Calypso ("The Concealer"). She fell in love with the handsome castaway and, after giving him food and wine, seduced him. Calypso held Odysseus prisoner on the island for seven years, but he soon grew tired of her and would sit staring forlornly out to sea, longing for home.

Athene Secures the Hero's Freedom

On Mount Olympus the gods noticed Odysseus's plight. All felt sorry for the hero except Poseidon, who hated him for blinding his son Polyphemus. When Poseidon went to faraway Ethiopia to receive a sacrifice, Athene seized the opportunity presented by his absence. She persuaded Zeus to help Odysseus. The father of the gods dispatched his messenger, Hermes, to Ogygia. Hermes gave Calypso the message she had long been dreading: Odysseus had suffered enough and Zeus was ordering her to let him go. Unwillingly, she helped Odysseus build a ship and gave him provisions for the journey. Odysseus had grown fond of her, but he had never forgotten his goal of returning home to his wife. He was glad to set sail again.

Eighteen days later, as Odysseus sailed past the land of Phaeacia (modern Corfu), Poseidon returned from his prolonged revels in Ethiopia. Enraged at the sight of his enemy in full sail, he seized his trident, stirring up an immense storm which smashed Odysseus's ship and would have killed him if a sea-nymph had not taken pity and helped him to shore. Poseidon vowed to punish him again another day. Naked and scratched from being dragged over jagged rocks, Odysseus finally clambered ashore by a stream. There, exhausted, he fell asleep under some bushes.

Rescued by a Princess

He woke to the sound of shrieking girls. Covering himself with a branch, he crept out from under the bushes to find a young princess playing ball with her maidservants. The other girls fled at the sight of the grimy, naked stranger, but Athene made the princess stand firm while Odysseus threw himself at her knees, asking for pity. She gave him food and fresh clothes, and while he washed and dressed himself, she whispered to her maids that such a handsome man would make a perfect husband. Then, raising her voice, she told Odysseus that she was Nausicaa – daughter of Phaeacia's king, Alcinous – and invited him to the palace. She said he could walk with her until they were close to the city, but then, to avoid malicious gossip, she should go on ahead while he approached the palace as a stranger. When he arrived there, she said, he should go straight in to her mother and clasp her knees in supplication.

Odysseus did as Nausicaa told him, impressing the queen and King Alcinous with his noble bearing and speech. Following local custom, the king offered Odysseus a ship in which to sail home. The next day, while sailors were preparing the vessel, Alcinous entertained Odysseus at a magnificent feast. There was a display of sports and dancing, and then the blind bard Demodocus stepped forward to entertain the diners with songs of the Trojan War. When the bard recounted Odysseus's own adventures, the hero wept.

A beach scene at Corfu, where Odysseus was washed ashore. He was welcomed by King Alcinous and his family, who feasted him and eventually sent him home to Ithaca in a new ship.

Still not suspecting his true identity, Alcinous asked Odysseus who he was. In a long and moving speech, Odysseus told the guests of his adventures since he had left Troy. Although the whole world marvelled at his exploits, he said, he was in reality a wretched man whose only desire was to return to his island home of Ithaca. When Odysseus finished his tale, there was silence throughout the shadowy hall. Finally, Alcinous spoke up, promising to send the hero home.

Odysseus Sleeps All the Way Home

The next morning, laden with gifts, Odysseus set sail from Phaeacia. He was so exhausted that he fell asleep on the voyage, and when the ship reached Ithaca the Phaeacian sailors laid him down on the beach, still slumbering.

When he awoke the ship was gone, and Athene appeared to tell him that he was in Ithaca. Warning him to keep his true identity secret, she disguised him as a ragged beggar and sent him to stay with his loyal servant Eumaeus. Odysseus pretended to be a refugee from Crete when he arrived at Eumaeus's hut, and he received a warm welcome. Eumaeus told the stranger that more than 100 princes, presuming that Odysseus was dead, had invaded the king's palace and remained there, eating his food, drinking his wine and pestering his wife Penelope to marry one of them. At this moment Odysseus's son Telemachus, back from Sparta (see box, opposite), appeared in the doorway of the hut. Odysseus was moved to see Eumaeus embrace Telemachus like a son.

Eumaeus hurried away to tell Penelope of Telemachus's return, leaving the father and son alone. Then Athene removed Odysseus's disguise,

Telemachus Sets Forth

Odysseus's son Telemachus was a baby when his father left for the Trojan War. He grew up into a fine young man, but he could not control the suitors who invaded his father's palace and pestered his mother Penelope to marry one of them.

The goddess Athene arrived at the palace of Ithaca disguised as a foreign king and told Telemachus to send the suitors home. Then he must sail to Pylos and Sparta in search of news of his father. After she had finished speaking, Athene vanished through the roof – and Telemachus, realizing who she was, was greatly heartened. He summoned the suitors and berated them about their conduct, begging them to go home. The suitors' leader, Antinous, retorted that they would not leave until Penelope agreed to marry one of them.

Telemachus decided to set off secretly to Pylos. Athene went round the city to find a ship and recruit the crew. Then, assuming the form of Odysseus's old friend Mentor, she led Telemachus to the ship and joined him on board.

Telemachus and Athene, in Mentor's disguise, soon reached Pylos, where they were received by King Nestor. He regaled them with tales of Odysseus's bravery, but knew nothing about his fate. Nestor gave Telemachus a chariot and his best horses, with his son as companion. Athene turned back, while the young men drove on to Sparta.

There Menelaus entertained his guests to a feast. When Helen entered the room she knew at once that Telemachus must be Odysseus's son. Telemachus asked Menelaus if he knew what had become of his father. Menelaus said that on his return from Troy he had become stuck in Egypt (see box, page 227) where Proteus, the Old Man of the Sea, told him that he had seen a tearful Odysseus trapped on an island with Calypso.

The suitors back on Ithaca sent another ship to ambush Telemachus on his return journey and kill him. But Athene was able to warn the prince and he came home by a different route to find his father, disguised as a beggar, already home.

and told him to reveal himself to his son. At first Telemachus thought that Odysseus was some god and would not believe him, but then he was overcome by tears and the reunited pair embraced tenderly. They made plans to avenge themselves on the suitors, and Telemachus returned immediately to the palace.

Odysseus again disguised himself as a beggar so that when Eumaeus returned he still did not recognize his master. But Eumaeus agreed to take Odysseus to the palace to beg,

The loyal Eumaeus, seen in a 5th-century BC terracotta image, had royal blood – he was a prince who was sold into slavery.

which was a common practice at the time. This gave Odysseus the chance to find out what kind of men he was up against. He soon discovered that they were low and cowardly. The suitors' ringleader, Antinous, grossly insulted the newcomer, striking him on the back with a stool.

Later that afternoon Penelope made an announcement. To the delight of her suitors, she said that she had at last accepted that her husband Odysseus must be dead, and would marry one of them. After a long evening of feasting and boasting, the suitors finally retired to bed. Odysseus and Telemachus now began to put their plan into action, taking down all the weapons and armour which hung around the walls of the hall.

Odysseus Keeps up the Deception

Penelope came downstairs and sat by the fire to question the visitor for news of her husband, confessing that she had used a device to avoid marrying the suitors. She said that she would only remarry when she had finished weaving a shroud for Odysseus's father, Laertes. She had made this task last for three years, unpicking at night what she sewed by day. The beggar told her that he had fought at Troy, and had seen Odysseus. Tears flowed down her cheeks, but Odysseus managed

with an effort to hold his own emotions in check. Now Odysseus's old nurse Eurycleia brought a bowl to bathe the guest. He turned away from the light to avoid recognition, but she noticed a familiar scar above his knee. With a gasp she upset the bowl and spilled the water. She was about to call out to Penelope when Odysseus clamped his hand over her mouth and made her swear to keep his identity secret.

The next day, Penelope announced that she had devised a test to select her new husband. She would marry whichever man could string Odysseus's great bow and shoot an arrow straight through a row of twelve axes. A vast feast was laid out, the bow was carried in and the contest began. One after another, the suitors tried but could not even bend the bow, let alone string it and shoot an arrow. Odysseus, still in disguise, asked if he might try the bow.

While the suitors laughed and abused him, Telemachus sent his mother and the other women to their quarters, with instructions to lock their doors and ignore any sounds from the hall. While loyal servants took up stations barring the exit doors, Odysseus weighed the massive bow in his hands, turning it this way and that.

He strung the bow effortlessly. Unhurriedly, Odysseus fitted an arrow to the string and fired it. The arrow passed right through the twelve axes. As Telemachus appeared by his side in full armour with sword and spear, Odysseus fired a second arrow. It pierced Antinous in the throat, just as he was lifting up a golden cup, and his life-blood gushed from his nostrils as he kicked over his table and fell choking to the floor.

There was uproar in the hall. Thinking that Odysseus had killed Antinous by accident, the suitors jumped to their feet. Their blood ran cold as they saw that the weapons on the walls had disappeared. Odysseus spoke out in a ringing voice, revealing his true identity. The desperate suitors pleaded with him, offering him compensation for all the food and wine they had consumed, but Odysseus was implacable. He fired again and again, his sure shot felling them one by one.

Telemachus, Eumaeus and another loyal servant were at Odysseus's side as he slowly drove the surviving suitors down the hall, massacring them till they lay in heaps like fish on a beach. Then they rounded up the servants who had been disloyal and executed them. The nurse Eurycleia ran upstairs to tell Penelope that her husband was back. But Penelope was still too shocked to believe her. She came downstairs, wondering whether to remain aloof or to rush forwards and kiss the man whose identity she still doubted. She sat down quietly on the far side of the hall, gazing at him as he, too, sat in wary silence.

Odysseus spoke first, saying that if his wife would not talk to him at least she could make up a bed for him to sleep alone. But now the shrewd Penelope put him to the test. She called to her servants to move out the great bed that Odysseus had built himself. Odysseus leaped to his feet, reminding her that the bed could not possibly be moved because he had constructed it around a living olive tree – a secret that was known only to the two of them.

Realizing that her husband had returned, she flung her arms around him, saying she had been afraid of being deceived. They went joyously to bed, and after making love they recounted the difficulties they had endured during their long years apart.

Knowing that he had to win the forgiveness of Poseidon, the sea god, Odysseus travelled inland, as instructed by Tiresias. He came to a place far from the sea, where he sacrificed a boar, a bull and a ram to the god. His task accomplished, he returned to his palace and lived happily with Penelope into great old age.

Penelope fails to recognize her husband, disguised as a beggar. This 5th-century BC terracotta relief was found on Melos, an island renowned for its artworks.

Aeneas, Founder of the Roman Race

The Trojan prince Aeneas was a son of Aphrodite, known to the Romans as Venus. Before he was born, the goddess prophesied that her son would come to rule over the Trojans and would found a great and undying dynasty. He was a leading Trojan warrior in the war against the Greeks, but when Troy was sacked he fled the city's smoking ruins and set out across the seas to fulfil his destiny, recounted by the Roman poet Virgil in his *Aeneid*.

On the night Troy fell, the Greek soldiers rampaged through the city like marauding wolves, spreading panic and death. Aeneas fought desperately, but when he saw the Trojan king Priam killed, he realized that the city was lost. Taking his young son Ascanius by the hand he lifted his father Anchises onto his shoulder and carried him out of the blazing ruins. Aeneas's wife Creusa followed, but was lost in the turmoil and confusion. When, in desperation, Aeneas went back to look for her he saw a vision of Creusa in which she told him to give up the search and flee to safety.

After a stay on Mount Ida, near Troy – where they built ships and prepared for a sea voyage – the Trojans set out for Thrace. There Aeneas was met by the ghost of Priam's son Polydorus, who told him he had to leave. They carried on to Delos to consult the oracle of Apollo who told Aeneas that he must find the "ancient mother" of his people. Anchises said that the oracle must mean Crete – homeland of Teucer, an ancestor of Troy's founder.

When they reached Crete Aeneas had a dream revealing that the oracle actually referred to Italy, home of Dardanus, another of his ancestors. The next stop for the Trojan ships was Epirus on Greece's western coast, where a Trojan prophet, Helenus, advised Aeneas to travel on to

Sicily. They sailed on past Scylla and Charybdis, the twin monsters that threatened the wandering hero Odysseus on his travels (see page 232), but when they reached Sicily, Anchises died, worn out by the long and arduous voyage. Stricken with grief, Aeneas buried his father at Drepanum, close to Eryx, where a shrine already stood in honour of his immortal mother Venus.

The Goddesses Interfere

The goddess Juno had learned that Aeneas was destined to found a race so great that it would one day destroy Carthage, a city on the shores of Tunisia, northern Africa, that she favoured above all others. When Aeneas's fleet set sail from Sicily, heading for mainland Italy, she ordered Aeolus, the keeper of the winds, to release hurricanes. Aeneas watched in despair as many of his ships were sunk in a huge storm.

The survivors were driven to Carthage, where Queen Dido welcomed them with a vast banquet. After the food, Aeneas recounted his adventures, starting with the tale of the wooden horse and the fall of Troy, and describing all his wanderings since then. Venus, wanting to help Aeneas, sent Cupid to make Dido fall in love with him. The love magic worked. As she listened spellbound to Aeneas's narrative, Dido's veins began to burn and later, ablaze with passion, she rushed frenziedly about the city like a deer pierced by an arrowhead.

Juno saw that this was a chance to divert Aeneas from his destiny in Italy. The next day, as Dido and Aeneas set out on a hunt, the goddess sent a rainstorm. The hunt retinue scattered in the torrential downpour and Dido and Aeneas found themselves alone in a cave, where they made love. But Jupiter sent his messenger Mercury to remind Aeneas of his great destiny and instruct him to leave Carthage at once.

Aeneas did not know how to break the news to Dido. When she heard that the fleet was being prepared she flew into a rage, calling Aeneas traitor and threatening to hound him wherever he

Juno, the Roman version of Hera, hated Aeneas because he was a Trojan. Here she is depicted in marble by a follower of Praxiteles in the 4th century BC.

went. Aeneas was torn by inner conflict, but the call of destiny stiffened his resolve.

The grief-stricken queen asked her sister Anna to build a huge pyre, saying that she needed to burn every object that reminded her of Aeneas – in particular a sword that he had left behind. Later that same night Mercury told Aeneas in a dream that he must sail before daybreak. As Dido watched his ships slipping away in the dawn she cursed him to a hard journey and his descendants to a long history of future warfare with the city of Carthage. Then she climbed the pyre she had made of her lover's belongings and threw herself on Aeneas's sword. Her body was burned to ashes soon afterwards. Far out at sea, the Trojans looked back to Carthage and saw the thick column of smoke, without knowing its terrible meaning.

Aeneas Lands in Italy

When the Trojans came to Sicily once more, they stopped to stage funeral games in honour of Aeneas's late father Anchises. There Juno incited some of the Trojans to burn their ships and settle; they founded the city of Egesta. But the goddess could not prevent the remainder from pushing on to mainland Italy. They landed at Cumae, near Naples, where Aeneas sought out the Sibyl, an ancient prophetess. She warned him that a hard road lay ahead, with terrible wars in Italy. Aeneas begged to be allowed to visit the underworld, in order to see his beloved father once more. The prophetess warned him that the descent to Hades was easy, but the return was hard. She agreed to escort him to the land of the dead and told him to find a branch of the sacred mistletoe which would be their pass.

They set out in pitch darkness through the insubstantial shadows of the underworld. At length they came to the banks of the Styx, where they saw Charon the ferryman roughly pushing back the souls of the dead as they pressed forwards, desperate to be taken across. Charon agreed to carry Aeneas and the Sibyl, although their living weight made his barge sit dangerously low in the murky water.

Disembarking on the other side they first passed the spirits of those who had died in childhood, then the ghosts of suicides. Next they came to the phantoms of those who had died for love. Dido was there and Aeneas tried to tell her that he loved her and had been forced to leave her against his will in order to follow his fate, but she only turned away. The Sibyl drew Aeneas on, past the fields of war heroes, where he spoke with many friends, and past the river of fire that surrounded those condemned to an eternity of punishment.

Anchises Shows Aeneas the Future

Finally they reached the green and pleasant abode of the blessed, where the light was radiant and the air fresh. Aeneas's father Anchises saw him coming and cried out with joy. With tears running down his cheeks, Aeneas tried to embrace his beloved father – but his arms passed right through his ghostly body. Anchises explained the mysteries of death, purification and reincarnation, showing him

Mercury had to remind Aeneas of his destiny. The gods' messenger, depicted in this Roman bronze, was called Hermes by the Greeks.

a line of souls preparing to be born. These were Aeneas's own descendants who would one day carry Rome to glory (see box, page 242). His father told him that they would arise from his future marriage to an Italian princess named Lavinia. Aeneas gazed in astonishment before his father took him and the Sibyl to the gate that led back to the upper world.

Aeneas rejoined his crew and they sailed on to Latium, at the mouth of the River Tiber. The king, Latinus, had recently dreamt that a stranger would marry his daughter Lavinia, and that their union would give rise to a great nation. But Latinus had already promised Lavinia to Turnus, king of the local Rutulian tribe. However, when he received a messenger from Aeneas, he remembered his dream and offered the princess to him instead. Juno, still looking for opportunities to cause trouble for the Trojans, decided to work through the spurned suitor Turnus. She stirred up a brawl between Latins and Trojans in which two Latins were killed. The local tribes, including Latinus and his people, united under Turnus to expel the Trojan interlopers.

The Latin armies massed on the banks of the Tiber, and the watching Aeneas felt a great surge of despair, for the Trojans were heavily outnumbered. But then the god of the river advised Aeneas in a dream to visit Evander, the king of nearby Arcadia, and to make an alliance with him. Evander agreed to lend his support, undertaking to bring the Etruscans into the alliance. As a token of trust he sent his beloved son Pallas back with Aeneas, putting the youth under his personal protection.

As if to seal the bargain, Aeneas's mother Venus appeared in a clap of thunder to present Aeneas with a magnificent shield made by the divine craftsman Vulcan. This shield, she said, would make her son invincible in battle. Yet Juno was not to be thwarted. She warned Turnus that Aeneas was away, canvassing support. Turnus swooped down on the Trojan camp, and mounted a surprise attack. And so the battle began.

Aeneas returned with Arcadian and Etruscan reinforcements and the fighting continued. In a tragic moment, Turnus killed Evander's son Pallas – and exuberantly pulled the belt from Pallas's body and donned it himself as a trophy. Aeneas had no quarrel with Latinus, who had received him kindly and offered him his daughter, and suggested that, to save bloodshed, he and Turnus should meet in single combat. Turnus agreed, although Latinus's wife Amata tried to dissuade him. She was fond of Turnus and still wanted him to marry Lavinia.

Juno was still determined to do whatever she could to wreak havoc among the Trojans. She warned Turnus's sister, Juturna, that her brother would die in an encounter with Aeneas and

Rome's Debt to Troy

In Homer's account of the Trojan War, the Iliad, *Aeneas is not a major figure. When the Roman poet Virgil identified him as the founder of the Roman dynasty he was following a tradition dating from the third century BC, 200 years before his own day.*

In the *Iliad* the Trojan warrior Aeneas fought many times against the Greek heroes, but was always saved by the gods for a higher purpose. The Greek mythical tradition describes him as surviving the slaughter when Troy fell. "The Fall of Troy" – a cyclic poem, now lost – claimed that Aeneas left the city before it was overrun and took his family to Mount Ida. By the sixth century BC, he was widely depicted on vases carrying his father out of the ruins. There were various versions of his wanderings, but all showed him moving towards Italy. But the interlude with Dido is probably not traditional. It may have been invented by Virgil to explain Rome's hostility to Carthage, home of the great general Hannibal who waged war on Rome in the third century BC.

This gladiator's helmet is decorated with scenes from the sack of Troy, a tale that would have been familiar to every educated citizen of Rome. Fighters in the Coliseum would have been proud to identify themselves with the Greeks.

241

Aeneas, Ancestor of Augustus

In 31BC, after thirty years of civil war, Augustus defeated Anthony and Cleopatra and became the supreme ruler of the Roman world, giving himself the new title of Emperor. One of Virgil's aims in the Aeneid was to glorify Augustus. The poet represents Aeneas as the Emperor's political precursor as well as his ancestor; both men brought peace to an age that was exhausted by civil war.

Gaius Julius Caesar Octavianus chose the name "Augustus" – meaning "Sacred" – to boost his status. The Romans declared him "Father of His Country" in 2BC. When he died he was transformed into a god.

Virgil may well have found some aspects of Augustus's totalitarian rule distasteful, but he accepted his official patronage and portrayed the Emperor's reign as the culmination of 1,000 years of history and prophecy.

Aeneas, like Augustus, had a mission to make Rome glorious. When he met Anchises in the underworld, his father showed him the line of his descendants, among whom was Augustus Caesar. Anchises said that Augustus was a man of divine race who would establish a new golden age and extend the great Roman Empire as far as India, the Caspian and the Nile. Anchises declared that such greatness would be the fruit of Aeneas's actions if he settled in Italy.

It was a Roman's true destiny, he added, to rule over nations. The shield that Venus gave to Aeneas (see pages 240–241) before his combat with Turnus in Italy showed a pageant of all the great historical events of the future, culminating in Augustus's victory at the Battle of Actium. The poet remarks that Aeneas had no knowledge of the events depicted on the shield, but he revelled in their image as he lifted it up to his shoulder. Venus's gift of the shield echoes the action of the sea-nymph Thetis who, in the *Iliad,* persuaded the divine smith Hephaistos (known to the Romans as Vulcan) to make a shield for Achilles (see page 218).

exhorted her to save him by creating a distraction to avert the duel. Juturna disguised herself as a Latin soldier and roused the Rutulians, leading them onto the battlefield once more.

Aeneas tried to call his men back, but was hit by an arrow and forced to retire. Turnus exulted at the sight of Aeneas's wound and charged across the field in his chariot, killing many Trojans. As the battle rolled nearer, and Aeneas's doctor despaired of removing the arrowhead, Venus magically healed the wound with a herb. At once, Aeneas

surged forth at the head of his army and when Juturna saw him she remembered Juno's warning. Tipping Turnus's driver out of his chariot, she seized the reins herself and drove Turnus all over the battlefield, struggling in vain to evade Aeneas as he closed in for the long-awaited duel.

Amata, watching the chaotic movements from the city walls, thought that her favoured champion Turnus had been killed, and hanged herself in despair. Meanwhile, Turnus was tiring. He realized that the truce had been sabotaged by

A fresco from Pompeii shows Aeneas wounded in battle; Venus looks on anxiously. In some tellings of the myth, she rescued Aeneas's spear during his battle with Turnus when the weapon became stuck in a tree trunk.

his own sister and grew even more frightened. Finally, he was unable to hide any longer – and Turnus and Aeneas faced each other for the last time. Fate stood still because the gods, too, realized that the moment of resolution had come. Jupiter held up his scales and weighed the destiny of each man. He made the assembled gods, including Juno, give an undertaking that they would no longer interfere in the course of events.

First, Turnus struck at Aeneas, but his sword snapped in two. Understanding that fate was against him, he froze as if rooted to the spot. He felt the sensation of a person in a dream who wants to run, but whose limbs refuse to function. He could see no escape, but no way of attacking either; and he looked around in vain for his chariot.

In the moment that Turnus hesitated, Aeneas poised his fateful spear and hurled it with all his strength. It flew like a black hurricane, whistled through Turnus's armour and slashed open his thigh. The massive warrior sank to his knees, while the Rutulians let out a groan that echoed around the woods and hills. Humbled at last, Turnus stretched out his hand and accepted that Aeneas had won the right to marry Lavinia. He said that enmity between them should now end and begged Aeneas to send his body back to his father.

Aeneas hesitated, remembering his own father and touched by Turnus's words. He might even have spared his opponent's life, but then his glance fell on the familiar studs of the ill-fated belt of young Pallas. The sight filled him with blind anger and, seething with uncontrollable fury, he sank his blade deep into his enemy's chest. Turnus's limbs slackened and chilled. With a terrible moan, his life departed to the shades below.

Aeneas and Lavinia married and had many children. So says the *Aeneid,* all Romans have the blood of Troy running in their veins.

243

Romulus – First Builder of Rome

After Aeneas had triumphed over Turnus in single combat, he married the princess Lavinia and settled in Italy, founding the city of Lavinium in her honour. The local population and Aeneas's Trojan followers lived together peacefully and, over the years, became one people. But the conflicts that would give birth to the great city of Rome were not yet over.

Several generations after Aeneas's death, a quarrel arose among his descendants. Amulius seized the throne of Alba Longa – a city founded by Aeneas's son Ascanius – from his twin brother Numitor and sentenced Numitor's daughter Rhea Silvia to a lifetime of chastity so that she could not bear an heir. This judgement was later cited as the origin of the Vestal Virgins, priestesses who led the Roman worship of Vesta, the goddess of the hearth.

But by chance the god Mars saw Rhea Silvia when she came to draw water at a spring in his sacred grove and he made love to her. She bore him twin boys, Romulus and Remus. Amulius flew into a fury, threw Rhea into prison and gave orders for the babies to be drowned – but his men could not bring themselves to kill the infants and abandoned them on the bank of the River Tiber. A she-wolf who came to the river to drink found the pair, who stretched out their hands to her appealingly. She suckled them and they were later brought up by a shepherd.

Numitor is Restored to the Throne

In time the boys grew into strong young shepherds, who occasionally raided Numitor's herds to support their community. One day they were trapped by brigands. Romulus escaped, but Remus

Romulus and Remus, left to die by Amulius's soldiers, were nursed by a she-wolf. This wolf is an Etruscan bronze from the 5th century BC; the babies are Renaissance additions.

was captured and brought before Amulius, accused of stealing Numitor's cattle. Amulius sent the youth to Numitor who, in questioning him, realized that Remus was one of his lost grandsons. He released the young man, who rejoined Romulus; together they organized a rebellion, killed Amulius and restored their grandfather Numitor to the throne.

Romulus and Remus decided to found a new city on the spot where they had been rescued by the she-wolf. But the same brotherly jealousy that had torn Numitor and Amulius apart now surfaced between Romulus and Remus. There are different accounts of the quarrel, but the end result was that Remus was killed.

The Rape of the Sabine Women

The new city was named Rome (in Latin, Roma) after Romulus. But the population was composed largely of men, and the shortage of women threatened its survival into the next generation. Romulus sent messengers to many local tribes proposing marriage alliances, but with no luck. Then he hit upon a plan. The festival of the Consualia was due to be held in Rome and big crowds from neighbouring areas were expected to attend. Romulus knew that the men of the Sabine tribe would bring large numbers of their womenfolk with them. He called all the Roman men together and told them what to do to solve their problem.

When the festival began, the men of Rome ran through the crowd and seized all the young Sabine women. Each man kept the woman he managed to grab, although some aristocrats had also marked out the most attractive women and hired squads to capture them. The Sabine men were forced to leave, shouting and cursing, and promising that they would have their revenge.

The women, too, were angry and determined to resist. But Romulus himself went among them, reassuring them that the Roman men would treat them with the utmost courtesy and consideration, and do their best to win their love. In time,

A glass cameo from AD20 shows Aeneas surrounded by his descendants Julius Caesar, Augustus, Tiberius, Livia and Caligula. Germanicus floats above the group.

especially as they began to bear children, the Sabine women grew to love their husbands and to enjoy their lives in Rome. Nevertheless, their fathers, still furious, gathered an army to attack. They managed to enter the city and the Sabines and Romans faced each other for the decisive battle. The Sabine women, torn between love of the families in which they had grown up and their new-found love for their husbands and the fathers of their children, could not bear the prospect of what must surely follow. Tearing their clothes and loosening their hair, they ran into the midst of the two armies, begging them not to fight. Instantly the confrontation ended. The Roman and Sabine leaders made peace and the two communities were united into one state, with Rome as its capital.

IMPERIAL SUPERMEN

The Romans were attracted to the Greek hero myths not just as good stories but also as parables of power. So when, with the establishment of the Empire, supreme authority became vested in one man, state propagandists looked to the tales for role models to boost the imperial image. While poets ransacked Homer in search of epithets to eulogize the emperors, sculptors turned to antique models to portray them in poses recalling Theseus or Achilles. Some rulers even started believing the claims: Commodus (AD161–192) styled himself the Roman Hercules and gave public displays of his fighting skills.

Above: Commodus poses as Hercules with lionskin and club. When he carried his identification with the hero to the point of appearing naked in gladiatorial shows, his ministers judged him insane and had him assassinated.

Left: Rome's first emperor, Augustus Caesar (63BC–AD14) bestrides the world like a colossus in the huge 7ft-high statue known as the Augustus of Prima Porta after the location of his wife's villa, where it originally stood. The sculpture is now in the Vatican Museums.

Left: No emperor had a more heroic image than Hadrian, whose bearded visage adorns an *aureus* (Roman gold coin). Born in Spain, he travelled constantly around the empire, turning his life, in Edward Gibbon's words, into "almost a perpetual journey".

THE CELTIC, VIKING AND GERMANIC WORLDS

CELTIC DEITIES AND HEROES

Their hegemony extending at its peak over most of the continent of Europe, the Celts were a warrior people who worshipped an array of martial deities. Some of the fiercest of these were female, such as the Irish goddess the Morrigan (see page 257). The British queen Boudicca, or Boadicea, invoked Andraste, a goddess of victory, when she sacked Roman Colchester, London and St Albans in AD60. War goddesses spurred warriors on to victory, but also appeared in the form of a raven or crow, omens of death. For the Celts, every aspect of the natural and super-natural worlds was overseen by deities: thus Belenus, a sun god, fought with the storm god Taranis, the "Thunderer", to ensure that day followed night and

Below: **Deities were often thought to live in old tombs like this one at Kilcooley in Donegal. Such tombs were also said to be entrances to the Celtic Otherworld.**

that spring chased away the dark, barren winter. A clap of thunder, a flash of lightning, a sudden downpour – all were signs to the ancient Celts that their gods were displeased. Senior among the gods and goddesses found among the Celtic peoples was an ancestral deity called simply "God" or "Father": in Ireland, this was the Dagda ("Good Father").

Although the Romans gradually asserted their control over the varied societies of most of Celtic Europe, the old beliefs lingered. Julius Caesar reported on the gods of the Celts but interpreted them as local manifestations of Roman deities. The most popular god of the Gauls he identified as Mercury, revered as "the inventor of all the arts". The god he was referring to was probably Lugus, who gave his name to Lyon, and was no doubt related to Lugh ("Shining"), a divine warrior-craftsman of Irish myth. The Romans and Celts both had many martial heroes, as well as myths about powerful gods and the forces of nature. Ironically, it was the rich literary genres of early Christian civilization that enabled many, once oral, Celtic stories to survive, notably in Ireland and Wales.

Opposite: **The antlered fertility god Cernunnos was one of the most widespread Celtic deities. Here he is depicted on a 3rd-century BC cauldron found at Gundestrupp in Denmark.**

A Sacred World

From inscriptions and written texts we know the names of about 400 Celtic gods and goddesses. Probably three-quarters of these were local deities, because there does not appear to have been a pantheon universally recognized throughout the Celtic world, akin to the Olympian gods of the Greeks and Romans. Those deities who were widely worshipped were often referred to by simple titles – Dagda ("Good God" or "Good Father"), Matrona ("Mother"), Maponus ("Son" or "Youth"). Caesar said that the Gauls all claimed descent from a common divine ancestor whom they called simply "Father". For the most part, however, the divinities of the Celts were *genii loci*, "spirits of place", associated with a particular location.

This detail of a bronze votive wagon of *c.*650BC from southern Austria shows the stylized figure of a female deity, who supports what may be an incense burner. She is surrounded by mounted and dismounted male figures and two stags. The wagon, which stands nearly 12in high and 19in long, may have been used for some ritual associated with hunting.

It is small wonder that Caesar observed that "the whole nation of the Gauls is greatly devoted to religious observances": wherever they went, the Celts were likely to enter on the terrain of a god, goddess or spirit, to whom due respect had to be paid. Before the coming of the Romans, however, it was unusual for the Celts to build permanent shrines to their deities. If a god or goddess were to be appeased or appealed to for help in some matter, the necessary rituals would have taken place in the open air at the sacred spring, grove, tree, waterfall or other natural feature that was associated with the relevant deity. It was only after the Roman conquests that temples were constructed over such sacred sites as the springs at Nemausus (Nîmes) in France and Aquae Sulis (Bath) in England.

Nor, on the whole, did the ancient Celts make images of their gods. Although early stylized figures occurred and have sometimes survived, the idea of representing deities in realistic human form was another import from the classical world. In 279BC, just two centuries before the Roman conquest of Gaul, the Galatian leader Brennus mocked the human-like statues of the Olympian gods and goddesses that he saw during his participation in a Celtic invasion of Greece, indicating that the concept was clearly completely alien to the Celts. The idea must have become less strange, however, with the increasing contacts between the classical and Celtic civilizations in the following centuries.

Some ancient Celtic deities may have taken the form of animals, later to become more human figures – such as Cernunnos, the "Horned God" or

"Horned Sacred One", a widespread fertility god associated with forests, the vitality of nature and beasts both wild and tame, who was probably venerated as "Lord of Animals". Cernunnos came to be depicted as a mature bearded man with antlers or horns (see illustration, page 250). Other deities with close animal connections include the goddess Epona, who was associated with horses (see box, page 256), and the Morrigan, an Irish war goddess who could take the form of a crow (see page 257).

There are countless instances of humans being transformed into animal form and back, testament to the Celtic belief that many creatures possessed supernatural powers (see also box, page 261). To foretell events was one such ability, and druids, bards and seers observed many animals in order to make divinations. One bad omen widely understood was the alighting of a crow or raven upon a warrior's shoulder before battle, which heralded his death. A more positive avian association appears in the Welsh story of Bendigeidfran ("Bran the Blessed"), occupying the *Mabinogion*'s Second Branch. The tale may be the origin of the British tradition that states that,

should the ravens depart from the Tower of London, the kingdom will fall. Bran means "Raven" and at the climax of the story his severed head is buried under London's "White Mount" where it acts as a protective amulet for the island of Britain.

The Celts of Continental Europe

From Irish and Welsh writings we have some idea of the myths associated with the Celtic gods and goddesses as they were worshipped in the British Isles. However, as far as the Gauls and other continental Celts are concerned, the mythological record is patchy to say the least. Apart from votive monuments and a few coins, virtually the only clues are found on a single object: a silver cauldron found in 1891 at Gundestrupp in Denmark and dated to about 250BC.

Although the cauldron ended up in Denmark it was probably made in southeastern Europe by Celts who, to judge from various stylistic features, had contacts with Thrace and, through there, with Greece. The panels that make up the cauldron depict scenes and

Roman and Celtic gods

The Romans believed that most nations worshipped the same deities, although the names of the various gods and goddesses differed from land to land, and their functions also varied slightly according to local conditions. When Julius Caesar listed the most popular Gaulish deities in his *Gallic War*, he naturally gave them what he assumed to be their corresponding Roman names: Mercury, Apollo, Mars, Jupiter and Minerva. It is believed that "Mercury" refers to a god called Lugus. His cult centre, Lugdunum ("Fort of Lugus", modern-day Lyon), became the capital of Roman Gaul, and his festival, 1 August, was chosen as the feast

The god Cernunnos flanked by the Roman gods Apollo (left) and Mercury; from a Gallo-Roman relief found at Rheims in France.

of Augustus, the most important Roman holiday in Gaul. Many local gods were also identified with Mercury and became known by both their Roman and Celtic names, such as Mercury Artaios and Mercury Moccus. Likewise with Mars, who was not just a war god but also a guardian and healer: he was identified, for example, with Nodens, a healing god of southwest England. Another British healing deity, the goddess Sulis, was identified by the Romans with Minerva and known as Sulis Minerva. Such divinities generally remained unmistakably Celtic, as seen in their dress, torques and weapons.

253

The Great Hag

In Irish and Scottish myth, features of the landscape were often said to owe their existence to a land goddess, the Cailleach Bheur, who took the form of a giant hag.

Every night, after tending her cattle, the Great Hag went to the top of Ben Cruachan to block the spring that arose there with a huge boulder, so that it would not flood the plain below overnight. But one evening she fell asleep on her way up the mountain, and awoke to find the waters of the spring gushing out in a great torrent and cascading down the mountainside. In vain the Hag struggled to block the spring with the rock, but the force of the flood was too great even for her. Finally defeated, she looked down at the flooded valley and saw people and animals, dead and dying, in the floodwaters. She was so overcome with guilt that she turned into stone. The flooded plain became Loch Awe in Argyll.

A standing stone at Rossnowlagh in County Donegal, Ireland. Many such solitary stones were once worshipped as manifestations of the Great Hag.

divinities with parallels in other sources: the Horned God is there, sitting among animals, and there is a bull hunt and a scene that shows a giant tipping warriors into a cauldron. These and other scenes recall the Welsh story of Bran the Blessed and the cauldron of rebirth (Wales's greatest treasure that could restore the dead to health), the magic cauldrons of the Irish *sidh* (see page 260) and the action in the Irish epic *Cattle Raid of Cooley* (see pages 268–273), all recorded more than 1,000 years after the Gundestrupp cauldron was made.

Sacred Numbers

Numbers played an important part in Celtic mystical thinking. The number five represented the world – north, south, east, west, and centre, as reflected, for example, in the five provinces of Ireland. But the number three was paramount. The mystical quality of three was reflected in the three tiers of the universe – heaven, Earth and Otherworld, or sky, Earth and sea – and the three types of being who inhabited the cosmos – mortals, deities and the dead. Celtic society, too, seems to have had three main strata: warrior-aristocrats, druids and craftsmen (who included bards and farmers). The festival of Samhain (see page 261), which was a time when the frontier that normally separated the supernatural and natural worlds temporarily disappeared, was celebrated on the "Three Nights of Samhain".

Numerous Celtic deities possessed three manifestations, and images of such triple beings have been found all over the Celtic world. Among them are the *genii cucullati* ("hooded spirits"), fertility spirits which are depicted wearing long hooded capes. They are often found in the company of the triple mother goddess (see page 257). The triplication frequently implies great potency – very literally in the case of one statue of a Gaulish god, identified with the Roman Mercury, who is depicted with three phalluses. Many images of three-headed gods and animals also occur, and

Gaulish depictions of triple-horned bulls have been discovered by the dozen in many parts of France.

One of the most important Celtic concepts was the trinity of king, sovereignty and the land. Sovereignty was often personified as a powerful female deity, such as Queen Maeve of Connacht (page 270), who was probably a fertility goddess in origin. She is sometimes said to have been the lover of three times three kings (see also page 256).

In the myths, unusual phenomena tend to come in threes. The *Mabinogion* relates how, in the time of King Lludd, Britain suffered from three plagues, and the same work also refers to the "Three Happy Concealments", "Three Unhappy Disclosures" and the "Three Men Who Broke Their Hearts With Worrying".

Multiples of three were also of significance to the Celts. There is some evidence that the Celtic month consisted basically of three weeks of nine days each plus feast days. The Fianna, Ireland's élite warrior band, was made up of platoons of twenty-seven men, and the voyager Mael Duin was warned by a druid that he must carry a crew of no more than eighteen including himself. When this number was exceeded, Mael Duin's ship was carried off into the Otherworld (see pages 260–263).

The Mother Goddess

Among the most widely revered of Celtic deities were a range of powerful female figures who embodied the earth, fertility, fruitfulness and well-being. Shrines, statues and inscriptions to these mother goddesses have been discovered all over the Celtic world. They play an important role in Irish and Welsh mythology.

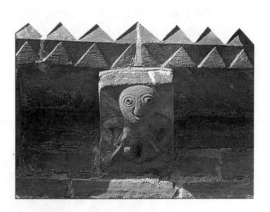

As a deity of fertility, the mother goddess was associated with promiscuous sexual activity – graphically seen in this pagan figure illustrating lust on a Norman church at Kilpeck in Herefordshire. She is known in Ireland as the Sheela na Gig.

In an age when most people did not live beyond early childhood, and when those who did spent most of their short lives in a constant struggle to avoid hunger and disease, the mother goddess was of central importance. She presided over all aspects of female fertility and childbirth, and was frequently depicted breastfeeding a baby. People appealed to her when they were pregnant or sick, and sometimes buried her image with the dead: one small statue of a mother goddess was found, poignantly, in the grave of a baby at Arrington in Cambridgeshire. Mother goddesses were also linked with the fertility of the land and individual prosperity, and could be shown dispensing apples, grapes, bread or coins to symbolize wealth and nature's bounty.

The Tuatha De Danann ("Children of the Goddess Danu"), the divine race of Irish myth, were said to be descended from one such goddess, Danu, who is probably identical to Anu, a goddess associated with the fertility of Ireland. Two round hills in County Kerry were once believed to be her breasts, reflecting her function as a divine mother; the hills are known to this day as "The Paps of Anu". She has a counterpart in the Welsh goddess Don, the divine matriarch of the *Mabinogion*.

Danu and Don are very much in the background of the myths, but other goddesses are more active. The Irish stories in particular feature a number of formidable divine matriarchs who embody

255

the sovereignty and prosperity of the land. According to ancient tradition, the fertility of the soil and, therefore, the well-being of the people were only assured if the king coupled with one of these divinities. In pre-Christian times, the High King of Ireland was ceremonially "married" to a mother goddess as part of his inauguration ritual at Tara. This tradition is strongly represented in the myths: Queen Maeve, for example, who represented the sovereignty of Connacht, was said to have married nine successive kings of Ireland. *The Book of Invasions* recounts that when the Milesians, the ancestors of the Gaels, first came to Ireland, it was ruled by three kings, whose consorts were the divine matriarchs Eriu, Banbha and Fodla. The Milesians named the land after Eriu (modern Irish *Eire*) in return for a pledge that they and their descendants would always govern the island. It was

A votive sculpture of a triple goddess from Burgundy in eastern France. This particular goddess was especially popular in the region. The three female figures are holding things that clearly associate the goddess with motherhood: a baby, a cloth that may be a napkin, and sponges for washing. Each of the goddesses has one breast bared for suckling.

A drawing of Epona, after a monument to the goddess found in France. She was often shown carrying a large key, which has been interpreted as a symbol of her ability to unlock the gateway to the Otherworld. This recalls stories such as the Irish tale of the fairy woman Niamh, who entered the Otherworld on horseback with the hero Oisin (see page 262).

Epona

The ancient Celtic goddess Epona was linked with horses and motherhood, and is no doubt connected with the Welsh goddess Rhiannon and the Irish goddess Macha.

Dedications to Epona, whose name derives from the Celtic for "horse", have been found all over the former Celtic world. The goddess was usually depicted with horses or ponies, often mounted on a mare and dispensing fruit, grain or bread. She was especially popular in Burgundy, a centre of horse-breeding and home to the only known sanctuary dedicated to the goddess. Epona was sometimes portrayed as a triple mother goddess.

All riders – whether warriors, heroes, or just ordinary travellers – revered Epona. Roman cavalrymen worshipped her, and she was the only Celtic deity to be honoured with a festival at Rome, which took place on 18 December. Epona's patronage of journeys had a profoundly spiritual aspect – she was connected with the journey of the soul from life to the Otherworld.

said that when a king was ritually married to Eriu, the goddess handed him a golden cup filled with red wine as a symbol of the sun and its benefits: the continued fruitfulness of the kingdom.

Other, even more formidable, Irish mother goddesses are closely associated with sexual potency, war and death. The most prominent of these is the Morrigan, who is said to have coupled with the Dagda, the tribal patriarch of the Tuatha De Danann. She also attempted to seduce the hero Cuchulainn, becoming his implacable foe when he

goddesses known as the Suleviae and associated with healing was worshipped as far apart as Hungary and Britain, where there were shrines at Cirencester, Colchester and Bath. Like images of individual goddesses, representations of the triple goddesses often show them bearing objects that symbolize motherhood or fertility, such as a baby, loaves or fruit. The triple goddess frequently appears alongside representations of the male triple god of fertility known to the Romans as the *genii cucullati* ("hooded spirits").

The central figure in this panel of the Gundestrupp cauldron is probably a mother goddess, perhaps one linked with war: a crow or raven perches on her hand and a fallen male lies at bottom right. The two smaller female figures may be aspects of the same deity.

rejected her advances. The Morrigan decided the fate of warriors, determining who would die in battle. Other deities representing this darker side of the mother goddess include Badb and Macha, and Maeve also has much in common with such figures. Both Badb and the Morrigan were able to metamorphose into a crow or raven, in which form they were said to hover over battlefields as harbingers of death to those fighting below.

Celtic mother goddesses are very commonly shown in groups of three, which the Romans called *Matres* ("Mothers") or *Matronae* ("Matrons"). Each of the figures in the triad represented a different aspect of the goddess, such as youth, maturity and old age, or birth, life and death. A trio of mother

The Second Branch of the *Mabinogion* is titled "Branwen, daughter of Llyr", although her role is less active than that of her brother Bran the Blessed (see page 253). She is described in the story as one of the "three matriarchs of Britain", which may be a reference to an old triple goddess of sovereignty. This may also be where the twelfth-century writer Geoffrey of Monmouth got the idea that the mythical King Leir of Britain, who is derived from Llyr, had three daughters. In Ireland, the goddess Brigit was sometimes said to have two sisters of the same name – in origin the three Brigits were probably different aspects of one goddess, just as the Irish war goddesses, such as Badb and the Morrigan, sometimes appeared in the form of triple goddesses.

257

Lords of the Heavens

The heavens played a central role in Celtic belief. They were the source of storms, alarming manifestations of divine power which also brought nourishing rain. Above all, the heavens were the domain of the sun, source of heat, light and growth. Several divine figures are closely linked with solar symbolism, such as Lugus, who is believed to be related to the Irish hero Lugh and the Welsh Lleu – all three names mean "Bright" or "Shining". Although Lugus may have been a sun god in origin, the Romans identified him not with Apollo, their god of light, but with Mercury.

A bronze Gallo-Roman statuette of the Hammer God from southeastern France. The style of the figure shows the extent of Roman artistic influence in this part of Gaul.

Apollo, on the other hand, was quickly associated with a popular Celtic deity called Belenus. One of Apollo's most important titles, Phoebus, means exactly the same as Belenus – "Brilliant" or "Bright" – and the Celtic god seems to have been allotted much the same range of functions as the Roman deity. Belenus was the lord of the sun, light and warmth, and may well have been the god who presided over the Celtic festival of Beltane (1 May), which celebrated the coming of summer. Like Apollo, Belenus was appealed to in times of sickness, reflecting the pervasive belief in the healing and sustaining powers of the sun.

Lugh and Lleu are not the only mythological heroes with solar connections. In Irish myth, Lugh is sometimes said to be the father of the Ulster hero Cuchulainn, whose hair was said to glitter "like the shining of yellow gold". At one point in *The Cattle Raid of Cooley*, he radiates so much heat that he melts the snow for thirty feet all around him. Gawain, perhaps the most distinctly Celtic of the Arthurian heroes, was clearly linked to sun symbolism: his strength was said to increase as the sun grew stronger, reaching its peak at midday, and then to decrease as the sun went down. Cuchulainn and Gawain are involved in many similar adventures – Cuchulainn, for example, appears in a beheading episode very like the tale of "Gawain and the Green Knight" – and one theory claims that the two heroes have a common origin, perhaps as a tribal sun-hero of northwestern Britain.

Many Celtic gods were assimilated to Jupiter, the supreme lord of the heavens and the head of the Roman pantheon. As the ruler of high places, Jupiter was sometimes connected with local mountain deities, such as the Celtic Alpine gods Uxellinus and Poeninus. But most often he was identified with Celtic sky gods. Some of the most striking images of Jupiter from the Celtic world are monumental columns upon which the deity is portrayed as a mounted Celtic god of the skies. Many remains of such columns survive, mainly in eastern France and the Rhineland, and they usually depict the sky god vanquishing a giant beneath the hooves of his horse. This scene has been said to symbolize the eternal battle between the forces of prosperity and

Another widespread deity associated with the weather was the Hammer God, who is always shown carrying a pot and a big double-headed hammer with a long handle. He is called Sucellus ("Good Striker") in one inscription, although this may be a description rather than the god's name. Lyon, the focus of the cult of Lugus, was also an important centre for the worship of the Hammer God, which may suggest an affinity between the two deities. The Hammer God was sometimes depicted with sun symbols and was particularly popular in wine-growing regions. According to one theory, the god was believed to strike the hard

A cauldron was an attribute of the Dagda, and many similar vessels feature in Celtic myth. This wheeled cauldron of c.800BC, found in Romania, is adorned with stylized birds and was probably for ritual use.

light, represented by the sky god, and those of darkness and death, represented by the giant.

The sky god often bears a wheel, one of the commonest Celtic symbols of the sun, and a thunderbolt, representing the sky god's role as a god of storms. The thunderbolt was also the chief weapon of Jupiter, and he was sometimes specifically linked with Taranis, a Celtic storm god whose name means literally "Thunderer". Taranis appears to have been a widespread deity, although little is known of his cult. He may have been simply a divine personification of thunder, or he could have had a wider role as a bringer of rain and therefore of fertility.

frozen soil at the end of winter, heralding the return of the warm sun and making the earth soft for cultivation once more.

The Hammer God may be connected with the Dagda, the patriarch of the divine race of the Tuatha De Danann in Irish myth. The Dagda's attributes were similar to the hammer and pot: he carried a large club, with which he could both kill people and revive them, and a cauldron from which he dispensed a never-ending supply of food. Both gods possessed the power to overcome death, and the Dagda was said to wear a very short tunic, a characteristic garment of the Hammer God.

The Otherworld

"It is the most delightful land of all that are under the sun; the trees are stooping down with fruit and with leaves and with blossom. Honey and wine are plentiful there; no wasting will come upon you with the wasting away of time; you will never see death or lessening. You will get feasts, playing and drinking; you will get sweet music on the strings; you will get silver and gold and many jewels. You will get everything I have said ... and gifts beyond them which I have no leave to tell of." Thus it was that the Otherworld, the mystical enchanted land of many Celtic myths, was described to the warrior Oisin by the fairy-woman Niamh of the Golden Hair.

In Irish myth, the Otherworld was created as the domain of the divine race of the Tuatha De Danann following their defeat by the Milesians (Ireland's fifth and last race of invaders). The Milesians, it was decided, would rule the visible parts of Ireland, while the Dananns took possession of the invisible regions below ground and beyond the seas. This Otherworld was accessible through caves, lakes and above all the *sidhe* or fairy-mounds, the countless prehistoric burial mounds of Ireland such as those .

of the Boyne in County Meath. The Dagda, the tribal patriarch of the Dananns, divided the *sidhe* among his people. According to one story, the Dagda gave each of his offspring a *sidh* except for Oenghus, his son by the goddess Boann. The Dagda had Oenghus raised by Oenghus's half-brother Midir at the *sidh* of Bri Leith. Later, Oenghus went with Midir to demand a *sidh* from their father. The Dagda said that he had given out all the fairy-mounds, but told Oenghus to go to Newgrange, the *sidh* of Nuadu, a Danann king, and ask to stay a night and a day there. Nuadu agreed, but at the end of his stay Oenghus refused to move and lived at Newgrange thereafter.

For most of the time, life in the Otherworld consisted of hunting and feasting, and those who lived there knew neither pain nor sickness. Nor did they ever grow old, for which reason the Otherworld was also known as *Tir na n-Og*, the "Land of Youth". Each *sidh* possessed a magic cauldron that dispensed an inexhaustible supply of food, and also boasted some special wonder. There might be magic apple trees continually laden with fruit that granted immortality; or food and drink that restored the dead to life; or pigs that could be slaughtered and cooked in a cauldron one day and come back to life the next, to be eaten again; or magic potions that bestowed great wisdom.

Manannan, the god of the sea, was said to have built invisible barriers to keep mortals out of the Otherworld. Nevertheless, there are many stories of heroes and other individuals crossing into the

The handle of this 1st-century AD bronze cup from County Leitrim is a stylized representation of the head of a bird, probably a swan. Swans are often linked with the Otherworld in Irish myth.

The Mystic Hound

"Of all the hounds he had seen in the world, he had seen no dogs the same color as these. Their color was a brilliant shining white, and their ears red." King Pwyll of Dyfed was right to wonder at these strange dogs, for their master was Arawn, the ruler of Annwn, the magical Otherworld of Welsh mythology.

Dogs are among the animals most often connected with the Otherworld in Celtic myth. They may be harbingers of death, as the red-eared hounds of Annwn are sometimes said to be – red was associated with death, as seen vividly in the story of Da Derga's hostel (see page 263). In this tale, Da Derga is said to possess a pack of nine white hounds: white is another color that indicates the supernatural in Celtic myth. Dog skeletons have been found at many sites, which suggests that they were involved in ritual sacrifice, possibly associated with the afterlife and the Otherworld. For the Celts, dogs were also believed to have magical healing qualities. It has been suggested that this is because they heal their own wounds by licking, but for whatever reason depictions of the animals are commonly found at Celtic healing sanctuaries. At one sanctuary, at Lydney in Gloucestershire, no fewer than nine canine images have been

A replica of a bronze hound found at a Roman-period healing sanctuary to the god Nodens at Lydney, Gloucestershire.

discovered as offerings to the British god Nodens. Visitors to the sacred healing springs at the source of the river Seine in France (see page 264) would sometimes offer up to the goddess Sequana images of a person carrying a dog. Dogs are often the companions of mother goddesses.

Otherworld by accident, or being led there by magic animals or fairy women. In the tale of Mael Duin, the hero's ship contains more than the magic number of eighteen men and in consequence drifts into the Otherworld kingdom of Manannan, which did not lie below ground but was a group of enchanted islands.

The Tuatha De Danann, however, could move freely between the mortal world and their own domain. The Morrigan was one Danann who regularly left her *sidh* to oversee the fate of warriors, most notably Cuchulainn. At the festival of Samhain (31 October–1 November), the boundaries of the Otherworld came down altogether, and its inhabitants left their *sidhe* to roam freely among mortals,

often causing havoc with their magic. For most ordinary folk, Samhain was a time to stay at home and hope to avert trouble. The hero Finn first came to the attention of the High King of Ireland by vanquishing an Otherworldly mischief-maker who regularly burnt down the royal seat at Tara. In later times, the gods and goddesses of the Otherworld became the fairy people of folk belief, just as the old Celtic feast of Samhain has survived down to the present day as Hallowe'en.

The land of Annwn, the magic underworld of Welsh mythology, is similar to the Irish Otherworld. It is a land of hunting, feasting, health and youth, ruled by King Arawn, who sometimes emerged into the mortal world on hunting expeditions with his

Oisin and Niamh

The visit of the warrior Oisin to the Otherworld is part of a tradition of stories in which heroes fall in love with fairy women. Niamh, an Otherworld princess, rode out of the mists on the shores of Lough Leane, where Finn and his warriors were hunting. "I have come for Oisin son of Finn," she declared. Oisin fell in love with Niamh at once and leaped onto the horse behind her. They rode off into the lough and entered the Otherworld.

Below: Lough Leane, one of the Lakes of Killarney in present-day County Kerry and the scene of Oisin's departure for the Otherworld with the fairy woman Niamh.

Oisin and Niamh married, had three children and enjoyed every imaginable pleasure. Oisin lived for three centuries in the Otherworld without growing a day older. But he missed Ireland and his father. Even though Niamh had told him that things would not be the same as they had been when he left, Oisin still wanted to go back, so she warned him that while he was there he must not set foot on Irish soil. With a promise to return swiftly, Oisin rode back into the mortal world.

Niamh had been right. Finn's castle was nothing but an overgrown ruin, and Finn himself lived only in folktales. Oisin's heavy heart made him careless and, forgetting Niamh's warning, he got off his horse to wash at a trough. The moment his foot touched the ground, he aged 300 years and fainted, a wizened man. He recovered consciousness in the arms of St Patrick, who had just arrived in Ireland. The saint tended the aged Oisin, who in his last years became a famous bard, telling stories of Finn that drew audiences from all over Ireland.

magical hounds. In the First Branch of the *Mabinogion*, King Pwyll of Dyfed exchanges places with Arawn for a year, and spends his time in Annwn "in hunting and song and carousal, and affection and discourse with his companions". After this there is a firm friendship between Annwn and the kingdom of Dyfed. According to the Second Branch of the *Mabinogion*, the first pigs to be seen in Britain came from Annwn and were given by Arawn to Pwyll's successor, Pryderi.

One of the treasures of Annwn was a magic cauldron of plenty. In one story, "The Spoils of Annwn", Arthur and three boatloads of his men entered the underworld in an attempt to steal the cauldron. The raid was a complete disaster, however, and Arthur escaped from Annwn with only half a dozen of his companions. Arthur's experience points to the darker side of the Otherworld. When mortals ventured into it deliberately, they tended to encounter demons, monsters and other perils, rather than the land of bliss that greeted those who strayed into it or were invited or conducted there by one of its true inhabitants.

A number of animal species are specifically associated with the Otherworld. In addition to pigs, both dogs (see page 261) and swans are prominent. In several myths in which magical Otherworld swans appear, they are metamorphosed humans, as in the stories of Midir and Etain, lovers who flew away together as swans, and Oenghus and the swan-maiden Caer, the daughter of a Danaan god who spent every day of one year as a beautiful woman and every day of the next as a swan on a lake in Connacht. Another story relates how the sea god Lir, the father of Manannan, went into self-imposed exile in a *sidh* in Ulster after failing to be chosen as king of the Otherworld. The successful candidate, Bobd Dearg, magnanimously presented Lir with his sister Aobh in recompense. Lir and Aobh were married and had two sets of twins (or three children in some variants). When Aobh died, Lir married her sister Aiofe, who was jealous of her stepchildren and turned them into swans. They were destined to remain swans for 900 years, until the coming of St Patrick, who freed them from the spell. When the saint restored them to human form they were very old, but lived just long enough to be baptized into the new Christian religion.

Life after Death

The discovery in Celtic graves of such things as food, cauldrons and other domestic artefacts, as well as objects symbolizing the sun, suggests that the ancient Celts probably believed in some form of life after death. In Irish myth, the Otherworld was also the land of the dead, who were ruled by a god called Donn, the "Dark One". He was said to be the eldest son of Mil, the leader of the Milesians, who fell foul of the goddess Eriu by not wanting to name Ireland after her. Donn was drowned in the sea off southwestern Ireland, but after his death he became ruler of the dead and went to live in a *sidh*, a small island that is still called Tech nDuinn ("House of Donn"). From here, it was said, the dead would begin their journey to the Otherworld.

Donn may be identical with the figure of Da Derga ("Red God"), who features in a myth called "The Destruction of Da Derga's Hostel". The "hostel" in question is one of a number of Otherworldly houses that appear in the Irish myths. According to the story, Conaire, the High King of Ireland, was predestined to die in this house. He journeyed inexorably towards it, despite various omens such as three riders in red on red horses. The climax of the story is a great battle in the hostel, during which Conaire is beheaded.

Conaire's champion, Mac Cecht, gave the severed head a drink of water, and it recited a brief poem before dying. There are echoes here of the Welsh story of Bran the Blessed, who was killed in a great battle and had ordered his followers to cut his head off in the event of his death and take it to London (see page 253). On the way, they sojourned for eighty years at Gwales, an Otherworldly island (perhaps Grassholm) off the Pembroke coast of Dyfed. Gwales recalls Donn's offshore *sidh* of Tech nDuinn. Here, as Bran had predicted, the head remained uncorrupted and talked as merrily as ever it did while he was still alive.

The Natural World

For the Celts, most features of the landscape were imbued with significance. Fires caused by lightning were sacred, bogs were evil, and there was not a mountain, tree, river or spring that did not have its own spirit. Amid such numinous surroundings it was unwise to tread carelessly, for fear of offending the gods, and respect was shown by making offerings.

The Celtic deities of the natural world were often synonymous with the places themselves. Rivers were particularly venerated as an essential source of life, and it is noteworthy that the Marne in eastern France derives its name from *Matronae* ("Matrons"), the title given to several mother goddesses (see page 257). Sequana, goddess of the Seine, was another Gaulish river deity. Swords, shields and helmets were often cast into such bodies of water as ritual offerings – as famously occurs with King Arthur's sword Excalibur.

The most sacred part of a river was the source, often a spring. These were places credited with great healing powers, and both Gaul and Britain abounded with such sites dedicated to various gods and goddesses. The source of the Seine was in Burgundy, at the Sequana Spring, while the chief sacred spring in Britain was Aquae Sulis ("Waters of Sulis", modern Bath), where a triad of Celtic goddesses called the Suleviae were among the deities venerated at the hot springs. Near Hadrian's Wall, the spring of Brocolitia (modern Carrawburgh) was the domain of the goddess Coventina, usually portrayed as a classical nymph.

The ancient veneration for springs and wells has survived in folklore, as seen in the widespread custom of casting coins into wishing wells. Many of the springs and holy wells that are now assigned to Christian saints were doubtless associated long ago with pagan gods, goddesses and spirits.

A Roman-period monument discovered at the spring of Carrawburgh, Northumberland. It bears the Latin dedication "To the Goddess Coventina" (*Deae Covventinae*).

Oak Trees and Groves

Trees were revered by the Celts as symbols of seasonal death and regrowth, and they also formed a bridge between the Earth and the heavens. The greatest tree of all was the oak, from which the druids collected their sacred mistletoe, according to the Roman writer Pliny the Elder (AD23–79). He describes the ceremony involved in gathering the plant: "They prepare a sacrifice and a holy feast under the tree ... a priest dressed in white climbs the tree, cuts the mistletoe with a golden sickle and catches it in a white cloak."

Oak trees feature strongly in Welsh myth, where they are often associated with magic. In the story of Lleu, oak blossom is one of the flowers used to conjure up Blodeu-wedd. Later, when Lleu is wounded by his enemy Gronw, he changes into an eagle that perches at the top of an oak tree. The tree is described as "a sanctuary for a fair lord" and appears to have magic properties, in that "neither rain nor heat affect it".

Among the holiest of all druidic sacred places were oak groves, and the word *nemeton* ("grove" or "sanctuary") is found in numerous ancient Celtic place-names, such as Nemetobriga ("Exalted Grove") in Spain, Drunemeton ("Oak Grove") in Galatia in Asia Minor, and in present-day Nymet and Nympton in Devon. Anglesey's sacred groves may also have been oakwoods – the scene, according to Roman sources, of ritual human sacrifice (see page 266).

The Washer at the Ford

At times rivers and streams possessed a sinister symbolism as the boundaries between life and death. One common theme is that of the Washer at the Ford – the war goddess who waited at a ford, sometimes in the form of a woman, sometimes as a crow or raven, and determined which of the warriors who passed would perish on the battlefield that day.

On their way to battle, a band of warriors stopped at a ford, where they beheld a terrible sight. A tall phantom woman, her eyes red and angry, glowered at them through grey, matted hair. At her feet, which were awash with blood, lay the mangled corpses of warriors, some so hideously disfigured that not even their mothers would have recognized them.

As the warrior band gaped in horror, the woman let out a hideous, shrieking laugh that sent a shiver of terror down their spines. Slowly, she raised her arm and pointed a bony finger at each man in turn. At last the chief of the band found the strength to approach the woman. With much effort, he forced himself to speak. "Who are you?" he asked.

"I?" she screeched, "I am the Morrigan, the Phantom Queen. Some call me the Washer at the Ford. I sleep on Mount Knocknarea, deep in the Cairn of Maeve. My work is to haunt all the streams of Ireland, washing away all the sins of men." "Who, then," asked the band's war-chief, "are the sinful men who lie in this gory heap before us? Are they those you have killed and maimed today?"

The Morrigan cackled again. "I did not kill these men, nor have I so much as harmed a hair on their heads!" She peered deep into the warrior's eyes. "Look again at these dead warriors. They are the very men that stand behind you, as they will be this evening, after the battle. I am merely washing the blood from their limbs."

The chieftain looked again at the corpses, and began to make out the features of some of the comrades accompanying him.

The Morrigan slowly bent down to rummage among her gory bounty, then held up an object for the chief to see. He turned to look and beheld, dangling by bloody locks, his own severed head.

A stylized bird, probably a crow or raven, drawn from a Spanish Celtic pot of *c.*100BC.

Ritual and Sacrifice

The twin functions of divination and assuring the future were the most popular of the druids' activities, and generally included some form of sacrifice. Much is often made of the Celts' propensity for sacrifice, which in Roman texts is distorted into wholesale massacres: Caesar claimed that the Gauls would build a huge wicker model of a man, fill it with victims then set the structure alight. People were sometimes sacrificed, but far fewer than the Romans claimed. Most sacrifices involved animals or the ritual destruction of a weapon.

Pliny noted that the Celts sacrificed bulls and oxen, and the practice is well attested. At Tara, the installation of the High King of Ireland involved a ritual called the "Bull-Sleep", in which a white bull was slaughtered. A druid consumed some of the bull's blood and flesh before going to sleep wrapped in the animal's hide. The dreams he had during this ritual slumber were said to indicate whether or not the correct person had been chosen as king.

Inanimate objects were also offered to the gods. Deep pits, perhaps conceived of as entrances

Below: The "skull gateway" to the Gaulish sanctuary of Roquepertuse in southern France. The skulls may be evidence of human sacrifice.

Above: The 3rd-century BC Gundestrupp cauldron. Cauldrons were used to catch the blood of sacrifice victims and for boiling flesh.

to the Otherworld, were filled with offerings of jewels, pottery and weapons which had been ceremonially broken before being thrown in.

Celtic funerals in particular were "magnificent and expensive", according to Caesar. Archaeological discoveries show that the Celts buried their nobles with chariots, jewellery, rich fabrics and vessels of various kinds. Some graves have yielded dogs, hares, birds and even whole teams of horses complete with cart. There is evidence that entire clans would gather for funeral banquets and ritual processions, at the end of which spears might be ceremonially hurled into the dead person's grave. Around 100BC there was a growing trend for cremation, so little evidence of funeral customs from after this time survives, except for the accounts of such foreign observers as Caesar. "They put on

Bog Burials

The Celts regularly made ritual deposits in bogs and marshes, perhaps to appease the gods or spirits who were thought to suck in unwary visitors. Among the offerings were cauldrons, weapons, chariots – and human beings.

Bodies of both men and women, mainly under forty years old, have been found in bogs. The most famous, from Denmark, is "Tollund Man", who had been ritually garotted and was found naked apart from a cap and girdle. He was probably a Celt, because the corpse of a similarly executed ancient Briton was recovered from Lindow Marsh near Manchester. He too was naked, except for a fox-fur armband. Both garottes had been knotted in the same way,

and an examination of the two men's stomachs revealed pollen of mistletoe, a plant sacred to the druids, who probably prepared a last ritual meal for victims. The Lindow man had been knocked out by blows to the back of the head, then garotted to death, before having his throat cut and being flung face down into the bog.

The body recovered from Lindow Marsh. The bog had preserved the body remarkably well, and his skin, nails and general health revealed that he was probably a high-status individual.

the fire everything they reckon to have been precious to the departed," he reported, "even living creatures." He adds that only a generation before he was writing, dependents and slaves might also have been thrown into the flames.

Such ceremonies may have been intended as an appropriately grand send-off to the Otherworld, where the dead would arrive equipped with the familiar objects and creatures that had been useful to them in the mortal world. Unfortunately, the unwritten lore attached to these splendid funerary rituals passed, with druidism, into oblivion. We are left to guess why, for example, the skulls of beheaded corpses were stored at the southern French sanctuary of Roquepertuse; or why, at other shrines, bodies were dismembered, decapitated, flayed and stripped of flesh before being piled up.

In peacetime, the Celts believed that it was impious to touch any valuables intended as a gift to the gods. Writing in the first century BC, Diodorus Siculus commented that in Gaul's temples "a great amount of gold is openly on show as an offering to the gods, and no one dares to touch it through religious fear." Much to the surprise of the Romans, Celts did not keep the plunder of battle for themselves but dedicated it to the gods. Any warrior who tried to keep his booty was punished with torture.

Military victories had their own ritual etiquette and the winners of a battle would sacrifice any living creatures they had captured. The glory, heroism and honour of war, its discipline and martial skill were given immortality in word and song, with some of the best examples to be found in the Ulster Cycle (see pages 268–273).

The Ulster Wars

In the Ulster Cycle, Irish myth moves to the world of mortal superheroes. The action centres on the disputes between the kingdom of Ulster and Queen Maeve of Connacht and her allies. The cycle comprises many texts, but its essence is encapsulated in the *Tain Bo Cuailgne* ("The Cattle Raid of Cooley") in which an attempt to steal Ulster's prize bull is defeated almost singlehandedly by the hero Cuchulainn.

The Ulster Cycle presents a fascinating picture of ancient Celtic society. The characters are nominally Christian, but their ways are largely untainted by alien cultures – here are Rome's "barbarians" portrayed in all their gaudy, bloodstained splendour, fighting, drinking, womanizing and going into fits of battle-madness. These stories highlight the matriarchal nature of Celtic society: the power of women is often presented not only as equal to that of men but, as in the case of Maeve, exceeding it. The tales also reflect the directness which the Romans found so disturbing in the Celts. Sex, bloodshed and even defecation are described with relish. In one episode of the *Tain*, Cuchulainn beats his opponent so furiously that both are enclosed in a cloud of the man's excrement; thereafter, the text adds gleefully, his bowels were never quite the same.

Whether any of the characters really existed is doubtful. The topography, however, is authentic

and it is possible to follow the progress of *The Cattle Raid of Cooley* on a map of Ireland. The spirit of place was very important to the Celts – the twelfth-century *Dinnshenchas* ("History of Places") gathers together much of the Irish lore on the subject – and the *Tain* is heavily laden with tales of how various physical features got their names.

The story begins in the time of Fergus mac Roich, mythical king of Ulster and, legend has it, author of the *Tain*. Fergus was a giant in every sense of the word. He had the strength of 700 men and he could consume at one sitting seven deer, seven pigs, seven cows and seven vats of alcohol. It took seven women to satisfy his rampaging sexual appetite. In battle he wielded a sword that was as long as a rainbow.

Above: Navan Fort in County Armagh, the Emhain Macha of the Ulster myths. It was the capital of the historical kings of Ulster.

Fergus wished to marry his brother's widow, Nessa, who accepted on the condition that her son, Conchobar (Conor), be king for a year. Fergus agreed, but Conchobar proved so popular that when the year was up the people of Ulster refused to have Fergus back. He was not too unhappy, however, being glad of the free time to go hunting.

Under Conchobar's reign, Ulster was a powerful province, famed for its warriors. At the forefront stood Fergus and two other heroes, Conall Cernach and Cuchulainn. These last two were grandsons of the druid Cathbad, the king's chief adviser. Despite this strength, Ulster was overcome by a weakness that even Conchobar was unable to remedy.

It originated with Macha, a divine queen who had once been married to Nemed, one of Ireland's original invaders. Appearing in human guise, she married an Ulsterman, Crunnchru, and became pregnant with twins. Shortly before they were due, her husband bragged that Macha could outrun the king's fastest horses. Conchobar summoned her to a race at his capital and ignored all her pleas for the event to be put off until after she had given birth. And so Macha raced the horses and beat them, but as she crossed the finishing line she died, giving birth to twins at the same time. This is said to be the origin of the name of Conchobar's capital, Emhain Macha ("Twins of Macha"), present-day Fort Navan.

Deirdre of the Sorrows

The story of Deirdre and Naoise occurs in a manuscript dating from the ninth century. It was added to The Cattle Raid of Cooley to explain why Fergus supported Connacht in the raid rather than his native Ulster.

Deirdre was the daughter of Fedlimid, Conchobar's chief storyteller. The druid Cathbad predicted that she would be the most beautiful woman in Ireland but that she would also cause many Ulster warriors to die. The men of Ulster wanted to kill the child at once, but Conchobar intended to marry her and hid her away with only a nurse for company.

One winter's day, when she was at the age to marry, Deirdre saw a raven drinking the blood of a slaughtered calf. "I could love a man with hair like the raven, cheeks like blood and skin like snow," she said. "There is such a man," the nurse said, "Naoise, son of Usna." One night, Deirdre went to meet Naoise, and they eloped to Scotland with two of his brothers. Word of this seeped back to Ulster. Conchobar was furious, but sent a peace offer to the sons of Usna. They agreed to return if Fergus accompanied them as surety for their safety. Conchobar agreed, but had Fergus delayed on a pretext, so Deirdre, Naoise and Naoise's brothers arrived at Emhain Macha without him. Conchobar at once asked one of his followers, Eoghan, to kill everyone except Deirdre. Naoise, his brothers and Fiacha, a son of Fergus, were all slaughtered. When Fergus learned of this treachery he left Ulster and offered his services to the queen of Connacht. Deirdre lived with Conchobar for a year but in the end her grief was so deep that it drove her to suicide: she hurled herself from a chariot and split her head on a stone. Her sorrows were at an end. As the druid had prophesied, those of Ulster were about to begin.

With her last breath Macha cursed the men of Ulster: whenever the kingdom was threatened they would be afflicted for five days with unbearable pangs, as agonizing as childbirth. The curse would last for nine generations and the only exemptions were women, children and Cuchulainn, perhaps due to his partly divine origin (see box, opposite).

Conchobar may have been an able ruler but, as the story of Macha shows, he had an unpleasant streak. This trait was to initiate a damaging divide within the kingdom. The flashpoint was his love for the beautiful Deirdre, who eloped with another man (see box, page 269). To get her back, Conchobar resorted to methods that outraged Fergus's sense of honour and left his son Fiacha dead. Fergus consequently deserted to the rival kingdom of Connacht, taking with him 3,000 of Ulster's best warriors. This switch of allegiances brought about the deaths of many Ulster warriors in a great conflict between Conchobar's kingdom and the formidable Queen Maeve of Connacht.

The Jealousy of Maeve

The war between Ulster and Connacht centred on two bulls of supernatural power: the White Horned Bull of Ai and the Brown Bull of Cooley. Famed for their size and strength, these animals were purportedly sent to Ireland by the gods in a deliberate attempt to incite war and bitterness. If so, the gods' purpose was amply fulfilled.

It all started with a bedtime argument between Ailill, king of Connacht, and his wife, Maeve, over who was the wealthier. Ailill won by a narrow margin, citing his unrivalled bull, Finnbhennach Ai, the White Horned Bull of Ai. Maeve was determined not to be outdone and eventually she learned of Donn Cuailgne, the Brown Bull of Cooley. Cooley, however, was in Ulster, and the bull's owner did not want to part with it. Maeve therefore decided to steal it and summoned to her aid not only the men of Connacht but also warriors from all the other provinces of Ireland except Ulster.

In origin Maeve was probably a goddess of fertility and sovereignty. She was a formidable woman – a strong leader and brave fighter with a ravenous sexual appetite. Even Fergus, who became her lover after his defection from Ulster, was no match for her: on one tryst he lost his sword, a piece of symbolism which greatly amused his fellows. Maeve was single-minded and selfish – the only reason she married Ailill was that he was generous and turned a blind eye to her love affairs. She was a born intriguer, happy to use deceit to achieve her ends.

Two bulls confront each other on this 2nd-century BC silver-plated iron torque found in southern Germany. Weighing some 14 pounds, it was no doubt made as a votive offering to a god rather than as something to be worn.

The Life of Cuchulainn

Of all the Ulster champions none was more illustrious than Cuchulainn. With his divine connections, supernatural powers, magical weapons and short but brilliant life, he was the epic hero par excellence. His mother, Dechtire, was the daughter of the druid Cathbad. His father's identity, however, was a mystery, although in one story he was the god Lugh, the hero of the Dananns.

Cuchulainn in his battle-fury, wielding the *gae bolg*, his personal lethal weapon.

Lugh is said to have made Dechtire pregnant in a dream while she was staying with King Conchobar and his hunting party by the river Boyne. Her child was named Setanta, but became known as Cuchulainn ("Hound of Culann") at a young age, after he had killed the fierce watchdog of Culann the smith and had taken its place until Culann had reared a new one. As a boy, he routed Conchobar's youth brigade and entered the Ulster king's service. He was trained in arms in Scotland by a female warrior, Scathach, who taught him such heroic feats as standing on a lance in flight and also gave him a vicious weapon called the *gae bolg*. A sort of spear, when it struck home its head sprouted thirty darts that coursed through every part of the victim's body, killing him instantly.

When his blood was up, Cuchulainn was gripped by a terrifying battle-frenzy during which his hair stood on end, his muscles bulged and his body rotated within its skin. One eye protruded from his head, the other sank into his skull and his battle-cry drove people insane. He had many lovers, but always returned to his wife Emer. Cuchulainn appears in many Ulster Cycle tales, most notably *The Cattle Raid of Cooley*. His death came seven years after the raid, when Maeve plotted to kill him with six sorcerers, the children of Calatin, a druid slain by Cuchulainn. King Conchobar knew that not even a superhero could combat such an array of magic power, and tried to keep the warrior out of harm's way. But the sorcerers conjured up an illusion of battle which convinced Cuchulainn that Ulster was being laid waste.

As he rode forth from his place of safety, he was struck by a magic spear thrown by one of the sorcerers. Mortally wounded, he tied himself to a rock so that he would be able to face his enemies with honour, standing up. For three days none of them dared approach him. In the end, Badb, a war goddess, landed on his shoulder in crow form. Cuchulainn did not stir, and so everyone knew Ulster's greatest hero was dead.

271

Having determined to seize the Brown Bull, Maeve sent spies into Ulster. Their reports filled her with joy: every warrior in the province except one, Cuchulainn, was stricken by a mysterious complaint – the curse of Macha – and would offer no resistance. With Fergus to guide them, her armies set out in the direction of Cooley on the Monday after the feast of Samhain.

Fergus, however, was troubled at the thought of fighting his old friend, the hero Cuchulainn. He sent him a warning, and when the Connachtmen reached the Ulster border they found their way barred by a wooden hoop in which was carved a challenge in ogham script. Cuchulainn had made the hoop from a living oak while standing on one leg and using one arm and one eye. The inscription challenged every invading warrior not to pass, on pain of dishonour, until he had made a hoop in the same way. "I except, of course, my friend Fergus," he added, and signed his name.

None could match the achievement and so the army made a detour, only to be met by another impossible challenge. And so the delaying tactics continued, until eventually Maeve ordered her army to ignore them and advance. Cuchulainn then fell upon her men, killing them first in twos and threes, then, as he grew angrier, by the hundred. The mere sight of Cuchulainn in his battle-frenzy was enough to make seasoned warriors die of shock.

Finally, through Fergus's mediation, a compromise was reached whereby Cuchulainn's slaughter and Connacht's advance could both be slowed. Cuchulainn promised not to lay into the Connacht troops, provided that he was met every day in single combat at a certain ford. While the fight was taking place, Maeve and her troops were permitted to advance, but as soon as it had ended she had to call a halt for the day. Maeve was confident that even if Cuchulainn could not be killed she would be able to find enough champions to keep him busy until her armies reached their destination.

At first plenty of heroes were willing to try their luck. But as each challenger was rapidly dispatched, Maeve had to offer increasingly large

Bricriu the Trickster

Tricksters – subversive and often hilarious characters who tend to get their come-uppance – appear in many cultures. In Irish myth, the most notable trickster is Bricriu, a bard with the nickname "Poison Tongue".

Bricriu was an archetypal mischief-maker who featured in many of the Ulster tales. Sometimes his cunning was helpful to Ulster; more often it was not. Yet his malevolence rarely caused serious damage and was usually humorous. In one episode, Bricriu tried to foment civil strife in Ulster by making three great warriors, including Cuchulainn, quarrel over who should receive the champion's portion – the greatest serving of food at a royal banquet, together with the privilege of sitting on the king's right hand.

To achieve this end, Bricriu invited the court to a great feast at his grand dwelling, threatening various calamities if they refused. The king and his men ignored his threats, however, until he finally swore that if they did not come he would make the breasts of their womenfolk beat together until they were black and blue. This did the trick, and the court, including the three heroes, headed for Bricriu's house. Once there, he provoked the quarrel, which turned into an almighty brawl that left his house a ruin. Bricriu ended up in a rubbish tip and emerged so filthy that nobody recognized him.

Bricriu met his end when he stepped in to judge between the Brown Bull of Ulster and the White Bull of Connacht. Ignoring his presence, the two bulls trampled him to death.

Cuchulainn belongs to an ancient tradition of heroes who combat warriors, giants and monstrous beasts. This heroic figure fighting a lion is on a golden brooch of *c.*250BC from Celtic Spain.

bribes to the others. Royal treasuries, herds of cattle, acres of land, the hand of Maeve's daughter – even the "friendly thighs" of Maeve herself – were promised. But no man who accepted a bribe lived to receive it. At one point Maeve managed to trick Fergus himself into meeting Cuchulainn. But the two had sworn that they would never fight each other. Instead, Cuchulainn pretended to run away, having first extracted a promise from Fergus that he would repay the favour on demand.

Finally, Maeve sent Natchrantal, a great champion, who put up a strong enough fight for Maeve to be able to launch a lightning raid and bring the Brown Bull back to Connacht. The raid should have ceased there, but Maeve continued to send men against Cuchulainn, among them Ferdia. Until now, Cuchulainn had killed each of his challengers with a clear conscience. Ferdia, however, was his best friend and was an equally adept fighter. The only thing he lacked was the secret weapon possessed exclusively by Cuchulainn: the *gae bolg*, an invariably lethal spear which, on entering its victim, sent tiny darts into every part of the body.

For three days the two men fought, with neither gaining the advantage, until on the fourth day, Cuchulainn was seized by his battle-frenzy and killed Ferdia with the *gae bolg*. In doing so, however, Cuchulainn himself was severely wounded.

For several days he lay unable to move, and during this time the Ulstermen recovered from Macha's curse and joined battle with Maeve's army on the Plain of Garach. For a while it seemed as if the Connachtmen might win the day. At one point Conchobar was at Fergus's mercy, but at the pleading of the king's sons Fergus diverted his stroke and lopped the tops off three nearby mountains.

The sound of battle reached Cuchulainn on his sickbed. When told that it was caused by Fergus's battle-fury, Cuchulainn rushed to the fray to demand that Fergus return his earlier favour by running away. Fergus obliged, leaving Maeve with only her own troops. The tide of battle turned, and Maeve's forces fled. Maeve escaped death only because Cuchulainn considered it beneath him to kill her.

Ironically, while all this blood was being shed, the two bulls were deciding which was superior. On reaching Connacht the Brown Bull of Cooley challenged the White Horned Bull of Ai with three mighty bellows. All day and all night they fought, in a gargantuan contest that took them all over Ireland. By morning the white bull was dead and its victorious opponent made its way back to Ulster, scattering fragments of its foe around the countryside. As it reached the Ulster border, however, the exhausted animal died in an explosion of black vomit. Many Irishmen had died – and for absolutely nothing.

273

SAGAS OF THE NORSEMEN

Around AD834, an important Viking funeral was held at Oseberg, near the Oslo Fjord in Norway. The corpse of a rich and powerful person was placed on the deck of a slender ship, which was then buried in a grave mound. Uncovered by archaeologists more than a millennium later, the ship burial opened a window onto the culture of large areas of pagan Europe, including Germany and England as well as Scandinavia.

By combining information from early writings and archaeologial findings such as this one, a picture emerges of a lifestyle and a philosophy that still have the power to excite the imagination. The stories explain the different levels of existence in the universe, including the place within that framework for gods and humans, and the purpose of the distinct classes that give form and order to society. The principal Norse gods are recognizably human, dominated by the cunning Odin and the sometimes brutish Thor. Always eager to feast and carouse, they conspire and compete with each other and their enemies in a series of vivid episodes played out against a setting that resembles the human world – one dominated by menacing elemental forces and a climate and terrain against which the gods must pit their wits and strength. In the human sphere of Midgard, mortals cohabit with gods, dwarves and giants, who are fearsome enemies who pose a constant threat.

In the harsh environment of northern Europe, where life itself was believed to have begun as a fusion of two extremes – ice and fire, it was necessary to have stamina and endeavour to survive the tests posed by the pitiless climate and relentless tribal violence. Such a life made the region's peoples intensely aware of the inescapable nature of fate. Without remorse, Odin selected those who were to die in battle, and an apocalyptic demise, even for the gods, was inevitable. All roads led to Ragnarok – the end of the world in which gods and humankind would be entirely destroyed, before the cycle would turn again and a new, more peaceful world would emerge.

Above, left: A silver pendant from Ostergötland in Sweden depicts a Vendel warrior, distinguished by his helmet with raised eyebrow guards (*c.*AD1000).

Opposite: A snow-capped mountain scene in Norway, with the Geiranger Fjord beneath. Such landscapes form the background to the myths of the Vikings.

275

The Creation of the Universe

Norse creation myths were permeated by the natural elements that were regular features of the people's environment. The engendering of life, the formation of the cosmos, and the establishment of the heavenly bodies were all seen as determined by the dramatic collision of heat with cold, most vividly typified by volcanic activity in a sub-arctic landscape.

The most important sources for these Norse beliefs are the tenth-century *Voluspa* and the thirteenth-century *Grimnismal* and *Vafthrudnismal*, three poems which the Icelandic chronicler Snorri Sturluson expanded upon from other unknown sources in his detailed account in the *Prose Edda*.

At the beginning of time, before the earth had been formed, there was nothing in existence – just a void called Ginnungagap. To the south of this was Muspell, a region which was bright and full of flames; to the north lay freezing cold Niflheim (which later became the land of the dead). In the midst of Niflheim was Hvergelmir, a spring from which flowed eleven rivers. As these rivers ran from their source, the poisonous lees that they deposited began to harden into ice. When the ice came to a halt the vapour rising from the poison froze into frost, layer upon layer, until it had spread right across Ginnungagap. Grim cold now emanated from Niflheim and that part of Ginnungagap that faced northwards, but the southernmost part was warmed by the sparks and hot wind from Muspell. As the frost met these gusts it melted, and from the moisture life began.

The drops formed a primeval giant, Ymir, who gave rise to a race of frost-giants. From sweat under his left armpit, Ymir grew a male and a female, while one of his legs begot a giant son.

A sense of foreboding, struggle and hostility pervades Norse creation myths, reflecting the harsh environment typified by this Norwegian landscape.

The World Tree

The axis of the universe was an enormous ash tree, Yggdrasill, also known as the World Tree, which formed a column linking the worlds of the gods, mankind, the giants and the dead. Its fortunes mirrored those of the universe it sheltered; as well as sustaining the world, it suffered in the same way as those who lived in it.

Nothing is known of the origin of Yggdrasill. It appears to have been timeless, existing before the beginning of the world and destined to survive Ragnarok (see pages 320–325).

A variety of creatures dwelled in or by the tree: a wise eagle who sat in its uppermost branches, with a hawk called Vedrfolnir between its eyes; a monstrous serpent, Nidhogg, who lay deep down in Niflheim, by its roots; a squirrel named Ratatosk who ran up and down its trunk carrying insults between the eagle and the serpent; and four stags, named Dain, Dvalin, Duneyr and Durathror, who lived among the tree's branches eating young shoots. To them and others the tree was a source of life. It dripped dew so sweet that bees made honey from it, and its fruit was said to be helpful to women in labour, hastening the emergence of the child.

As well as providing protection and nourishment for the world, the tree was said to suffer anguish and bitter hardships, caused by the very creatures it sustained. The stags and squirrel stripped it of new growth, and Nidhogg gnawed at its roots, as

The World Tree, Yggdrasill, was constantly gnawed by deer and other creatures, as depicted in this Viking-era carving from Urnes, Norway.

did countless other serpents. In this way the tree knew the tribulations of the universe at every level and suffered just as much as those who dwelled in it.

To counteract this damage and pain, the Norns (see box, page 281), who resided by the well of Urd, tended the tree every day by pouring water and mud over the branches so they would not rot away. The water was so holy that everything it touched immediately turned as white as the delicate film inside an eggshell.

As guardian to the whole world, Yggdrasill was the supreme example of a widespread belief in trees' protective qualities. In Germany, Scandinavia and the British Isles, particular trees beside buildings were venerated, and the welfare of the family or community was seen to depend on their health. Offerings were made to them; for example, ale was poured over their roots.

Temples also had guardian trees: Adam of Bremen, in his description of the temple at Uppsala, refers to a great evergreen growing close by. Details of his description are remarkably similar to those of Yggdrasill in Norse poetry: the tree's broad outstretched branches offered shelter to the temple, and there was a sacred well at its foot.

Further melt-ice created Audhumla, a cow, from whose udder there flowed rivers of milk for Ymir. For her own sustenance Audhumla licked the salty rime stones. After three days of licking on the stones a complete man had emerged. Again, life had grown out of the reaction of heat and cold on one another. This strong and handsome man, Buri, begot a son called Bor, who married Bestla, the daughter of a frost-giant called Bolthorn. They produced three sons: the gods Odin, Vili and Ve, who in time decided to kill Ymir. So much blood flowed when Ymir fell that the race of frost-giants was drowned. Only Bergelmir escaped, becoming the progenitor of a new race of giants.

The Origins of the World and of People

Odin and his brothers then created the world out of Ymir's body: the earth out of his flesh; rocks from his bones; stones and gravel from his teeth and shattered bones; and lakes and the sea from the blood that flowed from his wounds. From Ymir's skull they formed the sky and set it up over the earth, placing four dwarves, Nordri, Sudri, Austri and Vestri (representing North, South, East and West) at each corner to hold it up. Ymir's hair was used to create flora, and his brains were thrown into the sky to form the clouds.

The three gods took sparks and glowing particles emanating from Muspell and set them in the firmament above and below the Earth to become the stars in the sky. They gave positions to all of them, and ordained their courses. Some were fixed, while others wandered around and below the Earth the gods had constructed. The Earth itself was circular, and they placed a vast sea around it. Along the shore they allotted land to the giants, while inland they made a fortification against them out of Ymir's eyelashes, within which lay Midgard, the realm the human race was to inhabit.

Once the world had been established, the gods created people to live in it. As Odin and his brothers walked along the sea shore,

they came upon two tree trunks and created a man and a woman from them, named Ask ("ash tree") and Embla (possibly "elm", or "vine") respectively. The gods then gave them breath and life, consciousness and movement, and a face, speech, hearing and sight. From this first couple descended all those who lived in Midgard.

The credit for creating the social classes goes to the god Heimdall (see box, page 321), about whom little is known but who must have been important within the Norse pantheon. One day, using the name Rig, he came to a farmhouse

The Trundholm chariot dates from the Bronze Age. Day was believed to be driven across the sky in such a chariot by Sun.

Fire, Ice and Water

Although particular, recognizable places do not feature in the Norse stories of the origin of the world, specific sites or natural features can be identified which may have provided the inspiration for important aspects of the creation myths.

It was in Iceland that most of the myths took the shape in which they have survived until today. The idea of intense heat meeting cold to generate life could well have originated in a place where this unusual juxtaposition is commonly seen: Iceland's ice-covered volcanoes erupt, spewing out boiling lava, flames and steam, and the ice caps melt flooding the valleys below.

Other elements of the creation myths may be associated with a place that the Roman historian Tacitus described as holy to the Germans. At the salt springs of the River Saale, near Strassfurt, people obtained salt by pouring water over piles of burning wood. Tacitus noted that this process involved uniting two opposing elements, water and fire, thereby apparently presenting the same conditions that engendered life in the story of the cow Audhumla.

where he was received by a couple, Ai and Edda ("great-grandfather" and "great-grandmother"), who gave him coarse bread and beef broth to eat. He stayed to rest with them, remaining for three nights and sharing the couple's bed. Nine months later Edda bore a son, a swarthy child with dark hair and dull eyes. Named Thrall, he was condemned to spend his life performing hard labour. He married an unattractive woman and from them descended the race of slaves.

At another house, Heimdall was received by the more affluent Afi and Amma ("grandfather" and "grandmother"). Rig was given a trencher full of meat, and again he stayed three nights. Nine months on Amma had a son. Called Karl ("freeman"), he had a ruddy complexion and bright eyes. He grew up to farm land and build houses, and from him came the race of free men.

Rig finally came to the home of a third couple, Fadir and Modir ("father" and "mother"), who laid out a sumptuous meal of bread, meat, poultry and wine. As usual, Rig stayed for three nights and nine months later a boy was born, who was named Jarl ("earl"). He had flaxen hair and a fair complexion, and his eyes glittered like jewels.

Jarl grew up accomplished in all aristocratic pursuits: skilled in the use of weapons, and in riding, hunting and swimming. Heimdall eventually acknowledged him as his own son and taught him about the runes. Jarl became rich, and was married to a beautiful woman. The nobility descended from their children.

279

The Three Levels of Existence

The cosmology of the Norse mythological world as it emerges from the later myths is not easy to reconcile with that depicted in the creation stories, and it is certainly impossible to draw up a precise picture using evidence from them. The best that can be done is to paint a heady image of varied landscapes and vast distances – even in the real world, the Vikings considered a good knowledge of regions and inhabitants to be more important than a map.

Yggdrasill

ASGARD
Realm of the Aesir

The Well
of Urd

VANAHEIM
Land of the Vanir

VALHALLA
Hall of the Slain

Bifrost

The Well
of Mimir

MIDGARD

JOTUNHEIM
Land of the Giants

The World Serpent,
Jormungand

Spring of
Hvergelmir

NIFLHEIM
World of the Dead

HEL

The Dragon, Nidhogg

The creation myths present a flat world, with Asgard, Midgard and Jotunheim all on one level surrounded by the sea. In all other Norse myths, however, the world seems to consist of three different levels, stacked one above the other like a series of plates. On top was Asgard, where the gods lived in their magnificent halls, as well as Vanaheim, abode of the Vanir, and Alfheim, the home of the light elves. Here, too, lived those who died in battle, feasting in one of Odin's halls, Valhalla, or Freyja's hall, Sessrumnir. On the level below was Midgard, the world of men and the underground homes of dwarves and dark elves, and Jotunheim (Giantland), the mountainous land of the giants.

Asgard and Midgard were connected by the flaming bridge Bifrost, which appears to mortals as the rainbow. Snorri describes it as very strong, with three colors, and says that it was built by the gods with more skill than any other structure.

Down below, on the third level, was Niflheim, world of the dead, which included Hel, where those who died of sickness, old age or accident were judged. It was named after its guardian, Loki's monstrous daughter.

The different worlds were linked by the central column of the World Tree, the great ash

In the creation stories the world appears to be flat, but in other Norse myths it was divided into three levels, Asgard (home to the gods and light elves), Midgard (where humans, dark elves, dwarves and giants lived) and Niflheim (the realm of the dead). All were linked by Yggdrasill whose roots penetrated each level.

Yggdrasill, whose three roots reached all three levels and whose branches extended above them all providing shelter and sustenance. One root was embedded in Asgard, under which was the well of Urd ("fate") where the gods held their council every day. The second root delved into Jotunheim, and sheltered the well of Mimir, the repository of wisdom where Odin was to leave one of his eyes in return for a knowledge-giving drink. The third root extended down into Niflheim, and beneath it was the spring of Hvergelmir, the source of the rivers that contributed to the world's creation.

This bronze amulet is believed to be a representation of a priest of the cult of Odin, ruler of Asgard (c.AD800).

Various stories of the gods' travels give an impression of the distances and type of terrain thought to lie between each world. Hermod's journey from Asgard to see Hel (see page 318) takes him downwards and northwards, through valleys full of darkness and over almost impassable mountains and rivers, for a duration of nine nights. The road from Asgard to Jotunheim led eastwards, and it was necessary to cross the ocean in a boat and then, on land again, to navigate huge forests before reaching it. Thor made this journey regularly. For example, he planned a journey to Utgard in the summer, so that he could test himself against the giants (see pages 302–306).

The Norns, Shapers of Destiny

Norns were female supernatural figures who were thought to determine the destinies of individuals. Three particular Norns lived by the well of Urd, but there were other Norns as well, both benevolent and malevolent, who could reverse a person's fortune at their whim.

Of the three principal Norns who lived by the well of Urd ("fate"), situated beneath one of the roots of Yggdrasill, one was actually named Urd, while the others were Verdandi ("being") and Skuld ("necessity"). They were said to determine the lives of men and allot their lifespans. According to the *Voluspa*, they "cut on wood", which may refer to the action of carving magical runes. However, the word used for wood in the poem also refers to a large plank, and it was customary in Norway to record dates and numbers of days and years by cutting notches into the wooden walls of the home. So this term may just mean that they recorded the days in an individual's life.

Other Norns were thought to visit each child as it was born to determine events in its life. A runic inscription found in a church in Borgund in Norway reads: "The Norns determine good and bad things and they have brought great sorrow to me." These Norns differed in their origins. Some were divine, some were of the race of elves, some of the race of dwarves. An individual's fortune and quality of life were explained by the origins of the Norn that was believed to protect him or her. Good Norns, of divine lineage, were thought to influence lives favourably, but misfortune was associated with malevolent Norns, thought to descend from baser ancestry.

Norns were also sometimes pictured allotting destiny by spinning: in the poem *Helgakvida Hundingsbana* ("The Lay of Helgi, the Slayer of Hunding") the Norns are depicted spinning and weaving the threads of Helgi's fate.

The Aesir

The Norse gods lived together in the realm called Asgard, beyond and above the human world. Here they held heated debates about their various dilemmas – how to regain hostages from the giants, how to deal with the evil progeny of Loki, how to protect their magical treasures. They interacted with each other like any other social group, and were characterized by superhuman strength rather than by moral absolutes.

Asgard was originally inhabited by the Aesir alone. Another tribe of gods, known as the Vanir, coexisted with them in the separate upper realm of Vanaheim. But the two groups subsequently fought a long, bloody war (see pages 314–315), after which members were exchanged and a few of the Vanir came to live in Asgard.

Little is known of this war, but we are told that the most important of the Vanir who came to Asgard were Njord, god of the sea, and his twin children: the god Freyr and the goddess Freyja. Whereas the Vanir were deities of fertility, presiding over land and sea, the Aesir were associated with war, magic and the sky. The magician Odin was their chief and Thor, protector of Asgard, was second-in-command. Adam of Bremen, an eleventh-century historian, reported that Odin made wars and blessed men with bravery in battle, while Thor ruled in the sky, governing thunder, lightning, the winds and the rain.

These three standing figures from a woven tapestry of *c.*1100 have been identified as the trio of primary gods worshipped by the Norse people – Odin, Thor and Freyr. Odin, with one eye, stands on the left wielding not a spear but an axe, while the central figure gripping a hammer is probably Thor. The third figure holds an ear of corn or a piece of fruit – symbols of Freyr's role as a fertility god.

Sacred Places

The Norse deities were not always worshipped in elaborate temples and holy buildings. Sites of natural beauty were sometimes chosen as idyllic settings in which to venerate the gods and frequently they were not even marked by a monument.

This beautiful lake at Thingvellir in Iceland was probably held to be sacred since the island's "Althing" (an annual assembly of free men) met nearby during the Viking era.

The Roman historian Tacitus described how the Germans did not confine their worship to a domestic forum, but also consecrated open forests and groves. Many Scandinavians, particularly those who settled in Iceland, also chose natural venues as their sites of worship. Literary sources tell of sacrifices brought to groves, rocks and stones, which were believed to represent patron gods. In the poem *Hyndluljod*, Freyja tells how her human protegé, Ottar, set up a cairn in her honour.

Sacred places might be chosen for their outstanding beauty. One such site, Helgafell (Holy Mountain) in Snaefellsness, western Iceland, is mentioned in the *Eyrbyggja Saga*. Thorolf Mostur-Beard, a devoted follower of Thor who emigrated to Iceland, held this mountain to be so sacred that no one was even allowed to look at it if they were unwashed, and no living creature, man nor beast, was to be harmed there.

The same Thorolf also held sacred the place where the pillars of his high seat (removed from a previous site and brought on the journey) had washed ashore (see page 298). Deeming this to be somewhere holy that Thor had divinely guided them to, Thorolf gave orders that it should never be desecrated with either bloodshed or excrement.

Unsurprisingly, the site was indeed desecrated after Thorolf's death. Following an assembly held there, a rival family declared that they were going to follow their normal custom and relieve themselves – they then proceeded to do so with much show. Thorolf's son and his men attacked them for this affront; a fierce fight ensued, with blood spilt on both sides, defiling the holy ground even further. After this incident, the temple and the assembly were removed to a fresh venue.

The bridge between Asgard and Midgard, the immortal and mortal worlds, was called "Bifrost". Snorri describes it as the rainbow, consisting of three plaited strands of fire.

Snorri, the Icelandic chronicler, tells that all the other Aesir, mighty as they were, deferred to Odin like children to their father. Odin was a formidable and frightening character, rather less concerned with the protection of his subjects than with the accumulation and exercise of his own magical powers.

Odin's wife Frigg, was, like him, credited with the ability to foresee the future. She was queen of the gods and first lady among the goddesses. Stately and bountiful, she also had a maternal aspect accentuated by her concern for her son, Balder. In this capacity she was invoked by women during childbirth and by those wishing to conceive. Frigg and Odin's other children included Hod, who was to play an unwitting role in Balder's fate, and Hermod, who was to prove himself in an act of outstanding bravery (see page 318).

Many of the gods were said to be Odin's off-spring. Thor was his eldest son, although not by Frigg but Jord (Earth), with whom Odin had an extra-marital liaison. Thor in turn was married to Sif, a golden-haired goddess, although he also had two sons, Modi and Magni, by a giantess, Jarnsaxa.

Asgard, Realm of the Gods

The Norse people envisaged a world divided into three different levels, one above the other (see pages 280–281). At the top, Asgard lay above Midgard, the world of men surrounded by vast oceans. Beneath Midgard was Niflheim, the land of the dead presided over by Loki's daughter, Hel, who gave her name to the realm's citadel.

It was in Asgard that the gods had their impressive abodes. Odin's two halls were called Valhalla, hall of the slain, and Valaskjalf, which contained his high seat Hlidskjalf. Sitting on Hlidskjalf Odin could preside over the whole world, with a view of each level and all that went on in it, and only he and his wife, Frigg, were allowed this high privilege. Thor's hall, known as Bilskirnir, in the region of Thrudvangar, was said to be the largest building ever constructed, while there was no more beautiful place than Balder's hall, Briedablik, except perhaps the hall Gimli, which stood at the southernmost edge of the realm. Gimli was considered to shine more brightly than the sun, and it was believed that this building would remain standing after the end of the world. Gods were to live there at peace with one another after Ragnarok.

Also on this top level were Vanaheim, home of the Vanir, and Alfheim, realm of the light elves – supernatural beings who were thought to be more beautiful than the sun. Midgard was home not only to humankind but also to the the giants, who lived in Jotunheim, and the dark elves, said to be blacker than pitch, who lived underground. Elves were therefore alluring as well as dangerous. The different levels were linked by a rainbow bridge and the parts of the cosmos by the World Tree or Yggdrasill (see box, page 277 and pages 280–281).

Asgard was protected by a wall which was razed during the war against the Vanir, leaving the realm defenceless. A builder approached the Aesir and offered to construct a mighty barrier that would be completely secure against giants. In payment, he requested the goddess Freyja as his wife, and the sun and the moon for his own. The Aesir decided to agree to the builder's demands on condition that he complete the wall before summer – which gave him six months – but if it was at all unfinished on the first day of the new season they insisted that his price would be forfeit. They felt sure that he could not possibly finish such a task in that time, and they secretly hoped to gain the best part of a wall without cost. Furthermore no one was to aid him in the work. However, the builder asked that he might have the help of his stallion, Svadilfari and, ever-mischievous, Loki (see pages 307–311) persuaded them to consent.

The Aesir were amazed at the size of the rocks that the stallion was able to pull, and the builder's work rate increased threefold with its assistance. As winter wore on, the team's progress continued apace and the wall rapidly became so high and strong that it could never be breached. Contrary to the Aesir's anticipation, the builder had almost completed his task a full three days before the allotted time.

Somewhat alarmed, the gods met to discuss tactics. They asked each other who had been responsible for this impetuous bargain which could end in the loss of Freyja, the sun and the moon. Blaming Loki for having persuaded them to agree to the use of the stallion, they seized him and told him to resolve their predicament. Loki promised to do so.

That night, when the builder went to fetch stone with Svadilfari, Loki, disguised as a mare, cantered out of the wood and drew near to Svadilfari, easily distracting the stallion. As the mare ran away Svadilfari raced off into the wood after it. All night the horses chased each other among the trees, leaving the hapless builder powerless to finish his work. Realizing now that he would not fulfil the Aesir's ultimatum, the builder flew into a monstrous rage. At this his guise slipped and the gods could see that he was in fact a giant. They called for Thor. He appeared immediately with his hammer raised to reward the giant not with Freyja, the sun and the moon, but with a smashed skull. Then the impostor was sent to Hel. Meanwhile, Loki, who had taken the mare's form, was to give birth to a magical horse called Sleipnir.

Picture stones such as this were first used in Gotland as monuments to the dead. This example, from the Germanic Iron Age, is incised with an image of the sun and vignettes of hunting.

285

Odin, God of War and Magic

Perhaps the most complex of all the Norse Gods was Odin. Presented in the sources as foremost of the Norse pantheon and known as "Allfather", he was not, however, a benevolent father-god – he was as fickle as he was powerful, as treacherous as he was generous, and although respected and worshipped, he was never entirely to be trusted.

The supreme deity Odin is depicted in a medieval manuscript with his two raven companions Hugin and Munnin. Hugin is believed to represent memory, whereas Munnin personifies thought. Each day Odin would send them out into the world and they would return bearing news of events. Odin is typically represented with only one eye and wearing a dark hat.

Odin cut a terrifying figure: one-eyed, he travelled among mortal men wearing a dark, wide-brimmed hat that cast a shadow over his face. As a god of magic, war and wisdom, he visited Midgard to distribute knowledge and victory in battle. He had many names which hint at his various roles, and the diversity and fickleness of his character. He was known as Alfodr ("Allfather"), but also as Valfodr ("Father of the Slain"), Hangagud ("God of the Hanged"), Haptagud ("God of Prisoners") and Farmagud ("God of Cargoes"). Snorri lists another forty-nine names that Odin was reputed to have called himself, which also reflected aspects of his character. Among these were Harr ("High One"), Grimr ("Masked One"), Svipall ("Capricious One"), Hnikarr ("Inflamer"), Glapsvidir ("Swift Tricker"), Sigfodr ("Father of Victory"), Blindi ("Blind One"), Baleygr ("Shifty Eyed"), Gondlir ("one with a magic staff"), Vidurr ("Destroyer") and Yggr ("Terror").

Odin was invoked by his followers for victory in battle, and to give or deny victory was within his power. But he could be faithless, suddenly turning against his favourites and causing their rapid downfall, and he was sometimes accused of awarding triumph unjustly. It was in his interest, as a god of war, to promote strife, and it was said that he sometimes boasted of being able to incite nobles against each other so that they would never be reconciled again.

Odin was a master of magic and went to great lengths to further his supernatural powers. He was said to have only one eye because he had pledged the other in payment for a drink from the well of Mimir, which was situated beneath a root of the World Tree. The water in this well promised

Odin Wins the Mead of Poetry

When Odin wanted to take the mead of poetry from the giant Suttung and give it to the gods he had to call on all his powers of cunning and guile.

Disguised as Bolverk, Odin persuaded Baugi to bore through a mountain to help him gain the mead of poetry.

Disguised as a mortal and calling himself Bolverk ("evil-doer"), Odin took up lodgings with Suttung's brother, a giant called Baugi, who had owned nine slaves, all of whom Odin had ruthlessly murdered. He offered to do their work, and as his price requested a drink of Suttung's mead of inspiration. Although it was not in his authority to agree to such a request, Baugi yielded.

When winter arrived, and he had completed his work, Bolverk demanded his reward and so the two of them set off for Suttung's mountain home. When they arrived, Suttung flatly refused to take any part in Bolverk and Baugi's pact. So Bolverk found an auger (an instrument for boring), and ordered Baugi to bore a hole into the mountain, which he believed contained the mead.

When a tunnel had been created, Bolverk transformed himself into a snake and slid into it. There he discovered Gunnlod, Suttung's daughter who guarded the precious liquid. He lay with her for three nights, for which she granted him three tastes of the drink. He drained the pot called Odroerir with the first drink, and in the next two sips he emptied the two vats Bodn and Son.

Odin then turned himself into an eagle and escaped to Asgard. Furious, Suttung also took the shape of an eagle and followed in pursuit. When the Aesir saw Odin flying towards them they quickly placed special containers in the courtyard, so that as he flew overhead he could release the mead into them. Suttung, however, was so close behind his opponent that he caused Odin to spill a little of the mead of inspiration outside the walls of Asgard, and ever since that time any mortal who so wishes has been free to partake of it there.

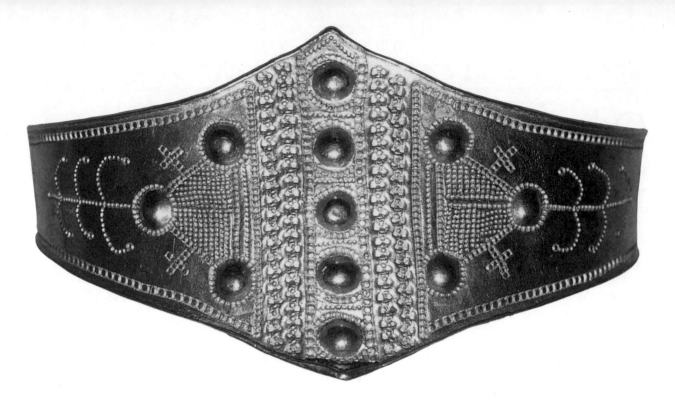

This golden armring (*c.*AD900) from Jutland in Denmark is elaborately decorated with a pattern symbolizing Yggdrasill, the World Tree. This giant ash tree was the axis of the Norse mythical world. Odin hung upon it for nine days and nights without sustenance in order to learn the secrets of the universe.

inspiration and knowledge of the future to whoever drank it. Another version, however, claims that Odin gained wisdom and information from the head of one of the gods, Mimir, the oldest and wisest of the Aesir, which he kept for himself after it had been cut off by the Vanir (see page 315). He was able to consult the head whenever he wished to obtain occult knowledge.

Odin could also change his shape at will, often flying through the air in the form of an eagle, and his spirit could be instantly transported to distant lands as any other bird or creature, while his body lay as if asleep. His magical abilities made him a formidable opponent – with mere words he had the power to both calm or stir the sea, extinguish fires or change the course of the winds.

It was also said of Odin that he only spoke in verse, and that poetic ability and inspiration were gifts that he alone bestowed. For example, he blessed one of his favoured subjects, Starkad, with the ability to compose poetry as fast as he could physically speak the words.

The source of poetic inspiration was the mead of poetry, which Odin stole, to the benefit of humankind as well as himself. This magical liquid came into being after the war between the Aesir and the Vanir (see pages 314–315), when the two sides sealed their truce by simultaneously spitting into a vat. The Aesir then took this spittle, which symbolized peace, and, not wishing to waste any, formed it into Kvasir, a man who was so wise that there was no question that he could not answer.

Kvasir travelled far and wide imparting his knowledge to others until eventually he arrived at the home of two malicious dwarves, Fjalar and Galar. Unwitnessed, they killed Kvasir and poured his blood into two vats, called Son and Bodn, and a pot, called Odroerir, before adding honey to create a rich mead. The resulting liquid conferred the ability to compose poetry or pronounce words of wisdom. To placate the gods, who bemoaned the loss of their companion, the dwarves explained that Kvasir had suffocated in his own intelligence.

The dwarves were undone by the giant Suttung whose parents had been needlessly murdered by Fjalar and Galar. Faced with the threat of death, the two offered him the precious mead as compensation. Odin, as is fitting for the god of magic, then gained the priceless drink from Suttung's daughter, Gunnlod (see box, page 287).

Odin, the World Tree and Sacrifice

Although it would appear to be an important part of his story, the myth of Odin hanging on the World Tree survives only in one enigmatic passage from the *Havamal* ("Words of the High One"). This tells how he underwent great suffering to win the runes, the source of wisdom and magical lore.

In the poem Odin himself narrates how he hung on a windswept tree identified as the World Tree, Yggdrasill, for nine full nights without food or water, slashed with a spear and sacrificed – "given to Odin, myself to myself" – until, screaming, he was able by virtue of his suffering to reach down and seize the magical runes. By this heroic deed Odin also learned nine magical songs from the son of a giant named Bolthor and his wisdom became so great that he was able to master eighteen magical spells previously unknown to any man or woman.

There are obvious similarities between Odin's hanging on the World Tree and Jesus Christ's sacrifice on the cross: Christ hung on the Rood Tree, without food or water, and he was also pierced with a spear as was Odin. Christ cried out before dying as Odin cried out when he seized the runes during his self-sacrifice. Christian influence on the *Havamal* cannot be entirely discounted, but crying out, hanging and stabbing are also ancient elements of Norse myth that are particular to the cult of Odin.

Lord of the Spear

Gungnir, Odin's spear, was specially crafted by the dwarves. It was his favourite weapon, and he used it to incite or reduce discord. Those who died by spear-wounds were sacred to Odin and went to serve him in Valhalla.

One of Odin's many epithets was "Lord of the Spear" and his own magical spear, Gungnir, was unstoppable in its flight.

Odin ruled over the point of no return – the moment at which the spear leaves the hand and cannot come back. An aspect of this was the initiation of war by the hurling of a spear above the opposing army. Sometimes it was said to be thrown by the war god himself, standing behind the host. Enemy armies could also be dedicated to Odin by flinging a spear over their heads, and if they fell they became an offering to him.

Those who were killed by a spear became part of the Einherjar, his troop of warriors in Asgard. Thus, human sacrifices to Odin were stabbed with a spear, ensuring that they would be received by him after death. A dying nobleman, free of battle-wounds, who wished to go to Valhalla instead of Hel (the citadel for those who died in their beds), could have himself lacerated with the point of a spear.

Odin with his spear and a raven confronts the wolf Fenrir on this panel from a Viking-era cross on the Isle of Man.

Bodies of those sacrificed to Odin, having been hanged or killed with a spear (see box, page 289), have been recovered from bogs. Adam of Bremen, in his *History of the Archbishops of Hamburg-Bremen*, also describes the bodies of men and animals hanging in the trees near the temple at Uppsala, where a festival was held every nine years in honour of the gods. Prisoners of war were often hanged as offerings to Odin.

Gautreks Saga has an account of a sacrifice to Odin involving one of the god's particular favourites, Starkad, whose destiny was shaped by the favour of Odin and the enmity of Thor. He was in the service of Vikar, the king of part of southern Norway, when the king's war-fleet lay becalmed near an island, and it was decided that the sailors must offer a human sacrifice to Odin to rouse a favourable wind. To everyone's horror, the lot of victim fell to King Vikar himself. That night Odin came to Starkad and led him into the forest to listen to a dispute with Thor concerning his own fate. Then Odin dismissed Starkad, saying that he expected repayment for the many favours he had shown him, and he wanted King Vikar in sacrifice. As Starkad left, Odin handed him a spear that appeared to be nothing more than a reed.

Next morning, Vikar's men decided that their best plan was to make a mock sacrifice of their king on the island, and Starkad offered to arrange it. He took a length of soft, raw calf-gut from the ship's cook and tied a noose in it, which he looped round Vikar's neck. He tied the other end to the slender twig of a sapling fir and made the king stand on a tree-stump; then he struck him in the chest with the reed, crying "Now I give you to Odin!" At once the stump rolled from beneath Vikar's feet, the reed became a spear, the gut a strong rope, and the twig a sturdy branch on which the king swung aloft to die a horrible death, simultaneously pierced and hanged.

Starkad had obeyed Odin, but at the cost of treachery which filled him with shame, especially because Vikar had been his lord and blood-brother, one of the most sacred bonds in the heroic code of honour.

Warriors killed by the spear were received by Odin in Valhalla. This Gotland memorial stone probably depicts Odin on his eight-legged horse, Sleipnir, hailing a dead soldier who will join his warrior group, the Einherjar, in Asgard.

Odin did not need food and lived on wine alone. He threw his portion of meat to the two wolves, Geri and Freki, who sat at his feet. Odin also had two ravens, Huginn and Muninn, whom he sent out every day over the world to bring him reports of what was going on. In the evening they would sit on his shoulders and tell him about all that they had seen. Ravens are traditionally linked with battle and death, both poetically and in reality, as they were commonly found on the battlefield in the aftermath of war, scavenging among the corpses.

Odin's other animal was the extraordinary offspring of Loki and the stallion Svadilfari (see page 285). This creature, Sleipnir, had eight legs and was the fastest of all horses; he bore Odin through the sky at the head of the Einherjar. Sleipnir could leap the walls of Niflheim, and Odin used him for all his errands. The stallion was once lent to Hermod, who rode him to Hel in an attempt to save his brother Balder (see page 318).

Valhalla

In Valhalla each day the slain warriors put on their armour and ventured to the courtyard to fight one another. At dinnertime, all those who had fallen in the fighting rose again to sit together through the evening, carousing, feasting and drinking, at peace with the whole company.

The Einherjar were sustained by a never-ending supply of mead from the udder of Heidrun, a goat that stood on top of Valhalla, plucking and chewing leaves from a tree named Laerad. Every day she was milked to fill a vat so big that all the Einherjar could drink from it to repletion. Their food was the meat of the boar Saehrimnir, which was cooked daily in a special pot called Eldhrimnir and magically became whole again in the evening. The flesh of Saehrimnir was always sufficient to feed all the Einherjar, regardless of their number.

Those who were to join the ranks of the Einherjar were brought to Valhalla by special envoys, the Valkyries. These seem originally to have been ferocious female spirits who revelled in bloodshed and devoured victims on the battlefield. In some versions of myth there were only three Valkyries, all thought to live for ever, while in others there were twenty-seven, or thrice nine as the sagas put it, only a few of whom were thought to be immortal. Later in the Viking era they became more dignified and were portrayed as beautiful golden-haired female spirits who waited on the Einherjar in Valhalla, and went down to the battlefields both to grant victory according to Odin's decree and to lead the slain to Asgard.

Valkyries are of primary importance in the stories and poems about the legendary heroes, for they conducted worthy warriors to Valhalla and there brought them mead. Occasionally Valkyries are portrayed as supernatural beings who snatched heroes from mortal danger. In other versions they were said to be protective spirits who blessed kings and princes who paid due respect to Odin, and received them as their husbands following a heroic warrior's death.

These two objects represent Huginn and Muninn, Odin's two ravens, cast in the form of gilt and bronze harness mounts from Gotland, c.AD700.

From Wodan to Odin

Evidence suggests that the cult of Odin is very old. By the time of the Romans the Germans already had a protective deity, Wodan, who was invoked for success in battle, and also exhibited Odin's sinister and fickle nature. In pagan England, a god named Woden was patron of kings and princes and the god of war and magic.

The first-century Roman writer Tacitus describes a German god, Wodan, whom he identifies with the Roman god Mercury. He places him as the chief god of the Germanic peoples to whom human sacrifices were made. There has been little evidence found to differentiate this Wodan from the later Odin – he was god of the dead and of battles, and was associated with the spear, the wolf and the raven.

Understood to inspire his followers with a battle-frenzy, Wodan rendered them immune to fear or pain. He was also regarded as the primogenitor of kings, and received monarchs and nobles into his halls after death. Wodan was connected to trade and the economy: he was referred to in inscriptions as "Mercator" or "Negotiator", just as Odin was sometimes described as "god of cargoes".

In pagan England the Anglo-Saxons worshipped a god called Woden. The Anglo-Saxon royal dynasties looked upon Woden as their divine ancestor and traced their lineage to him. In certain genealogies Woden has a son named Baeldaeg, who has been identified with Odin's son Balder (see pages 316–319).

English place names with the meaning "Woden's barrow" suggest that Odin was originally associated with burial sites or mounds. Influenced later by the Scandinavian invaders, English homilists often used the Norse name Odin instead of Woden, which further attests to the link between the two gods.

The Capricious God of Kings

There are many stories in Saxo Grammaticus's thirteenth-century, sixteen-volume *The History of the Danes* and the "Family Sagas" and "Sagas of Ancient Times" which illustrate the volatile nature of Odin's support for his favourite kings, princes and nobles. He would give them weapons, yet it was thought that he could deliberately cause any of them to die unnecessarily so that the slain warrior would be forced to join Odin's army in Valhalla and be available to support him at the final destruction of the world. Sigmund the Volsung, King of the Huns, for example, received a magnificent sword which Odin himself had brought to the hall of King Volsung and thrust into the trunk of a tree that stood in the centre of the building. Yet during Sigmund's last battle Odin came onto the battlefield and fought against him, shattering the sword with his spear. The battle turned against Sigmund and he was killed.

Odin also gave his followers valuable advice. He taught Sigmund battle spells, and he showed Hadding, another of his favoured followers, how to array his troops to give himself full advantage on the battlefield. And it was said that Odin himself stood behind Hadding's troops and shot ten arrows as one.

Odin appeared throughout Hadding's life, to rescue him, and to give him strength and spells to break his bonds when he was captured by enemies. He prophesied that he would never die at the hands of a foe but only by his own hand. Eventually the hero did hang himself – an appropriate death for a warrior who worshipped Odin.

It is told that Odin also taught the secret of arranging troops in a special formation to Harald Wartooth, King of the Danes, and pledged that he too would never be harmed by wounding. In return Harald promised Odin the souls of all those that he killed in battle. Odin granted the king victory for most of his life, but turned against him in his old age. In disguise, Odin bred enmity between Harald and his nephew, King Hring, and eventually caused a war. During this he betrayed the secret of Harald's battle formation to his enemy. When Harald realized that his opponent had anticipated the formation, he knew that only Odin could have imparted it, and that the god had deserted him. Finally, as he drove across the battlefield, he became aware that Odin had taken the place of his charioteer. He begged him for one more victory, but Odin paid no heed to his pleas, threw him from the chariot and slew him.

It was not only technical skill and resourcefulness in warfare that protected Odin's favoured armies from defeat – the god's magic also played a part. No human to whom he was opposed had the capacity to combat his cunning. Odin was able to blind, deafen, paralyze or strike panic into entire enemy armies and to blunt their weapons so that they were redundant. On the other hand, he was able to increase the strength of favoured armies and make them impervious to wounding.

Inspired by Odin, a group of warriors known as Berserks would fight naked and in a maddened state, unaffected by fire or weapons. Familiar historical figures in Norse literature, they served famous kings (such as King Harald Fairhair of Norway and King Hrolf of Denmark) as elite bodyguards, or roamed freely, seeking trouble either alone or in groups. In *Heimskringla* Snorri describes how these men went into battle as wild as dogs or wolves. They bit their shields and were as strong as the most ferocious bears or bulls.

This mould, found at Torslunda on the island of Öland in the Baltic, would have been used for making helmet plates. The figures were probably intended to bring luck in battle – the dancing youth in the horned helmet is thought to be a follower of Odin and the animal-like warrior may well represent a ferocious Berserk. It dates from the 6th century AD.

THE ART OF WARFARE

It was the right of all free men in the Viking Age to carry weapons. In the often violent times in which they lived, not only kings and nobles were involved in war; people of all ranks might find themselves called upon to fight in support of their lord, to travel with a band of raiders, or deal forcefully with a feud at home. Their favourite weapons, never far from their sides, were swords and spears – the latter sacred to Odin – and, in later times, the battle axe.

Left: The sword was often a status symbol denoting the rank of the warrior. Tales of the heroes often speak of marvellous swords, such as the one belonging to Sigurd, given to his father by Odin. This decorated hilt is from the 11th century.

Swords were known as "fires of Odin" while axes (*left*) were often named after trolls. This weapon, however, from a high-ranking grave in Mammen in Jutland (*c.*900–1000) is inlaid with silver and had a ceremonial function. The cap of the 7th-century helmet (*top*), from Vendel, Sweden, depicts a procession of warriors.

Right: This 12th-century ivory chessman was carved in Western Norway and found in the Outer Hebrides, illustrating the extent of Norwegian migration. It depicts an armed warrior mounted on a horse and wearing a helmet similar to the one shown opposite. Horses were used by the Vikings to transport their warriors, but all surviving accounts of warfare show that they dismounted once on the battlefield and fought on foot. Even Sleipnir was not used by Odin in battle.

The popular image of Vikings wearing horned helmets, such as this one (*right*) from Bronze-Age Denmark, is not borne out by archaeology – no examples survive from the Viking period. However, some helmets are embossed with figures wearing crested and horned headgear. It is more than likely that these figures had symbolic significance, perhaps representing deities of war.

Thor, God of Thunder

Thor was the best loved of the Viking pantheon. A mighty figure with colossal strength, a huge red beard and thick brows over glowering eyes, he strode about the cosmos, fighting giants and trolls. He was the protector of Asgard and the gods could always call upon him if they were in trouble. Life was simple for Thor – the giants were his enemy and he spent much of his time killing them.

Found on a farm at Akureyri in Iceland, this small bronze figure is just over 3in high and was probably made around AD1000. It represents Thor gripping his hammer.

Just as Odin was complex and crafty, Thor was straightforward and physical – the brawn to Odin's brains. Although Odin was the chief of the gods, Thor was no less revered; in fact there is some evidence to suggest that he was held in higher esteem. According to Adam of Bremen, it was Thor's statue that dominated the Uppsala temple, centrally positioned between those of Odin and Freyr. Whereas Odin was favoured by nobles and kings, Thor was beloved of farmers and their families who made up the majority of the population.

That he was held in high regard is demonstrated by the wide proliferation of names with the first syllable "Thor" that are still in use. Personal names such as Thorkel, Thorir, Thorgeir and Thorbjorn were common among men, while Thorgerd, Thorbjorg, Thordis or Thora were often chosen for women. Literature also provides several examples of men having their names changed in honour of Thor. Similarly, place names beginning with the element "Thor" are distributed throughout Iceland: Thorshofn (Thor's Haven) and Thorsnes (Thor's Headland) can be found in at least five different locations. Norway has another Thorsnes, as well as Thor's Rock (Thorsberg), Thor's Island (Thorsey) and a number of places called Thor's Temple (Thorshof).

Thunder was said to be the sound of Thor's huge chariot driving across the sky, and his eyes were red, fierce and flashing, as befitted a god of thunder and lightning. His power over storms rendered his blessing vital for those making sea crossings. Although the other gods rode to their daily assembly, Thor had to walk, wading through rivers and striding over plains, because he was so

Thor Loses his Hammer

When his hammer Mjollnir – crucial to the gods' security in Valhalla – was stolen, Thor had to suffer great humiliation to retrieve it. His comical attempt at cross-dressing endangered its recovery.

When Thor discovered that his hammer was missing, he shook with fury, roused Loki, and told him the news. "Come with me" said Loki urgently, and led him to the home of the goddess Freyja. They asked to borrow her feather coat, which transformed the wearer into a bird, in order to travel swiftly to foreign lands. "I would give my gift even if it were made of gold or silver to find Mjollnir," said Freyja.

Loki flew off and found Thrym, Lord of the Giants, who asked him why he had come. "Have you hidden Thor's hammer?" Loki asked immediately. "Yes," replied Thrym. "I've hidden it eight leagues underground, and no one shall have it unless I am given Freyja as my bride."

When Loki and Thor told Freyja to prepare herself as Thrym's bride, she flew into a rage and would not hear of it. In consternation, all the gods met together to discuss the dangerous situation. If Freyja would not marry Thrym, how could they retrieve the hammer?

Heimdall came up with a solution: "Let us dress Thor in bridal clothes and send him to Thrym in place of Freyja." Thor protested hotly but Loki reminded him of Asgard's fate if

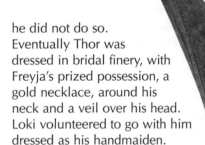

he did not do so. Eventually Thor was dressed in bridal finery, with Freyja's prized possession, a gold necklace, around his neck and a veil over his head. Loki volunteered to go with him dressed as his handmaiden.

Thrym was very pleased to see Freyja, and ordered a great feast to be prepared. Thor ate a whole ox, eight salmon and all the other delicacies, washed down with three horns of mead. Thrym was aghast; he had never seen a maiden consume so much. "Freyja has eaten and drunk nothing for eight whole nights, so eager was she to come to Giantland," explained Loki.

On hearing that, Thrym was so pleased he went to kiss Freyja, but reeled back in fright. "Why are Freyja's eyes so red and fierce?" he gasped. Loki quickly replied, "Freyja has not slept for eight nights, so eager was she to come to Giantland."

As gullible as the other giants, Thrym was satisfied and eager to proceed with the wedding. He ordered the hammer to be brought in to hallow the couple. As soon as it was laid on the bride's lap, Thor leaped up, grabbed Mjollnir and tore off his veil. Armed once again, he crushed all the giants in the hall, choosing Thrym as the first of his victims.

Many tiny silver hammers such as this have been excavated across Scandinavia. They are believed to symbolize Thor's hammer and were probably worn as amulets.

colossal. Inevitably, his strength was matched by an enormous appetite. He easily devoured more than a whole ox during the course of a meal, and special drinking goblets had to be kept aside for him to accommodate his mammoth thirst.

Thor owned three important material possessions. Foremost was his precious hammer, named Mjollnir. This weapon struck fear into the hearts of giants or trolls, for it could never fail or miss its mark, whether raised aloft or thrown, and would always return to the hand of its owner, rather like a boomerang. Mjollnir also held the power to sanctify, and was raised for the purpose of hallowing on several different occasions: Thor had two goats, named Tanngnjost and Tanngrisnir according to Snorri, who not only drew his chariot, but could also be killed for food and resurrected by holding the hammer over their skins in blessing (see page 302). Secondly, Thor owned a magical belt that doubled his already formidable strength whenever he wore it. His third possession was a pair of iron gloves, without which he was unable to wield the mighty Mjollnir.

He actively sought out giants, with the express intention of annihilating them, seldom hesitating to raise his hammer in preparation for an attack when he encountered them. However, there were some occasions when he saw giants as allies, or at least had some use for them: he even had two sons, Modi and Magni, by the giantess Jarnsaxa.

The most detailed account of the worship of Thor is given in *Eyrbyggja Saga*, which tells of a chieftain in Norway named Hrolf, who was a close friend of Thor and kept a temple dedicated to the god. So devoted was he that he became known as "Thorolf". When Thorolf emigrated to Iceland he took the timbers of his temple with him,

A 9th-century Viking carving depicting Thor's ominous glare. His bushy eyebrows and beard are distinctive facial features.

together with the earth from beneath Thor's altar. As he approached the coast of the country he threw overboard into the ocean the pillars from the temple, one of which had the figure of Thor carved on it, and declared that he would settle wherever Thor chose to beach them. Once onshore, Thorolf soon found the pillars on a headland, which he named Thorsnes, as the place is called to this day.

In due course Thorolf built a large temple dedicated to Thor in the land in which he had settled. The door of the temple was in one of the side walls, and just inside it stood the high seat pillars. Beyond these the building was considered a sanctuary. In the centre of the temple was a raised platform like an altar, upon which lay an armring (worn by a priest during public occasions) and a sacrificial bowl, which held the blood of animals killed as offerings. People swore oaths on this altar. All the local farmers had to pay tax to the temple and support the temple priest in all his religious undertakings. The priest, in turn, was responsible for the maintenance of the temple and the organization of sacrificial feasts.

Other marks of Thor's popularity are the many memorial stones dating from the ninth, tenth and eleventh centuries found in Denmark and southern Sweden. These bear inscriptions such as "May Thor hallow these runes" or "May Thor hallow this memorial", or sometimes just "May Thor hallow". Some stones appeal for Thor's protection merely with a carved image of his hammer. The hammer motif also appears in the shape of miniature amulets (some of them are barely an inch long) made of silver or base metal, which have been found placed in graves. Several have loops attached to them, which suggests that they may have been worn as pendants, and perhaps represent a pagan equivalent to the miniature cross worn by Christians.

Thor and the Giants

On one occasion, Loki mischievously persuaded Thor to visit the giant Geirrod without his hammer, belt of strength or iron gloves. The journey was long and Thor needed to take lodgings for the night. He stopped at the home of a giantess called Grid, who told Thor that Geirrod was cunning and difficult to deal with. She lent Thor another magical belt, some iron gloves and her staff, warning that he might be in need of their protection.

As Thor approached Geirrod's court he came upon a river. Before attempting to cross it, he fastened on the borrowed belt, then waded through the water with the help of Grid's staff. But the flow of the river proved formidable and by the time that he had struggled to the middle he was almost out of his depth. At this point, he looked up and saw Gjalp, Geirrod's daughter, standing astride the river urinating to increase the torrent. Thor picked up a huge stone and threw it at the giantess to distract her. Then he made a rush for the bank and was able to grab onto a rowan tree and haul himself out to safety.

When Thor arrived at Geirrod's court, he was shown to a goatshed where he was to lodge for the night. Inside was just a single chair, which Thor sat upon, and as he did so it lifted up beneath him, pushing him almost to the ceiling. He was in danger of being crushed, but he resisted a collision by lodging his staff against the roof. There was a great crack, and a chilling scream. Thor looked down and saw that the giant's two daughters were under the seat beneath him. Their backs were broken.

Geirrod then called him into the hall. As Thor entered, Geirrod picked up a lump of molten iron and flung it at him. Catching it with the help of the borrowed iron gloves, the god raised it in the air, taking aim as he did so. Geirrod ran behind a pillar to protect himself, but Thor was unperturbed: he hurled the glowing lump through the pillar, whereupon it hit Geirrod and continued straight through the wall.

Not all of Thor's foes were so cunning as Geirrod. Sometimes, as in the story of his battle with Hrungnir, he had only to contend with brute strength. Even so, there were hidden surprises in this contest that Thor could not have anticipated.

The story began one day when Thor was away in the east, destroying trolls. Odin became involved in a horse race with the giant, Hrungnir. The two were racing so hard that the giant unexpectedly found himself inside Asgard. The Aesir treated him with hospitality and invited him to join

An exquisitely decorated silver cup from Fejo, Denmark (c.AD800). It would have been used by kings and their followers in carousing – a favourite activity of the gods too.

299

Thor Fights the World Serpent

Jormungand, the Midgard serpent, was Thor's adversary. The god's meeting with a giant gave him an opportunity to destroy it, which he greatly desired to do.

Thor was travelling across Midgard, having adopted the appearance of a young boy. During this journey he took lodgings at the home of a giant called Hymir who was about to undertake a fishing expedition. Seeing this as an opportunity to confront the world serpent, Thor enquired if he could accompany him. The giant looked him up and down and replied dismissively that he would not be much use as he was so small. Thor, mindful that he needed the boat, had to restrain his temper. Hymir ordered his companion to find his own bait, so Thor tore off the head of the largest ox in Hymir's herd.

The pair launched a boat and rowed fast, until Hymir said that they had reached his usual fishing ground. Thor insisted that they continue further, so they took up the oars again. When Hymir suggested that it would be dangerous to go any further because of Jormungand, Thor ignored him and rowed on. Hymir was now very uncomfortable. Finally, Thor chose a strong line with a huge hook on the end, to which he fastened the ox-head before throwing it overboard.

Deep under the sea the Midgard serpent went for the bait and swallowed the hook. It pulled away so violently that Thor was flung dramatically against the side of the boat. Summoning up all his strength, he pushed his feet through the bottom of the boat and braced them against the seabed. Then he pulled up the serpent. He was about to lift his hammer to strike the monster when Hymir

The giant Hymir watches Thor attack the world serpent with his hammer in this medieval manuscript.

grabbed his knife and cut Thor's line so that the creature sank back into the sea. Thor threw his hammer in after it and some say that the serpent's head was struck off, but most people say that it lived on and still encircles the world.

them in a drink, for which they brought out the goblets that Thor usually drank from, as no others were large enough. The giant drained all of them and, as he became drunk, he began to boast, saying that he would destroy Asgard and kill the gods – all except the goddesses Freyja and Sif, whom he would carry off. After a while the gods began to feel frightened, and called for Thor. He appeared immediately and demanded to know what right a giant had to drink in Asgard. Hrungnir defended himself, saying that Odin had welcomed him personally, and it would be no credit to Thor to kill him while he was unarmed. Instead, he suggested a duel. Thor rose to the challenge at once, as he had never before been so blatantly provoked.

Hrungnir went home to retrieve his weapons, and at the appointed time and place the two met. The giants were all extremely anxious about the outcome of the duel, for Hrungnir was the strongest among them, and they felt sure that if he were to be killed Thor could do as he pleased.

Hrungnir had a whetstone as his weapon, and a stone shield with which he intended to avert Thor's blows. Thialfi, Thor's servant, ran to Hrungnir and told him that he was a fool to hold his shield in front of him, for Thor would attack from beneath. Because giants are not very intelligent, Hrungnir naively took Thialfi's advice and put the shield on the ground so that he could stand on it, holding the whetstone ready in his hands. Suddenly Thor appeared not from below but as a blaze of lightning in front of him. He hurled his hammer at Hrungnir who simultaneously threw his whetstone, with the result that the two weapons met in mid-air. The whetstone was shattered by Thor's invincible hammer, which went on to smash the giant's skull.

Thor was triumphant, but during the fray a shard of whetstone had lodged in his head. Having scarcely given himself time to savour his victory, he went in search of a sorceress called Groa, the wife of Aurvandill the Bold, whom he hoped would assist him in removing the fragment. Groa sang spells over Thor until the piece of stone began to loosen. Thor was so pleased that he wanted to offer her something in return, so he told her that her husband would be home soon: the god had waded through the river Elivagar – the collective

Two goats, perhaps representing his own goats Tanngnjost and Tanngrisnir, flank a "thunderstone" (a fossilized sea urchin considered sacred to Thor) in this Viking-period brooch from Birka, Sweden. Thunderstones were believed to have dropped to earth during a storm.

name for the eleven rivers flowing from the spring of Hvergelmir in Niflheim – carrying him in a basket on the return journey from Jotunheim. Thor said that one of Aurvandill's toes had stuck out of the basket and had frozen, so he had broken it off and thrown it into the sky where it became the star known at the time as Aurvandill's Toe (modern commentators have identified it with the morning star, Venus). However, Groa was so delighted to hear of his return that she forgot her spells, and the shard remained lodged in Thor's head.

Thor's Humiliation

The giants were helpless in the face of Thor's mighty strength, but magical art could always get the better of him. A straightforward soul, he was not wily and versed in sorcery like Odin. But even when things did not go well for him, the giants found themselves forced to retain respect for his courage in the face of adversity.

One day Thor set off in his chariot with Loki. At nightfall they arrived at a peasant's house and were given lodgings for the night. At dinnertime Thor slaughtered and skinned his goats, put them into a pot, and when they were cooked invited the peasant family to join Loki and himself for a meal. Thor placed the goatskins on the floor and gave strict instructions to the family to be sure to throw the bones onto the goatskins after they had eaten. Thialfi, the peasant's son, forgot this, and in his hunger took one of the goat's thigh bones, splitting it open to enjoy the marrow.

Before dawn, Thor rose and dressed himself, raising his hammer Mjollnir to bless the goatskins. At that the goats stood up, alive again, but one of them was lame. Thor flew into a rage when he realized that the family had not obeyed his orders: the god's brow lowered, his eyes flashed and he gripped his hammer menacingly. The peasants wept, begged for mercy and offered all their possessions as reparation. When he saw their fear, Thor softened and accepted their two children, Thialfi and his sister Roskva, as recompense. They became his servants and attended him diligently.

Thor left his goats with the peasants and continued on his journey with Loki, Thialfi and Roskva. Eventually they entered a huge forest, and walked through it all day, until at nightfall they came upon a building with a large entrance at one end, where they decided to sleep. In the middle of the night they were awoken by a great earthquake that shook the ground and the building. They got up and, groping around, found a smaller chamber off to the right of the main building, where Thor positioned himself, while the others, terrified, cowered behind him. At dawn Thor went outside and realized that the disturbance had been caused by an enormous giant, asleep and snoring loudly beside them. At that same moment the giant awoke and stood up. He reached so far into the sky that even Thor was afraid.

Thor asked the giant his name. "My name is Skrymir. But I have no need to enquire about you – I can see that you are Thor of the Aesir. But have you taken my glove?" As Skrymir reached down and picked up his glove, Thor realized that the glove was where they had sheltered the night before – they had thought it was a building, but the chamber in which they had cowered was in fact the glove's thumb. Skrymir asked if he could accompany Thor and his companions on their journey, and Thor, not wanting to appear cowardly, consented. The giant then suggested that it would be a good idea to pool their food, and Thor agreed, so Skrymir gathered their provisions in one bag and put it on his back.

In the evening the giant fell fast asleep and Thor took the provisions bag so that he and his companions could eat, but try as he might, he could not open it. Already tired and hungry, he was now also very angry and grasped his hammer in both hands. He brought the hammer down hard on the giant's head, but the giant simply woke up and asked whether a leaf had fallen on him.

At midnight Skrymir was snoring loudly again, and Thor approached him once more. He swung his weapon hard and it sank into Skrymir's crown. Skrymir awoke once more and said "What's happening now? Did an acorn fall on my head?"

How the Gods Gained Treasures

Dwarves were the craftsmen of Germanic mythology. Although they jealously guarded their skill and their gold, the artful Loki persuaded them to make six treasures which he then gave to the gods, to the especial benefit of Thor.

The dwarves helped Loki out of trouble by forging six treasures for the gods, including Thor's hammer, Odin's ring and Freyr's shining boar.

As a mischievous prank, Loki decided to cut off all of Sif's golden hair as she lay asleep. When she awoke and discovered her loss she was distraught. When Thor heard of Loki's treachery he threatened to break every bone in his body. So, in terror, Loki promised that he would convince the dwarves to fashion a new head of hair from gold.

The dwarves agreed to help him out of trouble and please the gods. They not only made the head of hair for Sif, but also crafted the ship *Skidbladnir*, which, when its sail was raised, would always get a fair wind and could be fitted in a pocket when out of use. As if this was not enough, they also forged the invincible spear Gungnir.

But Loki could not resist further scheming. He made a bet with two dwarf brothers that they could not make treasures as precious as the first three. They duly produced three more, successfully ignoring Loki who, as a fly, tried hard to distract them.

Loki took all the treasures to Asgard. He gave the hair to Sif, and it took root on her head. Then he gave Skidbladnir to Freyr and Gungnir to Odin, and both were greatly pleased. Next, he handed over the last three treasures. The first was the gold ring Draupnir for Odin. It is said that eight rings of equal weight and value dripped from it every ninth night. Second, for Freyr, was a golden boar which ran across the sky and sea faster than any horse and shed light in the darkness from its bristles.

The third was a magical hammer, Mjollnir, which would never fail to strike its target and always returned to its owner – this was given to Thor.

The gods thus owe their greatest treasures to Loki, although, in deciding that the protective hammer was the best gift, the gods stated that the dwarves had won the wager with Loki, which he reneged on.

Thor backed off quickly, explaining that he had unexpectedly awoken and must have disturbed Skrymir, but it was only midnight and still time to be asleep. He decided that if Skrymir slept again he would strike a third blow, hard enough for Skrymir never to wake up.

Just before dawn, Thor roused himself and rushed at the sleeping giant, bringing down the hammer with all his strength. He struck Skrymir's temple, and the force of the blow was so powerful that the weapon sank deep into the giant's flesh. Skrymir simply stroked his face and said, "Are there birds in the tree above me? I am sure something fell on my face as I woke up."

Later that morning, when they were ready to move on, Skrymir took the bag and turned away back into the forest. Relieved to see him go, Thor's party continued until it came to an imposing castle which dominated a flat plain. The huge gates were shut, but everyone was able to enter by

squeezing themselves between the bars. As they did so they saw a great hall, filled with giants who were seated on benches. On his throne, at the head of them all, was their king, Utgarda-Loki.

Thor's party approached Utgarda-Loki, who demanded to know what feats they could perform, "as no one can stay here with us who does not have some particular skill or talent at which he is better than other men". Loki confidently proposed an eating contest, "for no one can eat faster than I". Utgarda-Loki approved and called for a giant called Logi to compete against Loki. The two sat at either end of a vast dish filled with meat and began to eat as quickly as they could, eventually meeting in the middle. Loki had eaten all the meat off the bones, but Logi had eaten all the meat, the bones and even the dish itself. It was agreed that Loki had lost the contest.

Utgarda-Loki then turned to Thialfi and asked how he would prove himself. Thialfi was a very

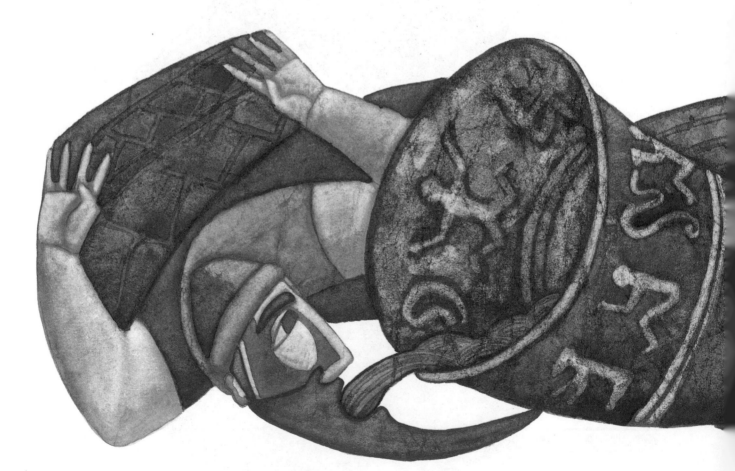

fast runner and offered to compete in a race. Utgarda-Loki asked another giant called Hugi to run against Thialfi. In the first race Hugi was so far ahead that he turned around and met Thialfi face to face. The second race was merely a repetition of the first. Thialfi tried for a third time, certain that he could triumph over his opponent, but when Hugi had reached the end of the track Thialfi had only run half its length. The outcome of the contest was decided.

When it came to Thor's turn, he agreed to take part in a drinking contest. Utgarda-Loki bade his manservant bring out the special horn that his men used for such events. He explained that it was considered admirable to empty the horn in one draught, although some people took two – no one was such a poor drinker that they could not drain it in three draughts. Thor looked at the horn, which did not seem very big to him, despite being rather long, and as he was very thirsty he drank in

great gulps, expecting to empty the horn effortlessly. But when he ran out of breath the mead's level had hardly changed.

Utgarda-Loki said that he would never have believed anyone who told him that Thor of the Aesir could not drink more than that, but he was sure that Thor would achieve his task at a second attempt. Saying nothing, Thor put the horn to his mouth, determined to swallow a larger draught. He struggled for as long as he could hold his breath, but still he could not raise the horn as high as he would have liked. "What is the matter Thor?" asked Utgarda-Loki. "You'll be lucky to drain the horn even the third time around. Maybe you should try a different contest." Thor was infuriated, and he tried again. This time he made some impact on the level in the horn, but still failed to empty it. "Do you want to try something else?" said Utgarda-Loki, "You are obviously not going to get anywhere with this." "I will," said Thor. "What do you

The giant Utgarda-Loki challenged Thor to empty a drinking horn in no more than three draughts. Unbeknown to Thor, the other end of the horn was dipped in the sea.

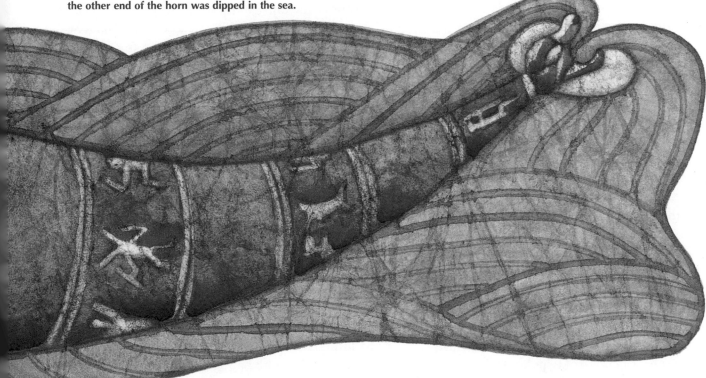

A replica of a golden horn found at Gallehus, Denmark, in the 18th century. Thought to date from AD500, the horn bears a particular rune suggestive of Swedish origins.

suggest?" "This may not sound like a very great feat, but the young boys here try to lift my cat above the ground. I would not even have mentioned this to you if I had not already seen that you are a much less impressive person than I thought."

At this, a big grey cat ran into the hall and Thor grabbed it beneath the belly and tried to raise it. But the cat's back simply arched and Thor was only able to raise one paw off the ground. Utgarda-Loki watched and said, "Just as I expected. It is a big cat, and Thor is small compared to us."

Thor was now in a violent rage and, intent on proving his courage and might, he offered to fight someone. Utgarda-Loki looked around and said, "I don't see anyone here who wouldn't think it beneath themselves to fight with you, but perhaps you could take on my old nurse, Elli." Utgarda-Loki ordered the old woman to wrestle with Thor, yet the harder Thor fought the firmer she stood. Eventually, Thor lost his footing and fell to one knee. Utgarda-Loki brought the fight to a halt, saying there was little point in Thor continuing with further contests against his people.

The next morning, Thor and his group departed. Utgarda-Loki accompanied them some of the way, and asked Thor what he thought of his visit. Thor replied that he had suffered great humiliation. "Furthermore, I know you will say that I am a man of little consequence, which irks me."

Then Utgarda-Loki spoke: "Now that we are outside the castle I will tell the truth. While I am alive you will never set foot in my castle again: I swear that if I had known before that you had sufficient strength to bring us so close to disaster, you would never have entered in the first place.

"I tricked you with illusions: it was I that first met you in the forest. I had fastened the provisions bag with magic bonds so that you could not open it. And perhaps you noticed a flat mountain near my castle with three valleys? Those were the marks of the three blows of your hammer. I cunningly set the mountain between myself and you.

"I also deceived you in the contests. When Loki competed at eating, he rivalled Fire, which devours everything in its path. In running, Thialfi competed against Thought, whose speed no one can match. The other end of the horn from which you were drinking was dipped in the sea, so you never had a chance of draining it.

"Lifting the cat's paw was a mighty feat, for the cat was the powerful Midgard serpent which encircles the entire world. And in the wrestling you contested with Old Age, who defeats everyone, despite their strength. Now we must part, and it will be better if we do not meet again. Be warned that I will always defend my castle with similar tricks."

As Thor listened to all this he grew extremely angry and automatically reached for his hammer, but just as he was about to bring it down on Utgarda-Loki's head he found that the giant had vanished into thin air. To his astonishment, when he turned towards the castle, he found it had also disappeared. So he had to return home, very dissatisfied with his expedition.

Loki, Companion to the Gods

Loki is an ambiguous character. He was listed among the Aesir as companion to the gods, yet he was destined to become their adversary at Ragnarok. In many of the tales, he is a typical trickster, possessed of a sense of mischief that the gods have to suffer. Yet this miscreant was also the gods' friend, often helping them out, and it was he who provided them with Thor's hammer Mjollnir, their most powerful weapon.

Although Loki inhabited Asgard he was not thought to be divine – in fact there is no evidence to indicate that he was directly worshipped at all. However, he was integral to the entire Norse mythological canon, for it was Loki who instigated the dynamic of life among the gods and became a cardinal figure because of his constant subverting of order, sometimes out of mischief and at other times because of some darker intent.

Constantly present, particularly alongside Odin and Thor, Loki took part in many of the gods' escapades. While it was Loki's tricks that were continually getting the gods into trouble, it was equally often his wiles that got them out of their predicaments. In the poem *Lokasenna*, Loki was even described as a blood-brother to Odin – a close bond that was considered sacred in the Norse community.

A furnace stone from Shaptun, Denmark, thought to show Loki with his lips sewn up by the dwarves. This is how they punished him for refusing to pay his forfeit after they had won a wager with him about whether they could make precious treasures for the gods (see box, page 303).

307

Loki Recaptures the Golden Apples

Ever the menace, Loki allowed his actions to threaten the gods with extinction. But it was also his resourcefulness that saved them.

Loki had the misfortune of being taken captive by a giant called Thiazi, who would not free him unless he promised to deliver to him the goddess Idunn and her precious apples of eternal youth. Always thinking of himself, Loki vowed to do this, so the giant released him.

Loki conceived a plan: he told Idunn that that she must come and see some apples in the forest which she was bound to think were precious. Once she had been lured beyond the safe confines of Asgard, Thiazi swooped down on her in the shape of an eagle and snatched her up so that he could take her to his home.

The gods were immediately affected by the loss of the youth-giving fruit and in a trice grew old and grey. Fearing for their lives, they met together to decide what to do. They discovered that Idunn had last been sighted with Loki, so they seized him and threatened him with death if he did not recover her and her apples. Loki promised to find her, and borrowed Freyja's falcon shape to fly to Thiazi's castle in Giantland. Luckily, he found Idunn there all alone, and quickly transformed her into a nut so that he could fly home to Asgard with her grasped in his claws.

When Thiazi returned and discovered his captive had escaped, he was furious and decided to pursue Loki: he adopted the eagle shape again and gave chase. The Aesir saw the falcon flying with a nut gripped in its claws and the eagle following closely behind. They acted quickly and built a fire in Asgard. The falcon flew over the wall and immediately dropped down to safety, but the eagle was not able to take evasive action straight away and flew directly into the flames, where it perished.

The Aesir had managed to kill the giant Thiazi, and Loki had once again wriggled out of a desperate situation.

The goddess Idunn with her magical apples was snatched up by Loki in the form of a falcon so that he could return her to Asgard. In pursuit, the giant Thiazi took the shape of an eagle.

Freyja owned a beautiful necklace, known as the Necklace of
the Brisings, which Loki, in the form of a flea, attempted to steal.
This 10th-century chain of beads (shown with pendants) is from
the Varby hoard, which is among the most magnificent Viking
treasures found in Sweden.

Even though people do not seem to have regarded Loki as a god to be invoked for assistance, he was the subject of many stories and played an important part in many myths.

Snorri tells us that Loki was handsome and witty, but also malicious, sly and evil. Describing him from a Christian perspective, he refers to him as the slanderer of the pantheon, the origin of all falsehood and the disgrace of everyone on Earth. By nature he was restless and easily bored, which led to his gradual decline until he became a miscreant who betrayed his companions. But in most of the myths he was content living with the gods, indulging himself by playing practical jokes.

As a shapeshifter he could take the forms of animals, birds and insects. He would often transform himself into an insect when he was enjoying his tricks; for example, he became a fly when he was trying to distract the dwarves making Thor's hammer, Mjollnir (see page 303).

Loki's monstrous nature, however, was eventually to prove too much for the gods. Their patience was finally stretched too far when Loki caused the death of Balder, setting in train an irreversible series of events that would culminate in the end of the world.

309

Loki's Evil Offspring

Descended from the giants Farbauti and Laufey, Loki was married to the goddess Sigyn who bore him two sons called Narfi and Vali. Loki, however, was unfaithful to the unfortunate Sigyn. Following a liaison with Loki, the giantess Angrboda bore him three monstrous children, all of whom play important roles in the myths.

The first of these offspring was Jormungand, a ferocious and venomous serpent. Next there was Hel, a female of unspeakably hideous appearance. Last came the fierce wolf Fenrir, who possessed a might that seemed indomitable. These three were no mere imps, but three of the most terrifying creatures in the Norse universe, and they were a significant threat to the occupants of Asgard. Indeed, Jormungand and Fenrir would be the destroyers of Thor and Odin respectively at Ragnarok (see pages 320–325).

The gods continued to tolerate Loki and his malign influence almost until the end of the world. They were unable to destroy his offspring, even when locked in combat. Although the three creatures posed a constant threat to Asgard, fate had ordained their continuing existence.

Instead, the gods had to do their best to defend themselves against Loki's mischief and his uncontrollable children. All of Asgard was alarmed when it was discovered that Loki had sired these three offspring and that they were being raised in Jotunheim, for the gods had heard prophecies of the great harm that these siblings would cause, and they felt sure that such predictions were true. The Aesir's fear of the creatures' inherent evil was confirmed merely by the evidence of their parentage – their giantess mother Angrboda was considered as heinous as their evil father.

Odin sent gods to locate the children and bring them to Asgard, so that he himself could determine their fate. He decided to deal with Jormungand, the serpent, by throwing it into the sea that lay around all the lands of Midgard. There, deep in the ocean, the monster grew until, biting on its own tail, it encircled the whole world. And in this position, it brooded endlessly on how it could one day get its revenge on the gods.

Hel, Loki's unspeakably ugly daughter by Angrboda, was described as being half dead and half alive, with a grim countenance and a body that was part normal flesh and part black and livid. This hideous creature was thrown into Niflheim, the land of the dead, where she was to hold authority. It became her responsibility to give food and lodging to all those sent to her – mortals who died of sickness or old age rather than in battle. Her realm became known as Hel.

The monstrous wolf, Fenrir, was raised by the Aesir. The only way to restrain the wolf was to fetter it – an act only made possible because Tyr was brave enough to risk his hand in Fenrir's jaws (see box, page 313).

Loki, companion to the gods, had all the qualities of a jester. Depicted in carvings decorating the stern of the Oseberg ship (discovered as part of a 9th-century boat burial in Norway), Loki writhes among mythical beasts.

The Ambiguity of Loki

Yet Loki, as ever, was not simply a producer of evil. In keeping with his ambiguous nature, Loki had other offspring who were a boon to the gods rather than a menace. In addition, he was able not only to beget children, but to bear them as well. He was the mother of Odin's marvellous eight-legged horse Sleipnir, sired by the giant stallion Svadilfari (see pages 285 and 291), which carried its rider effortlessly over land, sea or air.

Loki's maternal aspect in that myth reveals another aspect of his character – his ambiguous sexuality. Apart from giving birth to Sleipnir, it is also told in *Voluspa Hin Skamma* ("The Short Prophecy of the Seeress") that he once became pregnant by eating the half-burnt heart of a woman, and from this gestation came all female monsters. *Lokasenna* relates a verbal contest between Loki and the gods in which Loki was accused of spending eight years as a woman milking cows beneath the earth, where he bore children – an activity considered most effeminate and despicable by his challenger Odin.

To insult someone using words that implied passive homosexuality was punishable in Icelandic and early Swedish law by full outlawry. It may be that the sexual uncertainties surrounding Loki described in the myths were intended to darken his character.

With the approach of the final episode of Norse mythology, Loki's character becomes less mischievous and more overtly evil. He was destined to reveal his true nature by causing the death of Balder, an action regarded by the Aesir as the most wicked ever to have happened. Even then, they were unable to punish him exactly as they wished, because he was fated to take part in the events of the final cataclysm.

Found in Denmark (*c.*AD400–800) this bronze stallion expresses dignity and power. The Norse people held horses in high esteem, associating them not only with speed but also fertility. One of Loki's greatest gifts to the gods was the magical eight-legged horse, Sleipnir.

The Shadowy Pantheon

Asgard was inhabited by a multitude of diverse and colorful characters, but little information has survived about most of them. Some of the Aesir feature only briefly in individual myths, and no further details of their connection to the Norse pantheon or of their characters survive.

The most senior member of the Aesir, after Odin and Thor, was Tyr, a war deity and the bravest and most courageous of the gods. It was held to be wise for warriors to invoke him, as he wielded great power in battle and dictated its outcome. Men who were undaunted in combat were said to be as valiant as Tyr. He was also connected with runes (the earliest Germanic alphabet), magic and wisdom, and Snorri tells that a clever man was known as "Tyr-wise". A warrior who hoped for victory was advised to carve runes onto particular parts of his sword, and repeat Tyr's name twice, which may explain why a character in the runic alphabet is called "Tyr".

Balder, the son of Odin and Frigg, is one of the better known among the Aesir, mainly due to the myths of his death (see pages 316–319). He was considered the wisest, most beautiful and most beloved of his counterparts. According to Snorri, light shone from him, and the scentless camomile plant was once called "Balder's eyelash" because it was so white.

Balder had a wife, Nanna, who bore his son Forseti, god of justice. It was Forseti's role to settle legal disputes, and all those who came to Glitnir, his hall in Valhalla, which had golden pillars and a silver roof, left with their difficult legal disputes

resolved. Balder also had a brother, Hermod, who travelled to Hel in search of him (see pages 316–318).

The other sons of Odin included Vidar, Vali and Bragi, and a stepson, Ull. Vidar, the silent god, was said to have a strength almost equal to Thor's. He too was to feature in the battle at the end of the world (see pages 320–325), avenging his father's death. Vali, Odin's son by the giantess, Rind, avenges the death of Balder by killing Hod.

Bragi was, like his father, a god of poetry. According to the poem *Sigrdrifumal*, he had magical runes carved on his tongue. He was married to Idunn (see page 308).

An important god about whom little is known, was Ull, the son of Sif, Thor's wife. He was known as the ski god, the bow god or the hunting god, because his particular skills were archery and skiing. Beautiful to look at and an accomplished warrior, he was invoked by men engaged in single combat. The evidence of place names suggests that he was once a powerful deity, but sadly few stories about him have survived.

Although not much is known about Tyr, god of war, fighting men may well have worshipped him prior to battle. This 7th-century Frankish funerary monument depicts an armed warrior.

Binding the Wolf Fenrir

The gods were afraid that the huge wolf Fenrir would cause them serious harm, so they attempted to restrain it. But they could not have done it without Tyr's selfless bravery.

When the gods saw how huge Fenrir, one of Loki's malevolent offspring, was growing, they were alarmed and decided to bind the creature. They found a strong iron fetter, called Laeding, and suggested that the wolf pit his strength against it. Fenrir did not think much of the shackle, so he let them bind him and freed himself easily.

The gods forged another fetter twice as strong, called Dromi, and urged the wolf to try again. They said that Fenrir would become very famous if this one could be broken free from. Fenrir felt even stronger now and broke from Dromi with ease, again. The Aesir now feared that they would not be able to fully restrain Fenrir.

Odin then sent Freyr's servant Skirnir to the dwarves, and he bade them make another fetter, Gleipnir. It was smooth, soft and silky as a ribbon, but deceptively strong. The Aesir were very pleased. Fenrir looked at it carefully and said "I do not think I will gain much of a reputation by breaking such a thin ribbon, and if this band is made by magical art then, thin as it is, it is not going around my legs." Fenrir thought again and said, "If I cannot free myself I will have to wait a very long time before you free me. But, lest you think I am a coward, I will take part in this game if one of you will dare to put his hand in my mouth."

None of the gods dared take this risk until at last Tyr volunteered to put his right hand into Fenrir's mouth. At that the wolf allowed itself to be bound, but discovered that the harder it kicked the stronger the fetter became. The Aesir all laughed – except Tyr who lost his hand to Fenrir's jaws.

The pernicious wolf, Fenrir, was brought to Asgard at the command of Odin. The gods decided to bind it with fetters to control it.

The War Between the Aesir and Vanir

The deities of war, the Aesir, once lived completely separately from the gods and goddesses of fertility, the Vanir – the Aesir in Asgard and the Vanir in Vanaheim. Eventually, however, their happy accord was shattered and a war broke out between them. From ambiguous accounts in the poem *Voluspa* and Snorri's *Edda* we can piece together the strange story of the conflict between the two tribes of gods and their reconciliation.

The seeress who narrates the tenth-century poem, *Voluspa*, declares that she remembers the very first battle in the world, fought between the Aesir and the Vanir. She tells how it started when the Aesir tried to destroy Gullveig, a woman skilled in magic (particularly in a form of witchcraft called *seid*) who had provoked their animosity by practising sorcery. They stabbed her with spears and burned her three times, but each time she rose again from the flames. Eventually, resigned to her indestructibility, they accepted her into their community.

Traditionally, Gullveig has been associated with gold and wealth. Her very name means "intoxication with gold". It has been suggested that because of her attachment to riches Gullveig was one of the Vanir, and in particular that she may have represented an aspect of Freyja who was thought to weep tears of gold, and, in her enthusiasm for precious stones, gave her daughters the names of jewels. (Freyja had even acquired the glittering Necklace of the Brisings by agreeing to sleep with each of the four dwarves who made it.) Snorri tells two different myths about the conflict between the two tribes but does not clearly state its origins, although it is implied in his accounts that Gullveig was at the centre of the war. In one version, the gods met to discuss some disagreements between the two groups, and Odin hurled his spear into the enemy host at some point, signalling the beginning of hostilities. The war was prolonged. One side and then the other gained the upper hand, but the Aesir's stronghold was eventually shattered and the Vanir held the field. It was then agreed that members of the Vanir should live peacefully in Asgard.

In another myth, Snorri describes how Odin declared war against the Vanir, and how they defended themselves and their land vigorously. Each side

Gold, jewels and riches were the province of the fertility deities. The three-pronged gold mount from Norway (above) was probably worn by a warrior, whereas the Danish gold brooch (left) was purely decorative (c.AD1000).

Guardians of the Land

Land spirits were thought to dwell in features of the landscape such as rocks, hills or rivers. They were not considered divine, but nonetheless they had the power to protect the land and its fertility.

Although land spirits were believed to bestow benign power, they also represented a malevolent force that had to be placated.

The first clause of Icelandic law, established *c.*AD930 when the country had not yet adopted Christianity, prohibited ships with sterns adorned by dragon-heads from approaching the country. Such insignia had to be removed before the ships gained sight of the shoreline so that the spirits would not take fright and desert the land.

Belief in land spirits endured in Scandinavia long after the general conversion to Christianity. A late-thirteenth-century Norwegian law attempted to suppress the belief that land spirits lived in groves, mounds and waterfalls. Yet a fourteenth-century account reports that women continued to take food into caves or to stone piles (cairns) where they would consecrate the food to the spirits and then eat it. They did this in the belief that they would be favoured by them, and become more prosperous.

Particular features of the Norse landscape were peopled by protective spirits. This waterfall lies at the upper end of Norway's Saltdalen valley.

laid waste to the other's territory, and when at last they tired of this destruction, the two tribes met to negotiate a truce, whereby they agreed to exchange hostages.

The Vanir sent their leading members, Njord and his son Freyr, to join the Aesir. In return Honir, a handsome and accomplished figure accompanied by the wise Mimir, joined the Vanir. This part of the peace agreement proved unsuccessful: Honir was made a chieftain when he arrived at Vanaheim, but he either could not, or would not, make any firm decisions without Mimir at his side and for this reason he was considered a poor diplomat. The Vanir concluded that they had been cheated in the exchange of hostages, so they decapitated Mimir and sent his head to the Aesir. Odin embalmed the head and sang incantations over it so that he could consult it whenever he desired to gain occult knowledge.

The significance of the myth describing the war between the Aesir and the Vanir is difficult to determine, and the war itself is not described in any detail in surviving accounts. However, it appears to explain how the two types of gods, representing very different sensibilities, came to interact and coexist. It has also been suggested that the myth embodies a memory of a time when a warrior cult battled with a fertility cult for supremacy, and the two religions eventually fused. This theory is prompted by a passage in *Voluspa*, in which the established gods, the Aesir, are challenged by another race whose practices they find repellent. In the struggle for ascendancy, the Aesir eventually abandon their attempt to expel the challengers.

In stories of events following the truce, the distinctions between the gods become blurred: the warlike preoccupations of the Aesir merge to some degree with the Vanir's concerns with riches.

315

The Death of Balder

The death of Balder is probably the most famous of all the Norse myths. The event underlines the mortality of the gods and the limits on their power. Even Odin, who journeys to the land of the dead to discover Balder's fate, is unable to prevent the tragedy. Balder, the most beautiful and beloved of the Aesir, is the victim of malice, and his demise is the harbinger of far worse destruction – it indicates that evil has come among the gods. Their ultimate destruction in Ragnarok cannot be far away.

This silver amulet of a horseman is one of a pair found in a grave in Birka, Sweden, possibly depicting Odin or his son Balder.

When the young and noble god Balder had a series of nightmares, the gods thought them to be omens. Hearing this news, Odin decided to saddle up Sleipnir and ride to Niflheim to discover the meaning of the dreams. He sought the grave of a long-dead seeress. When he found it, he chanted spells that forced her against her will to rise up and speak to him about the future of the gods. She told Odin that Hel was preparing for Balder's arrival and that the blind god, Hod, was destined to be his unwitting killer. Sensing the ominous implications of her prophecies, Odin rode home with a heavy heart.

The Aesir met together to discuss this devastating news, for it was of great concern to them. Balder's mother, Frigg, decided to safeguard her son by extracting solemn oaths from all things animate and inanimate not to harm him. When this had been done, the Aesir amused themselves by persuading Balder to stand before their assemblies while they playfully threw things at him, knowing that none could harm him.

Loki grew jealous and conceived a plan. Changing himself into a woman he went to visit Frigg at her home, Fensalir. Frigg asked the woman if she knew what the Aesir were doing. The visitor replied that they were shooting at Balder, but he was not being hurt. "Neither weapons nor wood will harm Balder. I have received oaths from all things," said Frigg. The woman then asked if indeed every single thing in existence had sworn an oath not to hurt Balder, and Frigg replied that one plant, a small tree called mistletoe growing to the west of Valhalla, had seemed to her too young to make such a vow.

With this in mind, Loki went in search of the mistletoe, pulled it up and took it to the assembly. Restored to his usual form, he approached Hod, who was standing alone outside the circle of gods. Loki asked him why he was not shooting at Balder. "Because I cannot see him," replied Hod, "and I have no weapon." "I will direct your aim if you want to shoot at him with this stick," said Loki.

Hod took aim as the trickster directed. When the stick hit Balder it pierced him through and he fell down dead. This was said to be the unluckiest deed ever performed among gods and men. When the Aesir saw what had happened they were speechless with shock and could only weep. They were all certain that Loki was responsible for the death, but they could not punish him – it was forbidden to spill blood on the assembly ground.

Frigg eventually formed a plan. She sought a volunteer to ride to Niflheim to offer Hel a ransom

Opposite: **Balder died at the hands of the blind god Hod, who was tricked into shooting him with mistletoe. This drawing by Olafur Brynjulfsson illustrated a medieval version of the *Edda*.**

for Balder's release. Hermod, Balder's brother, came forward and agreed to go on Odin's horse Sleipnir. When he got to Hel she told him that the strength of feeling for Balder must be tested before she would release him: "If all things in the world will weep for Balder, then I will let him go."

When Hermod arrived back at Asgard and relayed Hel's condition to the Aesir, they sent messengers all over the world to ensure that Balder should be wept out of Hel. Everyone and everything complied, except a giantess called Thokk (thought to be Loki in disguise), who refused, saying, "Thokk will weep dry tears for Balder. I had nothing good from him dead or alive."

After this Loki ran away and hid on a mountain, where he built a house with four doors so that he could keep watch on all sides. By day he transformed himself into a salmon and sheltered beneath a waterfall. At night, sitting in his house, he wondered what sort of device the Aesir might use to catch him and laced together some twine, thereby inventing the first fishing net.

Then Loki noticed through one of the doors that the Aesir were nearby. He immediately threw the net into the fire, and rushed to the river. However, the Aesir noticed the shape of the net in the smouldering ashes and recognized its value. Having quickly made one for themselves, they threw the net into the waterfall. Thor held one end and all the other Aesir held the other, and together they dragged the net through the water. But Loki swam along in front of them, then squeezed himself between two stones on the riverbed so that he was unreachable. Then the gods weighted the net so that nothing could pass beneath it. Once again Loki swam before the net, but realizing that he would soon be in the open sea, he leaped over the net and swam back to the waterfall.

The Aesir made a third attempt to drag the river, and this time Thor waded behind the net. Loki now faced two alternatives: the mortal danger of entering the sea or the equal danger of confronting Thor. He decided to leap as quickly as he could over the net, but Thor caught him by the tail, which explains why the salmon tapers at its rear.

The gods were determined to punish Loki for his part in Balder's death. He was bound with his own son's entrails, as shown on this stone cross from Cumbria in England.

The Aesir were not about to forgive Loki: he was dragged to a dark cave where they set three stone slabs on edge. Loki's son, Vali, was transformed into a wolf and Loki was forced to watch him tear his other son, Narfi, to pieces. Then the Aesir used Narfi's intestines to bind Loki over the three stones. Skadi took a poisonous snake and fixed it over Loki's head so that venom dripped onto his face. Loki's wife Sigyn stood beside him with a bowl to catch the poison, but when it had filled up she had to empty it. To try to escape the venom, Loki yanked at his bonds so hard that he caused an earthquake. But he failed to break free, and there he was destined to lie until Ragnarok.

The Funeral of a God

All the Aesir were filled with grief at the demise of their beloved Balder, and so they gave him a magnificent funeral. The god was placed on his ship and it was launched, engulfed in flames, into the sea. In Viking times, this funerary custom was reserved for the elite – kings, princes or other affluent and favoured members of the community.

Beings of many kinds attended Balder's cremation: Odin with his ravens, Frigg with all the Valkyries, Freyr in his chariot drawn by the golden boar Gullinbursti, Freyja with her cats, and Heimdall on his horse Gulltopp. A great throng of frost-giants and mountain-giants were also present, together with elves, dwarves and the rest of the gods.

The Aesir were unable to launch Balder's ship, *Hringhorni*, the biggest one of all, so they had to summon a giantess named Hyrrokkin. She arrived from Jotunheim riding in a chariot drawn by a vicious wolf, using poisonous snakes for reins to guide her steed.

Hyrrokkin pushed the boat out with just a nudge while flames flew from the rollers and the earth quaked. Thor was so angry at being unable to accomplish the task himself that he raised his hammer to smash the giantess's skull. But the other gods begged for mercy on her behalf, and eventually placated him.

As Balder's body was carried on to the ship, his wife Nanna collapsed and died from grief, and was laid next to him on the pyre. Then the Aesir set the ship alight and Thor consecrated it with his hammer, Mjollnir. At the same time, an unfortunate dwarf named Lit happened to run in front of Thor's foot. The god kicked him onto the burning ship, where he perished.

The giantess Hyrrokkin, who arrived in a chariot drawn by a wolf, was invited by the gods to push Balder's funeral ship into the ocean.

319

The End of the World

The idea of fate infused Norse mythology; destiny was immutable. This concept culminated in Ragnarok, the coming destruction of the world whose inevitability was felt throughout Norse mythology. So precisely was it preordained that the details of what would happen were already known, and the gods prepared for it daily. But even though Ragnarok meant universal disorder, annihilation would not be total.

The word Ragnarok is a compound: the first element, *ragna*, means "organizing powers" and was commonly used to refer to the gods. The second, *rok*, means "fate" or "destiny". Thus the term as a whole meant the fate or destiny of the gods. The second element became confused, however, quite early in the study of Germanic mythology, with *rokkr*, meaning "twilight", and gave rise to the title of the conclusive opera in Wagner's *Ring* cycle, *Götterdämmerung*, "Twilight of the Gods".

Although it was to bring about their destruction, the gods could not halt the onset of Ragnarok. It had to come to pass as prophesied, and all they could do was show stoic bravery in the face of certain destruction. To the Norse people, fate was a fact of life, something that could not in any way be avoided or changed, and had to be met without fear. Even death, the ultimate end, was already decreed and needed to be encountered with brave acceptance. To laugh in the face of death was one of the greatest achievements that a Norse warrior could perform, and such a warrior was long remembered by his peers.

Ragnarok was described in the *Eddas* in imagery that, like the creation myths, appears to have been influenced by the natural phenomena of Iceland. The world was to be destroyed by fire and water, with steam and flames rising to the skies – a vision which could well have been inspired by the experience of volcanic eruptions.

The Norse people imagined the end of the world in terms similar to that of its beginning: the coming together of fire and water – a combination no doubt related to the activity of geysers such as this one in Langarvatn, western Iceland.

Heimdall the Horn Blower

Heimdall was a particularly enigmatic figure in the Norse pantheon, so much so that it is not certain whether he was a member of the Aesir or the Vanir. He was the watchman of the gods, and the blowing of his trumpet, Gjallarhorn ("Resounding Horn"), which could be heard across the three levels of the universe, would sound the onset of Ragnarok.

Heimdall's origin was unusual; he was said to be the son of nine sisters who all gave birth to him simultaneously. In some sources these nine maidens were identified as giantesses, while elsewhere they were associated with the waves of the sea, believed to be the nine daughters of Aegir.

According to Snorri, Heimdall was called the "white god" and was held to be very great and holy. He was also known as Gullintanni "Golden-toothed" and Hallinskidi (possibly meaning "One with Leaning Sticks", but used poetically to refer to a ram). His horse was named Gulltopp ("Golden Top").

Heimdall dwelled in the hall called Himinbjorg, beside the bridge Bifrost that connected Asgard with Midgard. His role was to sit at the border of Asgard every day guarding the bridge against attempted crossings by giants. Heimdall was well suited to his position as watchman because he possessed marvellous eyesight: he could see for a distance of 100 leagues, equally as well by night as by day. His hearing was just as extraordinary: he could hear grass springing from the ground or wool growing on sheep. He was also ever-wakeful, and needed less sleep than a bird. These qualities were essential to the gods because he was alert to the events that would mark the onset of Ragnarok, which could occur at any time. At its first signs Heimdall was expected to raise Gjallarhorn aloft and sound it, signalling to the gods to prepare for the last great battle.

Heimdall was the mortal enemy of Loki, just as the Midgard serpent was the particular enemy of Thor. Loki and Heimdall were destined to fight one-to-one and destroy each other during Ragnarok, but an earlier conflict between them is also described in a myth. Taking the shape of seals, the two gods fought over a beautiful "sea-kidney", which Snorri identified as the Necklace of the Brisings. From this story it could be deduced that Heimdall may have been a shape-changer.

Heimdall was also said to be the progenitor of the different classes of men (see pages 278–279), and the seeress-narrator of *Voluspa* referred to men as the sons of Heimdall. It is not clear why Heimdall rather than the all-father, Odin, should have been considered the begetter of human society, but the claims made for him in this respect at least attest to his importance in the pantheon, even if we know little else about him.

The horn is symbolic of the point of no return – when events have gained an unstoppable impetus. It is the sound of Heimdall's horn, Gjallarhorn, which will announce the arrival of Ragnarok. This late Bronze-Age example, known as a *lur*, was found in a peat bog in Denmark.

Descriptions of major incidents involving volcanoes bear a marked resemblance to the sequence of events during Ragnarok: mountains are shaken by earthquakes, the sun disappears due to the clouds of smoke, and ash, flames, smoke and steam fill the sky. Melting ice can cause floods of water to run alongside rivers of burning lava. The long Icelandic winter must also have helped shape the vision of Ragnarok's summerless years.

The Vision of the Apocalypse

Snorri describes the events of Ragnarok in great detail. First, he claims, fierce battles will rage throughout the world for three years. Motivated by greed, brothers will kill each other. No mercy will be shown and the ties of kinship will not even prevent fathers from killing their sons.

A terrible winter will prevail, called Fimbulwinter; snow will drift from all directions and great frosts will cover the land. Biting winds will be constant and the sun will fail to shine. Three such winters will follow, with no summers. The wolf believed to chase the sun will finally swallow it, to everyone's horror. A second wolf will then catch the moon, and that will be equally disastrous.

There will be a huge earthquake – trees will be uprooted, mountains will crash to the ground, and all fetters will break. At the same time, both the wolf Fenrir and Loki will be loosened from their bonds. The Midgard serpent will fly into a giant rage and make its way to shore, causing the ocean to surge over the land.

The ship *Naglfar*, made from dead men's nailclippings, will float loose from its moorings. (It was important that no one in the Viking world

Left: **Although during Ragnarok a huge earthquake will cause devastation and all other trees will be uprooted, the World Tree, shown here in a medieval manuscript, will remain standing.**

Right: **In the final battle, Surt will carry his flaming sword aloft, burning everything around him. A ship bearing Loki and the giants will arrive on the shores of Midgard and the Midgard serpent will rise up from the sea.**

should die with untrimmed nails, for those who did contributed greatly to the construction of this ship, and both gods and men hoped to defer its completion for as long as possible.) Laden with giants, *Naglfar* will be carried along in the flood of the surging ocean, with Loki at the helm and a giant called Hrym as its captain.

Fenrir will advance with his mouth gaping so wide that his upper jaw will rest against the sky and his lower jaw against the Earth – it would gape even wider if there were more room. Flames will flare out from his eyes and nostrils. To one side of him will be the Midgard serpent, which will spit so much poison that it will bespatter the sky and the sea. In all this turmoil the sky will open and from it will ride the sons of Muspell. Surt, who has been stationed throughout time at the frontier of Muspell, will ride at the head of the group brandishing his flaming sword, which will shine brighter than the sun. Everything around him will be burned. As Muspell's sons ride over Bifrost into Asgard the bridge will break under their weight. They will advance to Vigrid, a plain stretching 100 leagues in each direction where the last battle will take place. Fenrir will also arrive there, as will the Midgard serpent, and Loki accompanied by Hrym and the frost-giants.

When all this happens, Heimdall will stand up and blow mightily on Gjallarhorn, to awaken all the gods. They will hold counsel together. Odin will ride to Mimir's well and consult Mimir on his own and his people's behalf. The ash Yggdrasill will shake, and nothing in heaven or on Earth will be without fear. The Aesir will put on their armour and take up their weapons, and so will all the Einherjar, and they will advance onto Vigrid.

Odin will ride in front wearing a golden helmet and a beautiful mail-coat, carrying his spear,

This gilt-bronze bridle mount from Sweden, dating from the 8th century, depicts a winged serpent or dragon. In the final battle of this creation, the Midgard serpent, who up until this time has dwelled in the depth of the ocean, will surge onto the shore and bespatter the sky and sea with poison.

Gungnir. He will choose as his foe the wolf Fenrir. Thor will advance at his side but will be unable to help him for he will have his hands full fighting the Midgard serpent. Freyr will battle with Surt for a great length of time, but will eventually succumb because his good sword has been given away to Skirnir, who secured for him Gerd as a wife.

The snarling hound Garm, an evil creature, will also become free. It will battle with Tyr, and they will struggle to the bitter end. Meanwhile, Thor will vanquish the Midgard serpent, but will retreat only nine paces before he is mortally wounded by its deadly venom. Fenrir will swallow Odin, killing him. But Odin's son Vidar will immediately avenge his father, while wearing a shoe that has long been prepared for this moment. Throughout time, material for this shoe has been collected from the pieces of waste leather left over when people make or repair shoes. Anyone keen

to assist the Aesir in their time of need must make sure that they throw these pieces away rather than keep them for later use. In the final battle, Vidar will put one foot over the wolf's lower jaw and, grasping its upper jaw, he will tear Fenrir apart.

A 12th-century glazed pottery egg from Sweden intended as a symbol of rebirth.

Loki will battle with Heimdall, and they will both fall. After that Surt will fling fire over the whole Earth so that it burns. Flames, smoke and steam will shoot up to the firmament. The sky will turn black and the stars will disappear. The Earth will sink into the engulfing sea that will rise up.

When at last the fires have died down and the seas have subsided, the Earth, now grown fair and fertile, will rise again from the sea. Crops will sprout unsown and harvests will be abundant. Odin's sons Vidar and Vali will still be alive, and so will Thor's sons Modi and Magni, who will have possession of the hammer, Mjollnir. Balder and Hod will arrive from Hel, and they will all sit on the grass in the place where Asgard had once been and discuss what happened in former times. These gods will rule the world anew and will tell one another tales of the old gods and of Fenrir and the Midgard serpent.

The sun will also have begotten a daughter, no less fair than herself, just before being swallowed by the wolf, and the daughter will follow the path of her mother', wending her life-giving way across the sky. The human world will be repopulated by two people, called Lif and Lifthrasir, who will have remained hidden in the ash tree Yggdrasill throughout Ragnarok. Thus the end will contain the germ of a new beginning, and the cycle will start again.

325

THE
EASTERN
WORLD

INDIA'S ETERNAL CYCLE

The vast number of Hindu gods and goddesses can be bewildering, but beyond this variety lies unity, expressed in the unchanging, indestructible divine reality known as *brahman* that, according to Hindus, exists in all things. Everything in the universe, every creature and plant, is a manifestation of *brahman* and thus contains an element of the divine. The multiplicity of gods merely reflects different aspects of the divine unity,

and a symbol of the underlying connection is the *trimurti*, or triad, of the gods Shiva, Vishnu and Brahma. These gods are sometimes shown as three faces on a single statue symbolizing three distinct functions: Brahma as the creator, Vishnu as the preserver and Shiva as the destroyer of all things at the end of each cycle of time. Significantly, each deity derives his power from his goddess consort – Sarasvati, Lakshmi and Parvati, respectively.

Present-day India, as diverse in cultures and topography as ever, is imbued with ideas that can be traced back through millennia. There are few distinctions made between mind and matter, or humankind and nature. Hinduism, the most widespread religion in India (although just one of seven major faiths with Islam, Buddhism, Jainism, Sikhism, Christianity and Zoroastrianism), is at once also a science, a lifestyle and a social system.

The key to understanding Indian philosophy's different schools of thought lies not in logic but in the convention of *vidya* (unitary thought), which seeks to understand phenomena as a single system in which God and humankind are one. Enlightenment is believed to lie in realizing infinite harmony with the universe. One of the later Hindu sacred texts, the *Upanishads*, expresses it as: *atman* (the vital force in all things) is *brahman* (absolute truth).

In the Indian tradition, time is seen as non-linear – past, present and future co-exist in each generation. This theory underpins the doctrines of *karma* and *samsara*, the cycles of causality and rebirth. Indian religion has evolved over many centuries – its gods and goddesses have not been discarded but modified, and their attributes and roles have become fluid. It is this fluidity that has resulted in a rich body of stories and one of the world's oldest unbroken traditions.

Above: Shiva is at once protector and destroyer, dancer and ascetic. Here he rides his faithful bull Nandi in a temple mural from Bundi, near Ajmer.

Opposite: The Jain temple complex at Junagadh looks out across the Gujarat plains. Such sites offer a focus that is as much social and cultural as spiritual.

329

Creation and Sacrifice

In Indian origin myths, the creator god does not, strictly speaking, create. Rather than make the universe out of nothing, he rearranges pre-existing matter – often in an act of ritual sacrifice. Order emerges from chaos as the Earth is set apart from the waters and the sky.

India's earliest religious texts are the four *Veda*s ("books of knowledge"), which date from *c*.1000BC and may have derived from the oral traditions of semi-nomadic peoples who moved into northern India *c*.1500BC. Two hymns of the *Rig Veda* attribute the creation to a great being filled with wisdom and strength and with eyes, mouths, arms and feet on all sides. He is Visvakarman, "Maker of All". His act of bringing things into order is a ritual

Two women on a terrace make ritual offerings to Brahma, in this watercolor from Khambavati Ragini, *c*.1725. The importance that ritual came to assume in the Vedic age enhanced both the mystery of creation and the prestige of local priests.

sacrifice like that performed by priests, but he is also the sacrifice itself. The composers of the hymns make it clear that no one can really know the true nature of Visvakarman's sacrifice but the result, the separation of the Earth and sky, is clear enough for all to see. The hymns also liken the way in which Visvakarman produced order from chaos to a farmer churning milk to make butter.

Towards the end of the Vedic period, *c*.1200–*c*.900BC, when the Vedic hymns were collected, priests began to emphasize the power of ritual sacrifice. They claimed that their sacrifices were re-enactments of creation and that their rituals did more than simply propitiate the gods – they served to maintain the very order of the universe.

The image of sacrifice as creation exists elsewhere in the *Rig Veda* in the story of Purusha, the vast primordial man who had 1,000 heads, eyes and feet. The gods and sages issued from Purusha and they pinned his body down for a sacrifice. In their rituals, Vedic priests gathered around a sacrificial fire and made offerings of oil, grain and clarified butter – a practice explained in the hymns, which say that when Purusha was sacrificed, the butter thrown into the fire became the season of spring, the fuel that burned was summer and the act of offering, autumn. The result was a great supply of clarified butter, which the gods formed into all the birds and animals that fill the Earth and all the forms of sacred verses known to priests.

Then Purusha was cut into many pieces, from which the entire universe was created: the sky came from his head, the Earth from his feet and the air from his navel. The moon issued from his soul and the sun from his eyes. From his mouth came Indra, king of the gods (see pages 338–341), and Agni, the god of sacrificial fire; his breath

Prajapati's Tears

One creation myth from the Taittiriya Brahmana, c.900–c.700BC, tells how Prajapati willed the universe into being, producing smoke and fire which condensed into a vast sea.

Prajapati emerged, but as soon as he was conscious, the Lord of All Creatures wept, for he could see no purpose in his existence. As he cried, his falling tears became the Earth. The tears he wiped away became the air and those he brushed upwards became the overarching sky. He wanted offspring and settled down to practise religious austerities. He gave birth to demons, then put aside his body which became night. He created himself anew, made men and women and cast his body aside, which became the moon. He then assumed a new self, creating the seasons from his armpits and the dusk and dawn from his body. Finally he made the gods from his mouth and when he put aside this next body it became the day.

In some versions of the Prajapati creation myth, the Lord of All Creatures emerged not from a fiery miasma but from a lotus bloom that had been floating on the primal waters.

became Vayu, the god of wind. The four classes of ancient India also came from Purusha: the *brahmin* or priests from his mouth; the *kshatriya* or noble warriors from his arms; the *vaishya* or traders and farmers from his thighs; and the *shudra* or servants from his feet.

The Purusha tale was also applied to Brahma (see pages 332–335) who was then generally considered to be the source of the class, or caste, system. Visvakarman was later linked with Prajapati ("Lord of All Creatures"), who is also identified with Brahma, Shiva and Tvastr (see pages 342–345).

In another version of the Purusha story, told in the *Satapatha Brahmana*, c.800BC, the universe was the soul of Purusha and he came into exis-

tence when he became conscious and said "I am". Overcoming his initial fearfulness, he desired company and willed himself into two pieces, male and female. His two parts made love and from their union humankind was born.

The female Purusha was overcome with shame because their love was incestuous. She fled from her father-husband, turning herself into a succession of beasts. But each time Purusha also changed, caught up with her, and made love to her again. In this way, the two of them made all the animals on Earth. Purusha also created Agni (god of fire) from his mouth and hands. In the version of this myth in the *Brihandaranyaka Upanishad*, c.700BC, Purusha is linked with Brahma.

The First of the Gods

Brahma is often cast as the first of the gods. A personification of *brahman*, he is the consciousness that existed before anything else and which, in the first act of creation, willed itself into being. Brahma's essential roles are as creator god and giver of boons, or favours, to petitioners who perform acts of austerity.

One of the vast array of Indian creation myths tells how, in the first days, Brahma emerged from a golden egg to begin creation. According to this tale, when the universal consciousness, *brahman*, felt the desire to create living creatures it willed first the waters into being and then a seed to float on them. The seed became a golden egg which shone with the brightness of the sun. It contained Brahma, also known as Narayana because he was born of the waters, or *nara*s. For one year Brahma existed inside the egg until his meditative power split it open. Coming forth, Brahma made the sky and the Earth from the two halves of the egg, and then began creating the rest of the universe. This account is given in an early Hindu text, the *Laws of Manu*, written during the first and second centuries BC. In this period Brahma was understood as a personal form of *brahman*, the reality underlying and preceding the universe. According to some scholars, the idea of a personal creator god developed first in the popular imagination and was only later accepted by the priests as spiritual history.

Brahma was therefore seen as the essence of all things. The entire universe existed through him. He was believed to be present both at the creation and the destruction of the universe which, according to Hindu cosmology, is destroyed and then recreated in a never-ending cycle.

In this conception, Brahma experiences time very differently from mortals. Each day, or *kalpa*, in his life is equivalent to 4,320 million Earth years. At the end of each of his days, Brahma sleeps, and his night is exactly the same length as his day. When he goes to sleep, the universe dissolves into watery chaos; when he awakes Brahma recreates the universe. All living creatures which have not found liberation from the eternal cycles of birth, death and rebirth are reborn in the new universe according to the *karma* they have accumulated over their previous existences.

Each *kalpa* is divided into 1,000 *mahayuga*s ("great ages") and each of these is split into four *yuga*s ("ages"), with particular characteristics. The Kritayuga was a golden age, lasting 1,728,000 years. Humans were happy and virtuous and worshipped a white god. In the Tretayuga, which lasted 1,296,000 years, virtue fell away by one quarter; humans were dutiful but they were sometimes in conflict. They worshipped a red god. In the Dvaparayuga, lasting 864,000 years, virtue half disappeared; there were many quarrels and much dishonesty but many people still did right; the god was yellow. The current age, the Kaliyuga, will last for 432,000 years. People are dishonest and wicked, they crowd into vast cities and live like beggars. Natural disasters are common and rulers are tyrannical; only one quarter of virtue remains; the god is black. At the end of this age, Vishnu will appear on Earth astride his white steed Kalki. Everything will be destroyed and the universe prepared for the new creation which will begin at the start of the next cycle.

This cycle is embedded within a still larger one. After 360 *kalpas*, Brahma is said to have lived one year, and his life lasts for 100 of these years – a total of 155,520 billion Earth years. At the end of that vast epoch, Brahma himself will join in the general dissolution, and after a further 100 divine years of chaos, a new cycle will be inaugurated by a new Brahma. At this point Brahma as creator god will separate from *brahman* as divine reality, for while Brahma can die and be reborn in a new

Three of Brahma's four heads are visible in this 10th-century sandstone statue. Each face represents a different facet of the creator god. He once had a fifth head, so he could see his beloved consort Sarasvati wherever she went, but it was destroyed by Shiva after an argument.

form, *brahman* always exists. Hindus believe that there is no end or beginning to the cycle of time, which is likened to a wheel eternally spinning, with the unmoving axis at its centre, representing the impersonal divine reality or *brahman*.

There is great conflict between Brahma and Shiva, however. This reflects the competition between the worshippers of the two gods. As far as scholars can tell, there was never a cult of Brahma, although one may have existed and been lost to history. As Hinduism developed over the centuries, though, strong cults grew up around the gods Vishnu and Shiva, and Brahma's role diminished. He remained a creator deity but he was no longer seen as the personal form of *brahman*, for

this honour passed to either Vishnu or Shiva. Moreover, many myths were reworked to highlight Brahma's inferiority to these other gods, some even suggesting that Brahma was created by one of them, and not from the divine waters from which sprang the beginnings of the universe.

One popular version of the creation story, told by Vaishnavites, followers of Vishnu, casts Brahma as the creative force of Vishnu. They identified Vishnu with *brahman*, asserting that he had

This Pahari school painting, *c.*1760, shows Vishnu reclining on the snake of eternity with Brahma, cradled in a lotus flower, representing his creative energy. As Vishnu meditates with his consort Lakshmi, he orchestrates the birth of the world.

existed before anything else. Using his *maya*, or creative power, he created a vastness of primordial waters and then rested, lying on the 100-headed serpent Ananta-Shesha, who represented eternity. As Vishnu meditated, or in some accounts even as he slept, his creative energy came forth from his navel in the form of a delicate lotus blossom. It rose, wavering, up in the air, and in its petals was Brahma. By the power of Vishnu, Brahma brought forth order and the universe was created. This creation takes place at the beginning of each cycle of time. In some versions, the serpent Ananta-Shesha represents the accumulated *karma* of the lives lived in the previous *kalpa*, which determines the form of the new creation.

The Superiority of Shiva

In an important myth told by Shaivites, followers of Shiva, Brahma and Vishnu are forced to recognize Shiva's great status and his superiority over them. One day Vishnu and Brahma were disputing which of them was the prime creator and thus the most worthy of reverence. Back and forth their arguments went, as each countered the other. But finally they were silenced when, suddenly, a vast, fiery pillar reared up before them on the all-encompassing primal waters.

Brahma and Vishnu were astonished by the pillar's vast size and the brilliance of its flames, and they agreed that they must find its source. Brahma transformed himself into a swan and flew upwards along the column for 1,000 years, while Vishnu became a boar and plunged into the waters, travelling down along the column for the same period. Neither found the end, and they returned, aching and speechless with weariness, to their starting point. Then Shiva appeared to them, from inside the pillar, and they realized that the awesome column was Shiva's *lingam*, or life-giving sacred phallus. (With one of Shiva's aspects being as a god of fertility, worship of the *lingam* is a central part of his cult. Predating Hinduism, which incorporated it in about 200BC, the *lingam* seems to serve as an image of Shiva's power and all-pervasiveness.)

Cycles of Creation

Just as there are many versions of the creation, so there are varying descriptions of the Hindu cosmos. All, however, rest on the tension between eternity and rebirth.

The snakes on this 18th-century gaming board lead to hellish states, while ladders climb to moral ones. Celestial squares above complete the picture of the Hindu cosmos.

The Earth is composed of seven circular continents, the central one set in a salty sea from whose centre rises Mount Meru. To its south lies Bharatavarsa, the old name for India. Below repose demons and snakes amid the seven vertical layers of hell while above shine the seven layers of heaven, at the top of which is *brahman*, the abode of perfect souls. Before the souls that escape the torment of hell stretch two paths: for perfected souls lies the Way of the Gods, which follows the northern course of the sun to the eternal peace of *brahman*; the Way of our Fathers charts the southern course of the sun, eventually returning its souls to Earth where they are reborn. Thus the cycles of creation and destruction, of birth, death and rebirth reflect the journey of both the soul and the universe itself.

335

Four-headed God of Wisdom

Images of Brahma show him with red skin and white robes astride a goose or sitting on a lotus. He has four heads, indicating the four directions of the compass, and four arms, representing the four Vedas, the most ancient scriptures. Once, however, a burning desire led him to create a fifth head.

As guardian of the *Vedas*, Brahma is the god of wisdom; he is also revered as the greatest of all sages. One of his names is "Grandfather", because of his status as creator and source of all. But there are several explanations as to why he has four heads. One story tells how Brahma created a female consort, Sarasvati, from his own great energy. Her beauty was so delicate that he felt a powerful longing for her although she was his own daughter. He turned his passionate gaze on her, but the goddess's natural modesty made her flee from him.

She skipped away to Brahma's left and then to his right, then ran lithely behind him, but each time the god grew a new head so that he could feast his eyes upon her. Unable to escape on Earth, she leaped into the sky, but Brahma sprouted a fifth head to follow her with his eyes. Then the god caught hold of his daughter and made love to her. She gave birth to the first people.

Brahma lost his fifth head in a quarrel with Shiva. One day Brahma was drunk and filled with illicit desire for his own daughter, Sandhya, who was married to Shiva. When he approached Sandhya she understood his lecherous intent and fled in the fleet form of a deer, but Brahma transformed himself into a strong-legged stag and galloped after her. Shiva saw Brahma pursuing his wife across the inky blue sky, and he felt anger rage within himself. Roaring with divine wrath, he seized a bow and quiver and loosed an arrow that flew so fast and so accurately that it cut off the stag's head at a single strike. Then the animal turned back into Brahma, with four heads, and the god abandoned the unseemly chase, humbly paying his respects to Shiva.

Shiva fires the deadly arrow which severs Brahma's fifth head. Shiva was angry because Brahma lusted after Sandhya, Shiva's wife.

Brahma, with his *shakti*, Sarasvati, rides the cosmic goose Hansa which, like Shiva's bull and Vishnu's eagle, carries him throughout the world. Although the god eventually lost his status as the primary deity, this 1820s' watercolor from Trichinopoly in southern India shows him in all his glory.

From that day, Brahma and Vishnu accepted that Shiva was without equal among the gods. They had come from him, they saw, and must therefore pay him homage. In another version of the myth, Brahma returned from his journey claiming that he had found the end of the *lingam*. But it soon became clear he was lying, and for this act of dishonesty he lost the right to be worshipped.

In later times Brahma's status diminished to such an extent that he came to feature in myths primarily as a granter of favours, or boons, to petitioners. Sometimes he was even forced to grant a boon because of the great spiritual power that the petitioner had gained through meditation or the performance of austerities – acts of physical self-denial and mental concentration. For example, in the tale of the Triple City of the demons (see pages 344–345), when the demons ask Brahma for permission to build their cities and to be made invincible for a limited period, he has to allow it, even though it is against the gods' interests, because of the power they have gained by strict austerities.

The petitioners are filled with *tapas* ("heat") and so cannot be denied. The power of *tapas* is derived from meditation and austerities. It is so strong that demons and even ordinary humans who possess it can overpower the gods. Throughout the *Mahabharata* (see pages 360–367) men and demons cause trouble for the gods. This is an unfamiliar concept for Western readers accustomed to the mythological world of the Greeks and Romans in which gods occasionally descend to help or punish humans but in which humans seldom, if ever, affect the lives of gods.

337

The Bringer of Plenty

The hymns of the *Rig Veda* praise Indra again and again for his power and virile strength. Quick to act, he had a vast golden body, great arms bursting with muscles and a distended belly swollen from his delight in the gods' intoxicating drink of *soma*.

A wall-painting of Indra from Balawaste, *c.*7th–8th century AD. The great storm god may have declined in importance since the Vedic age, but his influence is still felt among the newer deities.

Indra's role as storm god, master of the rain-clouds, won him the adulation of a people saved from drought and famine by the welcome onslaught of the monsoon rains. A divine warrior, a storm divinity armed with thunderbolts, as well as a god of fertility and the life-giving waters, he occupied the supreme position among the gods of the Vedic age. His status later diminished, but he remained an important Hindu god and, as Shakra, became a significant Buddhist deity (see box, page 385).

According to the *Rig Veda* myths, within moments of his birth Indra, the great ruddy-faced warrior, took up the powerful *vajra* ("thunderbolt") and, afire with the force of the divine drink *soma* (see box, opposite), sprang into action to defend men from drought. The demon Vritra had rounded up the raincloud cattle and imprisoned them in his ninety-nine fortresses. Drought had already taken a deadly grip on the Earth, bringing men and women closer to starvation each day. Ceaselessly they appealed to the gods for help.

The divine response was quick to come. Indra was born, son of Dyaus (sky) and Prithivi (Earth). The infant at once grabbed the *soma* that men were offering to the gods, and drank a vast amount of it. He was filled with divine power and in that instant he became lord of the three worlds of Earth, sky and the air between.

He seized the thunderbolt that belonged to his father Dyaus and leaped into a golden chariot. At his side were the Maruts, spirits of tempest and thunder who were to become Indra's stalwart followers. The Maruts took the form of fearless youths in golden armour equipped with axes, bows and arrows and dazzling lightning spears. In chariots drawn by deer they rode out with Indra against Vritra and, like a shower of rain that comes with the onrush of a violent storm, they scattered forth across the sky chanting songs of war.

338

Vritra watched Indra approach, and roared as the young god drew near. The demon was complacent because he thought no god or man could hurt him. But Indra, fired by the divine drink, proved deadly with his fearsome thunderbolt, finding the monster's weak spots and quickly dispatching him. On galloped the Maruts and set the cloud cattle free in a great stampede, so that the waters gushed down from the sky to the Earth below. As the thunder rumbled, lightning flashed and the storms broke, men and women danced for joy on the parched ground and hailed Indra who had saved them from the drought.

Vibrant with triumph, Indra then turned against his father Dyaus. Taking him by the ankle he flung Dyaus to the ground and killed him, ignoring his mother Prithivi's pleas to spare her husband. Taking his father's fearsome thunderbolt as his own, Indra, although still only newborn, proved his status as one of the great gods.

Dyaus was often associated with Varuna ("All-Encompassing"), another god of the Vedic era, and

Drink of the Gods

Indra's heroic exploits were fuelled by the divine intoxicant soma, a strong milky liquor that was a key part of religious sacrifices in the Vedic period.

The vital life-sustaining liquid, the drink of the gods also known as *amrita* (see box, page 340), was believed to make all who tasted it immortal.

In time, the sacred liquid was personified as the god Soma. Like Indra he was a warrior and because Indra relied on the drink for his strength, Soma was sometimes said to rank higher among the deities than the storm god himself. Soma assumed Indra's role as god of waters and fertility and became associated with the moon and the moon god Chandra. In some myths the *soma* of the gods was kept in the moon, which waned and waxed as it was drunk or refilled.

Soma may have derived from a hallucinogenic mushroom, fly agaric. It is not found in India, but it may have come to Vedic-era India from Afghanistan.

The eagle Garuda, shown here in a teak carving dating from the 17th century, incurred Indra's wrath when he stole the divine *amrita*.

The Churning of the Milk

The great powers of Indra were waning because he had been cursed by a powerful sage. The gods were worried that if their leader grew weak they would be overcome by their enemies the demons. So Vishnu instructed them to churn the Ocean of Milk to create the divine drink soma, *or* amrita.

So great was the undertaking that Vishnu ordered both gods and demons to bring the great Mount Mandara to the ocean's edge to stir the waters with. They balanced it on the back of the king of tortoises, Kurma, one of Vishnu's ten incarnations (see pages 348–351), and used the great serpent Vasuki, or Ananta-Shesha, as a churning rope to twist the mountain and so stir up the waters. They soon tired, but lightning burst from Vasuki's mouth and unleashed a welcome, cooling rainstorm. Trees on Mount Mandara were torn from their roots by the

This Pahari school watercolor, *c.*1760, shows Vishnu and the serpent, Vasuki, churning the milky ocean to produce the divine drink *soma*.

motion and, rubbing against each other, burst into flames. Soon the entire mountain was ablaze and all the animals and plants that lived on it were destroyed. When Indra put the fire out with rain, juices from the trees and plants flowed into the ocean and over the gods, making them immortal.

As the gods and demons churned, the moon arose, followed by the sun; then the

goddess Lakshmi, who became Vishnu's wife, appeared. Next came Vishnu's white steed and the white elephant Airavata, which Indra claimed. A flood of blue poison rose up, but before it could devastate the Earth, Shiva gulped it down, keeping it in his throat, which is why he is called Nilakantha ("Blue Throated"). Finally the divine physician Dhanwantari rose up from the ocean, holding a cup full to the brim with *soma*.

The cunning demons turned against the gods and stole the *soma*. Vishnu, dressed as a seductive woman, managed to return it to the gods, but the demon Rahu, disguised as a god, at last got a taste. The sun and moon warned Vishnu and although Rahu was killed, the demon's head and neck were infused with the *soma*, rendering him immortal. He flew up into the sky and to this day wages war on the sun and moon, and sometimes even swallows them, causing an eclipse.

Then the demons and gods fought a tremendous pitched battle. Thousands upon thousands fell as the gods triumphed. They returned Mount Mandara to its proper place, and trooped home, rejoicing loudly. The wondrous Vishnu became guardian of the *soma*.

the tale of Indra's parricide thus echoes his triumph over Varuna. At one time chief of the gods, Varuna was revered as guardian of the cosmic law and judge of human actions. He was the life of the universe he created, the wind was his breath and the sun his eye, and like Indra after him, he was the giver of waters. Varuna punished mortals for their wrongdoing, and images of the god show him carrying a rope with which to tie up sinners. But in the course of the Vedic age, Varuna's authority diminished and he lost his pre-eminent position. In later times Varuna became a god of rivers and seas.

Indra's conflict with Varuna is a reflection of the clash in the Vedic age between the *brahmins* (priests), whose loyalty was to Varuna, and the *kshatriya*s (warrior class) whose special god was Indra. The active Indra seized the initiative, representing the power of the warriors' actions as opposed to the cosmic law embodied by Varuna. Indra's thundering progress across the heavens with the warlike Maruts make him symbolic of the raiding warriors of the Vedic age. In the tale of Vritra, he and the Maruts round up the cloud cattle just as bands of nomadic warriors would have raided the cattle of other tribes.

Indra assumed many of the characteristics of Varuna and he was even praised as the creator of the universe in one of the *Rig Veda* hymns. According to this account, he built it in the form of a simple wooden house: first he took the measure of space and the sun, then he built four corner posts on which he hung the walls of the universe; and finally he set the sky on top as the roof. Two of the doors of the universe-house opened to the east and each morning Indra flung them wide to let the sun in. At the end of the day Indra took the sun and hurled it out of the world's west-facing doors, into the surrounding darkness.

The Guardian of Fertility

As source of the life-giving waters, Indra was also revered as a fertility god. One story tells how the demons, seeing that the gods were sustained by the ritual sacrifices of priests, defiled the plants that the priests used so that their sacrifices would be spoilt. The plants withered and all the fruits turned to foul-tasting mush; men and their animals grew idle and listless and famine descended on the land. Then the gods struck back, making their own purifying sacrifices which banished the poison and restored the fertility of the Earth. Men and animals could eat once more and make offerings to the gods. Happiness at last returned to the Earth and a great festival of thanksgiving was planned to celebrate the famous victory.

But among the gods, there was a disagreement as to who should be first to accept the offerings of the grateful people. The deities arranged a race and declared that the winner should assume the honour. The victors were Indra and his brother Agni, the fire god, and it was they who were duly honoured. Ever afterwards Indra was celebrated as a fertility god. Offerings of the new crop were made to the two sibling deities each and every year at the autumn rice harvest and the spring barley harvest.

This 17th-century dagger is decorated with elephants, animals associated with Indra (above) in his manifestation as god of war.

341

God of Destruction, Lord of Life

With Brahma the creator and Vishnu the preserver, the third god of the Hindu *trimurti* or triad is Shiva, whose primary aspect is as the destroyer. But he is an enigmatic god with many attributes that frequently seem contradictory.

Shiva is both mountain mystic and erotic dancer, kindly protector and fierce destroyer. He is worshipped in the form of the *lingam,* or phallus, but also possesses female energy and is sometimes seen as the androgynous god-goddess Ardhanarishvara.

He has five principal aspects, each with many forms. The first is an ash-smeared ascetic, who sits in his heaven on Mount Kailasa, in the Himalayas. His devotions are the source of all his power and maintain the entire universe.

The second is Nataraja, Lord of the Dance, who embodies and celebrates the movement and energy of the universe and the rhythm of life. His is both a dance of joy – his footsteps relieve the suffering of his worshippers – and the terrible *tandava*, the dance of destruction that returns all to chaos at the end of each *kalpa* (see page 332). Sometimes the dance is said to represent the rhythm of the individual's consciousness in which illusion and knowledge are in perpetual conflict.

The third aspect is a fearsome destroyer. As Bhutesvara, Lord of Ghosts, Shiva is said to loiter in cremation grounds bedecked in terrifying snakes and hideous human skulls. Animal sacrifices are made to appease him. (In this aspect he also has the form of Bhairava, demon-destroyer.)

In his fourth aspect he is a fertility god. Common images of fertility such as snakes, bulls,

In this 18th-century painting, the symbol Om (top left) denotes Shiva, whose meditations on Mount Kailasa nourished the universe. He is attended by Parvati and devotees.

soma and the crescent moon are associated with him. He is attended by a bull, Nandi, and has an image of the crescent moon on his forehead.

The fifth aspect is a benign protector, god of medicine, healer and giver of long life. He uses his hair to prevent the force of the River Ganges causing devastation as it tumbles down from heaven (see pages 346–347). He is the loving consort of the goddess Parvati and together they symbolize wholeness. When he is worshipped as the phallic *lingam* (see page 335) it is in conjunction with the encircling *yoni* (which represents both the vagina and the womb). The union of *yoni* and *lingam* represents the harmony between matter and spirit as well as male and female. By uniting with his *shakti*, or female energy (see page 368), sexual difference is resolved into wholeness.

Shiva's Appearance

This god is sometimes represented as a fair-skinned man, with five faces smeared with ashes. These stand for the directions north, south, east, west and the zenith – for Shiva's power is all-encompassing. His hands represent balance, between life and death, and good and evil. His hair is usually in matted locks, sometimes curled on top, and he often wears snakes around his neck, with one curled in his hair. His throat is blue because as the protector he swallowed the blue poison that was produced when the Ocean of Milk was churned (see box, page 340). Shiva carries the *trisula*, or trident, representing lightning, a sword and a bow, which he used to destroy the dreaded Triple City (see pages 344–345), and a club with a skull at the end.

He has a third, fiery eye in his forehead (see page 374) which appeared one day when Parvati came up behind him and in loving jest covered his two eyes. But when Shiva could not see, darkness flooded through the universe, and the third eye appeared to ward off chaos, sending flames into the dark. It burned Parvati's father Himalaya and all the creatures in the universe. But Parvati begged Shiva for mercy and he brought Himalaya and the creatures back to life.

Shiva and Rudra

Shiva's terrible aspects are derived from his links to Rudra, fearsome Vedic god of cattle, storms and medicine.

The name Shiva ("Auspicious One") was used as a title for Rudra until the end of the Vedic era. Rudra ("Howler"), with both destructive and life-giving aspects, was seen as a wild man riding a bull. He was also god of sacrifices and song, the gods' physician and guardian of healing herbs. In addition, he was identified with Agni, god of sacrificial fire, and offered protection against Varuna the mysterious judge of men (see page 341). Shiva inherited these characteristics from Rudra, and he may have had links to Vedic deities, such as a figure depicted in a yoga-like posture on seals of the Indus Valley civilization. Another influence was the Lord of the Beasts, to whom animal sacrifices were made. This god contributed to Shiva's aspect as both fearsome destroyer of the universe and benign fertility god.

Agni, the Vedic god of fire, was a protector figure against Varuna, once the punisher of mortal wrongdoing, who is depicted here at the Brahmesvara temple, Bhubaneshwar.

The Destruction of the Triple City

Shiva's role as destroyer inspired the tale of his attack on the Triple City of the demons. The three cities represented the three worlds of Earth, air and sky, and Shiva's annihilation of them reflects his destruction of the universe at the end of each *kalpa* (4,320 million years).

One of the unfortunate effects of Brahma's granting boons was that a demon, Taraka, became invincible in combat with all the gods except a future son of Shiva. Vishnu fought Taraka for 30,000 years until, unable to harm him, he abandoned the fight. Only after Shiva was persuaded to produce an heir (see pages 374–377) with Parvati did it become possible to defeat the mischievous Taraka – when the young man had grown up he killed the demon. But shortly after these battles, Taraka's three sons Tarakaksa, Kamalaksa, and Vidyunmalin took themselves to a mountain top and built up a great store of *tapas*-power by practising meditation and austerities. Then they visited Brahma to ask for a boon of their own.

The temple at Mahabalipuram on the Coromandel coast, built in AD700–728 and the sole survivor of seven, has two shrines – the larger one on the right celebrating Shiva, that on the left Vishnu.

Their first request was to be made immortal. As this went entirely against *dharma*, the universal law, Brahma was able to turn it down. Then the demons asked for three cities in which they could live for 1,000 years, until Shiva came to destroy them at the appointed time. Brahma granted their wish and the trio asked the demon Maya to construct their cities. The first, of gold, he built in heaven, for Tarakaksa. The second, made of silver, hung in the air; its king was Kamalaksa. The third, of iron, stood on the Earth and was Vidyunmalin's.

All were wondrous to behold and the three demon kings ruled them for many years. As their reputation grew, millions of demons went to live there.

King Tarakaksa's son, Hari, then won a boon from Brahma. Hari asked for a lake with the power of restoring life to demon warriors who had died. With the powers that Brahma granted, the demons ravaged the Earth. Fearless, they were now unstoppable in battle and soon began greedily taking possession of the entire celestial realm.

Even fearsome Indra, attacking the demon cities with the Maruts, could not break down their defences. The gods, despairing, asked Brahma for help. He listened kindly and told them that because the demons had gone against *dharma*, they could be destroyed, but he added that only a single arrow fired by Shiva could bring the Triple City down.

The gods at last persuaded Shiva to fight for them. He asked for a chariot, bow and arrow with which to do battle. Shiva then leaped into the chariot and, with Brahma at the reins, set off for the Triple City. When he was within sight of the demons, Shiva loosed an arrow – the demons and their city were consumed in a wall of fire. Shiva paused and told the flames to cease because it was not yet time for the end of the universe. But all the gods, people and creatures gave thanks to Shiva, who had saved them from the demons.

Tvastr, the Divine Artisan

The divine artisan Tvastr, creator of Shiva's chariot, made weapons for the gods, including Indra's fearsome thunderbolt. He was also the architect of celestial palaces.

For Varuna, god of waters, Tvastr (also known as Visvakarman) fashioned a dwelling place that floated like an island far out to sea. He raised a white-walled hall and surrounded it with trees made of precious jewels. Here Varuna held court, adorned with flowers and attended by the Adityas, sons of the goddess Aditi, who were a source of prosperity. Varuna's other servants were *nagas*, hooded snakes, and a host of giants and demons who won release from death and rebirth by making vows of loyalty. In the many rooms and spacious seats of the great hall lived the spirits of seas, rivers and mountains. Day after day the halls resounded with dancing and hymns in praise of Varuna.

For the storm god Indra, Tvastr built a heaven named Swarga, fashioned like a chariot, and for Yama, god of the dead, an assembly house the color of glittering gold, filled with sweet smells and gentle melodies.

Holy Waters, Blessed Earth

Hindus believe that the Ganges is a holy river that can purify those who bathe in it. One myth relates that the Ganges flowed only in heaven until Shiva helped it run upon the Earth, releasing thousands of souls who had been punished by the gods.

On Earth, Sagara, King of Ayodhya, was desperate for his two wives to conceive because he felt incomplete without offspring. He performed rites of abstinence and other austerities, after which his first wife produced one son but his second wife, Sumati, gave birth to 60,000. These were called the Sagaras. But they grew up to be such unruly children that the gods complained to Vishnu, who decided to punish them.

One day, Sagara chose his finest stallion to make an *ashvamedha*, or ritual horse sacrifice, as an expression of his great power and wide dominion. For a whole year he wandered the Earth with his horse, challenging all he encountered. He even wished to fight Indra, but the great god, angry at such pride, seized the horse, and drove it to the realm of Patala, far beneath the Earth.

The proud king ordered the 60,000 Sagaras to dig towards the centre of the Earth in the hope of discovering Patala. Eventually they came to a place far underground where the horse was grazing, guarded by Kapila, a sage who was a partial incarnation of Vishnu. The Sagaras mistook him for Indra and began insulting him. But they angered Kapila too much, and in revenge he reduced all 60,000 young men to a pile of ashes.

Sagara was distraught and sent his grandson Ansuman to beg Kapila for mercy. The sage relented, and said that the Sagaras would be raised from death on the day the sacred Ganges left heaven and descended to water the Earth. Many years later Ansuman's grandson Bhagiratha Raja

The sacred Ganges streams through Shiva's hair and out into the fields. This picture from the Punjab Hills in Rajasthan, *c.*1730, reflects the belief that while the river's source is Vishnu's toe, it is through Shiva that the waters flow from heaven to Earth.

The Sacred Ganges

The Ganges rises in the Himalayas and flows for more than 1,500 miles to the Bay of Bengal. It is the holiest of the three rivers of Hinduism.

According to myth, the Ganges flows from Vishnu's toe through heaven, Earth and the underworld. The three streams meet at Benares, or Varanasi, the most sacred city in India, also called Kashi ("City of Light") and said to be the home of Shiva himself.

The beautiful goddess Ganga, personification of the river, was said to be a daughter of Himalaya, god of the mountain range. She was first a consort of Vishnu but he considered one wife to be enough and passed her on to Shiva. She also married a mortal king, Shantanu. The eight *vasus*, gods of day, wind, fire, water, dawn, light, moon and the Pole Star, had been cursed to be born as mortals; Ganga promised to be their mother and to kill them as soon as they were born so they could return to immortal life. She kept her promise for the first seven *vasus* but then her earthly husband stopped her hand. The eighth survived to become Bhishma, one of the heroes of the *Mahabharata*.

The peaks of Bhagirathi Parbat tower over the Ganges headwaters in the Indian Himalayas.

won a boon from Brahma and Shiva, so he asked the gods to allow the Ganges to flow on Earth. The great gods agreed, but they saw that the force of the celestial river might cause devastation on Earth if it was not dissipated in some way. Shiva then offered to check the power of the river by letting it flow through his matted hair. This divided the waters into seven rivers – the Ganges itself and its tributaries. The life-giving waters ran quickly across the grateful Earth, but did not flood it. They filled the deep hole left by the 60,000 Sagaras, creating the ocean (also called *sagara*). The waters cascaded into the underworld where they covered the ashes of the 60,000 Sagaras. In that instant the young men's souls rose to the heavens.

The Great Preserver

Images of Vishnu in his ten incarnations or avatars are popular with Hindus, and he is widely worshipped in these different forms. The concept of his many incarnations has allowed followers of Vishnu to incorporate into their worship a wide range of legendary heroes and popular deities.

This 18th-century wooden figure shows Vishnu in his first incarnation as the fish-man Matsya. He saved Manu from the flood and then killed the demon Hayagriva.

Vishnu took some terrifying forms in the course of his incarnations on Earth. But in every case it was his overriding role as protector and preserver that inspired him to take flesh as an animal or human. He came to Earth to avert a catastrophe or right a wrong – and so maintain *dharma*.

The number and kind of Vishnu's manifestations varies in different sources and is said by some to be beyond counting, but the generally accepted number of the principal incarnations is ten. The avatars reflect the evolution of life on Earth – beginning in the waters as a fish and ending at the terrible end of the current age of disintegration with Kalki the Destroyer.

The Animal Avatars

At the dawn of the present age, Vishnu was incarnated as Matsya the fish-man. He came to save Manu Vaivasvata, the father of the human race, from a great deluge and to kill a demon named Hayagriva ("Horseneck") that had stolen the sacred *Veda* from Brahma while the god slumbered.

Matsya first appeared to Manu as a tiny fish in a handful of water that Manu had scooped up to perform his early morning devotions. As he watched, the fish grew. Manu put it in a jug, but still it grew. He transferred it to a large bowl, but it continued growing until he put it in the sea. Then the fish spoke, warning Manu that at the end of seven days a great flood would cover the land, and that he must build a ship, taking on board the religious sages, his family, animals and plant seeds. He should tie the boat to a horn on Matsya's back and Matsya would tow them all to safety.

When the flood came, Manu did as he was told and the fish's prophecy came true. Using the snake Sesa, Manu tied the boat to the fish's horn and the fish towed Manu to a high Himalayan peak where he and his companions waited for the flood to subside. Then Matsya killed the demon Hayagriva, and took the *Veda* back to Brahma.

In his second incarnation, as Kurma the tortoise, Vishnu helped the gods and demons recover the *amrita* from the Ocean of Milk (see box, page 340). The *amrita* and certain other sacred objects had been lost when the universe was reduced to chaos at the end of a previous age, and Vishnu came to Earth in order to help recover them.

The gods and demons used Mount Mandara as a churning stick to stir up the ocean, and Kurma swam to the seabed so that they could rest the heavy mountain on his back while they did so. The churning was a great success and as well as the *amrita* several other treasures were recovered from the ocean, including the goddess Lakshmi, or Sri, who became Vishnu's wife; Chandra, the moon; and the astonishing white elephant Airavata who became Indra's mount.

Scholars believe that pre-Vedic Indians worshipped the tortoise. They are thought to have seen the animal as an embodiment of the universe – with the upper shell standing for the sky above and the lower shell standing for the Earth below, while the soft body of the tortoise in between represented the atmosphere.

Vishnu's third avatar was Varaha the boar, who rescued the Earth from the floor of the primordial ocean, where the demon Hiranyaksha ("Golden Eye") had taken it. The demon had performed great austerities, which had persuaded Brahma to grant his plea that no man, animal or god would be able to kill him. Delighting in his invulnerability, Hiranyaksha ran riot, attacking men and women, provoking the gods, stealing the

Body of the Gods

Images of Vishnu often show him with dark blue skin, representing endlessness or infinity.

Vishnu is usually shown either seated on a lotus or lying on the 100-headed serpent Ananta-Shesha, afloat on the cosmic waters. He takes this form after the universe has been destroyed and before it is recreated (see page 335).

One of his four hands is empty, its open palm representing generosity. In another he holds a discus which symbolizes the sun, the source of life. The discus is sometimes replaced by a wheel, standing for the cycle of life, death and rebirth.

In the third hand he holds a conch shell, the source of the five elements. His fourth hand holds a lotus, signifying creative power or sometimes a club, standing for time. The god wears a golden garment that signifies the holy *Veda*s or scriptures. He also carries a bow and a sword. As the great preserver, Vishnu flies on the back of the fearless golden-breasted bird Garuda. His consort is Lakshmi, goddess of prosperity and wealth.

An early 19th-century painting of Vishnu as Visvarupa, in whom he represents the universe and all the Hindu gods.

A 19th-century bronze statue of Vishnu as Kalki, from south India. In this, his final incarnation, Vishnu will descend to the Earth at the end of time to restore moral order. The figure has four hands holding the attributes of Vishnu: a wheel, symbol of the cycle of existence; a conch, the source of all things; the lotus flower, representing creativity; and the club, symbolizing time.

350

sacred scriptures from Brahma and as a final insult hurling the Earth to the bottom of the ocean.

But the demon had one vulnerable point: when dealing with Brahma, Hiranyaksha had had to recite the names of the animals that would be unable to hurt him – and he had forgotten the boar. Vishnu therefore assumed the form of a vast boar with a roar louder than Indra's thunder and flaming eyes brighter than lightning. Shining like the sun, Varaha the boar swam to the seabed, killed Hiranyaksha and rescued the Earth, setting it floating once more on the surface. Vishnu incarnated as the man-lion Narasimha to kill yet another demon. Hiranyakasipu was the brother of Hiranyaksha, and he too stole the Earth and won a similar boon from Brahma. In his case, no god, man, or animal could kill him, by night or day, neither inside a building nor under the open heavens.

Like his brother, Hiranyakasipu was driven to wild behaviour by the knowledge that he was immortal. He set himself up as the one god and banned all other forms of worship. But his own son, Prahlada, was a devoted Vaishnavite and refused to abandon his god. This drove his father into a frenzy of rage, and – snorting and spitting – he vowed to kill his son. However, no matter what the attack mounted against Prahlada, the young man always walked away unhurt.

Again and again, Prahlada refused to abandon Vishnu and insisted that the god was all around them. At dusk one day Hiranyakasipu angrily asked Prahlada whether Vishnu was inside a pillar at the doorway of his temple. Prahlada replied that he certainly was; and Hiranyakasipu, yelling that he would murder the god there and then if he could, kicked the pillar. Narasimha-Vishnu then stepped out of the pillar and ripped the demon king to pieces. He did not break the terms of Brahma's boon as it was dusk – neither day nor night; he was in the temple doorway – neither inside nor outside; and he had taken the form of a man-lion – neither god, man nor animal.

Vishnu's later avatars saw him take human form. When the gods lost their heavenly kingdom to an ambitious earthly king, Bali, Vishnu became Vamana the dwarf, son of Aditi and the sage Kasyapa, to win it back. Vamana, exploiting Bali's reputation for kindness, asked the king for as

This 5th-century sandstone figure from Maharashtra shows Vishnu as Vamana the dwarf. When King Bali offered him as much land as he could cross in three paces, Vamana grew to a great size and took Bali's entire kingdom.

much land as he could cover with three strides. Bali agreed happily but then watched in horror as Vamana expanded in size and strode across his land, taking all except the underworld, Patala, which he gave to Bali in recognition of his kindness in granting the boon. Vishnu then came to Earth as Parasurama, son of a *brahmin* named Jamadagni. This was at a time when the *kshatriya*, or warrior-king class, was abusing its position and tyrannizing other people including the *brahmin* priests. Vishnu's aim was to restore order and bring the priests back to an eminent position.

The seventh incarnation was Ramachandra, righteous and courageous hero of the *Ramayana* epic (see pages 352–359). The eighth was Krishna, cowherd, teacher and prince, and an important figure in the *Mahabharata* (see pages 360–365). The ninth was Gautama Buddha, at the start of the present age. Some say that Vishnu's purpose was to mislead the wicked and arrogant by diverting their attention from the sacred scriptures; but others suggest that he took the form of the Buddha out of a desire to ease the sufferings of animals and to stop religious sacrifices. Clearly Buddhism was a rival to Hinduism. The Buddha was incorporated into the worship of Vishnu either to demean Buddhism and assert Hinduism's superiority or to absorb the faith into the Hindu mainstream in the same way that many Vedic and pre-Aryan deities had become Hindu gods.

The tenth and final incarnation, Kalki, has yet to occur. At the end of the present age, Vishnu will appear clasping a burning sword and mounted on a powerful white steed. The world will then be destroyed before a new creation. This idea may have been influenced by the Buddhist doctrine of the Maitreya Buddha. In the *Mahabharata*, Kalki is a *brahmin* who will judge men and women, rewarding the good and punishing the evil. In southern India, Kalki is shown as a horse – possibly a survival of a pre-Vedic horse-worshipping cult.

351

Prince Rama and the Demon King

Vishnu took the form of the handsome warrior prince Rama to save the Earth from
the wicked demon king Ravana. He combined gentleness and virtue with courage and
physical beauty with vast strength, making him one of the most enduring Hindu heroes.

The tale of Rama's heroic exploits is told in the
Sanskrit epic the *Ramayana*, which is still performed in India by professional storytellers. The
epic was fashioned into its surviving form over the
years between *c*.200BC and AD200. It is said to be
the work of a hermit-poet named Valmiki, who
appears at the end of the narrative, although in
reality it has evolved over generations.

The *Ramayana* was originally an account of
the warring adventures of a historical tribal chief
named Rama. As in the poem, he was son of King

Dasaratha, who lived sometime between 1000 and
700BC. It became increasingly devotional over the
years as passages on gods and religious ritual were
added. The first of its seven books, which scholars
have shown to be among the last composed,
claims that Rama is an incarnation of Vishnu.

**The lovers Rama and Sita as seen by the Deccan artist
Rahim Deccani who painted this scene on the side of a
lacquered jewel casket, *c*.1660. Sita was an incarnation
of Vishnu's consort Lakshmi.**

An Unconquerable Demon

Ravana, the fearsome ten-headed demon king of the island of Sri Lanka, was all-powerful. One day, filled with the heat of *tapas* after great austerities and penances, he asked Brahma to make him so strong that no god or demon could beat him in combat, and Brahma was forced to grant this boon. Like many demons before him, once Ravana knew he was invulnerable, he ran riot – defiling priestly sacrifices and even capturing the wind god Vayu and Agni, god of the sacrificial fire. Indra and the other gods begged Brahma to help them and he took them to see Vishnu.

When the lesser gods explained why they were distressed, the great protector calmed them and said that the terms of Ravana's boon did not protect him from men or apes. The gods should descend and take the form of apes, he said; while he would be born in the form of four princes.

Meanwhile, Dasaratha, the king of Kosala in northern India, longed for a son and performed a horse sacrifice to propitiate the gods. A fine black stallion was released, accompanied by a priest, and wandered for a full year to fulfil the rules of ritual sacrifice. When it returned priests chanted mantras while Kausalya, the king's principal wife, killed it herself with a sacred sword.

In time, each of Dasaratha's three wives gave birth to sons, and all of them were incarnations of Vishnu. The first to be born was Rama, Kausalya's child, who had half of Vishnu's nature. The second wife, Kaikeyi, was the mother of Bharata, who was filled with one quarter of the great god's spirit. The third wife, Sumitra, then gave birth to twins, called Lakshmana and Satrughna, each of whom had one eighth of Vishnu's being.

As the boys grew up they acquired great learning, wisdom and military prowess. But Rama was the most beautiful of the children. Rama and his half-brother Lakshmana were inseparable, and loved to play and learn together. When Rama was sixteen, he helped the great sage Vishwamitra dispatch demons that had been interfering with religious sacrifices. As a result he was granted heavenly weapons with which to fight. The sage also took Rama and Lakshmana to the kingdom of Mithila to witness a sacrifice being made by Janaka, king of that realm.

Janaka had a beautiful and gentle daughter, and princes came from far and wide seeking her hand. She was an incarnation of the goddess Lakshmi, Vishnu's heavenly consort, and she took the name Sita ("Furrow") because she was born

Rama appears with pendulous ears adorned with jewellery in a 13th-century bronze statue from southern India. This popular hero and his wife Sita together embody incorruptibility and fidelity.

from the earth of a ploughed field. After his daughter, the king's most prized possession was a bow that had once belonged to the great god Shiva. It was so vast that mere mortals could not lift it and it could only be moved on an eight-wheeled iron chariot pulled by many strong men.

When Rama and Lakshmana came to court, Janaka greeted them courteously. They asked to see the bow and when it was wheeled into their presence Janaka declared that any man able to bend Shiva's bow could marry Sita. Rama picked up the bow, strung it and with his great strength bent it so far that it snapped in the middle. As it broke, it made a sound like thunder and the mountains and fields seemed to tremble.

Janaka declared that Rama was surely without equal and was worthy of Sita's hand in marriage. Rama and Sita were married and Dasaratha soon declared that he would pass the throne to Rama. Everyone rejoiced, welcoming his decision.

Lakshmana looses an arrow aimed at the demon Surpanakha who, disguised as a beautiful woman, had tried to woo both him and the faithful Rama, and so undermine the purity of their souls. From a 17th-century Rajput dynasty watercolor.

But on the day before the coronation, one of Queen Kaikeyi's servants poisoned this happy atmosphere by stirring up resentment in Kaikeyi that Rama, and not her own son Bharata, was to be king. Many years before, Kaikeyi, had cured Dasaratha when he was close to death after being hurt by a demon and the king had promised her two boons. Now Kaikeyi went to see Dasaratha and reminded him of his promise.

The king, mindful of how she had saved his life, said again that he would give her whatever she desired. So Kaikeyi demanded that the king send Rama into exile for fourteen years and give his throne to Bharata.

Dasaratha was horrified. Kaikeyi had tricked him. The king rolled his eyes and sighed deeply, for he had to keep his word and grant her wish. But when Dasaratha told Rama, the prince remained calm: he was happy to obey his father's orders. Dasaratha wept and, as the news spread, grief swept through the land. Sita insisted on going with Rama into exile and although he tried to dissuade her, she would not give way. Lakshmana was also determined to accompany his beloved brother Rama. And so, on that very day, Rama, Sita and Lakshmana set out for the forest.

Within a few days Dasaratha, who could not bear the loss of his eldest son, died of a broken heart. When Bharata returned to Ayodhya and discovered what had happened he cursed his mother. He did not want to profit from his brother's loss. He considered striking her down, but he realized that even after what she had done he must still honour her as his mother.

Bharata went to the forest to ask Rama to return and take up his rightful position, but Rama would not go against his father's decree. Bharata gave Rama a pair of precious sandals decorated with gold, but Rama refused them, saying he would live a simple hermit's life wearing his hair matted like a sage and a rough suit of bark. Bharata returned sadly to Ayodhya and placed the sandals on his throne to signify that his realm rightfully belonged to his elder brother.

The exiles travelled southward, and from time to time helped sages who were troubled by demons, until they settled peacefully in a hut on the banks of the Godavari River in southern India. Years went by and Lakshmana and Sita were a great comfort to Rama. The time came when just six months of their fourteen-year exile remained.

Then one day a hideous demon-woman named Surpanakha happened to pass through that corner of the forest. When she saw Rama's handsome lotus-blue body she was filled with longing for him. Surpanakha transformed herself into a beautiful maiden to approach the prince. She flattered him, and offered him the rule of a great kingdom if he would come with her. Rama declared that nothing could tempt him to abandon Sita but that Lakshmana was in need of a wife. So the demon tested her wiles on Lakshmana, but he did not treat her seriously. At once she flew into a rage and tried to attack Sita. Rama pushed her roughly back and Lakshmana drew his bow and shot her in the nose and ears. The screaming Surpanakha fled.

One of Surpanakha's brothers was the demon Khara and she flew to him, demanding revenge. Khara acted at once, marching into the forest at the head of an army of 14,000 demons. But Rama killed the entire army and its leader in a single day. So Surpanakha fled to another of her brothers, the demon Ravana, king of the island of Sri Lanka. She told him of Rama's violence against their fellow demons and advised the king that the best way to hurt Rama would be to take away his beloved Sita.

The king and another demon brother, Maricha, at once travelled to the forest, hauled through the air in Ravana's great chariot by a team of panting demons. Maricha took the form of a breathtakingly beautiful deer and wandered up to the fair Sita as she was gathering wild flowers from the carpet of blooms on the forest floor.

This Sindhi sword, with a hilt of silver and gold and a blade of Iranian steel, dates from the 17th century. The warlike endeavours of the heroes of India's epic texts, the *Ramayana* and the *Mahabharata*, recall the battles fought by the warriors of the pre-Vedic age. Victory in battle symbolized a triumph of good over evil.

Rama's greatest desire was to make Sita happy, and when she said that she longed to possess the deer's soft hide he seized his bow and went after the animal. It took a long chase, but Rama finally shot the deer and the demon leaped out of its body. It imitated Rama's voice and sent up a great cry, calling to Lakshmana and Sita for help.

Back at the hut Rama's companions heard the cry and Sita begged Lakshmana to go and help him. At first he refused, for he was only too aware that it might be the work of bewitching demons who could take many forms and imitate any voice. But Sita was so upset that eventually Lakshmana went off to investigate. As soon as Lakshmana had gone, Ravana disguised himself as a sage and approached Sita through the trees.

Sita greeted him courteously and told him the story of her wandering with Rama. Then Ravana told her who he truly was and tried to tempt her to abandon Rama and come with him to Sri Lanka as his glorious queen. Sita looked at him dismissively. Rama was her lion, she said, and Ravana a mere jackal who should turn tail and flee.

Ravana, smarting, reverted to his true form as king of the demons, seized her and flew off towards Sri Lanka. Sita screamed for Rama and Lakshmana to help her, to no avail. But Jatayus, king of the vultures, was asleep on a nearby peak and did hear her cries. He flew straight at Ravana, like one of the great Indra's thunderbolts.

In the raging battle that followed Jatayus smashed Ravana's chariot and killed his horses but Ravana dealt Jatayus a mortal blow with his sword. The demon king then took Sita and flew high beyond the vulture's range and on towards Sri Lanka. As they passed over a place named the Mountain of the Apes, Sita, still calling forlornly to Rama and Lakshmana, threw down her jewellery. Far below, the apes saw her, heard her cries and found the ornaments she had dropped.

Jatayus, king of the vultures, tries in vain to rescue Rama's wife Sita from the clutches of Ravana, the demon king, in an illustration of the *Ramayana*, c.1760. Before he died, however, Jatayus was able to tell Rama what had happened to his wife.

In the forest, Rama was overcome with grief when he found Sita gone from the hut. He hung his head: Sita was his life, he said, and without her he had nothing. All night he and Lakshmana wandered through the forest, searching for her in vain.

When dawn broke, they found the vulture Jatayus where he had fallen to the ground after being hurt by Ravana. He told the brothers how Sita had been carried off to the south by the demon. Then he died in Rama's arms. Rama respectfully burned the vulture's body, and its soul flew up to Vishnu's heaven.

Then Rama and Lakshmana travelled on toward the south, but encountered a horrid demon blocking their path. They fought for all they were worth and succeeded in slicing through the monster's arms. Lying twitching on the ground before them, the demon begged the brothers to burn his body, in return for which, he promised, he would tell them how to recover Sita.

They did as he asked and the demon was transformed into a glorious celestial being called Kabandha. He told them that Sita had been carried off by Ravana and advised them to seek the help of the monkey king Sugriva who lived high up in the mountains of southern India.

Land of the Apes

The brothers bid Kabandha farewell and went in search of Sugriva. The king greeted them and showed them the ornaments he had seen thrown from the sky. They filled Rama with sadness and fuelled his desire for revenge. But, with the coming of the rainy season, he was condemned to wait with Lakshmana as Sugriva's guest.

Far away in Sri Lanka, Ravana would not rest from his attempts to seduce Sita. But she was always loyal to her husband. She thought only of Rama and took pleasure in nothing.

When the rainy season came to an end, Rama asked Sugriva to help him in his search for Sita. The monkey king agreed readily, and assembled a great army of bears, apes and monkeys for the campaign. One of the apes was Hanuman, son of the wind god Vayu. He had many powers, including the ability to fly, and he soared across the sea from India to Sri Lanka in his search for Sita.

Hanuman found the princess in Ravana's palace and told her of the planned attack. She gave him a ring to carry to Rama as a sign of her faithfulness and undying love. Hanuman left her but before he returned across the water he set about making mischief in Ravana's city. He killed many soldiers and destroyed many fine buildings but finally was captured. Ravana decided to injure the ape and then send him back in order to frighten the monkey army. He ordered that cloths soaked in oil be tied around Hanuman's tail and set alight. But the moment this was done Hanuman escaped and ran through the city setting fire to many buildings. Then he flew back to Rama and told him that he had found the princess.

Rama and Lakshmana rejoiced loudly at the news. Then they led their army southwards and set up camp on the Indian shore opposite Sri Lanka. Here they were joined by Ravana's brother Vibhishana, who had been banished from the demon king's court because he had tried to persuade Ravana to make peace with Rama. But there was no way across the waters for this great army.

Rama then found the craftsman Nala among the monkey hosts. He was an incarnation of the divine artisan Visvakarman or Tvastr (see box, page 345), and knew how to build a bridge across the straits. In just five days, Nala built a line of rocky islands to link India and Sri Lanka – which can still be seen today. Before setting out on the dangerous expedition, Rama won the favour of Shiva by setting up and worshipping an image of Shiva's all-powerful *lingam* (see page 335).

Then the army formed into lines. Rama climbed on to Hanuman's back, Lakshmana clambered on to the back of another monkey, Angada, and they made the crossing, leaping from one island to the next. They reached Sri Lanka and set up their camp opposite Ravana's city. Out from the city came the demon army, mounted on lions, wolves, elephants and other animals amid a cacophony of thumping drums and blaring horns.

357

Hanuman the Immortal Monkey

Rama's loyal general Hanuman was a golden-bodied monkey with a ruby-red face and a devastating roar. Strong enough to lift a mountain, he also had magical powers to shift shape or become invisible. He could also fly because his father was the wind god Vayu.

Hanuman was born to help Rama in his battle against Ravana, for Vishnu had told the gods to father a race of monkeys to fight the demons.

When King Dasaratha performed his horse sacrifice in the hope of becoming a father, he distributed cakes to his three wives. But the youngest, Kaikeyi, refused hers because she had been handed it last – and a bird carried it away. Deep in the forest the bird dropped it and Vayu with his soft breath blew it into the hand of a monkey named Anjana. She held the cake for a few moments, turning it over and over in wonder, and then Shiva himself appeared to her, ordering her to consume it. As she ate it she became pregnant with Rama's loyal friend.

Hanuman had the great appetite of a god and Anjana was unable to pacify his extreme hunger. When Hanuman one day caught sight of the sun in the sky, he mistook it for a golden fruit and using his father's power of flight he jumped up to seize it. The sun fled but Hanuman followed. In Swarga, Indra's heaven, Indra attacked the monkey with a thunderbolt and Hanuman fell back to Earth. But Vayu saw what had happened and in a rage for revenge he swept into the bodies of all the gods, torturing them with burning indigestion. Then Indra made peace with Vayu and the wind god persuaded him to grant Hanuman the ultimate boon of immortality.

In other versions of the Hanuman myth, Rama made the monkey general immortal as a sign of his gratitude. After their victory over Ravana, Rama offered Hanuman anything he wished, and the monkey asked only to live for as long as men talked of Rama – and Rama's fame will live for ever.

Hanuman, the monkey god, adorns a silver altarpiece from the Chamundi Hills, in Mysore. The monkey's devotion to Rama was such that he became revered as a god in his own right.

According to the legends of the *Ramayana,* the islands between Sri Lanka and the Indian mainland were made by the craftsman Nala to form a bridge so that Rama could cross the water and bring his armies to the gates of Ravana's stronghold.

The battle raged for three whole days, until the climax when Ravana and Rama fought mightily against one another. Rama eventually seized a divine weapon provided by Brahma himself and with this he shattered the iron heart of the demon king. Ravana swooned, fell down and died. Rama's task was accomplished.

The remnants of the demon army fled, and Rama declared Vibhishana king of Sri Lanka. Then he gave orders that Sita should be brought to him. She was carried to him across the flower-strewn plain crying softly with happiness. But Rama treated her coldly. She had been in Ravana's palace and shame had attached itself to her since it was possible that she had been unfaithful.

Sita protested her innocence, but Rama said nothing. Then Sita asked Lakshmana to build a funeral pyre and, to demonstrate that she was free of sin, she flung herself into the flames. Rama felt deep regret, for he realized that she was indeed innocent. But in that instant the flames parted and Agni the fire god came forth carrying Sita. He gave her to Rama, saying that she was free of guilt. Then Rama and Sita embraced joyfully.

They went quickly back to Ayodhya, where Bharata was overjoyed to see them and delighted to return the throne to his brother. Rama was crowned king. But over the weeks and months that followed, the people of the city began to whisper against Sita again, doubting her innocence. Rama felt driven to appease them, although he loved Sita still, and he sent her into forest exile.

Sita found shelter with Valmiki – the poet of the *Ramayana* – and gave birth to twin boys, Lava and Kusa. Years later the boys returned to Ayodhya and Rama recognized them. He sent messengers asking Sita to return and when she did he asked her one last time to swear her innocence. But she was weary of so many doubts cast on her fidelity, which had in truth never wavered for an instant. She called on the earth – her mother, for she was born of a furrow – to reclaim her as a final proof that she had been faithful, and she was swallowed into the ground according to her wish.

Rama was maddened by sorrow, for he had lost his true consort. He continued to mourn her for the rest of his days and, shortly after, abdicated in favour of his sons. At the appointed time Garuda, Vishnu's faithful mount, descended to Ayodhya for him and Rama rose to heaven. There, once again in the form of Vishnu, he found Sita in the form of Lakshmi, and they were at last reunited in glorious and eternal happiness.

359

The Spirit and the Sword

The *Mahabharata*, the great epic of India, tells of the conflict between two groups of royal cousins and probably grew out of hero-songs hailing the feats of warriors on the plains of northern India *c.*1000BC. Krishna plays a key role in the tale, because he is a cousin of both the warring sides, the Pandavas and the Kauravas.

Arjuna's armies attack the Kaurava lines, watched by Brahma and other deities, in this Mughal watercolor, *c.*1598. The role of the gods in the *Mahabharata* was a complex one since their loyalties were often divided. Some, like Shiva, resolved the dilemma by switching sides before the battle's end.

The *Mahabharata*, the longest epic poem in the world, was written between 300BC and AD300. The lineage of its heroes starts with the goddess Ganga. In accordance with a deal she had made with the *vasu*s, Ganga had killed all her children except the last-born, Bhishma. But she left her husband, Santanu, king of Hastinapur in northern India, and he fell in love with the nymph Satyavati.

To win Satyavati's hand in marriage, Santanu promised her father that their children would inherit his kingdom; Bhishma, the existing heir, agreed to this and promised never to father any children. Before she met the king, the nymph had had a son, Vsaya, after being seduced by a powerful sage, but Vsaya's existence was a secret.

Santanu and Satyavati had two sons but both died and the youngest left two young childless wives, Ambika and Ambalika. According to tradition, the closest surviving male was honour-bound to sleep with the wives in order to father an heir. Bhishma refused because he had promised to have no children. The next closest relation was Vsaya, and Satyavati prevailed upon him to do his honourable best. But because no one knew of his existence Satyavati had to mislead the wives, convincing them that the tall, good-looking Bhishma was in their chamber. When they saw Vsaya, who had the wild eyes and unkempt appearance of an ascetic, they were horrified. Ambalika blanched with fear and her son was called Pandu ("Pale"). Ambika shut her eyes tight and her son, named Dhritarashtra, was born blind.

Pandu inherited the kingdom of Hastinapur and took two wives of his own, Kunti and Madri. Pandu could father no children because he had been cursed by a sage burning with the power of

Demons

In the Mahabharata, the Danavas were said to be both the gods' brothers and their eternal enemies. The gods were caught in a seemingly endless conflict with the forces of evil, who were powered by the boons granted by Brahma.

The demons' boons, won from meditation or practising austerities, enabled them to come close to matching the gods in power. They were feared as disrupters of ritual, and those who neglected religious rites were often their prey. Agni, the Vedic god of sacrificial fire, became a celebrated slayer of demons.

The commonest name for the demons was *ashura*s. In the early Vedic period *ashura* meant god. Varuna, who in this era was the chief god, was hailed as "wise Ashura" in the *Rig Veda*. But by the later Vedic period *ashura*s signified evil demons and giants.

Other types of dangerous beings included *raksha*s or *rakshaka*s, beasts who assumed

A 17th-century mural of marauding demons, from the Lakshmi Narayan temple in Orchha, Madhya Pradesh.

fierce forms as dwarfs, giants and animals. The *naga*s were demon snakes, ruled by Ananta-Shesha (also known as Vasuki). The *pisacha*s were frequenters of cemeteries and were believed to feast on decaying flesh.

tapas, but his wife Kunti had been granted a boon by another sage: she could consort with the gods themselves five times. Her first child, Karna, was born after she made love to the sun god Surya. Her second son, Yudhisthira, was fathered by Dharma, god of duty and the law. The next was conceived with the wind god Vayu, and named Bhima. She also bore a warrior son, Arjuna, by the storm god Indra. Her fifth and final chance she passed to her husband's other wife, Madri. She slept with the Ashvins, horsemen of the sun, and gave birth to the twin boys Nakula and Sahadeva.

Karna was to forsake his brothers so the five boys, Yudhisthira, Bhima, Arjuna, Nakula and Sahadeva, became known as the Pandavas ("Sons of Pandu"). They were set to inherit the throne of Hastinapur, but shortly afterwards their father died and their blind uncle Dhritarashtra became regent. He had 100 sons of his own, who were known as the Kauravas ("Sons of Kuru") after a king who was an ancestor of both sets of cousins.

Dhritarashtra treated his nephews as members of his own family and the two groups of cousins grew up alongside each other. The *brahmin* Drona, who had abandoned the life of a priest in order to prove his prowess as a warrior, taught them the arts of war. It soon became clear that the Pandavas – and especially broad-chested Arjuna, son of Indra – were particularly talented.

The Kauravas watched and grew jealous, led in this as in all things by the eldest brother, Duryodhana. One day a practice bout between Duryodhana and Bhima grew so serious that Drona had to haul the scrabbling warriors apart. Another time Drona, as a test, sent his charges out against his old enemy Draupada, Draupadi's father. Duryodhana and the Kauravas were defeated and sent home, but the Pandavas led by Arjuna captured the king and brought him to Drona. These and other humiliations were too much for Duryodhana. He and his brother Kauravas became sworn enemies of the Pandavas.

361

Exile and Treachery

The feud between the Kauravas and the Pandavas grew more bitter with every passing year. When Dharma's son, Yudhisthira, came of age and inherited the throne of Hastinapur, the jealous eldest Kaurava, Duryodhana, was ready with a plan to undermine his rule.

Duryodhana was his father's eldest and favourite son. It was easy for him to persuade his father, Dhritarashtra, to refuse the throne to the eldest Pandava and instead give it to him. He even won Dhritarashtra's approval for a murder plot to do away with the Pandavas once and for all.

He invited his cousins to a celebration at a remote house set deep in the countryside. But he had his servants baste the walls of the house with butter for he had issued orders that the house be burned down, to kill the Pandavas and make their deaths look like a terrible accident. Before they went to the house, the Pandavas were warned of the plot. They fled with their mother Kunti to a distant forest; the house burned down and Duryodhana believed his cousins had been killed.

The Pandavas disguised themselves as wandering *brahmin*s and had many adventures. In the course of one, Arjuna won an archery contest whose prize was the hand of the beautiful princess Draupadi. But when he returned to his mother and told her that he had won a fine prize, she – not realizing what it was – told him to share it with his brothers. He had to follow her wishes, and she could not go back on what she had said, so the five brothers shared Draupadi.

In the course of the archery contest, however, Arjuna had been recognized despite his disguise, and the news travelled fast to the Kauravas that their cousins were still alive. The Kauravas could not agree how best to do away with their great rivals. In the end, however, the *brahmin* Drona persuaded his brothers to invite the Pandavas home and offer them half the kingdom.

The Pandavas returned to the Hastinapur region and took over a desert area named Khandavaprastha. They built a splendid new city named Indraprastha (near modern Delhi) and invited the Kauravas to see it and to attend a consecration ceremony. The consecration was so splendid, and the sacrifices so grand, that Duryodhana felt sick with envy and left more determined than ever to bring his cousins low.

The Kauravas' first act of reprisal was to build a new hall filled with crystal glass and adorned with lapis lazuli and gold. It had 1,000 columns

the end of the game, he had bet and lost his own personal possessions, the Pandavas' kingdom, their freedom and even his beloved wife Draupadi.

Duryodhana drained his cup and laughed openly. Then he sent his brother Dushashana to fetch Draupadi from an adjoining chamber. Dushashana dragged her in by her hair, taunting her that she was now his slave girl and he could do what he wished with her. In front of the roomful of jeering, laughing Kauravas he began to tear at her clothes. But Draupadi prayed chastely to Vishnu to save her modesty and the god protected her. Each layer of clothing that Dushashana tore off was instantly replaced by another.

Duryodhana was maddened by his triumph and pulled Draupadi into his lap, scrabbling at her clothes. Bhima burnt with righteous fury and pledged that he would kill Dushashana and drink his blood and then smash Duryodhana's thigh in revenge for this indecency.

At that moment, King Dhritarashtra heard a bloodcurdling jackal's howl, and he knew with awful certainty that it prefigured the downfall of the Kauravas. He spoke kind words to Draupadi, offering her three boons as a small recompense for her mistreatment. For the first two, the princess asked for her own freedom and for that of her five husbands. Then she spoke proudly to her tormentors, saying that in order to thrive in the world her husbands only needed liberty – and she contemptuously rejected the third boon.

Duryodhana managed to persuade his father to allow one more throw of the dice. He said that the animosity between the two sets of cousins was now so intense that the only way to avoid violence was for them to part. Whoever lost the dice game, he said, should go into forest exile for thirteen years. The two sides agreed. The Pandavas lost. Wearily disguising themselves as wandering beggars, they set off for a forest hermitage.

But outside the city, Arjuna separated from his brothers. A sage had told him to travel to the mighty Himalayas and seek the help of the gods, and so he told his brothers he would meet up with them later on in their travels. He found the god

and 100 doors and was just as splendid as the Pandavas' palace. Duryodhana invited his cousins to an opening party at which he approached Yudhisthira and challenged him to a dice-throwing session. But it was all carefully planned – for he had devised a plot with his devious uncle Shakuni, who knew all the tricks there were for enticing an opponent into rash bets.

Yudhisthira accepted the challenge although he was not a gambler. They began with small sums of money and jewels, but the betting escalated – and all the time Yudhisthira lost steadily until, by

Shiva and managed to obtain his favour. Shiva gave the great warrior the *pasupata*, a heavenly weapon, and other gods also gave Arjuna arms. Then he met his father Indra, who welcomed him into Swarga, his heaven. Arjuna stayed there for many months preparing for battle. Finally he returned to Earth in a vehicle driven by Indra's charioteer, Matali, and met up with his brothers.

During their exile the brothers performed many great feats. In the last year of their exile, the Pandavas travelled in disguise to help the king of Virata, who had been attacked by the voracious Kaurava armies. Arjuna single-handedly defeated an entire Kaurava detachment, and in gratitude the king of Virata offered to help the Pandavas regain their kingdom of Hastinapur. So fate moved a full-scale conflict between the two sides ever nearer.

Both sides turned to Krishna, who was a cousin to both the Pandavas and the Kauravas. He said he would join one side as an adviser and provide a vast army for the other. Arjuna had first choice and opted to have Krishna's counsel.

Later the Pandavas sent Krishna to speak to Duryodhana in an attempt to avert the conflict. But Duryodhana had his heart set on bloodshed and he refused to negotiate. While in the Kauravas' court, Krishna took care to speak to Karna, suggesting that he switch sides in the war. Karna refused, but promised not to kill any of his brothers in the heat of the battle.

The scene was set for conflict. The two vast armies drew up on the plain of Kurukshetra, prepared to follow their duty as warriors and fight to the death to defend the honour of their family.

A Fateful Game of Dice

Nala, husband of the divinely beautiful Damayanti, gambled away his wealth and his kingdom just as Yudhisthira had done. And as a result Nala, too, almost lost his beautiful bride.

One day Nala, handsome ruler of Nishadha, caught a wondrous speaking swan whose strong wings were dusted with gold. The bird offered to fly to Damayanti, the beautiful princess of neighbouring Vidarbha, and praise the prince to her. In this way, the couple fell in love before they ever met.

Shortly afterwards Damayanti held a ceremony to pick a husband and chose Nala. The pair lived together in great happiness for twelve years and had two beautiful children. But one day Nala made a small error in his purification rituals. Kali

swept into his body and drove Nala to challenge his brother Pushkara to a game of dice in which Nala lost everything but his wife. He left the city, but Damayanti followed him.

They wandered in the forests, until Nala – still driven by Kali's evil urgings – abandoned Damayanti while she slept. When she woke, she wandered far and wide, looking for him in vain. Eventually, she was given refuge in a palace at Chedi.

Nala meanwhile had rescued the serpent Karkotaka from a sage's curse. In return the snake bit him, transforming him into

the dwarf Vahuka and causing Kali enough pain to drive out the wicked deity. As Vahuka, Nala became chariot driver for Rituparna, king of Ayodhya.

Some time later Damayanti was recognized by a wandering priest and returned to live with her father. Then Bhima sent priests out to look for Nala with a message from Damayanti, begging him to return. One of them became suspicious when he met Vahuka, so Damayanti held another ceremony inviting Rituparna so Vahuka would come too. When, at the feast, she called Vahuka to her, he confessed his true identity. He became once more the handsome Nala and the loving couple were reunited. Before they parted, Rituparna instructed Nala in dice-playing. Nala then challenged his brother to another game of dice and defeated him. He had it in his power to destroy the man who had brought him so much misery, but he forgave him and allowed him to live at peace in his kingdom.

The impulsive Nala falls in love with Damayanti as the swan describes her legendary beauty which had enchanted many, including several of the gods.

Eighteen Days at Kurukshetra

The insulting behaviour of Duryodhana and his Kaurava brothers came back to haunt them during their epic battle with the Pandavas at Kurukshetra. Warriors gave their all as the conflict swept back and forth for eighteen days before coming to its dreadful conclusion.

Despite his age, Bhishma, commander of the Kaurava army, carried the battle to the Pandavas. As son of the goddess Ganga, he found no equal on the battlefield. But Bhishma knew that he would die at the hands of Shikhandin, one of the Pandavas' brothers-in-law, whom he had grievously insulted in a previous incarnation. And when Shikhandin stepped forward with Arjuna, the mighty general Bhishma was slain.

The *brahmin* Drona then took up the Kaurava cause, and at once dispatched Draupada, his oldest enemy (see page 361). But Drona too

The Battle of Kurukshetra, the dramatic climax of the *Mahabharata*, captured the imagination of generations of Indian artists. This cotton wall-hanging, showing the battle at its height, was executed for the Rajah of Chamba in the 18th century.

was soon slain by the cunning Pandavas. So Karna, son of Surya, the eldest of the Pandavas, came forward and sought out Arjuna. They became locked in fierce combat, both wielding weapons of the gods. Arjuna used those given to him by Shiva when he had visited the Himalayas at the start of his exile from Hastinapur. Karna had a javelin that Indra had given him. The two fought long and hard as equals until Karna unleashed the power of his javelin. When it missed his foe he knew that he was doomed and, cowering in the shadow of Arjuna's chariot, he begged for mercy. The Pandava general only laughed. Honour, he scoffed, had meant nothing to Karna on the day that Draupadi was insulted. He killed Karna and the sky over the battlefield grew black as Surya mourned the death of his son.

The tide of battle turned decisively against the Kauravas. One by one they fell, and revenge was sweet for the Pandavas. The cheating dice-player Shakuni wept and begged for his life before he was killed by Sahadeva, the youngest Pandava. Dushashana, who had torn Draupadi's clothes in his lustful desire to see her naked, died at the hand of Bhima. The victorious warrior swelled with triumph as he fulfilled his threat (see page 363) by drinking Dushashana's life-blood.

As dawn rose over the bloodstained battlefield, there was only a handful of Kauravas alive and the air was thick with vultures. Duryodhana was hiding in a lake, but Yudhisthira tracked him there. Duryodhana was by now a broken man. He sobbed and offered Yudhisthira the entire Kaurava kingdom. But Yudhisthira insisted on fighting. Finally, Duryodhana emerged and agreed to single combat with each Pandava. Forward stepped Bhima who struck him down, then watched him crawl back to his own lines.

The battle had been won. But Drona's son, Ashvatthaman, was still thirsty for revenge. He crept into the Pandava camp where, in the shadows, he encountered the terrifying form of Shiva.

Ashvatthaman fell down in awe, but the great god declared he could no longer protect the Pandavas and swept into the soldier's body. The killer went on his way, and everyone he encountered that night in the Pandava camp was slaughtered. Dhrishadyumna, brother-in-law of Draupadi, and her five sons were among the victims – but the Pandavas themselves were not there, since they were looting the Kaurava camp.

At first light Ashvatthaman raced across the battlefield and woke Duryodhana to show him the heads he had taken – for he thought they were the Pandavas themselves. Duryodhana felt a welcome wave of triumph, but then he looked more closely and saw that these were not his enemies' heads. Duryodhana's joy soured and turned to bile. He fell down in bitterness, and died.

After so much bloodshed, peace did eventually settle on this troubled family and across the bloodstained land. The Pandavas reached an agreement with their blind uncle Dhritarashtra. Finally, Yudhisthira acceded to the throne of Hastinapur – as he should have done years earlier. He was a good king, under whom people prospered and enjoyed the fruits of plenty.

THE LIVING GODDESS

Prehistoric worship in India was founded on the cults of fertility and the Mother Goddess. While male deities came to dominate religious belief in most other cultures, the veneration of female energy remains central to Hindu ritual. No Hindu god can function without his female consort, and the thousands of local folk deities found throughout the Indian countryside are mostly female. One figure dominates goddess worship, however: Kali the merciless destroyer, whose power gives life to the universe, activates the potential of the gods and rids the world of demons intent on bringing chaos to the harmonious structure of the cosmos.

Top Left: This shrine at Gwalior in Uttar Pradesh shelters an archetypal image of *shakti*, female energy, images of which are common in the countryside. There is no recognizable female form, only a smooth block of stone, covered in crimson paste signifying femininity. On to this are pasted strips of silver foil reflecting the fact that *devi*, the general term for *shakti*, derives from the Sanskrit *div*, which means "to shine".

Above: Among the oldest artefacts in India are figures of an ancient Mother Goddess, like this 3rd-century BC grey terracotta example from Mathura. Evidence for the worship of goddesses can be traced back to *c.*3000BC.

Left: This 18th-century diagram from a *Hatha Yoga* text book shows an *asana*, or divine position, which recalls the *yonic* triangle. The hole in the rock behind, and the lotus flowers in the foreground, complete the female imagery.

Above: A stone statue of Kali stands in a clearing in a forest in Bihar, in north-eastern India. In this part of India, the form of goddess worshipped is the black-skinned Mahavidya Kali who has been the centre of a cult since the 15th century or earlier.

Right: The goddess remains a central focus of worship for men across India. Many seek unity with her by adopting her likeness. Here a devotee dresses as Kali for the festival procession to the Bhagavati temple in Kerala.

Forces of Fertility and War

Archaeological finds at places such as Mohenjo-Daro in the Indus Valley suggest that the people there worshipped fertility goddesses nearly 5,000 years ago. Although belief in a supreme female divinity declined in Vedic times, faith in goddesses of fertility or war became a major element of Hinduism.

Aspects of the goddess encompass two clear opposites: the gentle mother of procreation and beauty, and the murderous avenger. Here Kali, an example of the latter tendency, beheads a man, in this watercolor from Bundi, *c*.1650.

Vedic religion centred on a cluster of male divinities. In the *Veda*s, goddesses were essentially subordinate to gods and were viewed as their consorts. The goddesses were generally personifications of natural features and forces or related to objects associated with ritual worship. Ida was the goddess of food offerings, Vach the goddess of speech. Sarasvati, later wife of Brahma, began life as a Vedic river goddess alongside Ganga and Yamuna (see box, opposite). The ever-youthful Usas, was a personification of the dawn and was widely popular; there are several entrancing hymns in her honour in the *Rig Veda*.

But one of the goddesses, Aditi, was in some sense a Vedic version of the all-encompassing Great Goddess. Aditi represented infinity as the upholder of the Earth and sky. She was benevolent and associated with light, and also linked to the

cow – for she was the source of life in the universe as a cow is a source of nourishing milk. Aditi's sons, the Adityas, included Varuna and were often said to be twelve in number, representing the months of the year. However, in the original myth of the Adityas there were eight, seven of whom the goddess loved while the eighth she threw away. The divine smith Tvastr took the eighth child and made him into Vivasvat, the rising sun. The parts he did not use tumbled to Earth and came to life as elephants who, because of their origins, had a divine element within them. Aditi's role later expanded to make her mother of all the gods.

A Temperamental Muse

Brahma's wife Sarasvati is the embodiment of his power, the instrument of creation and the energy that drives his actions. She is revered as the goddess of the creative arts, and particularly of the sacred pursuits of poetry and music.

Sarasvati is identified with the Vedic goddess of speech, Vach. She is the source of the holy scriptures and is said to have created Sanskrit, the ancient and sacred language of the Hindus. The holy *Veda*s may have emerged from Brahma's head, but it was her energy that formed them.

From the earliest times, Sarasvati has been goddess of the Sarasvati River, a once westward-flowing stream that emerged from the Himalayas in northern India. Now dried up, the river retains a symbolic presence and is said to run underground and flow invisibly into the mighty Ganges.

Scholars believe that Sarasvati's link with riverside hymn-making and religious ritual led to her identification with Vach. It was Vach who was originally named "Mother of the *Veda*s" and this epithet passed to Sarasvati. Viraj, the female energy that is part of Purusha in some versions of his myth (see pages 330–331), is also identified with Sarasvati.

The goddess was renowned for her quarrelsome nature. According to one story, Vishnu once had three wives – Sarasvati, Lakshmi and Ganga – but the trio argued so much among themselves that Vishnu grew weary and decided to offer two of them to his fellow gods. He gave Ganga to Shiva and Sarasvati to Brahma. But Sarasvati was soon responsible for Brahma's lack of devotees: one day Brahma summoned his new companion to attend an important religious sacrifice, but she told him to wait because she was not yet ready for it. In his fury he married Gayatri, a sage's daughter, and when Sarasvati found out, she cursed Brahma to enjoy just one day of worship each year.

This 12th-century marble statue from Pallu in Rajasthan shows Sarasvati as goddess of learning. She is usually white-skinned and is sometimes shown riding a swan or peacock, or standing on a lotus flower. She is often depicted with a lyre.

A Widow's Sacrifice

Sati made the ultimate act of self-sacrifice in burning herself to prove her husband Shiva's worth. Her name was forever linked with widows who made a similar gesture of devotion when their husbands died.

At one time, in certain communities in India, a living widow would be burned on her husband's funeral pyre. Some cases may have been voluntary but most were enforced by custom.

The Sanskrit noun *sati* – derived from *sat*, meaning true or good – was applied to the cremated wives, and European missionaries later gave the name to the act itself. The British anglicized the word as "suttee".

Scholars do not know when the practice began. In the Vedic era it was only symbolic – the wife lay down on the pyre with her husband before it was lit, and was then helped away by mourners. *Sati* was most evident among the *brahmin* class from the late seventeenth century in Bengal, and was given added momentum by a legal code that allowed widows to inherit property. The practice was banned in British India in 1829, but it continued in some Indian states until the middle of the nineteenth century.

A ritual that began as a purely symbolic gesture eventually saw wives consumed in the flames of their husband's funeral pyre. This watercolor of a *sati* ceremony is from Tanjore, southern India, c.1800.

By the fifth century AD the worship of the Great Goddess was playing a significant part in Hinduism. This revived religious impulse combined the ancient fertility cults with the personified goddesses of the Vedic pantheon. Shakti now took many forms. Devi ("Goddess"), the feminine form of *deva*, was a generic name that encompassed them all.

At various times Devi is known as Parvati, Lakshmi, Uma, Durga, Kali and many other names. The goddess could be benevolent like Parvati, or fiercely malevolent like Durga and Kali. But even in her fierce forms she is said to continue to nourish her devotees. Many local and tribal deities were assimilated in the goddess. Village goddesses still widely worshipped today are understood to be aspects of her (see page 368).

Shiva's First Wife

From around the seventh century AD, Devi was often portrayed as the wife of Shiva. The god first married her in the form of Sati, daughter of Brahma's son Daksha. Sati was a devotee of Shiva, but Daksha disapproved of the god because of his unkempt appearance. So when Daksha held a *swayamvara* ceremony to choose a husband for his daughter, he invited all the gods save Shiva. But Sati would marry no one else, so she focused all her energy on him and when she flung her garland in the air the god himself suddenly appeared to catch it and claim her as his wife.

The feud between Daksha and Shiva worsened. Eventually, at a sacrificial ceremony, Sati decided to prove her husband's great worth to everyone present. She hurled herself into the firepit and gave her body up to the flames.

Far away, Shiva knew at once what had happened and he stormed into the sacrifice, driving the other gods before him and striking off Daksha's head in his fury. Then he tenderly picked up Sati's body and began a sad dance through the world, spreading suffering as he went. Vishnu followed, and to ease Shiva's pain he cut away at Sati's body as Shiva danced. It fell to Earth in fifty-one pieces and, wherever a part of Sati landed, a holy site was set up by Shakti's devotees.

The temple at Kamakhya in Assam marks the spot where Sati's *yoni* is said to have fallen. One of her toes supposedly landed near the Ganges and is marked by the Kalighat temple. The place became known as Kaliksetra ("Place of Kali") and in its anglicized form is called Calcutta.

Devi next returned to Shiva as the moody but beautiful Parvati and another benevolent form of the goddess was golden-skinned Uma, with whom Shiva is often shown enjoying domestic bliss.

Principal among the malevolent forms were Durga and Kali. Many-armed Durga was a terrifying slayer of demons and she was often honoured with sacrifices. Goats and other animals were sacrificed to her each autumn at a festival in Calcutta. Until the middle of the nineteenth century, human sacrifices were also part of her cult.

Kali was often said to have sprung from the forehead of Durga. She first appeared in the Hindu pantheon as a form of Devi in around AD500 in the *Markandeya Purana*, her black body horribly thin, a necklace of fifty human skulls around her neck. Like Shiva in his Bhairava form, Kali frequented graveyards and cremation grounds. Sometimes she was Bhairavi, a feminine aspect of Bhairava.

Karni-Mata, shown here on a brass temple door from Bikaner in Rajasthan, was an incarnation of Durga. The 14th-century shrine was dedicated to the worship of rats which are believed to be the souls of Mata devotees and carry Durga on visits to Earth.

The Daughter of the Mountains

Shiva was distraught and inconsolable at the loss of Sati, but she returned to him as Parvati, daughter of Himavan, spirit god of the Himalaya mountains.

After a punishing journey through the towering Himalayas, the sage Narada paid a visit to the mountain god Himavan. He prophesied that Himavan's daughter would marry the great god Shiva. Pleased at the prospect, Himavan arranged for Parvati to wait on Shiva high in the mountains. But Shiva was too preoccupied with his searingly powerful meditation to take notice of the beautiful maiden.

At this time the gods, who had been driven from heaven by the demon Taraka (see page 344), learned from Brahma that only a son of Shiva could save them. So they sent the love god Kama to awaken Shiva's interest in Parvati, hoping he would then produce an heir. Although Kama hit home with his arrow of love and made Shiva notice Parvati, he also awoke Shiva's anger and was consumed by fire from his target's third eye. Shiva, wounded by the arrow, looked longingly at Parvati for a few moments, but he quickly regained his self-control and settled once again to his meditation.

Now Parvati decided that if her beauty could not seduce the great god, she would turn to religious austerities in the hope of winning Shiva's heart. She settled in a grove near the peak on which he meditated and tried through rigorous self-denial to escape the rule of her physical senses. She starved herself of food, froze her body in icy pools and slept with nothing but the hard mountain ground for a bed. One day a wandering priest passed by, and seeing the fair young goddess engaged in such austere pursuits, stopped in the grove to talk to her. He asked her why she was being so hard on her beautiful flesh and laughed

Shiva with Parvati as golden-skinned Uma, 10th-century copper-gilt inlay from Nepal.

when she said she was performing austerities because she had set her heart on marrying the lord Shiva. The priest began to deride Shiva, calling him a foul-smelling hermit beggar who wore snakes wrapped around his body and daubed his skin with ashes. Parvati said she loved Shiva for all his oddities. Then the priest mocked Shiva again as a quick-tempered haunter of cemeteries. Parvati could stand no more and covered her ears, but in that instant the priest revealed himself as Shiva in disguise. The god said that he had been moved by her devotion, and he begged Parvati to be his wife if her father would allow it. Shiva and Parvati were soon married and the gods were overjoyed, believing that now a warrior would be born who could rid the world of Taraka.

A Matter of Love and Death

After the blast of flame from Shiva's third eye destroyed the love god Kama, the Earth became a barren place. But, as Kama lay dead, the love god's faithful wife Rati persuaded Parvati to help.

Parvati begged Shiva to bring Kama back to life, and he was reborn on Earth as Pradyumna, a son of Krishna and his favourite wife Rukmini. But he was snatched from his cot by the demon Shambhara – who had been warned that the child would one day murder him – and thrown into the sea.

Pradyumna was swallowed by a fish. The fish was then caught and Shambhara unwittingly bought it at market. That night his wife, Mayavati, prepared the dinner. And when she gutted the fish she found the child inside.

Now, Mayavati was an incarnation of Rati, and as she stood in the kitchen she had a vision of the sage Narada who told her that the baby was her husband Kama. He then enabled her to make the boy invisible, so she could raise him in secret.

When Pradyumna was young she tried to seduce him, but he was unwilling for he believed her to be his mother. Mayavati then explained to Pradyumna that their souls were those of Rati and Kama. Soon they were lovers and Mayavati became pregnant. When Shambhara began to mistreat her, Pradyumna attacked and killed the demon. Pradyumna and Mayavati then lived as man and wife, but later Pradyumna was killed in a fight. Back in the celestial realm he resumed his form as Kama and faithful Rati came quickly to join him.

Shambhara throws the child Pradyumna into the ocean to rid himself of his future assassin. Little does he know that the child will return to destroy him.

A Child to Save the Gods

Shiva and Parvati had a great love for each other but for many years they did not produce a son. The gods, still desperate to be rid of Taraka, sent Agni, the fire god, to see Shiva in the Himalayas. His arrival interrupted Shiva and Parvati as they were making love, and when Agni complained that the gods were longing for a child, Shiva took some of his seed and threw it on to the ground. Agni at once transformed himself into a bird and gobbled it up, then flew off to find Indra.

Agni's belly burned fiercely and the fire god had to drop the seed he had eaten. It fell into the sacred Ganges, but the river could not contain it either and threw the seed out into the rushes along its banks. There it settled, and was transformed into a beautiful baby boy, luminous as the moon.

Six heavenly nymphs came to the river to perform their devotions and found the baby, who looked up lovingly at them. All the young women were overcome with longing for the boy and they began to squabble over him. But the child developed six heads with six mouths so all six women could suckle him. On that day the sound of drums was heard in heaven and flower petals fell gently from the sky to indicate the gods' approval. High in the Himalayas, Shiva and Parvati felt an unexplained joy and Parvati found milk flowing from her breasts. In time the child, Karttikeya, was brought to Parvati, who raised him as her own son. In later life he became a great warrior and fulfilled Brahma's will by defeating the demon Taraka.

Most of the many versions of the birth of Karttikeya (also known as Skanda) emphasize the power of Shiva's seed, which was too strong for lesser gods to carry. In the Shaivite version related in the *Shiva Purana* (compiled between the eighth and fourteenth centuries AD), all the gods travelled to the Himalayas to remind Shiva of the need for a child and all ate his seed when he cast it on the ground. None, however, could bear it and they had to vomit it up. Agni then carried some away and impregnated the wives of seven sages. But the sages' wives were abandoned by their husbands, who were angry at their mysterious pregnancies. The seven women produced just one embryo between them, which they then left in the Himalayas. The power of Shiva, which fed the growing child, was too great for the mountains, and they cast it into the Ganges. The river could not bear the infant's power either and cast it out on to the bank where it was transformed into a handsome boy.

Peacocks, such as this 14th-century bronze Deccan example, were favourite images in early Hindu art. They represented immortality and acted as mounts for many gods including Karttikeya, god of war, who rode a peacock named Paravani.

376

Shiva, Parvati and their first son Karttikeya rest at home on Mount Kailasa. The holy family are often shown in a setting of domestic bliss, although persuading Shiva to raise a family, and provide a son to kill the demon Taraka, proved far from easy.

Karttikeya became the Hindu god of war and leader of the celestial army. He has twelve arms and six heads and is usually shown riding a peacock named Paravani. He is often described as a bachelor and thought of as a god of chastity. In some versions of the myth he is the son of Agni rather than of Shiva. These accounts tell how Agni made love to Swaha, a daughter of the sage Daksha. She took his seed and placed it in sacred Ganges water where it grew into a baby.

Shiva's role as god of the *lingam* often conflicts with his ascetic guise, in which his goal is to escape passion. This tension, however, not only shows his ability to combine opposites, but also illustrates his dependence on the female sex. He is often described making love to Parvati: in the version of Skanda's birth told in the *Shiva Purana*, Shiva's erotic exertions were so energetic that the other gods feared that the universe would be shaken to pieces. But his lovemaking with Parvati was often interrupted and neither of his children was born by natural means from Parvati's womb.

Shiva's and Parvati's second son was the elephant-headed god Ganesha, a very popular object of worship. There are many different stories describing his birth and explaining how he came by his unusual appearance. One of the most popular tells how Parvati grew tired of Shiva's habit of walking in on her when she was bathing and so fashioned a child from soap suds to stand guard at the door and stop the god entering. When Shiva arrived he did not know who the child was; he flew into a fury when the boy tried to block his entrance and, seizing a sword, cut off the child's head. Parvati heard the noise and leaped from the bath. She came running out and when she saw her son's headless body she wept and wailed at Shiva. The god took pity on his consort and promised her that he would cut off the head of the first animal he saw and use it to repair her son's body. At that moment an elephant passed by and Shiva kept his word, decapitating the animal and placing its giant head on the boy's neck. Parvati was entranced by her son's odd but charming appearance.

Another version tells how, when Parvati begged Shiva for a son, he told her that as an ascetic he had no desire for children. She continued to pester him, however, and he made her a son from the red cloth of her gown. He was making fun of her, she thought, but her desire for a child was so great that she remoulded the cloth baby and brought it to life. She hugged the baby boy and suckled him. Overcome with love, she wept tears of joy. But when Shiva took the child in his arms the baby's head fell off.

377

Parvati was distraught and she would not let Shiva rest until he promised to bring her boy back to life. Shiva sent his bull Nandi to find a new head, and on his travels through the Earth and heavens, Nandi encountered Indra's great elephant Airavata. He tried to cut off its head, but Indra and his fellow gods came forward to defend the beast. Nandi, however, was too strong for them and took the head back to Shiva. In their heroic struggle one of Airavata's tusks was broken off. When Shiva placed the elephant head on the boy's shoulders, a beautiful four-armed god with three eyes and a splendid pot belly came into being. Indra came to Shiva to beg forgiveness for having been unwilling to give up his elephant to make Shiva happy. Shiva accepted his repentance and told Indra to cast Airavata's headless corpse into the ocean, predicting that one day Airavata would rise again from the waters with a new head (see box, page 340).

Child of the Ocean

In their married life the couple had many quarrels. After one, Parvati left her husband and performed such remarkable austerities that she was remade in dual form as the golden-skinned Uma and the terrifying black-skinned Kali. Another quarrel began when Shiva found that Parvati had fallen asleep while he was reading to her from the holy *Veda*s. He was involved in a complex explanation of ritual, and it enraged him that she had lost her concentration. But when Shiva reprimanded her, she

Shiva lost Parvati after an argument over her religious devotion. He won her back after defeating a shark that had been eating the fish in the coastal village she was staying in. Watercolor from a copy of the *Gita Govinda*, Mewar, Rajasthan, c.1550.

denied that she had been sleeping and said that she had simply closed her eyes to help her think. Shiva tested her by asking a question about the scriptures he had been reading and Parvati could not answer. Then he cursed his wife to leave the Himalayas and be born a mortal.

With Parvati gone, Shiva sat down eagerly to resume his meditation, but he found that the image of her delightful body disturbed his concentration. The more he tried to cast her from his mind the stronger the fascination grew, and at length he resolved to fetch her back. On Earth Parvati had been born in an Indian coastal village where the people made their living by fishing. Her beauty made the young men of the village view her with awe, and she had no offers of marriage.

Shiva sent his bull attendant Nandi to Earth to track Parvati down, and he took the form of a fierce shark scouring the coastal waters. He discovered Parvati in the village and began to haunt the sea nearby, eating the fish and tearing the fishermen's nets to shreds. The poor seamen were facing ruin. They had caught a few glimpses of the shark and in the stories they told each other it grew bigger and fiercer with every telling. They were too frightened to challenge this beast of the sea themselves but they announced that whoever could rid them of it would win the hand of Parvati, the most beautiful maiden on the coast.

When Shiva heard this he descended to Earth and disguised himself as a fisherman. In the blue coastal waters he was able to subdue Nandi and he dragged the shark back to the village behind his boat. Parvati recognized her lord and they were married. The village men and women said farewell to the couple, and Shiva and Parvati travelled back to their home in the Himalayas.

The Cult of Ganesha

Parvati's son Ganesha, the plump elephant-headed god, is the centre of a popular cult. He brings good fortune to all kinds of activity.

Hindus number Ganesha among the five most important gods – with Brahma, Vishnu, Shiva and Devi. His combination of animal and human attributes is said to reflect the merging of qualities that occurs when a worshipper's soul achieves unity with the divine.

Ganesha is a god of beginnings. His image stands at the entrances of houses and temple sanctuaries, where he acts as a protector. He is always honoured first, before devotees embark on their worship of other gods. He has the power to do away with obstacles, and those who worship him make offerings to win his favour for any project they are about to undertake – from composing a letter to making a journey or constructing a new building.

Writers often invoke his name at the start of books because he is a god of wisdom and is also renowned as a skilled scribe. His elephant's head and the rat or mouse on which he rides are emblems of sagacity and it is said that he wrote down the *Mahabharata* at the dictation of the scribe Vsaya. Before beginning, he made Vsaya promise never to stop and never to use words that were difficult to follow, which explains the accessible quality of the epic.

Ganesha's name means "Lord of Hosts" and another of his roles is as the general of Shiva's army. He has a pot belly because of his great fondness for sweets and fruits, which are his favourite offerings. One of his tusks was broken off when his head was taken from Airavata (see main text) and he carries it in one of his four hands. He is said to use the tusk as a writing implement.

As god of wisdom and good fortune, Ganesha is always worshipped before all other gods. The marigolds and lotuses that adorn this marble statue in southern India have been given as offerings to him, and sometimes the sweets that gave him his pot belly are included too.

Parvati's Golden Skin

A lovers' quarrel between Shiva and his black-skinned goddess, Parvati, brought about their separation. She left their mountain home in a fury, intent on performing austerities that would win her the boon of a golden skin to satisfy her companion.

High in the Himalayas Shiva jested with Parvati, embracing her and speaking softly. Her skin was so dark, he said, that when she laid herself against his pale body it was like a black snake climbing a sandalwood tree. Parvati pulled sharply away and anger made her eyes glow red. Shiva quickly tried to calm the goddess, withdrawing what he had said, but she continued to rail at him. Soon Shiva himself grew angry and as the lovers traded insults Parvati declared that if her body was so loathsome, she would abandon it through meditation.

Parvati then left, her anger blazing. On her way from Shiva's Himalayan home she instructed Nandi to guard her husband's door and not let any other women in – for she knew his nature well. She told him she was going to practise asceticism in order to gain a golden skin. Her son Ganesha begged to go with her and they set out together.

On the way they met a mountain goddess named Kusamamodini. Parvati asked her to keep watch over Shiva's palace and warn her if any other woman went in to see the great god. Kusamamodini promised to do as she was asked, and Parvati and Ganesha continued on their way until they found a perfect place to practise austerities. Then the goddess lost herself in meditation while the elephant-headed boy guarded her.

This 20th-century gouache shows Parvati with golden skin. Although this form reflects a softer aspect of the goddess, it was acquired in anger, after the goddess had argued with her husband.

The moment Parvati was gone, a demon by the name of Adi made his way to Shiva's palace. Adi's father, Andhaka, had been hurt by Shiva and Adi was seeking revenge. Adi found Nandi standing sentry at Shiva's door, but he slipped past the bull by taking the form of a slithering serpent. Then he stepped into Shiva's bedchamber in the form of a golden goddess. Shiva hurried to embrace the woman, for he was thrilled by her perfect form and complexion and he thought that she was Parvati returned from her devotions. But as he talked to her and embraced her he became suspicious. He examined her body closely, but he could not find the lotus mark that Parvati had on her left side. Then Shiva knew that Adi was a demon. Summoning the power of his anger, he dispatched Adi with the spite that he deserved.

Meanwhile Kusamamodini had used a mountain breeze to send news to Parvati that Shiva had been seduced by a golden-skinned visitor. Parvati grew mad with jealousy and anger, and from her mouth her fury emerged in the form of a lion. But then Brahma came softly pacing across the mountainside and asked Parvati what she desired, as he was the giver of boons and her austerities had been great indeed. She said that she wanted a golden skin, because her husband had mocked her. And Brahma then granted her wish.

The Devotees of Death

For hundreds of years until the mid-1800s, thuggee *assassins robbed and murdered travellers in central and northern India – and sacrificed them to the goddess Kali.*

The *thuggee*s' preferred way of killing their victims was garroting – a method they said had been taught them by Kali herself using a clay dummy. They would befriend travellers on the road, then turn upon them and strangle them with a noose or handkerchief. On the sacred Ganges River between Benares and Calcutta they posed as boatmen, offering to take pilgrims across the water – but when far from shore they would rob and kill their victims.

On the Ganges the victims were generally thrown into the water, but on land the corpses were buried in pits ritually dug using a sacred pickaxe. One third of the robbery proceeds, as well as the bodies, were offered to Kali, in curious rituals that included sacrifices of sugar to the goddess. All the victims were men as the goddess did not desire female sacrifices.

The cult of Kali lives on in the form of painting known as Kaligat. The style, demonstrated in this 19th-century image, still thrives today, focusing on lurid representations of the avenging black-faced goddess.

The movement took its name from the Sanskrit *sthaga* or "thief". The *thuggee*s' origins, however, are not known. Some members were Muslims and they claimed to be descended from seven different Muslim tribes. Some accounts say they were preying on innocent pilgrims and travellers as long ago as the seventh century AD.

The British authorities made a concerted effort to stamp out the *thuggee* movement during the governorship of Lord William Bentinck (1834–1835) and more than 3,000 were captured in the 1830s. By 1861, *thuggee*s were a thing of the past, but they left one lasting legacy in the form of the word "thug", meaning a violent criminal.

381

Goddess of Good Fortune

Another form taken by the Great Goddess was Lakshmi, wife of Vishnu. She is still worshipped under the name Sri, goddess of beauty, prosperity and good fortune, and she has long been associated with the principal gods. In the *Vedas*, Sri was wife of Varuna, chief of the gods, and sometimes of the golden-haired sun god, Surya.

Lakshmi emerged from the Milk Ocean when the gods churned it to produce *amrita* and she at once became Vishnu's consort (see box, page 340). In most accounts, she was originally the daughter of a sage named Bhrigu, but hid in the ocean after the gods were driven out of heaven.

She is pictured as an ideal of slim-waisted, full-breasted feminine beauty. In some accounts of the churning of the Milk Ocean, when she emerged – one of fourteen precious things that were the happy by-products of the process – both Shiva and Vishnu were entranced by her beauty and disputed the right to marry her. But because Shiva had already claimed the moon when it rose from the ocean, Vishnu took Lakshmi. Shiva was so upset that he swallowed the poison that was produced during the churning and so saved the whole of creation.

As Vishnu's *shakti*, or female energy, Lakshmi played an enabling role in his acts of protection and preservation. Some Vaishnavites conceive of god and goddess linked as Lakshmi-Narayana to form the personal and approachable face of *brahman*. When Vishnu took flesh as the upholder of *dharma*, she also incarnated as his companion. She was the devoted, ever-faithful Sita when Vishnu was born as righteous Rama, and when the god became Krishna, Lakshmi was both the passionate and beautiful cowgirl, Radha, and Krishna's favourite wife Rukmini. Their union is seen as an image of the soul's relationship with god.

Male devotees of Vishnu sometimes dress as women in order to gain greater spiritual intimacy with the deity. Towards the end of his life, the renowned sixteenth-century mystic Sri Chaitanya identified more and more strongly with Radha and regularly wore women's clothes. Mystery surrounds his death as he is said to have simply disappeared, but his followers claimed he had been a full incarnation of Vishnu's eighth *avatar*, Krishna.

In the myth of the churning of the Milk Ocean, Vishnu assumed female form to become the bewitchingly beautiful Mohini who seduced the demons into giving up the *amrita* after they had snatched it from the gods.

Bringer of Wealth and Fertility

As Sri, Lakshmi is said to reside in sweet-smelling floral garlands which bring fortune and wealth to the wearer. But because good fortune can disappear as quickly as it appears – and despite her great faithfulness as Sita – Lakshmi is sometimes referred to as changeable or fickle and her good will is eagerly sought.

She also has a role as a fertility goddess and is particularly linked to the richness of the soil. Because of this, she is sometimes known as Karisin ("rich in dung") a variation which is naturally popular in the countryside.

The love god Kama was Lakshmi's son, fruit of her union with Vishnu. She is particularly associated with the lotus flower, a common Indian symbol of fertility, and another of her names is Padma, which means "Lotus". She is shown either seated or upright on a lotus, sometimes with Vishnu. In the popular image of Vishnu reclining on the serpent Ananta-Shesha, Lakshmi is depicted soothing her lord by rubbing his feet with ointments. Her image is usually golden-skinned.

Lakshmi and the Washerwoman

This tale is told about the autumn festival of lights, Diwali, which is held in Lakshmi's honour. Householders light lamps to attract the benevolent goddess to their home; if she visits, they believe she will bring them prosperity in the coming year.

One year, at Diwali, the king of a northern Indian realm gave his wife the most wonderful necklace of pearls. But when she went for her morning swim, leaving her necklace and clothes by the shore, a crow swooped down from the sky and snatched the precious pearls.

To comfort his distraught wife, the king at once dispatched his servants to announce a generous reward for their return.

The crow, meanwhile, had dropped the necklace over the poorest part of a city and it had been found by a washerwoman. When she heard the desperate proclamations about the reward, she made her way to the palace, where she proudly handed the necklace to the king.

He was delighted with the woman's honesty and offered her a purse heavy with coins as a reward. But the woman refused. Instead she asked the king to grant her a favour. That night, when the celebrations for Diwali were due to begin, she wanted her humble hut to be the only lighted house in the kingdom. She asked the king to forbid the lighting of any other Diwali lamps for this one night. It seemed a small thing to the king, who did not take Diwali very seriously anyway, so he willingly granted the washerwoman her wish.

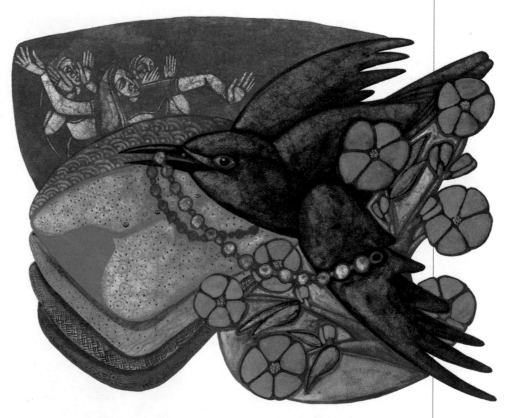

The queen cries out as a passing crow flies off with the precious pearl necklace she had left with her clothes as she went for her morning swim.

But Lakshmi was not pleased when she came to the kingdom to inspect the displays of Diwali lamps. At first she thought no one had bothered to light any lamps at all, but then she saw the washerwoman's house in the distance. She walked swiftly there and knocked on the door. The washerwoman greeted her, but would let the goddess inside only if she promised to stay for seven generations.

Lakshmi was pleased that the woman was so devoted to her, and she agreed. On that day the washerwoman's luck changed and she was never to know poverty again. Her sons and daughters, and their children and their offspring, enjoyed lasting prosperity and good fortune – the gift of Lakshmi – for seven long generations.

383

The Birth of the Buddha

While Hinduism may now be India's dominant faith, the early influence of Buddhism is often overlooked. For its founder, Prince Gautama Siddhartha, the luxury and privilege of his royal background were as nothing to him compared with the beauty of truth.

The boy who was destined to be the Buddha was born in the foothills of the Himalayas, in what is now the province of Terai, Nepal. His father was a noble warrior, Suddhodana, the king of Kapilavastu, head of the Gautama clan of the Shakya tribe; his mother, Mahayama, was a royal princess. One night, as Mahayama slept peacefully in the royal palace, a great white elephant came to her bedside and entered her womb. As the months went by, a desire for solitude and silence came increasingly upon her, and finally she took herself off into the forest where she could meditate alone. Lying down beneath a sal tree, she finally gave birth, not to an infant but to a miniature man, the future Buddha. Where his foot first touched the ground the earth thrust forth a lotus plant, and as he looked about him to each of the points of the compass, gods, goddesses, men, women and demons saluted his sanctity. Eighty thousand joyful relations flocked together to celebrate his coming, and at a splendid ceremony he was given the name of Siddhartha. A hundred and eight *brahmin*s were present to bless his birth and 100 godmothers promised her their help. Overwhelmed by her joy, her life's dearest ambitions all accomplished, Queen Mahayama died only two days later, to be reborn among the deities. Siddhartha was looked after by his mother's sister, the princess Prajapati.

*Buddha*s mark the entrance to the Swayambunath temple, near Kathmandu, the place where Siddhartha emerged from the lotus flower to take his first steps on his road to *buddha*hood. Several hundred steps lead from this gateway to a temple beyond.

It was prophesied that the boy would become either a great king or a *buddha*, or "Enlightened One". Suddhodana had ambitions of worldly glory for his son. As long as he protected the boy from ever seeing the unhappiness of human life, his advisers told him, Siddhartha would accept his royal destiny without question. Suddhodana accordingly built three special palaces for his son, and here the pampered prince grew up in unimaginable luxury, lulled by soft music, delighted by gentle fragrances, his every wish anticipated by 1,000 willing servants. So, ignorant of his alternative destiny, the young Siddhartha grew from boyhood to youth, his education that of a future king.

As Siddhartha emerged into manhood, a rivalry developed with his cousin and companion Devadatta. One day Dandapani, father of the lovely Yasodhara, Siddhartha's intended bride, demanded that the young prince prove himself in manly arts. A tournament was arranged, in which Siddhartha might match his skill, strength and intellect against those of Devadatta and another young warrior, Sundarnand. Devadatta strove implacably to outdo the young prince, and as the tournament started, he went all out to win in every event. Yet Siddhartha was not only victorious in the more artistic events such as music, mathematics, elocution and recitation, but also outdid his more warlike rival as horseman and charioteer. In archery, and even in wrestling, he held Devadatta to a draw. Only in the fencing contest did Devadatta at last prevail. It seemed natural that Siddhartha would be awarded the garland, but when he was, Devadatta looked on in outrage.

Siddhartha's sense of well-being was only enhanced by the joys of matrimony. Guards kept the realities of the outside world at bay, while within the palace walls were only luxury and pleasure. Increasingly concerned that Siddhartha might come to look beyond his blissful confinement, Suddhodana had the royal apartments filled with beautiful women, poetry, music and every kind of delight. So it was that the young prince reached a man's years without ever so much as dreaming that existence might have its less agreeable

A Divine Cosmology

The form of the Buddhist cosmos was of little interest to a mind set on an abstract state of enlightenment beyond mere earthly concerns. Yet the faith's rapidly growing following required a less rarefied way of grasping its salient points. And into the vacuum left by "pure" Buddhism spilled innumerable influences from Hinduism and Jainism.

At the centre of the Buddhist universe, Mount Meru rises from an endless plain. Beneath lie 136 hells, each marked out for the punishment of a particular sin. Mount Meru's peak provides the foundation for the realms of the Four Great Kings, Dhritarashtra, Virudhaka, Virupaksha and Kubera, who rule the east, the south, the west and the north. Above these kingdoms lies the heaven of Shakra, the Buddhist equivalent of the Hindu god Indra. There are forty-four further heavens, each with its own deities and delights for rewarding virtue, and beyond these lie the heavens' topmost tiers: where *buddha*s dwell in abstract formlessness, having transcended time and self.

Above: **Rooftop decorations stand before the *stupa* at Bodnath, Kathmandu, one of Buddhism's holiest shrines.**

385

aspects. In time, however, Siddhartha grew curious about what might lie beyond the walls of his palace. Ignoring his father's pleas, he resolved to visit the world outside. Guessing at his son's intentions, Suddhodana did his best to replicate his carefully contrived illusion in the city outside. He had the streets surrounding the palace all scrupulously swept, and the facades of their buildings appealingly decorated. Any sick, aged or ugly people, and any sight which might rock the unquestioning complacency of his son was banished from the vicinity. Yet the gods did not wish the king's sleight to succeed: Siddhartha's outings from the palace were to change him for ever. In all he would make four excursions in the course of

which he would see the "Four Sights". The first of these was a stooped, wizened man, shuffling awkwardly along with the aid of a stick. This, his charioteer Chandaka told the astonished prince, was the appearance of old age. All human beings were destined to this decrepitude, he said, even the youthful Siddhartha. On their next outing the pair found the beauties of the city scene disfigured by another sight of suffering: a man racked by disease and pain. This too, said Chandaka, could happen to anybody, even to a king's son such as Siddhartha. Still more shocking, however, was the sight of a corpse, encountered during their next excursion. Nothing had prepared the prince for the thought that his life must one day end. Filled with

The Buddhist Pantheon

If the cosmos imagined by Buddhists reflects that of India's ancient Hindu tradition, so too does its array of deities.

All the great gods and goddesses of the Hindu tradition have their counterparts in popular Buddhism, though their names and their functions have often been changed. Hence the Hindu god Indra, supreme among deities, has his equivalent in Shakra, the heavenly king. Buddhists recognize the rule of the deathly Dharmaraja, or Yama, in the underworld, but demote the great Shiva and his wife Parvati to the role of doorkeepers to the Buddha. The Hindu earth god Kubera, renamed Jambhala, is bodyguard to the sage. Demons suck the 500 dugs of Jambhala's dreadful wife Hariti, terrifying both in her ferocity and her fertility. The goddesses of the Buddhist

pantheon are not on the whole distinguished by their gentleness. The dawn goddess Marishi has none of the benignity of the Hindu Ushas. Not all the Buddhist deities are so terrible, however: Sarasvati, goddess of teaching, and Prajna, the goddess of knowledge, are kind. Nor, indeed, are they all borrowings from Hindu tradition. Tara has made the opposite transition. Once the "Mother of all the *Buddhas*", she has been absorbed into Hindu lore.

Left: A 10th-century stone image of Tara, mother of the *buddhas*, protector of people and bestower of long life. This "supreme mother" typically embodies wisdom and compassion as female attributes.

confusion and gloom, he wondered whether it could be worth living at all. Next time they ventured forth, however, they met a monk out begging with his bowl. This man, said Chandaka, had willingly forsaken family, home and comfort in order to seek peace and spiritual fulfilment in a life of poverty and prayer. Moved beyond anything he had ever experienced by the sight of such unworldliness, Siddhartha returned home resolved to emulate the monk's example, and to set out himself upon the road of renunciation. The luxuries of the palace seemed as nothing to him now, and although the sight of his sleeping wife and baby did tug at his heartstrings, he stiffened his resolve. He stepped briskly from their chamber, went out to where Chandaka was waiting with his horse Kanthaka and took off into the world.

Soon they came down beside the Anoma River, where Siddhartha took leave of his faithful charioteer. Taking off his royal jewels and his rich clothes, and cutting off his beautiful black hair, he handed them to Chandaka, bidding him to take them back to his family at the palace, along with his farewell message. Siddhartha said he was setting off to seek an end to old age and suffering, and would vanquish death or die himself in the attempt. If he were successful in his quest, he would return home in triumph.

For six years Siddhartha dedicated himself to asceticism. Yet no spiritual benefits seemed to flow from his suffering: the road to enlightenment seemed as elusive as ever. Instead, the *bodhisattva* (*buddha* in waiting) determined to pursue his own path, a "Middle Way", as he called it, between luxury and asceticism. Physical self-mortification, he realized, merely made an obsession of the hurting, hungering human flesh. Escape from the body and its preoccupations would require an inward, contemplative journey. So, accepting the gift of food

387

that a young woman gave him, he sat down beneath a tree, resolving to remain where he was until he had attained enlightenment. Alarmed to see that a new and irresistible heavenly enemy was on the point of coming into being, Mara, king of the demons, summoned up all his forces and gathered all his energies to prevent the *bodhisattva* from becoming a *buddha*. Mara hurled all the elements at his command at the holy man, but his evil was no match for the other's supreme good. His lightning bolts became lotus blossoms and wafted gently down around the peacefully praying Siddhartha; the clouds of earth and ashes he launched were turned by his enemy's righteousness into sweet-smelling sandalwood, while all the darkness Mara could muster could not dim the surpassing brightness of the *bodhisattva's* glowing soul. Thunder filled the heavens and the Earth shook, cleaving the universe. Mara and his demons fled in panic, leaving Gautama Siddhartha meditating still, the calm victor in possession of the field.

Their way now safe from evil spirits, a host of more benign gods and goddesses gathered to witness the *bodhisattva's* final transformation through *dhyana* or deep meditation. Through three long watches of the night, Siddhartha moved slowly by stages through the limits of earthly reality. Finally, in the fourth watch, he saw how man's restless destiny might be transcended, and freedom and stillness at last attained in a state of *nirvana* which extinguished all earthly attachments as one might blow out a candle. The man's moment of extinction was the birth of the Buddha. In that ecstatic instant, Siddhartha saw the possibility of eternal salvation. But he did not seize it for himself. He decided that his place was in the world, among his fellow men and women. And so, starting with two merchants, with whom he shared a meal, the Buddha began to gather round him a group of disciples. Retracing his steps in the hope of recruiting the companions of his ascetic years, he found his way barred by the Ganges, and a ferryman who insisted on cash payment which the Buddha was unable to provide. Undaunted, he flew across the mighty river, coming to earth on the other side,

The Bodh Gaya *stupa*, which marks the place where the Buddha achieved true enlightenment. The bodhi tree which grows at the site today is held to be a direct descendent of the pipal tree under which Siddhartha resisted Mara's onslaughts.

where he found his old companions still striving after salvation through self-abnegation and austerity. At first derisive they soon became devoted disciples, persuaded despite themselves by the Buddha's insightful teaching, and impressed by his miraculous powers. Soon hundreds and thousands were flocking to follow this great teacher. His quest successfully concluded, the Buddha could now keep his promise to his family, and return home to Kapilavastu. Yet his homecoming was not to be quite what his father had imagined. Begging for his bread in the streets of the city, the great prince was returning a monk. Suddhodana was at first appalled but eventually he was won over by the Buddha's words of wisdom, and soon the whole royal family was converted.

But there remained people who distrusted Siddhartha's sacred message, and they found a ready leader in Devadatta, his boyhood rival. Devadatta dedicated himself to the task of bringing down his old enemy, but all his stratagems ended in failure. In despair, Devadatta fell seriously ill. When he recovered, he let it be thought that he had repented. He went to see the Buddha to ask for forgiveness, but his murderous intentions were apparent to the gods. Flames billowed forth from the ground and burned him up where he stood.

For forty-five years the Buddha's mission continued, but at last he decided that he had lived long enough. Making his way to the country of Mallas, he lay down in an enchanted grove. Great rulers gathered to take their leave of the teacher. He comforted them, explaining that his own work was now complete and that the rest would be up to them. Then he fell unconscious and died. Though men and minor deities mourned, the great gods rejoiced at the Buddha's passage to *nirvana*:

they understood the necessity for this progression beyond the world. Deep darkness filled the sky, broken only by bolts of lightning. The Earth was thrown into tumult, and the rivers appeared to boil. His disciples built a pyre for their departed leader which burst into flames of its own accord at the moment the heavens appointed. When the flames had died down and the smoke cleared, his remains were divided up among eight princes, who set off to bear these sacred relics through all the world. The Buddha's body may have departed in death, but his spirit endured among the living; his holy life may finally have been over, but a great world religion was only beginning.

The reclining Buddha on the verge of *parinirvana*, the final departure from the cycle of rebirth that he achieved on his death. A 12th-century statue from Polonnaruwa, Sri Lanka.

CHINA'S HEAVENLY MANDATE

For more than three millennia, the emperors of China, rulers of the most populous nation on Earth, offered prayers and sacrifices to the gods and ploughed the first furrow of each new agricultural year. Known by the title Son of Heaven, the emperor served as a living link with the heavens and addressed his celestial forefathers on behalf of the Chinese nation. Politically, he dominated China, a tightly governed nation in which the gods themselves sometimes seemed like divine bureaucrats whose powers mimicked imperial rule on Earth. Some texts even described a heavenly Ministry of Thunder, with a staff of emissaries waiting, for all the world like the emperor's own officials, to carry out the edicts of the bird-headed Thunder God.

Yet this ordered cosmology was only part of a many-faceted world of myth almost as multifarious as the Chinese people themselves were numerous. In the confusion of conflicting beliefs, some strands stand out. Among the earliest ingredients was ancestor worship, posited on the belief that a part of the human soul survived death; if sustained by sacrifices, it would repay kinfolk by bringing good fortune to the family and providing guidance through divination. Another was the brand of ritual practised in early times by *wu* shamans and subsequently taken up by Daoist priests, who sought the way to achieve harmony with the physical universe. In later times, too, Buddhism would bring its own distinctive philosophy.

The most substantial corpus of myth, however, emerged before recorded time began. Using the fourth-century BC text *Questions of Heaven*, Han-period (206BC–AD220) scholars gave structure to the mass of formless myth and fragments of surviving stories by compiling a pseudo-historical body of new gods and authority figures which reflected the earthly dynasties whose rule people were subject to. So the pageant of Chinese legend – often not dissimilar in content to other Asian stories – merged with the actual past. Mythical kings – such as the serpent-bodied Fu Xi and the Yellow Emperor, established by Sima Qian (*c.*145BC–*c.*86BC) as the propagator of Chinese culture – took their place in a dynastic line of rulers that was to continue until the last emperor was forced to abdicate in 1912.

Above: A 19th-century greenish-gold Dragon Robe of embroidered silk. The splendour of the robe suggests an owner of high status.

Opposite: The Great Wall was first built in 214BC, just seven years after China's unification. At more than 2,500 miles, the wall is one of the longest structures ever made and links a series of older walls built to protect against marauding nomads.

391

From the Vapours of Chaos

In Chinese mythology, the act of creation was understood as a matter not of bringing something out of nothing, but of turning formlessness into an ordered pattern. The universe came into being when existing elements, previously mingled in chaos, were set apart in an arranged fashion. The ancient Chinese imagined the primeval chaos as a cloud of moist vapour, suspended in darkness.

In one account there was no creator as such, simply a mysterious coming into being. According to this version, before the beginning of time everything was contained in the vast cloud of moisture; all was one, until the act of ordering transformed the unity of chaos into the duality of opposites: yin and yang (see box, opposite), heaven and Earth, light and darkness. Then the interaction of opposites led to the variety and multiplicity of the universe.

In another account, from the *Huai Nan Zi* text of the mid-second century BC, two nameless gods were said to have emerged from chaos and then made the sky and Earth. The gods were so immense, stretching from the lowest depths to the utmost heights, that their size was beyond any human comprehension. The pair divided into the elements yin and yang and gave form to hardness and softness as well as the variety of all living things found in the universe.

The most commonly told tale, however, was that of Pan Gu, a late addition to the body of Chinese myth which some scholars date to the third century AD and others to the following century. It assumed great importance and came to overshadow earlier creation myths featuring the mother goddess Nü Wa (see pages 400–403). The concept of a cosmic egg and the transformation of a primordial man into the natural features of the universe are also found in Hindu mythology and many scholars argue that the Pan Gu myth was probably influenced by tales from Central Asia.

The story of Pan Gu tells how, before heaven and Earth were separated, there was chaos – vast and unknowable – containing all the elements of creation. It took the form of moist darkness within a giant egg. At its heart Pan Gu, the Creator, slowly came to life. For 18,000 years Pan Gu slumbered in the midst of formlessness, growing all the time. Finally, he awoke. He had the shape of a stout man, short in stature but with strong arms and shoulders; in one hand he held a chisel and in the other an axe. In the darkness he flailed about him with these tools, splitting

The legend of Pan Gu provides the first comprehensive Chinese account of the origin of all things. Some believe it to have been devised by the Daoist Ge Hong in the 4th century AD to give accessible form to abstract philosophical accounts of universal order. This 19th-century illustration shows Pan Gu holding the egg of chaos composed of the intertwined symbols of yin and yang.

Yin and Yang

Pan Gu's creative power separated the elements into yin and yang, Earth and heaven. In traditional Chinese thought these opposing but complementary forces are believed to permeate not just all life but the entire universe.

Yin is associated with female, absorbing qualities: passivity, darkness and the moon. Yang is linked to male, penetrating qualities: activity, brightness and the sun. In the realm of beasts, yin is the tiger and yang the dragon; in the landscape, valleys are yin and mountains yang. A broken line and even numbers are yin, an unbroken line and odd numbers are yang. Throughout the universe the two qualities are in constant fluctuation – one giving way as the other expands, so that, for example, light gives way to dark, heat to cold, and vice versa. Their interaction is understood to be the very process of life, and yin and yang are shown together as the dark and light surfaces of a circle.

The first development of the concept is lost to history but by the third century BC Daoist philosophers – led by Zou Yan – were presenting yin-yang as a theory of everything underlying history and cosmology. Zou Yan is traditionally also credited with developing the notion of the Wu Xing, or Five Elements – earth, wood, metal, fire and water – that were linked to yin-yang. This proposed that history and the universe were patterned by the interactions of the agents and that these were themselves aspects of the yin-yang fluctuation.

In Daoist thought the yin-yang opposition is a manifestation of the transcendent unity of Dao (the "Way", a philosophy emphasizing yieldingness – to "go with the flow"). Daoism also associates yin and yang with the two souls each individual possesses – the material soul (yin) and the heavenly soul named *hun* (yang). When the two were united, a person would enjoy good health, but conflict or division between them may result in illness or even death.

This amulet shows a tiger (the king of beasts and identified with the west) below a circle representing yin and yang, the opposing and complementary principles of the universe. The eight trigrams, or *Ba gua*, depicted around the circle are the key to knowledge, having been invented by Fu Xi, the first of the Three Sovereigns (see box, page 398).

the egg open and sending the elements of creation flying through space. The lighter, purer parts, or yang, flew upwards and became heaven, while the heavier ones, or yin, sank to take shape as the Earth. In one place heaven and Earth were linked but Pan Gu worked away at the join until they were separated.

The creation myths tell how various parts of Pan Gu's body became magically transformed into the five sacred mountains that are such a central part of Chinese mythology. These peaks were the source of all power and were also associated with the Five Elements. The pine-clad hillsides seen here are the Huangshan ("Yellow Mountains") in the province of Anhui.

Pan Gu stood with his feet on the Earth and the sky resting on his head. He found that the yin and yang elements continued moving apart with the force of the blows he had struck. Every day the sky grew higher by one *zhang* (ten feet) and the Earth grew one *zhang* thicker; Pan Gu increased in size at the same rate. For another period of 18,000 years he resolutely kept his place, for he feared that if he did not keep them apart sky and Earth would fall back into each other's embrace and order would collapse into chaos. By the end of this time Pan Gu was vast almost beyond imagining, stretching like an endless pillar from the ground to the furthest reaches of the sky.

Eventually Pan Gu could see that his task of separation was done. Exhausted by his toils, he lay down upon the Earth and died – and his vast body was transformed. When alive his virile action had brought order and difference out of chaotic unity, and in death he gave the plain Earth a wealth of new and beautiful forms. His breath became the winds, his voice the blast of thunder, his left eye the sun and his right eye the moon, his bristling hair and beard the glittering stars of the night sky and his sweat the rains. His hands and feet became the four corners of the square Earth, and his body the five sacred mountains that were homes to the gods (see pages 396–399). His life-blood became the rivers and streams that water the Earth, his flesh was the fields, his body-hair the grass and slender trees, his teeth and bones minerals and rocks, his semen and bone marrow precious pearls and jade. The fleas on his body transformed into the human race.

In some myths, Pan Gu controlled the weather, bringing sunshine when he was happy and storms when he was angry or sad. Despite the fact that he grew to such a size, images of Pan Gu show him as a dwarf wearing a bearskin or a dress of leaves, often with a horned head and holding the chisel and axe that he used for the creation. In some earlier versions of the myth, his head became the Eastern Mountain, his feet the Western Mountain, his left hand the Southern Mountain, his right hand the Northern Mountain and his stomach the Mountain of the Centre.

Allegory of the End of Chaos

An alternative allegorical account of the creation of order from chaos was given in the fourth century BC by the philosopher Zhuangzi. According to this version, the Emperor of the Southern Sea, Shu, and

A clothes pin which dates from the early part of the Qing dynasty and consists of two jade *bi* discs entwined with ferocious looking dragons. According to myth, jade is derived from the bone marrow of Pan Gu; and the material is considered by the Chinese to have magical and curative properties. *Bi* is the symbol for the circular sky or heaven and the hole at the centre corresponds to the *lie kou* through which the lightning flashes. The *bi* was used ritually by the king who had bestowed on him by heaven the mandate to rule on Earth provided that he remained virtuous – hence the title "Son of Heaven".

the Emperor of the Northern Sea, Hu, often met to discuss and compare their realms. Each was willing to travel halfway to encounter the other and they met in the land of the Emperor of the Centre, Hundun ("Chaos").

Hundun always made the other emperors most welcome and attended to all their needs while they were visiting him. But he suffered because he did not have the seven holes that humans have in their heads – and so could not breathe, see, hear or eat. The emperors Shu and Hu wanted to make a gift to Hundun because he was so attentive and generous to them, and suggested that they would make the holes in him to improve the quality of his life. Hundun accepted their offer happily, so Shu and Hu set to work. Each day they drilled one hole in Hundun's head; for the first six days, all went well, but while they were drilling the seventh and final hole Hundun died. In that moment, the universe was born.

The two emperors' names combined, *shu-hu*, mean lightning and, clearly, one interpretation of the allegory is that it was the electrical energy of lightning that transformed chaos. In traditional Chinese cosmogony there was said to be a hole in the top of the sky named *lie kou*, and through this aperture lightning sent its fiery darts. Hundun was sometimes thought of as a bird, and owls, in particular, were associated with chaos.

395

The Square Earth

The ancient Chinese believed that the Earth was square and unmoving, surrounded by seas on all four sides and overarched by a circular, turning sky. The life-giving rain that fell on the land ran off into the seas.

According to one cosmology known to predate the Qin era (221–207BC), the sky was like an upturned bowl, circling around the still point of the Pole Star. When Gong Gong (Spirit of the Waters) blundered into the Buzhou Mountain (see page 402), he not only made a hole in the firmament but also caused the whole sky to tip so that the Pole Star was no longer in its centre. The square Earth was yin and the circular sky was yang. The structure of the universe was often likened to that of the Chinese chariot, which had a square carriage beneath a circular umbrella; however, while the chariot umbrella stood on a central pole, the sky was usually said to be upheld by four – sometimes eight – mountains or pillars.

An alternative cosmology proposed that the universe was like a vast egg standing on end: the Earth floated on a great ocean, filling the bottom of the shell, and the stars and planets moved across the inner shell that arched overhead.

The Chinese dragon – seen here in a 16th-century frieze – was a benevolent creature embodying wisdom and strength. The First Emperor chose it as his imperial emblem.

Within the real landscape lay a mythical one with five sacred mountains – one for each point of the compass and a fifth in the centre. Each of the cardinal directions was linked to an animal, a season and an elemental force (see box, page 393). East was associated with the Green Dragon, the season of spring and the element of wood; west with the White Tiger, autumn and metal; south with the Red Phoenix, summer and fire; and north with a black tortoise-snake hybrid named the Dark Warrior, winter and water. The fifth point, the centre, identified with China itself, was associated with the color yellow and the element of earth.

It is said that the north was feared in earliest times and was not worshipped, but the emperors of the Han dynasty (206BC–AD220) claimed to hold power under its protection and made sacrifices and devotions in that direction.

The two mountains of the east and the west were particularly important. The Eastern Mountain, Taishan, was near Qufu in northeastern China. From the second century BC on, Taishan was widely believed to rise above an underworld where souls resided after death. Only great rulers

Heavenly Bodies

Ten suns and twelve moons lived at the eastern and western edges of the Earth, taking it in turns to cast light on the toils of women and men. The watery moons were yin, the fiery suns yang.

At the far east of the square Earth ten bright suns existed in the Valley of Light, where they were cared for by their gentle mother. Near the valley's edge was a lake on whose banks a hollow mulberry tree towered high in the heavens. Each morning the suns' mother washed them in the lake, then the sun whose turn it was to cross the sky climbed to the top of the tree while the other nine followed as far as the lower branches. The chosen sun rode across the heavens in a chariot controlled by its mother and hauled by strong dragons. At the end of the day, in the far west, the sun found another vast tree and returned to Earth by way of its branches. Red flowers covered the western tree and shone softly in the near dark, casting a glow across the evening sky; some people said these were the stars.

Like the suns, the twelve moons – one for each month – were cared for by their mother. They lived in a lake at the Earth's western edge and also took turns to cross the sky in the chariot.

A moonlit evening depicted with some classic elements of Chinese art, including mountains, trees and water.

were able to perform religious sacrifices on this peak. Chroniclers of the Han era set out to glorify their own emperor by telling how the Qin ruler Shi Huangdi tried and failed to perform a sacrifice there because bad weather, presumably controlled by the wind god, drove him to the lower slopes.

Sacrifices on the five mountains were a way of demonstrating wide dominion and a dynasty's right to rule. A body of stories grew up in which ores from the mountains were used for making dynastic swords. The smith became a mysterious figure and his handiwork was imbued with magical power, a little of which was thought to go into each weapon.

One such tale was told of the King of Wu near the mouth of the Yangtzi River. He ordered two grand swords from a smith named Gan Jiang. The smith set off with his pregnant wife Mo Ye,

The Three Sovereigns

The mythical history of ancient China recounts that after the death of Pan Gu, the land was governed by three rulers in turn, the last of whom ushered in the "Ten Epochs" during which men and women learned essential skills, including hunting and farming.

The first of the three rulers was the sinuous Lord of Heaven, who took the form of a great serpent with the feet of a wild animal and lived in the Kunlun Mountains in northwest China. He was a mighty creature with twelve heads who reigned for 18,000 years. His successor, the Lord of Earth, had an identical appearance and ruled for the same length of time, but he took up residence in the Dragon Gate Mountains (thought to be peaks in Henan Province). The third

was the Lord of Man, who settled in a place named Xing Ma (probably in modern Sichuan). He presided over the first of the "Ten Epochs" detailed by the ninth-century AD historian Sima Zhen, who based his work on very old sources that have since been lost.

Shen Nong (right) taught the people of China to plough the land and harvest crops. With Fu Xi, he was reinvented during the Han period as a "historical" ruler.

and travelled far and wide in the Five Mountains to find suitable ores. After he had gathered the minerals, he carefully plotted a propitious time to cast the swords – when yin and yang would be in ideal conjunction. But he found that no matter how well he planned, no matter how expertly he prepared his furnace and heated the ore, the material would not give up its metal.

He told Mo Ye that many years earlier, when faced with a similar problem, his old master and the master's wife had flung themselves into the flames, and two superb swords had been the result. Inspired by this, Mo Ye threw pieces of her hair and clippings from her nails into the furnace and Gan Jiang cast two wonderful swords, a male one that he named after himself and a female one he called after his wife. In some versions of the tale, Mo Ye also hurled herself into the furnace to enable the swords to be made.

He hid the male sword and gave the female one to the king but the king discovered the decep-

tion and slaughtered Gan Jiang. Just before he expired, however, the smith told Mo Ye that their child would grow up to avenge him – and it came to pass as he had predicted. The son cut his own head off with the sword named after his father; a stranger took it to the king, who threw the head into a furnace, and when it would not melt he was persuaded by the stranger to cut off his own head. This was cast into the flames and then the stranger decapitated himself; his head fell into the furnace, and the three human heads solidified into a single piece of metal with marvellous properties.

In the far west lay the towering Kunlun Mountain, where four rivers rose to water the four quarters of the land; and in the east, at Guixu far out in the Eastern Sea, lay five holy mountains which were home to the immortals. Kunlun was a mythical peak but was associated with the actual Kunlun mountain range in northwest China. In some versions those who found Kunlun and drank the vivid red waters that flowed from it became immortal. As the source of life-giving waters, Kunlun Mountain plays a very similar role to the Hindus' Mount Meru – and the two are often linked by scholars.

Kunlun stretched from Earth to sky, and downwards beneath the Earth's surface for the same distance. It rose through nine levels and from doors in its sides the winds blew. The east-facing door of light was guarded by a fabulous creature with nine human heads and the body of a fierce tiger. The Lord of the Sky made his home there, and the birds of Kunlun did his bidding.

The majestic palace of Xi Wang Mu, Queen Mother of the West (see box, pages 422–423), was located on Kunlun's wonderful slopes, and the mountain was also home to the Lord of the Rain, usually seen as an armour-clad warrior who used a sword to flick water onto the needy Earth. In a tale told of Shen Nong (see page 406), the Lord of the Rain used a branch to sprinkle water and save the world from a terrible drought ushered in by the god of the burning wind. One story cast the Lord of the Rain as the chrysalis of a silkworm accompanied by a magical long-legged bird. The bird appeared at the court of Qi and danced before the courtiers on one leg; when the prince sent to Confucius asking what the sighting could mean, the wise one said it was a sign of coming rain. In the storms that followed Qi was the only state not to be flooded.

Kunlun was said to be the source of the great Yellow River. Its presiding god was He Bo, known as the Count of the River, once a mortal man who had tied stones to his back and thrown himself into its waters, thereby gaining immortality and wonderful powers. His cult centred on annual sacrifices held at Ye and Linjin.

For many years until the end of the Zhou era (1030–221BC), a young woman was each year offered as bride to the Count of the River. After celebrations and ritual preparations, she was tied to a marriage bed and sent to her death on the gushing waters. After human sacrifice had ended, travellers who could afford it made offerings of precious jade ornaments to He Bo before venturing onto the river.

This boulder of jade is 16in high and has been deeply carved on both sides in the form of Red Cliff, an idyllic mountain, cleft by rushing waterfalls, its ledges dotted with pagodas and pines.

399

Mother of the World

Mother deity Nü Wa was called to save the Earth and its people when the sky threatened to fall in after a dispute among the gods. She appeared in many guises, sometimes as a beautiful goddess or a child, at others as a human-headed serpent. Fu Xi, her brother or husband, accompanied her in later versions of the myths.

In a tale from the Han dynasty (206BC–AD220) Nü Wa created the first human beings. According to this account, after Earth and heaven had come into being, Nü Wa roamed the land. The sky was filled with stars and the waters with fish, while the fertile countryside was teeming with animals – but Nü Wa felt lonely. Pausing at a pond, she looked into the waters, saw her own reflection and thought sadly how much pleasure a few companions would give her. Then it struck the goddess that she could use her divine powers to create companions in her own likeness.

Stooping low, Nü Wa took a handful of mud from the water's edge and began to mould it into shape, fashioning a tiny body with two arms and two legs. As soon as she set it down, it took life and capered on the grass before her. Nü Wa was pleased with the being she had created and set to work to make more. The creatures she made were the first people.

Nü Wa laboured until the sun in its chariot drawn by dragons had finished its journey across heaven and the night sky was sparkling with stars; then she rested, laying her head on a rock. In the morning she carried on as before. The goddess

Creator goddess Nü Wa and her husband Fu Xi are depicted coiled around one another in this Chinese silk funerary banner, which dates from the 6th or 7th century AD; their yin-yang partnership re-established cosmic harmony. The wings are indicative of immortality.

made scores of little people, desiring to fill the Earth with the creatures, but it was slow work. After some time she paused, looking about at the towering mountains and endless plains, and understood that at the rate she was going she would never be able to make enough humans to fill the Earth. So she took a rope or builder's cord, dipped it into the mud and swung it about her so that drops of mud fell on the ground all around. As the clods landed they turned into more people like those she had so laboriously moulded with her hands. In this ingenious way Nü Wa made countless humans, enough to populate the Earth in all its vastness.

Pan Gu Creates the First People

An alternative account of the first days combines the myths of Pan Gu and Nü Wa, claiming that Pan Gu himself made the first people out of clay.

The Creator Pan Gu separated heaven and Earth, and then brought plants and animals into being. But he felt unhappy with his handiwork, because none of the birds and beasts had the power of reason; he decided there ought to be one creature with the ability to care for and make use of other living beings.

With his strong, skilful hands he began to mould the first people from mud, and as he finished each figure he set it to dry in the sunshine. Some of the creatures he filled with the female qualities of yin and fashioned into women, others he endowed with the male qualities of yang, turning them into men. He worked all day beneath the hot sun, piling up his people against a rock outcrop.

As the sun went down he straightened his aching back and looked up at the sky, where he saw a bank of dark stormclouds. Some of the clay people had not yet dried and he realized that his handiwork would be obliterated if the storm broke over the figures. He hurried to move them into the shelter of a nearby cave, but as he worked a great wind arose, whipping up the clouds until they filled the sky. Pan Gu cried aloud with anguish as the thunder cracked and the rains poured down while he was still moving the figures. Those damaged were the ancestors of people with unusually shaped bodies or disabilities.

The phoenix, or *feng huang*, indicated happiness and luck – a sign of heaven's favour. Just as the dragon was identified with yang and the emperor, so the phoenix was associated with yin and the empress. The phoenix was the symbol for the cardinal direction of south – often being referred to as The Red Bird of the South – and represented drought, the element fire and the season summer.

According to many versions of the myth, the people Nü Wa made by hand were aristocrats and rulers, while those she flicked from her twirling rope became the "black-haired", a common name for peasants. The rope was sometimes said to be a reed or vine she had plucked from the bank beside the pond. The goddess was usually depicted as a human-headed dragon or snake, so clearly she did not create humans exactly in her own image. She was also said to have taught her creatures to marry and breed, for she realized that if she had to replace all the humans who died her creative task would be without end.

For many years Nü Wa's creatures lived a happy life, watching their children and grand-children grow to maturity, but then calamity struck. The overarching sky was damaged follow-ing a bitter dispute among the gods.

In some accounts the quarrel was between Gong Gong, Spirit of the Waters, and Jurong, Spirit of Fire. They fought in the far north of the country at the foot of Buzhou Mountain, a mythical peak that, according to the tales, lay northwest of the Kunlun Mountains and was one of the pillars that held the sky in position. Gong Gong sent flood-waters but they were driven back by Jurong's rav-enous fires. This defeat drove Gong Gong wild with rage. He blundered into Buzhou Mountain like a maddened boar, reducing it to rubble.

Without the mountain peak to support it, the northern sky tilted towards the ground. Half the sky tumbled in, and great cracks opened up in the Earth; the sun, moon and stars fell into the path that is familiar today. Waters poured out of the chasms in the ground, covering the plains, but on higher land, flames ravaged the forests. As a con-sequence of the shuddering impact, the northwest reared up and ever afterwards rivers and streams ran away to the southeast where they gathered to form the seas, found there to this day. Maddened by fear, wild beasts rampaged far and wide, attacking and devouring the fleeing people, while sharp-beaked birds desperate for food swept down from the skies to peck the last flesh off the bones of corpses. The seasons fell out of their proper order.

Nü Wa Repairs the Damaged Heavens

Nü Wa acted swiftly to repair the damage caused by Gong Gong. First she took some boulders from a river swollen with floodwaters and set a fire so fierce that it melted the stones to a thick liquid. She used this as a paste to patch the pieces of the ravaged sky back together. Next the goddess looked around for something to support the heav-ens and stop them falling in again, and her gaze fell on a tortoise. She took the beast, sliced off its four legs and erected them as supports for the sky at the four corners of the square Earth (see pages 396–399). She drove away the fierce beasts that had been preying on people, especially a black-skinned dragon that patrolled the Yellow River valley, whipping up floods. She controlled the floodwaters by building dykes made from the ashes of burned reeds.

Nü Wa's work was done. Order returned to the universe, and a new era of comfort was ushered in for her people. Wild animals lived peaceably alongside humans, and food crops grew quickly in the fertile soil. Nü Wa was delighted and, according to some myths, she rewarded the survivors with the first musical instrument, a thirteen-piped instrument named the *shenghuang*; in most accounts, however, it was Fu Xi who taught people how to make music (see box, page 405). Content at last, she laid herself down to die and, as with Pan Gu (see page 395), new wonders emerged from her dead body. In one account, ten gods sprang from her intestines and took up position as guards of the land of mortals.

There are many versions of the linked myths of Nü Wa and Gong Gong. In some, the skies fell in – for unknown reasons – and Nü Wa repaired the heavens long before Gong Gong came to Earth and caused further damage. Sometimes Gong Gong, rather than fighting the fire god, was said to have led a revolt against the mythical Emperor Zhuan Xu – ruler of gods and men who reigned from 2513BC to 2435BC. Some scholars

identify Nü Wa as an ancient mother deity; certainly her myth predates that of Pan Gu by several centuries. She is mentioned in texts of the fourth century BC, some 700 years before Pan Gu made his first appearance.

The myth of the toppling sky and the rearing Earth explains the topography of China, accounting for the fact that mountains rise in the northwest and there are flat, river-fed plains in the southeast. Another version of the same story, told in the *Classic of Mountains and Seas* (*c*.400BC–AD100), used the tale to explain the creation of day, night and the seasons. According to this account, after Gong Gong's collision with the mountain had torn a hole in the northwestern sky, the sun's place was taken by a red-skinned dragon with a human head. When the dragon breathed out it was winter and when it breathed in summer reigned. If its eyes were open, it was day, but when it closed them night fell. Its breath was also responsible for the wind.

The tortoise was a familiar symbol of stability for the ancient Chinese. The animal also had sacred associations: its shell was used in divination rites and its four legs were used as pillars by Nü Wa to prop up heaven, thus establishing it as a link between heaven and Earth. This bronze dates from the Han dynasty (206BC–AD220) and is inlaid with gold and silver.

The Great Flood

In later myths Nü Wa's role as great mother was modified to allow for a masculine contribution to the origin of people. According to one tale derived from the myths of the southern Yao and Miao peoples, Nü Wa and Fu Xi (sometimes called Brother and Sister Fu Xi) were peasant children who married to produce a new race of humans.

On a stormy day, dragon-bodied Thunder himself came down to Earth and was captured and caged by the peasant father of a boy and a girl. His crops ruined, the peasant decided to serve Thunder up as a meal. He needed to go out to market but told the children they would be quite safe as long as Thunder was not given any water. But while he was gone the girl became concerned by Thunder's groans and flicked a little water into his mouth. Thunder shouted for joy, then burst out of the cage with a terrible bang.

Thunder gave the children a fang from his mouth, telling them to bury it and harvest the plant that grew from it. When the peasant returned and saw what had happened he set to work building an iron ship – for he guessed that a great flood was on its way.

Meanwhile the planted tooth grew in a single day into a vine that produced a giant calabash, a kind of gourd. The children sliced off the top and found rows and rows of sharp teeth like the one they had used as a seed. They pulled them out and created a small, soft sailing boat with room for both the girl and her brother. The storm then broke and the peasant jumped into his boat and

This 9th-century Buddhist painted silk depicts a thunder-bearer. A Tang-dynasty piece, it is from an important collection of such works found in caves in the Valley of the Thousand Buddhas at the Chinese end of the Silk Road.

his children clambered into the calabash as the floodwaters rose. Little by little the mountain peaks disappeared and before too long the boats had risen so high that they reached the Ninth heaven, abode of the gods. The peasant knocked at the gates of heaven to demand entry, angering the Spirit of the Waters, Gong Gong, so much that he forced the flood to retreat with such speed that the calabash and boat hurtled downwards. The soft calabash bounced safely, but the iron boat shattered on impact, killing the peasant.

The two children were alone in the world, for all the other people had drowned. Yet they learned how to survive by planting and growing food. Because the soft fruit had saved them, they took the name Fu Xi, from the word for calabash, calling themselves Brother and Sister Fu Xi.

Eventually they married and in due course Sister Fu Xi became pregnant and produced a meatball from her womb. They chopped the strange object into many pieces and wrapped it in paper, but a sudden gust of wind swept it away and scattered the fragments, which fell to the earth where they took form as humans. A new race grew up to people the Earth.

Fu Xi Scales the Heavenly Ladder

One account of Fu Xi's life made him the son of a country maiden and the god of thunder. He had a divine nature and could come and go between Earth and heaven on the tree of Jianmu that linked the two realms.

The mythical territory of Huaxu was an earthly paradise where people lived to a very great age. They enjoyed a blessed life without fear of fire or water and could follow the invisible paths of the sky as if they were roaming on the ground. A maiden of this land was one day wandering through the swamp of Leize, when she came across a giant's vast footprints in the soft ground. Curious, she stepped into the indentation, which was the footprint of the god of thunder. She felt strangely warmed in her belly and later discovered she was pregnant. In due course she gave birth to a healthy boy, whom she named Fu Xi.

The child had the nature and attributes of a god, and he could come and go between Earth and the heavenly realm. He went by way of the tree of Jianmu which grew at the very centre of the Duguang plain in southwest China. It had long and tangled roots, but above ground grew straight up without branches for miles into the sky. No mortal could find a grip on the smooth, soft bark. At the very top, far above the Earth, there was a proliferation of branches.

The plain of Duguang where the tree of Jianmu grew was said to be the very centre of the Earth and was itself a paradise – a place where plants and trees never dropped their leaves and a wonderful and diverse menagerie of beasts and birds had assembled.

Fu Xi, traveller between heaven and Earth, taught mortal people many wonderful things. Among other things, he showed them how to make fire by rubbing sticks together, and how to use it for cooking. He made a stringed instrument and showed men and women how to make music. Inspired by the intricacy and effectiveness of the spider's web, Fu Xi also made a net that people could use for hunting and fishing.

Master of the Harvest

Ancient peoples, having been taught how to hunt and fish by Fu Xi, learned the skills needed for a more settled way of life from his successor Shen Nong, the Lord of Earth, who taught people how to plough and harvest in the same era.

When Shen Nong was born on Earth, nine wells surrounded his place of birth. They were all fed from one spring, so if water was drawn from any one it affected the levels in all the others. In this era there were many people in China and they struggled to find enough food to meet their needs, surviving by eating plants, fruits, insects, shellfish – whatever came to hand. Shen Nong was inspired to teach people how to plough the land, sow seeds and harvest plentiful food crops. He showed them the qualities of different soils, that some were fertile and that others were barren. They hailed him as the god of agriculture.

Images of the deity show him with a human body and a bull's head, associating him with the ox that pulled the farmer's plough. The ox was originally a star divinity who was dispatched by the Emperor of Heaven to reassure people on Earth that if they worked hard there would always be enough food to eat. But the deity made a mistake in delivering the message – and as a punishment was outlawed from the heavens and required to stay on Earth to help farmers.

An early 15th-century water buffalo carved out of green jade. Shen Nong is often depicted in ways that link him to fertility.

Gift of the Five Grains

One day as Shen Nong was demonstrating how to plough and plant, a bank of sandy brown clouds appeared and unleashed a storm of seeds. After the clouds had passed, Shen Nong gathered the seeds and carefully planted them. Months later a rich and varied crop covered the fertile land in all directions. The seeds he gave to humans were said to be the Five Grains – traditionally, barley, two types of millet, hemp, and vegetables such as peas and beans. On another occasion when he was instructing the black-haired peasants, a remarkable red bird flew across the plain, carrying in its beak a nine-eared plant that shed seeds as it went. Shen Nong ran about collecting the seeds and then planted them. The plants that subsequently grew from them had marvellous powers to heal and banish hunger and death.

Shen Nong also appeared as god of the fiery wind. Some scholars suggest that in this role he may have been linked with the primitive technique of preparing land by burning vegetation prior to planting seeds in the ash-rich soil. When this was superseded by more settled farming methods such as ploughing, the deity took on the attributes of a god of agriculture. One myth tells how during the fiery god's rule as emperor, there was a terrible drought and humankind was saved by Chi Songzi who took a bowl of water, dipped a small branch in it and flicked water on the ground, thereby magically summoning stormclouds that released a needed deluge. Chi became Lord of the Rain. Another of Shen Nong's achievements is said to have been the conversion of the Eight Diagrams invented by Fu Xi into the sixty-four hexagrams contained in the *Yi Jing* (*Book of Changes*).

How the Sea Defeated Jing Wei

Shen Nong's favourite daughter was the delicate, slender-necked Nü Wa, who shared her name with the great goddess who created the first people at the dawn of time. But to his dismay she drowned in a boating accident and after death she vowed to avenge herself on the sea that had killed her.

Shen Nong's daughter loved the sea and took pleasure in rowing on the deep waters far from land, watching the sea birds swoop through the buffeting winds or skim low over the waves. But one day a squall caught her boat and she was swept overboard and drowned. When she did not return that evening, Shen Nong wailed loudly in the echoing dusk – but for all his divine strength he had no power over death and could not restore his lost one to her former shape.

For her part, Nü Wa was filled with a frenzy of anger towards the cruel sea that had ended her life before its time. Her soul took the form of a white-beaked bird with a many-colored head and red feet. Named Jing Wei, the bird looked like a cross between a crow and an owl. It nested on Fajiu Mountain, a northerly peak also known as Fabao or Luge, in modern Shaanxi Province.

From Fajiu the bird flew to the Eastern Sea carrying a pebble or twig in its white beak – and dropped it into the rolling mass of water. Then the girl's spirit told the waves that she would fill them up with wood and stones and make the great ocean into nothing more than a marsh to prevent it robbing any more young people of their lives. But the sea only laughed, and told her she could never achieve her goal, no matter how hard she might try.

Jing Wei turned her back contemptuously on the proud water. She flew back to Fajiu Mountain, picked up another twig and returned to drop it into the sea. From that day on the bird known as the *jing wei* has laboured ceaselessly to fill the sea, but despite its efforts the waves still roll and crash upon the shore.

The Yellow Emperor

In traditional Chinese histories, Huang Di ("Yellow Emperor") was revered as the greatest of the sovereigns said to have ruled China in the third millennium BC, during its legendary ancient past. Hailed as the ancestor of the entire Chinese race, he was also the most significant of all the culture heroes.

According to tradition, Huang Di created the wheel, boats and oars, and taught people to build roads and cut passes through forbidding mountain ranges. He invented handwriting and introduced the arts of pottery and music to China, although in some accounts Fu Xi, Nü Wa or Di Ku was credited with developing the first musical instruments (see pages 403–405). He also devised the first calendar, and gave people instruments with which to measure the movements of the stars and planets.

Huang Di also taught the selective breeding of animals and the seasonal planting of crops and trees – so building on the legacy of his predecessor and rival Shen Nong, who had introduced agriculture to China (see page 406). Huang Di was said to have driven away the wild animals that preyed on humans, although this was also credited to Nü Wa.

One of Huang Di's gifts to the Chinese people was boats. This carved coral model shows a typical fishing vessel, with one fisherman hauling his full net from the sea and another putting some of the catch into a wicker basket.

Victory over Chaos

The Yellow Emperor made the first armour, and in the earliest surviving myths he was a warrior deity who triumphed in a series of conflicts. He fought the Fiery Emperor Yan Di, a god of war Chi You, the single-legged deity Kui and others. It was emphasized that Huang Di did not go to war out of a love of violence, but in order to restore order when it was challenged. Around him grew up a mythology depicting him as a great general who won prolonged and heroic battles against his half-brother Yan Di and other foes (see pages 410–415).

After defeating Yan Di, Huang Di became chief of the gods, assuming overall authority as God of the Centre. His defeated rival became God of the South; his great ancestor Fu Xi was God of the East. Huang Di then sent Shao Hao to be God of the West and Zhuan Xu to be God of the North. Huang Di had four faces, one facing each of the cardinal points. He could not be outwitted or defeated because he could see in all directions at once. In one myth, preserved in the third-century AD text *The Myriad Sayings of Master Jiang*, the four emperors of the cardinal directions rose up against him, but he defeated them without trouble.

Immortal Secrets

The Yellow Emperor was also said to have been the first ruler to establish and organize religious ceremonial in China. According to some accounts,

Mythical Emperors

The early historians gave China's nine mythical emperors dates of reign, an order of succession, and names and titles (listed first and second respectively, and translated where possible). The dates, were, of course, also mythical, and since most of the rulers were originally gods, their activity tended to move between Earth and heaven. The first three are often called the Three Sovereigns or Three Emperors, the last three are the Sage Kings, of whom Confucius had a high opinion.

c.2900BC   **Fu Xi, Tai Hao (Great Brilliance)**
Divine being with a serpent's body. Brother and/or husband of Nü Wa who discovered the oracular diagrams. Taught people to cook and fish with nets.

c.2800BC   **Shen Nong, Yan Di (Fiery Emperor)**
Divine being with a bird's head and a human body. He invented the cart and the plough, and taught people to clear land to grow crops. Tried out medicinal plants on himself.

c.2700BC   **Xian Yuan, Huang Di (Yellow Emperor)**
Wise ruler and great warrior who invented wooden houses, boats, bows and arrows and writing. According to Daoists he dreamed of a land where people lived in harmony with nature. Regarded as ancestor of the Chinese people.

c.2600BC   **Jin Tian, Shao Hao (Lesser Brilliance)**
Son of a weaver goddess and the planet Venus whom she met while rafting on the Milky Way. Shao Hao introduced the twenty-five-string lute.

c.2500BC   **Gao Yang, Zhuan Xu**
Grandson of Huang Di, nephew of Shao Hao. Harsh ruler who ordered the link between heaven and Earth to be destroyed. Established male supremacy.

c.2400BC   **Gao Xin, Di Ku**
Cousin of Zhuan Xu. Encouraged musical composition and ordered the musician You Chui to develop many new instruments.

c.2300BC   **Yao, Tang Di Yao**
Model emperor praised by Confucius who lived frugally and cared for the people. His ministers were wise and able but not his son, so he chose his son-in-law Shun as his successor.

c.2300BC   **Shun, Yu Di Shun**
Praised as "sage emperor" by Confucius. Protected from hardships by heaven which sent birds to weed his crops and animals to pull his plough. Standardized weights and measures, regulated rivers and divided China into twelve provinces.

c.2200BC   **Yu, Da Yu (Yu the Great)**
Founder of the Xia dynasty. Son of Gun who was appointed by Yao to control the floods. With the aid of dragons, he completed the work begun by his father.

Huang Di, or Xian Yuan, was given a pill that granted immortality by Tai Yi Huang Ren, the spirit of a mountain in Sichuan Province. Huang Di visited the peak with Chi Jiang Ziyou, who stayed on to serve the mountain god, surviving on the flowers that grew on the gently sloping sides of the peak and gradually losing his earthly body in favour of a heavenly one. This Chi Jiang Ziyou later became the divine archer Yi (see pages 418–419) and performed many heroic feats. Xian Yuan was the name of an early deity of uncertain attributes who was linked to the Yellow Emperor; in a similar way, Fu Xi was sometimes named Tai Hao and the identities of Shen Nong and Yan Di mingled. The alternative names had enduring appeal: in his Tang-era (AD618–906) work *Seven Tomes from the Cloudy Shelf*, Wang Chuan called the Yellow Emperor Xian Yuan. (Legends about Di Ku, Di Jun and Shun also have so many similarities that it is likely they were three names for the same figure, perhaps drawn from the conflicting versions of three different peoples inhabiting China in prehistory.)

Huang Di revealed the key to eternal life in a book about medicine; he also knew how to make gold, for the tablet of immortality brought with it the secrets of alchemy. With Fu Xi and Shen Nong, he was sometimes viewed as a god of healing and medicine. His young empress Lei Zu was traditionally credited with being the first human to breed worms for silk; in some accounts she was given silk and instructed in the method by the goddess Lady Silkworm (see pages 416–417).

A 6th-century terracotta figure playing the lute or *qin*, an instrument thousands of years old. In the 3rd-century BC text, *Annals of Master Lu*, Di Ku commanded a divine craftsman to make the first musical instruments. Di Ku then showed people how to play music so wonderful that the pheasants and phoenixes danced and capered with delight.

A Battle of the Elements

Strife rocked heaven, and Huang Di and Yan Di, divine rulers who shared authority over the universe, resolved to do battle to achieve total supremacy. The Yellow Emperor, fearless in conflict, prepared to defend natural order against his half-brother.

Huang Di and Yan Di drew up their vast armies on the Zhoulu Plain, now in Hebei Province. Wild beasts swelled the ranks on both sides, while hawks and vultures darkened the skies over the battlefield. But the conflict was quickly over, for Yan Di was already an old man who lacked energy and resourcefulness while Huang Di was a virile warrior god, full of wiles and bursting with vitality. Yan Di fled to the south.

In the earliest accounts, the clash was an elemental one, for Yan Di (Blazing Ruler or Fiery Emperor) was armed with fire while the Yellow Emperor fought with water, and water inevitably won. After his victory, Huang Di established order throughout the universe, taking up position as God of the Centre, assisted by four gods of the cardinal directions (see page 408). But he had to face many challenges to his authority.

When Gu, a fierce dragon god with a human face, teamed up with another deity named Qin Pi to kill the god Bao Jiang, Huang Di acted swiftly. Gu and Qin Pi were summarily dispatched by Huang Di's executioners. But upon his death Qin Pi was transformed into a monstrous osprey with tiger's feet, who ever afterwards brought strife and bloodshed wherever he went. Gu meanwhile

became a hideous yellow-spotted owl with blood-red talons, bringer of drought and famine.

On another occasion, a minor god named Wei dared to kill Jia Yu, a divine serpent with a man's face, but Huang Di was quick to punish the upstart. Wei was captured, dragged ignominiously to Shushu Mountain, in the west, and tied to a tree. Huang Di, who had knowledge of death and possessed the pill of immortality, brought Jia Yu to the Kunlun Mountains and restored him to life. Unfortunately, Jia Yu was transformed into a fierce beast who preyed on humans until the divine archer Yi dispatched him.

Glorious Victory Procession

After his resounding defeat of Yan Di, Huang Di drove in a victory procession to make sacrifices on the holiest of all mountains, Taishan. His ivory chariot was pulled by a team of sure-footed elephants and guarded by six flying dragons on each side, while red phoenixes capered in the sky overhead. Winged snakes also attended. Tigers and wolves went ahead of the vehicle, together with the wind god Feng Bo and the master of rains Yu Shi who cleaned the dusty mountain road as the emperor approached.

At the very head of the procession was the strongman Chi You, who had been a follower of Yan Di but now had to answer to Huang Di. This tall, broad-chested god of war was one of eighty-two brothers from the south. These fearsome giants had unbreakable heads of bronze, with sharp horns and foreheads of iron. The hair on their metal scalps stood up straight and sharp like the blades of knives and they each had four eyes. Their feet were hooved like those of a strong ox. Their teeth were unbreakable, too, for their diet consisted of iron, sand and pebbles.

Chi You was as obstinate as the ox he resembled and he did not take kindly to being forced into Huang Di's procession. The Yellow Emperor

An 11th-century painted handscroll depicting the cataclysmic conflict between the forces of Huang Di and Chi You and their use of fire (right) and wind (left) respectively. Huang Di's army came under attack from the wind god Feng Bo, fighting for Chi You alongside the rain god Yu Shi, and the storm drove them back. This forced Huang Di to make use of unconventional military strategies and he sent his daughter Ba, bringer of droughts, to scorch the enemy into submission. The ruse worked, although it had detrimental results for Ba herself who was forced to live on Earth thereafter.

411

himself, meanwhile, was aware of Chi You's resentment and so he ordered Feng Bo and Yu Shi to watch over him. These deities often talked with the war god and in time he won them over, persuading them to help him escape. Then, rejoicing in his freedom, he returned to the south, where he tried to rouse Yan Di to further revolt – without success, for Yan Di was old and tired of conflict. Chi You's eighty-one brothers, however, were always spoiling for battle and he was also able to win the support of the Miao people, who felt that Huang Di had mistreated them. At the head of a clamouring army, which was boosted by a force of monsters and demons who also hated Huang Di, the god of war marched northwards, declaring his undying hatred for the Yellow Emperor.

Huang Di was saved in battle by Feng Hou's compass-like device. This mariner's instrument dates from the 19th century, but basic lodestones were used from the 11th century.

Failed Peace Talks

Huang Di heard of Chi You's approach and set out to try to reason with him, for the Yellow Emperor was renowned as a peacemaker and was skilled in arbitration. But the talking failed to deflect Chi You from his violent purpose, and the two armies drew up on Zhoulu Plain, which was still littered with the bones of warriors who had fallen in the conflict between Huang Di and Yan Di. In the Yellow Emperor's ranks were slavering wolves, tigers, swift foxes, jackals and bears with claws sharp enough to shred a man's skin. He also had the dragon Ying Long and his daughter Ba ("Drought") as well as several other deities on his side.

But for all his strength, Huang Di was bested in the first exchanges, particularly after Chi You used magic to envelop the battlefield in thick fog. While the animals and monsters in Huang Di's army circled helplessly, thrown into a panic by the

thick white blanket. Chi You and his fearless warriors moved purposefully about, stealthily bringing death to their enemies.

Huang Di ordered several charges to try and break free of the fog, but everywhere his men went the mist seemed to follow and they soon lost their bearings entirely. Then the Yellow Emperor was saved by an ingenious old man named Feng Hou. Huang Di saw this man with his head bowed deep in thought and rounded on him, assuming he was sleeping. But Feng Hou was close to a solution to their problems. Despite the roar of battle and the clamour of the frightened animals, he concentrated his mind in creative thought and invented a device like a compass that could show each of the cardinal directions. He set it in the front of Huang Di's chariot in the form of a statue of a fairy whose arm forever pointed to the south. With the help of this wonderful instrument, the emperor and his army burst out of the encircling gloom.

Huang Di now turned to his divine ally and subordinate, Ying Long, who had the power to unleash devastating rainstorms. He ordered the dragon to attack Chi You's army with water, but before Ying Long could act, the wind god Feng Bo and the master of rains Yu Shi – who were fighting on Chi You's side – let loose a devastating storm and Huang Di's vast army was driven back. Pondering yet another defeat, Huang Di thought of his daughter Ba who had the power of scorching heat at her disposal, and asked her to launch an attack. It was devastatingly effective, but it was the undoing of Ba herself, for she lost the power to climb to heaven and was forced to dwell on Earth. Ba was an unwelcome guest, disliked as a bringer of drought and insulted wherever she went.

Mythical Beasts

Jia Yu's transformation into a terrifying beast, with a tiger's flesh-ripping claws and a dragon's fiery breath, is just one of many examples of the strange animal hybrids that feature in Chinese myths.

Many were peaceable creatures. The *qilin* was one whose appearance is invariably a propitious omen. The name itself combined the characters for male and female, making the animal a living embodiment of the complementary junction of yin and yang.

As the legends would have it, individual *qilin* (often the head of a unicorn with other animals' parts: a horse's hooves or an ox's tail, for example) have cropped up throughout Chinese history, always to indicate the presence of some great man. One was found in the garden of Huang Di, the Yellow Emperor, and a pair were seen in the time of the great Emperor Yao. Two were spotted in Confucius's lifetime, one just before he was born, the other presaging his death when it was knocked down by a charioteer. So when, in AD1414, the Sultan of Malindi in East Africa sent a giraffe – the first ever to be seen in China – to the imperial court as a gift, it seemed only natural to present it to the reigning emperor, Yong Le, as a fine example of a *qilin*.

During Huang Di's procession to Taishan, after his victory against Yan Di, a host of immortal spirits followed his chariot, taking many remarkable forms – some with the heads of horses or birds, others with the bodies of dragons and serpents.

A strange enamelled mythical beast from the Ming dynasty that appears to be part dragon and part feline.

413

Divine Strategy

Chi You suffered heavy defeats following the intervention of Ba, but soon afterwards the rebel forces were strengthened once again by the arrival of some members of the Kua Fu, a tribe of giants from the far north, who had been persuaded to support Chi You. The tide of the war seemed to be turning once more, and Huang Di was at a loss what to do. He put General Li Mu in charge of the imperial troops and travelled alone to the sacred peak of Taishan, where he took to his bed. But new hope came to him there in the form of a visit from a divine fairy named Xuan Nü who offered to teach him military strategy. He was delighted to accept, and over the following days learned many battlefield manoeuvres. Then he mined a magic copper from the Kunlun Mountains with which to make new swords.

Huang Di's troops, equipped with these peerless weapons and directed by the emperor with his newly acquired military expertise, soon brought Chi You's warriors to the brink of defeat. The imperial army trapped the rebels in the centre of the plain and surrounded them. The flying dragon Ying Long was a terrible sight, sweeping down from above to exact revenge, killing several of the Kua Fu giants.

Swift Justice

Finally, Chi You was captured and brought in chains before the emperor – and Huang Di ordered the rebel's immediate execution. Even in victory, however, Huang Di's followers were terrified of Chi You's awesome strength and they kept him chained and handcuffed until after he had been put to death. Ying Long himself performed the execution. Then the chains and handcuffs, drenched in the blood of a god of war, were hurled out onto the plain, far from any dwelling. As they landed they were transformed into a grove of maple trees, whose reddish leaves are whipped against each other by the wind and seem eternally to complain of the war god's cruel death.

After the battle, Ying Long, like Huang Di's goddess daughter Ba, found that he had lost an essential element of his divinity and could no longer climb to heaven. Despite his great contribution to Huang Di's victory, the dragon was cursed to live forever on Earth. He travelled sadly to the far south where he still roams among the peaks and mountain lakes.

Chi You was renowned as the first to mine metal and to introduce metal weapons to humankind. In some accounts, he was linked with a deity who tried to race against the sun but died of thirst and exhaustion; the connection characterizes Chi You as an overreacher, whose false pride made punishment and death inevitable. He was sometimes seen as a primal rebel, the first to flout authority – but later mythological treatments viewed him with sympathy. It is characteristic of the Chinese tradition that rulers or deities who rise up but are defeated – such as Chi You or Yan Di – are viewed in the myths with respect and sympathy, despite their failure.

Zhou-period bronze swords, tinged green with age, closely resemble the image conveyed of Huang Di's Kunlun copper swords. It was said that the ore was fire-red but when cast as a weapon it turned green and transparent like a fragile jewel. It was tough enough to slice through jade, and it gave off an eery white light as if cold death itself were seeping out from the blade, searching for its victims.

Huang Di and Xing Tian

After defeating Chi You, Huang Di was faced with yet another challenge to his authority. A vast giant named Xing Tian arose in the south, determined to do away with the Yellow Emperor, and the two fought a titanic struggle which began in heaven and ended on Changyang Mountain.

As he marched north, Xing Tian shook with fury, for he was a long-time enemy of Huang Di. He had once been a minister of Yan Di, and when the old god was defeated (see page 410) Xing Tian fled south with him. He had wanted to join the revolt led by Chi You, but Yan Di would not allow it. But when Chi You was vanquished, too, Xing Tian set off to confront Huang Di – then in residence in heaven.

The giant shrugged off the challenge of one guard after another until he came face-to-face with the Yellow Emperor himself. Xing Tian contemptuously challenged Huang Di to fight – and the emperor rose at once and seized his best sword. A mighty conflict ensued, in which the two warriors tested their strength to the utmost and the air around them shook with their cries.

Without noticing, they left heaven behind and fought their way across the slopes of Changyang Mountain in western China. Here Huang Di saw his opportunity and with a single stroke sliced off the giant's head. From the top of his vast body it crashed to the ground, making the mountains themselves shudder. But Xing Tian did not fall, for the blow had not killed him: headless, he could not see but still had strength for the fight.

The giant lowered himself onto his haunches and groped around on the slopes for his head. As his huge fists smote here and there, they smashed whole cliffs and entire forests. Huang Di meanwhile had the advantage. He saw where the head had landed and quickly cut open the adjoining mountain so that it rolled into the crevice. Then he sealed the mountain once more and the giant's head was encased in rock.

Lady Silkworm

Huang Di marked his victories over Chi You and Xing Tian with a celebration in his palace. While songs of triumph rang out, the exhausted emperor rested on his throne, secure in the knowledge that he had restored order to the world.

Then, in the midst of this merry-making, came a strange apparition: Can Nü ("Lady Silkworm"), the goddess of silkworms, appeared wrapped from head to toe in horsehide. She bowed to Huang Di and offered him two delicately colored reels of the finest silk, one golden and the other silver.

There were various accounts of the life of the silkworm goddess and of how she first made silk. In one the goddess was a star deity named Jian Si; in another she was identified with Huang Di's empress, Lei Zu (some sources say Xiling Ji). But in the most complete account, she was the beautiful and faithful daughter of a mortal man.

According to this tale, Can Nü's father left home and travelled far away; for an entire year his daughter pined for him and cared for the home. One day as she groomed the family horse, she murmured that she would willingly marry anyone who could find her father and bring him home. In that instant the horse bolted and Can Nü could only watch in despair as it galloped away.

Within a few days the resourceful stallion had tracked down the young woman's father. He was living at his ease in a distant place, without a thought for his daughter's needs. The stallion approached him and by stamping its feet and waving its head indicated that it wanted to return home at once. The father, wondering if his daughter was in trouble, leaped onto the horse's back.

The young woman danced with delight when she saw her father returning. They embraced tenderly and she told him how much she had missed him and how the horse, perhaps sensing this, had

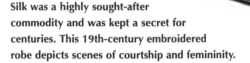

Silk was a highly sought-after commodity and was kept a secret for centuries. This 19th-century embroidered robe depicts scenes of courtship and femininity.

left one day to bring him home. From that day on, the father lavished care upon the horse, providing regular grooming and extra hay. But the creature was distressed and whenever it saw Can Nü it stamped its feet and and neighed as if in pain.

After some time the father asked his daughter if she could explain the horse's behaviour and she told him of the promise she had made – to marry anyone who brought her father home. The father ordered that the affair be kept a secret, and then he shot the horse with an arrow.

Now he thought his troubles were over. He skinned the animal and laid its hide out to dry. Then he had to go away again. That day his daughter and a friend were talking in the yard and Can Nü kicked the animal skin and laughed at it.

But as she turned away, still laughing, the skin rose up like a ghost, wrapped itself around her and whipped her away into the countryside.

Terrified, the friend ran after them but she could do nothing. When the father returned and learned what had happened, he searched far and wide for several days. Eventually, he found Can Nü, still wrapped in the skin, hanging in an unfamiliar tree. The poor man cried out: she was no longer his fair daughter, for she had been changed into a worm. As she wriggled she moved her head like a horse, and a fine thread spewed from her mouth.

Can Nü's friend named the tree "mulberry", a word derived from "mourning" (*sang*). People experimented with the thread and found they could use it to make fine cloths; they took tree cuttings and planted them, and, in time, learned how to breed silkworms for the thread.

The Fruit of the Worm

Chinese sericulture – breeding worms and producing silk – is so ancient that its origins are swathed in myth, but by the middle of the third millennium BC it had already been discovered that the silkworm's cocoon could be unravelled and woven into a soft cloth.

All that was needed to do this were the worms and the mulberry trees on which they fed – each day eating several times their own weight in leaves. Sericulture became a thriving cottage industry in rural China, with one of its bases in Henan Province in the north of the country.

For hundreds of years, the methods used were kept completely secret. Silk was not exported from China until the first millennium BC. Later, under the Han dynasty (206BC–AD220), a major trade in silk with Europe became established.

The cloth travelled along the Silk Road – a caravan trail which ran almost 800 miles from Shanghai on the China Sea through Ankara and Byzantium (Istanbul), across the Adriatic to Italy and then along the Mediterranean coast to the port of Cadiz in southwestern Spain. Han rulers made diplomatic presents of silk garments and used the luxurious cloth to pacify raiders.

Tussah silk, a less fine cloth that is made using wild rather than domesticated silkworms, was produced in India from c.1400BC. But the secret of how Chinese silk was made was kept until the mid-sixth century AD, when two Persian monks smuggled silkworms and mulberry seeds in bamboo canes to Byzantium at the request of the emperor, Justinian I, and sericulture was subsequently established in Europe. It had spread to Japan in the third century AD when, according to traditional accounts, a group of concubines secretly exported the Chinese method.

417

The Time of the Ten Suns

The first recognizably human emperor was Yao, the first of the three Sage Kings who were eulogized by Confucius for devoting themselves to bettering the lot of their long-suffering people. The greatest challenge Yao faced came when ten suns rose together in the sky.

"Why did Yi shoot the suns?" an ancient riddle asked. "Why did the ravens shed their feathers?" Most schoolchildren knew the answer, for the tale of the heroic bowman sent from heaven to help rid the country of a murderous drought was one of the best-known of all Chinese legends.

The story started with a portentous event that threatened to bring catastrophe on an apocalyptic scale. One day the people of the Middle Kingdom (China) rose as usual at sunrise, only to find an hour or so later that an angry red glow on the horizon portended the arrival of a second sun. Before long a third orb was mounting the sky, and then a fourth. Throughout the day new suns kept rising until no fewer than ten were spaced out equidistantly across the blazing firmament.

Down below on Earth, the heat was intense. People cowered in their huts, trying to find shelter. Crops shrivelled in the fields, and lakes and ponds dried up. Animals collapsed from exhaustion, and all activity ceased.

Faced with the greatest crisis of his reign, Yao prayed to Di Jun, God of the

A glazed earthenware tile in the form of a celestial archer on horseback, dating from the Ming dynasty. According to another myth, in addition to the nine suns Yi also shot the Celestial Dog, one of the animals which was said to devour the moon in times of eclipse.

Eastern Heavens, for aid. The emperor knew that if anyone in the celestial sphere could help, it was he, for he presided over the distant valley where the great Fu Shan tree grew. This was a giant mulberry in whose branches the ten suns, which in those days normally took turns to light up the sky, nested during the hours of night.

The suns chose to take their rest among the boughs for inside them were mystic birds, the jun-ravens, whose pinions carried the suns on their daily journey across the sky. These birds – indeed, the suns themselves – were the offspring of Di Jun and the goddess Xi He. Each morning she would bathe one of her children in the Sweet Springs which flow in the Sun Valley before sending it off on its life-giving journey.

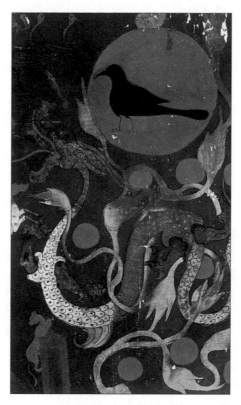

A jun-raven is depicted within a sun in this hanging silk, dating from *c.*200BC, which portrays the nine suns of legend destroyed by Yao's divine archer, Yi.

Now, however, for reasons that no one ever understood, all ten suns had decided to rise at once, and only divine intervention could prevent the entire world from burning up. Realizing the extreme gravity of the situation, Di Jun heard the emperor's plea and sent his most valued assistant to help undo the damage. This was Yi, the greatest bowman on heaven or Earth.

There was nothing unearthly in the appearance of the strapping young man who strode into Yao's presence, offering his services. Yao greeted his divine assistant eagerly, then took him to a window so he could see for himself the damage that was being done.

Yi had hoped, on first learning of his mission, to be able to settle the matter peacefully, but a single glance at the scorched land was enough to convince him that desperate measures were needed. Grasping his bow, he asked to be taken to a high tower from which he would have an unimpeded view of the heavens.

There he fitted an arrow to the string and took aim at the easternmost sun – the last of the suns to have risen. The shaft sped straight to its mark, striking the sun like a bird in flight – and, sure enough, as its light was snuffed out, a shower of black feathers fluttered down to Earth from the jun-raven within it.

Yi fired off a second arrow, then a third, and other suns fell. Word of his presence spread, and knots of anxious people began to appear on the roads and rooftops. The first cries of hope arose as the fourth and fifth suns were extinguished, and after Yi had taken aim at the sixth and seventh a roar was swelling from the now-crowded streets.

By the time he had shot down the eighth, the sky was darkened by the swirling rain of black feathers, and a glorious coolness began to spread across the land. Buoyed up by the cheers of the rescued people, Yi fitted a final arrow to his bow and sighted along its shaft at the ninth sun. As it in its turn exploded into blackness, he finally dropped the great weapon, leaving the last, westernmost sun to complete what was left of its journey to the horizon unmolested.

Yi had killed nine of the ten suns, leaving just one to illuminate the world for all future time. He had made himself a hero of humankind and had won the eternal gratitude of Emperor Yao. But time would tell that he had done so at the cost of making enemies in heaven. He would have cause to rue the divine wrath in time to come.

419

The Elixir of Life

Banished from heaven by Di Jun for killing the sun-birds, Yi went in search of the magic potion that could restore the immortality he had consequently lost. But the drug ended up in the wrong hands, and Yi had to undertake a fearsome quest to try to undo the damage.

When Yi had shot down the nine suns, he quickly learned that his task on Earth was far from completed. For all Emperor Yao's best efforts, the Middle Kingdom remained beset by such a catalogue of calamities that it seemed as though the world was returning to its primal state of chaos. Only the hero Yi could put things to rights.

Yi's Heroic Missions

And so the bowman set off on a series of missions that rivalled the Labours of Herakles in their epic scope. First he had to deal with storms that were sweeping across China, uprooting crops and tearing down houses in their path. Using his divine power to travel on the wind, he tracked the gales back to their source, which turned out to be Taishan Mountain, far to the east. Yi then knew his adversary, for the mountain was the home of Fei Lian, the Count of the Winds, a fearsome spirit who generally took the form of a one-eyed bull with the tail of a serpent.

Using sheets to divert the wind, creating a corridor of calm air through which he could climb the mountain, Yi confronted the troublemaker in his lair. Fei Lian had shapeshifting powers, and at first Yi saw nothing but a seemingly innocuous sack standing in front of a cave's mouth when he reached the summit. For a moment the hero was fooled, but then he saw that the sack was straining at the seams under the pressure of the winds contained within it. Fitting an arrow to his bow, he fired at it. At once the bag burst asunder and in its place stood Fei Lian himself, bellowing.

420

A moonlit night in northern China evokes thoughts of eternity, for the Chinese myths related that it was on the moon that the white hare or rabbit resided that was believed to prepare the potion of immortality.

Seeing Yi reaching for another arrow, Fei Lian ran back into the cave, drawing his sword as he went. But Yi followed him and loosed a shaft that struck the wind god in the knee, dropping him to the ground. Wounded, he lost the will to fight, and grudgingly offered his submission.

With the threat of storms removed, Yi set off next to tame a river that had burst its banks. Suspecting that some turbulent river god was behind the trouble, he loosed an arrow at random into the swirling waters. Sure enough, the flood receded, revealing a white-garbed figure riding a white horse, surrounded by a dozen attendants. Before the spirit could escape, Yi fired again, wounding him in the eye, whereupon he whipped on his horse and fled, leaving his companions behind him.

Instantly, Yi took aim at the nearest figure. In the nick of time he realized his target was a girl and swung the bow so that the arrow whistled harmlessly through her hair. In gratitude she flung herself at his feet, and he learned that her name was Heng E and that she was a sister of the vanquished water god. Startled by her unworldly beauty, Yi asked her on the spot to be his wife, and Heng E accepted.

Yi's troubles were still far from over, for a plague of monstrous creatures had also chosen this time to maraud through the Middle Kingdom, spreading devastation in their wake. There was Chiseltooth, a fearsome giant with a single huge incisor protruding from the top of his mouth, which he used to rend his victims' flesh. A monstrous water serpent was disrupting the calm of Dongting Lake. The Windbird was a gigantic peacock that could cause storms merely by flapping its wings. All these menaces Yi dispatched with his bow, winning for himself from a grateful Emperor Yao the illustrious title of Marquis Pacifier of the Country.

An 8th-century Tang-dynasty tile showing a fierce creature which matches the description of Chiseltooth, a giant with a huge tooth used to rip his victims apart.

The Banishment of Yi

But if Yao was pleased with Yi's triumphs, Di Jun was not. Yi had killed the sun-birds, his errant children, instead of merely bringing them to heel; and for that the god could not easily forgive him. In his anger, he let it be known that he was banishing the bowman from the heavens; since Yi cared so much for the well-being of Earth, he could live there as a mere mortal.

The news left Yi dumbstruck. Searching for a way to regain what he had lost, he could think of only one possible course of action. He would travel to the palace of Xi Wang Mu, the Queen Mother of the West, on Kunlun Mountain where Huang Di himself lived. There he would seek of her the elixir of immortality, distilled from the

421

wonderful peaches that grew nowhere but in her garden (see box, below).

Yi set out at once. Using his magic power of flight he travelled westwards to the fairy queen's palace, soaring effortlessly over the vast moat and the ring of fire that protected it. Once inside, he sought out Xi Wang Mu and humbly begged for the elixir, offering in return to serve her faithfully in any way she might choose. Pleased by his courtesy, the queen decided to favour his request. Knowing that he had great skill as an architect, she asked him to build her a summer palace in exchange for the drug.

For many months he laboured, creating a residence fit for a goddess, its floors made of glass and its walls of translucent jade. When it was finished it pleased the queen, and in payment she handed over a distillation of the elixir in the form of a tiny pill so potent that it glowed with a soft, evanescent light. Before Yi left, she warned him that he must not take it at once; to benefit from the potion's mystical powers, he must first prepare himself by prayer and meditation.

The Immortality of Heng E

Yi returned in triumph with his trophy. But on his arrival he found that Emperor Yao had urgent tasks waiting for him, and he had to leave home again without delay. Fearing that the pill might be stolen while he was away, he hid it in the rafters of his house.

He had hoped to be back before long, but he was mistaken. There were dangerous wild boars

Mystic Mistress of a Western Paradise

Xi Wang Mu, the Queen Mother of the West, was the fairy goddess of Chinese myth, and at one time people looked to her in hope of personal salvation. Yet there may have been fragments of historical truth behind all the tales of her magical fruit and golden palace.

According to the legends, Xi Wang Mu lived in a palace of pure gold set high on the summit of Mount Kunlun, a mythical peak in the west that may reflect distorted reports of the Hindu Kush. The walls that ringed it were 1,000 *li* (approximately 330 miles) in length and were topped with battlements of precious stones. There she lived surrounded by a celestial entourage that included the five Jade Fairy Maids. Whenever she left her paradise, she travelled on a white crane and used a flock of bluebirds as her messengers.

to be hunted down and a dragon that was terrorizing the Yellow River valley had to be confronted. Weeks dragged into months, and still his wife had no news of him.

Left on her own once more, Heng E pined for her absent husband. In her boredom she wandered the house alone, until one day her eye was caught by a strange light glowing from the roof-beams. Going to investigate, she found the magic pill wrapped in a silk covering.

She realized at once that the pill had special significance and she knew that she should leave it alone. But curiosity got the better of her. Taking it from its hiding place, she carried it downstairs to study it further. She was still holding it when, hearing a commotion outside, she stepped out of the house to find that, without warning, her hus-

band had at last come home. Panic-stricken, she swallowed the pill.

At once an extraordinary sense of lightness came over her. Escaping the pull of gravity, she found herself helplessly drawn upwards. Yu saw her plight but was at a loss to know what was happening – until he noticed the pill's silk wrapping lying discarded on the ground. Too late, he tried to seize Heng E, but she was already well beyond his reach, soaring heavenwards at an ever-faster rate.

She continued her ascent unimpeded until she reached the moon. It proved a desolate place, with no vegetation but a cassia tree. The only living things there were the white hare that the Chinese, like other peoples around the world, see in the markings on the moon's face, and the

In the palace gardens grew the Peaches of Immortality, mystical fruit that took 3,000 years to grow and a further 3,000 to ripen. Whenever one of the fruit matured, the goddess served it as the centrepiece of a feast whose other courses included monkeys' lips, dragons' liver and phoenix marrow. Guests were entertained by music from invisible instruments and songs from fairy tongues.

For a time around the end of the first millennium BC, a cult formed around the queen and her western paradise, though before long it was supplanted by the greater attractions of the Daoist and Buddhist heavens. Yet in the earliest references the Queen Mother of the West was treated not so much as saviour or goddess as a real-life ruler of some unidentified western state. According to a history of the

Zhou dynasty, written in the second century BC, she is said to have received the Emperor Mu Wang in 985 BC at a place called the Jewel Lake. Possibly it was that evocative place-name that inspired the later fantasies of the poets.

The gathering of the immortals at the golden palace of Xi Wang Mu by the banks of the Jewel Lake.

The moon (left) and the sun (right) from an 11th-century handscroll, personified as female and male respectively. In the story of Yi and Heng E, Yi represented the warm male principle of yang, and resided accordingly in the palace of the sun, while Heng E represented the female principle of yin and lived in the palace of great cold, situated on the moon. Thus, natural and cosmic balance occurred.

his story in silence, then told him the gods' judgement on his actions. They had taken pity on him for the misfortunes that had afflicted him in return for the great labours he had undertaken on Earth. They had decided that he should take his place again in their own ranks, only now he would occupy the palace of the sun. In so doing, he would lend it a male, yang presence to counterbalance the yin of Heng E's residence on the moon.

As Yi was leaving, the immortal handed him a leaving gift. It was a small red cake inscribed with a lunar talisman. It would, he was told, give him the power to visit Heng E, though she would never be able to come to him. That is why, Chinese people used to say, the light of the sun illuminates the moon but the moon cannot light up the sun.

So Yi took up his heavenly residence, relying on the experience of the sole surviving sun-bird to keep the orb moving on its diurnal course. It was not long before he first made use of the immortal's gift to visit his wife, who received him with rapture after her long spell of solitude. The two agreed that he should in future call on the fifteenth day of every lunar cycle. And so he still does, bringing yin and yang together to make the moon shine with an extra brilliance in the night sky at that time.

three-legged toad which was believed to devour it during eclipses.

And there she stayed, cursed with an immortality she had never wanted. In later times, she would be worshipped by the Chinese as Chang E, the Moon Goddess, and people would think sadly of her isolation as they gazed at its brightly shining orb on frosty winter evenings. (Her name was changed officially in *c*.2BC because Heng E broke a taboo concerning the emperor's own name.)

Yet she was not forgotten by her husband Yi. He sought in vain for a way to follow her up into the highest heavens, and finally decided to visit Xi Wang Mu's consort, a mighty being known as the King Father of the East. The immortal king heard

The Death of Yi

According to some accounts, Yi never regained immortality after his wife took the elixir of life. Instead, the great archer finally fell victim to the jealousy of a human rival he had chosen to befriend.

Feng Meng's skill at archery was surpassed only by that of Yi himself. Yi did his best to encourage the young hunter, teaching him the finer points of the bowman's art: how not to blink when aiming, the special skill of learning to see small objects as if they were large.

Under Yi's tuition, Feng Meng's talent blossomed. Soon he began to consider himself a rival even for his divine master. One day he challenged Yi to a shooting contest, taking aim at a flight of geese high up in the sky.

In an instant he had shot down three of the birds as they flew in line, each one with an arrow through the head. Before Yi could draw, the rest of the flock scattered across the skies, creating a seemingly impossible target. Even so, Yi brought down another trio just as neatly as his pupil, convincing Feng Meng that he would never outdo him.

In his bitterness, the hunter planned to kill Yi, knowing him to be now as mortal as any other man. Taking cover in a forest, he sought to ambush him, but each time that he sent an arrow whistling through the air, Yi countered with another that struck its shaft in mid-flight.

Thwarted at bowmanship, the assassin resorted to cruder methods to achieve his goal. Accompanying the unsuspecting Yi on a hunting trip, he waited until his companion had set aside his bow to pick up a bird that he had downed. Then he leaped upon him, bludgeoning him to death with the peachwood rod he used to carry home the game.

Yao Finds an Heir

Hard-pressed to find an heir to succeed him, the Emperor Yao finally settled on a humbly born farmer called Shun. His elevation to the highest office in the land was testament to the worthiness of virtue and filial piety, that is behaving respectfully towards parents.

Yao had been worn down by waging an unceasing battle against catastrophic floods and needed a right-hand man to help him. In the back of his mind, too, was the search for an heir, for he already knew that his son Dan Zhu (see box, opposite) was not up to the job. So he called a grand council and asked the wise men of the realm to suggest a suitable candidate. Each name put forward was rejected for various reasons. Finally, in despair, Yao asked for a fresh suggestion, adding, "It doesn't matter whether he's a gentleman or not, just so long as his virtue is adequate." At once several recommended Shun. Yao replied that he had heard the name, but asked to know more of him.

Shun's mother had died young and his father had remarried. His stepmother, who Shun had vowed to love as dearly as his late mother, had a son of her own, Xiang, and she did not reciprocate Shun's affections – instead, she plotted wickedly against him in favour of her child. Although treated terribly unjustly, Shun accepted the situation and was favoured by the gods for his forbearance. He never disowned his family and later gave them help when they needed it most. Yao listened to the tale of Shun's tribulations in silence, then said bluntly, "I will try him."

And so the young man was summoned to court and offered high office. An amazed Shun protested that he was unworthy, but the emperor insisted – while making it clear that Shun was on trial and would face instant dismissal if he proved unfit for the responsibilities placed upon him.

For three years Yao watched Shun's every action. He devised difficult challenges to test his mettle, but Shun overcame

Wooden Ming-dynasty figure of an aged Chinese dignitary wearing full robes and an official's hat. Such men offered advice in court and wielded considerable influence; indeed, it was such people who proposed Shun to Yao.

The Preposterous Dan Zhu

Emperor Yao chose not to pass on his throne to his son Dan Zhu, who for later generations became the archetype of the irresponsible heir unfit to inherit high office.

Dan Zhu's selfishness and insensitivity knew no bounds. He loved to go on boat trips even when drought gripped the kingdom, forcing sweating minions to carry the craft along the dried-up riverbeds. When his father taught him chess to keep him harmlessly occupied, he chose to play it in the most extravagant way, planting an entire plain in a chequerboard pattern of groves and open spaces and using live rhinoceroses and elephants to serve as the thirty-two pieces.

In time his excesses so alienated Yao that the emperor determined to banish him to the far south. There the angry prince stirred up trouble, raising the flag of revolt among disaffected border tribes. But he had no talent as a military leader, and soon he and his supporters were fleeing for their lives from the emperor's armies, halting only when they reached the sea. There, in his despair, Dan Zhu

killed himself by leaping into the waters. But it was not the end of him, for his spirit took the form of a bird called the *zhu*, shaped like an owl but with human hands. In later times it showed itself only in lands that were badly governed, its appearance a sure sign that high officials were about to be dismissed.

---

them and the emperor's admiration for him grew steadily. Eventually he paid Shun the ultimate compliment – giving him two of his daughters in marriage. Yao, his health failing, knew that at last he had found his man. Finally, he summoned Shun to the audience chamber before all the the dignitaries of the realm. "Approach, Shun," he said, stepping down from the throne. "For three years I have compared your deeds with your words, and you do what you say. Ascend the Dragon Seat!"

The entire court bowed low as Shun stepped up, first to reign jointly with Yao as regent and later, when the old emperor died, to rule alone. He proved a fit successor in every way, showing the same virtue and wisdom. And even in his new eminence, he never forgot his duty to his family, conferring on his stepbrother Xiang a high position at the court. Xiang proved so grateful for the mercy shown to him that he forgot all his earlier grudges and became a most loyal subject.

427

Yu Mounts the Dragon Throne

After reigning for many peaceful years, the dying Shun named as his successor his faithful regent Yu, who had completed the task of taming the floods. As emperor, Yu started China's first dynasty, the Xia, and a pattern of hereditary monarchy that lasted for millennia.

Once he knew that he was not much longer for this world, Shun confirmed that Yu was his heir and passed on some advice to his successor that the *Book of History* faithfully recorded: "Be reverent. Behave carefully on the throne which you will occupy, and respectfully cultivate the virtue expected of you." Then the wise old emperor died.

After observing a three-year official period of mourning for Shun, who was deified once he had passed over into the spirit world, Yu flung himself energetically into the task of governing the Middle Kingdom. Etched in Yu's mind was an extraordinary encounter he had had years earlier with the god Fu Xi inside a mountain during a hydrological tunnelling project. Fu Xi had encouraged him to see the flood-control work through and predicted that Yu would one day bring political order to China. Fu Xi had then presented him with two jade tablets to help him measure and map the kingdom.

As emperor, Yu now passed the tablets on to two officials, one of whom travelled from north to south and the other from east to west. Once back at court, each reported an identical distance: 233,500 *li* and 75 paces, or approximately 78,000

An undated scroll depicting the building of dykes during the reign of Kangxi (1661–1722). Dykes efficiently complemented channels as a means of controlling floodwaters, and during Yu's reign some spectacular drainage tunnels were built through the Wu Shan Mountains in Sichuan.

Benevolent Monsters

Unlike their malign counterparts in European tradition, Chinese dragons were usually regarded as auspicious beasts.

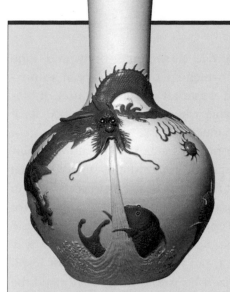

A detail of a 19th-century ceramic dragon spouting water from high in the clouds, reflecting the dragon's traditional role as a bringer of rain.

In Chinese myth, dragons seem to have had their origins as rain deities, and the connection with water always remained strong. They were usually thought of as living in lakes and rivers; some authorities also think they had a connection with the Yellow Springs, the underground stream through which the sun was held to travel in the night-time hours. They were regularly invoked in time of drought, and the Dragon Dance that is still performed at Chinese New Year festivities today originated as a ritual designed to encourage rain.

Though they were powerful creatures capable of doing great harm, dragons were generally portrayed as protectors, guarding treasure, or even heaven itself, keeping watch over waterways and the clouds and winds. Their image of beneficent power was appreciated by China's rulers, who appropriated the dragon as an imperial symbol.

miles – confirming the ancient Chinese view that the world was square (see pages 396–399).

Yu himself resumed the peripatetic lifestyle he had known as the flood-tamer, journeying constantly to every quarter of his realm. On his travels he saw many wonders. One was Yuqiang, god of the ocean wind, who lived at the world's northernmost limit. Said to have a bird's body with a human face, it was he who had been delegated to moor the five holy mountains that were home to the immortals to a fixed position in the Eastern Sea at Guixu – a task he achieved using turtles.

Much of Yu's time now was spent on problems of administration as he strove to provide a framework of just government for a land still reeling from its long history of natural catastrophe. He ordered a population census and a survey of the fields. Officials checked all the openings through which underground springs had bubbled up in the time of floods. They listed almost a quarter of a million sizeable vents, all of which were adequately blocked up. But the smaller outlets, less than eight paces across, were innumerable, and it was considered impractical to fill them all. That, ancient writers claimed, was why small-scale flooding continued in China to their day, even though cataclysmic inundations no longer occurred as they did in Shun's time.

As part of a general reorganization, Yu divided the Middle Kingdom into nine provinces, each with a governor and an appointed tribute of lacquers and silks. Ores sent from the regions were used to make nine magnificent tripod cauldrons, each decorated with insignia representing the people and products of the relevant district. These vessels were passed down from ruler to ruler and became important symbols of imperial power. It was said that the tripods increased in weight when China was well governed and grew lighter in times of bad rule. So when Yu passed them on to his son Qi, it took ninety oxen to move one, but in the last, decadent days of the Xia dynasty a single person could carry it away.

For all his successes, Yu remained profoundly humble, all too aware of the limitations of his achievement. On one occasion, while out riding he met a criminal in chains and is said to have burst into tears, protesting that the existence of crime in his kingdom was proof that his own virtue as a ruler was insufficient. On another

429

occasion, he submissively sat through a homily from his chief minister, who reminded him of the duties of a good king – not to have preconceived notions, to listen to the views of all, to aid the helpless and support the poor. Listening to the list, Yu threw up his hands in despair, protesting "Only the Emperor Yao could maintain that standard" – to which the minister replied that Yu would not have been granted the Mandate of Heaven if his virtue had not been up to the job.

Yu Fights the Serpent with Nine Heads

Although peace had returned to the Middle Kingdom, threats still arose from time to time that required all Yu's old courage and initiative. One such occasion occurred late in his reign, when word reached him of a monstrous creature called Xiangyao that was ravaging an outlying district of his realm. It came as no surprise to learn that the scourge was an emissary of Yu's old flood-era enemy Gong Gong, the water spirit, sent to spread misery and desolation in the newly ordered lands.

The beast had a serpent's body and nine heads, each of which spat forth a venom so noxious that it laid waste all the land around. It was huge in size, and when at rest it wrapped itself round nine separate hills.

At first Yu hoped to take the creature by surprise, but he quickly realized the futility of that plan. Even as it rested, its heads were constantly in motion, scanning every point of the compass for food to eat or enemies to kill. For a time the old emperor was hard pressed to come up with a way of confronting it, but then he had a flash of inspiration. He realized he would once more need the services of an old ally, the Winged Dragon. They would ride together for a final time.

What Yu had noticed was that the serpent never looked upwards, apparently assuming that no danger was to be expected from that source. So Yu mounted the dragon, sword in hand. Together the pair soared up and circled round until they were directly above their prey. Then they dropped almost vertically upon it as its reptilian eyes unsuspectingly scoured the horizon below.

Yu's sword flashed in the sunlight, and two heads were gone before the monster had time to react. Then it made a fight of it; its remaining heads bobbed and weaved like flails threshing grain. But the dragon was nimble and Yu's aim was unerring. As the final head was lopped off, the great body shook convulsively and lay still.

Yet the harm the beast caused did not die with it. From its mouths a steady flow of venom trickled, blighting the fields where they lay. Yu gave orders for the heads to be covered over with earth, but the poison in them found its way into the ground water, spreading to the land around.

The same thing happened when the remains were dug up and interred together in a single huge mound. Eventually the only solution proved to lie in burying them on an island in an artificial lake, whose waters served to soak up the remaining toxins and to insulate the neighbouring district from their virulence.

Yu had reigned single-handedly for only eight years when he killed Xiangyao, but he sensed that his time was almost up. He decided to go on a final tour of his realm. It was on this trip that death came to him, suddenly but peacefully while he was visiting Kuai Ji Mountain where, many years earlier, he had summoned the spirit army to do battle with Gong Gong. His body was buried in a great cave on the mountainside that in later times would become a place of pilgrimage. The historian Sima Qian visited it as a young man in Han dynasty times more than 2,000 years after Yu's death, paying his respects to the hero as part of a grand tour of his country's antiquities.

It was Sima Qian, too, who reported that Yu nominated his chief minister, Bo Yi, to succeed him on the Dragon Throne, but that the lords of the land refused to accept his candidate. Instead they pledged allegiance to Yu's son Qi, thereby establishing the hereditary principle that was to survive in China through all its various dynasties. Qi duly took up office as the second ruler of the Xia dynasty; and the oppressive weight of the nine bronze cauldrons throughout his reign can be taken as evidence that he did his best to follow worthily in the footsteps of Yao, Shun and Yu.

A dramatically fierce-looking, serpent-like dragon, in gold thread, decorates this 17th-century *kesi*, or silk tapestry. The dragon is depicted with all the traditional elements: a reptile's scaly skin, a stag's horns, long feline whiskers and four claws (five signified an imperial symbol). There are clouds and waves too, connecting the dragon to both water and sky, its two principal domains.

The Fall of Dynasties

In China's moralistic view of history, dynasties collapsed when their rulers misbehaved. Just as the virtues of the Sage Kings promoted their subjects' well-being, so the wicked ways of two notorious tyrants guaranteed trouble and the Heavenly Mandate was withdrawn.

If the early histories are to be believed, the Xia dynasty took its course peacefully for almost 500 years through seventeen successive rulers. The last of these, however, was a tyrant who bled the people dry to cater for his own pleasures.

Jie would waste a fortune on a whim. One of his concubines liked the sound of tearing silk, so

bale after bale was shredded for her pleasure. And he was as cruel as he was extravagant. He once set tigers from the royal zoo free in a marketplace, simply for the pleasure of seeing the people running for their lives.

Unsurprisingly, he was much hated, and when Tang, the Lord of Shang, raised the standard of revolt against him, people flocked to join his cause. The defeated emperor fled south, where he died shortly afterwards, a lonely exile dreaming of his lost powers.

The Shang dynasty brought China out of the era of myth and into history. Yet there was one Shang ruler about whom legends would accumulate, and once again he was the last of the line.

Zhou Xin was a despot in the mould of Jie. He was strong and he was intelligent, but it was said of him that, "With his eloquence he refuted good advice, and with his wit veiled his faults."

When one of his vassals, the Prince of Zhou, showed signs of discontent, Zhou Xin arrested him and took his son hostage. At a banquet one night, the emperor remarked drunkenly of the prince: "They say he's a wise man and knows many things. Do you think he'd be clever enough to recognize the taste of his own son?" Upon which, he gave orders for the son to be killed and boiled in a broth, which was duly served to his prisoner. Zhou Xin laughed uproariously when he heard that the prince had unsuspectingly drunk it.

This barbaric act was an error the emperor was to live to regret. The prince's heir, Wu, raised

A depiction of Emperor Wu by an unknown artist. Wu was the first ruler of the Zhou dynasty on whose behalf many gods had fought to overthrow the despotic regime of the last Shang emperor, Zhou Xin.

the standard of revolt, and rebels flocked to his side from across the kingdom. And according to the story-tellers the Prince of Zhou had divine aid too, receiving the help of the gods of the rivers and the seas and the deities of wind and rain.

The two sides finally met at the decisive battle of Mu in 1027BC. Historians record that Zhou Xin's soldiers quickly turned tail and fled. In the myths, however, the earthly struggle was accompanied by an epic combat, the Battle of Ten Thousand Spirits, in which gods joined the fray to rout the forces of evil in heaven as on Earth.

The defeated Zhou Xin then made his way back to his palace, dressed himself up in his most splendid robes and set fire to the building.

In the centuries that followed, the fates of Jie and Zhou Xin became object lessons for philosophers and historians, illustrating the evils that descended on the kingdom when its rulers abandoned virtue for sensual delights. The two became the obverse of the Sage Kings, dire warnings to later generations whose fates showed all too graphically that the Heavenly Mandate could be withdrawn if sovereigns ruled without consent.

Zhou Xin the Shang Sadist

Zhou Xin was said to be intelligent, though in a highly perverse way. He satisfied his inquisitiveness with horrific experiments.

To judge from the stories, he had a particular interest in the workings of the human body – one that he indulged in a vicious manner. Seeing some peasants wading through a stream in mid-winter, he had their legs cut off so he could study the effects of the cold on their bone marrow. When his uncle, Prince Bi Gan, once reproved him for his failings, he replied, "You're said to be a sage, and I have heard that sages have seven openings in the heart" – whereupon he ordered that the prince be killed and cut open so that he could check if the claim was true.

A CITY OF SYMBOLS

For the last five centuries of imperial rule, the hub of Earthly power was a walled complex of residences and audience chambers in the heart of Beijing's inner city. There resided China's emperor, the occupant of the oldest throne in the world, the Son of Heaven and the "Lord of 10,000 Years" with a divine right to rule known as the Heavenly Mandate. Following the principles of geomancy, the Forbidden City was laid out on a north-south axis with its four gates oriented to the cardinal points of the compass. Lined up in the centre were the great ceremonial buildings: the Hall of Supreme Harmony, from which state edicts were promulgated; the Hall of Perfect Harmony, where the throne stood; and the Hall of Protective Harmony, in which scholars and diplomats were received. In each, care was taken to ensure that the emperor always sat facing south, a propitious direction associated with the yang principle. The layout of the complex reflected ancient Chinese ideas that the world was square, with China itself – the Middle Kingdom – at its sacred centre.

Throughout the buildings and court-yards of the Forbidden City, animal symbols abounded in the form of cranes, lions, turtles and other beasts, many of them designed to protect the emperor and his entourage from evil spirits. One, however, dominated: the dragon, the symbol of authority, fertility, goodness and strength and the benevolent bringer of wealth and good fortune, was omnipresent. The emperor occupied the Dragon Throne, wore Dragon Robes and even slept in the Dragon Bed. The ordinary people of China sometimes referred to themselves as Children of the Dragon. In addition to the animals, there was an important use of color: azure, red, yellow, white and black constituted the Five Colors. Red and yellow were particularly prominent in the Forbidden City. The temples and palaces were red to bring good fortune, for it is the color associated with summer, fire and the south; while many of the roof tiles were glazed yellow, symbolic of earth, and the imperial shade that represented the Middle Kingdom.

Above: A painting on silk of the city by Zhu Bang. Only senior figures could enter the three-arched Meridian Gate, whereupon they crossed one of five bridges, numbered for their symbolism.

Top left: A bronze dragon, the animal most associated with imperial power.

Left: The Hall of Supreme Harmony, or Tai He Dian, with its "bird-wing" roof, was where the emperor celebrated the New Year and the winter solstice, appointed generals and read out the names of those who had passed their exams to gain entry to the civil service.

A Bureaucracy of Gods

The priests of China's earliest organized religions – native Daoism and imported Buddhism – gradually incorporated a host of folk beliefs. As the structures of the faiths evolved, their many gods meant they resembled heavenly versions of imperial rule on Earth.

The founders of Daoism recognized no gods at all. Laozi's *Dao De Jing* (*Way and its Power*) and Zhuangzi's *Zhuangzi* spoke only of the Dao itself, the ineffable wellspring of all being. The Dao, they said, had no name, for the act of naming involved differentiation while it was in everything as the primal force. The individual's goal was to live in tune with the Dao, which meant learning to go with the grain of the physical world rather than trying to impose a pattern. In practice, Daoism favoured spontaneity over planning, the unconscious over the conscious mind. Politically, it stood for laissez-faire government rather than state intervention; the highest ambition of a ruler should be not to be seen to be governing. Daoists stressed the impor-

tance of yielding ground in order to advance and sang the praises of non-interference and inactivity.

These concepts quickly struck a chord in China, serving to complement the activist, socially minded views of Confucius. While Confucianism appealed to the rational, organizing instincts, Daoism became a magnet for darker, more instinctive forces, touching a vein of native mysticism.

In time too it became the mouthpiece of popular religion. Since time immemorial, the mass of the Chinese people had worshipped a multiplicity of gods, some of the soil, others of the elements, many more tied to a specific locality. To this day no one has ever tried to catalogue all these multifarious deities, which varied from place to place.

The Examination God

The crowded Chinese pantheon had many niches. One of its most popular denizens was the deity who supervised success in examinations.

Kui Xing was the most brilliant scholar of his day, but, unfortunately, he was also physically repulsive. When he took the examinations for entry into the imperial civil service, he got the highest marks. Custom demanded that, as top scholar, he should receive a golden rose from the hand of the emperor himself. But the ruler took one

look at Kui Xing's ugly face and refused to present it.

The young man was devastated. In his distress, he went to the coast and flung himself into the sea, intending to kill himself. But a strange beast – some say it was a fish, others a turtle – rose from beneath the waves and carried him to safety. Subsequently he ascended to

A Divine Hierarchy

The Daoists inherited this teeming mass of gods and set about organizing them. They modelled the divine hierarchy directly on the political world they knew, providing heaven with an emperor, ministers and minor officials just like China itself.

At the pinnacle of power was Yu Di, the Jade Emperor. Although he was a relative late-comer, dating from the eleventh century AD, he drew on the authority of earlier celestial rulers. These included Shangdi, the Shang era's ruler of the natural world, and Tian or "Heaven", the Zhou era's less personalized concept of supreme godhead.

Yu Di had lived on Earth before attaining perfection as a god. Long childless, his royal parents had asked the priests to pray that they might have a son. Next night the deified sage Laozi appeared to the queen in a dream, carrying a baby in his arms, and she subsequently found she was pregnant with the infant Yu. He later inherited the throne, but gave it up to follow a contemplative life. Attaining perfection, he devoted the rest of his time on Earth to healing the sick.

His cult dated from the reign of the Song emperor Zhen Zong, who seems to have introduced it as a way of boosting his own standing following a humiliating military defeat. Although all sectors of Chinese society accepted the new supreme god, he was always more popular in court circles than among the public at large. For the most part it was only the monarch himself who prayed directly to Yu Di, making sacrifices to him annually at the Altar of Heaven in Beijing. Just as on Earth most people considered themselves too lowly to send a petition to the emperor in person, so on the divine plane they preferred to address themselves to some intermediary god.

There was plenty of choice, for beneath the Jade Emperor was an entire civil service of lesser deities. There were court officials such as the Transcendent Dignitary, a sort of celestial door-keeper. There were masters of the elements, including a Count of the Winds and a Lord of Lightning. One particularly exalted figure was the Supreme Ruler of the Eastern Peak, supervising a ministry of seventy-five departments. Another

heaven and took up residence among the stars in the Great Bear constellation.

From that time until the imperial examinations came to an end in the early twentieth century, he was their presiding deity. Candidates would keep his image, holding a writing brush and an official seal, in their home, and across China many millions of anxious prayers rose up to him in the tense days before the final assessment.

Kui Xing, the distraught scholar, is carried from the ocean to safety on the back of a strange sea creature.

437

七殿泰山王

powerful deity was the bird-headed Thunder God, who was responsible for punishing serious crimes through the emissaries of his Ministry of Thunder.

The Local Gods

If these gods filled the upper ranks of the celestial hierarchy, millions more operated on a purely local level. Among the most influential were the Cheng Huang, literally Gods of Wall and Moat, who were in charge of cities and rural districts. Like their earthly equivalents in the imperial administration, they received petitions from local officials and were thought to report to the Jade Emperor on the daily activities of the areas under their control.

These celestial posts were often filled by deceased mortals, for the boundaries between the worlds of the living and the dead were always fluid. The Chinese had no problem imagining exemplary individuals continuing to provide posthumous service in the celestial sphere, rather like Christian saints in heaven.

One example was Yue Fei, a real-life hero who in Song times led the imperial armies against invaders who had occupied northern China. Having won some notable victories, he sought to push on and reclaim the conquered lands, but was opposed by a peace faction eager to end the war. Gaining the upper hand, they had Yue Fei executed. After his death, however, he came to be revered as a hero of national resistance and was recompensed for his untimely end by being worshipped as the city god of Hangzhou, the capital to which the Song emperors had retreated.

Like magistrates on Earth, the Cheng Huang had many junior officials reporting to

Hell was a concept introduced to China by Buddhism, and Yama, the Hindu ruler of the dead, was the inspiration for Yan Luo, the prince of the Fifth Court of Hell, seen judging in a 14th-century painting. Those who stirred up enmity between relatives were sentenced to be gnawed by dogs.

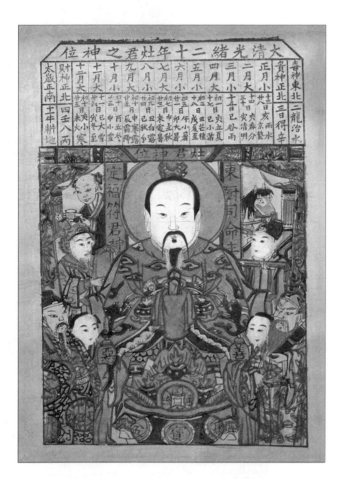

The Kitchen God, Zao Jun, decorates this 1895 calendar. An image of this popular deity is traditionally put up over the stove every New Year, the old one being taken down the week before and burnt using alcohol to make the god happy and try and ensure a favourable household report in heaven.

them. Chief among these were Bai Lao-Ye and Hei Lao-Ye, Mr White and Mr Black, who kept watch by day and night respectively. Below them was a whole district administration of local deities with specific responsibility for each street, temple, bridge or village.

The process of supervision did not stop outdoors. Inside the house was the domain of the Five Genii, responsible respectively for the front and back entrances, the well, the inner courtyard and the aisles around which traditional Chinese homes were constructed. The front doors in fact had two tutelary deities, the Men Shen, one for each panel. Pictures of the guardians, typically dressed as fearsome warriors, were pasted in place each New Year. Legend traced their origins to a Tang emperor who fell ill as a result of the attentions of a spirit; to drive it away, two army officers kept vigil at his door day and night, until he had the idea of having their pictures painted on the panels to let them get some sleep.

Most intrusive of the domestic spirits was Zao Jun, the Kitchen God. Each year he went to heaven to make a detailed report on the behaviour of the household over the previous twelve months. To avoid censure, each family member had to abide by a dizzying number of rules and regulations that stretched from avoiding blasphemy through showing proper respect for elders to maintaining high standards of hygiene. Bribery could also help: on the eve of the god's departure, he would be offered glutinous sweets and rice in the hope that his lips would stick shut.

For the pious, these reports were highly significant, for they were taken into account when each individual was judged after death. Beliefs about what happened in the afterlife varied considerably by region, and were further complicated by Buddhist notions of reincarnation. In general, however, it was thought that the soul of an individual who had behaved fittingly and whose memory was cherished with proper ritual observations would live on happily in the spirit world.

A very different fate attended those whose allotted lifespan was cut short unnaturally or who had no relatives to tend their graves. They risked turning into *gui*, restless ghosts condemned to wander the Earth for the balance of their given days. *Gui* of people who had committed suicide were especially feared, for they were believed to tempt others to follow their example so they could steal their bodies for reincarnation.

Thronged with gods, Immortals, ghosts and demons, the spirit world was above all crowded. And for believers it was ever-present. The numinous was never further away than the nearest roadside temple or household shrine, and the divine hierarchy was quite as intrusive as the earthly civil administration that it resembled.

Tales of the Eight Immortals

Daoists taught that those who achieved perfect union with life's essence could achieve immortality. The stories of eight, otherwise very ordinary, individuals who had attained that goal helped to popularize the message.

The secret of eternal life preoccupied the Chinese from the earliest times. Ancient myths spoke of two separate paradises in which the laws of ageing did not apply. One lay in the faery domain of the Queen Mother of the West, in whose garden grew a miraculous peach tree whose fruit brought immortality (see box, pages 422–423). The other was on five islands in the Eastern Sea (see page 429), the best-known of them vase-shaped Penglai. The First Emperor was sufficiently convinced of Penglai's existence to send an expedition in search of it in the year 219BC; none of the noble youths and girls who went on it were ever seen again.

The Daoist Disciplines

It was left to the Daoists to make the quest for eternal life a central tenet of their faith. Over the centuries devotees set their minds to finding practical ways of achieving the necessary mystical union. They devised a range of techniques designed to lengthen life and, ultimately, to enable adepts to win immortality through spiritual perfection. The methods included meditation, breathing exercises and diets aimed at avoiding foods that encouraged the "three worms" of disease, ageing and death.

Perhaps the oddest of all the disciplines were techniques designed to give adepts control over their sexual energy. These were inspired by the belief that people lost a little of their vital essence in each orgasm – a process of attrition that could be avoided only by practising non-orgasmic sex or

A wooden carving of Shou Lao, God of Longevity and a former star deity, holding a peach as the symbol of long life.

else by sharing synchronized climaxes with partners of equal spiritual power.

In the game of sexual entropy, the uninitiated could suffer. Chinese folklore had many stories of shapeshifters who took the form of beautiful young seducers, both male and female, while seeking to drain unsuspecting victims of their sexual essence. They thereby prolonged their own lives at the expense of their partners, who wasted away to an early death.

True Daoists condemned such behaviour, regarding it as a criminal attempt to find a short cut to a state properly achieved by years of spiritual discipline. Those who practised it, they maintained, could expect short shrift from the law-enforcing emissaries of the Ministry of Thunder.

Even so, tales of sexual vampires caught the public imagination more easily than abstract concepts of mystical union. It was probably in an attempt to popularize the Daoist message that stories of the Eight Immortals first started to circulate. Representing a cross-section of Chinese society, the octet brought home the message that victory over death was within anyone's grasp provided they had the motivation and will-power necessary to attain it.

No one knows for sure when the eight were first linked, though it seems to have been quite late in mythological terms, perhaps not before the fourteenth century. They soon caught the popular imagination, not least because they were portrayed in an approachably human way; several, for instance, had a partiality for wine. In time their images became ubiquitous, shown on every kind of decorated object from tableware to fans and wall-scrolls. They were generally depicted as a jolly group, contentedly enjoying for eternity the merited fruits of their labours.

Although the chronology of the group was always vague, the first to attain immortality seems to have been Li Tieguai, invariably depicted as a cripple with a crutch. After living an ascetic life for forty years, he was visited by the spirit of Laozi, the founder of Daoism, in human guise. Laozi tempted him with the pleasures of the flesh, and when the sage disdained them he was rewarded with immortality.

Some commentators claimed that Li had been born a cripple, but a more popular tale maintained that he acquired his crutch in the course of his initiation. In this version, Li told a disciple to look after his body while his spirit went to answer a summons from Laozi, instructing him to burn it if he did not return within the week, for he would in that case have finally become pure spirit. For six days the young man kept vigil, until word reached him that his own mother was dangerously ill. Not wishing to leave the body of his master unattended, he decided to proceed with the cremation a day early, assuming that his master had attained the immortality he sought.

But Li's spirit did return, only hours after the young man had left, and found only a pile of ashes where its human home had been. Looking around for an alternative to the body that had gone up in smoke, Li found an old beggar who had died on the mountainside a few hours before and he gratefully took up residence in the corpse, only to find to his chagrin that his host not only looked disreputable in the extreme but also had a lame leg. Seeing Li's discomfort, Laozi gave him in recompense a golden headband and the crutch that was to become his symbol.

Li held no grudge against his erring disciple. Proceeding at once to the young man's house, he found preparations already in train for the mother's funeral, but was nonetheless able to revive the corpse with his ever-present medicines. In later years pharmacists adopted him as their patron in recognition of his healing powers, and his image often adorned their shop signs.

If Li Tieguai represented China's sick and disabled, Zhongli Quan was a soldier and a man of action. After rising to be a Marshal of the Empire

An Unlikely Journey

Usually the Eight Immortals flew on clouds or white cranes from their island home of Penglai. But on one occasion they decided to travel by sea, borne on a strange variety of different objects.

Each of the immortal eight used their own particular emblem to carry them over the waves.

Thus equipped, the cripple Li Tieguai straddled the crutch that had been given to him by Laozi, while the pot-bellied Zhongli Quan floated luxuriously on a feather fan with a horsehair tassel. Lü Dongbin, who is the best-known of all the Eight Immortals, surfed from Penglai on his magic sword, and Zhang Guolao trotted amphibiously on his paper mule, a magical beast that could travel thousands of miles in a day, yet when not required could be folded up and stored in a wallet like a piece of paper. The scholar Han Xiang, being associated with the ability to create blooms, paddled across in a flower-basket, while He Xiangu, the only woman, was wafted gently on a lotus leaf. Most improbably of all, the street musician Lan Caihe perched precariously on a pair of castanet-like clappers, while Cao Guojiu was borne very authoritatively on the official tablet that guaranteed the right of admission to the imperial court.

Chinese artists enjoyed exploiting the humorous aspects of this bizarre flotilla, which became a favourite subject for paintings and illustrations.

Story-tellers subsequently adorned accounts of the trip with tales of hostile encounters with dragon-kings and sea monsters, and in time the expedition even provided a popular theme for opera.

These 19th-century southern Chinese tiles depict two of the Eight Immortals: He Xiangu (left) who lived off powdered mother-of-pearl and moonbeams, and Lan Caihe, theatrical patron, travelling on castanets (right).

in Han dynasty times, he retired to the mountains to pursue a hermit's life. As he was meditating in his cave one day, its stone walls split asunder to reveal a jade casket. Inside, Zhongli found documents of magic formulas which revealed the secrets of immortality. He followed the instructions they contained while the cavern around him filled with sweet sounds and multi-colored mist. Then a white crane arrived to carry him to his new home on the island of Penglai.

Lan Caihe was the most ambivalent of the octet, a wandering street musician sometimes depicted as a man and at others as a woman; in the theatre, he was usually played by a male actor wearing female dress. On Earth he earned his living as a mendicant street musician, dressed in rags and wearing only one shoe. He acted like a madman, but the songs he sang showed him to be a holy fool, singing of the vanity of life and all its pleasures. Often he would throw away the money he was given, leaving it for those poorer than himself. He finally attained immortality in a fittingly bohemian way, passing out drunk in a tavern in Anhui only to be wafted off to the Island of Immortals, leaving behind his shoe, robe, belt and musical instruments.

The fourth Immortal, Zhang Guolao, seems to have been based on a real-life hermit of that name who lived in the seventh century AD. Word of his sanctity reached the Tang emperors, two of whom summoned him to appear at court, though on each occasion he refused to go. Eventually he was persuaded by Empress Wu, only to fall dead at the gates of a temple as he entered the capital.

In the world of Daoist sages, however, death was not necessarily final. Although witnesses maintained that they had seen his body decay, he nonetheless turned up again not long afterwards back in the mountains. He took to claiming that he was immemorially old, having served as a minister of the legendary Yao almost 3,000 years previously. Called to court once more by Emperor Xuan Zong, who acceded to the throne in AD712, this old man of the mountains performed various magical feats that included making himself invisible, drink-

A woven silk rank badge from the early 16th century, worn on the coat to signify an official of the first rank. The bird depicted is a white crane, the animal that symbolized longevity and happiness. White cranes were normally used by the travelling Eight Immortals on their journey from Penglai.

ing a cup of poisonous aconite and felling birds and flowers simply by pointing a finger at them.

In 735 Zhang was elected Chief of the Imperial Academy at Luoyang in Henan Province. At about that time, the emperor asked a celebrated Daoist, Fa-shan, to reveal the secret of Zhang's extraordinary longevity. Fa-shan protested that to do so would be more than his life was worth. When the emperor insisted, he agreed only when promised that Zhang himself would be brought to revive him. The Daoist then just had time to reveal mysteriously that Zhang's true form was that of a primordial white bat before apparently expiring, as he had predicted. Zhang subsequently agreed to restore Fa-shan to life – a feat he accomplished by sprinkling water on the face of the corpse. Shortly afterwards Zhang returned to the mountains, where he himself finally died, though when his disciples opened up his tomb they supposedly found it empty.

In art, Zhang is usually shown riding on a magical donkey. In later years he was venerated by married couples as a guarantor of fertility.

443

The only woman among the eight was He Xiangu. As a girl she was instructed by a spirit in a dream to powder and eat some mother-of-pearl. She did so, simultaneously taking a vow of chastity, and thereby gained the power to float in the sky at will. She spent her days in the mountains picking herbs and berries that she took home each evening to her mother, having herself lost the need to eat. Like Zhang she was summoned to court by Empress Wu, but she disappeared en route, having achieved immortality.

Lü Dongbin represented the administrative class among the Eight Immortals, and his legend reflects Daoist views of the vanity of pursuing a career. The story went that he came from a family of high officials; his father had been a government prefect. He went to the Tang capital of Chang'an to study, and graduated with honours. He was destined for high rank in the civil service when a chance encounter in an inn outside the city changed his life for ever.

There he encountered the Immortal Zhongli, dressed in human guise as a retired army officer. The two men struck up a conversation, ending up drinking together late into the evening. Eventually the alcohol and the heat of the inn made Lü drowsy. As his companion warmed another bowl of rice wine, he drifted off to sleep and had a remarkable dream.

In it, his future career seemed to unfold before his eyes. He saw himself rising from an obscure provincial posting to attain high office. He proved a wise and just administrator, and was rewarded with great honours. After many years' service he was looking forward to a contented retirement when one day someone complained to the emperor about some misdemeanour he had committed. To his horror, he saw himself disgraced

Empress Wu Tian, first empress of China from AD624 to 705, was an imperial concubine until her marriage to Emperor Tang Gaozong. She summoned two of the Eight Immortals to court, Zhang Guolao and He Xiangu.

and sent to live out his old age in lonely exile. Worse still, his entire family was summarily executed.

At this terrible moment Lü woke up in a panic to find that his companion was still heating the bowl. This "rice-wine dream", as it became known, was enough to convince the young man of the futility of the course he had previously set for himself. Instead he gave up everything to follow Zhongli. Having passed all the spiritual tests his master set for him, he was rewarded with a magic sword with which he travelled around China fighting the forces of evil and helping the oppressed.

One tale of his wanderings tells how he took the form of an oil-seller to seek out just individuals, intending to reward all customers who proved honest in their dealings. Sadly, everyone he came into contact with turned out to be either venal or grasping, until eventually he met an old woman who was content with the measure he gave her and did not try to cheat on the payment. In recompense, he cast a handful of rice into her well, which from that day ran with fine wine, making her wealthy.

The best known of all the Immortals, Lü was credited with the authorship of many treatises and was even honoured as the legendary founder of a Daoist sect. Artists often portrayed him with a male child in his arms and, ironically enough, couples came to venerate him in the hope that their children, unlike him, would turn out to be successful government officials.

Han Xiang, the seventh of the group, was also a scholar. He studied under Han Yu, a famous Tang dynasty statesman and poet who was reportedly his great-uncle, and soon came to excel his master; one story tells how Han Yu scoffed at Han Xiang's claim to be able to make flowers bloom instantaneously, only to be silenced when Han magically produced blossoms from a clod of earth. On the leaves, a verse appeared in golden letters predicting Han Yu's fall from favour – a prophecy that came true in real life, for the scholar ended his days in exile. Han Xiang subsequently attained immortality with the help of instruction from Lü Dongbin, receiving as his emblem a basket of the flowers he had miraculously created.

The last member of the group was Cao Guojiu, an aristocrat normally depicted in official robes, bearing a tablet indicating his prerogatives as a courtier. As a young man he was at best thoughtless, and allowed himself to become involved in the misdeeds of a wicked younger brother who ended up by implicating him in a sordid murder case. Lucky to escape execution, he renounced the life of a spoiled aristocrat to take refuge in the mountains, where he devoted himself to meditation. In so doing he attracted the attention of Zhongli Quan and Lü Dongbin, who revealed the secrets of eternal life to him and welcomed him into their fold as the eighth Immortal.

Complete at last, the group retired to the Island of Immortals in the Eastern Ocean. Over the centuries, poets and story-tellers embroidered their legends, and devotees came to venerate them. In time they became the models of a long and happy life; the very number eight, by association, came to be a lucky one.

With their fondness for drink and helping deserving causes, the Eight Immortals were widely loved by the people and this was reflected by their prominence in popular art. Here, all of the Immortals are portrayed on a 19th-century tile wearing their distinctive garb and holding their respective emblems.

Lords of the Waters

No account of Chinese mythology would be complete without mention of the irascible dragon kings that ruled its seas, lakes and rivers, where they lived in the winter. Yet they could be friendly to those who paid them respect, bringing rain during spring and summer.

One old tradition linked the kings with sexual potency, for the dragon was considered to be the epitome of the male principle, yang. They were also held to be the ancestors of the emperors of ancient times (see pages 434–435). A curious story told how a king of the legendary Xia dynasty once collected foam from the mouths of two of his forbears who appeared to him in dragon form. For many centuries the saliva was locked away in a box. When it was finally opened by the tenth ruler of the Zhou dynasty, it spread out magically through the palace. Recognizing its procreative potential, the emperor ordered all of his wives to strip naked in its presence, and several of them subsequently became pregnant, thus creating a direct link between the existing ruling family and the monarchs of China's remote past.

Equally ancient was the notion that dragons could mount the clouds to bring rain. During droughts, peasants would take images of the dragon kings from the temples to show them the damage being done to their crops. In Han times, their images in clay would be taken out to the fields to encourage precipitation. They could also help harness rivers in time of floods; as late as 1869, an imperial edict giving thanks that an impending catastrophe had been averted reported that, "When the dykes of the Yellow River were in imminent danger of collapse, the repeated apparition of the Golden Dragon saved the situation."

The most powerful dragons were those who ruled the seas, rivers and lakes, and the mightiest of all were the sovereigns of the five oceans. Like the serpent-kings of Indian myth, they were thought to live in crystal palaces beneath the waves, feeding on opals and pearls. Once a year they travelled to heaven to report to their celestial overlord, the Jade Emperor. Yet for all their powers, they were not invincible; Chinese myths were full of stories of heroes such as Monkey (see pages 448–451) who stole a march on them but managed to avoid retribution.

Only exceptional individuals ever met the sea dragons face to face, but lesser mortals occasionally encountered their counterparts in the lakes and rivers. A story from the fifth century AD

A water dragon decorating the screen wall of the Palace of Peaceful Longevity in the Forbidden City. The king of all scaly creatures, the dragon is said to live under water half the year, rising into the sky during the spring when the constellation of the Dragon is at its height.

The Foolish Dragon

Dragons were powerful beasts, but the legends also often portrayed them as stupid. One told how a sea creature on a mercy mission was easily outwitted by a monkey.

One day a dragon living in the ocean saw that his wife was unwell. Hoping to restore her health, he asked if there was any particular food that she would like to eat. At first she refused to answer, but when pressed confided that she had a craving for a monkey's heart.

The husband was at a loss to know how to satisfy her whim. Still, not wanting to see her suffer, he made his way to the shore, where he spied a monkey in the tree-tops. To tempt it down, he asked if it was not tired of its own forest, offering instead to carry it across the ocean to a land where fruit grew on every branch.

Easily persuaded, the simian climbed onto the dragon's back. It soon had an unpleasant surprise, however, when the dragon dived down into the ocean depths. Panic-stricken, it asked where they were going, at which point the dragon explained apologetically that he needed a monkey's heart for his sick wife.

"Then you'll have to go back to land!" shouted the monkey desperately. "I left my heart in the tree-tops!"

Obediently, the foolish dragon did as he was told, swimming back to the shore and letting his prey scamper back to the trees. Scrambling rapidly to the safety of the topmost branches, the monkey thought to itself as it watched its former captor waiting in vain below: "What simpletons dragons must be to fall for a story like that!"

described how a girl gave shelter to a homeless old man one stormy night, only to find subsequently that she had become pregnant. She eventually gave birth to a formless lump of flesh which, when she threw it into a nearby lake, turned into a white dragon. The shock killed her, though her memory was kept alive in future years at the White Dragon Temple in Jiangsu Province.

A parallel tale told how, in Tang times, an individual named Liu Yi met a young woman mourning by the roadside. When he stopped to question her, she revealed that she was the youngest daughter of the dragon king of Dongting Lake, in northeastern Hunan Province. She was unhappy because she had been repudiated by her husband, the son of a river god, and had had to take human form. Learning that Liu Yi was heading towards the lake, she gave him a letter for her father to inform him of her plight.

In his palace on the lakebed the monarch read the missive with deep concern. Instantly a dragon was dispatched to rescue the maiden, returning with her within moments. It turned out that the girl's husband had died in the interim so, in gratitude to Liu for bringing news of his daughter, the monarch offered her to him in marriage. The couple returned to the human world to live together as man and wife.

The Monkey King

The irreverent and hilarious saga of the monkey who ends up as a *buddha* is possibly the Chinese tale best known in the outside world. It received the ultimate accolade when its hero, Monkey, became the stuff of countless popular legends.

The story of the Monkey King has no parallel in world mythology. To begin with, it is the work of a known author, even if little is recorded about him other than his name, Wu Cheng'en, and the fact that he was writing in the sixteenth century. Then again his book, *The Journey to the West*, has an odd pedigree, borrowing its title and its basic premise from a factual work of the same name written centuries before.

This first *Journey to the West* described the actual pilgrimage made by the monk Xuanzang to India in the seventh century AD to bring Buddhist scriptures back to China. Wu Cheng'en's reworking was very different – a wildly comic fantasia spanning the entire mythological cosmos, including heaven and hell, in which the monk acquired some very unlikely travelling companions. By a final irony, the most resourceful of these – a monkey with vast supernatural powers and a human body – became so popular throughout China that he himself became an object of veneration; images of him even cropped up in temples.

The plot of the book – best known in the West through an English version, *Monkey*, prepared by the poet and translator Arthur Waley – is so thickly packed with incident that no summary can do more than sketch its outlines. It starts with the birth of Monkey – no ordinary simian, for he emerged from a stone egg high up on the Mountain of Flowers and Fruit. The Jade Emperor

A Ming-dynasty jade monkey. *The Journey to the West* **is an allegory in which Monkey represents human failings.**

himself gave him special powers that soon caused him to be declared king of the monkeys. But after ruling his kingdom for many years, Monkey decided to go in search of wisdom. He met up with a Daoist Immortal, who took him on as a disciple and taught him how to fly through the air and to transform himself into seventy-two different shapes. He also learned how to cover 30,000 miles in a single leap, and to create 100,000 duplicates of himself simply by pulling out some hairs and crying, "Change!"

Armed with his new powers, he returned to the monkey kingdom and organized his subjects into an army 47,000 strong. But he still wanted a weapon for himself, and to find one he went to the court of the Dragon King under the Eastern Sea. There he tricked the monarch into giving him a magic wand that could change its size at its owner's behest. It could swell into a mighty pillar stretching to heaven or shrink to the size of a needle that Monkey could conveniently store behind his ear.

The Dragon King complained of the theft to the Lord of Hell, who sent minions to arrest Monkey while he was drunk at a feast. When he came to, he was less than happy to find himself in the infernal regions, and threatened to use his wand to destroy them unless he was set free at once. He made such a nuisance of himself that his captors were glad to let him go, even though he insisted on removing the pages of the *Register of*

the Living and the Dead containing the entries for himself and all his monkey subjects before he left.

Monkey was making powerful enemies by his raucous behaviour. Now the Lord of Hell joined the Dragon King in presenting a formal complaint to the Jade Emperor. Pusillanimously the Ruler of Heaven decided that the best way to keep his obstreperous subject out of further trouble would be to give him a menial post in the heavenly kingdom itself. So Monkey was summoned to the royal presence and granted the fine-sounding title of Grand Master of the Heavenly Stables.

He accepted the post with gratitude, but it did not take him long to realize that his only task was to feed the emperor's horses. Outraged at the

The Four Kings of Hell correspond to Buddhism's Four Diamond Kings of Heaven who guarded the *Register of the Living and the Dead* that Monkey stole when he was carried off to hell.

offence to his dignity, he stormed off back to Earth, where he proudly proclaimed himself to be the Great Sage, Equal of Heaven. To punish his presumption, the Jade Emperor sent an army to arrest him, but this was repulsed. Monkey then threatened to invade heaven unless his new title was recognized. Alarmed, the emperor sought to buy him off with a grander position. This time he was appointed Grand Superintendent of the Heavenly Peach Garden.

449

The Queen Mother of the West astride a sacred phoenix and holding one of her peaches, in a detail from a *kesi*. Appointed to watch over the peaches, Monkey ate all the best ones.

This posting, too, turned out to be a disaster. First, Monkey ate all the best peaches of immortality the Queen Mother of the West had been growing for the Peach Banquet she gave once every 3,000 years. Then he gatecrashed the festivities themselves before any of the other guests arrived, eating and drinking all the finest delicacies. Finally, tipsy and bloated, he found his way to the palace of Laozi, the deified founder of the Daoist religion, where he swallowed the golden pills that contained the Elixir of Life.

Now doubly immortal, Monkey escaped back to Earth with all the hosts of heaven pursuing him. He led them a merry dance, but eventually he was taken. Yu Di's rage knew no limits, and he gave orders that the miscreant should be executed immediately. But that proved impossible; the pills and peaches had made him invulnerable as well as immortal, and warriors hacked at him with axes, poked with lances and smote him with swords to no effect.

Eventually Laozi himself offered to get rid of him in his alchemical furnace. But that too proved ineffective; even after forty-nine days, the crucible did no more than make Monkey's eyes smart.

In despair, Yu Di handed his charge over to the Buddha, and here at last Monkey more than met his match. When he boasted that he was powerful enough to rule heaven itself, the Buddha challenged him to prove it by a simple test; all Monkey had to do was jump out of the Buddha's hand.

The task seemed easy enough. Monkey used all his powers to soar upwards for nearly 35,000 miles. Eventually he came to five huge pillars reaching up into the sky. Assuming that they marked the furthest limits of the universe, he left evidence of his presence by urinating on the base of one of them. Then he returned in triumph. But the Buddha only laughed to see him back. The five pillars had been the Buddha's own fingers, and the smell emanating from one of them was proof enough that Monkey had never left his grasp.

Thereafter, Monkey was imprisoned for his misdeeds for thousands of years, trapped under a mountain range. He was released through the intercession of Guan Yin, Buddhist Goddess of Mercy, only on condition that he fulfil his destiny by accompanying the monk Xuanzang to India to bring the Buddhist scriptures back to China. To restrain his natural violence, the goddess put a band on his head that tightened on command, instantly giving him a splitting headache.

The story of the journey quickly turned into a serio-comic epic. Along the way the monk and Monkey acquired two unusual travelling companions. The first, Pigsy, had been banished to Earth from heaven for violating a daughter of Yu Di, and had been reincarnated as a monster with a man's body and a pig's face. The second, another fallen celestial official, had taken the name of Brother Sand and supported himself by waylaying and murdering travellers until offered the chance to redeem himself by joining their quest.

This unlikely quartet endured no fewer than eighty separate adventures between them on the journey to "the West", surviving them all through the combination of Xuanzang's holiness, Monkey's sharp intelligence and the brute strength of Pigsy and Brother Sand. Eventually, after fourteen years, they reached their destination and collected the scriptures from the Tathagata Buddha himself. In completing the pilgrimage, Xuanzang acquired the power of flight, which considerably shortened their return journey; they were able to make their way back to the Chinese court in just eight days.

There they delivered the holy books to the emperor, and heaven and Earth joined to proclaim the success of their mission. As Xuanzang read from the scriptures, the four, plus Xuanzang's white stallion, slowly levitated into the air, while the courtiers fell to their knees in wonder.

They ascended into the presence of the Buddha, who pronounced the fates awaiting them.

Pigsy was appointed Head Altar-Cleaner to the gods – a post that, as the Buddha reminded him, would give him plenty of opportunities to finish off the scraps of ritual offerings. Brother Sand, who had shown real signs of reformation, became a saint in heaven. As for Xuanzang and Monkey, they received the greatest accolade of all, winning the status of *buddha*s.

Monkey was left with only one concern: to be rid of the migraine-inducing band that Guan Yin had put around his head. When Xuanzang asked him gently if it had troubled him recently, he raised his hand to his temples. Only then did he realize that it had disappeared of its own accord along with the last traces of his animal nature.

A Close Shave

Journeying in search of the Buddhist scriptures, Monkey and his companions faced many dangers. One requiring special ingenuity was the Land that Hated Priests.

On learning that the inhabitants of the land they were entering killed all priests who crossed their borders, the four Buddhists first tried to disguise themselves by donning native clothing. To assure their safety further, they spent the night locked inside a wardrobe in a roadside inn. But robbers came and stole the cupboard, only to abandon it soon after when challenged by policemen.

The travellers' plight now seemed desperate; their true identity was sure to be revealed by their priestly tonsures when they were found the next day. But Monkey, thinking fast, found a solution. Using his magical powers, he created 1,000 monkeys just like himself and provided each one with a razor. Between them they shaved the heads of all the land's leading citizens while they slept. In a land of bald-headed men, the pilgrims' own bare scalps subsequently went unnoticed.

JAPAN'S REALM OF THE RISING SUN

In Japan, as in China, there is a large pantheon of gods, but whereas the Chinese mirror the bureaucracy of Earth in heaven, the Japanese pay homage through their state religion of Shinto to a sun goddess, Amaterasu. Shinto followers believe that almost 3,000 years ago Amaterasu sent her grandson down to Earth to be Japan's first ruler, thus making the emperors of Japan her direct descendants – an actual divine family and not just a divinely chosen one.

The persistence and survival of Shinto beliefs are remarkable phenomena in a country in which the majority of people are practising Buddhists. In part Shinto owes its longevity to political factors – it has been used periodically to bolster the authority of the state. Equally significant, however, is the way in which Shinto beliefs are meshed into the very fabric of Japan: into the physical landscape as well as the mental hinterland of traditions. For Shinto (literally "The Way of the Gods") has its roots in ancient nature worship: its first deities were the innumerable spirits, described as "800 myriads of gods" – the *kami* or "beings of higher place" – that resided in mountains and waterfalls, or sacred groves of trees. Over time, human interpreters imposed order on this formless world, giving the faith a royal family of gods that parallelled, even linked with, the earthly imperial dynasty.

Yet even now, when the emperors have renounced their claim to divinity, the gods have retained a place in Japanese affections. Partly they have survived because the stories about them are memorable, populated by a cast of characters as passionate in their quarrels and reconciliations as Greece's Olympians. But the Japanese gods also draw from their local roots a continuity that entwines them inextricably into the nation's oldest traditions: their escapades explain the importance of ritual purity, the origins of flora and fauna, or feature tales of warrior heroes whose selfless sacrifice and loyalty exemplified the deferential code of rigid social etiquette. While, today, most of this mythology is consumed as entertainment, there is nevertheless a sense in which for many Japanese it forms an important part of national identity.

Above: A 17th-century Buddhist *sharito* or reliquary in the form of a bronze pagoda.

Opposite: One of the best-known symbols of Japan, the red Akino Miyajima Great Torii rising out of the sea, as seen from the window of Itsukushima Shrine, Miyajima Island. The shrine is dedicated to the divine daughters of the storm god Susano.

The Shape of the Cosmos

In Japanese mythology, the cosmos took form spontaneously from chaos. The primeval universe was a fluid, seething mass in the shape of a giant egg. The lighter elements floated upwards and formed Takama-no-hara (the "High Plain of Heaven"), the abode of the gods, while the heavier ones settled and became the solid Earth.

Then, from a white cloud, emerged three sky *kami*. The first-born was Ameno-Minakanushi ("Lord of the Centre of Heaven"), next was Takamimusubi ("August High Producer") and then Kamimusubi ("August Divine Producer"). Below, the Earth had not taken shape, for it was in constant motion like a darting fish or a patch of oil floating on the ocean. Yet from it sprang the first plant, a translucent reed shoot that forced its way up to the endless sky. There it became Umasiasikabipikodi ("Pleasant Prince Elder of the Reed Shoot") and Ameno-Tokotati ("Everlasting Heaven Stander"). Now there were five divinities inhabiting the wide spaces of the sky. All were invisible, fluid spirits without physical form.

The five were followed by seven further generations of deities, each appearing in male-female pairs as brother and sister, husband and wife. The last of these was the couple Izanagi and Izanami (see pages 456–457).

There are many different genealogies of the first gods, given in sources such as the early eighth-century AD *Kojiki* ("Record of Ancient Matters") and *Nihongi* ("Chronicles of Japan"). In the forms that have survived, Japanese creation myths appear to have been influenced by Chinese tradition. Scholars of Shinto argue that the primeval division of the universe into lighter and heavier elements is alien. In Chinese stories the universe came into being when primordial chaos

divided into its complementary principles of yin and yang. Some scholars believe that it is only with the exploits of Izanagi and Izanami that the myths reflect authentic, ancient Japanese tradition.

A legendary *tengu* – an elfish trickster – emerging from an egg. The Japanese concept of the primordial universe as a vast egg may have originated further afield in Asia.

Cosmology

Gods continued to be created and the vast population of *kami* was divided into celestial divinities, *amutsu*, and earthly ones, *kunitsu*. The High Plain of Heaven supported a fertile landscape filled with blossoming trees and stern mountains – a fragrant territory like that of parts of Japan itself. Across it ran a wide river, Amano-Gawa, through whose twinkling waters a bed of pebbles could be seen. From Earth up to heaven above there once rose a walkway or bridge, Amano-Hashidate. But the bridge disintegrated in the winds, tumbling into the sea far below and creating an isthmus to the west of Kyoto.

The Earth was called the Central Land of the Reed Plain. Deep beneath it lay Yomi, the dark land of the dead, where demons congregated, living in palaces or humble cottages according to their station in that world. The inhabitants of this underground hell were not paying the price for past sins: in the Shinto tradition there was no conception of a place of punishment after the death of the body; this came into Japan with Buddhism.

A Multitude of Worlds

Japan's Buddhist movements believed that the universe held worlds beyond number, populated by harmful or helpful spirits. While Shinto promised neither punishment nor reward after death, Buddhists could look forward to one of many paradises provided by buddhas to save their faithful followers from the cycle of rebirth.

Standing sentinel over the universe to vanquish demons were four guardians, each of whom was concerned with a quarter of the cosmos: in the east was Jikoku ("Watchman of the Lands"), while the west was protected by Komoku ("Widely Seeing"); in the north stood Bishamon ("Widely Hearing") and in the south arose Zocho ("Patron of Growth").

Different paradises were associated with the numerous Buddhist sects, each of which had its own *butsu* or *buddha*. The largest was the Tendai school founded by Saicho at Mount Hiei in the late eighth century. Its paradise was Ryoju-sen, a Japanese form of Vulture Peak, a mountain in India. There, by tradition, Shakyamuni (Shaka-nyorai was the Japanese name for the Buddha) preached the sermon that was recorded in the *Lotus Sutra*, a Buddhist scripture best known in Japan through Tendai and the later creed of the thirteenth-century monk Nichiren. This paradise could be reached by Buddhists before death by meditating on the truth of the Lotus.

The glories of Gokuraku Jodo ("Western Paradise"), given form by Buddha Amida, were often celebrated and were well known to Japanese devotees of Jodo, the Pure Land tradition. There,

jewels adorned the ranks of trees that ranged in orderly lines along the mountainside, and colorful, singing birds created a celestial harmony. On a deep pond brimming with ambrosia floated sacred lotus plants. Caressed by breezes, the *butsu* and his followers rested serenely on the soil; above, angels released flower petals onto them from the blessed air.

The twelfth-century monk Honen, a former Tendai devotee, taught that entry was open to anyone who devoutly repeated *nembutsu* in praise of the Amida.

A third paradise, Tosotsu-ten ("Paradise of Contentment"), belonged to Buddha Miroku (or Maitreya), who is destined to come to Earth far in the future. Devotees believed that Tosotsu-ten lay in the celestial realm; from time to time believers were transported there in a vision.

Bishamon, guardian of the north. Wooden statue, 18th century.

455

Begetting the World

The seventh august generation of celestial deities to stand forth on the High Plain of Heaven were Izanagi ("He Who Invites") and Izanami ("She Who Invites"). Their divine destiny was to establish the fair, sea-kissed islands of Yamato (Japan) in the unruly waters far below.

The older sky *kami* gave Izanagi and Izanami a magnificent spear with a bright blade and cold handle of sea coral adorned with glittering jewels. The couple ventured forth onto the majestic rainbow known as the Floating Bridge of Heaven and Izanagi used the spear to agitate the restless ocean on whose surface the shapeless Earth still floated like oil. The waters began to thicken and when Izanagi lifted the spear a drop from it solidified, forming Onogoro ("Spontaneously Coagulated"), the very first island.

Divine Union

Down the steep and elegant staircase of the heavenly rainbow came Izanagi and Izanami to test the land. They built a sacred pillar and a fine dwelling place worthy of august *kami* such as they.

Then god and goddess looked upon one another with desire. In some accounts they did not know how to achieve sexual union until they saw a pair of wagtails shaking their tails energetically; Izanagi and Izanami copied the birds and joined their bodies together. In the version recounted in the *Kojiki*, Izanami told her brother-husband that there was one place in which her body was lacking; he replied that his body had a place where there was too much and they agreed to unite these two parts. Their divine intention was to bring forth new lands and new generations of divinities from their partnership.

They devised a propitious ritual to celebrate their marriage: she would circle the holy pillar from the right while he did so from the left; when they met they would be one. When Izanami rounded the pillar and encountered Izanagi she exclaimed in pleasure at the sight of him. He, seeing her beauty, also cried out with delight – but he reminded her that it was improper for a member of her sex to speak first in this way.

The Progeny of Izanagi and Izanami

The first fruit of their union was not happy. Izanami gave birth to a malformed child shaped like a leech or jellyfish. The troubled couple laid the infant tenderly in a boat of reeds and set it floating on the water.

Sometimes the leech child is associated with the god Hiruko; in one Japanese account Hiruko's name is said to mean "child-leech". Hiruko may have been an ancient sun god whose cult was replaced by that of Amaterasu when the Yamato clan became dominant from the third century AD.

Izanagi and Izanami climbed to the wide High Plain of Heaven to try to discover the reason for the monstrous birth. After performing divination, the other sky deities revealed that the cause was the polluting effect of Izanami's error in speaking before her husband during their ritual at the pillar. So the couple returned and repeated the ceremony, only this time, Izanami kept her silence until spoken to by her husband.

Now their lovemaking bore fruit in the shape of the eight largest islands of Japan. At the same time the smaller islands of the archipelago and foreign lands far and wide formed from bubbles in the unruly ocean. When Izanagi saw the islands swathed in fragrant morning mists he inhaled deeply and cleared the air – his breath became the deity of the wind. Hunger troubled the couple, so they created the *kami* of rice. They made the gods and goddesses of the mountains, of the sea, of rivermouths and of trees.

But when Izanami came to give birth to the fire god, Kagutsuchi, she was terribly burned. Izanagi gasped with horror to see his beloved cast down, beyond comfort, on the ground. He realized she would die and railed bitterly against her cruel fate. But even her death and his furious grief resulted in the birth of many *kami*. The myth's many different versions give various names for these deities. According to one account, before she died Izanami gave issue to an earth goddess and a water goddess and to a deity named Wakamusubi ("Young Growth") from whose belly grew rice, corn, millet, hemp and pulse. Another account claims that poor Izanami vomited, spewing forth the goddess Kanayama ("Princess Metal Mountain"), and both her urine and excrement were also transformed into deities.

The tears shed by Izanagi in his anger also turned into gods and goddesses. Bitterly regretting the birth of Kagutsuchi who had deprived him of his beloved sister-wife, he drew his sword and sliced the child into three (some say, five) pieces – and each one became a god. The many drops of the child's blood that he spilled became stones in the wide river flowing across the High Plain of Heaven and can still be seen as the stars in the Milky Way. In another account the fire god's dismembered body became five great deities associated with revered Japanese mountains.

Izanagi and Izanami stand on the Floating Bridge of Heaven. Izanagi is dipping his jewelled spear into the primeval ocean. Late 19th-century hanging scroll by Eitaku Kobayashi.

457

Journey to the Underworld

Izanagi, distraught with grief, determined to follow his beloved to Yomi, the "shadowy land of the dead". In the underworld he discovered a land not unlike that above, but a heavy gloom hung over everything like a pall. Although the inhabitants were accustomed to the darkness, for anyone used to the sun-ripened territory above, Yomi was a place of horror.

Izanagi could only drive his feet forward into those deathly shadows by remembering his wife's delicate form and graceful manner while alive. At length he discovered Izanami. He knew her by her voice, but he could not see her due to the darkness in that corner of Yomi. At once, in trembling tones, he begged her to return with him to the land above. But she spoke harshly to her husband, blaming him for having delayed in seeking her out; she had, she told him angrily, eaten the dark food of the underworld, thus bonding herself with the dead; she could no longer return to the land of the living.

Izanami said she was about to lie down to rest and begged her husband not to disturb her as she slept. But Izanagi, maddened by grief and angry at her refusal to return with him, waited until she was asleep, then took the comb with which he secured his long hair, broke off the end tooth and set it alight. His torch sent up a burst of light that startled the shadows and crowding demons, sending them scurrying.

He saw his wife's recumbent body in the gloom and, lifting the torch higher, was sickened to see Izanami as she had become in that place. For her body was swollen and rotting, home to crawling maggots; slavering over her were eight foul thunder gods, incarnations of the underground thunders heard in earthquakes.

Izanagi cried aloud with horror. Then when he could bear to look no more, he threw down the torch and ran, blundering into the thick and filthy darkness. He was pursued by Izanami's shrieking curses, for she had been woken by his shout of despair and was enraged and ashamed that he had exposed her to light. She sent eight wild *shikome* ("foul women") clamouring after him. Their keening threats and curses rang out in that cavernous place, making Izanagi's skin crawl with horror.

Brandishing his sword, Izanagi ran for his life. Then he stopped and flung his headdress down onto the mulchy ground. It became a bunch of black grapes on which the hideous women

Demonically depicted Raiden, one of the eight gods of thunder. His drum was used to beat out the terrifying noise of earthquakes as well as storms in the sky. Wood and ivory carving, early 19th century.

458

Heavenly Illumination

The Nihongi *features a variant myth of the creation of Amaterasu and Tsukiyomi in which Izanagi produced the* kami *of the sun, the moon and the underworld from mirrors prior to his first act of procreation with his sister-goddess.*

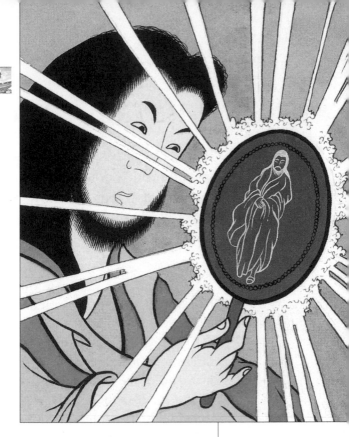

Izanagi stood alone in Onogoro and declared his intention to create offspring who would rule the world.

To this end he took a mirror of white copper in his left hand and, merely by gazing into it, divinely brought forth a deity named Ohohirume (probably a pseudonym for Amaterasu, for it means "Great Noon Female", a time when the sun is at the height of its power).

Then Izanagi lifted an identical mirror in his right hand and with his gaze gave form to Tsukiyomi. Using exactly the same mirror but this time looking sideways at it, he next created the god called Susano.

The first two divinities cast a bright light all about. Izanagi set them in the firmament to illumine the Earth far and wide: Tsukiyomi would shine with a pale light by night, while Ohohirume's fierce rays would be seen by day. But the third deity, Susano, proved almost at once to be dedicated to ruin, a bringer of destruction. Therefore Izanagi dispatched him to govern the underworld of Yomi, home to foul hags and demons.

ravenously fell, but they consumed them almost at once and continued their pursuit. Then Izanagi threw down his comb which became a clump of bamboo shoots and delayed the harridans once more. Izanami, seeing this, herself gave chase.

Izanagi was now almost safe, for he had reached the boundary of Yomi. The *Nihongi* version recounts how he stopped to urinate against a tree, giving issue to a great river that delayed his pursuers still further. In another account he was chased by Yomi's infantrymen, but kept them at bay by throwing peaches that he found growing on his path. Then he took a boulder and used it to block the passage between the worlds of the living and the dead. He heard Izanami arrive panting on the other side, but she could not reach him.

The huge rock's cold weight lay between god and goddess as Izanagi declared that he would divorce Izanami. She answered that if that came to pass she would destroy 1,000 inhabitants of the land of the living every day. He furiously countered that he would give life to 1,500. And so it was that death came into the world; but men and women, protected by Izanagi, still prosper, for they bring more lives into the world than are lost to the cold fury of proud Izanami.

In the bright light on Earth Izanagi saw the polluting mark of the underworld on his skin. He threw down his staff, shoes and clothing in horror, and they became deities. He plunged into a sweetly flowing river and then the wide sea to purify himself. (By ancient tradition mourners at a Japanese funeral would ceremonially wash themselves to rid themselves of the taint of death.)

Later Izanagi bathed his left eye and the goddess Amaterasu came forth; from his right eye sprang the deity Tsukiyomi. He flooded his nose with waters in a bid to flush out the dread odour of the land below and in so doing he brought forth the god Susano.

459

Amaterasu and Susano

Izanagi was restored and cleansed by his ablutions after the horror of his ordeal in the underworld. Addressing himself to the principal deities to which he had given form, he took his precious and holy necklace and handed it to the goddess Amaterasu as a sign that she would have dominion over the sky as the sun goddess.

To pale-skinned Tsukiyomi Izanagi gave rule of the night sky and the moon. In this account, sun and moon were devoted wife and husband, but when Tsukiyomi killed the food goddess (see box, page 463) they fell out – and for this reason they are rarely seen together. Susano, meanwhile, became guardian of the restless seas, or in some accounts of the Earth (although he was later assigned the underworld as a punishment – see page 466).

Susano Climbs to Heaven

Amaterasu and Tsukiyomi, then, occupied their allotted stations on the wide High Plain of Heaven, but in the Central Land of the Reed Plain, as Earth was called, Susano caused nothing but trouble. Without stop he howled and railed against Izanagi; in some versions – which identify him as Lord of

the Earth – he neglected his duties, and the foliage drenching the steep mountainsides and the fair blossom on the clustering trees withered during his period of rule.

When Izanagi asked what was the matter, Susano loudly complained that his station on Earth was not to his liking, for his only desire was to follow his mother to the land below where she had perforce now to dwell. Angrily, Izanagi granted his son's wish and banished him to Yomi.

Now Izanagi – his destiny fulfilled – elected to retire. One version has it that he climbed to heaven and lived in close proximity to his daughter in the Palace of the Sun. Others say he took up residence at Taga on the island of Honshu, where he is still worshipped to this day.

Then Susano declared that, before descending to the land of the dead, he must climb to the

Echoes of an Ancient Sibling Struggle

Some scholars believe that the myth of Amaterasu's conflict with Susano may preserve the ancient memory of an actual struggle between a priestess and her brother in prehistoric Japan.

There is a record in the annals of the third-century AD Chinese Wei dynasty of civil wars in Japan which followed the death of Himeko, priestess and queen of the kingdom of Yamato.

According to the Chinese historians, when Himeko's younger brother took the throne it sparked a conflict which was

ended only when Himeko's daughter took his place as ruler of her late mother's realm.

It is more likely, however, that the myth reflects a clan conflict in early Japan. Amaterasu was the great goddess of the Yamato clan and was revered as an ancestor of Japan's legendary first emperor, Jimmu. Susano, on

the other hand, was worshipped especially by the Yamato clan's enemies in the Izumo region. When the myths of Susano and Amaterasu were recorded, the Yamato clan had vanquished those in Izumo and were seeking to legitimize their superiority by establishing Amaterasu's seniority over Susano.

High Plain of Heaven in order to bid farewell to his fair sister Amaterasu. As Susano began the journey, his great and virile energy caused the vast seas to boil and the Earth to shudder and gape in a massive earthquake.

In heaven above stood Amaterasu. Hearing the commotion and seeing Susano approaching through the tall clouds and shifting mists, she concluded – knowing all too well his violent temper – that her brother was coming to her with evil intent. Her face grew dark; she convinced herself that envy drove him to climb up to steal her celestial realm. Girding herself for grim battle, she tied up her hair and her skirts, winding the string of dark jewels around her head and wrists. Then, picking up her great quivers, her bow of war and her sword that glimmered with the light of heaven, she stepped forth as a warrior. Her strength was so great that, when she stamped, her mighty legs sank into the ground as will a galloping stallion's into the foam at the ocean's edge.

Mount Fuji, the pre-eminent sacred peak in Japan, rises above autumnal suzuki grass, evoking an ancient image of the Central Land of the Reed Plain. Fujiyama or Fuji was also home to Sengen-Sama, goddess of blossoms.

The Competition of Procreation

Amaterasu challenged her brother in bold terms, but Susano reproached her, saying that he came only to pay a final visit before departing forever to the grim underworld of shadows and the dead. She demanded he prove that his motives were pure and he suggested that they compete in bringing forth divine children. The one who produced red-blooded male offspring, he said, would be shown to be in the right.

Amaterasu took Susano's mighty sword, and she handed him the *magatama* or string of beads she wore in her hair. Piously they washed the blade and the jewels in the Ameno-Mana, the deep heavenly well. Then Amaterasu bit into the sword,

461

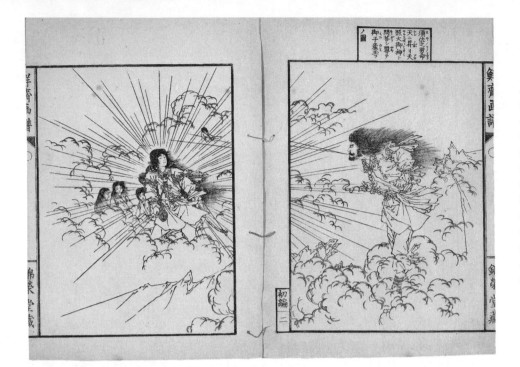

A 19th-century print illustrates the cosmic confrontation between the two elemental forces represented by Amaterasu and Susano. Here, Amaterasu stands alongside some of her handmaidens with whom she worked in the heavenly weaving hall, creating the divinities' garments – or even the very fabric of the universe itself.

crunching it in her strong jaws, and breathed out a bright mist that gave issue to three lithe goddesses. Susano chewed the beads and blew forth a cloudy breath that condensed into five strong gods.

The quintet of deities produced by Susano from Amaterasu's jewels were destined for a glorious future as guardians of the celestial realm, while the trio of goddesses that Amaterasu made from her brother's sword were dispatched to watch over the land of Japan in the Central Reed Plain. Between them, the eight children would in later ages be revered as ancestors of Jimmu, Japan's legendary first emperor, and of Japan's leading families.

Susano was not slow to point out that his triumph had proved his motives to be pure in the eyes of all heaven. But Amaterasu quarrelled with him, saying that since the gods had come from her beads, she was in truth the victor in the contest.

Susano's wild nature drove him to a violent campaign of vengeance. Chaos swept at his heels through heaven like a great thunderstorm punishing a country plain. He burst into the celestial rice fields, stamping on the soil and ruining the irrigation ditches and waters. Then, in the hall where the inhabitants of the celestial plain gathered each autumn to celebrate the harvest, he defecated and smeared his foul-smelling excrement.

Susano Attacks the Weaving Hall

According to some accounts, Amaterasu remained calm in the face of Susano's provocations and even made apologies for her brother to the other deities. But his next act was an outrage beyond excuse. He attacked the heavenly weaving hall in which Amaterasu and her maidens were at work.

It was part of the goddess's function to provide splendid garments for the deities of heaven, and she had many female attendants to help her in this task. According to some accounts, the weaving maidens also made the clothes that were worn on Earth by priestesses of the imperial sun cult; other scholars suggest that their creation was the universe itself, which expanded little by little as they laboured at their looms.

On this day the workers were rudely interrupted in their sacred task by wild Susano, who captured and tortured a pony, tearing its bright and dappled skin from its back and hurling it into the hall (some scholars believe that the pony's dapples refer to the stars). One of Amaterasu's loyal servants died in the assault, for she was so frightened that she started forwards, injuring herself fatally on the shuttle of the loom at which she laboured. A terrified Amaterasu fled from the hall and hid herself in a cave known as Amano-Iwato ("Heavenly Rock Cave").

A Wondrous and Fulsome Harvest

Amaterasu, the great goddess of the sun, sent her brother Tsukiyomi, the god of the moon, to pay court to the food goddess Ogetsuno. Their divine encounter led to violence, but was not without a productive outcome.

Ogetsuno lived in the Central Reed Plain, where mortal men and women would one day settle, and Tsukiyomi descended from heaven to visit her. Seeing the approach of so august a visitor, the goddess produced foods with which to welcome and entertain him.

When she pointed her head towards the land she gave issue to rice, while on setting her face towards the waters of the ocean she produced the many fish and other sea creatures. She faced the forbidding, snow-capped mountains and all the many creatures of the land, soft of pelt or covered with hard bristles, issued from her bodily orifices.

Tsukiyomi was disgusted that she was offering him food from her own body, and he drew his sword in anger. With a single stroke of the blade he brought the goddess down and returned to heaven buzzing with satisfied anger. But the great Amaterasu was displeased when he spoke of his adventure and from that day forwards, the sun and moon were rarely seen together.

Amaterasu then sent another celestial deity, Amekumabito ("Heaven-bear-man"), to see the food goddess; scholars believe he may have been meant to represent a cloud, for clouds were often divine messengers in Japanese tradition. He found that the food goddess was indeed dead, but from her body, like a fertile field supporting crops, came a wondrous harvest of good things. On her forehead grew millet; on her stomach, rice; in her genitals wheat and beans; in her eyebrows were silkworms; while circling her head were the ancestors of those hardy animals of the field, the ox and the horse.

The Return of the Sun

With Amaterasu gone, darkness fell across heaven and upon Japan below. Life abandoned a soil deprived of the sun's warm rays, and the crops failed; day and night were as one. The "800 myriads of gods" saw the need to restore order and they gathered on the banks of the heavenly river to seek a way of enticing the sun goddess out of her hideout.

The gods appealed to Omohi-kane, celebrated for his practical wisdom. On his advice they collected some cockerels, the sun goddess's sacred birds which – in normal times – herald her new coming each dawn. They then petitioned Tamahoya to make a great string of jewels, and Ishikori-dome to fashion a splendid, eight-sided mirror.

Next they brought a holy sakaki tree that had grown to maturity in rarified air on the high shoulder of a mountain and placed it near the cave in which Amaterasu had taken refuge. From its branches they hung the mirror clear as sky, the glittering jewels and long strands of colored cloth. Several deities gathered round; they performed devotions and sacred rituals. Then Ameno-Tajikarawo, who was known for his great physical strength, concealed himself close by the entrance to the rock cave.

The dawn goddess Amano-Uzume came forwards, clad in scanty clothing made from plants and streamers. She overturned a small tub and placed it opposite the cave door, next to the sacred sakaki tree. She lit holy fires, then, according to some versions, spoke a propitious incantation. The mirror, the strands of cloth that adorned the tree and the fires that the goddess lit were all later reproduced in Shinto shrines.

Amano-Uzume climbed onto the tub and began a lewd dance, as if her task was to seduce a haughty warrior or priest. Slowly she ground her hips and rolled her sleek belly, stamping her feet on the resonant tub. The assembled gods looked on with delight. She caught at her clothing, revealing her breasts, and then ripped away her undergarments, exposing herself completely. To the gods, her nakedness seemed a comic matter and they shouted with hearty laughter, so loud that heaven shook as if it would turn itself inside out. At the same time the cockerels that the gods had gathered crowed mightily.

Amaterasu emerges from her cave, Ama-no-Iwato in southern Honshu, and restores sunshine to the world. The story perhaps has its origins in an ancient eclipse. Triptych, 19th century.

The Reflections of Perfection

Mirrors are common at Shinto shrines, constituting one of the religion's three main emblems alongside a necklace and a sword. By venerable tradition the mirror used to tempt Amaterasu out of the rock cave is the very one that is worshipped in the goddess's primary temple at Ise in Mie Prefecture.

The clearness of a mirror's surface and the sharpness of its reflections represent an ideal for worshippers, who are encouraged to clear distorting clouds of passion from their minds and hearts so that they present untroubled images of their souls to the deity.

The *Kojiki* recounts how Izanagi himself gave a mirror to his divine children and instructed them to view themselves in it morning and night; if they fixed their minds on the celestial and pure while driving out wickedness he said they would see a pure consciousness reflected.

A mirror was often said to hold the very soul of its owner. In one celebrated story a dying mother left a mirror to the daughter who had nursed her through a long illness that destroyed her good looks. The mirror was a marital gift from the dead mother's husband – the girl's father – and the faithful daughter was later comforted by the mirror's reflection, in which she believed she saw her mother with her youth and beauty restored.

465

Amaterasu was enticed from her hiding place with a mirror, and because of this association bronze mirrors have long been one of the three symbols of Shintoism. Lotus-form, bronze mirror decorated with auspicious birds and butterflies, from the Muromachi period, 15th–16th century.

could not retreat into the cave. Another deity darted forward and tied a *shirukume* – a magical rope made from rice straw – across the entrance to the cave.

Light flooded from Amaterasu and, under her warm caress, fertility returned to the rice fields of the heavenly and earthly dominions. Order was restored, and two august deities, Ameno-Koyame and Futotama, presented themselves to Amaterasu, asking her humbly to remain with them henceforth and never again to shut her bright glory away in darkness.

Then the gods passed judgement on Susano. Their anger with him was great, for he might have caused a disaster in heaven and on Earth. They fined him heavily, ordered his beard to be shaved and the nails to be cut from his hands and feet. They made him recite propitious phrases used in purification rituals and make offerings of his mucus and spittle. Finally, the gods barred Susano forever from heaven and, warning him not to rest on Earth, then dispatched him to the dark and unwelcoming underworld.

Deep within her cave refuge, Amaterasu heard the cockerels and felt the vibration caused by the gods' laughter. She could not understand what could have provoked such rejoicing, for she knew that without her brightness the wide expanses of both heaven and Earth would be submerged in gloom and deprived of fertility. She opened the door to listen, then called out, asking what was the cause of such a commotion. Amano-Uzume answered craftily that the gods were rejoicing for they had found a mistress better than Amaterasu. Then curiosity proved too much for the sun goddess. She looked out and saw the mirror that the gods had hung in the sakaki tree and, captivated by its bright image, came further forwards – looking intently at the reflection of her own great glory, which she had never seen before.

In that instant the mighty Ameno-Tajikarawo leaped forward and caught her hand so that she

Order and Chaos

Some scholars read the episode of Amaterasu's disappearance as a mythological account of a solar eclipse, while others – pointing to Susano's desecration of the hall used for the autumn festival – see it as a myth of winter and returning spring. In many cultures sexual licence and impropriety are associated with agricultural fertility rites; Amano-Uzume's lewd dance may be part of a rite intended to lure the sun back from winter exile.

Amano-Uzume, who coaxed the sun to reappear, may well have been an import of Buddhism. Some writers identify her as a distant relation of the dawn goddess of Indo-European myth, who became Eos in Greek tradition (see box, page 169) and was lyrically celebrated as Usas in the ancient Indian scripture the *Rig Veda* (see page 370).

The divine quarrel between Amaterasu and Susano also represents a clash, familiar from other mythological and religious traditions, between universal order in the form of the great sun goddess and the force of chaos – Susano, unruly as a whirlwind or a thunderstorm. The Japanese myths were first collected in the *Kojiki* in AD712 to glorify the emperor, and in this context the triumph of Amaterasu may be meant to symbolize the glory of lawfulness and sound government established by the imperial dynasty in ancient times.

The Romantic Star Festival of Tanabata

There are few stories about stars in Japanese mythology. One tale – which is a version of a story imported from China – concerns the creation of the Milky Way and is celebrated in the festival of Tanabata held every year on 7 July.

This romantic tale concerns a brawny herdsman who fell in love with a beautiful girl weaver of delicate artistry. The weaver was a goddess – in the Chinese original her grandmother was the divinity Xi Wang Mu (see pages 422–423). In the Japanese version the weaver's father was the God of the Sky, who was displeased by her dalliance and whisked her off to the heavenly realm. Her devoted herdsman followed; then the father created the great celestial river of the Milky Way to keep the herdsman at bay. But the young man's devotion was such that in the end the god relented and allowed the two lovers to cross the river once a year – on the seventh day of the seventh month – over a bridge formed by magpies. Then they dwell in each other's loving company for one short summer night.

The girl weaver was called Tanabata and was associated with the constellation known to the Japanese by that name – and to Westerners as Vega in the constellation Lyra. On the night of Tanabata, the women and girls who primarily celebrate this festival of romantic love suspend paper streamers and twisted wool or cotton threads from tree branches. On the papers they have devotedly written poems about the celestial lovers or petitions for their own success in affairs of the heart. They also pour out water in a shallow dish and observe the reflection of the stars in the water; then they cast leaves of the kaji tree into the bowl, seeking in the movements of the water and of the leaves a divine signal as to their own chances in love.

Tanabata is explained to a young girl in this 18th-century print by Utamaro.

Susano in Exile

Susano, driven out of heaven, descended to the Izumo region in western Honshu. There he paused next to a river, seeking to calm his troubled soul. When he saw chopsticks floating in the water he guessed that there must be people living nearby and set off upstream to find them.

Before long he came upon an odd grouping – a young, beautiful woman and an elderly couple. All three were crying, railing loudly against fate. Susano asked what was the matter. The old man revealed himself to be Ashinadzuchi ("Foot-stroke-elder"), of divine lineage – a grandson of Izanagi and Izanami (and therefore Susano's nephew).

The couple explained that they had once had eight daughters, but one day Yamata-no-Orochi, a huge snake with eight heads and eight tails, had come from the Koshi district to prey upon them. Each year it returned and ate one of their daughters, until now only the youngest, Kusanada-hime ("Rice Paddy Princess"), remained. Before the day was out the snake would arrive and dispatch her, leaving them without a comforter in their old age.

The princess's beauty made Susano quicken with desire and he respectfully told the elderly pair that as brother of the great sun goddess he too was of divine lineage, and thus a relation. Then he calmly offered to kill the serpent in return for their daughter's hand in marriage. The parents promptly agreed and Susano swept her up, transformed her into a comb and hid her safely in his long locks. He asked the parents to bring him a great draught of sake rice wine. This he poured into eight deep bowls, which he laid out to tempt the snake. Then they hid themselves close by and waited.

Susano slays the eight-headed serpent Yamata-no-Orochi, shown here by the artist as an unpacified dragon coming up out of a raging sea. Hanging scroll by Kawanabe Kyosai, 1887.

The Divine Origin of Charms

There is a Japanese custom of charms and talismans, or **omamori***. Some are worn, while others are pinned up on the gateway of a house to offer protection against contagions. One explanation for this protective practice attributes Susano with power over disease and foul plagues.*

The tale recounts how one stormy night Susano wandered across the lands of the Central Reed Plain, his poor clothing offering him scant protection from the elements. At the house of Kotan-Shorai, Susano knocked and asked for shelter. But Kotan-Shorai was unimpressed by the stranger's scruffiness and refused to grant him entry.

Then Susano went to a nearby house, that of Somin-Shorai, Kotan-Shorai's brother. Opening his door Somin saw a sad traveller with the wind howling at his back and at once asked him in. He fed his guest and gave him sake to warm him, then showed him into a sleeping area to rest. The next morning, when Susano came to leave, he revealed his true identity and pledged that to the end of time Somin and his descendants would be free of the wicked spirits that cause disease, as long as they hung a sign at their gatepost to ward off the spirits. And since that day the Japanese have displayed notices on their gateposts identifying them as descendants of Somin-Shorai.

Susano Slays the Snake

When Yamata-no-Orochi appeared, the parents shivered with fright. The beast was as long as eight great hills divided by eight plunging valleys; its red eyes glowered and along its back grew trees. It lowered its eight heads to the bowls of sake and drank greedily. Soon its long eight-tailed body lost strength and it slumped down in a drunken stupor. Then Susano stood tall, drew his sword and sliced the beast into eighty pieces. As Susano chopped at one of its middle tails he struck hard metal. When he investigated he discovered a great sword hidden in the flesh. It was a weapon fit for a goddess and Susano afterwards delivered Murakumo ("Assembled Clouds") to his sister Amaterasu as a gift. This sword became a symbol of the imperial clan's rule and, renamed Kusanagi ("Mower of Grass"), it was the weapon later used by the heroic prince Yamato-takeru (see pages 476–479).

Susano and Okuninushi

The princess's parents rejoiced as Susano drew the comb from his hair, restoring the maiden to human shape. Then at Suga, in Izumo, he raised a palace with eight tall walls and took up residence with his new wife and parents-in-law. There they lived a blessed life. Fittingly for a deity associated with fertility, he fathered many children, one of whom, Okuninushi, became the hero of a myth cycle.

Youngest of eighty-one brothers, Okuninushi was murdered by his own siblings who were jealous at his success in marrying Princess Yagami-hime of Inaba, who they had set their hearts on. However, their enjoyment was short-lived, for their mother, Kusanada-hime, petitioned the deity Kamimusubi (see page 454) to restore Okuninushi to life, which two celestial princesses duly did.

Okuninushi was urged by his mother to flee to his father's underground realm for safety. He did so, and there he met and fell in love with Susano's daughter Suseri-hime – his own sister, whom he then married. Susano was displeased, but pretended to welcome his son in order to test his mettle. A series of challenges ensued, each of which Okuninushi met, and a thwarted attempt on his life by Susano. Finally, he fled from the underworld with his new wife, taking his father's bow and sword. Unable to apprehend him, Susano urged Okuninushi to use the weapons to humble his brothers and become ruler of Izumo, with Suseri-hime as his senior wife. All duly came to pass.

469

The Battle for the Reed Plain

Following his struggles with Susano, Okuninushi had to contend with the great sun goddess Amaterasu, who wished to enlarge her celestial kingdom to encompass the territory occupied by men and women in the Central Land of the Reed Plain.

The gods in the celestial realm were only too aware of the strife among the inhabitants of the Central Land of the Reed Plain. In this era, according to one myth, the plants, rocks and trees of Japan could speak and regularly disturbed the calm of night by sending complaints up to heaven.

Amaterasu dispatched Amano-Ho, one of the sons born of her contest with Susano (see page 462), to investigate, but on arriving he forgot his mission and settled on Earth without sending word back. Then she sent Amano-Ho's son, but he too failed to report. Next she sent a deity named Ameno-Waka-hiko, armed with a divine bow and arrow, who was famed for his fearlessness and prowess in battle. But even he proved unreliable: he seduced Okuninushi's daughter, Shitateru-hime, and settled in Izumo.

After eight more years of silence, Amaterasu next dispatched a divine pheasant to Earth to seek out Ameno-Waka-hiko. It alighted on a cassia tree near the god's dwelling and there it stayed, waiting for its chance to talk to Ameno-Waka-hiko. When one of the women of the house complained that it was an evil omen, Ameno-Waka-hiko drew one of his divine arrows and shot the pheasant. The projectile passed through the bird and winged its way directly to heaven, where the deity Takamimusubi deflected it back to Earth – and it dealt Ameno-Waka-hiko a fatal wound as he slept.

Shitateru-hime was distraught at her husband's death and her wailing and cries of grief could be heard even in heaven. The gods sent down a sweet wind that carried Ameno-Waka-hiko's body back to the divine realm. There they built a mortuary house, laid the body reverently in it and joined Shitateru-hime in her mourning. For eight days and nights they watched over the body, crying and lamenting the death. An earthly friend of Ameno-Waka-hiko by the name of Ajishiki went to console Shitateru-hime but because he looked so like the deceased, all the members of the household cried out and swarmed around him, declaring that he was in truth Ameno-Waka-hiko returned to life. Ajishiki was angered and with a great sword attacked the heavenly mortuary house in which his friend's body lay. It fell to Earth where it took the form of Mount Moyama.

The Goddess's Ultimatum

Now Amaterasu sent the deities Takamimusubi and Kamimusubi (see page 454) to inform Okuninushi that he must surrender his realm to her. In a gesture asserting sovereignty, the two divinities each took a glittering sword and sunk the handles into the crest of a breaking wave off Inasa beach in Izumo. Here, sitting cross-legged on the sword-tips, they materialized before Okuninushi. They informed him that the land of men and women was destined to be ruled by offspring of Amaterasu and demanded a swift response.

Okuninushi declined to answer, saying that his son Yakoto-shironushi would speak in his stead. The son was summoned and advised submitting to the illustrious deities. Some scholars believe that Yakoto-shironushi represented a priest or god of ritual language and for this reason he was the one summoned to communicate with the divine messengers.

Shortly afterwards another of Okuninushi's sons, the combative Take-minakata, appeared on the beach, balancing a great boulder on his fingertips as a show of strength and demanding the chance to contest the decision with the deities. He tried to grasp the arm of the deity Takamimusubi, but he could not grip it for it changed into an icicle that glittered in the morning sun, then into a sleek, sharp sword. Then Takamimusubi seized Take-minakata's arm, and it was changed into a frail reed that the deity easily crushed and cast aside. Take-minakata fled but after a wild chase the gods caught him. He breathlessly promised to submit and accept the decision of Okuninushi regarding the future governance of the Central Land of the Reed Plain.

The Will of Heaven

The fight between Okuninushi's son and Amaterasu's divine representatives is read by some scholars as a mythical rendering of the conflict between the people of Izumo and the Yamato clan. Others have suggested that it is an account of a religious ritual. In ancient Japan, the use of ritualized conflict – known as *sumapi*, a direct ancestor of modern sumo wrestling – was a widely accepted way of determining the will of heaven in a dispute.

Okuninushi consented to the decision made by his first son and agreed to hand control of the Central Land of the Reed Plain to majestic Amaterasu. Afterwards he built the great Taisha Shrine of Izumo. The divine emissaries Takamimusubi and Kamimusubi returned to the calm of the celestial realm to report to Amaterasu that they had succeeded in bringing order and peace to the unruly lands below.

A 19th-century boxwood carving depicts a wrestler performing a *kawazu* throw. Such bouts are said to have originated as divine contests.

471

Jimmu, the First Emperor

Amaterasu next sent her grandchild Honinigi to rule the Central Land of the Reed Plain as the representative of her divine family. His sons included Hikohoho, grandfather of Jimmu, who was raised on the western island of Kyushu. As an adult, Jimmu called his family together and announced that he would continue the heavenly task begun by Amaterasu and extend the glories of imperial rule to the region of Yamato, on the island of Honshu.

In the *Kojiki* Jimmu is presented as a historical figure. In reality, he was legendary, and scholars cannot agree on the facts behind the myth. The traditional date given for Jimmu's accession is 660BC. Actually, the clan from which the imperial dynasty emerged rose to prominence in the third to fifth centuries AD; they are referred to as Yamato from the Honshu region of that name. Some historians argue that the story of a migration from Kyushu reflects an actual movement by the ancestors of those who established rule in the Yamato region; others believe the dynasty rose to power there without any migration. More controversial is the theory that the invasion commemorated in the Jimmu legend was a historical one by Altaic-speakers from Central Asia.

According to the *Nihongi*, the emperor was forty-five when he began his journey of conquest and settlement. From Kyushu he proceeded resolutely by land and sea. On the waves Jimmu, at the head of a large fleet, met a deity astride a tortoise's back, who agreed to be his guide along the sea routes. In places Jimmu was welcomed and feasted by local rulers who pledged themselves to his service. Many harbours, rivers and settlements in Japan took their names from events that occurred on Jimmu's march. He met and subdued many deities who subsequently became the ancestors of important Japanese clans.

At the Hill of Kusaka Jimmu's troops encountered a fierce force, well led by Nagasunekiho, a local prince. It was a brutal battle, the armies were evenly matched, and Jimmu's elder brother Itsuse was wounded. Jimmu resolved to retreat, for the sun was low in the sky and his army was fighting into the sunlight, which was not fitting for a descendant of the sun goddess. He planned to attack at a later time in another place with the sunlight at their backs. It would symbolize for his men the great power of the goddess's dynasty.

The army accordingly withdrew and moved on. All this time, Itsuse was suffering keenly from his deep arrow wound. He did not pity himself, however, but donned heavy armour so that all could witness his bravery and recognize his steadfast spirit. But his strength continued to dwindle and finally, when the army came to Mount Kama, he died and was buried with great honour. Some

Servant of Jimmu during his long trek, the tortoise is a symbol of longevity and a guardian of the northern signs of the Japanese zodiac. Late 18th-century bronze sculpture by Murata Seimin.

472

The Divine Lineage of the Emperor

By tradition Jimmu and his imperial descendants can trace their ancestry right back to the first days of creation, for Jimmu's ancestor was great Izanagi himself. Jimmu was linked to him through the descendants of Amaterasu, Izanagi's daughter, completing the confirmation of his legitimacy to rule.

Amaterasu's grandson Honinigi was sent to Earth bearing the emblems of imperial power (the sword Murakumo, the beads or *magatama* and mirror). He fathered the prince Hikohoho, who travelled to the seabed and wed Toyotama, the dragon daughter of Watazumi, the sea god. Their son – born on the beach and abandoned at birth by his mother – later wed his nurse, Tamayori, who was Toyotama's sister and therefore another daughter of Watazumi. They produced many children, one of whom was Jimmu.

Wedded Rocks, at Futamigaura in Ise Bay, which gave shelter to Izanagi and Izanami. The sacred straw ropes symbolize the sanctity of marriage.

scholars believe that in ancient tradition Itsuse may have been Jimmu's predecessor as emperor. (The ideogram used in the *Kojiki* to describe the moment of his death is the one reserved for the death of an emperor. Also, the fact that several generations intervened between Honiningi and Jimmu reflects a period of consolidation by the invaders in Kyushu before they went eastwards.)

Futsu-no-Mitama, the Wonder Sword

The army observed the proper period of mourning, then travelled resolutely on. After surviving a storm at sea, they came to the region of Kumano. There, as the men set up camp, they saw a bear prowling close by; its roar made them shiver. That night weakness afflicted the soldiers and their emperor,

as if their food or the air they breathed had been poisoned. In truth the region's unruly gods had created a vapour that drained the men's strength.

But help was at hand from the army's celestial patron, Amaterasu. A man named Takakuraji had troubled dreams that night. He saw Amaterasu and a thunder deity, Take-mikazuchi, in conference on the heavenly plain. The goddess noted that her descendant was struggling in his divinely ordained task and urged her fellow deity to descend to Earth and pacify the emperor's enemies. Take-mikazuchi replied that he did not need to go down there himself for he could send his sword Futsu-no-Mitama; it would bring unstoppable force to the imperial army. Then he instructed the dreamer to look in his storehouse on waking the following morning, for he would find the sacred sword there.

473

Takakuraji did as he was told and sure enough found a great sword. Just as with the dual divine visitation to Okuninushi at Inasa (see page 470), the sword was somehow balanced on its hilt with the blade – sparkling with heavenly light – pointing upwards. He took it and brought it to Jimmu, who at that moment awoke from his slumbers. With the wonder sword the local deities were vanquished. Swiftly the army returned to strength and massed once more to march.

The Divine Sun Crow and the Dynasty

Jimmu's force climbed high into the mountains, but the route was so treacherous that they had to call a halt. Then Amaterasu intervened, appearing in a dream and promising to send Jimmu a divine guide in the shape of a red bird with three claws, named Yatagarasu or the "Sun Crow".

The crow descended and guided the imperial army across the peaks and slopes to the region of Uda, governed by two brothers named Ukeshi. Here Jimmu was greeted by the younger of them, who prostrated himself and revealed that his older brother was plotting to resist. He said that Ukeshi the Elder had raised an army, but on seeing the size of the imperial forces had been frightened and turned back. Now he had built a hall that concealed a murderous machine. His plan was to invite Jimmu to dine and then lead him into the room, where the device would end his life.

Jimmu sent a loyal soldier, Michi-no-omi, to reconnoitre. He encountered Ukeshi the Elder and denounced him for his treachery; then, enraged, Michi-no-omi drew his weapon and charged, driving the dishonourable Ukeshi into the hall he had prepared. Ukeshi blundered into the deadly machine and was killed. Michi-no-omi dragged out the body and hacked off its head, releasing a river of blood that lapped up to his ankles before draining away. Ever after the place was known as Uda-no-Chi-hara ("The Bloody Plain of Uda").

Ukeshi the Younger then laid on a feast of beef and sake for the troops, and Jimmu entertained his men by singing a traditional humorous song describing how each man gives his youngest wife the finest cuts of meat and expects the old wife to make do with a meagre serving.

Jimmu proceeded on his way, violently overcoming opposition and imposing the rule of law wherever he went. Finally, when he had routed all the enemies of order, he built a wonderful palace at Kasipara in Yamato. There he married a local beauty, Apirahime, but he still sought another maiden to be his principal wife.

One day he heard tell of a young woman named Isuke-yori-hime who had divine blood in her veins. The story was that her mother's beauty had drawn the attention of the god Omononushi. He could not forget her and followed one day when she went to relieve herself. Transforming himself into a red arrow, he fell into the water and was washed up beside her. She carried the arrow home, and that night she discovered that it had become a young man. She took him as her husband and their child was Isuke-yori-hime.

Another day, Jimmu met Isuke-yori-hime near the palace and was deeply impressed with her modesty and beauty. They began a courtship and in time she became his honoured wife, bearing him three fine sons. Many years later, after Jimmu's death, Isuke-yori-hime had to save their sons from the evil attentions of their half-brother, Tagishi-mimi, a son by Apirahime, who wanted to remove the boys to Yomi so that he could take power on Earth.

Unable to speak out openly, Isuke-yori-hime warned the children to be on their guard by singing songs about brooding nature and the massing of dark clouds on the mountain. One son, Take-nunakawa, then killed Tagishi-mimi and thereby saved the legitimate imperial line. As Emperor Suisei he succeeded Jimmu and consolidated the dynasty, which, according to tradition, has continued unbroken down to the present day.

Jimmu, with his divine crow guiding the way, delivers his people to their new homeland. Crows were revered in ancient Japan as messengers of the sun goddess. 19th-century Japanese print.

Named in a Brigand's Dying Breath

With the imperial dynasty established, many of Japan's other tales concern mythic heroes – as befits the land of the samurai (see pages 482–483). Yamato-takeru, the son of an emperor, was such a hero – and an ambiguous one: by turns a chivalrous noble and a cunning cheat.

Among all the Emperor Keiko's eighty children, the two youngest – twin boys – stood apart in their nobility and their beauty. Identical in all respects, having shared even the same placenta, only a difference in character distinguished them. For the courage of the younger, though equal to his twin's, was rough and ruthless, and at times impetuous. So it was that one day, the elder twin having missed dinner several times in succession, their father asked the younger where his brother could be. He bade the boy tell his brother of his displeasure, and his insistence that he thenceforth be present at every dinner without fail. Mealtimes were important opportunities for the emperor to hold court before his family and vassals: in treating them casually, the young prince was delivering a significant slight.

Five days later, however, the truant had yet to appear: his father's fury could now scarcely be contained. Calling the younger twin before him, the emperor asked him whether he had spoken to his brother as instructed. He had indeed, replied the boy, and in no uncertain terms. Feeling a dark foreboding at these words, his father asked him what exactly they meant. He had waylaid his errant brother, the boy explained insouciantly, in the palace privy when he had come in to relieve himself first thing in the morning. Catching him unawares and helpless, he had killed him, torn up his body and done

away with it. The ungrateful miscreant would never treat his father with disrespect again.

Taken aback at his son's brutal loyalty, the emperor determined to find it some more appropriate outlet. There and then he resolved to send him down to Kyushu to put down the brigand bands which were disrupting the peace of that southwestern island. Before his departure, the prince offered sacrifice at the shrines of Ise,

Tales of Yamato, a collection of 10th-century stories, from the series "Ten Designs of Old Tales". Woodblock engraving by Yashima Gakutei, *c.*1820.

begging Amaterasu to smile on his undertaking. His aunt, high priestess at one of the temples there, was delighted to hear of his mission. She gave him a richly woven robe of the finest silk and told him to keep it close by him wherever he went to ensure good fortune.

And so the youth set off to do battle, his fine wife Ototachibana beside him, a group of armed supporters in the rear. Down to Kyushu they went, only to find that their task appeared overwhelming, so strong was their enemy and so unaccommodating the island's rugged terrain. A pitched battle was out of the question, the prince saw: outnumbered – and, like as not, on such unfamiliar ground, outmanoeuvred – his little force would quickly be cut to pieces. His only conceivable option was to strike secretly at the heart of the rebel leadership. Yet this too was more easily said than done: the brigand chief Kumaso could be with any one of a score of scattered bands which roamed the island's impassable interior. By a stroke of luck, however, the hero learned that the enemy had been building a hall for feasting and were just about to open it with a massive banquet.

In Kyushu Yamato-takeru used the beguiling disguise of a pretty maiden to lower his enemy's guard. A portrait of a woman on a veranda tuning her *shamisen*. Toyokuni, 1769–1825.

Seeing his chance, the prince had his attendants bring him the robe his aunt had given him. Having bathed and anointed himself in fragrant oils, he then had his wife, Princess Ototachibana, help him put it on. Letting down his hair, he stuck it through with a pretty comb: a few jewels, a dab of make-up and – the man was a maiden! Three well-armed ranks of brigands formed a ring round the banqueting hall – but a force which would have frightened an army held no fears for an attractive young woman. Such a fair creature

needed no accreditation: she was welcomed unquestioningly to the celebration, Kumaso indeed insisting that she should wait upon him personally. Well schooled by his wife in the alluring ways of womanhood, the prince had practised the teetering steps of a delicate maiden. With fluttering eyelashes and demure downward glances he drove the brigand chief into a frenzy of desire.

Completely enthralled by this beguiling stranger, Kumaso could not rest without her presence: he kept draining his cup and recalling her just for the pleasure of seeing her standing by his side. Soon, inevitably, he was as intoxicated with alcohol as he had been before by the stranger's beauty. Only slowly did the rush of excitement give way to apprehension, therefore, when he saw the supposed maiden opening her gown. Craning forward eagerly to glimpse a woman's snowy breasts, he saw instead a naked weapon being drawn from his charmer's bosom. As the long knife glinted momentarily in the candlelight of the feast, Kumaso came groggily to the realization that he had been outwitted. Too late – the blade was buried deep in his body. Sensing that his life's end was upon him, Kumaso asked his killer who he was and where he had come from. When told that he was the emperor's son, the dying brigand asked if he could bestow upon him a new honorific name. Until that day, he told the prince, he had been held by all – including himself – to be, beyond comparison, the bravest and strongest man in all the country. Now, in his final moment, he knew that he had been wrong: from that time forth the prince should be named "Yamato-takeru", bravest man in all Japan.

Yamato-takeru's Twilight

After ruthlessly crushing rebels in the eastern provinces with the magic sword Kusanagi, the flawed hero Yamato-takeru's story was completed by two tales of self-sacrifice. First, his much neglected wife followed what she felt was the right path of dutiful marriage; then a chastened and mournful Yamato embarked on his final, redemptive mission.

Yamato-takeru's courage in battle was never matched by chivalry at home: he treated his wife with indifference. In birth and in beauty Princess Ototachibana was one of the greatest ladies of her age, but Yamato-takeru regarded her with contempt. She bore his disdain with all humility and patience, never complaining at the daily slights, but merely striving harder to win his love.

Her husband's constant attendant through the years of campaigning, Ototachibana felt her youth ebbing away inexorably as the harsh sun of 100 route marches blasted the unsurpassed beauty

from her face. A kind word or a tender gesture would have more than made up for all that she had lost – and yet not even these were forthcoming. Ototachibana's bravery was equal to her sadness, however, and she always managed a smile.

Even when, on his way to put down another rising in the east, her heedless husband fell in love with Princess Miyazu, Ototachibana succeeded in keeping her sufferings from the world. Miyazu had all the girlish grace and beauty which once had been Ototachibana's own, and Yamato-takeru's admiration for her broke Ototachibana's heart. Yet still she smiled stoically on as her husband promised Miyazu he would soon return to take her for his second wife. First, however, he had a hero's work to do – and for that, of course, he needed the long-suffering Ototachibana.

At Idzu's shore they saw the Strait of Kazusa stretching out before them. They needed to get to the other side if they were to reach the rebels' lands. His companions were nervous about the crossing, but Yamato-takeru derided their fears: this was no more than a little trickle, he told them – they could practically hop across. Shamed by his arrogant scorn the party put to sea without further delay, but scarcely had they left the shore than the spirit of the strait made his displeasure felt. A fearful storm arose out of nowhere to teach the boastful prince a lesson: mountainous waves washed over his craft; the wind shrieked dementedly, the lightning crackled and the thunder roared. To quell such a tempest a human sacrifice was required.

Yamato-takeru's lack of respect angered the spirit of the strait and it sent a powerful storm to endanger his frail craft. This woodblock print of a surging sea is by Hiroshige, 1853.

An Ignoble Deed?

Yamato-takeru's accomplishments, although undoubtedly great, frequently fell far short of modern ideas of courageous nobility.

His victory over one brigand chief, Izumo-takeru, was achieved by what now seems shabby subterfuge, the prince having contrived to get close to his quarry with protestations of undying friendship.

The infamous outlaw's confidence thus won, Yamato-takeru secretly fashioned a wooden sword, which he wore in his own scabbard in place of his real one of hardened steel.

One hot afternoon when the sun beat down without respite, Izumo-takeru suggested that they go swimming together in a nearby river. It was the moment for which the cunning hero had been waiting. As Izumo plunged heedlessly in, Yamato-takeru – who had lingered on the bank – went to the brigand's scabbard and switched swords with him. Their dip over, the prince suggested a fencing contest – just for fun. Izumo stood there waving his wooden weapon uselessly, while his "friend" ruthlessly cut him to pieces.

That her husband had caused the storm did not deter Ototachibana for a moment; nor did his years of ill-treatment. No sacrifice could be too great, she told herself, to save the man she had loved so thanklessly: she would give up her own life willingly, rather than have a hair of his head harmed. The mission for the emperor also had to be considered: its outcome must not be jeopardized, whatever might befall. And so the brave princess offered herself to the storm aboard a ritually laden raft which was consigned to the roaring sea. The waves rose to receive her and drew her down swiftly into the deep: no sooner was she gone than the seas subsided and Yamato-takeru's ship was able to make its way to the Kazusa coast.

But it was a different prince who put ashore. Awed at his wife's self-sacrifice, he was struck by how little he had ever given up himself. The rest of his life would be passed in the deepest mourning for her – but, as the fates would have it, his time was not to be long. Sent out by the emperor to free the people of Omi from the attentions of a monstrous serpent, the hero dealt with it easily enough. Having strangled the snake with his bare hands, Yamato-takeru thought his work done; but the serpent was no more than a minion of a more formidable demon. That fiendish master had by no means finished with the hero: filling the sky with darkness and rain, it sent a sickness stealing through the prince's body. His strength draining steadily away as he went, he headed homewards to report to the emperor one last time, but as he crossed the Plain of Nobo he knew that his end had come. Time flashed by, he said sadly, like a four-horse carriage past a crack in a wall. He was never, he sensed, to have sight of his father again. He died in that desolate spot, his life given up for his country and its people, an all-too-human hero rendered magnificent by his own courageous self-sacrifice. Grief-stricken at the loss of his favourite son, the emperor had a tumulus built for him on the plain where he had died, but soon afterwards his body took the form of a great white bird and flew back to Yamato, the land of his birth.

Lord of the Rice Bale

The tale of how the hero Hidesato acquired the name of Tawara Toda, by which he would become known to posterity, is one of the strangest and most stirring in all Japanese mythology, involving the two ever-fascinating themes of dragons and monster-slaying.

One day as Hidesato was making his way round the edge of Lake Biwa, he found his way blocked by a river that had the lake as its source. The river itself was spanned by a bridge; more of an obstacle, however, was the sleeping serpent, vast and ugly, whose coils sprawled across the path before him. But Hidesato was not a man to let some monstrous dragon concern him: climbing up its slumbering form, he jumped down the other side and simply continued on his way.

A voice behind him causing him to look back, he saw instead of a sleeping snake a strange humanlike figure, with wild red hair on which a dragon-shaped crown rested regally. This unlikely apparition explained he was the Dragon King of Lake Biwa, and he needed Hidesato's assistance in a heroic task. For many years he had assumed his dread dragon form at the approach of any human stranger, but until now every wayfarer who had seen him so had run away. Hidesato, however, had proven himself a man without fear: he begged him, therefore, to stay awhile and help him free his kingdom from the tyranny of a huge centipede dwelling deep within nearby Mount Mikami. It came down daily to snatch the king's subjects, dragging them off to be killed and eaten. Even the royal palace was not safe: his children and grandchildren were being abducted by the monster. It could not be long before he himself was taken.

Accompanying the king to his home beneath the lake, Hidesato was staggered at the opulence of it all: its magnificent chambers seemed to shimmer in the soft underwater light. At the heart of the palace was a vast and luxurious hall, where the hero was invited to eat the choicest delicacies. As he supped the sweetest sake and picked at crystallized lotus flowers, a troupe of goldfish danced sensuously to the eerie music of a band of carp.

Entranced and slowly surrendering to the sake's embrace, Hidesato was suddenly jerked to alertness by what sounded like a mighty thunderclap. The king beckoned urgently, summoning Hidesato to a window that he abruptly threw open, ushering the hero on to a balcony from which Mount Mikami might be seen.

Might have been seen, that is, had its slopes not seethed from top to bottom in the thrashing coils of a giant centipede. Its 100 feet glowed like lanterns while the twin fireballs it had for eyes lit up the hideousness

A detail from a 17th-century scroll by an unknown artist showing Hidesato killing Mukade, the centipede of Mount Mikami. Part of his reward was an inexhaustible rice bale.

was broken only by jagged flashes of lightning. Fearful thunderbolts shook the earth and a terrible storm raged all night long, but the next morning's sun finally rose upon a scene of peace and beauty.

Hidesato was acclaimed as the saviour of the Dragon King's people. For many days and nights there were celebrations, but finally the hero announced that he must take his leave and resume his journey. The king would not hear of his departing before he had accepted certain gifts: a bale of rice, a roll of silk, two bells and a cooking pot. The hero donated the bells to a nearby temple to commemorate his achievement; the rest of the gifts he decided to keep for himself. And priceless presents they proved to be: the pot would cook without ever being placed near a fire, while the roll of silk disgorged the finest fabric without ever reaching an end. Best of all, however, was the magic bale of rice: year after year it yielded its rich grain without any sign of nearing exhaustion. That remarkable gift made Hidesato's fortune and gave him a new name: Tawara Toda, Lord of the Rice Bale.

of its giant head for all to see. Hidesato grabbed his bow, snatched an arrow from his quiver and sent it swishing through the water. To his surprise and consternation, however, it glanced harmlessly off the monster's head. He took aim again: once more the dart was beautifully placed – but once more it spun off without inflicting injury. The hero was growing anxious when he suddenly remembered an old story he had once been told about human saliva having magic powers: with this in mind, he licked his last arrow before loosing it at its target. This time the shaft sped straight to its mark and stuck fast; in dying agony the monster collapsed into a heap of lifeless coils. As the lights in its head and feet were extinguished, so too the sun's light disappeared from the sky: the blackness

Heroic Hidesato rescued the Dragon King of Lake Biwa from the travails of a giant centipede. Iron dragon produced by Myochin Kiyoharu, 18th–19th centuries, a member of a famous family of armourers.

481

THE WAY OF THE WARRIOR

Japan is a land of extremes: topographically varied and breathtakingly beautiful yet violently volcanic. For 600 years it was ruled by clan-based shogunates drawn from the samurai warrior class, men whose ethos derived from centuries of militarist values first articulated in the traditional mythic tales of warring clans, heroic leaders and feats of valour and endurance – particularly the idealized role-model provided by Yamato-takeru. They glorified war and fearlessness, emphasizing selfless sacrifice and total loyalty to one's lord or *daimyo*. But at the same time artistic culture was gradually encouraged to flourish and a governing class was set in place which enabled modern Japan to emerge.

The samurai class took centuries to emerge, but by the twelfth century the struggle for land ownership and clan dominance had resulted in rival, warring fiefdoms inspired by stories of their own historic actions. The First Shogunate (1185–1333) marked the onset of the samurai's domination of Japan. By the Third (Tokugawa) Shogunate *daimyo* power was being curbed by Ieyasu from the centre; at the same time a rigid four-class social structure was instituted, under the supervision of the emperor, with the upper class constituted by the samurai, presided over by the shogun. *Bushido,* a code developed in the mid-1600s, emphasized the duty of everyone to respect and honour those above them in the social pyramid. It built on Zen meditation's philosophical strands; advocating concentration, discipline and sudden inspiration, Zen had a natural appeal for men who made ready for battle by preparing the mind to transcend the fear of death. However, the total triumph of central control and consolidation of national unity sowed the seeds of the shogunate's destruction, for there were no battles left to fight. Slowly the system ossified before collapsing in the nineteenth century, although the tradition remained deep-rooted enough in the national psyche for the Mongol-defeating *kamikaze* or "divine wind" to be an inspiration into the twentieth century.

Above: Typical curving roofs and gables of a *tenshu* – a large tower of storeys of decreasing size built within a central compound – at 16th-century Matsumotojo Castle in northern Honshu. The *daimyo* protected their powerbases with the construction of vast castles or *shiro*, particularly during the Sengoku-jidai or Age of the Country at War (1490–1600). Early castles were built of wood, bamboo and earth, but prolonged war and the introduction of Western techniques of fortification led to increased use of stone and moats.

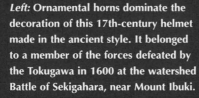

Left: Ornamental horns dominate the decoration of this 17th-century helmet made in the ancient style. It belonged to a member of the forces defeated by the Tokugawa in 1600 at the watershed Battle of Sekigahara, near Mount Ibuki.

Right: A 17th-century portrait scroll of Tokugawa Ieyasu, shogun from 1603 to 1616. He moved the centre of power from Kyoto to Edo and consolidated the Tokugawa clan's hold on power. During the Tokugawa shogunate – a period lasting 265 years until the Meiji restoration in 1868 – the samurai dominated Japanese society.

THE NEW WORLD

NORTH AMERICA'S MOTHER EARTH, FATHER SKY

"The Great Spirit is our Father, but the Earth is our Mother. She nourishes us; that which we put into the ground she returns to us ..." Spoken by Big Thunder of the Wabanaki nation in Maine, these words bear eloquent testimony to an awareness of the cosmos that is shared by all the native cultures of what is today Canada and the United States. According to this tradition, there is no separation between the spiritual and the material, between the real and the supernatural, or between the animate and the inanimate, because everything and everyone is endowed with spirit power, or "medicine". Big Thunder was describing a spiritual kinship, a relationship between humanity and the universe that is not negotiable. The notion of owning anything that comes from the land is as absurd as it is presumptuous. To live on the Earth, to breathe and drink and feed from its resources, and to be among the plants and animals, is to be part of a sacred cosmic unity.

In this view, the Earth itself is holy, with a sacred history that explains how – in an innumerable variety of myths – the world arose, how the species of animals were created, how the first people came into being and how each tribe came to occupy its particular place on the land. The animals on which humans depend for food and warmth have the same spiritual value as their hunters – they are companion species and their spirits must be acknowledged and respected, even when they are dead. The sky is a part of the cosmos, and as such it is crowded with spirits: those of the sun and the moon and the stars, those of the wind and the sea. Every natural phenomenon – forests, mountains, rocks, rivers, lakes, plants – has its own spirit. Myths tell of the diverse origins of different spirit "personalities" – the behaviour of the sun, the rhythms of the seasons, the movements of animals – but cosmic harmony depends on a balance being struck between them all.

In a predominantly hunter-gatherer society, survival depended on local knowledge about the land, seasons, animal behaviour and where useful plants might be found. This affinity resonates deeply through the stories and ceremonies of Native North Americans, revealing and affirming their kinship with the sacred totality and its varied life-forms.

Above: Among the Sierra Nevada Mountains by the German artist Albert Bierstadt (1830–1902). This landscape was sacred for the local Maidu people.

Opposite: The face of Nass-Shaki-Yeil, a creator god in Northwest Coast culture. He was the hoarder of light and the grandfather of the trickster Raven. This frontlet was made *c.*1850 by a Tsimshian craftsman.

487

Earthdivers and Creators

In many Native American cultures, tribal stories were told about how the world rose from the primal waters with the magical help of diving animals – a duck, a grebe, a beetle or a crayfish, among others, plunged into the murky depths to bring up grains of sand or mud, which then grew vast and became the terrestrial world.

Up in the sky, before the world was made, people lived in a village at whose centre grew a tree with huge white flowers. These blossoms gave light to the people in the sky, and when they fell, the sky grew darker. In the course of time a woman had a dream. In it she received a message: "The tree must be uprooted!" After some discussion in the village, the sky-folk agreed to pull the tree up, but as they did so, the tree sank and disappeared. Angrily, the chief called the woman into his presence, and, as she approached the hole left by the tree, the chief pushed her through it.

The woman fell and fell and, as she looked down, she saw the lower world, the world as we know it. But the form of the lower world had not been finished. The earth was not made. All she could see was water. Swimming on the water and flying above it were enormous numbers of birds. As the woman continued to plummet through the sky towards the water, a duck raised its head.

"How shall we make a resting place for this falling being?" cried the duck. And one after another, the birds began diving to see if the water had a bottom. Eventually the hell-diver bird went deep enough and brought up some earth.

The chief of the birds said: "Put the earth on the turtle's back!" So the beaver pounded the earth on to the turtle's back, and when the woman arrived through the air, they laid her on it. Here, mysteriously, she gave birth, and from her children came all human beings.

This Seneca story from New York State describes the creation of the world in ways characteristic of many Native Americans myths. First, at the beginning of time, there are the "sky-people". These are neither real people, nor spirits, nor gods. The sky-folk are vague beings, ancestors of that "first mother" who falls to the lower world, and are similar to the later people on Earth. Next, the lower world itself is a vast mass of water, populated by birds and animals. As in most stories from Native American hunting societies, these creatures can think and speak. Typical, too, is the animals' desire to complete the world, which is still only partially created.

As with many of these stories, a diving bird achieves the task. Sounding the depths of the primal waters, the diver brings up earth which is then plastered on the back of the turtle. And the whole world is thus understood to be an island resting on the back of that original turtle, and surrounded by the original waters.

In some "earthdiver" stories, as they are called, there is competition between the diving birds and the animals. The strongest and most skilful divers, such as the loon (great northern diver) or the duck, often win the day, but in other tales it is a small and insignificant animal who succeeds. Among the Cherokee people, originally from the southeast, the victorious earthdiver is a water beetle; while the diver in the creation story of another

This 19th-century beaded, buckskin purse is in the form of a turtle, the Earth-holding animal of many origin stories. Turtles have female associations and this one probably contained a girl baby's umbilical cord, serving throughout life as a protective charm or amulet.

This 19th-century Tlingit shaman's rattle takes the form of a grebe with two smaller birds on its back. Grebes and other waterbirds are often cast as the heroes of earthdiver creation stories. They dive into the primal waters to bring up the first fragments of earth that make the creation of people possible.

originally eastern tribal group, the Chickasaw, is a crayfish. In these myths, existence begins with animals who are at home in water and air. The first project for these creatures is the creation of the earth so that terrestrial beings, humans, can join them in a new world. As soon as there is dry land, there are people to walk upon it.

Native American stories explaining creation usually account only for the territory known by the particular society that owns the myth. Indeed, sometimes creation myths narrate only the origin of limited, albeit significant, parts of a tribal homeland. In northwest Alaska, for example, there is a thin, sandy peninsula called Tikigaq, which projects twenty-five miles into the Arctic Ocean. This low-lying, fragile-looking land was slowly formed before the last Ice Age out of sandstone deposits from local sea-cliffs. The Tikigaq Inuit, who have inhabited the peninsula for more than a millennium, have a story about the origin of their ancestral land that accounts for its geological structure.

According to this myth, the existing but incomplete world was inhabited by people and by beings who were half human and half animal. One of these beings was Tulungigraq ("someone like a raven"), a magically created man with the head of a raven (*tulugaq*, "raven"). Tulungigraq's creation work consisted of two main tasks. He was to bring alternating periods of night and day to a world still plunged in darkness, but before doing that he had to hunt down a whale-like beast that lived in the dark primal waters off the yet unformed Alaska. So Tulungigraq set out with his harpoon and travelled by kayak until he heard the great beast breathing through the night. Singing magical songs, the raven-man came alongside the animal and harpooned it. The sea creature sank, and as Tulungigraq secured it with his line, the animal rose again and transformed into land. This new stretch of earth became Tikigaq *nuna* (land): the peninsula which has since been the home of the Tikigaq people.

Like the Seneca earthdiver story, this Tikigaq tale explains how the Earth arose from the primal depths, but this time the agent of creation is a bird-man. These mythical agents of creation work their own magic. No mention is made of a supreme, omnipotent creator.

Raven, the trickster hero of Northwest Coast myths, who brought daylight and fire to the world, forms the handle of this 19th-century Tlingit ladle. Made of horn, bone, copper and abalone shell, the ladle may have been for ceremonial use.

489

Of Seasons, Seals and Cereals

The huge variety of natural phenomena, the rhythms of the days and the changing seasons, all provide themes for a wealth of origin stories. In some of these myths, the act of creation is a side-effect arising from a conflict between animals; in others, tricksters, such as the keen-eyed Raven or the subversive Coyote, come to the aid of struggling primordial humans.

Throughout Native American myth, large-scale phenomena, such as day and night, the seasons (see box, page 505), water, buffalo and whales, frequently emerge from something tiny and inconsequential. Not only that, but in the process of creating the larger phenomena, the tiny creators themselves sometimes change. One Iroquois tale explains how Chipmunk and Bear quarrelled over the question of daylight. Chipmunk, wanting day and night to alternate, sang: "The light must come. We must have light!" Bear, on the other hand, sang: "Night is best. We must have darkness!" When day began to dawn in response to Chipmunk's song, Bear was angry and chased his rival up into a tree.

His paw grazed Chipmunk's back, leaving an imprint, the two black stripes which stand out on the chipmunk's fur to this day. But he had escaped and his wish that night and day should follow one other has prevailed for all time.

The Tahltan people of the Northwest Coast describe a quarrel between Porcupine and Beaver over the length of the seasons. To indicate the numbers of winter months he wanted, Porcupine held up five claws. But Beaver held up his tail and said: "Let there be many winter months like the many scratches on my tail!" Angry at being contradicted, Porcupine bit off his own thumb, held up his hand and cried: "Let it be four months!" Beaver gave in, and since that time the winter in that region has lasted four months, and porcupines have four claws on each foot.

In many stories animals have simply existed from the beginning of time, but among the central Inuit of Arctic Canada sea mammals were said to have arisen from the mythical woman Nuliayuk (also known as Sedna or Takanakapsaluk), murdered by her own father. Her dismembered finger joints turned into the seal, walrus, whale and others, and Nuliayuk became the major sea deity, exercising control over all sea creatures from her home on the seabed.

A story from the Comanche people of the southern Plains explains how the great herds of buffalo came into being. Back in myth time, they were all owned by an old woman and a little boy. The animals were kept penned up in the mountains and none of the people could reach them.

This snuff box from western Alaska mimics two seals. The first seals were believed to have been formed from the fingers of the sea deity, Nuliayuk. Men smoked tobacco but women chewed it or took it as snuff.

Coyote, an animal trickster credited with many mythical interventions, held a council with the Comanche, and together they decided to send a tiny animal into the buffalo keepers' hideout. The boy, they reasoned, would adopt the animal, and it would in turn help to release the buffalo. Twice the plan failed; but the third time, despite the old woman's objections, the child kept his new pet. That night the creature escaped from him and, making its way to the buffalo enclosure, started howling. Terrified, the buffalo broke through their gate and rushed onto the Plains.

The notion that some powerful being, in the distant past, was hoarding something that people needed occurs also in stories about natural phenomena. The peoples of the Northwest Coast and the Inuit of Alaska describe how the "keeper of the daylight" kept light in a bag, which the trickster Raven stole. When Raven pecked the leather bag, daylight streamed forth. The Tlingit and Haida also describe how Raven stole water and sprinkled it over the Earth as he escaped, thus creating the great rivers and lakes of the region.

A widespread myth among the southern farming peoples attributes the origin of corn (see also box, page 507) and beans to a magical woman. The Natchez told how Corn Woman lived with twin girls. Whenever their supplies ran out, Corn Woman went into the corn house and came out with two full baskets. One day, the twins spied on her. Disgusted by the sight of Corn Woman making their food by shaking and rubbing her body, they ran away. Then Corn Woman told them: "From now on you must help yourselves. Kill me and burn my body. When summer comes, plants will come up where you have burned me. These you must cultivate; and when they have grown to maturity, they will be your food."

The emergence myths of the southwestern peoples mirror their lives as farmers and pastoralists. Corn emerged, like the first people, from a dark, underground realm. The spirit of corn is flanked by two holy persons in this 19th-century Navajo blanket.

491

The Circle of Heaven

In Native American belief systems the celestial world is alive – sky spirits manifest themselves in the various heavenly bodies, and in the wind, thunder and storms. There are many myths revealing the origins of these spirits, their location and their role in creation, with the different Native peoples' cosmologies emphasizing a range of celestial bodies.

The mythical firmament of Native North America has a variety of "geographies". For Californian peoples, the sky is like a roof, supported by pillars of rock which sometimes collapse with age and wreak havoc on Earth, whereas, for the Ojibway and the Pueblo peoples, the upper world is a sequence of layers, one above the other.

The Pawnee Sky Hierarchy

The Pawnee people of the Plains have a highly detailed conception of the firmament. The sky world that is described in their myths consists of three layers, or circles. At the level of the clouds is the "circle of visions". Above that is the "circle of the sun"; and, highest of all, is the circle of Tirawa ("Father Heaven"). Tirawa, the Great Spirit who created and informs every other spirit, is the husband of the female spirit who presides over the vault of the sky.

Before he made people, Tirawa specified the place and purpose of each heavenly body. The sun and the "Great Star" of morning (Venus) were placed in the east; the moon and the "Bright Star" of evening (again, Venus) were located in the west. The pole star, in the north, was ordained by Tirawa as the "Star-chief of the Skies", while the "Spirit-star" (Sirius), which was designed to be occasionally visible, was placed in the south. The four stars of the quartered regions – northeast, northwest, southeast and southwest – were positioned so as to hold up the heavens. Tirawa's stars were also required to manage other phenomena – the spirits of clouds, winds, lightning and thunder. Having given these forces their roles, Tirawa dropped a pebble into their midst. It rolled about in the clouds and then the waters of the lower world appeared. It was from these waters that the Earth itself emerged.

This Tsimshian mask has a moon face. The moon is important in all Native American mythologies, but in those of the Tsimshian and other peoples of the Northwest Coast region it is understood to be the major source of light.

Thunder Spirits

The Pawnee conception of a balanced hierarchy of celestial spirits contrasts with the Cherokee idea of a dense sky world – one made of rock, above which live the spirits of thunder.

The sun, as in Pawnee myth, lives in the east, the moon in the west. Above the sky vault

The War with the Sky Folk

According to a story told by the Kathlamet people of the Northwest Coast area, the unruly spirits who lived in the primal sky plagued the first inhabitants of the Earth with destructive storms. Eventually, their earthly victims decided it was time to retaliate.

Below on Earth, in the early time when people and animals were one and spoke the same language, tempests were perpetually wrecking houses and canoes, and making everyone miserable. So Blue Jay said: "We will sing the sky down." He sang for five years, but nothing happened. "Call all the people!" Blue Jay ordered. They all sang incessantly, but the sky did not move. At last Snow Bird began singing. The sky began to tilt. It tilted till it touched the earth. They fastened it to Earth and all the people climbed up into the sky.

Once in the sky, the animals began to wage war against the sky-folk. By cutting the bow-strings of their enemy, they routed the sky warriors. Then, headed by Eagle, the birds of prey attacked the southwest winds. The four elder winds were killed by the birds, but the youngest, the wind of the southwest, escaped – the only survivor. Their mission accomplished, most of the invaders returned home and the sky sprang back into place. But some of those who had ascended remained in the sky: Woodpecker, Skate, Elk and Deer stayed there and became stars.

This richly carved and painted pole, the work of a Northwest Coast Haida sculptor, depicts Thunderbird, a sky-dweller imbued with great power. From Thunderbird's eyes lightning flashed and his wings beat out thunder; he was also widely believed to have been instrumental in creation.

dwells the Great Thunderer and his two Thunder Boys, beautifully garbed in lightning and the rainbow. Other thunder spirits inhabit the mountains and cliffs of the sky; they travel on invisible bridges from mountain to mountain where they have their houses. Some of these auxiliary thunder spirits are benign, responsive to prayers and appeals from people, but other weather spirits are less sympathetic. According to some Cherokee story-tellers, the moon is a ball that was thrown into the sky in a mythical game. Long ago two villages were playing against one another when the leader of one team broke the rules that forbade contact between hand and ball, and picked it up.

Trying to throw it into goal, he tossed it so high that it hit the solid sky and stuck there as a reminder not to cheat.

For the Cherokee, the sky-vault was not only solid, but came down to the ground at "the sunrise place" where it could be touched. Once, a party of young men decided to visit this place and gain access to the sky. They travelled east for a long time and eventually reached the spot where the sky meets the ground. There they found that the sky was a dome of solid rock that was suspended above the Earth and swung up and down. Each time it swung up, an opening appeared, which promptly closed as the dome swung down again.

At sunrise, the sun appeared through this gap and proceeded to rise up the inside of the dome. The young men had waited for this moment to climb up on to the outside of the dome. But the first to attempt the feat was crushed by a falling rock. The others gave up and began their long trek home.

The Importance of Daylight

In the cosmology of the Inuit in the Arctic, as well as among the Tlingit and Tsimshian peoples of the Northwest Coast cultures, the sun is relatively unimportant. As confirmation of this status, the sun is a female and plays a comparatively minor role in myth and belief.

Many of the myths of the Northwest Coast which describe how daylight was created also explain how the stars and moon came into being. These stories usually focus on two main characters, a raven trickster and a being who hoards the light craved by all living creatures.

A Tlingit myth tells how the bird-man Raven sneaked his way into the light-hoarder's house by magically making the man's daughter give birth to himself. And this is how, once he had been born, Raven managed to see the bundles that hung on the walls of his grandfather's house. As the growing raven-baby, he crawled around, weeping and pointing at the bundles. This lasted for some days, until the grandfather cried: "Give my grandchild what he is crying for!" With that the boy was given a bag containing the stars. Rolling it about on the floor, he suddenly released his grip on it and let it float up through the smoke-hole of the house. The stars rose through the sky and scattered, arranging themselves as they have always been since. Raven then repeated his ruse, and the next bag contained the moon.

Daylight, the grandfather's prize possession and the prime object of Raven's desire, was kept in a securely bound box. Knowing by this time that a supernatural force was attacking his household, the grandfather reluctantly ordered the box to be untied. When the raven-baby had the box

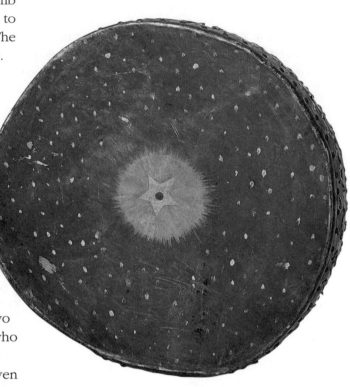

This painted rawhide hand-drum probably belonged to a follower of the Ghost Dance religion, which swept through the tribes of the Plains in the 1890s. The instrument is decorated with stars and dots that symbolize the spirits of the wider cosmos. Through their ceremonies, Ghost Dancers honoured the sacred spirits of the sky, whom they saw as allies in the struggle to restore Native American ways of life.

in his hands and let the daylight out, he uttered his raucous raven cry, "Ga!", and flew up through the chimney. This was how daylight, or sunshine, arrived on the Northwest Coast, together with the moon and the stars.

By contrast, among the Blackfeet of the northern Plains and the Navajo of the southwestern deserts, the sun is seen as much more than just the giver of light: all living and growing things require the energy that is provided by the mighty sun deity. This vital celestial body was also worshipped and propitiated by the Cherokee (see box, opposite) and other southeastern peoples.

A Spider's Quest for the Sun

A Cherokee story from the southeast begins in the shadowy gloom of primordial myth time. In their quest for light, the people are aided by a succession of brave animals.

At first there was no light anywhere, and in the darkness everyone kept bumping into each other. "What we need in the world is light!" they all agreed, and so they convened a meeting. The red-headed woodpecker made a suggestion: "People on the other side of the world have light, so perhaps if we go over there, they will give us some."

After much argument, Possum said: "I'll go and get light. I have a bushy tail and can hide the light inside my fur." So he travelled east, screwing up his eyes against the brightness. When he arrived on the other side of the world, he found the sun, grabbed a piece of it and hid it. But the sun was so hot it burned all the fur from his tail, and when he came home, he had lost the light.

Next, Buzzard went on the quest. On reaching the sun, he dived out of the sky and snatched a piece of it in his claws. Setting it on his head, he started for home, but the sun burned off his head feathers, and Buzzard also lost the light. When Buzzard returned home bald, everyone despaired.

Suddenly they heard a small voice from the grass. "You have done the best a man can do, but perhaps a woman can do better." "Who is that speaking?" the animals shouted. "I am your Grandmother Spider," replied the voice. "Perhaps I was put in the world to bring you light."

Then Spider rolled some clay into a bowl and started towards the sun, leaving a trail of thread behind her. When she was near the sun, she was so little that she wasn't noticed. She reached out gently and took a tiny piece of the sun. Placing it in her bowl, and following the thread she had spun, Spider returned from east to west. And as she travelled, the sun's rays grew and spread before her, across the world.

To this day, spiders' webs are shaped like the sun and its rays. And spiders always spin them in the morning, as if to remind people of their divine ancestor.

Made of buckskin in the shape of a rising sun, this Hopi shield was worn on a priest's back during a ritual.

The Details of the Universe

More common than those stories which describe the creation of major celestial bodies are those Native American myths focusing on the minutiae of the universe. Thus, one Lillooet story explains the moon's irregular surface in terms of the presence of three squatting frog sisters. Similarly, the star cluster known as the Pleiades is seen in an Iroquois myth as a band of children dancing at night.

"In the beginning the Great Medicine created the Earth, and the waters upon the Earth, and the sun, moon and stars." The creation story of the Cheyenne from the Plains, which opens with these words, proceeds to human beginnings without further mention of the origin of the cosmos. In some Native American cultures, this treatment of the celestial lights is preceded by a quiet, poetic vision of how things were at the beginning of time. Once the origins of sun and moon have been mentioned, the narrative often hurries on to a description of life on Earth and legends of the first people. The Lenape of Delaware have one such story: a deity known as Kishelamakank, at the very beginning of time, existed alone in space and silence. Suddenly he had a vision: he saw space filled with stars,

Morning Star, a deity who was associated with the well-being of humanity, decorates the headrest of this 19th-century Plains cradleboard.

sun, moon and Earth. Then, in keeping with his vision, the Earth sprang to life, followed by human existence in all its variety. But one god's thought was not enough to create the universe. The lonely creator therefore summoned help for his great task. He brought into being four Keepers of Creation and with these four spirits he conspired to produce the stars, sun, moon and Earth. Gathering strength, as if by chain reaction, the sun with its heat and the moon with her powers of fertility then brought life to the world. Once this had been accomplished, the Lenape creation story moves on to a description of "things as they are and have always been". The world of people and nature takes over.

If large cosmological events are sometimes passed over, what may seem minor aspects of creation are often explained in rather elaborate detail. Thus, a myth from the Lillooet people of the Northwest Coast describes how three frog sisters refused the advances of Beaver and Snake who came to court them. Beaver's disappointed weeping brought on rain. Threatened with a flood, the sisters escaped to the house of the moon. When the moon invited them to warm themselves by the fire, they insisted on sitting on his head. Jumping onto the moon's face, they spoiled his then unblemished beauty, and are still there to this day.

Similarly, the precise position of the sun is the subject of a Navajo creation myth. When "the first people" had arrived at their final home in this the "fifth world", after voyaging upwards through four dark underworlds, Sun-man and Moon-man who accompanied them on their ascent were hurled by their fellow travellers into the sky. The sun, which

The board around the "face" of this 19th-century Inuit dance
mask represents the air; the hoops are the different levels, or
layers, of the cosmos; and the feathers are the stars.

at first burnt too hot, gradually withdrew as the people made sacrifices to the power of heat and light. Thereafter, the sun moved in an orderly way from east to west every day, and the moon reigned over the night sky.

Perhaps because stars appear to be ordered in groups, the myths sometimes describe particular ones as families or little societies. The seven stars that make up the Pleiades have inspired many origin myths. One story, told by the Onondaga, of the Iroquoian confederacy of New York State, explains how some people settled in a favourite hunting area. The place was pleasant, game was plentiful, and while the adults constructed their lodges, the children organized some dances of their own.

Time passed and the children continued to dance every day. One day, however, a strange old man appeared and ordered them to stop. But they did not obey his instruction and kept on dancing. Then a small boy suggested that next time they met they should bring food from their parents' lodges and enjoy a feast together. But their parents refused their request. Undaunted, the children continued their merry-making – still happy, though hungry. Then one day as they danced, light-headed with hunger, they found themselves rising up into the sky. "Don't look back," their leader warned them. As they floated up, their parents ran out of their lodges laden with food to tempt the children back to Earth. But it was too late. One child who glanced down became a shooting star. The others, when they had ascended to the heavens, became the Pleiades star cluster: a band of happy children dancing through the night.

497

The Peopling of the Earth

Often, the first people are much the same as animals, sharing the same food and land and speaking the same language. Some myths tell of this early era as an age when life is perfect – until, that is, a trickster makes life the way later humans have always known it.

People, many stories suggest, have been here all the time – as, in many myths, have animals and semi-divine tricksters. While people and animals may take on different roles in particular tales, their natures are not too dissimilar. At the dawn of time the beings who existed combined human nature with that of the creatures whom later Native Americans knew and often hunted.

In a rare example of a Native American "dreamtime paradise", which may have been influenced by Christianity, the Cheyenne of the Plains describe the early people as having been placed by their creator, Great Medicine, in a "beautiful country" where people, animals and birds "who were all friends and had a common language" came into being at more or less the same time. The people went naked and were never hungry until floods and earthquakes struck. The ancestors were then forced to dress in skins and hunt for food. Great Medicine eventually took pity on them and provided corn to plant and buffalo to hunt.

Many origin stories describe the first people as helpless beings, physically deficient or technologically naïve. Sometimes an all-powerful creator brings people to perfection; in others, the people have to sort themselves out, or their survival depends on the outcome of a struggle.

A story from the Yana of northern California says that the shape of early people was not finally determined and gender was changeable. There were just thirty women and thirty men. The men went out to hunt deer while the women pounded acorns for bread. The men returned with nothing. "What shall we do?" the women asked. "There is no meat. Let us make women from men, and men from women." So the men became women and vice versa. The new men went out and killed many deer, while the new women stayed at home and pounded acorns. In that way they prospered and grew.

But Coyote, the trickster, did not like it. "There are too many women and too many men!" Opposed were Cottontail Rabbit, Grey Squirrel and Lizard. They knew about death but did not want it to be final, and they argued with Coyote about whether it should claim people. The animals then disagreed with Coyote about hands. In those days people's hands were round and fingerless, like Coyote's. "Let us cut through their hands," said Lizard. "They need fingers to shoot arrows and to pound sunflower seeds and acorns." "They can use their elbows," said Coyote. "Why do you talk about changing things?"

"We don't like them as they are," said Lizard and Rabbit. Then Lizard went off and sat in the sun. He leaned against a rock and, picking up a flint, he cut through his hands, making fingers. "Well, well!" whispered everyone when Lizard showed them his hands. Then he fixed their hands and now they could hunt deer with arrows of flint; they could fish for salmon and pound acorns. "When women have children," Lizard said, "they'll all have fingers." Only Coyote had no fingers. He sat by the lodge hanging his head.

An Inuit comb (c.500BC) incised with an image of an archer – perhaps a creator god – standing over a prostrate man and a variety of animals.

The Giver and the Watcher

According to this Tututni myth from southwest Oregon, two creative beings, the Giver and the Watcher, emerged from the purifying steam of their sweatlodge and collaborated in the making of humanity.

In the beginning there was no land. The Giver and the Watcher sat outside their sweatlodge. One day the Watcher saw land beginning to emerge from the waters which surrounded them. The Giver took some tobacco. He smoked and the land became solid. Five times the Giver smoked and discussed how the world and people might be made. He worked for days. Then day and night came, trees and grass appeared and the ocean withdrew.

Now it was time to make the first people. The Giver took some grass, mixed it with mud and rubbed it in his hands and made two figures. After four days two dogs, one male and one female, appeared, and the dogs bore a litter. Then the Giver went to work again. He fashioned two figures out of sand. This time the Giver had made snakes.

Soon the Giver thought, "How can I make people? I've failed twice!" The Watcher spoke, "Let me smoke tonight, and see if people emerge from the smoke." For three days he smoked, and from the smoke a house appeared with smoke coming from it. After a while, a beautiful woman emerged. The Giver was glad, and said: "Now we'll have

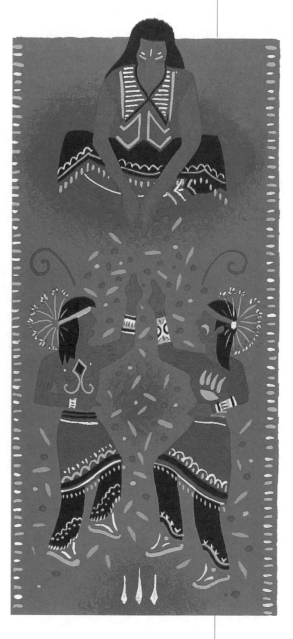

no trouble making people." The woman could not see the Giver and Watcher. But after nine days she grew sad and wondered who her kinsfolk were.

One day the Giver said to his companion: "Stay here and take this woman as a wife. You shall have children and be the father of all people. I'm leaving this world. Everything on it shall belong to you." The woman became pregnant. Even then she still couldn't see her husband, and when her son was born, she still did not know his father. So she wrapped up her child and went on a journey.

The woman and her son travelled for ten years. At last the boy asked, "Mother, where is your husband?" She replied: "I've dreamed of my husband." Then the Giver said to his companion: "The woman is home now."

At dusk the next day the Watcher, now a man, came in and the boy exclaimed: "My father has come!" The Watcher duly told them all that had happened. Meanwhile, the Giver brought order to the world and made the animals. He told the couple to have many children: "You, your wife and children shall speak many tongues. You'll be the parents of all the tribes."

"The Earth is my Mother"

Every phenomenon and every aspect of creation within the Native American cosmos has a spiritual dimension, but the Earth is regarded as having special sanctity. Stories about the Earth's origins are as various as the peoples, but there is unanimous agreement that this bountiful place is like a mother. The numerous myths and rituals that surround this figure bear witness to an ancient and indissoluble sense of kinship.

The Earth, which is home to all living and growing things, is regarded as being extraordinary bountiful, its fecundity providing evidence of its femininity. Native American stories show this mythical Earth Mother as having many faces, as numerous as her diverse landscapes, and all of her children affirm their kinship with her. Early in the nineteenth century, the visionary Shawnee chief Tecumseh tried to rally a number of tribes against the incursions by European settlers. In 1811, he declared: "The sun is my father, and the Earth is my mother; on her bosom I will rest." Tecumseh saw himself as an Indian first, and a Shawnee

The Great Serpent Mound, a huge coiling earthwork, was built some 2,000 years ago by an Ohio valley culture. It has been seen as affirming the Native tradition of reverence for the Earth.

second, and when he spoke of the Earth as his kin, he was speaking on behalf of all Native Americans.

Many Earth creation stories explain how this came to be so. In Algonquian tradition, the Earth was created by Gluskap, a mythic hero who made the whole known world from the body of his own mother. Similarly, the Oglala Sioux, who often speak of the Great Spirit, Wakan Tanka, as the grandfather of all things, also talk of the Earth as the grandmother of all things. Some mythologies provide this female Earth with a mate. For the Yuma people of the southern California desert the Earth's husband is the sky. After a primal embrace between the Earth-woman and the Sky-man, the Earth conceived and gave birth to twin sons. As their first task, the twins rose up from their mother's body to lift up the sky.

Away from the desert, the divine geometry of the world is less readily imagined as a division between Earth and sky. In the myths of the Algonquian peoples of the northeastern woodlands, the cosmos is pictured as a sequence of realms. Flat Earth is surmounted by a world of winds and clouds. Above it is the circle of the upper sky, where the Great Spirit dwells. But the sky is only the floor of the topmost heavenly world, which contains representations of all the things that exist beneath it. And the Earth below is the roof of an underworld, from which emerge the waters and plants that sustain life.

Defending the Sacred Relationship

As they saw the immigrants' frontier creep ever further west, Native Americans defended the integrity of their sacred Earth against alien ways. In the 1850s, Smohalla, the Wanapum holy man whose prophecies anticipated the Plains culture's revivalist Ghost Dance movement (see illustration, page 494), reminded his people of their sacred pact with the Earth. To save themselves from ruin,

---

The Sacred Home of the Choctaw

This story from the Lower Mississippi tells how the Choctaw people, when they moved their village, not only established a new connection with the Earth, but were guided by it.

The Choctaw elders gathered and chose two men, twins, who would lead them into new territory. But first a shaman told these men to cut a young, slender tree, and to strip it down into a pole. Then the shaman painted it and set it in the earth. "Whichever direction the stick points in the morning," said the holy man, "there you must travel." The following day, the stick was leaning towards the southeast and so the people began their journey in that direction, taking the pole with them. For years they travelled. Children were born and people died. And the remains of those who died on the way were carried in pots to their future settlement. Every night the people set up the pole, and every morning they consulted it. One morning, it stood upright, so then the people knew they had reached the land where they should settle.

"And where," they wondered, "shall we leave the remains of our loved ones?" "Let us place them

A painting by Paul Kane (1810–71) of a Native American village. Spiritual concerns were often important in influencing the choice of a camp site.

in this sacred mound of earth," the twins said. "The place of the Fruitful Mound is our home for ever."

That was how the Choctaw's sacred place came to be at Nanih Waya – at least until they were dispossessed of their land along the Mississippi, the River Beyond Age.

501

Smohalla's followers had to reject the habits of these strangers. To plough, dig mines and fence the land was not simply destroying natural habitats, it was murdering a cherished body. "You ask me to plough the ground! Shall I take a knife and tear my mother's bosom? You ask me to dig for stone! Shall I dig under her skin for bones? You ask me to cut grass and make hay and sell and be rich like the white men! But how dare I cut off my mother's hair?"

A similar anguish caused Young Chief, the leader of the Cayuse in the then Washington Territory, to ask: "I wonder if the ground has anything to say? I hear what the ground says. The ground says, 'It is the Great Spirit that placed me here. The Great Spirit tells me to take care of the Indians, to feed them properly.' The water says the same thing. The grass says the same thing. 'Feed the Indians well,' the ground says, 'the Great Spirit has placed me here to produce all that grows on me, trees and fruit.' In the same way the ground says, 'It was from me man was made. The Great Spirit in placing men on earth, desired them to take good care of the ground and to do each other no harm' ...."

Again and again, the Native American belief in the indivisibility of land and human existence is proclaimed. In 1900, nearly a century after Tecumseh's testimony, Big Thunder of the northeastern Wabanaki nation declared: "She [Mother Earth] nourishes us; that which we put into the ground, she returns to us, and healing plants she gives us likewise. If we are wounded we go to our mother to lay the wounded part against her to be healed." History rode roughshod over the landscape of Native America, but in the myths and ritual that continue to tell of its sacred past, the Earth lives on as the ultimate cosmic gift.

Sunset glows over the marshland of Bosque del Apache National Wildlife Park in New Mexico. The Native American attitude to the natural world is highly complex. Landscapes and skyscapes are not merely suffused with beauty; they also form part of the spiritual cosmos.

Old Man Arranges the World

Some myths describe how the Earth's sacred identity derives from the fact that the creator was once physically present. The mountainous western landscape of the Blackfeet bears the imprint of Napi, "Old Man", the mythical creator of the Earth.

The Blackfeet origin story tells of Old Man moving through primal territory, creating the features and the inhabitants of the rugged mountainous land that was to become the cherished homeland of the Blackfeet nation.

All the animals of the Plains at one time knew Old Man. He came from the south. He made the mountains, prairies, timber and brush. So he travelled, arranging the world as we see it today. Everywhere that Old Man went, he made new things. And all these things were connected to each other and were mutually useful. Old Man covered the Plains with grass for the animals. And when things were not quite right, he was prepared to adjust them. The prairies, for example, did not suit the ways of the bighorn. So Old Man took those animals by the horns and led them to the mountains. "This is the place that suits you," he said. He did the same when he made the antelope, leading them down from their first home in the mountains to the prairie. In this way, particular terrains and the creatures living upon them became suited to one another.

As he went about his primal, earth-moving and animal-arranging labours, the Old Man of the Blackfeet was often challenged by other great spirits, such as those of the sun and thunder, but his engaging and agreeable personality won through. He liked to rest from his labours every now and then, and he had a keen sense of humour. A lighthearted episode in the Blackfeet origin story describes how the creator sat on a steep hilltop and surveyed with some satisfaction the country he had made. "Well, this is a fine place for sliding," he mused, "I'll have some fun." He promptly began to slide down the hill; the marks he made while doing so can still be seen today in Montana at a place known as Old Man's Sliding Ground.

A World of Powerful Forces

Spirits of nature in Native American belief vary considerably in their power and significance. Some are seen as vast and even universal potencies, while others may hold sway over more specific aspects of the world, such as the wind, the sea, the rain or the animals. Still other spirits may be minor ghosts or sprites, appearing infrequently and only in restricted localities.

According to the Ojibway people of the northern woodlands, when the Earth was made four major spirits were put in place for the benefit of humankind. These spirits lived in each of the four directions and also held up the corners of the heavens. The spirit of the north brought ice and snow, which helped people to track animal footprints. The spirit of the south provided the climatic conditions that were favourable for the cultivation of pumpkins, melons, maize and tobacco. The western spirit was responsible for rain. And the spirit of the east brought light by commanding the sun to travel round the world.

This fragment of throat armour, made of shell by an ancient Mississippian artisan, is incised with crested woodpeckers, spiritual guardians of the four directions, and symbols of war.

Other Native American people also attributed spirits to the four cardinal points. Ga-oh, the Iroquoian wind giant, had four different animals – a bear, a panther, a moose and a fawn – at the mouth of his cave. When the north wind blew, the Iroquois said that the bear was at large in the sky. If the west wind blew, the panther was whining; the east wind was the moose "spreading his breath"; and the warm south wind was the "fawn returning to its doe".

Some spirits, such as the malevolent spirits of place that crop up in the hostile landscape of the Alaskan Inuit, are best avoided. If resting travellers have mysteriously disappeared beside a certain rock, then future travellers will take care to make their camp at a safe distance from the evil spirit inhabiting that rock.

Other spirits are benign, such as those accorded elaborate honours on the occasion of the Green Corn Dance, which was held every autumn by the Seneca of the northeast. During the dance one of the prominent tribal elders would address the servants of the "master of life" who had sustained the people through the year. This long speech began with an expression of collective happiness "because we are still alive in this world". The thanksgiving continued: "Besides this act, we give thanks to the earth, and we give thanks also to all the things it contains. Moreover, we give thanks to the visible sky. We give thanks to the orb of light that daily goes on its course during the daytime. We give our thanks nightly also to the light orb that pursues its course during the night. So now we give thanks also to those persons, the Thunderers, who bring the rains. Also we give thanks to the servants of the Master of Life, who protect and watch over us day by day and night by night."

Sometimes, a thoughtless or selfish individual can offend a spirit of nature and affect everyone's welfare, but a spirit's wrath need not be experienced as a general, communal crisis. The nature

Nipinouke and Pipounouke: Two Spirits of the Seasons

The eternal cycle of the seasons that is repeated every year is described in this Inuit story as a partnership between a couple of powerful spirit beings – Nipinouke brings spring and summer, while Pipounouke brings autumn and winter.

The Arctic's seasons stem from two spirits known as Nipinouke and Pipounouke. These spirits divide the world between them, each keeping to his own side for as long as he can. But eventually the time comes when they have to change places.

When Nipinouke comes, he brings with him warmth, birds, green leaves and fresh grass. But as summer wanes, Nipinouke must give up his place.

Pipounouke then arrives, bringing autumnal decay and the winds, ice and snow of winter. He destroys all that Nipinouke created. In this way there is *achitescatoueth*: succession in nature and balance in the world.

spirits of southwestern Pueblo myths, known as *kachina*s, will remind individuals of their obligations towards the whole community. A Tewa story describes a day when everyone was told to gather onions. But two girls felt lazy and decided to do something else. Towards evening they thought better of their disobedience, and had just begun to gather onions when the sun started setting. Suddenly one of them heard a noise. A *kachina* spirit appeared. It held two long yucca blades. "You don't obey the chief," said the *kachina*, and drew out its whip. "We'll go with you!" cried the girls, assuming the *kachina* was a human being. "No, I did not come to bring you home," said the *kachina*, and started to whip them. The girls ran, followed by the spirit. As they ran, they scattered the onions; the laces of their moccasins broke; their leggings came off; their shawls and belts dropped to the ground. The *kachina* then said, "Don't do it again! When people go out, they should all go together. This is what happens to disobedient girls. Now go home." They went home without any onions, and without their moccasins, belts and shawls.

Native American communities were frequently conscious of a great multitude of invisible forces at work. The Inuit myth world provides a dramatic example of how complicated this spirit

505

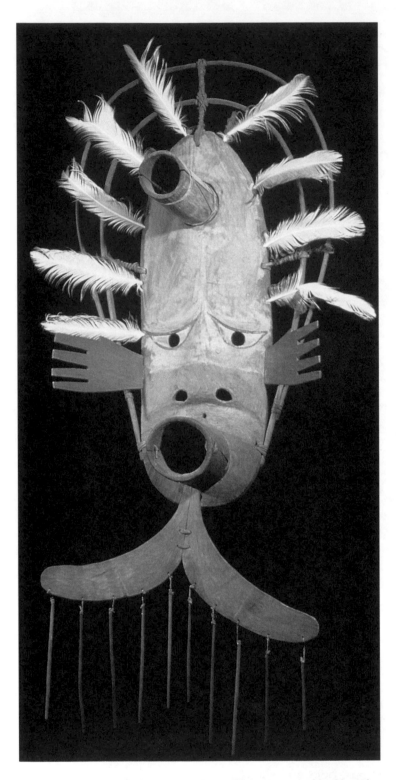

The Inuit wind-making spirit Tomalik is represented in this 19th-century shaman's mask. The winds of summer and winter blow through the tubes fitted in the mouth and forehead; white feathers evoke clouds and seabirds; and the lower pendants represent air bubbles rising from submerged seals.

life could be. In the Canadian Arctic, three major spirits ruled: the mother of the sea beasts (see page 491), the moon spirit and the spirit of the air and weather. If a man spoke too assertively about his hunting skills, he risked offending the spirit of the air and weather, and bringing on a chastening blizzard. Similarly, if a woman violated a taboo by preparing seal meat during her menstrual period, the offended mother of the sea beasts might withhold seals or walrus from the tribe.

Of primary importance to the hunters and fishermen of the Arctic and the Northwest Coast were the spirits of living animals. Successful hunters did not simply slaughter their prey. Animals would ignore a hunter if he did not promise to acknowledge their spirits by offering them the appropriate death rites. Among the Alaskan Inuit, the whale's soul, which lay in its head, had to be returned to the sea with the head intact, otherwise the soul could not return to its place of origin and be reborn. Other large or significant animals, such as caribou and wolves, had to be ritually butchered to allow their spirits to escape from their lodgings in the neck. Provided that men and women performed these rites, the animals would help them by "lending their bodies" – that is, by allowing themselves to be hunted.

There was a multitude of other spirits: those of ancestors which dwelled near village graves and camp sites; spirits of place inhabiting lakes and rocks; and spirits invisibly roaming the air which might approach an individual who showed mystical susceptibility and make a shaman of him or her. Many traditional Native American belief systems attributed powerful spirits to animals, plants and other natural phenomena. One of the first native words learned by missionaries and explorers in the northeastern woodlands and Great Lakes was the Algonquian term *manitou*, meaning "power, spirit, mystery". *Manitou*s were simultaneously forces in their own right and spirits inhabiting animals, places and the forces of nature. These powers were both helpful and vindictive. Even the shamans who controlled and interpreted spiritual forces were subject to their influence.

The Corn Spirit

To ensure a continuation of their divine blessings on hunting grounds and gardens, the spirits of nature had to be honoured appropriately. The northeastern Tuscarora people harvested and stored corn as their staple crop, and they learned the hard way how important it is to acknowledge the spirit of corn.

In a village where the corn harvest had always been rich, people became lazy and careless. They forgot to weed and left corn to be trampled. They let the dogs eat the surplus and stored their seed in poorly dug holes and damaged baskets. Worst of all, they neglected to give proper thanks to the spirit of the corn.

Assuming that they could continue to get more food by hunting, the men roamed the forest for game. But the animals had vanished. The hungry people dug up their baskets. But their stores had rotted or been eaten by mice. Only one man, Dayohagwenda, had given thanks for his harvest and stored his corn securely.

Walking in the forest one day, Dayohagwenda came upon an elm bark lodge surrounded by weeds. Seated there was an old man. Dirty and ragged, the old man was weeping. "Grandfather, why do you weep?" asked Dayohagwenda. "Because your people have forgotten me," replied the elder. As Dayohagwenda pursued his questions, he realized that the old man was the spirit of the corn, and that he was dirty and ragged because the people had become careless and ungrateful. The spirit of corn was weeping because he thought that he had been forgotten.

Dayohagwenda returned to the village and found the people on the verge of starvation.

Recounting what he had seen, he warned that the spirit of the corn might leave them for ever. If, however, the people began honouring him again, the spirit would help them. Then Dayohagwenda dug up his own supplies and found that the spirit had increased them.

From that time on, the people honoured the spirit of the corn. They carefully planted, weeded, harvested and stored. And they always gave thanks to the spirit who blessed them.

This modern painting honours Selu, the first woman of Cherokee myth, who produced the first beans from her breast and gave birth to corn after rubbing her stomach (see also page 491).

Tricksters: The Unpredictable Spirits

The jokers in the mythic pack, tricksters are found in the stories of all Native American peoples. Mischievous and capricious figures who deceive and exploit their fellow creatures for their own gratification, tricksters commonly appear as semi-divine but largely amoral presences at the creation of the world. In the guise of Raven, Coyote or Hare, they may permanently transform an animal's appearance or the course of a river. But just as often as they fool others, tricksters will themselves be duped and humbled. And however selfish and coarse they are, their antics provoke affectionate laughter, while their quick wits and mythic power inspire awe.

The generic term "trickster" was introduced by European and American writers – wherever a trickster figure appears in Native American myths, it was known only by a local name. Stories abound of tricksters in the form of Coyote, Raven or Hare, but they also appear in human (usually male) or semi-human form. Among the Ojibway and Menomini, the trickster was essentially the same being as the hero Manabozho, who was the product of a union between a woman and the spirit of the male north wind. And in Inuit myth, the male spirit of the moon, Alingnaq, who became master of the game animals, was exiled there for violating the taboo against incest after deceiving his sister into having sex. He is thus a creative and a destructive being.

Among the most famous series of trickster stories was that related by the Siouan-speaking Winnebago of central Wisconsin. In these tales, a chief breaks tribal taboos and then goes on the warpath. Talking nonsense and renouncing his social status, the ex-chief is shunned as a wicked person.

Many animal spirits are depicted on this Kwakiutl cedarwood totem pole. One of the principal Native American trickster figures, the Raven, is second from the base.

He then embarks on a solitary journey, "calling all the objects in the world younger brothers" and speaking to them in their own tongues. At this point, the chief becomes a trickster and a series of loosely connected tales relates how he roams the world, sometimes transforming things for the good, but mostly interfering mischievously in the affairs of animals and people. The exploits of this "Older Brother" are variously feared, marvelled at or viewed with indulgence and humour by his fellow beings. The trickster himself is regarded by turns as cunning, intelligent, foolish or unlucky.

The Two Sides of Manabozho

These contrasting character traits emerge clearly from two stories told by the Ojibway about the trickster and wonder-worker Manabozho. In the first, his skilful subterfuge brings him success in hunting. One day, Manabozho enticed a lone moose by claiming to be its estranged brother. As the animal drew near, he asked it whether it had heard the news about the person who killed its brother. Not realizing that the trickster was alluding to the moose's own impending death, it was caught off guard and Manabozho promptly slew it.

The other side of Manabozho's character emerges from a story relating how he once fell asleep, having ordered his rear end to guard some fowl roasting on a fire. When the birds were stolen and no alarm raised, he foolishly set his own hindquarters alight as punishment.

Nihansan's Foolish Dive

Many stories show the trickster as a victim of his own false perceptions. In an Arapaho legend, a figure called Nihansan dived into water to gather fruit that were merely reflections.

One day, Nihansan was walking by a stream when he spotted some juicy red plums under the water. He desperately wanted to eat them, so he undressed, dived into the water and groped about on the stream bed, trying to collect the fruit.

He emerged from the stream empty-handed, but resolved to try again. Taking some stones, he tied them to his wrists and ankles to weigh himself down under water. He plunged in for a second time, and searched the bottom in vain. Eventually, when he could hold his breath no longer, he released the stones and floated up to the surface.

Looking up, he suddenly noticed plums hanging on a tree above him. "You fool!" he said to himself, and climbed out of the water. He went to the tree, where he ate some of the plums and picked some more for his onward journey.

Many Ojibway stories about Manabozho portray him on the move, in search of fun and gratification. Yet however dissolute and wilful he allows himself to be, his transforming power is always present. One story recounts how he persuaded a group of swans, geese and ducks to dance for him with their eyes closed. Beating his drum with one hand, he broke the necks of these waterfowl with the other. Only the loon opened its eyes and escaped, for which Manabozho punished the bird by giving it its characteristic red eyes.

The Transformer and the Hare

Several Winnebago stories end with the trickster undergoing a character change and becoming a transformer after a series of mishaps. In one such tale, the trickster is weary of his life on Earth. He suddenly recalls why Earthmaker sent him to the world. As a last sign of his nobler disposition, he travels round removing hindrances to humans, for example by altering the course of rivers and clearing mountain passes of obstacles. Then he retires to heaven, leaving Hare in charge of the Earth.

509

In Winnebago stories, Hare is born of a virgin who dies, leaving him in the care of his grandmother. As he roams the world, he acts as both benefactor and clown. His grandmother, who represents the spirit of the Earth, often has to rescue him or excuse his bungling mistakes. In one tale, similar to a Manabozho story, Hare plans a snooze while roasting some duck and orders his anus to watch the fire for him. But foxes steal the meat and when he wakes up he punishes his anus by inserting a firebrand, whereupon he yells in pain and curses his own stupidity. As he hobbles away he picks up and eats a lump of fat he finds en route, until he quickly realizes it is part of his intestines that has fallen from his damaged behind. He effects a repair by pulling things tightly back into place, thereby creating the anus's wrinkled appearance.

Raven, the Creator and Mischief-maker

Raven was a highly important trickster figure and for peoples of the Northwest Coast, the Arctic and the Subarctic, he was, and still is, a heroic creator. Countless myths describe how Raven created the world, yet he is also treated as the supreme trickster. This seeming paradox may ultimately derive from conflicting attitudes towards the real bird – for example, the Koyukon Indians of central Alaska regard ravens as clever birds, but also consider their behaviour unpredictable and comic. Moreover, while ravens appear quick-witted and keenly aware of human behaviour, they are actually lazy scavengers, living off the food that animals and people have made efforts to hunt.

As a creator, Raven made the world twice over. The first world was idyllic: meat was plentiful and rivers flowed in both directions, so people never had to paddle their canoes. But Raven thought this world too easy for humans, and so remade it in its familiar form, with all its hardships and woes. This primal Great Raven is revered among Northwest Coast peoples as the "grandfather" figure to whom people attribute creative and healing power and to whom they pray for luck in hunting, good health and prosperity.

Yet Raven has a negative dimension to his character, which emerges in his reputation for selfishness and greed. Both real ravens and Raven the trickster are thought to lead an easy life, and some contempt attaches to them accordingly. Myths describe Dotson'sa (the Great Raven creator) as sleeping in dogskin blankets, whose foul smell and roughness were repellent to people.

The paradox of Raven's character, and of the ambivalent attitudes shown towards him, is expressed in a multitude of myths and legends from the Northwest Coast. To the region's peoples Raven is a creator and transformer, but also a buffoon and dupe. The Haida call him Power-of-the-Shining-Heavens, because he made both day and night. Likewise, he created the great rivers, the forests that

A 19th-century Tlingit emblem hat, worn for ceremonial occasions by members of the Raven clan. Throughout North America, Raven was a widespread trickster hero, held responsible for many things, including bringing light to the Earth.

The trickster figure Hare is shown in this Navajo weaving.
Hare is both a benefactor and a clown, and, like
other tricksters, can effect transformations.

teem with wildlife, the useful trees and berries and the sea with all its fish and mammals.

Alongside accounts of these achievements are comic tales of Raven's mischief-making and humiliation. In a story told by the Nootka of British Columbia, some old people were sitting watching a woman with eight braids of hair who was walking on the beach. She carried with her a stick, and began to dig up clams. Soon a tall figure with black hair appeared. The people recognized the pair as Octopus and Raven, and knew that Raven would begin to pester Octopus. Raven duly sat on a rock and asked her, "Octopus, are you digging for clams?" Octopus woman continued in silence. Raven repeated his question, but still got no reply.

Suddenly, after he had asked for a fourth time, Octopus's braids turned into tentacles. Wrapping four around Raven and four around the rock, she said, "Raven, I'm glad you asked that question. Yes. I am digging clams. These are clams. And I am digging them." Raven struggled. The tide was coming in. "You have answered my question, Octopus. Thank you. Now please let me go." But, as the water became deeper, Octopus kept repeating her answer and held Raven fast. The water rose over his head, and the people saw him drown. They were unconcerned, however, as they knew he would come to life again. And indeed, the very next day, Raven was back. But he refrained from asking Octopus any more questions.

Respecting the Animals

The relationship between humans and animals was fundamental to all aspects of Native American life. For most peoples, survival without animals would have been impossible. Meat, skin, bone, sinew, feather and ivory supplied almost all the essential needs of daily existence.

An Alaskan Inuit shaman's mask combining a spirit being's face with the image of a seal, one of the principal sea animals hunted by the peoples of the Arctic and Subarctic regions.

It was essential for humans to understand the animal kingdom. From childhood, people acquired a store of wisdom about the natural history of their locality, including a knowledge of animal behaviour, feeding and breeding habits, and migratory cycles. Combined with this was a repertory of specialized hunting techniques. Consummate hunters knew where and when to stalk prey, and the precise moment to strike in any given weather conditions. Moreover, this body of practical know-how was underpinned by a rich fund of myth, legend, songs and rituals, which placed a hunter's actions in context. To hunt meant infinitely more than killing; it was an act of spiritual significance with rules of conduct. Although animals were revered as holy beings, there was no contradiction in the view that the sacred and beautiful must also be killed.

Native Americans believe that all creatures are under the control of a guardian spirit (see box, opposite), understood either literally, as the father or mother of every animal in a particular species, or figuratively, as the species' collective spirit, comprising the souls of all its individuals. Some animals – notably the buffalo, eagle and bear – had powerful spirits that could help people or harm them according to how they were treated.

It was widely thought that animals and their spirit owners sacrificed themselves willingly to hunters who accorded them the proper "respect". However, this was far from straightforward, since correct hunting behaviour was fraught with taboos. For example, the Cherokee claimed that when a hunter shot a deer, the chief spirit of deer asked the dying animal whether it had heard the hunter pray for pardon. If not, the deer spirit would track the hunter to his tent and cripple him with rheumatism.

Sometimes, a hunter's skill derived from having had a close kinship with an animal. A myth of the Mistassini Cree of Quebec tells how a bear adopted a boy, sharing with him its diet of beaver, porcupine and partridge. The boy grew up to be a successful hunter, with a special understanding of the ways of bears. Peoples also believed that an individual or clan could form a special relationship with a particular species, which then acted as their guardian animal. The Iroquois proscribed the hunting of their clan totem species, such as the turtle and wolf, but among Great Basin peoples it was permitted if the person meant to assimilate the animal's power. In many areas it was the practice to dress up like the animal patron, wear its mask, or keep parts of its body in a sacred bundle.

512

Summoning the Buffalo to Aid the Hunter

For a major undertaking such as a buffalo hunt, the peoples of the Plains undertook spiritual preparations that were as meticulously detailed as the tactics of the chase itself. Plains Apache hunters were typical in the care they took over the correct hunting and butchering techniques.

The Plains Apache would begin their preparations for hunting by praying that the guardian spirit of the buffalo would ensure a plentiful supply of animals. The hunters lit a sacred pipe and petitioned the animal's spirit with the following wish: "There will be many. There will be much meat. We will camp among them."

The people would then sing and dance in honour of the buffalo, mimicking the animal's horns by putting their hands to their heads.

At times when the herds were scarce, the Plains Apache observed a special hunting ritual, conducted by the community's shaman. A piece of level ground was prepared, on which the shaman would scatter dung and pollen. As the people prayed, he performed four songs and imitated the bellowing of buffalo.

At the conclusion of a successful hunt, butchering had to be conducted according to a stringent procedure, lest the animal's soul be offended and its companions avoid future hunters. First, the hide was cut along the right shoulder. The foreleg and shoulder were then severed. A slice of fatty meat was cut from the back and thrown towards the east as an offering to the animal's spirit. The remainder of the animal was turned into food and clothing.

Care and reverence were shown even in dealing with the rest of the carcass. The feet, in particular, were treated with great respect, for fear of incurring the wrath of the spirit and being trampled by the herd's hooves on the next hunt.

A painting of a Buffalo Dance among Plains peoples by the artist George Catlin (1794–1872).

MESOAMERICA'S GODS OF SUN AND SACRIFICE

In November 1519, a battle-weary group of Spanish soldiers led by Hernán Cortés caught sight of the Aztec capital, Tenochtitlan. Founded in 1325 and laid out on islands in the middle of a vast lake, Tenochtitlan was a metropolis of some 200,000 people, much bigger than the largest European city of its day. What Cortés and his compatriots were gazing at was the culmination of 3,000 years of continuous cultural development.

The Aztecs (or more accurately, the Mexica) were heirs to a tradition that had begun in the mid-second millennium BC with the Olmecs and had been carried forward by a succession of peoples, including the Zapotecs, Mixtecs, Toltecs and, particularly influentially, the Maya. These peoples' imposing cities, temples and palaces resembled in many ways those of ancient Mesopotamia and Egypt. Yet, unlike those cultures, Central American civilizations developed without cross-currents of influence from elsewhere. Because the Aztecs were the dominant group in the region when the Spanish arrived, most of what we know about Mesoamerican myth comes from them. But as relative newcomers to power (their empire was only a century old when the Spanish arrived), the Aztecs had sought legitimacy by borrowing their gods from the succession of civilizations that had held sway in the Valley of Mexico for a millennium before them. Aztec myths were, for the most part, the shared myths of the region.

Above: **The pyramid called Temple I at Tikal has nine giant steps, symbolizing the levels of the Maya underworld.**

Opposite: **A limestone lintel from Yaxchilan depicts Lady Xoc as she lets blood, while her husband King Shield Jaguar holds a torch over her. Glyphs record the date of this ritual as October 28, AD709.**

Despite the immense destruction that was wrought during the ensuing Spanish Conquest, sufficient evidence survived – including a copy of the Quiché Maya's sacred *Popol Vuh* – for later scholars to gain an understanding of the region's civilizations and religions, the daily importance of which was recorded in stone and in paint. The picture that emerges is one of beliefs and patterns of thought that, in general, strike us as alien. Both the Maya and the Aztecs saw the world and humankind's role in it as forming part of a continuous cycle of destruction and regeneration. Within each cycle a cosmic disaster loomed as an ever-present danger, one they thought could be averted only by an offering of blood – human blood – to honour the gods.

The Maya Universe

For the Maya, the universe was fundamentally unstable yet predictable: living creatures occupied preordained positions and the world and its inhabitants were believed to exist within an alternating pattern of origination and destruction, each cycle of which lasted 5,200 years. This universe was a tripartite structure, with an uppermost layer of existence, or heaven; an Earth; and a fearsome underworld.

In Maya cosmology, the realm of heaven was one of permanence; its stability was assured by massive cosmic trees that anchored it in place. This sphere of existence was divided into thirteen distinct levels, each of which was presided over by a god. The Maya believed that a person had to have met a violent end if they were to enter heaven in the afterlife. Each stratum was reserved for a particular kind of violent death; thus, sacrificial victims inhabited a layer of their own, while those who had been struck by lightning or drowned resided in the level that was ruled by the rain god Chac.

So deeply ingrained was this conception of a stratified universe among the Maya that their temples and shrines were most commonly built on top of pyramids or on the summits of mountains, in order that religious observances and rituals could be conducted as close as humanly possible to the divine realms of the sky.

At the base of the cosmic structure lay the gloomy underworld kingdom that was known to the Quiché Maya as Xibalba ("Place of Fright"). It had nine layers and its own complement of deities. One god particularly identified with the underworld was the screech-owl Muan, who was also associated with maize and rain. In many cases the underworld gods resembled, or represented certain aspects of, deities of the Earth and sky.

Xibalba was the destination of the great majority of people after death. In all Mesoamerican societies, no notion of human morality was attached to the afterlife; unlike hell in Christian cosmology, the Maya underworld was not reserved for sinners, but was simply the final home of everyone who had not come to a violent end. Thus it was that kings, priests and noblemen who

An effigy from Tikal of the Old Fire God, one of a number of gods constantly revered in the Maya pantheon.

passed away peacefully were interred in imposing nine-layer pyramids – such as Temple I at Tikal, the Castillo at Chichén Itzá in the Yucatán peninsula, and the Temple of Inscriptions at Palenque – which symbolized the levels of Xibalba.

Once a person had entered the underworld, they were faced with a series of trials in which they were required to outwit the repellent gods who held sway over this realm. If victorious, the deceased person would ultimately ascend into the sky as a heavenly body. For the Maya, the epitome of how to negotiate the ordeals of the underworld successfully was the conduct of the Hero Twins, who thwarted the Lords of Xibalba at every twist and turn (see pages 528–533).

The Maya worshipped an extensive pantheon of deities. These are extremely difficult to categorize, as many gods appeared in a number of guises. For example, a particular deity might possess male and female characteristics, and have the capacity to be both old and young, and to assume either spiritual or corporeal form. In addition, many supernatural beings displayed animal characteristics, or combined human and divine attributes. Thus, the Hero Twins of the *Popol Vuh,* who left the upper world and descended into the depths to subdue the lords of the underworld, were themselves demigods.

Similar confusion surrounds the question of the supreme god of the Maya. At the beginning of Maya civilization (the Formative Period, *c.*200–*c.*100BC), two major deities, Itzamna (the god of writing, curing and divination, who was also known as Hunab Ku, or "Only Spirit") and Seven Macaw (Vucub Caquix, a bird deity), occupied this position at various times. Later, during the Preclassic Period (*c.*100BC–*c.*AD300), Seven Macaw rose to prominence and was thought to exert a powerful and benign influence over people's lives. By the time the *Popol Vuh* ("Council Book") of the Quiché Maya came to be written, however, he had been reduced to the role of a boastful impostor. For their part, the Quiché Maya revered a patron deity called Tohil (see page 535) as the Supreme Being, while the Postclassic Period (*c.*AD900–1535)

witnessed the growth of cults to central Mexican gods such as the Plumed Serpent, Quetzalcoatl. Likewise, the agricultural deity Xipe Totec ("Our Lord the Flayed One") had gained a large cult following by the time of the Spanish Conquest.

While the identity of the highest deity thus changed over time, other long-established deities in the Maya pantheon, such as the rain god Chac and the maize god (who corresponded to the divine hero One Hunahpu), were consistently revered. The trees that held the cosmos in place at its four corners, together with a central World Tree, were common features of the mythology and

The putrid Lords of Xibalba cavort in this ceramic pot painting. The figure on the left is feline. The central lord has a fleshless skull, while the stomach of the figure on the right is distended by disease and he has insect-like wings on its shoulders.

religion of several Mesoamerican cultures. The *Books of Chilam Balam,* sixteenth-century accounts of history, myth and prophecy from the Yucatán, describe the establishment of the trees aligned to the four cardinal directions as the first act of creation following the destruction of the old cosmos. Every tree and direction had its own color – white for north, yellow for south, red for east and black for west, while the central tree was green. Similarly, all the birds and plants associated with each tree were of the same color.

The Earth is Born

The *Popol Vuh*, the sacred hieroglyphic text of the Quiché Maya, opens with a description of how the gods of the sea and the sky joined forces to create the world in its present form. This momentous event took place amid great stillness and resulted from language: when the creator gods whispered the word Earth, it came into being. According to Maya calculations, creation took place recently – at the beginning of the current universal cycle, in 3114BC.

Prior to the act of creation, there was a dark void, containing nothing except the sky and the sea. There were no rocks, meadows or forests, nor were there any people, animals, fish or birds. Yet great creative potential was latent in this emptiness, in the shape of several gods who resided either in the sea or the sky.

Eventually, two of the principal deities, one from each realm, joined together to instigate creation. The sky god creator was called Heart of Sky, or Hurricane, and manifested himself as lightning. His partner was a sea god known as Sovereign Plumed Serpent, or Gucumatz. According to the *Popol Vuh*, these two deities were "great knowers and thinkers", and life began as soon as they engaged in dialogue.

The gods' first task – to shape the Earth from the vast and silent waters – is compared to the way that a farmer prepares a field of maize.

The importance of maize to the Maya was signified by the numerous gods associated with it. This statue of a maize god is from Honduras.

This agricultural metaphor anticipates the gods' long-term plan to create the present human race, or "people of corn".

The gods professed themselves happy with their work. The waters had receded, mountains arisen and trees grown. Over their new creation stood the vault of the sky. However, the Earth's silence still troubled them. Clearly, they needed to create animals. So they brought to life deer, birds, jaguars and serpents, then assigned them their places in the forest.

Believing that these creatures would naturally have the power of speech, the gods told them to announce themselves. But the only noises that they could utter were inarticulate screeches, grunts, howls and bellows. This greatly displeased the gods, because they had failed to fashion creatures who could pay them the respect that they felt was their due. In their anger and disappointment, the gods ordered the animals never to stray beyond the limits of the forest and to be subservient to the human beings who were to come.

Mud People and Wooden People

In Maya mythology, there is no sovereign deity who makes perfect beings in its own image. Rather, before humans arrived on the scene, the creator gods attempted several times to people the world with beings who could reflect their glory. When these proved inadequate, they were obliged to destroy them and try again.

Disappointed that the animals – their first animate creations – did not speak a comprehensible language, Gucumatz and Hurricane decided to create another species. What they required on Earth were beings who could call on them by name, pay them homage and feed them with regular sacrifices.

Thus they set about fashioning bodies out of earth and mud. But no sooner were they made than the creatures seemed utterly wrong; they were too soft and fell to pieces easily, their faces were lopsided and they could not articulate their words properly. Moreover, these mud people had no conception of how to honour the gods by assigning them particular days of worship within a calendar. In the absence of this, no proper relationship could be established between the divine beings and their creations.

The gods then tried for a second time. On this occasion, they made people out of wood. The males were hewn from the wood of the coral tree, while the females were made out of the fibrous cores of bulrushes. At first, these wooden people seemed to be a success. Their appearance and language were correct, and they were able to procreate. But two major defects soon became apparent. First, their minds were devoid of thoughts and their hearts were empty of feelings; as a result, they had no memory of or devotion to their creators. Second, they did not develop physically. Their skin was dry and crusty, their movements uncoordinated and their bodies were wont to warp.

So Hurricane called forth a mighty flood and drowned the wooden manikins. The only reminders of these prototype people, according to Maya belief, are the forest monkeys, who resemble underdeveloped humans.

The First Genocide

The *Popol Vuh* and other Mayan texts contain graphic portrayals of how Hurricane brutally exterminated the race of wooden people that he and his fellow creator god Gucumatz had made. After he had ruthlessly killed most of the people with a flood, Hurricane visited a series of gruesome fates upon the survivors.

To rid himself of the last of his failed creations, Hurricane first called on the services of two fearsome monsters: one, called Gouger of Faces, plucked out the wooden people's eyes, while the other – Sudden Bloodletter – ripped off their heads. In addition, the help of two monstrous jaguars, known as Crunching Jaguar and Tearing Jaguar, was enlisted – and they tore people limb from limb and ate their flesh.

Pictorial Maya codices show in gory detail some of the results of unleashing these monsters. For example, in the *Madrid Codex*, Gouger of Faces is portrayed as a king vulture diving on a seated wooden manikin. In its beak, the monstrous bird holds one of its victim's eyes, which remains attached to its socket by the optic nerve.

The *Popol Vuh*, though lacking in illustrations, gives a vivid description of the holocaust that overtook the wooden people. It relates how molten pitch rained down from the sky onto them, and how they were then crushed and hammered, until their flesh and bones were reduced to dust. The text goes on to tell how survivors were relentlessly hunted down in a permanent nightmarish twilight where rain falls incessantly. All the

A fearsome animal lurks on the far left of this detail of a page from the *Madrid Codex* – also known as the *Codex Tro-Cortesianus*. This and the other surviving pictorial Maya codices contain many depictions of the dreadful beasts which were let loose by the creator gods Hurricane and Gucumatz to eradicate the inadequate wooden people they had created.

accounts and images of this genocide in the codices bear witness to the sheer fury of the gods' attack on their flawed creations for their dullness and incompetence.

The onslaught continued unabated. Animals burst into people's houses, bringing wild nature into what had been domestic calm. The belief persists in modern Maya society that wild animals or birds which suddenly irrupt into a human dwelling are a warning of the gods' displeasure.

Domestic Chaos

Then new heights of terror were reached as the natural order was turned completely upside down. While the wild animals burst into the wooden people's homes, their possessions – animate and inanimate – began to speak. The domestic animals, such as dogs and turkeys, rebuked their former masters for having mistreated and eaten them. In a horribly violent image, the dogs proclaimed their revenge, snapping out that "today you people will taste the teeth in our mouths! We shall eat you instead!"

Likewise, the previously dumb, inanimate kitchen equipment came to life. Water jars, grinding stones and tortilla griddles all sprang into action. The grinding stones complained how their faces had been ripped and rubbed all day. "At first," announced the stones, "we did you service. But now the boot's on the other foot!" As they said this, they joined Hurricane in pounding the wooden people to dust.

The cooking pots then took up the theme, upbraiding the people for constantly scorching their faces and making their mouths sooty. "In return," they declared, "we shall burn you!" Finally, even the hearth stones came flying right out of the fireplace, like stones shooting out of a volcano, and rained down upon the wooden people's heads, crushing their faces.

Dogs were an integral part of every Maya household; as well as guarding the property, they could provide a meal for the family every now and then. This vessel in the shape of a dog may have been used ritually.

In the face of this fearsome attack, the wooden people ran for their lives in all directions. Some climbed on to the roofs of their houses, but these structures gave way and collapsed. Those who clambered up into the trees to escape the terrifying onslaught were instantly shaken down to the ground by the branches themselves. Others rushed to seek shelter in caves, only to see huge boulders roll into the cave entrances behind them, entombing them forever. Thus the fate of the unfortunate wooden people was sealed and their destruction was complete.

The Arrogant Impostor

Prior to the dawning of the present era, a monstrous bird known as Seven Macaw presumed to set himself up as the principal deity presiding over the gloomy twilight world that was left behind after the universal flood. This earthly pretender to power and his vain offspring had to be destroyed before the human race could be created.

Seven Macaw was characterized above all by his boastfulness and arrogance, and the way that he basked in his own delusions of grandeur. Chief among these was his claim to be both the sun and the moon. At this early stage, night and day had not yet become separate. Instead, a kind of "sun–moon" shone dimly through a mantle of cloud, creating a state of permanent twilight.

This Classic Period (c.AD300–c.900) tripod vase depicts the bird deity Seven Macaw, or Vucub Caquix. The bird is shown in characteristically proud posture, with its wings outstretched and wearing a necklace which is thought to signify power.

had the power to "bring down the sky". Yet in the very arrogance of these beings lay the seeds of their own destruction, for such exorbitant claims constituted a direct challenge to the authority of the founder gods (see pages 518–521). Clearly, this family of monsters would have to be done away with and more modest beings created in their place if the gods were to receive the respect they demanded.

In these crepuscular conditions, Seven Macaw was far and away the brightest being. "My light is great," he crowed, "I glow, I glitter, I shine." And, indeed, his physical appearance was nothing short of spectacular. His splendid plumage was made of precious metals and gemstones. His face was framed by jewel-encrusted, burnished metal plates, while his teeth were gleaming blue sapphires. Even the nest he lived in was built of dazzling metal. His proud boast was that his great white beak "shone into the distance like the moon".

Seven Macaw's vainglory even extended to claiming that he had dominion over time, since he fancied that he represented all the days and months of the year. His two sons entertained similar conceits: Zipacna dubbed himself the "maker of mountains", while Earthquake believed that he

Accordingly, Seven Macaw and his sons were engaged in combat by the Hero Twins Hunahpu and Xbalanque. These important characters appear in the *Popol Vuh* as the offspring of the union between the god Hun Hunahpu ("One Hunahpu") and an underworld maiden known as Xquic ("Blood Moon"). Their brave exploits, which they undertake in order to avenge the death of their father and his brother in the underworld (see page 528), all centre on vanquishing the evil forces that ruled the early world and on preparing the ground for the advent of human beings.

The first confrontation between Seven Macaw and the Hero Twins is described in terms of a hunting expedition. First, the Hero Twins lay in wait beneath the fruit tree where Seven Macaw habitually appeared to feed. At length, when he came, they opened fire with their blowguns. Hunahpu scored a direct hit that dislocated the bird's jaw. Stunned by the surprise attack, Seven Macaw plummeted to earth behind the tree.

But as Hunahpu rushed up to finish off his quarry, the bird seized his arm in its powerful beak and wrenched it from his shoulder. Hunahpu was left with a bleeding wound. The first engagement between Seven Macaw and the Hero Twins thus ended in stalemate. Evidently, an even greater effort was required to rid the world of the conceited monster.

In the next phase of the battle, the Hero Twins employed subterfuge in preference to direct assault. The scene opens with the slow progress home of Seven Macaw, who was carrying Hunahpu's arm and nursing his injured jaw. He told his wife about being ambushed by the Hero Twins: "They shot me with their blowguns and dislocated my jaw; now my teeth are all loose and I've got a terrible toothache." Yet despite being in excruciating pain, Seven Macaw hung Hunahpu's arm over his fire and dared the boys to come and retrieve it.

The Powers of Birds and Beasts

Animals and birds played a prominent role in Maya religion and myth. Certain species were identified with gods and celestial bodies, or were assigned social or calendrical significance.

The jaguar, revered as the top predator of the Maya rainforest, naturally came to be associated closely with the principal heavenly body, the sun. In addition, the Maya venerated a wide range of jaguar gods, variously identified with the underworld, the night, caves, stealth and hunting.

Another clear association was that between the wrinkled reptilian caiman and the old supreme deity of the Maya, Itzamna. Less obvious was the widely perceived affinity between the rabbit and the moon; a rabbit's profile was thought to be visible in the full moon.

Animals and birds also had a major symbolic function in the naming of people, clans and days and years on the sacred Maya calendar. Two of the first four human beings were called Jaguar Quitze and Jaguar Night. The harpy eagle was the personification of both the 20-year *katun* and the 400-year *baktun* calendrical cycles. The divine twins One Monkey and One Artisan (see pages 530–531) together were used to signify the eleventh day (Chuen), of the Maya calendar, on which shamans divined the future. Children born on this day were thought happy and fortunate.

masquerading as travelling shamans who specialized in curing toothache. The elders pronounced themselves happy to take part in this charade, and so the four set off for Seven Macaw's house.

Seven Macaw's Defeat

The monster sat wracked with pain by the toothache that the jaw injury had caused. Nevertheless, when the elders arrived, he observed the custom of greeting them with elaborate courtesies. He then enquired after the identity of the old couple's "children", and was told that they were orphans who travelled around with them, living off their leftovers.

Satisfied with this answer, Seven Macaw then asked the elders what "poisons" they could cure. In a comically self-pitying speech, he gave vent to the agony that his teeth were putting him through. "It's unbearable," he moaned, "I can't sleep and my eyes are sore. My teeth are all loose and I can't eat anything. Take pity on me!" "Very well, your lordship," replied the elders, "our diagnosis is that a worm is eating your jaw bone." (Interestingly, the Quiché Maya still believe that toothache is caused by worms.) The elderly couple then told Seven Macaw that, in order to get the worm out, they would have to extract his teeth; this remedy would also, they claimed, cure his eyes.

Vain as he was, the bird was alarmed at the thought of losing his beautiful teeth, but the elders reassured him that they would replace them with false teeth in "ground bone" of the very finest quality. Seven Macaw was thus persuaded, and the bogus shamans set to work, removing the monster's teeth of exquisite blue gemstones. However,

Meanwhile the Hero Twins approached two venerable white-haired elders to help them retrieve Hunahpu's arm and finally vanquish the monster. The first elder was a grandfather called Great White Peccary, the second a grandmother by the name of Great White Coati. The twins contrived a deception that involved them posing as the elders' orphaned grandchildren. The two old people were to approach Seven Macaw

they did not substitute them with ground bone teeth as they had promised, but only with kernels of white corn, and then proceeded to strip the area around his eyes of its precious metal. While the elders went about their task, the bird felt no pain and suspected nothing.

The image of the bird's dislocated jaw in this myth is thought to allude to the peculiar shape of the beak of the real scarlet macaw, with its large upper mandible and smaller lower one. Similarly, the removal of the metal discs around Seven Macaw's eyes is believed to explain the origin of the featherless white patches around the eyes of the real scarlet macaw.

The supposed "cure" applied by the elders simply succeeded in robbing Seven Macaw of all the signs of his prestige. And since his status rested entirely on outward show, he was nothing once divested of his gold and jewels. He promptly wasted away before their very eyes.

The episode thus concludes with total victory for the Hero Twins and with great rewards being bestowed on their helpers. As well as inheriting the huge amounts of wealth that Seven Macaw had amassed, the elders (who really were gifted doctors when they wanted to be) even managed to fit Hunahpu's severed arm back into its socket and make it as good as new.

Seven Macaw in the Heavens

Despite his depiction as an absurd and foolish figure in this tale, Seven Macaw had profound mythological and astronomical significance for the Maya people. They associated him with the seven stars that comprise the constellation of the Plough or Big Dipper, the rising and falling of which mark the beginning and end of the hurricane season in Central America. So according to some scholars, Seven Macaw's fall from the tree after being hit by

Hunahpu's blowgun pellet represented the descent of the constellation during the month of July.

Furthermore, the sequence of events as described in the *Popol Vuh* had a particular symbolic resonance. Seven Macaw and his two sons came to prominence in the immediate aftermath of the universal flood that Hurricane summoned up in order to sweep away the wooden people (see box, page 519). The Maya would probably have associated the onset of the torrential tropical rains that accompanied the rise of Ursa Major every year with this great mythological deluge.

The legend of Seven Macaw and his sons also had a clear didactic purpose, acting as a cautionary tale about the perils of overweening pride and personal vanity. Above all, the Maya valued modesty in their heroes; in common with many of the other characters in Maya mythology, it is the total absence of this quality in the monstrous bird and his offspring that seals their fate.

The ambush which leads to the final defeat of Seven Macaw is seen in this ceramic pot. In the foreground kneels the Hero Twin Hunahpu, who aims his blowgun at the bird deity.

Zipacna and Earthquake

Having destroyed Seven Macaw, the Hero Twins still had to deal with his two sons Zipacna and Earthquake, who had inherited their father's insufferable arrogance. The elder son, Zipacna, called himself "the maker of mountains", while his brother Earthquake styled himself "breaker of mountains".

The Hero Twins' defeat of the offspring of Seven Macaw is prefaced by the story of an earlier attempt to destroy his first son, Zipacna. In this tale, a group of proto-humans called the Four Hundred Boys enlisted Zipacna's help in carrying a huge tree trunk, but became alarmed at his enormous strength. So, they plotted to murder him by dropping the tree on top of him as he dug a hole for them. But Zipacna realized what was afoot and quickly excavated a side tunnel, which he scrambled into in the nick of time. In order to convince the boys that he was dead, he then cut off pieces of his nails and tufts of his hair and gave them to ants to carry to the surface. By and by, when the boys had drunk themselves into a stupor in celebration, Zipacna burst out of the ground, collapsed the hut and killed them all. The boys ascended to heaven and became the Pleiades.

The Hero Twins were deeply saddened at the loss of the Four Hundred Boys, and resolved to

One of the Hero Twins presents the head and body of Zipacna – packed neatly in a jar – to the Maya's major deity Itzamna on this roll-out of a Maya burial vessel.

kill Zipacna. Taking flowers and a large flagstone, they constructed a fake crab as a decoy to lure the gluttonous monster to his death. They placed it in a deep canyon, and told Zipacna about the juicy meal awaiting him. On reaching the canyon Zipacna let himself down to eat the crab. But the rock that made the false crustacean's back had been balanced in such a way that it rolled on top of him the instant he touched it. He struggled free, but immediately returned. At this point, the story leaves it unclear whether Zipacna fell headlong down the canyon and broke his neck, or choked to death on the "crab". In any event, the incident spelt the end of him; now it only remained for Hunahpu and Xbalanque to conquer Earthquake.

Earthquake's Downfall

Seven Macaw's second son, Earthquake, grew larger and heavier than even the sun. As this threatened to disrupt the divine order, the founder god Heart of Sky ordered the Hero Twins to end Earthquake's existence.

Like his gargantuan brother Zipacna, Earthquake spent his time roaming the world destroying things, including his brother's work. Thus, where Zipacna had raised a mountain, Earthquake would knock it flat.

Once again, Hunahpu and Xbalanque used guile to approach Earthquake. Passing themselves off as simple hunters, they excited his curiosity by telling him about a new mountain they had seen rising in the east. Earthquake told them to take him there, boasting that he would destroy it.

They set off in single file, with Earthquake walking between the two boys. On their journey, the Hero Twins shot birds with their blowpipes. Their hunting prowess impressed their companion, as did their skilful preparation of the wildfowl. Before cooking the birds, the boys smeared them with plaster ground from rocks dug from the soil. What Earthquake did not realize, however, was that they were practising magic: in smothering the birds thus, the Hero Twins were anticipating Earthquake's own enclosure in the soil after his death.

Earthquake ate greedily and they went on their way. But just as they arrived at the mountain, the monster's strength left him; the magic coating on the birds had taken effect. He instantly fell down dead. The two brothers then bound his wrists and ankles and buried him in the Earth. Thus the world was finally rid of the last of the monsters.

The Birth of the Hero Twins

The *Popol Vuh* interrupts its narrative of the adventures of the Hero Twins to recount their genesis and early life. Like their later exploits, this is a story of unrelenting conflict and turmoil. In particular, their campaign against misrule of the Earth must be seen in the light of the destruction of their father and uncle by the Lords of Xibalba (the underworld).

The twin deities One Hunahpu and Seven Hunahpu – respectively the father and the uncle of the future Hero Twins – had one abiding passion: the ballgame. So noisy was one of their hard-fought contests that it drew the attention of the main lords of the underworld realm of Xibalba, One Death and Seven Death. They resolved to summon the twins to attend them, kill them and annex their ballcourt. Accordingly, they dispatched four owls to lead One Hunahpu and Seven Hunahpu down into the bowels of the Earth. On their way down, the twins had to traverse deep canyons, cross rivers of blood and pus, cross barriers of spikes and fight armies of scorpions. They survived these hardships, and eventually arrived in Xibalba. Here, they were set three tests by the underworld lords. First the lords dressed up manikins to look like themselves; when One Hunahpu and Seven Hunahpu greeted these counterfeits respectfully, the real lords laughed derisively. Then they fooled the twins into sitting on a hot stone. Finally, each twin was given a lighted torch and a cigar, with the instruction that they must be returned in the morning "just as they look now". On failing this final, unpassable test, they were executed and buried in the underworld ballcourt.

Before interring the twins, the underworld lords severed One Hunahpu's head, changed it into a gourd and placed it in the fork of a tree. The tree promptly bore a great crop of fruit, which no-one was allowed to touch. But a young woman, Blood Moon (Xquic in Mayan), daughter of the lord Blood Gatherer, tried to pick the gourd that had once been One Hunahpu's skull. As she did so, the gods ordained that the gourd spat into her hand, making her pregnant with Hunahpu and Xbalanque. When Blood Gatherer learned of his daughter's indiscretion, he flew into a rage and ordered her sacrifice. But Blood Moon persuaded the messenger owls sent to conduct her to her execution to spare her. They deceived the underworld lords with a lump of red cochineal resin in the shape of Blood Moon's heart. This ruse gained her enough time to reach the upper world.

The birth of the Hero Twins, whose mother Blood Moon was impregnated by a gourd, was a momentous event in the history of the Quiché. This terracotta figure of a pregnant woman is from the Guatemala highlands.

The Deadly Ballgame

The ballgame was played throughout Mesoamerica. The ball was made of solid rubber and the game usually took place in a masonry ballcourt. Although the exact rules are not known, some elements of the game have been reconstructed from artistic depictions, early Spanish accounts and archaeological evidence.

The Mesoamerican ballgame may have been somewhat akin to rugby or American football, the object being to get the ball into the endzones. At some courts, however, stone rings have been found on top of the side walls, suggesting that a player scored by hitting the ball through the rings.

Players were forbidden to use their hands or feet; instead, they hit the ball with their knees, elbows and hips. Depictions of the game show players wearing extensive padding on these parts of their bodies.

Ballcourts were generally shaped like a capital "I" and had either vertical or sloping side walls. Court sizes varied enormously; while some could accommodate only one or two players per side, others are on a grand scale (such as the court at Chichén Itzá, which measures some 550 feet in length).

The ballgame was not just a focus of entertainment. In some cultures, it became a symbolic re-enactment of conflict, and incorporated ritual human sacrifice. Along the side walls of the court at Chichén Itzá is a long stone frieze depicting the aftermath of a game. The captain of the defeated team kneels on the ground, his head severed, with blood gushing from his neck. At the centre of the ball is a skull. This calls to mind the scene from the *Popol Vuh* where Xbalanque is forced to play the game using his brother's head. To the Maya, the ballgame would have been seen as a recreation of the battle between the Hero Twins and the Lords of Xibalba (see pages 524–525).

The ballgame is thought to have been played by the earliest Mesoamerican cultures, such as the Olmec. It was more than a sport; such was its importance that courts, like this one at Copán, were often built as part of ceremonial complexes.

Once there, Blood Moon sought out Xmucane, the mother of One Hunahpu and Seven Hunahpu. Xmucane set the girl an impossible task to test her credentials: she was told to bring home a whole netful of maize from just one plant. But as the gods wished to ensure the safe birth of the twins, they intervened to help Blood Moon, and so she was accepted by Xmucane.

Hunahpu and Xbalanque's Childhood

When the Hero Twins were growing up, their grandmother Xmucane spurned them. They also had to contend with the jealousy of their half-brothers – the twins One Monkey and One Artisan. The Hero Twins had to hunt for the entire family, but thrived on the outdoor life. By contrast, One Monkey and One Artisan stayed at home, currying Xmucane's favour with their musical and artistic skills. When the Hero Twins returned laden with game, Xmucane prepared food only for herself and the older boys, leaving the providers to live off leftovers.

At first the Hero Twins put up with this contemptuous treatment, but eventually they rebelled. Returning one day empty-handed, they reported that the birds they had shot had got entangled in a high tree. Their half-brothers foolishly agreed to come and help retrieve them. As they shinned up the tree, Hunahpu and Xbalanque made the trunk grow, leaving them stranded, and then called up to them: "Undo your loincloths and let the ends dangle behind you!" The brothers obeyed, and were instantly turned into forest monkeys. The only sounds these two great singers could now make were howls and shrieks. Even their grandmother, who was distraught when she heard what had happened, could not help laughing when she saw their absurd new guises.

The Hero Twins later came upon their father and uncle's ballgame equipment and taught themselves how to play. Like One and Seven

This ceramic ballplayer wears a garment made from a full jaguar pelt draped around his waist, as protection against the rough stone surface of the court. His necklace is made, in part, from the skulls of beaten opponents.

One Monkey and One Artisan

The first twin sons of One Hunahpu were One Monkey and One Artisan. They had been present at the fateful ballgame when their father and uncle were led away to the underworld. Unlike the unselfconscious "doers" Hunahpu and Xbalanque, the elder twins are portrayed in the Popol Vuh *as reflective thinkers.*

Skilled and industrious, One Monkey and One Artisan became the patron gods of art. This Classic Period frieze is decorated with a row of dancing spider monkeys.

One Monkey and One Artisan are depicted as lazy "stay-at-homes", with an evil streak in their characters. They made two failed attempts on the lives of their infant half-brothers, the Hero Twins, by abandoning them on an anthill and in a bramble thicket. The elder twins' resentment only increased as they saw the Hero Twins grow up to become active, carefree adolescents.

Yet the elder twins also had positive traits. They were diligent, accomplished in many forms of art and gifted with prescience. They were venerated throughout Mesoamerica as the patron deities of all artists, musicians and dancers. The Aztecs believed that those lucky enough to be born under the day-sign One Monkey would become singers, dancers or scribes.

Hunahpu before them, they were summoned by the Lords of Xibalba, yet the Hero Twins proved more cunning and resourceful than their forbears. They circumvented the graven images by creating a mosquito that bit the real lords and made them cry out. Similarly, they won through the ordeal of the torches and cigars by extinguishing them and substituting red macaw feathers for the torch flames and fireflies for the glow of the cigars.

On subsequent nights, the pair endured ordeals in the House of Knives, the House of Cold, the House of the Jaguars and the House of Fire. Their final sojourn was in the House of Zotz the Killer Bat. Throughout the night, they held the bat at bay, but when Hunahpu peered out in the morning, he was decapitated and his head was carried off to the Xibalbans. Xbalanque then devised a plan to resurrect his brother. He first took a squash and carved it into a likeness of his brother's features. He and the headless Hunahpu then returned to the ballcourt for another match against the gods, only this time using Hunahpu's real head as a ball. During the game, Xbalanque deliberately hit his brother's head into the woods, where he switched it for the squash. When play resumed, the squash burst, and the tricked gods were defeated. Hunahpu's head was restored to his body and he was made whole again.

531

The Defeat of the Underworld Gods

The Hero Twins – Hunahpuh and Xbalanque – had to undergo a series of ordeals that the evil Lords of Xibalba devised for them. But they had learned from the mistakes of their forefathers. Every time, by their cunning, courage and perseverance, the pair succeeded in outwitting the malevolent underworld gods. Nevertheless, it was not enough for the Hero Twins to survive: they had to win. To truly avenge the cruel deaths of their father and uncle, the brothers had also to bring about the annihilation of the lords One Death and Seven Death. In other words, they had to overcome death itself.

Underworld creatures take part in a macabre dance of death along the side of a cylindrical funerary vessel. The central figure has skull-like features and prances gleefully in front of a sacrificial altar. On the far right sits a dog, grinning because he has been brought back to life. Above him hovers the firefly that the Hero Twins used to light their cigars. Such comic-grotesque images of Xibalba were common in Maya art.

The next test set for the Hero Twins by the Lords of Xibalba involved them having to leap over a pit of fire. Faced with this ordeal, the boys flung themselves straight into the flames. The gods thought that the two had perished, so they rejoiced and scattered their ashes in the river. But Hunahpu and Xbalanque's bodies were reconstituted in the water. Five days later they emerged in the form of beautiful young fish-men.

The Hero Twins then disguised themselves as ragged, itinerant performers and went back to Xibalba. At first they entertained the commoners, but news of their wonderful show soon reached One Death and Seven Death, who summoned them to perform in their palace. The brothers began their act there with various animal dances, and went on to demonstrate a number of miracles. They burned down a house full of lords and restored it to new again without injuring a single person. They repeated this trick with a dog. But even these spectacular feats failed to satisfy the gods, who begged the duo to provide them with bigger thrills. "Sacrifice someone without killing them!" they yelled. The twins accomplished this easily, and the gods, now whipped up into a frenzy, cried: "Do it to yourselves!" So, Xbalanque ripped out his brother's heart and revived him on the spot. "Now do the same for us!" demanded the two principal lords. "But of course," replied the crafty twins suavely, "what is death to the gods?"

And so they killed One Death, the chief lord of Xibalba. At this, the other great lord, Seven Death, suddenly grew meek and begged for mercy. But Hunahpu and Xbalanque marched him and all the lesser lords to a canyon and hurled them to their deaths. Then the Hero Twins revealed their true identities to the people of Xibalba, and invoked the names of their father and uncle. The terrified Xibalbans expected to be executed, but the twins agreed to spare them on condition that they no longer demand human sacrifice.

The final act of the victorious brothers in the underworld was to disinter the remains of One and Seven Hunahpu from the ballcourt. They reassured their forbears that future generations would honour their memories. After reporting that they had "cleared the road of death, loss and pain," they ascended to the upper world. Their duty done, the Hero Twins were taken up into the sky, where one of them became the sun and the other the moon, though Maya myth is unclear as to which brother becomes which celestial body.

Ceramics for the Dead

The Maya custom of burying food and precious objects, such as jade or obsidian carvings, for the dead in pottery containers provided a convenient medium for detailed depictions of the underworld and its sometimes outlandish denizens.

On this Maya funerary vessel, the skeletal Lord of the Dead (*centre*) dances with his bizarre menagerie.

Some of the most spectacular Mesoamerican imagery of the Late and Postclassic periods is found on painted pottery left in Maya graves. Sites range from elaborate tombs in temples at Tikal or Copán to simple burials under the floors of houses.

From the island of Jaina off the Campeche coast, which may have been used as a necropolis, come elegant miniature figures depicting nobles and gods. Even more striking are polychrome pots painted in the so-called "codex style". The loose style sometimes calls to mind the free-flowing graphic invention of 20th-century comic-books.

The painters' subject-matter is often the underworld, known to the Maya as Xibalba, the "place of fright". Some authorities have suggested that these scenes may have derived from a now-lost codex detailing the soul's journey through Xibalba after death rather in the manner of the Egyptian *Book of the Dead*. The treatment is often comical, reflecting the Maya's ambivalent relationship with death – part fascination and part derision.

The sometimes hallucinatory nature of the imagery may have reflected genuine experiences of altered consciousness: one recurring motif shows participants receiving ritual enemas, possibly of an intoxicating liquor or the hallucinogen peyote, administered from a leather or rubber syringe-bag fitted with a hollow bone tube.

The First Human Beings

The final stage in the Maya legend of creation concerns the emergence of human beings. For their third, successful attempt at making people, the founder gods Hurricane and Gucumatz chose maize as their raw material.

After their first two abortive attempts at fashioning human beings, Hurricane and Gucumatz prepared carefully when they tried for a third time. Only when the human race emerged would the gods be properly honoured and the sun, moon and stars make their appearance.

To assist them in their endeavour, the creator gods solicited the help of some of the animals they had already put upon the Earth. Four species – the fox, the coyote, the parrot and the crow – were sent out to scout for a suitable location for this new act of creation. At length, they came upon a mountainous site called "Split Place" or "Bitter Water Place", where useful plants grew in abundance. Many delicious fruits were there for the harvesting, such as cacao (chocolate), custard apples and sweet plums. Most important of all, however, were white and yellow strains of maize, which would form people's staple diet. The animals gathered the maize and took it to Xmucane, the grandmother of the Hero Twins. She ground up the grain, and then mixed it with water with which she had washed her hands.

Then she passed the mixture on to Hurricane and Gucumatz. Out of this dough-like paste they moulded the first human beings. At first they were just four in number; these were the ancestral forefathers of the Quiché Maya lineages. Their names were Jaguar Quitze, Jaguar Night, Not Right Now and Dark Jaguar. These first humans were known as "mother-fathers", for in future ceremonials they came to represent both the male and female parents of all their descendants, a tradition which continues to this day.

The mother-fathers were highly satisfactory. Unlike their failed predecessors, they could express themselves lucidly and comprehend well. They were pleasing to the eye and worked vigorously. One especially remarkable attribute was their supernatural vision, which allowed them to observe everything on Earth and in the sky. They could even see inside rocks and mountains and far into the ocean depths. At first, their creators approved of their thirst for knowledge, and encouraged them to investigate their surroundings to the full; in return, the humans were grateful to their benefactors.

But gradually, humans' boundless curiosity and comprehension threatened to rival the creator gods' own omniscience, and they began to regard their creations with less indulgence. They decided to put a limit on people's abilities. So, as if breathing on a mirror, Hurricane clouded their sharp vision, making them able henceforth only to see things that were relatively close at hand. Having been put in their place, people were sure to remain loyal and subservient to the gods.

Next the gods made four women as wives for the men. Their names were Red Sea Turtle, Prawn House, Water Hummingbird and Macaw House. These "ladies of rank" gave birth to the many tribes that made up the Quiché people. Even before the advent of the sun and the beginning of recorded history, these early people multiplied and flourished. Their skins were of many colors and they spoke a variety of languages. Yet what united them was their shared anticipation of the first sunrise. Without exception, they were devout believers who prayed fervently to their creators, beseeching them to safeguard their children's future. They humbly implored the gods to give them light and a safe place to live, and to ensure their prosperity and well-being. As well as paying homage to the gods of heaven, the first people worshipped the divine hero One Hunahpu and his ancient mother Xmucane.

As they conducted their prayer and fasting, the first people kept a constant lookout to the east. They knew that the first sunrise would be preceded by the ascent of the planet Venus, and looked forward to the "dawning and sowing" that would confirm their place on Earth. When the sun finally did appear, life-giving heat would permeate throughout the Earth, and the people's lives would take on a new coherence and purpose. However, the first dawn was so long in coming that the people became downhearted. They wandered around aimlessly in the darkness, with no sense of belonging to a place and with no conception of social order.

Migrating ceaselessly across the land, they eventually settled at a place known as Tulan Zuyua ("Seven Caves, Seven Canyons"). At this site, they acquired their patron deities; the most important was the one-legged god Tohil. As a bringer of fire, Tohil was a great benefactor to the people, but he also demanded regular human sacrifice. His character soon became evident when a hailstorm suddenly extinguished all the fires in Tulan Zuyua. The tribes were half-paralyzed with cold, so Tohil offered to restore the gift of fire to them by grinding his heel into his sandal. Yet this help came at a price; the people had to agree to the principle of humans being "suckled on their side" by the god. This meant that victims' hearts would be cut out through a hole in their ribcage. According to the Quiché, this was the origin of human sacrifice. Still yearning for the rise of Venus and the sun, the people soon began to migrate away from Tulan Zuyua towards the east. Dignified and resourceful though these early people were, they had no

Although this figurine of a Maya woman is thought to represent a courtesan, it displays the stateliness and dignity that this culture regarded as essential feminine virtues.

535

possessions and were dressed in animal skins. They endured great hardships; stumbling around in the darkness, they could find nothing to eat and were gradually becoming parched with thirst.

In the midst of this suffering, the "mother-fathers" climbed up a mountain called Place of Advice, and there resolved to turn the mass starvation into an act of penance. Tohil and the other gods were moved at this, and responded by ordering Jaguar Quitze and his companions to keep their sacred images safe. Accordingly, although they were exhausted by their long vigil, the forefathers searched high and low for secure places in which to conceal the images of the deities. For example, the effigy of the god Hacauitz was hidden on a mountain peak, attended by his adherents as they waited for the first dawn. And suddenly, the dawn began. First the "sun carrier"

Venus became visible above the horizon. In their happiness, Jaguar Quitze and his fellows "cried sweetly" and burned incense in gratitude. Then the sun itself came up. As it did so, all the birds and animals rose up from the valleys and lowlands and watched the joyous spectacle from the mountain tops. The birds spread their wings in the new warmth of the sun's rays and the first human beings knelt in prayer. However, so intense was the sun's power that the old gods were turned to stone, along with the first dangerous wild animals, the forerunners of the modern puma, jaguar, rattlesnake and fer-de-lance. Just one small god,

A new day dawns over the imposing site of Chichén Itzá on the Yucatán peninsula. On the left stands a figure of a standard bearer, while on the right is the Pyramid of Kukulcan.

How the People of Corn Started Farming

The development of Mesoamerican culture from hunter-gatherer societies into great urban civilizations was founded on the cultivation of four crops – beans, squashes, chillis and maize. Of these, maize was of paramount importance.

An early cultivated form of maize was first grown in the Tehuacan valley in Puebla in central Mexico around 5,000 years before the Spanish Conquest. Some 2,000 years later, during the Formative Period, hybridization of this crop with a related wild grass known as *teosinte* had produced larger, more productive strains. The domestication of maize was highly significant, since it formed the basis of settled arable farming in the region. As a result, the population of central Mexico grew dramatically and began to congregate in large villages. Early people's diet of corn was supplemented with beans and chillis. Together with several varieties of squash and tomato, these provided essential vitamins and proteins.

The central role played by maize in the rise of Mesoamerican civilization is reflected in the mythology of the Maya. A variant of the myth of One Hunahpu in the *Popol Vuh*, who was decapitated by the Lords of Xibalba (see page 531), portrays him as the god of maize. His severed head is represented as a corn cob, whose seeds sprout and rise from the "underworld" (i.e. below the Earth). In this account, then, the Hero Twins' descent into the underworld to retrieve their father's remains clearly symbolizes the human quest for corn as the staple of life. Nor can it be a coincidence that this text describes the first human beings as having been created from maize (see pages 534–535).

Finally, there is an episode in the *Popol Vuh*, immediately preceding the defeat of the underworld gods, which describes how the hunters Hunahpu and Xbalanque were charged with tending their grandmother Xmucane's garden. Wishing to avoid any exertion, they used magic to make their tools do their work for them. According to Mesoamerican scholars, this brief

This stone effigy of a maize god shows a human figure surrounded by the cobs of corn that formed the main food crop of all Mesoamerican societies.

interlude may symbolize the change from a society based purely on hunting to one reliant on a combination of game hunting and domesticated vegetables and grains.

Although maize was the main food crop throughout Mesoamerica, the Maya, who traced their origins to the "people of corn", had a particular affinity with it. Artefacts often depict corn cobs as human heads; conversely, the Maya are thought to have practised cranial deformation to mimic the elongated form of maize.

White Sparkstriker, fled into the shade and so avoided being petrified. The sun that rose at the first dawn is described in the *Popol Vuh* as being "like a person with a hot face". Its rays were so concentrated that the Earth's surface – which had been wet and muddy – dried out completely. However, gradually, as time passed, the power of the sun's rays lessened, making life on Earth more tolerable for all living beings.

When the tribal forefathers witnessed the first dawn, they performed a solemn act of remembrance for those who had not survived the arduous journey. They also gave thanks to the gods Tohil, Auilix and Hacauitz. Because they were poor, they mixed in scraps of resinous bark and marigolds with the refined copal incense burnt in this ritual. The spirit of Tohil then spoke through his stone image and commanded the people to make sacrifices of deer and birds to the gods. So, on their hunting expeditions, although the people killed many deer and birds, they ate only the larvae of hornets, bees and wasps. When they returned home, they poured the blood of these mammals and birds into the mouths of their gods' effigies. At this time, the people of the "mother-fathers" avoided others and lived secretly in the forest. Whenever other groups passed by, they concealed their whereabouts by imitating the calls of birds and animals. Presently, however, their patron gods became

dissatisfied over the question of sacrificial offerings. They reminded their chosen people of the pledge they had made to perform human sacrifice. To meet their obligations, therefore, the ancestors of the Quiché began to ambush small groups of hunters from other tribal groups. They cut open their victims' sides, offering up their hearts and blood to the gods.

At first, the tribespeople whose members had been waylaid and ritually slaughtered thought that wild animals were responsible for their disappearance. But when the truth dawned on them, they determined to capture the images of the gods for themselves. They tried first to track down the worshippers of Tohil, Auilix and Hacauitz, but the ancestors of the Quiché were too clever for them. However, they did come across the spirits of the gods, who had taken on the guise of three handsome youths bathing in the river. The tribespeople devised a plan to trap the boys, by sending three lovely young women down to the river to seduce them. But the spirits of the gods realized immediately that this was a trick and, spurning the lovely girls' advances, sent them straight back to the tribal chiefs with a gift of three cloaks, exquisitely embroidered with motifs of a jaguar, an eagle and hornets. The tribal chiefs were delighted with the fine cloaks and put them on, whereupon the embroidered creatures came

A seated man prepares for a bloodletting rite. The *Popol Vuh* traces the origin of auto-sacrifice to the earliest days of the Maya.

This roll-out image of a vase painting shows lords resplendent in their ceremonial regalia. The figure on the far right is wearing a hornet-covered cloak like the one given to the tribal chief in the *Popol Vuh*.

to life and attacked them. The angry tribesmen were humiliated by having fallen for this ruse, and prepared to make war on their enemies.

In the great conflict that ensued, the tribespeople gathered for an assault on the capital of the forefathers of the Quiché. They donned their full battle regalia and marched on the city. However, on the way, the army was entranced and fell into a deep sleep. The defenders stole up on the sleeping tribespeople and humiliated them again by plucking out their beards and eyebrows and stealing their war trophies. Then the Quiché returned to their citadel where they set up wooden manikins along the ramparts. Tohil advised them to collect wasps and hornets, and fill four big gourds with them. When the attackers finally arrived in full cry, they were deceived by manikins moving on top of the citadel walls. Then suddenly the defenders unleashed the contents of the gourds on the tribespeople. Agonizingly stung on their arms and faces, they were in no fit state to resist when the ancestors of the Quiché emerged from the city and cut them down with bows and axes. The survivors were spared on condition that the tribespeople pay tribute in perpetuity.

This triumphal episode of Quiché mythic history ends with the death of the ancestral forefathers. When they realized death was approaching, the forefathers began to sing a lament. They announced that the "time of our Lord Deer" had come, namely that the current solar year would soon be replaced by one beginning with the day named after the deer. They explained that their work was complete and that the time had come for them to return to their place of origin.

Jaguar Quitze then bestowed on his people a sacred object called the "Bundle of Flames"; this carefully secured artefact would, he explained, represent his continuing presence and power among them after his death. Then the ancestors vanished, never to be seen again. A holy day was instituted in remembrance of the "mother-fathers" – the Day of the Lord Deer, which also became known as the Day of the Sacred Bundle.

The Quiché People

The first men, Jaguar Quitze and his brothers, had three sons – Noble Two, Noble Acutec and Noble Lord. These founders of the major Quiché patrilineal families embarked on a pilgrimage to the east to seek the place of their fathers' origin.

As the leaders of the tribe, the three nobles realized that their skills and wisdom would be missed while they were away, and so reassured their people that they would return. Not long after they set out, they were received by a monarch in the Yucatán called Nacxit, who conferred on them the collective titles Keeper of the Mat and Keeper of the Reception House Mat. The first title is thought to refer to council leadership, and the second to tribute or tax collection.

Nacxit also gave the lords various emblems that would enhance their power when they returned home. According to the *Popol Vuh,* these were: "canopy and throne, bone flute and bird whistle, sparkling powder and yellow ochre [used as cosmetics], puma's paw and jaguar paw, head and hoof of deer, leather armband and snailshell rattle, tobacco gourd and food bowl, and finally parrot feathers and egret feathers."

Farther east, the lords were given manuscripts. This episode probably alludes to the original hieroglyphic *Popol Vuh*, for the eastern

Most of the buildings of the Quiché have been reduced to rubble. But Maya sites elsewhere give some idea of what the architecture must have been like. This magnificent palace in northern Yucatán was built by the Puuc Maya in the 9th century and is adorned with masks of the rain god Chac.

Yucatán was an important centre for the production of Maya codices. Returning to their citadel of Hacauitz, the nobles proudly displayed their new symbols. Their power had grown considerably, and they resumed their dominion over their own people and all the neighbouring tribes.

After the lords' journey to find their roots, further migrations ensued, and resulted in the founding of successive citadels, named "Thorny Place", "Bearded Place" and "Rotten Cane". Of these, Bearded Place was the greatest settlement. Here the Quiché were at peace, and civic life flourished. Their civilization was hallmarked by magnificent splendour, tempered with modesty; there was no foolishness, envy, arrogance or quarrelling in the city until a tribe called the Ilocs rebelled; they were roundly defeated and punished by being enslaved or sacrificed.

By the time Rotten Cane was founded, five generations had passed since the advent of light. Apart from its physical security on a rocky outcrop, Rotten Cane (or Quiché, as the town came

Pedro de Alvarado, the Spanish conquistador, subdues the Maya. Alvarado arrived in Mexico with Cortés and then struck out on his own to conquer lands to the south. His reputation for savagery is recorded in the *Popol Vuh*.

to be called) was renowned for the devout nature of its inhabitants. Its lords engaged in long penances and partial fasts which could last for up to a whole solar year. During these devotional activities, they would refrain from sexual activity and observe strict dietary restrictions. One important result of these austerities was a return of the clear vision and foresight that the first people had enjoyed before the gods clouded their vision (see page 535). The shaman lords also addressed the gods in a series of elaborate songs, praising Heart of Sky for the gifts of life and prosperity, and praying for continuing good fortune.

At the time that the *Popol Vuh* was written, eleven generations of lords had ruled peacefully over the Quiché Maya. Then, in the twelfth generation, during the rule of Three Deer and Nine Dog, a new name suddenly appears in the manuscript – Tonatiuh. This appellation, which means "he who travels getting hot", was given by the Nahuatl speakers of Mexico to Pedro de Alvarado, the notorious Spanish conqueror of Guatemala. Having begun by recounting the creation of human beings, the authors of the sacred text ended their mythical history poignantly with the destruction of their nation. "That is enough about the being of Quiché," the text concludes, "since it is no longer to be seen."

541

TEOTIHUACAN

Teotihuacan was the great metropolis of the Classic era, and in its heyday around AD500 was one of the world's biggest cities. Orderly residential neighbourhoods crowded with tenement blocks stretched away from a central ceremonial artery, which became known to later peoples as the Avenue of the Dead. There, temples and palaces flanked an imposing sequence of open spaces and plazas culminating in the 196-feet-high Pyramid of the Moon.

Right: The Pyramid of the Moon was shorter than the Pyramid of the Sun, but it was built on higher ground so the summits of the two structures were level.

Far right: A carved serpent's head from the Temple of Quetzalcoatl typifies the florid decorative touches that enhanced many of the city's monuments.

Above: A mask from a burial cache illustrates the serenity of Teotihuacan art, with its taste for what have been called "clear, anonymous faces, neither male nor female, young nor old".

Above: Seen from the top of the Pyramid of the Moon, the ruins of Teotihuacan stretch into the distance along the Avenue of the Dead. To the left, the Pyramid of the Sun – Mesoamerica's largest ruin – rises more than 200 feet above the surrounding plain.

Right: The most pervasive feature of Teotihuacan architecture in the so-called *talud-tablero* profile of the facades of the major buildings. This consists of a vertical rectangular face *(tablero)* and a sloping one *(talud)* which alternate with each other.

The Aztec Universe

The Mexica, or Aztecs, inherited the rich traditions of a range of predecessor cultures and it is perhaps unsurprising that, like the Maya, they recognized a three-layered cosmos. But of all the pre-existing strands, the one this warrior aristocracy most emphasized was that of human sacrifice, an act they felt was vital to pleasing the gods and averting disaster.

As elsewhere in Mesoamerica, the Aztec cosmos was believed to have four directions emanating from a fixed centre. The directions were the cardinal points of north, south, east and west, whose meridians quartered the Earth. Many cultures believed that a tree grew in the centre of the world, rising up through the layers of heaven and sending roots down to the underworld, but for the Aztecs the centre was their capital city of Tenochtitlan built on an island in the middle of the great Lake Texcoco.

This horizontal concept of the universe had its vertical counterpart. The world inhabited by human beings was a huge flat space, surrounded by the sea, and at a certain point, the sea curved up to become the sky; the upper air consisted of "sky waters" which might at any time fall and obliterate the Earth. Such a catastrophe was believed to have happened to the world four times already

Ometeotl, the Lord of Duality, was both man and woman. This sculpture shows him/her as master of fate with a headdress bearing the mask of the star dragon.

(see pages 546–549). Apocalyptic disasters were typical of the Aztec cosmos, which though unstable was nevertheless capable of regeneration.

How the World Was Made

Ometeotl, the supreme being, existed beyond time and space. As was common with Aztec mythological beings, Ometeotl had a dual nature, being at the same time both male and female, as signified by his/her alternative title of Lord of Duality. He/she dwelled in the highest of the thirteen heavens in a paradise known as the Place of Duality. The two-sexed god was also known as two separate deities, Tonacatecuhtli and Tonacacihuatl, meaning "Lord of Our Sustenance" and "Lady of Our Sustenance", who were locked in coition. This mysterious concept of duality within unity was recurrent in Aztec cosmology. Ometeotl was the parent and source of all creation, and as Tonacatecuhtli is said to have brought the Earth to life with his breath. In the words of the Aztecs, the universe lay like a drop of water in the creator's hand, and people lay like a grain of seed within that droplet.

Thirteen Layers of the Sky

The Aztec heaven extended upwards from the Earth's surface in thirteen hemispheres, the uppermost of which was called Omeyocan, where the supreme being Ometeotl lived, eternally creating, organizing and sustaining the world with his/her holy breath.

At the centre of Tenochtitlan lay the Great Temple, as shown on this 16th-century Spanish map.

Below the Earth's surface lay Mictlan, the underworld, which was created by Omeyocan's sons. The three levels of the cosmos – the heavens, the underworld and the Earth's surface – converged at the centre of the world, the Aztec capital city of Tenochtitlan.

"Who would conquer Tenochtitlan? Who could shake the foundation of Heaven?" one Aztec poet cried, as if to say that were Tenochtitlan to be captured or destroyed, the universe itself would collapse. At the sacred centre of this sacred city stood the double temple of Huitzilopochtli, the Aztec national god, and the ancient god of rain, Tlaloc.

Ometeotl created the gods, but there his/her work ceased and all further creative activity was carried out by the other deities, some 1,600 in all. Ometeotl was not, however, so ineffable and awe-inspiring that he/she could not be given a visual identity in Aztec sacred art. To emphasize the deity's primordial status, he/she was portrayed as an ancient being with a sagging jaw. The female half of Ometeotl was also associated with fire and the Pole Star. This connection with fire further associated the female Ometeotl with the fire goddess Chantico, who was herself the consort of the fire god Xiuhtecuhtli. Fire, which for the Aztecs included the pole of heaven, thus provided Ometeotl's connection with the Pole Star.

Tonacatecuhtli and Tonacacihuatl ordained further creation through their four sons, whose number corresponded with the four sacred quarters of the Earth. At the same time as being separate deities, these sons were all aspects of an omnipresent god. The oldest of these was Red Tezcatlipoca or Xipe Totec, god of agriculture (see pages 568–569). The second and strongest was Black Tezcatlipoca, who became known simply as Tezcatlipoca (see pages 546 and 554–557). The third was White Tezcatlipoca or Quetzalcoatl (see pages 547 and 558–559). The youngest and smallest was Blue Tezcatlipoca, better known as Huitzilopochtli, the warrior god who protected the Aztec nation.

These brothers helped create the world, the calendars, fire, the first man and woman, Oxomoco and Cipactonal, and the gods of rain and water (see page 547 and 564–569).

The Five Suns

In four past ages, called "Suns", the world was destroyed when the sun itself was thrown out of the sky. Each age was presided over by a different god, who later destroyed it in an appropriate manner. For example, the goddess of water destroyed the Fourth Sun by flood, causing the heavens to fall down. The Fifth Sun was created when Ometeotl's four sons raised the sky.

The sun was commonly used as a decorative motif. In this gold pendant, dating from the Aztec period (c.AD1325–1521), it is represented as the bulbous god Tonatiuh.

The "Fifth Sun" was the age of the present, and the Aztecs performed constant rituals to ensure that the cosmic balance was maintained, for the world was a precarious place: one false move and it could tilt into chaos. Previous eras had been destroyed, and the next age always began when one of the other gods became the sun.

The four ages already past were named after the years in which they had ended. The first, for example, came to a close in the year Four Jaguar, and so the entire age took that name. Each of the four past ages was also associated with one of the elements of earth, air, fire and water. Likewise, each world age was identified with one of the five directions of the cosmos. Different peoples lived in each era and at its destruction, they were either killed or transformed. The Aztecs were very particular about the diets of each people, all of whom, until the Fifth Sun, lived on seeds.

The First Sun

The first age was associated with the element of earth and was ruled over by Black Tezcatlipoca, or simply Tezcatlipoca, the most powerful of the sons

of Tonacatecuhtli and Tonacacihuatl. One day Tezcatlipoca decided to turn himself into the sun. During this "Sun of Earth", the world was populated by a race of giants, so strong that they could rip trees from the ground if they pleased. They were vegetarians, living on a diet of pine nuts.

But the Sun of Earth ended exactly 676 years after it had been created. Quetzalcoatl, jealous of his brother shining so brightly in the sky, took his staff and struck Tezcatlipoca into the waters that surrounded the Earth. Then Tezcatlipoca turned into an enormous jaguar and devoured the entire race of giants. Later, he rose into the sky in the form of a mighty jaguar and became the constellation Ursa Major. Appropriately, this world met its end on the day Four Jaguar so it is also known as the Jaguar Sun.

The Suns of Wind, Rain and Water

The second world was created and ruled by Quetzalcoatl in his guise as the wind god Ehecatl. During this age, the "Sun of Wind", people evolved a little beyond the rudimentary habits of the giants, but they still lived simply on the seeds of the mesquite tree.

This time it was Tezcatlipoca's turn to strike down his rival Quetzalcoatl. All the people and their deity with them were carried away by a vast, dark hurricane that swept down on the Earth and blew them into the forest. The survivors of the wind were transformed into monkeys, the very ones – according to the legend – you can still see in the jungles of Central America today. This occurred in the year Four Wind, which gave its name to the era.

The third world, the "Sun of Rain", was presided over by Tlaloc, the god of rain and consequently also of fertility. This time, the human race discovered agriculture and began to cultivate a primitive form of grain. This world ended in the year Four Rain, when Quetzalcoatl created a rain of fiery ash, and the survivors were all transformed into butterflies, dogs and turkeys.

Chalchiuhtlicue or "She of the Jade Skirt" was the creator of the fourth world, the "Sun of Water". The wife of Tlaloc, she was the deity of running and still water: the oceans, rivers, lakes and streams. In this age the people of Earth subsisted on a seed called *acicintli*. The fourth world was destroyed when Chalchiuhtlicue made the waters under the Earth rush to the surface, causing a great flood. At the same time the sky collapsed and people were transformed into fish. This happened in the year Four Water.

The Fifth Sun

The current era is the Fifth Sun, created when the god Nanahuatzin sacrificed himself at Teotihuacan (see pages 542–543 and 562–563). Presided over by the fiery sun god Tonatiuh, whose name means "he who goes forth shining",

The fertility goddess Chalchiuhtlicue, shown in this Aztec codex suckling a child, was the deity who presided over the Fourth Sun.

Jnic. v. parapho ypan mitoa inque
nin mochichivaya Yҫeҫeyaca teteu.

paynal.

vitzilopuchtli.

(1)

(3)

Tezcatlipuca.

(2)

quezalcoatl.

chicomecoatl

chachalmeca

(4)

(7)

(10)

totochtin.

otontecuhtli

yxcoҫauhqui

(5)

(8)

(11)

tlaloc.

yacatecutli

ixtlilto.

(6)

(9)

(12)

How Life Was Created After the Fourth Sun

The Aztecs believed that they were living in the age of the Fifth Sun, which would end with a huge earthquake in the year Four Motion. Although no single source encompassed the way in which life had been recreated after the destruction of the preceding fourth world, a number of different myths described successive stages of the process.

The Fourth Sun was destroyed in an apocalyptic cataclysm in which the waters under the Earth rose to drown the world at the same time that the sky collapsed in upon it. Everything was drowned and washed away (see page 547). Afterwards chaos reigned until Ometeotl's four sons, the chief gods of the Mesoamerican pantheon, transformed themselves into trees to lift up the firmament, thereby creating a space in which creation could begin once more. Another version of essentially the same story had the brother gods, Tezcatlipoca and Quetzalcoatl, making the sky and the Earth out of the torn body of the fearsome ogress Tlaltecuhtli , who would only let crops flourish on Earth if she was fed with human blood. Putting aside their differences, the brothers decided to rid the world of her so as to permit creation to commence. They did so by turning themselves into giant serpents, which grappled with her and tore her in two. One half they threw into the sky, where it became the vault of the heavens; the remaining half, the other gods formed into the Earth.

A separate myth told how Quetzalcoatl was also responsible for restoring humans to the Earth. To do so, he had to travel to the underworld in search of all that was left of the fish people, their predecessors of the Fourth Sun: some bone in the possession of the sly, possessive Mictlantecuhtli, the skull-faced death god of central Mexico. Having succeeded in his quest, Quetzalcoatl took the trophies to the mythical Aztec paradise called Tamoanchan, literally "Land of the Misty Sky". There, Quetzalcoatl's fellow gods decided to co-operate, and ground the bones up like maize and moistened the bone flour with their own blood. Then they fashioned people from the sticky dough. In Tamoanchan, the gods nurtured the infant humans until they were big enough to be sent down to the surface of the Earth by themselves.

A variant account had humans emerging fully formed from the bowels of the Earth. The place of origin was Chicomoztoc, "Seven Caves", a legendary mountain in whose womb-like inner recesses the human race was thought to have been miraculously generated. This myth was particularly cherished by the nomadic Chichimec peoples of northern Mexico, many of whom traced their own origins to Chicomoztoc. Among them were the Aztecs (or Mexica) themselves, who included an account of a stopover there in the epic tale of the long trek that took them from ancestral Aztlan, somewhere in the north, to the Valley of Mexico.

it is the era of a fully evolved culture when the human race – and according to the myth the first people in this age were the inhabitants of Teotihuacan – at last cultivates maize, the Mesoamerican staple.

Bernardino de Sahagún included a visual guide to the gods in his work describing Aztec mythology, the *Florentine Codex*, which was written around 1570. In this detail, it is possible to pick out Tlaloc, Tezcatlipoca and Quetzalcoatl among others.

But war and disease also make their appearance during the Fifth Sun, and the world will eventually be consumed by earthquakes. After the earthquakes, time will come to an end forever. This event is inescapable, but can be postponed by satisfying the gods through the performance of ritual human sacrifices. All this, as Bernardino de Sahagún recorded in the *Florentine Codex*, will come to pass "when the Earth has become tired, when already it is all, when already it is so, when the seed of Earth has ended."

The Earth Mother

The Aztec Earth goddess was both horrifying and bountiful, hideous and radiant. In her character as the Earth itself she produced everything human beings needed to survive. In her celestial aspect she was the Milky Way, mother of the gods.

The Earth Mother was one of the oldest Aztec deities, known under several names and forms. As the Earth goddess, from whose body grew the essentials of the Aztec diet, she was known as Tonantzin ("Our Holy Mother") or Teteo Innan ("Mother of the Gods"). But she was less an active god with a history of deeds than an ancient spiritual presence: someone who had always been there, dwelling within the Earth from the very beginning of time (see also box, page 549).

In another incarnation she was Toci ("Our Grandmother"), a healing presence who was worshipped alongside Chicomecoatl in the annual harvest festival as the personification of nature's benevolence. Yet another avatar was as Yohualticitl ("Midwife of the Night"). This healing divine presence presided over sweatbaths, which in the Aztec world were small, womb-like structures heated by fires built against their outside walls. People in need of physical or spiritual purification would crawl inside and sprinkle water on hot stones with a brush of scented herbs, filling the interior with fragrant steam. Then, after they had recited the prescribed hymns and prayers required by tradition, they would dash out to immerse themselves in cold water, cleansed both in body and in spirit.

The most obviously appealing of all the fertility goddesses was Xochiquetzal, the epitome of feminine beauty and grace who was associated with the Eden-like Tamoanchan. A Venus figure who was sometimes said to be Quetzalcoatl's lover,

The goddess Tlazolteotl, "Eater of Filth", squats and unceremoniously defecates. Her association with sensuality and voluptuousness casts some light on the Aztec view of sex.

she was linked to the arts and all forms of pleasure. A goddess of the Earth's abundance, she was also reputedly the first mother of twins and retained an association with pregnancy and childbirth.

So too did a very different figure, the fearsome Tlazolteotl, who was often portrayed in the squatting position that Aztec mothers generally adopted to give birth. As the goddess of filth, she was similarly associated with excrement and with the sexual lust of which it was the symbol. One of the nastier Aztec customs took place in her name. Young girls might be forced into prostitution in the barracks for trainee warriors, only to be ceremonially killed once their career had reached an end, their bodies dumped as polluted refuse in the marshes of Lake Texcoco. Yet curiously this sinister, witch-like figure, identified with venereal diseases and the punishment of sexual excess, could absolve sin as well as inspire it.

The gap between the lovely and gracious flower goddess Xochiquetzal and the hag Tlazolteotl could hardly have been greater, but both represented aspects of the Aztec attitude to sexuality and the role of women in society.

Mistress of the Cycle of Birth and Death

The Mesoamericans were always ready to expand the ranks of the gods and goddesses. Coatlicue was a late incarnation of the Earth Mother worshipped by the Aztecs.

Coatlicue ("She of the Serpent Skirt") symbolized fecundity in her role as mother of the fire and warrior god Huitzilopochtli ("Hummingbird of the South"), of the moon goddess Coyolxauhqui, and of the stars, her 400 sons (twenty times twenty, meaning "innumerable"). But despite her fertility, she was also considered virginal by the Aztecs, who believed that Huitzilopochtli's conception was immaculate. This led certain Catholic commentators to associate this aspect of Coatlicue with the Virgin Mary.

But the goddess had a darker side to her. She was also associated with death and regeneration. Few representations of her survive, but in this aspect she is fearsome.

Coatlicue is the subject of one of the most celebrated of all Mexican sculptures – a giant statue excavated in 1790 next to the cathedral in Mexico City. A pair of snakes are where her head should be; she wears a necklace of human hands, hearts and a skull; and her skirt is made of rattlesnakes. Her feet are a pair of giant claws.

Pulque, the Divine Intoxicant

Pulque was an alcoholic beverage which the Aztecs made from the fermented sap of the maguey cactus and often drank in rituals. How pulque came to be made available on Earth is the subject of one of the Aztecs' most colorful myths.

The goddess Mayahuel wears a headdress decorated with green feathers, paper and rubber in the Aztec *Codex Magliabediex.*

The magnificent maguey cactus that grows so abundantly in Mesoamerica had many important uses in Aztec society. The leaves served as roofing material and produced fibre for weaving. Leaves and roots, rich in vitamins A and B, contributed to at least thirty different foods and drinks, the most ritually significant of which was the intoxicating beverage pulque (or *octli*).

A vivid myth involving Quetzalcoatl and the beautiful young goddess Mayahuel explains the origin of pulque. When the gods observed the early humans, they saw that they never danced or sang, so the deity Quetzalcoatl ("Plumed Serpent") decided that a stimulating drink like pulque would make them happier. Travelling to the heavens, Quetzalcoatl found the lovely Mayahuel, the granddaughter of one of the *tzitzimime*, a group of malevolent female spirits transformed into star demons who held a grudge against the living, and persuaded her to come down with him to Earth.

When they reached the Earth, the couple transformed themselves into a single gigantic tree. Mayahuel was one fork and Quetzalcoatl the other. When the grandmother *tzitzimitl* discovered that Mayahuel was missing, she was enraged. She summoned the *tzitzimime* and together they swooped down to Earth in pursuit of the errant granddaughter. As the star demons arrived on Earth, the tree composed of Mayahuel and Quetzalcoatl split in two. Recognizing Mayahuel in one of its great branches, the grandmother *tzitzimitl* ripped the offending bough to pieces and fed it bit by bit to the other *tzitzimime*. Sorrowfully, Quetzalcoatl buried what was left of the beautiful Mayahuel's fleshless bones, and from these sprang the original maguey cactus that would later produce the joyfully intoxicating drink pulque.

Pulque was also associated with another group of deities known as the Four Hundred Rabbits, for it was a rabbit that had discovered pulque when it nibbled the maguey plant. Images of these 400 rabbits were discovered buried at the base of the Great Temple at Tenochtitlan, leading some scholars to suggest that these gods were identified with the 400 brothers killed by the Aztec's national god Huitzilopochtli when he burst from his mother's womb (see box, page 551).

One of the gods of pulque, known by the date-name Two Rabbit, was especially revered in the vicinity of the birthplace of the last Aztec emperor, Motecuhzoma. The brutality and humiliation of the conquest had driven many Aztecs to the solace of pulque, which made the Spanish anxious to stamp out drunkenness. Assuming that Two Rabbit was the demon of intoxication, they smashed his image wherever they found it.

Although pulque, or *octli*, was sacred and used in many rituals, at the same time it was perceived by the Aztecs themselves as subversive. In the *Florentine Codex,* Father Bernardino de Sahagún recorded that even though "the god [Two Rabbit] was wine, he was considered to be full of sin. For the god hurled people off crags, he strangled people, he drowned people, he killed them. He was an awesome being, one not to be affronted, one not to be abused." Drink had to be taken with due care. This suspicion of pulque was reflected in civil legislation. The sale of the drink was strictly regulated, and only certain people – the sick, the nobility and those over fifty-two years of age – were allowed regular access to it. Three cups per day was the prescribed ration. Adults found drunk three times would on the first offence have their hair cut off, on the second offence have their houses demolished, and on the third be put to death.

Pulque was also freely used on ritual occasions, administered as a drug to prisoners who were going to be sacrificed. The captives, known as "children of the sun", were marched regularly into Aztec territory in long, weary columns. They were forced to drink pulque until they were intoxicated; then made to dance and sing as they entered the great city of Tenochtitlan.

Mayahuel, entertained by a dancer, nestles in an agave cactus. Above them a jar of pulque floats in the night sky, below her an ascetic dances under a serpent. A detail from the *Codex Borbonicus*.

Lord of the Smoking Mirror

Among the first four gods created by Ometeotl in the thirteenth heaven (see pages 544–545) was Black Tezcatlipoca. This restless, dark deity was described as "all-powerful and unequalled" and he could "see into the hearts of everyone".

"Tezcatlipoca", wrote Bernardino de Sahagún under the instruction of his Aztec informants, "was considered a true god, whose abode was everywhere – in the land of the dead, on Earth and in heaven." So impressed was de Sahagún with the stature of Tezcatlipoca, that he compared him to Jupiter, king of the gods in Roman mythology. Undoubtedly, Tezcatlipoca – as Black Tezcatlipoca was usually known – was quite unlike the God worshipped by the Christian conquistadors. "When Tezcatlipoca walked on the Earth," continued de Sahagún, "he quickened vice and sin. He introduced anguish and affliction."

So different was the Aztec "Jupiter" from the Christian deity that de Sahagún described him as the opponent of God: "This wicked Tezcatlipoca we know as Lucifer, the great devil who there in the midst of heaven, even at the beginning, began war, vice and filth." De Sahagún then succinctly summarized Tezcatlipoca's nature: "He created, he brought down all things." Tezcatlipoca, then, was the great god who could both create and destroy; he could bestow wealth, long life and happiness and then casually take them all away.

Among the most evocative and inscrutable aspects of Tezcatlipoca was his name, which meant "Smoking Mirror". The god carried one mirror at the back of his head and sometimes a second mirror replaced one of his feet, torn off when he was hurled out of heaven for seducing a virgin goddess. The history of Tezcatlipoca's mirror is as obscure as the images in its smoking surface. But mirrors clearly had magical qualities. Toltec legend talks of a mirror, whose surface was like smoke, that could predict the end of droughts. Tezcatlipoca is said to have stolen this mirror and hidden it, thus prolonging the famine. The mirror "smoked" because it was made of obsidian, a black volcanic glass that reflects darkly and often with distortions. Tezcatlipoca could see into the future with his mirror and into people's hearts. This magical clairvoyance, that he alone of the gods possessed, made him patron of shamans, for whom mirrors were tools of the trade.

The Warrior God

Tezcatlipoca was vividly illustrated in the Aztec codices, where he was usually depicted as a warrior. Bearing the *atlatl* (spear-thrower), darts and shield, he carried a war banner and wore in his hair the two heron feathers that were the usual headdress of the Aztec knights.

Tezcatlipoca had his opposite in both the gentler, life-giving Quetzalcoatl (see pages 558–559) and in the agricultural deity Red Tezcatlipoca or Xipe Totec (see pages 564–569). While Xipe was associated with the sun of the upper world, Tezcatlipoca represented the "dark sun" as it travelled at night through the underworld. These opposing principles of day and night, light and darkness, were represented symbolically in the ballgame (see box, page 529) that was played throughout Mesoamerica. At the end of the Fifth Sun, this will be the game that Tezcatlipoca must win. For at the end of the present age Tezcatlipoca will steal the sun and thus destroy the world, the gods and human history.

Tezcatlipoca was also known as "The Left-handed One", implying that he was sinister and untrustworthy. Father de Sahagún described Tezcatlipoca in this guise as the god who "cast his shadow on one, visited one with the evils that befall men. He mocked, he ridiculed men."

Even more inauspiciously, the "left-handed" god was also known as Yaotl ("Enemy"), who stirred up discord and presided over battles. Social or political humiliation of any kind was attributed to Tezcatlipoca. He would do no one the favour of taking sides. Indeed, he was the promoter of wars and god of weaponry, and the insignia woven on his tunic was the skull and crossbones. Warriors who fell in battle would – unlike civilians – go to a temporary place of glory before they descended to the underworld. But it was Tezcatlipoca who determined when and where they would fall. As god of battle, Tezcatlipoca performed a vital service to the entire Aztec pantheon, for it was only through war that a sufficient number of captives could be taken and transported to the temples of Tenochtitlan.

Tezcatlipoca's unpredictability was well illustrated by his association with certain animals. Many Aztec gods had a *nahualli*, or earthly double, often an animal whose character resembled their own. Tezcatlipoca excelled in assuming the form of his *nahualli*, and he was said to appear

This Aztec incense burner in the form of a turkey's claw, one of the symbols associated with Tezcatlipoca, is decorated with his sign.

555

The warrior god Tezcatlipoca wears a jaguar skin. Like the jaguar he was a creature to be feared, an implacable enemy and a fearsome fighter.

compared with the most powerful and awe-inspiring wild creature in the region. The reason for this was clear to friar Bernardino de Sahagún, who described the jaguar as: "noble, princely, the ruler of animals. It is cautious, wide, proud. By night it watches. Very clear is its vision. Even when it is very dark, it sees." The spotted jaguar's skin, which Tezcatlipoca habitually wore, represented the night sky to the Aztecs. Just as the jaguar was the all-powerful creature of the night, merciless to its prey, so Tezcatlipoca was the darkest and most implacable deity in the whole pantheon.

Tezcatlipoca's darkness was emphasized in other ways. For example, he was often identified with the countless ghosts and spirits who haunted the night. Thus he appeared as a horrifying demon called Night Axe, a headless man with a wound in his chest that opened and shut with the slamming sound of an axe striking wood. The priests of Tezcatlipoca sometimes painted their bodies with a mixture of ground-up narcotic mushrooms, tobacco, poisonous snakes and scorpions, a weird black paste corresponding with the deity's own dark violence.

on Earth as a skunk, a monkey and a coyote: all of them perceived as sly, mischievous and deceitful creatures. But the animal most closely associated with Tezcatlipoca was the jaguar, and in his manifestation as One Jaguar, the god was

Virgin and Seducer

Tezcatlipoca was also conceived of as a beautiful young man, and was thus the presiding deity of youths training to become warriors. He was the youngest of the gods – sometimes described as a virgin, sometimes as an irresistible seducer of women – and in some versions of his story he was reborn every year. As Telpochtli ("Young Male"), Tezcatlipoca was worshipped by the *telpochtiliztli*, a sect of young men and women. In honour of the deity, these devotees would dress in sumptuous costumes at night and sing and dance through the streets of Tenochtitlan (see also pages 578–579).

Although Tezcatlipoca was an unpredictable god who could bring misfortune and humble the successful, he also had his protective side. In one story, it was he who led the Aztecs in their search for a homeland. The dark god spurred them on by recounting the visions he could see in his super-natural mirror. Thus when the Aztecs arrived at Texcoco, across the water from their future capital of Tenochtitlan, the priests set up a mirror in Tezcatlipoca's temple, in which they saw the shad-owy and beautiful visage of the deity himself.

Tezcatlipoca is dressed as an Aztec warrior in this 15th-century codex. He wears heron feathers in his hair, knee straps made of skin from a jaguar and carries a banner. His body is painted black and his face golden with black stripes.

The Origins of War

As a warrior god, one of Tezcatlipoca's most important functions for the Aztecs was to ensure that there was sufficient warfare to provide them with a steady supply of the captives they would need to sacrifice to the gods.

The Aztecs did not generally regard peace as a virtue. Their interest in political dominion over their neighbours and their devotion to gods of battle such as Tezcatlipoca led them rather to value the pursuit of war. But according to myth, war had not always existed. Nor was it regarded as an indigenous Aztec practice. The Aztecs understood the pursuit of war to have come to them in early historical or mythological times

from a remote north Mexican hunting people called the Chichimecs.

Far from feeling ashamed that they had not invented war for themselves, the Aztecs believed that to inherit a skill from such a venerable source gave it a sacred ancestry. As one text declared: "Could we betray the teaching of ancestors such as the Chichimecs or the Toltecs? No, our hearts have received life from them!"

The Aztecs explained the origins of war as a case of sibling rivalry between the children of the sun and the Earth. The oldest brothers were loose-living and hard drinking, so the sun and the Earth sent five younger brothers to sort them out. A war ensued in which the decadent older brothers were thrashed by the clean-living younger ones. The archetype of a puritan, ascetic warrior was born.

The Plumed Serpent

Quetzalcoatl ("Plumed Serpent") was worshipped across central Mexico and he was certainly one of the most revered gods in the Aztec pantheon. Like so many of his fellow deities he had several incarnations. The most important of these were as a creator god, one of Ometeotl's four sons; as Ehecatl, the god of wind; as the Morning Star; and – uniquely among the gods – as a semi-human ruler, Topiltzin (linked to the city of Tula and a line of historical Toltec priest-kings admired by the Aztecs). The priestly Quetzalcoatl was often contrasted to his dark shamanic brother Tezcatlipoca. Throughout the myth cycle of the Aztecs the relations of the two brothers veer between enmity and alliance.

Quetzalcoatl's multifaceted character is suggested by the words that make up his compound name. While *quetzal*, meaning the quetzal bird's feather, refers to what is beautiful in Quetzalcoatl's nature, the word also means "precious". *Coatl*, the second part of the deity's name, also has a double meaning: "serpent" and "twin". The entire name could therefore mean both "Plumed Serpent" and "Precious Twin". This wordplay allowed the Mesoamericans to represent him sometimes as a snake with bright green feathers and sometimes in human form.

An Ancient God

Quetzalcoatl was one of the gods the Aztecs inherited from older civilizations in Mesoamerica. One of the earliest surviving representations of this great and exotic deity is at the third-century Temple of Quetzalcoatl at Teotihuacan (see pages 542–543), which represented the point where heaven and Earth met. This junction of the spheres, which Quetzalcoatl maintained, was necessary for the rain which brought agricultural prosperity to the Mexican plateau. Quetzalcoatl was associated with water, the sky – which the Aztecs believed was an extension of earthly waters (see page 544) – and, by extension, fertility and life itself. His power was regenerative and life-giving, because (to bring the rain) he linked the Earth with the sky. In one celebrated sculpture, Quetzalcoatl rises in great coils from a representation of the Earth Mother and joins the figure of Tlaloc, god of rain and lighting. Similarly, in his aspect as Ehecatl, the wind god, Quetzalcoatl was credited with the winds that brought rainclouds. In the *Vienna Codex*, he is shown as the wind god with his arms raised to support heaven. Quetzalcoatl is thus holding up the clouds, and in his role as wind god is also blowing the rain across the thirsty lower world. In this guise, the god was known as "roadsweeper to the *tlaloques*", the little rain gods, who lived in the mountains.

The Plumed Serpent devours a human being sacrificed in his honour, in a detail from the Codex Borbonicus.

558

Where Tezcatlipoca carried his obsidian mirror, the Plumed Serpent, in his guise as Ehecatl, wore a conch shell, his symbolic "jewel of the wind". In imitation of their deity himself, priests of the Quetzalcoatl cult wore conch shells cut in cross-section to show a concentric, whorled pattern that represented the movement of the wind. Many of the temples dedicated to Quetzalcoatl were also circular, signifying the eddying of the wind.

Quetzalcoatl was also often identified with one of the earliest of the Mexican deities: a dragon of the sky who could not only punish the human race with tornadoes and water spouts but also reward it by promoting agriculture. In this connection, Quetzalcoatl was also the beloved and ever-welcome deity of springtime and vegetation.

His primary connection with water was underlined in historical times when the conquistadors entered Quetzalcoatl's holy city of Cholula. During the Aztec era, Cholula was a destination for pilgrims who were seeking advice or prognostication from the local priests. Poignantly, the people of Cholula were convinced that if Cortés and his men were to desecrate the temple of Quetzalcoatl, the lord of waters would create a huge flood and drown the invaders. They soon discovered their beliefs were unfounded.

God of Priestly Wisdom

The Aztecs also identified the Plumed Serpent with priesthood: the two most important priests in Tenochtitlan were given the title Quetzalcoatl, and the *calmecac* school where young priests were trained was also dedicated to him. In this incarnation, Quetzalcoatl was represented as a bearded man painted black. His attributes include a conical hat with a sharp projection, from which came a penitential blood offering to the god's *nahualli*, the quetzal bird.

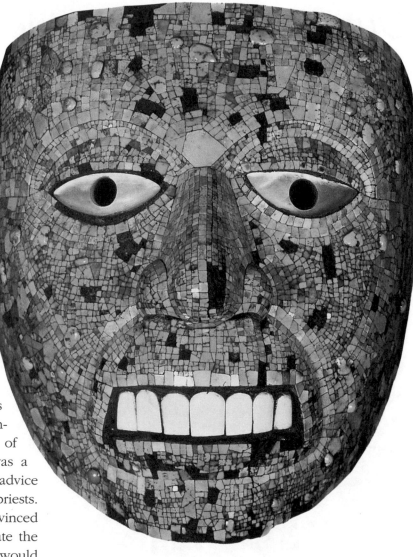

A mask – from around 1500 and decorated in turquoise and shell – represents Quetzalcoatl in human form. This type of mask was never intended to be worn over the face, but may have been worn elsewhere on the body. All Mesoamericans valued green materials – jade, turquoise or the green feathers of the quetzal bird – above any others. Cortés soon discovered this and exchanged Aztec gold for green glass beads.

In his semi-human incarnation, as the Toltec ruler Topiltzin, he was also high priest of Tula, where his cult was benign, without human sacrifice. Topiltzin initiated a peaceful, ascetic and spiritual era. His association with wise rulership meant that green quetzal feathers or stones were often worn as a sign of sovereignty by Mesoamerican rulers.

559

Quetzalcoatl as the Morning Star

One story tells how Quetzalcoatl, in his manifestation as the priest-king Topiltzin, sacrificed himself at the end of his reign, undermined by renewed support for Tezcatlipoca. Weeping, he arrayed himself in all his finery, including his turquoise mask, and then he stepped on to a pyre and lit it. As his body was consumed by flames, his heart rose into the sky to become the Morning Star. From his new place in the heavens, Quetzalcoatl promised that one day he would return to Earth and establish a lasting era of peace and harmony.

This winged image of Quetzalcoatl as the Morning Star was recorded soon after the Spanish Conquest. The resemblance to a Christian angel may have been deliberate.

Quetzalcoatl was a truly protean deity. Worshipped as both the Plumed Serpent and the god of the wind, he was also identified with the Morning Star under the name of Ce Acatl. The Morning Star, or Venus when it rises before the sun, was known to the Aztecs as "Lord of the Time of Dawn"; as a competitor to the sun – which rose when Venus faded – he was regarded with awe.

This mistrust of Venus derived from the deep antagonism in Aztec myth between light and darkness. Because the stars – even those which appear at dawn – represented the night sky, Ce Acatl and the sun were believed to be hostile to one another. Since the sun was obviously vital to life on Earth, the Morning Star was therefore regarded as inauspicious. Old people, children and rulers were particularly vulnerable to his anger. Paradoxically, while Quetzalcoatl in his aspect as the wind god was adored as the harbinger of rain, Ce Acatl in his dawn dominion was the enemy of rain and the bringer of drought.

But like so many other Mesoamerican deities Ce Acatl embodied a paradox: the mistrust was often mingled with gratitude. Although on the one hand the Morning Star was notorious for having assaulted, in his guise as the god of cold, the first sun to rise after the auto-sacrifice of the gods (see pages 562–563); on the other hand it was believed that the star also helped lift the sun on its journey into the sky each morning.

Despite these ambiguities, the myth of Quetzalcoatl's exile from Tula and his ascent into the sky to become the Morning Star was widely thought to prophesy a happy future, a prospect to which the Aztecs clung. This promise was contained in Quetzalcoatl's own prediction before his death that he would one day return, conquer his enemies and establish a new dominion of piety.

Quetzalcoatl's Ominous Return

As Cortés was making his way through Mexico towards Tenochtitlan, the Aztecs believed that this strange new figure was none other than Quetzalcoatl himself, returning to bring in a new era of peace and prosperity. In one of history's most bizarre coincidences, Cortés arrived in the city on the very day, One Reed, prophesied for the return of Quetzalcoatl.

The Aztecs and other Mesoamerican peoples were quick to adopt Christianity, with many seeming to have believed that it was simply another version of the rites of Quetzalcoatl. There seem to have been two main reasons for this eagerness to convert. Firstly, according to Cortés's companion Bernal Diaz, the Spanish missionaries resembled in appearance the Aztec priests of Tenochtitlan, who "wore black cloaks like cassocks and long gowns reaching to their feet. Some had hoods like those worn by canons, and others had smaller hoods like those of the Dominicans." More importantly, the Christian message of brotherly love seemed to be paralleled by the ideals of piety and good government represented by Quetzalcoatl in his aspect as the priestly ruler Topiltzin.

The story of Christ's death and resurrection was a further echo of the Aztec belief in Quetzalcoatl's second coming. In this way Jesus and the Mesoamerican deity became identified as one holy being. So while much of Aztec culture and religion was swept away by the onslaught of the Spanish conquistadors, the worship of the Plumed Serpent managed to survive, though in a barely recognizable form.

Quetzalcoatl in his guise as the Morning Star bursts out of the Earth, represented by a serpent, in this pre-Toltec stone carving.

561

The Creation of the Sun and Moon

Two gods of vastly different characters, Tecuciztecatl and Nanahuatzin – one all vanity and one all humility – are central to Aztec myth because they were to transform themselves into the lesser deity of the moon and the all-powerful god of the sun.

The creation of the sun and moon took place at the great ceremonial centre of Teotihuacan, about twenty-five miles northeast of modern-day Mexico City. After the fourth holocaust, in which the sun as well as the Earth had been annihilated, four gods met in the darkness at Teotihuacan to create a new sun. They agreed that the self-sacrifice of a god was required to bring it into being.

As the gods discussed who should die by fire to create the new sun, the vain and handsome Tecuciztecatl put himself forward "to carry the burden, to bring the dawn". But the gods decided to make him compete with the god Nanahuatzin for the position of sun or moon. Although an equally powerful god, Nanahuatzin was very humble, maybe because he was disfigured by running sores.

While the gods built a vast sacrificial bonfire, Tecuciztecatl and Nanahuatzin did penance on two mounds. The two gods now presented offerings that reflected their personalities. Where vain, boastful Tecuciztecatl brought quetzal feathers and gold, Nanahuatzin brought bunches of reeds. Where Tecuciztecatl offered awls of coral and jade, Nanahuatzin merely offered cactus spines anointed with his own blood.

Tecuciztecatl Fails

When, after four days, the sacrificial fire had become searingly hot, the two gods were robed for their ordeal: Tecuciztecatl in the richest garments, Nanahuatzin in a tunic of paper. The attendant gods, still taken in by Tecuciztecatl's pretensions, now called upon him to jump into the fire.

Tecuciztecatl ran towards the flames, but four times recoiled in terror from the intolerable heat. So the gods called on Nanahuatzin: "Daring, determined, resolved and with hardened heart, he shut his eyes. He did not falter or turn back. All at once he threw himself into the fire. His body crackled and sizzled; he burned." Spurred on by Nanahuatzin's heroic act, Tecuciztecatl too ran into the pyre. The gods now waited in the darkness for the birth of the new sun. But instead Tecuciztecatl rose as the moon, casting a blinding light. To subdue his brilliance, one of the gods threw a rabbit up into his face. This rabbit can still be seen on the face of the full moon.

Nanahuatzin now rose in the heavens as the new sun, but refused to move across the sky until he had been fed with the hearts and blood of all the other deities. Incensed at this demand, the Morning Star attacked the sun with his darts and spear, only to be defeated and hurled down into the underworld. The sun god was acknowledged as supreme, and all 1,600 gods now allowed themselves to be sacrificed.

The humble, ulcerated Nanahuatzin was thus transformed into the mighty sun god Tonatiuh, he "who blinded one with his light". The first day of the Fifth Sun had begun.

Birthplace of the Gods

The name Teotihuacan means the "Place where God was Created". The Aztecs, who only knew it as ruins, believed this city of plazas, palaces and pyramids in central Mexico was the very place where the Fifth Sun itself was created. They were awed by the evidence of a once great civilization that had been utterly lost.

Teotihuacan's Pyramid of the Sun (*c.*AD225), which is linked to the smaller Pyramid of the Moon (*c.*AD150) by the Avenue of the Dead. Both echo the shape of the nearby mountains.

Indeed, Teotihuacan was also said to have been where the whole pantheon of Aztec gods was brought into being. The *Florentine Codex* of Bernardino de Sahagún confirms that the Aztecs made it their first sacred centre when they arrived after their long journey from the north in search of a final home. At Teotihuacan the newcomers made offerings to the gods who had led them to safety, buried their leaders and built pyramids above their tombs.

Another Aztec legend claims that Teotihuacan's famous pyramids of the Sun and Moon (see pages 542–543) are the very mounds on which the gods Tecuciztecatl and Nanahuatzin did penance before sacrificing themselves to the flames and becoming the moon and sun.

Gods of the Natural World

Of the multitude of gods in the Mexican pantheon, none could match the popular appeal of those associated with the fertility of the land. To a primarily agricultural people, the harvest rather than conquest was the sign of the gods' munificence.

While intellectuals sought to explain the mysteries of the universe through cosmological speculation and in terms of sun and star deities, the mass of the population was more concerned with those gods whose activities touched their daily lives. In particular, concerns about drought and the fertility of the land lay at the heart of day-to-day Mesoamerican religion, while the 360-day calendar (see pages 570–571) was planned around the agricultural year, which began in February.

Mexico's climate is marked by long seasons of torrential rain followed by very dry seasons, so the propitiation of the rain gods was considered essential. The chief rain god was Tlaloc. But reflecting its importance, many other lesser deities were associated with rain or water. A whole host of gods were also linked to agriculture and in particular

with maize. Different gods represented different stages of the grain's development; for example, Xipe Totec, the "Flayed One", was associated with the first shoots of maize in spring, while growing maize was celebrated with a big midsummer festival to the maize goddess Xilonen, during which everyone feasted on maize porridge, tamales and tortillas wrapped around chillied vegetables.

These preoccupations with the natural world show through in one of history's sadder public statements, made when leading Aztec priests were informed after the Spanish Conquest that they would have to abandon their old beliefs.

Attended by a pair of acolytes, a goddess figure (centre) nourishes plants sprouting from her head and crawling with life-forms in this mural, from around the 8th century, at Teotihuacan.

Disputing the decision, they tried to explain just what their vast and complex pantheon meant to them and to their people. "It is through the gods that all live," they informed the Franciscan missionaries who brought them the news; "they give us our daily fare and all that we drink, all that we eat, our sustenance, maize, beans, amaranth. It is they whom we supplicate for water, for rain with which everything flourishes on the Earth."

This last reference was an eloquent one, for the most actively venerated figure in the Aztec world was the rain god Tlaloc. He is easily recognized in the codices, as much from his round goggle eyes as from the insignia associated with him: in one hand he holds a jade tomahawk symbolizing a thunderbolt or the writhing serpent of lightning, while in the other he carries a jug from which he pours out the rain. His other distinctive feature is his jaguar teeth, a connection that may have been suggested by a perceived resemblance between the sound of thunder rumbling and the big cat snarling.

Tlaloc was revered as an old god, with a long history behind him (he shared, for example, many traits with Chac of the Maya); the earliest known image of him comes from a vase made in the Valley of Mexico as early as the first century BC. He was an important figure at Teotihuacan, featuring prominently among the culture's leading deities. In Aztec mythology he was remembered as the being who presided over the Third Sun of creation, when he ruled a world of rain that was eventually destroyed by a hail of fiery cinders.

"She of the Jade Skirt", Tlaloc's consort, made the plants grow. This Aztec stone sculpture depicts her in her youthful incarnation as mistress of childbirth and the spring.

Mistress of Torrents and Whirlpools

While Tlaloc had responsibility for water as it fell from the sky, his consort Chalchiuhtlicue ("She of the Jade Skirt") was the presiding spirit of rivers, lakes and other places where rain is collected. She too had ruled over one of the ages of creation – in her case the Fourth Sun, the Sun of Water. As a goddess associated with growth and the beginnings of life, Chalchiuhtlicue played a significant role in the rituals surrounding the birth of babies.

In particular, she presided over a rite that fascinated Spanish churchmen because of its resemblance to baptism. A priest sprinkled water over a newly born infant to cleanse it of the spiritual uncleanliness passed down from its parents. The child was given its name and presented with miniature tools that symbolized the occupations it might take up in later life.

An imposing figure dressed in blue and white with a crown of blue reeds, Chalchiuhtlicue was by no means always the placid figure a connection with lakes and ponds might suggest. Known sometimes as the "Agitated" or "Foaming One", she was also associated with whirlpools and

565

Cults of the Jaguar

The jaguar was the top predator of the Mesoamerican rainforest. Feared for its nocturnal hunting skills, it became a symbol of silent power that kings and even gods sought to emulate.

A god emerges from the jaws of a jaguar in this Zapotec image from the 6th century.

From the start of Mesoamerican civilization, in the religion of the Olmecs, the jaguar played an important role. Images of were-jaguars – humans with the power to transform themselves into the beast – suggest that the connection may have gone back into the shamanistic practices of even earlier times.

In later years, the cult of the jaguar was strongest among the Maya, who inhabited the southern jungle lands where the animal lived. Among their gods was a Jaguar Baby, resembling the snarling infant figure common in Olmec art.

In the northern kingdoms of the Valley of Mexico region, the jaguar was equally respected, even though few of their citizens could ever have seen one. Teotihuacan had a Temple of the Jaguars, so called from depictions of the animal on its walls. The mysterious image of a netted jaguar also figured prominently in the city's religious symbolism.

One of the two great Aztec military orders was that of the Jaguar Knights. But the animal's main association in later times was with Tezcatlipoca, who often took the form of a jaguar. Silent, nocturnal and deadly, the great cat was in every way a fitting symbol for the most formidable of all the gods.

A harvest feast whose main dish is a meal of cooked maize is celebrated in honour of the god Quetzalcoatl, in a detail from an Aztec codex dating from before the Spanish Conquest.

The *tlaloques* also play a significant part in an Aztec myth that tells how maize was first given to the world. In the beginning the grain was known only to red ants, who kept it hidden deep inside Mount Tonacatepetl, a prominent local peak. To find out what they were concealing, Quetzalcoatl transformed himself into a black ant and made his way unseen to their secret storeroom. He took samples of the cereal back to the other gods, who tasted it and found that it was delicious. Chewing it into a mash, they placed it in the mouths of human babies, and discovered that it was just the food that the human race needed to grow up healthy and strong. But the rest of the store still had to be recovered from its hiding place if people were to benefit from its nourishment. To release it, Quetzalcoatl slung a rope round the mountain and tried to shift it, but it was too heavy for him. Perplexed, the gods took the problem to Oxomoco and Cipactonal, the divine couple who were the oldest of all the gods. They decreed that Nanahuatzin, the creator of the Fifth Sun, should be given the task of splitting the mountain open. He did so with the help of the *tlaloques*, who snatched up the grain inside and scattered it – and so were responsible for bringing the crop to humankind.

Altogether, just under half of the monthly festivals in honour of the gods were dedicated to those associated with water, either directly – as in the case of the festival of Tozoztontli when flowers were offered to Tlaloc – or indirectly. These water festivals started in February and carried on until November. They included the festival of the salt goddess Uixtocihuatl, sister of the rain gods,

torrents. Representations show her seated on a throne from which a raging flood surges forth, sometimes carrying struggling humans away.

Living at high altitude, the Aztecs associated rivers with mountains, which they considered to be the home of rain. Tlaloc himself lived on a peak to the east of the Valley of Mexico that bears his name to this day. On its summit, more than 13,000 feet up, stood a shrine to the god. Those heights were also the homes of the god's attendants, the *tlaloques*. Sometimes there were said to be many of these, but on other occasions just five were shown, each bringing a different kind of rain: fiery rain (possibly symbolizing drought), fungus rain, wind rain, beneficial rain symbolized by jade signs, and flint-blade rain, which was probably a reference to violent hail. Like Tlaloc himself, they were widely venerated and it seems likely that they were very popular. People made gruelling pilgrimages to visit the caves where they were supposed to dwell. Sometimes children were sacrificed to them, immured in caverns behind huge boulders. The priests who abandoned them there believed they were committing them to an earthly paradise in the heart of the mountain.

Macuilxochitl, god of gambling, challenges a few mortals to the game of patolli, "the game of the mat", in a detail from a 15th-century codex. According to the Spanish, the Aztecs were inveterate gamblers.

in June – when old women and young girls wearing flowers in their hair danced together. In September, Tepeilhuitl – the festival in honour of the mountains where clouds gather – was celebrated by making dough sculptures of mountains. Those who had passed away and gone to the tropical paradise presided over by Tlaloc (Tlalocan, on heaven's fourth level) were remembered at this time.

Gods of Maize

A body of legend surrounded Mesoamerica's staple crop, maize, and a cluster of divinities shared responsibility for its growth and fruition. Maya maize gods had elongated heads that recalled the shape of ears of the cereal; it is even possible that infants' skulls were deformed in imitation of them.

By Aztec days at least four separate deities were associated with the maize plant in different aspects of its growth. In its earliest stage, the tender green ear was symbolized by Xilonen, conceived of as a dancing maiden with a double ear of the cereal in each hand. There was also a male personification of the young plant in the shape of

Cinteotl, a young man colored yellow in the codices and sporting sheaves of maize in his headdress. The goddess of the harvested crop was Chicomecoatl, who received the gratitude of the populace for her bounty every August.

Cinteotl, maize's masculine personification, was closely associated in the people's minds with various other young male deities associated with sensual pleasure, the connection apparently lying in a link perceived between the fertility of the land and human sexuality.

One was Xochipilli (literally, "Flower Prince"). Portrayed as a handsome youth beating on a drum, he was the patron of flowers, dancing, feasting and all occasions on which people wore garlands on their heads. Less happily, he was also responsible for inflicting boils, haemorrhoids and venereal diseases on individuals guilty of sexual excess. Another young god associated both with pleasure and the penalties of excess was Macuilxochitl, patron of games and gambling.

Perhaps, the oddest of all the deities associated with the growing crop, however, was Xipe Totec, a god of springtime honoured when the maize seed first sprouted. For reasons still not fully understood, but most likely connected with a myth that is now lost, he was known as the "Flayed One", and victims were sacrificed to him in particularly bizarre and gory ways.

Some were tied to frames and shot with arrows, their blood being allowed to drip onto a round stone that symbolized the Earth. Others were condemned to the so-called "gladiatorial sacrifice", in which captive warriors wielding mock weapons edged with feathers fought fully armed Aztec knights. After they had duly bled to death from the wounds they received, the prisoners' bodies were flayed. Their captors then wore the skins, tied over their own naked flesh, for twenty days, during which time they ran around the city begging for alms. The religious symbolism behind this startlingly gruesome exercise was apparently connected to the way in which maize seeds lose their old skin when the new growth bursts forth, and therefore it was associated with the beginning of a new cycle.

Xipe Totec, a god of regeneration, often wore a human skin, in imitation of the way maize seeds wear a husk. This Aztec granite mask shows him as a fresh-faced young man.

569

Cycles of Destiny

The dangerous gods of Mesoamerica were the masters of time, dictating the fates of hapless humans according to capricious whim. In order to attempt to predict the next move in the gods' game of life and death, priests developed a complex system of two calendars.

From early on, the Mesoamericans had a solar year of 365 days, which they split into eighteen twenty-day months, each one reflecting the influence of a particular deity and including a festival in his or her honour. In the Aztec calendar, gods associated with the cultivation of maize predominated in the earlier part of the year, when agricultural activity was busiest. Later came festivals for warriors, hunters and women. The year ended with five so-called "nameless" days (The Barren Days), necessary to round up the 360 to 365. As these were under the protection of no particular god, they were considered ill-omened, and people avoided undertaking any major enterprise at this time.

The calendar was imperfect, however, for the mathematics of Mesoamerica lacked fractions, and so never came to terms with the fact that the actual length of the Earth's revolution around the sun is roughly 365 and a quarter days. So they had no equivalent to the leap year, introduced into European calendrics by Julius Caesar in 46BC. The result was that over time the Mesoamerican solar year wandered through the seasons. To keep any kind of agricultural relevance, it must have been corrected from time to time, though such amendments have gone unrecorded. Because of its imprecision, archaeologists refer to it as the Vague Year. Yet it had huge significance as the main measure of time for public events.

The 260-day Calendar

Alongside the 365-day calendar (Xihuitl to the Aztecs; Haab to the Maya), another of equal significance and possibly even greater antiquity was regularly consulted. This was a 260-day almanac, in which each day bore a number from one to thirteen and one of twenty names – for example, Alligator, Wind, House – which, like the numbers, rotated in a fixed order. So, in the Aztec version, the day named One Alligator was followed by Two Wind and Three House; once Thirteen Reed had been reached, the sequence continued with One Jaguar (Jaguar being fourteenth in the day-name sequence). One Alligator was reached again on the 261st day of this never-ending cycle.

Unlike the solar calendar, the 260-day count had no apparent link with the seasons or the

This 10-feet-wide Calendar Stone, found in Mexico City in the 18th century, depicts the 260-day annual cycle. Its size and magnificence show how significant the keeping of time was to the Aztecs. Glyphs of the twenty day signs surround the Earth Monster. The four panels represent the four worlds previously destroyed by the gods.

movements of heavenly bodies, which has led to much debate about how it originally came into use. A likely explanation is that it was devised by midwives as an aid to calculating the gestation of babies, from the time of the mother's first missed period to the birth. The facts that individuals in many parts of Central America took their names from their birthday as measured by the count and were reckoned at that time to have already completed one 260-day cycle – in effect, to have been born on their first birthday – point in that direction.

The origins of the 260-day calendar remain obscure, but the evidence suggests that it was in use throughout much of Mesoamerica by the first century AD. It played a central role in Maya life in the Classic Period just as it was to do in Aztec times 1,000 years later; in fact, many day-names were shared by the two cultures.

While the 365-day calendar served to measure the passing seasons, the 260-day cycle was primarily a guide to the future, providing a crucial tool for diviners to foretell private fortunes as well as the likely outcome of affairs of state. Every day

Even though they were associated with death and the night, owls were also linked with the Lords of the Day.

reflected the influence of gods and other forces that could be propitious or unpropitious. Firstly, the thirteen numbers of the sequence each had their divine patrons, the so-called Lords of the Day, who were associated with the thirteen levels of the heavens and with a similar number of flying creatures – hummingbirds, owls, butterflies, doves.

A Living Tradition

Despite the introduction of Christianity, some Mesoamerican beliefs have survived to the present day. In particular, the ritual 260-day calendar is still alive among highland Maya communities.

Among the Ixil, Quiché and other peoples of Guatemala and southern Mexico, shaman priests known as day-keepers still reckon the passing of time by the twenty signs and thirteen numbers of the Maya. Villagers turn to these community healers for reading omens, protection against ill health and advice on their future projects.

One of the biggest communal celebrations geared to the old calendar is the Eight Monkey Festival in the Quiché community of Momostenango in Guatemala. The festival is still held on that date of the 260-day year. Although nominally Christian, the feast clearly encompasses memories of the old faith.

On the appointed day tens of thousands of Indians gather at first light in company with a 100 or more shamans. They come to honour the god they call Dios Mundo (God of the Earth), praying for past forgiveness and future blessing around piles of broken pottery that serve as altars. To speed each prayer on its way, fresh shards are added to the piles – a distant echo of the human or animal sacrifices that in past times would have accompanied similar appeals to the gods.

Secondly, each of the twenty day-names came under the sway of a specific deity. And thirdly, the forces prevailing at the start of each thirteen-day period cast a lingering spell over the remaining twelve days. The result was a rich stew of associations that could be interpreted only by trained priests. Even so, some days were so obviously bad that children born on them were sometimes renamed on more auspicious ones.

The Aztecs called the 260-day cycle the *tonalpohualli* – literally, "counting of the day-signs" – and had a myth to describe how it had come into being. The first humans, they claimed, had felt the need for such a calendar and had taken their concerns to the oldest of all the gods, the divine couple Cipactonal and Oxomoco. Oxomoco chose a symbol for the first day. She selected the alligator, after which the other nineteen day-signs fell into place of their own accord. The first almanac of all the signs was then drawn up, and their grandson Quetzalcoatl passed the art of divining from it down to humankind.

The lessons that could be learned from a proper reading of the calendar were vast indeed. According to the chronicler Diego Durán, the *tonalpohualli* "taught the Indian nations the days on which they were to sow, reap, till the land, cultivate corn, weed, harvest, store, shell the ears of corn, sow beans and flax seed." It was equally indispensable to merchants setting out on expeditions or rulers contemplating policy decisions.

If 260 days had to pass before a given number and name – Twelve Reed, say – came round again on this cycle, a much longer period had to elapse before a Twelve Reed day coincided with a particular date in the 365-day year. Mesoamerican mathematicians worked out that it took a total of 18,980 days for the two year-counts to mesh – a period equivalent to fifty-two 365-day years and seventy-three revolutions of the 260-day cycle. This mathematical fact attained huge importance for various Mesoamerican peoples, for whom the Calendar Round – the name now ascribed to the fifty-two-year period – took on great mystical significance. The Aztecs referred to it as "the bundle of years", from the custom of storing a peeled stick

Each day in the 260-day calendar was associated with a particular god or myth, as this colorful detail in the *Codex Cospi* shows.

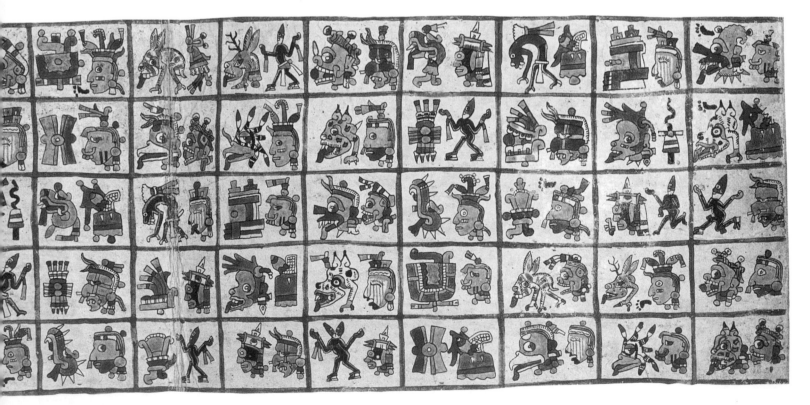

At the end of every 52-year cycle, people all over the Valley of Mexico waited on rooftops to see the sacred flame lit near Tenochtitlan. Then a courier carried the flame from house to house for the people to light their own fires.

to mark the passage of each solar year; the wands were then tied into a faggot and ritually burned once fifty-two had been collected. They awaited the moment with trepidation, for they believed that in a very real sense it represented the end of time, the instant when the gods might choose to destroy the world. As the fateful time approached, people shattered their household utensils, let their fires go out, abstained from sex, fasted, kept silence, and gradually abandoned all their daily activities.

On the night itself, a solemn procession passed out of the capital, headed for an ancient shrine on a nearby peak. There the assembled priests and dignitaries waited in utter silence until midnight, carefully watching the Pleiades. If this star cluster continued to move after it had reached its zenith, it was taken as a signal that the world was not about to end.

To celebrate the survival of the world, priests sacrificed an important victim – usually a captured prince or general – by cutting out his heart on an altar on the mountain top. A priest would then strike fire on a fire-drill within the cavity where the victim's heart had been. When the sparks had strengthened into a flame, they were used to ignite a great bonfire.

Then, people who had been waiting anxiously on their rooftops would raise a cheer at this confirmation that the end was not at hand. Subsequently the flame was carried to the Great Temple in Tenochtitlan itself. After months of tension, people could at last relax; their world was safe – at least for another fifty-two years.

573

A Universe Fuelled by Blood

The gods had set the world in motion and, through their magical calendar, had determined the fate of those who lived in it. They expected something in return from their creation – and the most valuable gift of all was blood.

To modern eyes, the most startling aspect of the Mesoamerican world was its emphasis on sacrifice and blood, yet to the people of the time the need for such offerings would have seemed self-evident. For the region's gods were not benevolent. They were as capricious as they were all-powerful, and human beings only survived on sufferance. Both the Mayas and the Aztecs believed that in past ages the gods had created and then destroyed several worlds. The world they lived in would only survive if people did all in their power to avert the anger of the gods. There were several mechanisms by which the gods could be appeased. Due care and attention was one

A captive is prepared for sacrifice with his arms tied behind his back and an incision above his heart in this Totonac carving from between AD500 and 900.

such method. According to the Maya chronicle the *Popul Vuh*, one earlier race of people had already been destroyed for failing to praise the gods. Subsequent generations took care never to repeat the mistake.

Images of the leading deities were carefully tended in their shrines, and were regularly paraded before the people at festivals. Offerings of all kinds were made to them, not just at the temples but also in sacred places including caves and mountaintop shrines. A whole cache of treasures, including food containers and artworks from conquered lands, was buried in the foundations of the Aztecs' Great Temple of Tenochtitlan, while the Sacred Cenote, or sink-hole, at Chichén Itzá in the Yucatán peninsula has yielded up many valuables, including gold discs and ornaments of jade.

More Precious Than Gold

Ultimately, however, the gods sought something more precious to them than gold, and that was blood. The blood of animals was an acceptable offering, and in Aztec times quails were slaughtered in large numbers, their heads torn off before the sacred images. Dogs and turkeys were also frequent victims, and on important occasions jaguars were sometimes killed; sixteen died to celebrate the accession of the sixteenth ruler of Copán, and a jaguar skeleton was uncovered in the Tenochtitlan temple foundations.

For the most part, though, human blood was the offering the gods most desired. The *Popol Vuh* recounts how Tohil, patron deity of the Quiché Maya, specifically rejected offerings of precious metal in favour of flesh. By Aztec times, the demand for victims had become so great that special wars were fought in which the aim was not to kill the enemy but to seize people who would subsequently end up on sacrificial altars.

Although evidence for earlier periods is slight, it seems likely that human sacrifice on a smaller scale went far back in the history of the area. But the quantity of killing seems to have increased greatly with the ending of the so-called Classic Period in the seventh or eighth century AD. By Toltec times, skull-racks for displaying heads of victims became a common feature of ceremonial centres. At Tenochtitlan, a huge skull-rack stood between the Great Temple and the ballcourt.

While most victims were prisoners-of-war or slaves, individuals of all ranks were also expected to contribute their own blood through the practice known as auto-sacrifice. This involved passing sharp implements – thorn-studded twine, stingray spines, spikes from the maguey plant – through fleshy parts of the body, including the earlobes, cheeks, lips, tongue and foreskin. The blood was then usually smeared on to paper and burned before statues of the gods.

The Origins of Human Sacrifice

Mythology provided explanations for these sanguinary obsessions. One Aztec myth described how the present world was created when Quetzalcoatl and Tezcatlipoca tore the Earth Monster Tlaltecuhtli in two, transforming one half of her torso into the sky and the other into the earth (see box, page 549). All growing things were fashioned from her body. At night, it was said, she could sometimes be heard howling for the hearts of men to eat, and her hunger had to be satisfied if she was to continue to provide nature's bounty.

Another story told how two gods sacrificed themselves to become the sun and moon (see pages 562–563). Both rose into the sky, but

A priest slaughters a captive in honour of the gods in this stela from Guatemala. Human sacrifice was an important part of Mesoamerican culture from the earliest civilizations.

It was common for victims to be sacrificed at the top of the temple steps. When the heart had been removed, the body was flung to the ground. Eyewitnesses described the steps streaming with blood. This graphic illustration is from the *Codex Magliabechiano*, which was painted by Aztec artists under the direction of Spanish friars soon after the Conquest.

remained there motionless. The sun god, Tonatiuh, declared that he would not move unless the other deities gave him their own blood as a sign of fealty. When the other gods agreed to have their hearts cut out, he began his journey. Ever after, humans had to repeat the gods' gesture if Tonatiuh was to continue his passage through the heavens.

In practice, sacrifice also served other, more practical purposes in Aztec society. The great majority of victims were prisoners-of-war, and the demands of the sacrificial altars provided a justification and a rationale for constant military activity. This in turn served the interests of the ruling warrior class, whose position at the peak of the social hierarchy rested on battlefield prowess.

If any one person's hand can be seen behind the upsurge in killing that marked the Aztec heyday, it was probably that of a nobleman called Tlacaelel, who served as adviser to three successive rulers in the fifteenth century. According to the Dominican chronicler Diego Durán, who drew his information from Aztec sources soon after the Conquest, Tlacaelel was not merely a great general, "bold and cunning in the trickery of war", but he also "invented devilish, cruel and frightful sacrifices". For although detailed figures are hard to

estimate, there seems to have been a quantum leap in the number of sacrificial victims under the Aztecs in the latter part of the fifteenth century.

Ritual killings formed part of most, if not all, of the festivals that marked the various months of the agricultural year. Special events could call for the sacrifice of thousands. The rededication of the Great Temple of Tenochtitlan in 1487 was said to have been marked by the mass slaughter of 20,000 or even as many as 80,000 victims.

The most common form of sacrifice in Aztec times was the cutting out of hearts. Four priests would hold the victim spreadeagled over a sacrificial altar while a fifth, equipped with a razor-sharp flint knife, would rapidly cut out the heart. The hearts themselves – still pulsating – were raised up towards the sun by the officiating priest. Then the blood-soaked body bumped slowly down the steps of the pyramid to land in a sodden heap at its base. Old men collected the bodies for dismemberment. Skulls were displayed on the skull-rack in the temple compound.

Bernal Diaz, one of the conquistadors who accompanied Cortés, wrote an account of his visit to the Great Temple of Tenochtitlan: "There were some smoking braziers of their incense, which they call copal, in which they were burning the hearts of three Indians whom they had sacrificed that day; and all the walls of that shrine were so splashed and caked with blood that they and the floor too were black ... The stench was worse than that of any slaughterhouse in Spain."

The bodies of prisoners-of-war were retrieved afterwards by their captors, and parts of them were consumed by members of their families in ritual feasts. These cannibal meals were solemn affairs, for the flesh of the victims was considered to be consecrated and was, in the words of one chronicler, "eaten with reverence, ritual and fastidiousness – as if it were something from heaven". As a gesture of humility, the warrior himself would refrain from eating in case he himself should end up in a similar situation at some future date.

Other forms of sacrifice, including beheading and shooting with darts, were also practised in the course of the monthly festivals, in which the victims were for the most part considered representatives of the gods (see pages 578–579). Those to be killed were treated with respect by their captors, and were promised a happy afterlife in the upper levels of the Aztec heaven.

Yet few free-born citizens ever volunteered for the honour. Death on the altars was almost invariably imposed by the powerful on the weakest members of society. The great mass of the population apparently stoically accepted human sacrifice as an institution that was sanctioned by both age-old custom and the divine order.

Rites of Confession

The sense of sin weighed heavily on several of the Mesoamerican peoples. To lessen the burden, they had recourse to self-mortification and to rituals of confession.

Post-Conquest accounts describe penitential rituals among the Zapotec and Maya. Zapotecs would pierce their flesh and allow the blood to drip onto maize husks as they recounted their transgressions. Certain Maya communities chose a scapegoat – usually an old woman – to bear the sins of the whole community. After hearing the confessions of each individual, the victim would be stoned to death, thereby winning atonement for the entire village.

The best-attested rites are those of the pre-Conquest Aztecs. Deeply puritanical in their attitude towards sex, they felt the need to purify themselves ritually of the stain it cast upon them. Men were given a single chance to do so by a once-in-a-lifetime confession to the goddess Tlazolteotl.

At a time of his choosing, usually in late middle age, the penitent would strip naked and confess his misdemeanours to a priest representing the goddess. He would then be offered absolution, but not before he had been forced to carry out a series of painful penances.

A Maya ballplayer is dressed in the simple clothes of a penitent. His bruised and swollen face drips with blood from a bloodletting ritual.

Impersonating the Gods

The concept that someone could become divine by dressing up in the regalia of the gods was an ancient one in Mesoamerica, and it was to provide the Aztecs with a rationale for some of their most bizarre and harrowing rituals.

Virtually all Mesoamerican peoples were used to seeing representations of the gods in pottery and stone. Given the theatrical nature of much of their public ritual, it was then a natural step to incorporate living images of the deities into festivals and other ceremonies in the form of humans splendidly adorned in their vestments traditionally associated with individual divinities.

For participants and spectators alike, the concept went far beyond any idea of play-acting. When Maya kings put on costumes that reproduced the traditional outfits of the maize god or the jaguar god of the underworld, they were thought to become temporarily divine themselves.

Under the Aztecs, the concept became linked with the cult of human sacrifice. In an extension of previous practice, victims known as *ixiptla* were dressed up, each as a particular god. Treated with the respect due to the divinity they were held to have become, they were then sacrificed to that same deity. All the gods of the Aztec months seem to have been celebrated in this way. But the concept of divine impersonation was expressed in its most extreme form in the shape of the young man – handsome, smooth-skinned and intelligent – chosen to represent Tezcatlipoca every year at the end of the month dedicated to the deity. For a whole year he was honoured as the living representative of the god.

During the day he was kept under guard in Tezcatlipoca's temple, where he was trained to dance and play the flute. At night he was released in the company of eight young warriors, who acted both as his attendants and as sentinels to check that he did not escape. As he walked through the deserted night-time streets, he played on his flute and rattled bangles attached to his arms and legs. Citizens who heard the sounds told

Sacred Bundles

One feature that Mesoamerican religion shared with some native faiths of North America was the veneration of bundles containing objects sacred to the cult of a particular god.

Examples of sacred bundles have been found in Maya artwork of the Classic Period, and the *Popol Vuh* recounts how the Quiché Maya carried one such pack representing an ancestor with them on their migrations. Chichemec peoples including the Mixtecs and Aztecs adopted the practice, which had obvious attractions for nomads forced to take their gods with them on their travels.

Aztec bundles purportedly included the gods' mantles, bequeathed to retainers in the legendary past when they had sacrificed themselves to bring life to the world; to these were added jade, jewels, skins of snakes and jaguars and other holy objects. The relics were entrusted to priests known as "god-bearers", who acquired special powers from them, including the ability to pronounce oracles.

A priest in the striped headdress of the maize goddess and flanked by other priests dressed as the rain god's assistants performs a ritual in a detail from a 16th-century Aztec codex.

each other that the god himself was passing; some would bring out sick children for his blessing, hoping to see them cured.

The adulation rose to a climax as the month sacred to Tezcatlipoca came round again. In those final twenty days the Aztec ruler himself came to the temple to dress the youth in the full regalia of the god. He was provided with four wives, themselves held to represent important goddesses. Five days before the end of the month, the emperor went into temporary retreat to indicate that the living Tezcatlipoca reigned supreme in the city. When the final day came, the youth was taken to the shrine of the god, where he bade his wives farewell. Then he mounted the pyramid. When he reached the top, he was sacrificed. The dead body was carried down to ground level, where it was butchered. The flesh was later cooked in a stew served to the ruler and other dignitaries at a banquet. One of the guests was the youth who had earlier in the day been selected to be the god's new representative – and next year's main course.

The Power of the Shaman

Mesoamerican religion may have had its roots in shamanistic rites imported across the Bering land bridge from Asia. Their influence was long lasting: shapeshifting sorcerers were feared long after the Spanish Conquest and spirit journeys are still part of popular myth.

The ability to enter trances, to fly supernaturally, and to cure spirits, plus the possession of animal spirit companions, are all features of the shaman. Hallucinogens that were known to later peoples, including narcotic mushrooms, morning-glory seeds and peyote, may also have been used from the earliest times to induce trances and visions.

By Aztec times, different terms were used to describe the two aspects of the shamanistic relationship between man and beast. In the Nahuatl language, *tonal* served to describe the animal familiar spirits associated with most individuals from shortly after their birth.

The technique of shapeshifting and the sorcerers who had learned its secrets were both denoted by the word *nahual*. Such individuals were greatly feared, as was their patron deity, the mighty but sinister Tezcatlipoca. While many Aztec divinities had the ability to transform themselves, he was particularly noted for his animal disguises.

Sorcery had become partly professionalized by the Aztec era. On the one hand, priests seem to have mastered various shamanistic techniques, which they were happy to apply as the occasion demanded in addition to their normal ceremonial duties. On the other, many other individuals seem to have made a living from magical practices.

The greatest demand was for diviners – a role partly filled by the priests who specialized in interpreting the 260-day almanac. Other individuals read the future in the patterns maize grains formed when scattered on a cloak. Fortune-tellers – often old women – would gaze into pots of water or mirrors of polished obsidian in search of clues, and prognosticate the likely outcome of diseases by knotting and unknotting lengths of rope. Some individuals used fasting and hallucinogens to enter trances in which they sought enlightenment. People also consulted spirit healers who claimed to cure ills with the aid of a pharmacopoeia of therapeutic plants alongside various magical techniques shared with North American medicine men. Some apparently used sleight of hand to remove supposed pathogens – typically pebbles or flint blades – from within their patients. Others employed incantations and private rituals as a prelude to "sucking out" the disease.

Entertainers and Illusionists

Public fascination with the supernatural created a demand for illusionists who performed apparently impossible feats as entertainment. Texts are vague about the details of their performances: some apparently were able to swing vessels filled with water from a cord without spilling a drop, but descriptions of others "who toast maize on their mantle", "who burn with flames someone's house" or "who dismember themselves" are less clear. All apparently performed tricks designed to amaze and mystify their audience.

Other *nahualli* had more sinister aims. Black magicians known as "human owls" – birds of ill omen – sought to bring harm on selected individuals by burning them in effigy or by surreptitiously touching them with blood. "Sleep throwers" carried with them the arm of a woman who had died in childbirth, which was believed to have the power to stupefy all the inhabitants of a house so that they could easily be robbed at night.

The Lady Xoc, in a shamanistic trance, has a vision of a warrior emerging from a serpent's mouth in this Maya stela dated AD725. For reasons unknown, the glyphs are in mirror writing.

581

SOUTH AMERICAN KINGDOMS OF GOLD

The towering Andes mountain range runs for more than 4,000 miles down the western side of South America. From Colombia in the north to Tierra del Fuego in the south, these imposing mountains overlook a dramatic range of landscapes. The grasslands, the dry coastal plains and fertile valleys, even the high, barren plateau of Callao in southern Peru, have seen several great civilizations rise and fall. It is in this majestic terrain that the Andean mythology is rooted, with the mountains acting as objects of great awe and reverence.

When the Spanish conquistadors arrived in the sixteenth century, the dominant power was the Inca empire. However, before the Incas' ascendancy, the Chimor civilization in Peru ruled for 500 years from Chan Chan. Then there was the city of Tiahuanaco, set high on the austere *altiplano* ("high plateau") near Lake Titicaca, where there flourished a culture that spread its influence for more than 1,000 years until it fell into decline after the first millennium AD.

Unfortunately, evidence of patterns of belief is sparse. No written records were made until Spanish priests began recording legends in the sixteenth century. Inca gods and myths have many antecedents, because local mythologies were adapted and subsumed wherever the empire spread. Yet by studying archaeological evidence it is possible to unravel some of the beliefs of earlier cultures. For example, the Inca god Pachacamac appears to have been a Chimu deity, and Viracocha seems to be allied to the creator Con Ticci (or Thunupa) worshipped by the Indians of the *altiplano*.

Cultures that had evolved over 10,000 years did not take long to destroy. The process began in 1527, when Pizarro and his men were welcomed as guests into the Inca city of Tumbes. They were amazed by its marvellously engineered aqueducts, a fortress whose walls were built of vast blocks of unmortared stone, and, most impressive of all, a temple clad with plates of gold and silver. In its garden were luscious fruits and vegetables – all made of precious metals. But gold proved to be the Indians' undoing. Motivated by the prospect of unlimited riches, Pizarro returned five years later with an army that quickly made itself master of the entire Inca empire. Within twenty years of his arrival, most of the continent was under European control and the influence of the Christian faith.

Opposite: **Gold was both the glory and the downfall of South American Indians. Invaders lusted after objects such as this cast gold Colombian flask in the shape of a seated woman, dated AD600–1100.**

Below: **The icons of the pre-Christian Indians, represented in pottery by early cultures such as the Chavin and Moche peoples, reflected the world around them. This pottery incense burner, depicts a puma and is from Tiahuanaco.**

Valleys of the Chibcha

The Chibcha inhabited the mountain valleys in modern Colombia, to the north of the Inca empire, where they created a great civilization that survived until the Spanish arrived in the sixteenth century. Three tribes – the Zipa, the Zaque and the Iraca – ruled the Chibcha lands. They believed that the universe was created by an all-powerful god named Chiminigagua.

With a pectoral such as this adorning his chest, a member of the Popayán tribe, neighbours of the Chibcha, would have displayed his wealth and power. This piece dates from AD1100–1500.

In the first days, the Chibcha told, the Earth was covered in darkness. Then the god Chiminigagua, who contained shining light within him, began creation by setting the light free. First he fashioned a flock of great black birds that carried his light inside them and instructed them to fly through the world. As they soared over the towering Andes, they released the brilliance, like falling moisture, from their beaks and the world filled up with light. It was only afterwards that Chiminigagua made the sun and set it in the sky, and created the moon to be its consort.

In some versions of the myth, the light that Chiminigagua released was originally hidden inside a vast house over which he had control. After some time, he decided there had been enough darkness and set the light free. Chiminigagua, the Chibcha said, was also filled with goodness – and the first Spanish chroniclers of the native myths identified him with God the Father in the Christian tradition. But although Chiminigagua created the universe, he did not make mankind.

The First Men and Women

A little while after light had settled on the Earth, a woman named Bachue ("large breasted") clambered from Lake Iguaque high in the Andes, carrying her young son in her arms. He was three years old and just emerging from infancy into childhood. With him, she settled nearby and lived quietly, watching proudly as he grew into a handsome young man. In time she became his lover and proved so fertile – each of her pregnancies resulted in between four and six children –

Chibcha chiefs from the region around Lake Guatavita in Colombia gilded themselves and dived into its waters to mark their accession. The ritual gave rise to the legend of "El Dorado".

that eventually the ever-multiplying family of her children and their descendants grew large enough to populate the entire Earth.

Bachue and her son lived with their people for many years, but one day they felt an urge to return to the sacred lake from which they had come. Bachue called some of her people together at the lakeside and bade them farewell. She handed down laws governing day-to-day life and told them to live together peacefully and to honour the divine order. Then before their eyes she and her son transformed themselves into serpents and slithered away into the lake. Ever afterwards the pair were worshipped – and were said sometimes to appear to their followers in a vision, as glistening snakes. Bachue – sometimes known as Furachogue ("kind woman") – became an Earth divinity, the Chibcha goddess of agriculture, harvest and water.

The belief that the first people came from a watery place – a sacred lake or stream – was common to many American peoples. In the Inca legends, for example, their dynasty's founder Manco Copac and his sister-wife Mama Ocllo are said to have been set down on the shores of Lake Titicaca in Peru by the sun god Inti. The myth of Bachue is also linked to another common body of legends in which people came from inside the Earth. Indeed, the Chibcha believed that at the point of death, people's souls returned to the centre of the Earth, carried along the course of an underground river on lightweight canoes made of spiders' webs. For this reason, spiders were highly regarded.

Boredom Breeds Creativity

The Chibcha also passed down a variant history of how the first men and women were made. According to this tale, two *caciques* – native princes – were alive in the time of darkness at the start of the world. The *cacique* of Sogamozo and his nephew, the *cacique* of Ramiriqui, were surrounded by a great fog of darkness and grew bored. To entertain themselves, they took some clay and a handful of reeds, moulding the first men from the clay and cutting the first women from the reeds. They told their creatures to worship them faithfully and then, to provide light,

585

The rectangular style of this red ceramic Chibcha mask is distinctively Peruvian. The beasts which decorate its edge reflect the animal world from which, as Andean mythology saw it, the human race had come.

climbed into the sky, the prince of Sogamozo becoming the sun and his nephew the moon.

An ancient rite thought to be connected to sun worship may have grown from this myth. The ceremony took place at Sogamozo, the sun's territory according to the legend. Twelve men dressed in red, perhaps representing the twelve months, danced around a man robed in blue, who may have stood for the sky or the sun. The dancers chanted a song recalling how people must die and be turned to dust but their souls would live on.

Chiminigagua created the universe, but he was not worshipped as the chief of the Chibcha gods. That honour fell to the sun deity Bochica, who was revered for giving the people civilization and knowledge of the arts.

According to legend, Bochica appeared from the east. He came in the form of an old man in full-length robes with long hair and a beard growing down to his waist. At this time the people were living almost as animals, without gods, buildings or even crops. Bochica taught them how to build huts and grow fruits, how to spin and weave and how to live together peaceably and sociably. He also instructed them in the worship of the sun god and persuaded them to lead chaste and sober lives. People flocked to hear him speak. At Cota he lived for some time in a cave and preached regularly to vast crowds of people.

But much of Bochica's work was undone by his beautiful wife Chia, sometimes known as Huitaca. A tall, comely woman, she followed him into the Chibcha lands, preaching the opposite of his doctrine. Where he encouraged the people to be chaste and sober, she told them to drink and dance, be merry and make love. It was a message the people liked to hear and many came round to her ways, but Bochica, naturally enough, was furious and prepared to stop her.

In some versions of the myth she provoked him even further by using her magical powers to make the Funzha River overflow its banks. It created a flash flood, which only a few people were able to escape by clambering on to the mountaintops. For his revenge Bochica banished her from daylight, condemning her to live only by night from that day to the end of time. Some histories relate that he turned her into the moon; others that he made her into an owl, which shuns the sun and must fly abroad by moonlight. As Huitaca she became the Chibcha goddess of drunkenness and self-indulgence.

Bochica remained on Earth for 2,000 years, living a life of self-denial and instructing the people in the ways of civilization. He established festivals, pilgrimages and sacrifices, and appointed a high priest for the cult of the sun. He also saved the people from a great flood (see box, page 589) and from the terrifying god of storms, Thomagata – who, like Huallallo Caruincho, a god of the Indians of the Huarochirí region of Peru, took the form of a fireball. When at length he departed, he either ascended to heaven or he left for the west, leaving his footprint in a rock.

Bochica was worshipped as the giver of laws, with precious sacrifices of gold, tobacco – and also boys. The victim, named the *quesa* ("wanderer"), was always taken from a particular village, now known as San Juan de los Llanos, that was connected to Bochica's cult. At the age of ten he was moved to a sun temple at Sagamozo and for five years he was treated with the greatest care and reverence. When he reached fifteen he was taken

Seeds of Life

One set of creation myths told by northern Andean tribes featured an all-powerful divinity named Sibu, who had the power to grow men and animals from seeds.

Sibu entrusted his precious seeds to the god Sura. But as soon as Sura's back was turned Jabaru emerged and seized the seeds and ate them. And then, when Sura returned, Jabaru cut his throat and buried him in their place. Some time later Jabaru returned to Sura's grave and found Sibu standing by a cacao and a calabash tree that had grown there. Sibu greeted him, then asked politely for a drink of cocoa made from the tree.

Jabaru took some beans to his wives who prepared the drink, using the hard shell of the calabash fruit as a cup. When Jabaru returned, Sibu insisted he drink first. Jabaru grasped the cup and drank thirstily. The fruit of Sura tasted good. But just then, pain coursed through his belly which swelled and swelled until it burst, scattering Sura's seed on the ground. Sibu, willing Sura alive once more, returned the seeds that would one day give life to men and beasts on Earth.

This Moche anthropomorphized maize cob, AD450–550, links humans to agriculture and also suggests the mountains that overlooked the fields.

in a splendid procession to a pillar erected in Bochica's honour and shot dead with arrows by priests. After he had died, the *quesa*'s heart was cut out and offered to Bochica and the child's blood was collected as a sacrifice to the god.

Bochica was also known as Xue ("Lord"), Sugunsúa ("disappearing one") and sometimes even as Chimizagagua ("messenger of Chimini-gagua"). The Spanish priest Pedro Simon, who in the seventeenth century recorded some of the myths and traditions of the Chibcha and other South American peoples, claimed that the cult of Bochica had grown from a folk memory of a visit by one of Christ's apostles.

Bochica is a type of divine figure common in South American myths. Called a "culture hero" by scholars, he teaches culture and social and survival skills to tribes that were previously primitive. He is comparable to Kenos, the establisher of order and who teaches the first people speech, in the myths of the Tierra del Fuego tribes, or the Chimu deity Pachacamac (see page 593).

A Disgraced King

Bochica's sojourn in the Chibcha lands was used by local mythmakers to support the notion of divine kingship and to validate the ruling dynasties' hold on power. In the same way, legends of the first Incas, Manco and Mama, were used further south along the Andean range in Peru.

The histories recount that at Sugamixi in the eastern part of the territories the ruler of the Iraca lands, Nompanem, warmly welcomed Bochica, and that the god established the laws and religious rituals in Nompanem's realm. Shortly afterwards the high priest Idacanzas founded a dynasty of priests for the sun cult – presumably with the visiting god's approval.

But Hunsahua, chief of Tunja, broke the divinely ordained conventions and suffered a terrible fate. He was overcome with desire for his own sister and found that she was all too willing to share the illicit pleasure. Flushed with happiness, the young lovers expected understanding from

their mother – but she flew into a rage, declaring that she would never allow them to be together.

Hunsahua and his sister eloped. But when, after another argument with their mother, they left for the far south of their lands, horror followed them. At Susa, moments after Hunsahua's sister had given birth to a healthy baby, the child was turned by divine magic into stone. They travelled on to Tequendema, where Bochica had created a vast waterfall – renowned as one of the wonders of the world – when he dissipated the flood created by the god Chibchachum (see box, opposite). Here they thought they might find solace for their pain and resolved to make their home, but they too were turned to stone where they stood in the middle of the fast-flowing river.

Divine retribution and death attended another Chibcha couple whose sexual appetites and pride brought them public shame. A chief at Lake Guatavita – where a temple stood to the serpent god who lived in the waters – discovered that one of his wives had been unfaithful to him with another man. In his rage, he ordered her lover's murder and then forced her to eat the dead man's sexual organs. He even paid musicians to sing songs about her faithlessness around the town.

The lady fled from the palace with her baby daughter and flung herself and the child into the lake. Now the chief regretted what he had done and he went to see his most powerful shaman and asked him to find a way of bringing her and the baby back to live with him. The shaman sacrificed to the lake god, then, after hurling heated stones into the waters, himself jumped into the deep.

The shaman discovered the lady and her baby alive and well on the bed of the lake, living with the serpent god of the waters, and he hurried back to tell the chief the wonderful news. When he heard this, the chief ordered him to go back and bring his wife and child home. For many hours the chief waited anxiously, but when the shaman finally returned it was only with the baby's tiny corpse. He told the chief that the serpent god in the lake's depths had eaten the child's eyes and so the baby had died.

The Anger of Chibchachum

The people of the Bogotá plain provoked Chibchachum, god of labourers and business, to a fury with their complaints and disobedience. In his rage, Chibchachum sent a great flood to wipe out the region, but the people appealed to the sun god, Bochica, to protect them.

Bochica appeared astride a rainbow that arched majestically over the local town of Soacha. He brought out the sun to evaporate the waters, then he took his gold staff and hurled it at Mount Teguendama, making a chasm in the rocks through which most of the flood flowed away. The magnificent waterfall that Bochica created still exists today, spilling into the sacred Lake Guatavita (see illustration, page 585).

Bochica was determined to punish Chibchachum and dispatched him to the underworld with the task of supporting the world on his shoulders for eternity. Some accounts tell how it had previously been held up by pillars; others that it was kept aloft by trees. From time to time, the weight becomes too much for Chibchachum and he shifts it from one shoulder to the other – causing the Earth to shudder and grind in an earthquake.

The rainbow had marked the Chibcha people's deliverance from the flood, and ever afterwards they worshipped it as the goddess Chuchaviva. They prayed to be saved from the curse of Chibchachum who from his underworld exile decreed that the rainbow's every appearance would also bring death. Bochica's wife Chia, who had tried to undermine his civilizing influence (see main text), may have lent her magic to Chibchachum to create the great deluge, for in other myths she is responsible for floods.

Creation and Deluge

All cultures have myths explaining how the world was created, but in addition the tribes of the Andes share tales of a great flood. Similar in essentials to the story of Noah in the Bible, the South American flood myths tell how one, two or sometimes a group of people escaped the deluge by climbing to the top of a mountain.

According to the Cañari Indians of Andean Ecuador, mankind was saved from total extinction by the intervention of a magic mountain. A great flood swept across the land and two brothers hurriedly gathered food supplies and fled the lowlands, taking refuge on Huacaynan peak. As they looked down fearfully at the mounting waters from their lofty perch, at first they could not understand why, although the flood was rising and other peaks were being submerged one by one, it appeared to be getting no nearer to them. Then the truth came to them; as the waters climbed, so Huacaynan grew taller to keep them safe. The brothers stayed on the mountain, surviving on their meagre supplies until the waters went down.

At first they were afraid to leave their place of safety, but they had eaten all their food and they had to go in search of more. They set off across the mountainside and walked until they dropped with exhaustion. They built a makeshift hut on the spot where they had collapsed and scratched a living gathering edible plants and roots. But every day was a struggle, for they never had enough to eat and were always hungry.

One evening, when they trailed home after a long day searching for food, they found a meal laid out in their hut together with beakers of *chicha* – corn beer. It looked like a feast prepared for a king and they ate and drank hungrily, once again unable to believe their good fortune. That night, for once, they slept deeply and well, without noticing the damp and cold of the mountain.

When they returned the following evening they found another feast, and again on the next

While the spectacular landscapes of the South American interior tend to dominate Andean mythology, cultures whose influence stretched to coastal regions, such as the Chimu, also looked to the ocean for inspiration. In this piece of Chimu pottery, a crew takes to the sea guided by a totemic figurehead.

day. The same thing happened for ten nights, and the brothers grew more and more curious as to the identity of their benefactors. After the tenth night, the two young men decided that they would set a trap. The elder brother volunteered to keep watch to see who came to prepare the food.

On the following day, when the younger brother left as usual to look for supplies, the elder one concealed himself in the building and settled down to wait. He fell into a reverie but he was disturbed by the flap of wings and, looking up, saw

The Mysteries of Nazca

Giant images of animals, birds and people can be found etched in the ground at several places in Peru. The most famous are those created on a plateau in the Pampa de Ingenio Desert by the Nazca, who thrived from c.200BC to AD600.

In the pebble and sand of the desert's thick white soil the Nazca etched their mysterious patchwork of zigzags and spirals. Some form recognizable patterns – a plant, a whale, a giant bird, a monkey – while elsewhere lie long straight lines which can run unbroken for up to five miles.

The lines were first discovered in the mid-1920s, but their meaning has remained hidden despite exhaustive research. German archaeologist Maria Reiche, encouraged by the American Paul Kosok, studied the lines for decades. Her theory, that the images were aligned with constellations and offered some kind of astrological guide to the seasons, remained popular until, in the late 1960s, the British astronomer Gerald Hawkins tested the theory with computers and found that very few corresponded with the stars.

Various theories have been devised to explain why the images can only be seen from the air. The most eccentric of these was put forward by the Swiss writer Erich von Däniken, who in the 1970s declared that the lines were landing strips used by alien spaceships – whose occupants, he claimed, set up a base at Tiahuanaco, a ruin of temples and palaces near the southern end of Lake Titicaca, some time around 600BC.

Some writers have suggested that the lines may have been connected to religious rites and used by shamans – priest-doctors whose spirits were believed to have the power of flight. Others claim the Nazca had developed a primitive glider or hot-air balloon which they used to look down on their designs from the air. But most modern studies have argued that the lines were made not for viewing from the air at all but for walking or running on, perhaps during religious rituals. People may have gathered to use them in ceremonies designed to draw life-giving water from the sacred mountains above.

Human figures, like this one etched into a hillside in the San José pampa, are rare among the Nazca figures. However, they are thought to predate the drawings of animals and birds.

Disguised as a macaw, one of two beautiful
bird-women flies down from her home in the
heavens. She and her sister secretly tended the
first men of the Cañari tribe – the only people
to survive the great flood. The men fell in
love with their tenderness and beauty.

two brightly colored macaws come to land before the hut. He quickly understood that magic was at work because the longer he gazed at them, the more the birds looked like women of his own tribe. It seemed to him as if the larger bird was wearing a cloak; then he saw her take it off and begin to prepare the food. Both birds had the faces of beautiful women. Suddenly he could bear it no longer and, overcome with longing, he burst from his hiding place in an attempt to catch them. But with an angry cry they flew away into the sky, leaving him alone and hungry.

When the younger brother learned what had happened, he was intrigued and insisted that he would lie in wait in his turn. For three days he kept watch but saw nothing. On the fourth his patience was finally rewarded, for he heard the beating of birds' wings and saw the macaws circle the hut and then come down to land. It was just as his brother had said – they looked exactly like beautiful Cañari women.

He watched as they went inside the hut and made the food. As soon as they had finished, he rushed into the hut, shutting the door to trap them. Both birds screeched in fury. He managed to grab hold of the smaller while the larger one burst past him, knocked the door open and flew away. Intoxicated by his captive's beauty, the man made love to her many times. She had grown calmer when she saw that he intended to treat her well. Soon she became pregnant and in time gave birth to six sons and six daughters.

Afterwards the brothers lived with the bird-woman on the mountainside for many years. They were able to grow crops from seeds that she brought back in her beak from far away. The twelve boys and girls were the ancestors of the entire Cañari race. Ever afterwards the Cañaris regarded Huacaynan as a *huaca* – a holy place – and they had a special regard for the macaw.

The Chimu Flood Tale

The Chimu Indians who lived on the coastal plain of Peru and northern Chile also told of a great flood that wiped out most of mankind. This flood story may be based on a real El Niño event – a weather phenomenon which periodically brings catastrophic floods to the South American coast.

In the Chimu myth, the only survivors were a handful of men and women who clambered high into the mountains and hid with their animals and supplies in cold, damp caves beneath the peaks. After some time, their food ran low and they sent out dogs to see if the waters had subsided. On the first few occasions, the animals returned clean so they knew that the land was still flooded; but one day the dogs came back spattered with mud and then the people knew that the flood had receded.

They crept cautiously down the slime-covered mountain and built a new settlement, determined to get on with their lives. But, cruelly, many of the survivors were killed by a plague of poisonous snakes that thrived in the mud and filth left behind by the departing waters. A few hardy folk escaped, killed the snakes and set to work repopulating the world.

The plain occupied by the Chimu is largely barren, but is punctuated by fertile valleys where precious water flows down from the mountains. Here the Chimu created the majestic city of Chan Chan, heart of the great Chimor civilization that finally fell to the Incas in the fifteenth century. The Chimu had to learn to make the most of their water supplies and developed complex irrigation systems. One of their creation myths explains how the land came to be as it is.

Con and Pachacamac

In the first days of the world, before men had been created, a god named Con came into the land from the north. Strong and lithe, he could move quickly over the most difficult terrain. Wherever an obstacle blocked his way, he simply removed it by the power of his will, decreeing that mountains should sink or valleys be filled as he desired. His father was the all-powerful sun.

But Con was lonely, so he created men and women and set them down in a pleasant, fertile land. At this time grain was easily harvested and fruits ripened quickly, and the first people had an easy life, wanting for nothing. But some of them angered Con and, swelling with divine indignation, he resolved to make their lives difficult.

He ordered the soft rains to stop so that the plush grasslands were transformed into a stony

Prominent noses and large eyes animate these ritual Chimu drinking vessels. Crafted from single sheets of silver, the cups, dating from between AD1359 and AD1476, were buried with a nobleman. It was believed that they would bring him sustenance after death.

593

The Wonder of Pachacamac

At the mouth of the Lurin River stood a temple whose cult proved so enduring that when the Incas stamped their authority across the Andean landscape, imposing their own code upon its disparate cultures, they decided to allow the cult of Pachacamac to remain, and drew it into their own great cult of the sun.

There were few unifying features in South America in early times. People lived in small communities, their identities shaped by their immediate environment. What cultural focus there was, however, came not from a political structure, but from the rituals at the great temples: Chavín de Huántar, Tiahuanaco and Pachacamac.

The influence of Pachacamac in particular spread far beyond its own Lurin valley. It was the only temple dedicated exclusively to the creator god of the same name and pilgrims would come with gifts from miles around to pay their respects or consult the shrine's revered oracle.

After crossing the inhospitable mountains, travellers would be awed by the temple, lying as it did on a man-made hill set within its fertile coastal valley. Fantastic murals covered the adobe walls and through its many doors access could be found to a series of plazas. The shrine itself was the preserve of nobles, priests and pilgrims who would have to fast for twenty days to gain admittance to the lower plaza – and for a whole year for entry to the upper. Above this inner sanctuary rose a terraced pyramid at the top of which was found the oracle

itself, the wooden idol around which the cult of Pachacamac was focused.

People would come to consult the oracle on all important issues, from the prospects of the year's harvest to matters of personal health and welfare. Failure to follow its advice would lead to all manner of natural disasters. But only priests could enter its chamber, consulting it on others' behalf, and even they were prevented from casting their eyes upon the idol by a cloth that hung before it. And the god was appeased by the blood of regular sacrifice.

From the lands that lay beyond the Lurin estuary would also come petitions for a local shrine to Pachacamac. And, if successful, the local community would be sent a priest. In return they would offer up a stretch of land, its produce used for offerings to the cult. Each new temple was seen as a child of the cult whose family, which knew no boundaries of culture or degree, survived the might of Inca domination.

The riches collected in the temple were buried to keep them from the plundering Spanish, and included this llama-wool cloth decorated with a bat motif. It pre-dates the Incas' rise to power.

desert and at a stroke turned their rich, generous land into a barren one where nothing would grow easily and quickly. But looking at his people labouring hopelessly over the hard, stony ground, Con felt a moment's pity and decided that if they were willing to work hard he would give them a little help. He decreed that at some places rivers would flow down into the plain from the mountains behind, bearing precious waters from the melting snow. The people learned quickly to dig irrigation canals and were able to scratch a meagre living from the soil.

But Con's reign was disturbed when a second god came into the land. This newcomer, called Pachacamac ("Creator"), was the child of the sun's union with the moon, and so one of Con's brothers. Pachacamac immediately began to challenge his brother's authority. After a tremendous struggle, he prevailed and drove Con out. Then Pachacamac wandered throughout the land he had won, deciding what he wanted to do with it.

Much of what he saw pleased him. But Pachacamac decided he was not impressed with the people that Con had made, so he transformed them into a breed of chattering monkeys and sent them off into the wilds. He then created a new people, and these were to become the worthy ancestors of the men and women who are alive today. He taught them all that they know – about hunting and farming and about the arts and the family. In return the people made Pachacamac their supreme god and worshipped him faithfully, building a great temple in his honour near the Peruvian city of Lima (see box, opposite).

When the Incas conquered the coastal kingdoms they imposed their laws and their culture, but they also took over some of the gods of the people they defeated. Pachacamac and his brother Viracocha were among these gods, and they both became important deities in the Inca pantheon. In some accounts Pachacamac is described as a tall, white man with the power to do magic and even work miracles, who proclaimed that people should show each other love. Spanish churchmen used to suggest that this myth – like that of Bochica (see

The nurturing of souls beyond the grave was an important feature of Andean life, as shown by this wooden figure found at a Chimu burial site. Several layers of plaster have been applied to its face, a sign of spiritual regeneration. In its hand is a *kero*, a ceremonial drinking vessel, further suggesting that the figure, dating from c.AD1000, was used in rituals.

pages 586–588) – may have had its roots in a visit to South America by a Christian apostle long before. They liked to suggest that Saint Thomas, who was long reputed in Christian legend to have visited India and made many converts there, made his way to the Americas from Palestine by way of eastern Asia.

In the Shadow of the Gods

The Huarochirí region covers part of the western flank of the Peruvian Andes, and the myths handed down by the local Indians were connected intimately to the landscape. Like other groups they viewed the mountains as sacred places; the name of their chief god, Pariacaca, is also that of a snow-capped peak that was revered as his home.

For many years anarchy ruled over the Earth. But while tribes battled for survival, with no great leaders or kings, five eggs quietly appeared on the highest slopes of Mount Condor Coto. They contained the great god Pariacaca.

In the lands beneath the peaks lived Huataya Curi. Although a poor peasant, only he knew about Pariacaca's appearance – for he was the god's son. One day, Huataya Curi was returning from the ocean when he grew tired and lay down to rest. In his sleep he heard two foxes talking about a rich man named Tamtanamka who had been taken ill and whom no one had been able to cure. According to one of the foxes, his wife had been unfaithful to him and this was why the man had fallen ill. She had been toasting maize when a grain had leaped out of the fire and burned her dress in the most intimate place. She had then given the grain to the man she desired and they had made love. That grain had spawned a hideous double-headed toad that lay hidden beneath Tamtanamka's grinding stone. And ever since their union two snakes had hung from the eaves of his house devouring all of Tamtanamka's strength.

Huataya Curi resolved to go and find the invalid and cure him. At the man's house he met a beautiful young woman who sadly told him she

The Llama

The llama was a great friend to the Andean Indians. It was a hardy pack animal, its wool kept men and women warm and its flesh fed them. They even made candles from its fat and shoes from its skin.

The Indians believed that the souls of the dead were sometimes reincarnated as llamas and they often sacrificed the animals to the gods. Llama wool, fat and even foetuses were used in sacrifices. Some Indians even believed that llamas had the power to see the future – as in one version of the deluge myth that was told on the Peruvian coast.

A shepherd took his llamas to a rich pasture, but they would not eat. He was troubled and when he asked them what was wrong, they said that a portent in the sky foretold that the sea would rise and flood the Earth for five days.

was the sick man's daughter. He told her his purpose and she took the stranger to her father.

Huataya Curi told Tamtanamka that he would cure him if he could marry his daughter. And the desperate lord agreed. Huataya Curi then told Tamtanamka of his wife's adultery and the creatures in his house. Kill these beasts, he said, and the sickness will depart; on recovery, worship Pariacaca, who would be born on the next day.

When Tamtanamka's servants found the snakes in the roof, his wife confessed. Then Huataya Curi found the toad under the grinding stone. Tamtanamka's illness left him and he at once allowed Huataya Curi to marry his daughter.

The Huarochirí saw the llama cast in the Milky Way, not as a constellation but in the dark spaces between the stars. This is just one of the many examples of their reverence of the animal, shown here represented in crimped silver sheet.

The Trials of Huataya Curi

But Huataya Curi's problems were not over. His new brother-in-law was indignant at the match. Vowing to humiliate the peasant who had married his sister, he challenged him to a contest. At this time Pariacaca appeared on Condor Coto and Huataya Curi travelled to meet his father. He told Pariacaca of the brother-in-law's challenge and Pariacaca said that he would help him. The

The shepherd asked his flock if there was any way of escaping the flood, and the llamas told him to gather enough food for five days and then to drive them to the top of the great Villacota mountain. He did as he was told and when they arrived at the peak they found that it was already crowded with animals, but no people. Too busy with their own concerns they had failed to spot the portents.

No sooner had the shepherd and his flock reached the summit than the waters began to rise. The fox could not keep his tail from getting wet, and it was stained black for ever. But after five days the waters subsided, as the llamas had predicted. The animals and the shepherd returned home, and from that lone survivor all the people in the world are descended.

In some versions of the myth the shepherd took his six sons and daughters with him to the mountain, and the peak – as in the tale of the brothers told by the Cañaris (see page 590) – rose higher and higher to escape the rising waters. This certainly makes it easier to explain the repopulation of the Earth after the deluge.

brother-in-law first suggested a music and drinking contest. Pariacaca told Huataya Curi where to find a fox's panpipes, a skunk's drum and a small-necked jar filled with *chicha,* corn beer, on the mountainside. With these implements Huataya Curi made such powerful music and provided so much drink that he was declared the winner.

When the angry brother-in-law next proposed a dressing-up competition, Pariacaca gave his son a fine suit of snow and he won again. And the same happened with a third trial – the wearing of exotic lions' skins. With Pariacaca's help, Huataya Curi soon appeared dancing in a magical red skin beneath a rainbow. The villagers gasped and applauded, and Huataya Curi was once again declared the winner.

In desperation, the wealthy man next suggested they race to build a house. He had many workers to help him, but Huataya Curi, for all his magic powers, only had his wife. The wealthy man's helpers almost completed the entire building on the first day while Huataya Curi had done no more than lay the foundations. But when the sun rose the next morning, there stood Huataya Curi beside a veritable mansion. In the night the animals, birds and snakes had helped him build it.

Now Huataya Curi declared that it was his turn to choose an activity. He challenged his rival and his wife to a dancing contest but they had barely begun to show their steps before he turned them into deer and set off in pursuit. He caught the wife and stood her on her head so that her skirt fell down, exposing her private parts. Then he turned her to stone and, ever since, passers-by have stopped to stare at her. And although the wealthy man escaped into the mountains, he was cursed to live out his life as a deer.

Pariacaca, God of Waters

Pariacaca emerged from the eggs on Mount Condor Coto in the form of five falcons. After flying far and wide, the birds returned and took human form. Some say the five people are Pariacaca and his four brothers, but others that they are different forms of the god.

Pariacaca was a deity of mountains, water and wind, and several stories describe him launching great floods. In one he destroyed a village with a deluge because when he passed through at festival time nobody offered him a drink. He also used water to seduce the beautiful maiden Chuqui Suso, whose maize was dying from lack of water. Pariacaca told her he would make water flow freely into her fields if she would make love to him. Later they walked together beside a canal named Coco Challa where she turned into stone. In May during the canal cleaning season even today Indians hold a festival of drinking and dancing in Chuqui Suso's honour.

The toad was one of the most poisonous beasts of the Andes, with a prominent place in the Indians' supernatural menagerie. This piece, from AD100–200, gives the toad jaguar markings.

Distant Shores of Paradise

The Huarochirí told tales of a time when their home was a fertile paradise – before the god Pariacaca drove them out into drier lands. Scholars believe that the Indians may once have lived in lush valleys nearer the coast but were defeated by invaders and driven inland to the harsher highlands.

The Indians in those days were ruled by two holy people or gods named Yana Namca and Tuta Namca, but a third being, Huallallo Caruincho, defeated them and took control. He imposed strict rules on the people. Each woman was allowed to bear just two children and was forced to choose between them, keeping one to raise and giving up the other to be eaten by Huallallo Caruincho. The lands were rich and filled with perfect, brightly colored parrots and toucans. Every seed that was planted ripened in five days. Similarly, when men or women died they returned to life after five days. But the people lived evil lives. Their easy life came to an end when Pariacaca emerged from the five eggs on Mount Condor Coto, and defeated Huallallo Caruincho. In the Spaniard Francisco de Avila's gloss on the legends, he comments that the lush lands were named Yunca or Ande, and that Yunca referred to the fertile valleys that lie towards the coast. In other versions they are called "anti lands", which scholars believe may have been a general term used to refer to warm lowland landscapes.

Working the dry soil of the continent's interior made life hard for many tribes. Myths recalling fruitful lands suggest that peoples such as the Huarochirí once lived in coastal valleys such as those near Paracas, shown here.

Shamans and Sacred Stones

Specifically Inca myths are few and far between, but studies of their customs reveal a world in which all living things and natural objects are revered, people turn to stone, boulders come alive, prayers are addressed to the mountains and the dead pay social visits.

When Spanish missionaries first arrived in Peru, they quickly learned that objects called *huaca*s were the focus of special devotion. From the start they had problems with the word, for the idea it represented had no exact Christian parallel. Most often they translated it as "idols", for many of the *huaca*s were cult-objects fashioned from wood or stone. Sometimes "shrine" seemed more appropriate, for the term also encompassed holy sites.

But the concept stretched much further than either of those European notions. The chronicler Garcilaso de la Vega, himself half-Inca, caught the full animist flavour when he wrote of people worshipping plants, flowers, trees, mountains, rocks, caves, precious stones, wild animals and some species of birds. A *huaca* could be anything that incited religious wonder. For the Andean peoples the natural world was alive with spiritual power.

The great temple of Sacsahuaman outside the city of Cuzco shows Inca stonework at its finest. Each block was individually cut to fit its neighbours. No mortar was used. When earthquakes, which shook the region regularly, struck, the stones simply shifted and then moved back into position.

Some features attracted particular veneration. Mountains were especially revered. Other focuses of devotion were large or oddly shaped stones.

The *huaca*s had their parallels in Inca mythology. Tales of the dynasty's founder, Manco Capac, told how at the end of his life he was turned into stone, a fate also supposed to have befallen his brothers at Huanacauri and the first race of humans. Sometimes the process happened in reverse. In the battle that saw the great emperor Pachacuti drive Chanca invaders back from the walls of Cuzco, the boulders on the hills above the old Inca capital were said to have been transformed into warriors who turned the tide of the fight. Later, Pachacuti spread the word that they were gods who put on flesh to help him as a secret weapon in all his subsequent campaigns.

On a humbler level, farmers set standing stones in the middle of their fields in honour of the Earth goddess, Pachamama, and would make

This Inca doll, wrapped in a colorful wool blanket, was probably never a plaything. It was found in a tomb and most likely had some sacred significance.

offerings to her for good crops. Similar monoliths protected irrigation canals, guarding them magically against leaks. At the top of mountain passes, cairns, called *apacheta*s, offered safeguards for travellers; to ensure a safe passage, they would add a rock or some other small object to the pile and say a brief prayer before passing on their way. Sometimes an offering of alcohol was made. This custom is still practised today.

*Huaca*s could also take the form of personal talismans, often in the shape of pebbles carved to resemble llamas, ears of maize or tiny human beings. In the home, too, there would most likely be some small object, wrapped in cloth or displayed in a niche. Sometimes the house would have another, odder guardian, for the Andean peoples combined ancestor worship with their veneration of the natural world. Archaeological discoveries over the past century or more have revealed that the practice of mummifying the dead stretched back perhaps as much as 5,000 years before the coming of the Incas, and it continued under their rule. Often, the process was left to nature; corpses were simply taken out to the high

mountains or to the coastal desert to dry out. More exalted individuals were treated by artificial techniques. Families would sometimes keep the preserved bodies of a deceased father or mother in the house, treating them with deference and parading them through the streets dressed in fine clothes on the occasion of the annual Festival of the Dead.

No one carried respect for their ancestors to greater lengths than the Inca ruling house. In Peru it was customary for the dead to retain their personal possessions, which were normally either buried with them or in places they had loved. In the case of royal mummies, that meant keeping their own palaces; their heirs were expected to build themselves new ones. There the preserved corpses would sit in state, cared for by clan groups known as *panaca*s. Vast estates were put at the *panaca*s' disposal so they could keep the dead kings – and themselves also – in the state to which they were accustomed. To maintain the illusion that normal life continued, the mummies would pay social calls on one another, and on important ceremonial occasions would be brought out to attend the festivities in Cuzco's main square.

This 9-in-high silver llama wears a royal blanket decorated in gold and cinnabar. No one knows the exact purpose of objects such as this but it has been suggested that they may have been either toys or little household huacas. The Inca calendar was punctuated with sacrifices of llamas.

could about these local sanctuaries. His *History of the New World* lists no fewer than 350 shrines within a radius of 20 miles around Cuzco, ranging from rocks and springs to battlefields. He reported that local people conceived of them as radiating out in spokes from the city's great sun temple, the Coricancha. There were forty-one of these lines and each one was the responsibility of a clan, that was expected to tend the shrines in their care and offer sacrifices on appropriate occasions.

According to Cobo, the attendants to whom the duties were delegated were usually old people past more active work. When questioned, they would explain the significance of their particular *huaca*, acting as a kind of oral memory-bank. They knew the correct formulas for making sacrifices and the offerings that were to be given, and would promise prospective worshippers, in Cobo's words, "high hopes of good luck, listing previous successes to boost the reputation of the shrine".

Even when Cobo was drawing up his catalogue he had to rely on the memory of his informants to identify the *huaca*s, for most had disappeared. Generations of priests before him had made it their business to remove what they saw as relics of idolatry. Many boasted of their successes, and the numbers they quote give some idea of the sheer quantity of the objects that the Indians held sacred. One missionary, for example, recorded that he had personally destroyed more than 30,000 "idols" and some 3,000 mummies during his career.

Among the first objects of the Spaniards' attentions were the oracles: holy sites to which rulers and commoners alike would go for advice

Ancestral Centres of Worship

Another form of ancestor worship was the respect paid to *paccarisca*s – the places where tribal ancestors were believed to have emerged into the upper world. These could be caves (the most important one being Pacaritambo, southwest of Cuzco), hills, lakes or springs, and they became important centres for public thanksgiving.

Nowhere had as many as Cuzco itself, where the Incas feted their own origins. Early in the seventeenth century, a Spanish priest called Bernabé Cobo took it upon himself to find out all that he

The Stone that Wept

A legend of Cuzco told of a massive boulder outside the city walls that wept tears of blood. Behind the tale lay memories of a real-life tragedy that marred the construction of one of the Incas' greatest architectural achievements.

Made of massive blocks of masonry, many of them weighing more than 100 tons, the fortress of Sacsahuaman overlooking Cuzco startled the conquistadors with its Cyclopean bulk, leading some to call it the eighth wonder of the world. But one of the largest boulders intended for its construction never reached the site. Instead it remained on the plateau in front of the fortress, so exhausted by its long journey from the mines, the Cuzcans claimed, that it had come to rest and wept blood.

The truth, according to Garcilaso de la Vega, was that the stone had been deliberately left by the Indians who pulled it there. They abandoned it following a disaster that occurred in the course of the journey, when the huge stone broke loose on a mountain road, crushing many of those who were dragging it. In the chronicler's words, it was these victims – he puts their number at an improbable 3,000 – who wept tears of blood, and the stone remained isolated and unused outside the Inca capital to serve as their lasting monument.

on important questions or to learn what the future had in store. In a world in which natural features were frequently imbued with numinous powers, oracles were commonly in the open air.

But the greatest of all the Andean oracles lay at Pachacamac, not far from modern-day Lima. Its reputation long pre-dated the Incas, who did not dare to tamper with it when they conquered the region in the late fifteenth century. Instead they contented themselves with building the largest sun temple in the kingdom next to it and with identifying its presiding deity, the eponymous Pachacamac, with their own god Viracocha (see pages 606–609).

In its heyday, people came from all parts of Peru as well as from southern Ecuador to consult the oracle, which was located in a chamber atop a stepped adobe-brick pyramid. The god who resided there not only offered advice to individuals, including the Inca emperor, but was also reputedly able to provide protection against bad weather, crop failure, earthquakes and disease.

In return the god expected tribute. Offerings in the shape of cotton, maize, dried fish, textiles and gold poured in, but they were not enough to satisfy the divinity, who also required the blood of sacrificial victims. Hecatombs of llamas and guinea-pigs were slaughtered to feed the idol, and in earlier times there

This silver maize cob dates from AD1430–1532. It was probably used as an offering. The palace of the ruling Inca had a whole garden of life-size, golden animals and plants similar to this one.

were human victims, too, to judge from the mummies of women with signs of strangulation found on the site in 1897 by archaeologist Max Uhle.

Presumably the officials in charge of the oracle had, like their counterparts at Delphi in ancient Greece (see box, page 185), a good grasp of politics that enabled them under normal circumstances to give appropriate advice. Yet they were far from infallible. When the conquistadors were holding the Inca Atahualpa as a prisoner, he received a visit from the priests of Pachacamac. His captors were surprised to see that he treated them with contempt, even suggesting to the Spaniards that they should put them in chains and let them see if their god could arrange their release. Asked to explain his hostility, he replied that the oracle was false, for on three crucial questions it had given bad advice. It had predicted that his father Huayna Capac would recover from his final illness if taken out into the sunlight, whereas in fact he had died; it had told Huascar, Atahualpa's rival for the throne, that he would succeed in the civil war that divided the two, but in reality he had lost; and it had advised Atahualpa himself to attack the Spanish invaders, assuring him that he would kill them all.

Despite such failures, the Andean peoples had a passion for divination that was not satisfied by the oracles alone. Soothsaying and promises of good luck were the principal stock-in-trade of the shamans who flourished in all parts of the Inca lands, much as they did further north (see pages 580–581). Although they had low social standing, they were consulted even by the nobility, and their advice was invariably sought before any major decision was taken. On a humbler level, local people turned to them whenever they wished to find lost objects or learn news of absent friends.

The diviners used a bewildering variety of techniques to predict the future. Some gazed at the ashes of charcoal fires; others studied cobwebs or interpreted dreams. The *calparicu* – literally, "those who bring good fortune" – inflated the lungs of sacrificial birds or animals and scrutinized them for signs of what the future would bring. There were practitioners, too, who cast lots with ears of maize, beans or pebbles; who studied the movement of giant spiders kept in tightly lidded jars; or who simply observed the flow of saliva spat into the palm of their hand.

Other, more sinister activities might also be involved, for among the ranks of the shamans were many sorcerers who practised black magic in secret and whose malign influence was widely feared. They were associated with spiders, lizards, snakes, toads and moths, and it was bad luck to see any of these creatures near someone's home. Even the Inca ruler feared enchantment; women attendants instantly swallowed any hairs that fell from his head lest they should fall into the hands of hostile shamans.

Such practices were the downside of a worldview that contained superstition alongside devoutness and wonder. Without a written faith or creed, the Incas saw divinity all about them and humbly acknowledged their own limited place in the natural world. Constantly chastened by life's menacing unpredictability, they moved respectfully and fearfully through a world of ever-present spirits.

On one side of this ritual drinking vessel, Incas bear sacks of offerings. On the other is a carved head. The vessel dates from C.AD1500.

Atonement for Sins and Misdemeanours

When Spanish priests first arrived in Peru, they were startled to find that the Andean peoples had their own rites of confession and were already used to the idea of doing penance for their sins.

Confessions were usually made to the priestly attendants, male or female, responsible for the upkeep of shrines. The worst sins were murder, theft, sacrilege or treason; in contrast, adultery and fornication were regarded merely as misdemeanours. If the confessor felt that the penitent was telling less than the whole truth, he or she might resort to divination to settle the issue and would use a stone to pummel the bent back of anyone considered to be lying.

Penances were apt to be severe, "especially if the man who had committed the sin was poor and could not give anything to the confessor", as one Christian commentator sourly noted. They almost always involved fasting, which in Inca terms did not mean going without food altogether but merely without meat and seasonings. A more peculiar punishment involved being beaten with nettles by hunchbacks who had

been specially employed for this purpose.

Any misfortune was taken as a sure sign of transgression, and when harm came to the Inca ruler the whole nation did penance. Even the ruler himself and his family were expected to participate. But they confessed their faults in secret to their father Inti, the sun god, for it was not considered fitting for the royals, the Children of the Sun, to reveal their weaknesses to any human intermediary.

Instructor of the World

Long before the coming of Christianity, the Incas and their Andean neighbours believed in a supreme creator god. They gave him many titles, among them Ilya Ticci Viracocha Pacayacacic – "Age-Old Creator Lord, Instructor of the World".

Many decades after their empire fell, the Incas still remembered a tale about Pachacuti, their finest ruler, who had made them a great power. They told how, as a young man, he was on his way to visit his father, the reigning Inca, when he came to a spring called Susurpugaio. As he passed, a flash of light caught his eye, and when he looked into the water he saw that a piece of crystal had fallen into it. Gazing intently at the glassy nugget, he was amazed to spot inside it a tiny figure with three bright rays like those of the sun radiating from its head. The apparition wore Inca-style earpieces and dress, and on its forehead was the *llautu*, a scarlet headband that was the Inca symbol of royalty. Yet the figure's kingship was obviously beyond the human realm, for serpents coiled around its arms, and Pachacuti could see lions' heads over its shoulders and between its legs.

Terrified by the sight, the future ruler took to his heels, only to be summoned back by a commanding voice. The figure told him not to fear, for he was Viracocha, the creator lord. He informed Pachacuti that he would conquer many nations, but must take care to honour his divine protector and remember him in his sacrifices. The vision then vanished, though the crystal remained. Pachacuti kept it and was said to be able to look into it and see the regions he would later subdue.

Pachacuti was so impressed by the apparition that he later had a golden statue prepared to his

The creator deity Viracocha was venerated by many tribes in the Andes. This stele, dated AD600–1200, is from Tiahuanaco, a city abandoned by the time of the Incas.

instructions to capture its appearance. The image was that of a bearded man – unusually, for the Incas themselves were clean-shaven. It was placed in Viracocha's temple in Cuzco, and was said to be about the size of a ten-year-old boy.

The god whom Pachacuti had been privileged to glimpse was acknowledged by all the peoples of the southern Andes as the creator of the universe. Although the details of the creation story often varied in the telling, all agreed in setting the events in the Callao region around Lake Titicaca and in the ancient, ruined city of Tiahuanaco nearby, which had been abandoned centuries before the Incas rose to prominence. Also common to each version of the story was a belief in an earlier race of beings that had been swept away in a cataclysmic flood.

In essence, the story told how Viracocha fashioned the Earth and sky in darkness, then set the sun and the moon in the heavens to give them light. He made humankind in his own image, first creating a generation of giants to inhabit the newly established world. But the giants displeased him, and he punished some by turning them to stone – a tale that apparently served to explain the presence of huge stone statues at Tiahuanaco, some of which are still there to this day. The rest of the giants were swept away in the deluge that then inundated the Earth.

Her Majesty the Moon

In the Andean scheme of things most gods, except the creator Viracocha, were paired off with female counterparts, and the sun and moon made an obvious couple. Mama Kilya – Mother Moon – occupied a special place in the pantheon of the Incas. As consort of the sun god Inti, she was the maternal ancestor of the royal line.

As Inti's partner, Mama Kilya had her own shrine in Cuzco's great Coricancha temple. It was decorated with sheets of beaten silver and served by its own priestesses.

Considered the ruling Inca's mother, just as the sun was his father, she was also identified with the Coya or the principal wife of the Inca (the title given to the aristocratic ruler of the people known as the Incas).

Throughout the Andes region, lunar eclipses were regarded with terror, for it was thought that some monstrous creature was trying to devour the moon. To scare the attacker away, people brandished weapons at the heavens and made all the noise they were capable of, even whipping their dogs to make them bark.

Although Mama Kilya was a revered figure, her position was not elevated enough for some of the peoples the Incas conquered. In particular, the Chimu of Ecuador, who had long venerated the moon as their principal deity, were less than pleased when she was forced to take on a secondary role. But the might of the Inca prevailed, and the Chimu too had to adjust their pantheon to give pride of place to the imperial Inti, the sun god who became pre-eminent throughout the Inca empire. This was despite the fact that the Chimu had traditionally regarded the sun as a hostile power.

This Inca-period pottery figure wears a ceremonial half-moon pendant. He or she carries several drinking vessels and may be performing some kind of ritual.

In a second act of creation Viracocha then reappeared on Earth, some said at Tiahuanaco and others at Lake Titicaca, either from the waters or on an island that later became the seat of a great temple. He caused the sun and moon, whose light had been dimmed, to shine once more, and they cast their first light from the mountains that backed the lake. It was then that he created all the different peoples of the Earth, giving them their distinctive dress and customs (see box, opposite).

Lord of Divination and the Seasons

Viracocha was widely venerated in the Inca world as the universal creator and master of all. Prayers addressed to him called him the Lord of Divination and the Seasons, omnipresent and omnipotent, able to grant the gift of life itself. When he was invoked in the company of other gods, his name always came first. Yet, for all that, he remained a remote and insubstantial figure. Although the Incas built temples to him, including a splendid one in Cuzco, he was overshadowed in terms of public ceremonial by other gods. No great estates were assigned to the upkeep of his places of worship as they were for other deities – an omission the Incas justified by claiming that, as he was the creator of everything, he had need of nothing.

Insofar as this faceless divinity eventually came to acquire a personality, it was through his identification with a separate figure of Callao legend, Thunupa. Andean tales of this culture hero described how, like Viracocha, he arrived mysteriously from the south on the banks of Lake Titicaca at a time when the sun had just returned after a long absence. He had magical powers to make water flow from stone and the imprint of his feet could be seen even in hard rock. He, too, was described as a bearded man, dressed in a long tunic, and stories told how he moved northwards

Tiahuanaco, which was established c.AD200, was the highest city in the ancient world, and more than a millennium later its ruins still awed the Incas. Huge monoliths such as this inspired legends about an ancient race of giants.

through the Andean foothills inspiring universal veneration and acquiring the name of Ticci Viracocha, or Creator Lord.

Because of their beards and their mysterious appearance apparently out of nowhere, the Spanish conquistadors found themselves referred to as "Viracochas" among the native people when they first arrived. The illusion did not last long. No one expressed the disenchantment that replaced it better than the Inca Titu Cusi, one of the last Inca rulers. "I thought they were kindly beings sent (as they claimed) by Ticci Viracocha, that is to say by God," he told his fellow nobles. "But it seems to me that all has turned out the very opposite from what I believed. For let me tell you, brothers, from proofs they have given me since their arrival in our country, they are the sons not of Viracocha, but of the Devil." Seeing their land ravaged and their people abused, few of his audience would have disagreed.

Why People Dress Differently

According to one myth, all the diverse Andean races could trace their origins back to the repopulation of the Earth after the flood, when the creator god fashioned them just as they were in Inca times.

The chronicler Cristóbal de Molina was told that the creator god Viracocha made the different peoples out of clay, and then painted on the garments that each group were to wear. Each was given its own language, songs and favourite foodstuffs – even a preferred hairstyle, long or short.

Then the creator sent them underground to make their way to the various regions to which he had assigned them – the caves, lakes and mountains from which they re-emerged into the light would subsequently be worshipped as holy places. The first generation was in due course turned into stone, and it too subsequently became an object of reverence.

The purpose of the tale seems to have been to explain the different clothes and customs of the various Andean peoples at a time when each ethnic group was most easily marked out by their distinctive garb. Even today there are recognizable differences between the traditional dress of adjoining valleys, and profound respect continues to be shown to rocks and stones.

609

The Giants from the West

Barely a century after Pachacuti had begun his work it was brought crashing down. When the first Spaniards appeared along the coast of the Inca empire, the locals did not know whether to fight them, fear them or worship them. For, quite remarkably, there existed an abundance of beliefs about mythical beings who might one day arrive from the west.

The peoples of coastal Peru inherited ancient legends of invaders from the sea. Long ago, one of the legends said, newcomers arrived, some dressed in animal skins, some stark naked, in reed boats which were as large as ships. Nobody knew where these people came from, but to the tribes who lived along the coast they were truly monstrous. The head of an ordinary man would only come up to their knees and their eyes were the size of plates. They landed at Santa Elena, and made an encampment there whose ruins could still be seen by the early Spanish explorers. The area was practically a desert, but because of their great strength the giants were able to dig wells deep into solid rock until they found water which, because it came from so far down, was always sweet and cool. However, the native peoples of the coast grew to hate their new neighbours who had appetites fifty times as great as those of normal men. In an area where food was often scarce they took more than their share of fish from the sea and game from the forest, and they would also steal food whenever they got the chance, leaving their bitter neighbours hungry.

The giants were especially loathed because they forced both the local women and the local men to submit to them sexually, and because of their great size they always ended up crushing their unwilling partners. But the natives were powerless to do anything more than pray for divine vengeance and hope for a day when the dreadful giants would leave them in peace. Then one day a pillar of fire roared out of heaven, revealing an angelic being with a sword of flame which consumed all of the giants, leaving nothing but a few of their skulls scattered on the ground.

Men from the Sea

Juan de Velasco, who wrote an early European history of Quito, speculated that the giants came to South America around the time of Christ. He also thought that other invaders arrived about 600 years later. The Cara came in *balsas,* log ships which could carry up to fifty men. After populating the coast they soon moved into the mountains, and ruled Quito until the Incas took it from them in the fifteenth century. Yet another legendary invasion was led by the god-chief Naymlap who landed on the coast near Santa Elena. As soon as his followers came ashore, they built a temple and erected a green stone idol to honour him. After reigning for many years, Naymlap grew wings and flew off into the sky, leaving his empire to its fate.

When the conquistadors came on their horses they might well have resembled the towering western invaders of myth. Their skin, clothes and weapons were strange enough to the people of South America, but their appearance was rendered even more remarkable by the animals they rode. Horses were awesome creatures which nobody in South America had ever seen before. To the Incas, it was not immediately obvious that the newcomers were hostile. They could have been emissaries of Thunupa who many years before, having brought culture and law to South America, was said to have walked away into the west across the Pacific Ocean. In the north, the Europeans were referred to as *gagua,* after the supreme god and giver of light Chiminigagua. However, as the list of their atrocities grew and the true nature of their mission became apparent, they were associated with the local devil, Suetiva, and their title was changed to *suegagua* – "demon with light".

The Patagonian Colossus

A popular belief in the gigantic stature of Patagonians survived in Europe for centuries after Antonio Pigafetta, who accompanied Magellan on the first voyage round the world, wrote a highly colored account of his adventures. After rounding Cape Horn, Pigafetta's ship put into a cove to escape the winter weather. This gave Pigafetta a chance to add another story to his collection of tall tales.

According to Pigafetta's account, a naked giant appeared one day on the shore, dancing, singing and leaping in the air while pouring sand over his head. When a party from the ship approached him, the giant seemed astounded, and pointed upwards, thinking that they had come from heaven. He was so enormous that the tallest of the sailors only came up to his waist. His huge face was painted red all over, except around his eyes where the skin was yellow. He had two hearts painted on his cheeks, and dyed white hair. When he was shown his own face in a steel mirror he was so terrified that he jumped back, knocking over four crewmen.

More giants arrived later. Two of the younger ones were put into chains, but their friends on the shore started firing arrows at the ship, killing one of the crew. Although the sailors had guns, they never hit a giant, because despite their bulk they never stood still, moving nimbly and running faster than horses.

Magellan's ship sailed past the Carro Paine Grande mountains in Patagonia, an unforgiving land far to the south. A long way from home, many European travellers recorded fanciful tales.

611

Fateful Tales of the Golden City

The legend of a lost city of gold, ruled by "men of metal", lured explorers and raiding expeditions to Peru from the early days of the conquest. Since then, there has scarcely been a country in South America that has not been claimed as the site of El Dorado.

When the Spaniards arrived on the west coast of South America, they heard stories from nearly all the peoples on the fringes of the Inca empire about a magical kingdom where the roads and buildings were made of gold. It was ruled by a powerful priest-king, called El Dorado ("the Gilded One"), because even his body was covered in gold. These legends were probably native hearsay about the great cities of the Inca, but even after the Spaniards had conquered and pillaged the empire, they refused to accept that they had found the fabled kingdom, and continued to search for it in the mountains and jungles beyond Peru.

As it happened, the tales had some foundation in fact. In pre-Chibcha times, "the Gilded One" was the new ruler of the region around Lake Guatavita in the Colombian mountains behind Santa Fe de Bogotá, who would make an offering of gold to the god of the lake to mark his accession to the throne. Before the ceremony, the ruler-to-be spent some time fasting in a cave, before marching to the lakeside where priests stripped him of his royal robes and covered his body in a layer of fine gold dust. The newly gilded king then sailed out into the middle of the lake to make his offering, accompanied by four local chieftains who were also dusted with powdered gold. In the centre of the lake, the new ruler dived into the water, washing off all the gold so the gods could take it. Gradually, El Dorado lost its original meaning, and instead of referring to a person came to be haphazardly applied to any mythical golden city.

"People of Metal"

The Guaraní, from the basin of the Plate River, told tales of a golden city that almost certainly derived from fifteenth-century raiding expeditions across the Chaco. They captured piles of gold and silver from peaceful tribes that were subjects of the Incas, and returned with stories about "people of metal" living to the north.

From these excursions, the idea of a golden land called Paititi spread throughout Paraguay. It was combined with existing myths. Eventually it came to be said that Paititi lay in a magic lake

Right: The discovery of jewellery such as this gold Tairona pendant, AD900–1550, led some conquistadors to believe that El Dorado was in Colombia.

Left: Tales of the legendary king, El Dorado, stimulated the imaginations of Western chroniclers. This 16th-century engraving shows him being painted with gold.

The Golden Condor

The Derrotero de Valverde (Account of Valverde) *contains detailed instructions on how to find a great Inca treasure in the mountains of Ecuador. But although exact copies of the original document still exist, nobody has ever been able to find the gold.*

In 1534 the young soldier Juan Valverde fell in love with a native girl and together they ran away to her home village, Pillaro, high in the Andes mountains. There they lived until a Spanish patrol arrived three years later. Valverde was terrified that he would be caught and executed as a deserter, and decided that he and his wife should return to Spain. To help pay for the journey, the village elders told him that the Inca general Ruminahui had hidden a store of gold in the mountains.

After three weeks, Valverde returned with treasures that included a golden condor, with emerald eyes and outstretched silver wings. But the village headman declared that the condor had to remain hidden until the Europeans had been driven from the Andes and the Inca empire re-established. The bird was returned, but even without it Valverde now had enough gold to make him rich.

When the half-illiterate conquistador returned to Spain laden with dozens of crudely formed gold bars, King Charles I (Emperor Charles V) ordered him to reveal the source of his wealth, or have it confiscated.

The *Account of Valverde* reveals that the great golden condor lies, with many other idols, in an artificial lake in the Llanganuti mountains. The route to it – through forests, along rivers and over daisy-covered hills – is described in detail, starting from the village of Pillaro. King Charles I sent several expeditions in search of the lake, all of which were defeated by weather, starvation and exhaustion. In the nineteenth century, the Spanish botanist Antonio Guzman found some ancient Inca mines in the area, but he could not locate the treasure. In the twentieth century, even helicopter reconnaissance has proved useless in the face of fog, high altitude and bad weather.

called Cuni-Cuni, which was the source of the Paraguay River and was guarded by a jaguar-lizard called Teyu-Yagua. According to the tale, all of the population wore gold and silver ornaments. In 1526, Sebastian Cabot sailed the Parana and Paraguay rivers to find them.

Other expeditions soon followed. In 1530, a German knight called Ambros von Alfinger set off inland from the Venezuelan coast. Instead of finding the legendary city, the knight became legendary himself – for his cruelty. His provisions were carried by native slaves, chained together by neck-rings. When these slaves became exhausted, von Alfinger beheaded them to save the trouble of unfastening the links. Eventually, the knight was killed by a native arrow.

Incredible cruelty, followed by the violent death of the oppressor became a feature of El Dorado expeditions. When Francisco de Orellana arrived at the Coca River in 1541, on the journey that would eventually lead him to sail down the Amazon, his intention was to join Gonzalo Pizarro (brother of the conqueror) on a quest to find El Dorado. He had set out from Quito three weeks after Pizarro, but had no trouble following his trail, because it was signposted with corpses. Pizarro left Quito with 400 Spanish soldiers, 4,000 native slaves, 2,000 dogs, 4,000 pigs for food and a herd of llamas. He returned a year later with eighty starving men, a sorry testament to his doomed search for Lake Guatavita.

A Legend of Lost Souls

The El Dorado of the Omaguas was thought to be in the upper reaches of the Orinoco River, near the mythical Lake Parima, said to lie on the Venezuelan-Guyanan border. Diego de Ortaz set out to find it in 1537. Decades later one of his men, called Juan Martínez, stumbled from the jungle, starved and exhausted, and swore with his dying breath that he had met the Gilded One. There is still a popular Chilean myth about the City of Caesars, which has solid gold streets and lies somewhere in the south of the country on the borders of a mountain lake. The city is named after an expedition to find it, sponsored by Sebastian Cabot and led by Francisco César. Not only are its exact whereabouts unknown, it is also invisible, and seems to contain elements of native ideas about the afterlife. The people who live there do not have to work, and they live for ever. Anyone

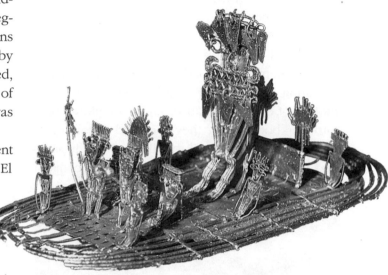

The ceremony at Lake Guatavita, depicted in this finely made pre-Columbian Chibcha gold *tunjo*, or raft, is believed to have been the source of all the tales about a mythic golden city somewhere in the South American hinterland. Beautiful gold objects such as this continued to inspire treasure hunters for centuries after the conquest.

who happens upon the City of Caesars by chance, however, forgets all about it, including the route back, once they leave. This enchanted city will only appear at the end of the world.

To this day stories are told of travellers lost in the jungle in search of the golden city. Many of them are probably apocryphal. The most famous disappearance of the twentieth century was that of the Briton Colonel Fawcett, his son and a companion. In the 1920s, they went looking for a lost city of gold in the Mato Grosso, deep in the rainforest. Fawcett was an experienced surveyor and explorer. They never returned, although for several years sightings were reported.

Spirits of the Mountains

Despite the efforts of the missionaries, some beliefs survived the conquest, among them a reverence for Pachamama, the ancient Andean goddess whose body is the Earth. Along with other old mountain gods, called *apus,* she is often worshipped on Christian holy days.

The Peruvians of the Ocongate say that once God had made the world he gave it to Pachamama and the *apu*s to develop as they wished and then retired to a distant place. Pachamama, who called herself "Saint Earth", had the task of creating and nurturing the land that God had made. She is the mother of everything, absorbing her children back into her body when they die, and according to herbalists it is her blood that flows through plants and gives them their healing powers. Pachamama

decreed that the people of the Andes should burn coca leaves and spread them over the Earth to please her, and that they should make sacrifices to her, especially on the feast days of Saint James, The Immaculate Conception and Our Lady of the Purification, at Christmas and New Year and on the Thursday before Ash Wednesday. On these occasions, Pachamama is offered anything from beer to plants to guinea-pigs, and people frequently sacrifice sheep and llamas to her as well. At one time the sacrifices included human life.

Whenever the Incas found a potato or an ear of maize with a peculiar shape, they made offerings to it as though it were a representative of Pachamama. They believed that she was usually asleep, but that during the period of Jujay, from July to August, her body opened up to receive new seed, as well as sacrifices and public adulation. During Jujay the Earth was not only alive, it was also ravenous or even angry, and liable to release evil powers into the world. At this time of year people would be careful not to incur her wrath.

Despite her fierce reputation, Pachamama is often compared to the Virgin Mary. In the mining communities of Peru and Bolivia, she is the gentle Virgin of the Mineshaft, who protects the workers from the devilish owner of the mines, known as "Uncle", and his demonic female companion. This view of mine-owners, and the beneficial influence of Pachamama, is reflected in a legend from the

Pachamama, mother spirit of the Earth to whom all human life returns on death, proved an enduring goddess. With the advent of Christianity, her worship was allied with that of the Virgin Mary, ensuring that in timeless places such as here, where the Illiniza volcano towers over an exposed mountain valley in Ecuador, the ancient spirits of the Andes lived on.

early days of colonialism. The Spaniards running one particular silver mine worked their native labourers to the point of collapse. The workers tried fighting back, but all their protests were mercilessly quelled. In desperation the workers prayed to the mountain for help and either the spirit of the mountain, or Pachamama herself, took pity on them and came to their aid. One night a native mule-handler, on his way to the mineshaft, met a man he had never seen before who told him the road was blocked and urged him to turn back. But the handler was curious, so he returned later and hid by the track. After a short while there appeared an endless line of mules, each carrying a load of silver slowly past him and away from the mine. Suddenly one of the animals collapsed and broke its leg. The handler rushed up and unpacked it, burying the silver by the roadside so he could fetch it later. But when he returned, the silver and the mule were gone. Where the mule had been lying was a beetle with a broken leg. The merciful spirit in the mountain had turned all the local beetles into mules to carry away every bit of ore in the mines, so that the Spaniards no longer had any reason to stay in the area, and would leave the natives in peace.

Just as the Incas absorbed much of the imagery of the cultures they conquered, so Christianity was influenced by local belief. This 18th-century painting shows the Virgin Mary in Cerro Rico, the rich hill of Potosí, Bolivia, echoing the ancient belief that the landscape was home to Pachamama.

A Cult of Santa Maria

The popularity of the Virgin Mary owes as much to the essentially feudal system imposed by the Spanish government after the conquest as to the spiritual orientation of native Indians.

The Virgin Mary was a popular figure for many of the early Spanish settlers. Mixing easily with the maternal cult of Pachamama, her image soon became widespread among the native Indians as well. As the Immaculate Protectress she was the natural refuge from the manifold tragedies of disease, death and social exclusion that came with the invasion.

In the Christian faith, Mary is subordinate to her son. As such she won the sympathies of a class kept in place by a rigid spiritual hierarchy. Native Indians and *mestizo*s were banned from the priesthood by the First Council of Mexico in 1555 and, three years later, from reading the scriptures altogether. This prohibition was not lifted until the end of the eighteenth century and the publication of the first vernacular translation of the Bible in 1790.

TREASURES FOR THE AFTERLIFE

One of South America's most compelling enigmas surrounds ancient practices of burial and ritual sacrifice. Tombs, often placed at *huacas*, or holy places, sometimes dug deep into the highest mountain peaks, suggest both mystery and terror: for the bodies found within them included not only princes and kings who had passed away, but, in some cases, people, even children, sacrificed for the greater good of their society. Such burials furnished a nobleman with the materials to live on in death as he had in life. By appeasing ancestors, they might also ensure a reign of peace for a new ruler, or a bountiful harvest for the nation. In addition, elaborate burials forged a spiritual bond between communities and the landscape and, in the case of the interment of the great Inca, offered a focus for disparate peoples spread out across the vast and distant plains.

Right: Gold and silver ornaments accompany the Old Lord of Sipan in the grave. The gold-and-turquoise warrior with owl headdress in the centre recalls his prowess in battle. Such examples of ancestor worship were as much for the benefit of the living as for the dead.

Above: The remains of these two adobe pyramids in the Lambayeque valley, northern Peru, mark an important Moche burial site. From AD100 to AD300, several generations of the Lords of Sipan were buried here amid an array of gold and turquoise objects which testified to a wealth they would keep beyond death.

Right: This wooden mask, with shell eyes, bound with a tapestry band, would have given human form to a mummified individual of status who, curled into a foetal position, would have been put in a crevice or other such natural grave. This Inca example dates from *c.*14th century.

Above: Figurines, such as this female form, *c.*1500, are common to Inca burial sites. Fascinated with an ideal other world, the Inca often rendered it in miniature; hence the sacrifice of children, who as small adults, were symbols of innocence and perfection.

Left: This wooden hand grasps a disc of the sun. It was found in a Chimu burial mound, dating from *c.*AD900–1500, and is probably less a religious symbol than a potent political one. Chimu rulers sought power and influence through conquest rather than industry. In overrunning areas that had flourished under the Moche, such as the Lambayeque valley *(far left),* they let irrigation canals fall into ruin while taking on local craftsmen to produce goods which offered prestige and political influence. The symbolism of the piece would have fitted a politically accomplished king.

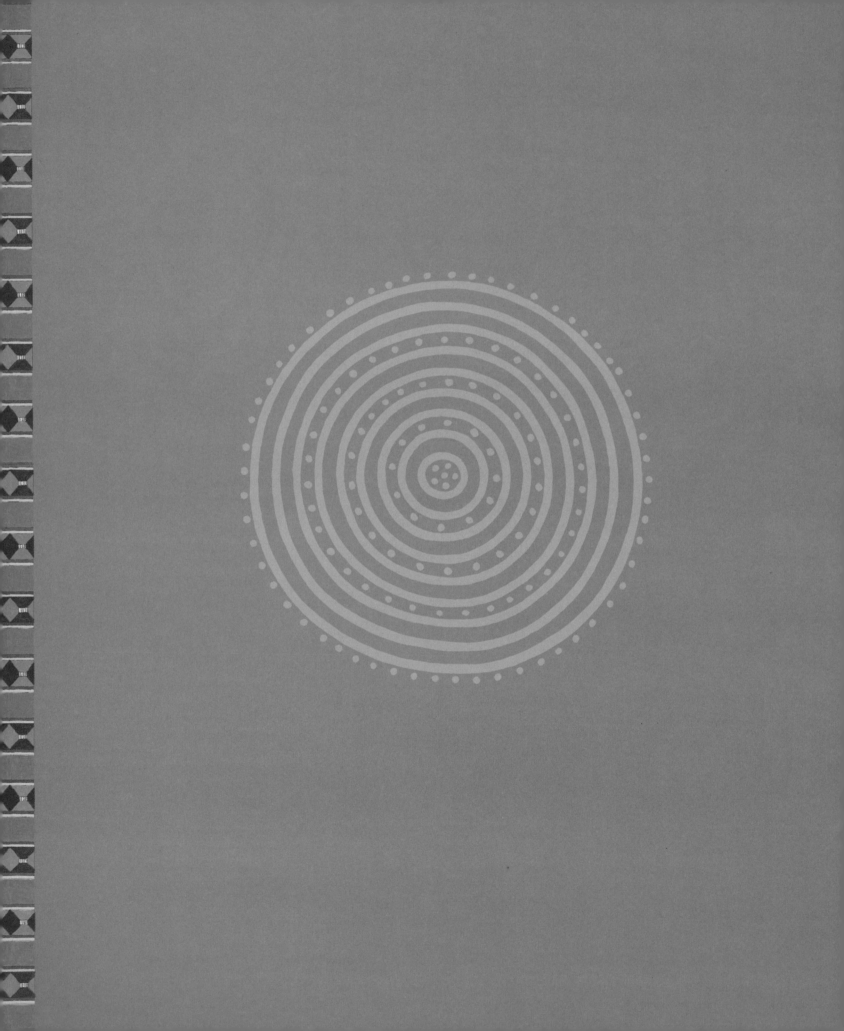

THE
SOUTHERN WORLD

THE ANCESTRAL VOICES OF AFRICA

The peoples of Africa – humankind's birthplace – ranged from the Stone Age San of the Kalahari to the urbane, city-state dwellers of the Indian Ocean coast. Every part of the world has well-preserved memories of the past, but in Africa they were and are particularly strong. In cultures where family ties were the dominant force and that for the most part were without writing, history was passed down orally from generation to generation. Under such circumstances, the narrator's urge to tell a story was combined with the chronicler's desire to record events. Embroidered to hold an audience spellbound or to honour the dead, the feats of famous ancestors were easily turned into the stuff of legend.

There were many great deeds to recall. Scholars are only now coming to appreciate the size and wealth of the empires that flourished in sub-Saharan Africa before the coming of Europeans. Much of the impetus behind the growth of these states, which developed from the ninth century AD onwards, came from contact with merchants from Islamic North Africa, who bought gold, leatherwork and slaves in return for salt and luxury goods.

Gold contributed much to the legends about Africa which circulated in Europe and elsewhere during the Middle Ages. The earliest known West African empire was that of Ghana, established by the Soninke people from the eighth century onwards in the area between the Senegal and Niger rivers. Other power centres developed later in the Yoruba city states and the Hausa lands. Greatest of all, perhaps, was the empire of Mali, founded by the Mande people, which was ruled over in the fourteenth century by Mansa Musa, whose fabulous wealth was evident when he went on a pilgrimage to Mecca in 1324.

Even older than the Sudanic states was the kingdom of Ethiopia, which traced its history back to Menelik I, supposedly the son of the Queen of Sheba. Its Christian faith separated it from the Muslim city states of the Swahili-speaking eastern coast, whose sultans grew rich on the Indian Ocean trade. Most mysterious of all were the little-known kingdoms of the south, particularly in the lake highlands, the equatorial rainforest and further south, where Bantu-speakers came together in federations with rulers thought of as gods.

Opposite: **A metal plaque showing the gateway to the palace of the *oba* of Benin, the great Edo kingdom of West Africa, *c.*17th century.**

Below: **Many African peoples attached significance to stools – among the Ashanti, for example, a king's stool represented his authority over the Earth, on which it stood. This beaded stool is from Cameroon.**

Oldest Tales of the San

The ancient creation myths of the San or Bushmen of the Kalahari Desert connect to a primeval era of irregular light and nights of total darkness. Their stories explain the first appearance of the antelopes and account for the arrival of the sun and moon in the sky.

The San's hunting lifestyle is representative of that of the earliest humans in Africa, intimate with the bush and the antelopes – springboks and heavier elands – that are among their prey. San mythology has central roles for the animals and insects of the bush, notably the praying mantis, a divine creator in many San myths.

According to San lore, the sacred mantis was married to the hyrax, a small mammal, and their daughter was the porcupine. In one story, the porcupine was the wife of Kwammang-a, a primeval ancestor whose discarded sandal the mantis used to create the first eland for the hungry San to hunt.

The mantis kept the eland in a cool water-pool surrounded by thick reeds, and brought it honey for food. Slowly the eland grew stronger and bigger until it was the size of a brawny ox. One day a young hunter went with the mantis to the waterhole and spied with the divine insect on this strange creature. Then Kwammang-a, hearing the hunter's account of what he had seen, took his bow and followed the path to the waterhole. In time the eland emerged cautiously from the reeds to drink and Kwammang-a fired a deadly arrow that brought the beast low. The mantis, far away seeking food for the eland, found that the honey had dried up and knew this to be a sign that blood had been spilled on the thirsty ground and that his majestic antelope had been brought to an evil end.

He hurried to the waterhole but when he called the eland it did not come, and the mantis wept. A dusty trail of blood led him to where the hunters were cutting up the beast for meat. Rage swept through the mantis and he tried to shoot the hunters with his own arrows. But all his shots missed and somehow came back towards him.

In the bush the mantis found the dead eland's thrown-away gall bladder hanging from a branch. When he split it open blackness flooded every-

Ancient San rock art from Kamberg, South Africa, of a hornless, heavily built eland antelope and human hunter figure.

How Things Got Their Hues

The sacred mantis brought honey to many antelopes, and according to the type of honey the animals took their varied complexions. To the upper rim of the rainbow the mantis gave his own hue.

The mantis brought honey to the first eland both as food (see main text) and as a refreshing balm. When he visited the eland in the sweetness of evening he would mix some of the honey with water and use the concoction to rub down the quivering sides of the great beast he had created. The eland has a dark fawn coloring because the mantis gave it dark-colored wasps' honey.

The mantis brought light-colored liquid honey to the gemsbok, and the animal is therefore white. The hartebeest was fed on the reddish comb of young bees; although the hartebeests of central and western Africa are brown, those in southern Africa are red. Brownish honey also accounted for the dark skin of the now extinct quagga, once a member of the zebra family. Springboks typically have a red-fawn coat because like the hartebeest they ate the honey of young bees.

Meanwhile, according to the San, in the colors of the rainbow yellow appears to arch over red because the yellow mantis lies above the red-brown of their ancestor Kwammang-a. In this instance the mantis is ascribed a yellow color, although most of the insects are green or brown in order to blend in with the foliage on which they perch, invisibly waiting for prey. However, there is one exotic species of African mantis with green-yellow wing markings that appear like eyes when it spreads its wings. The rainbow itself was sometimes called Kwammang-a.

where, driving the bright sun beneath the horizon. The mantis himself could not see momentarily and blundered into bushes. Once recovered, he took the gall bladder and threw it up into the sky – and it became the moon, which illumines the darkness of night for the good of the hunters.

When Sun Lived on Earth

The San also told a tale of the sun's first appearance in the sky. In the earliest days the sun lived among the tribes of the bush. He was like other men except that a brilliant light shone from his armpits when he raised his arms; then when he let his arms fall again, darkness swept across the Earth. A wise old woman instructed her grandchildren to creep up on old man Sun and hurl him into the sky so that the light he released could fall far and wide on all living things.

They waited until Sun had lain on the ground to sleep, then they crept towards him stealthily and in an instant they had seized him and flung him up high over their heads into the great cavern of the sky. They called out to him to stay put and to descend no more to Earth. Far away, across the bush, the children's relatives saw Sun appear as a golden sphere in the heavens and were pleased. Thus darkness was driven from the skies.

Making the Earth

The great mystery of how Earth, sky and ocean emerged at the beginning of time is linked in many African cultures with the first days of the tribe.

Nigeria's Yoruba people have a highly developed mythology of the creation of the world and of the kingdoms of Yoruba, with many versions featuring different members of a pantheon of spirits and gods. In one important myth, the great god of the sky Olodumare – or Olorun – looked down from his seat in the heavens and saw that the world was no more than a vast ocean. He summoned two of his sons, Obatala and Oduduwa, gave them a bag, a hen and a chameleon, and sent them down to the world. As they descended he lowered a great palm tree that settled on the waters: when the brothers landed, they did so in the tree's branches.

Almost at once Obatala began hacking at the bark of the tree and made a strong palm wine from its sweet sap. He soon became drunk and fell asleep. Oduduwa, meanwhile, climbed down and opened the bag his father had given him. Inside he discovered sand, which he sprinkled on the heaving surface of the water. Then he released the chameleon onto the sand; the creature advanced very slowly – as chameleons have ever since – and the land held firm. Looking deeper in the bag, Oduduwa found some dark earth which he scattered over the sand. He placed the hen down on it and this animal, scratching and pecking, flung the earth far and wide, where it settled to form the great continent of Africa.

Oduduwa walked proudly into his territory. From on high Olodumare dispatched Aje ("Wealth" or "Prosperity") to be Oduduwa's worldly companion. Olodumare also gave his son a sack of maize to sow in the ground, a supply of cowrie shells for him to use in trade with other peoples and three bars of iron to be made into weapons and agricultural tools. Proud Oduduwa was the

A sacred palm tree depicted in 17th-century Yoruba brasswork. Their creator of Earth varied: depending on the story, it could be Obatala or Oduduwa, sometimes Oranmiyan and even Ogun.

first king of Yoruba. He called the place where he had performed his act of creation Ile-Ife or "Wide House" – and it became a great city of the Yoruba.

Yoruba Created to Rule

Another version explained more explicitly why the Yoruba should exercise power over other peoples. In his great realm of the sky Olodumare created seven princes, then gave them a chicken, twenty iron bars, bags containing cowrie shells, beads and a mysterious substance wrapped in cloth. He sent them down to the world and, once again, created a great palm tree in which they landed. The six oldest princes – Olowu, Onisabe, Orangun, Oni, Ajero and Alaketu – took what they thought was valuable from the gifts of the sky god and left the youngest prince, Oranmiyan, with the chicken, the iron bars and the substance wrapped in cloth. Then they were gone, back to the heavens.

Opening the cloth, Oranmiyan found a black powder and threw it on the waters beneath the tree. The chicken at once flew down, and scattered it far and wide to make the land. When Oranmiyan settled in the land, the six older princes reappeared and demanded their share of the new world – but Oranmiyan refused, showing them the iron bars that he had transformed into an

awesome array of weapons. The six princes bowed low and Oranmiyan graciously granted them a small portion of the new land to rule, but only on condition that they and their descendants would be subject to his descendants for all time. So Oranmiyan, in this version the first king of the Yoruba, established the greatness of that tribe in the very first days of history. In some traditions he is known as Oranyan and is said – like King Arthur in Britain – to be living still, sleeping until a time of great trouble for the Yoruba when he will rise up in their defence (see pages 632–634).

The Shape of the Universe

Some African peoples understand the universe to be shaped like everyday objects such as a gourd or an egg.

To many cultures, the round calabash illustrates the shape of the universe.

The Fon people who founded the seventeenth-century kingdom of Dahomey (modern West Africa's Benin) saw the universe as resembling a split calabash, a round fruit whose hard skin can be used as a container for water or seeds.

The Fon used the image of a calabash cut in half horizontally to describe the universe: the top half contains the sky, sun and moon and the bottom half is full of water. The Earth, they said, is flat and floats in the waters held in the bottom half. For this reason, when people dig in the earth, they eventually hit water.

The top half of the universe rests on the bottom half, and the two halves meet at the horizon where sea and sky touch, in a wonderful place that people can never reach, no matter how far they sail. In the dawn of the world the creator placed a sacred snake around the

calabash to bind the join between the two halves. In some accounts, however, the divine serpent Aido-Hwedo lies beneath the Earth to prevent it sinking (see page 630).

The Dogon of Mali believe that the creator Amma took the shape of an egg (see page 628) and, according to one myth, he made the universe in the same

form – as his twin. Within the egg were four elemental parts and the divisions between the parts were the four directions of space. Altars to Amma are made of a vertical stone built up with clay into an egg shape. "Amma" means "to hold firm and keep in place" and one who repeats the name helps to maintain and sustain the universe.

Life Bursts Forth

The Kuba, who live in the abundant rainforest of Central Africa, call their creator god Mbombo and picture creation as a sudden eruption from his mouth. Once, according to their account, nothing existed but restless water lost in darkness – and Mbombo, a spirit who moved over the water. Then in the deep, dark hours of the first day, Mbombo was stricken by a sharp stomach pain and vomited, producing the sun, moon and a stream of bright stars. Light fell all around him. As the sun shone, the ocean became clouds and the water level fell, revealing hills and plains. Again Mbombo's stomach convulsed, this time sending forth a wonderful and various stream of life: the tall sky, the sharp-forked lightning, deep-rooted trees, animals in all their lithe power and the first man and woman.

The Yoruba god Obatala, who failed in his mission to create land on Earth because he fell into a drunken dream (see page 626), was credited with creating the sun. When the king of a forest tribe neglected to make the correct sacrifices, the gods sent a tree crashing down to destroy his house – but Obatala intervened, using divine magic to transform the wood into gold. He ordered the heavenly smith to make a boat and jar from the gold, then commanded his slave to take up the jar, climb into the glittering boat and pilot it up to the peak of heaven and on to the far horizon. He watched with great satisfaction as the sun journeyed across heaven for the first time. His father Olodumare, lord of the sky, decreed that the gentle moon should rise to complement the sun in the sky. Olodumare fashioned the pale moon as a flintstone with one thin and one rounded aspect. As it spins, ever obedient to Olodumare's command, it presents itself to the peoples of Yoruba in different aspects, from crescent to full.

The Power of Amma

The Dogon of Mali in West Africa revere a single god, Amma, who created all things. At the beginning of time he existed in the form of a great egg that contained the entire creation in potential form. The egg contained the elements fire, earth, water and air, and in a series of seven explosions these combined to make life. When the elements act upon one another, life follows – for instance, air blowing on fire creates sparks, while water falling on earth will make plants grow. In one account of the creation, Amma first designed the universe in his thoughts and drew a series of signs in space with water; then he sent forth the signs and they took form, becoming real. In another version, Amma's act of creation was likened to that of a potter. He cast the sun and the moon as pots and hung them in the sky; afterwards, he took a handful of small clay pieces and hurled them into space, creating the stars. The Earth he made female, also from clay, and laid her out flat, face upwards. Dogon craftsmen – especially ironworkers and blacksmiths – were held in the highest regard. Traditionally, they were not required to work the land, but were given food at harvest time; the iron they smelted provided a significant commodity to trade with.

A Dogon altar iron in the form of a dancing figure, used in ancestor worship. The first human blacksmith was a Dogon ancestor who had stolen a fragment of the sun from the heavenly smithy of the Nummo spirit twins.

The Power of Rain

Essential for agriculture, the regulation of life-giving water is overwhelmingly important. In a Fon tale of quarrels between the gods, the thunder god Hevioso refused to send rains to feed the crops until the Earth deity Sagbata accepted his authority to rule the sky without interference.

Sagbata was a son of the Fon's twin-faced creator goddess-god Mawu-Lisa; Hevioso, also male and female, was his brother-sister. According to one tale, Sagbata was sold into slavery by Mawu-Lisa and became Death's servant. He survived the ordeal and was sold on to another owner, but when he eventually escaped from slavery and returned home, he discovered that Hevioso had been made king of the tribe. The siblings quarrelled and Sagbata seized power from Hevioso, who took himself off to the sky.

Sagbata ordered his people to raise great crops of corn, but Hevioso looked down from the sky and resolved to withhold the rains. When the wet season was due and no waters fell from heaven to soften the hard ground, famine spread and many died. Then the people began to complain to Sagbata and the Earth deity saw that he had to act swiftly.

Sagbata called together all the peoples and animals of his kingdom. As his subjects watched, he took threads of black and white cotton, raised them to his mouth, whispered a soft command and then set the threads hanging in the sky as a ladder between Earth and heaven. Then he asked for volunteers to climb up to Hevioso and demand that the rains be restored. The eagle was the first to go: it soared halfway up the sky but then was struck down by Hevioso. Next the cat tried, but when it reached the same halfway point, Hevioso dispatched it with a thunderbolt.

At last it was the turn of the slow, sure chameleon – favoured creature of Lisa, the male half of Mawu-Lisa. The chameleon climbed so slowly that Hevioso grew bored and went away to deal with other matters. From time to time, Hevioso returned and flung a rasping thunderbolt down at the poor creature, but the chameleon hid behind the thread to which it clung. Finally the chameleon stood outside Hevioso's dwelling. He passed on Sagbata's message begging for rain – and Hevioso, seeing that Sagbata was accepting his authority in heaven, relented. Rain fell, and in Sagbata's land the corn grew tall. Some say that Sagbata had to submit entirely to Hevioso because the thunder god had possession of the two things essential to life on Earth: the water of the rains and the fire of celestial lightning.

Ancient Serpent Beings

Sometimes seen as the first and proudest of all creatures, the serpent was associated with royal power. In many traditions it had divine status as creator god or supreme being, considered ancient partly because of its ability to shed its skin and become young again.

The Fon of Dahomey said the snake was so old that it existed even before the Earth was made. As the divine male serpent Aido-Hwedo, he served the great creator Mawu. She rode in his mouth, and wherever she desired to go Aido-Hwedo took her. Her creation took a serpentine form, which explains why the Earth is not flat and plain but has winding rivers, deep valleys and steep slopes.

From time to time Mawu and Aido-Hwedo rested, and then the serpent's excrement piled up in vast mounds that became the sheer-sided peaks of mountain ranges. This waste contained mineral riches within it, and because the mountain rocks have solidified from it they hide great wealth in their depths which people have learned to dig out. Mawu's creation took the shape of a vast calabash, split in two: the lower half contained waters on which the Earth floated while the top half was wide sky, home of the life-giving rains and of light (see page 627).

Mawu understood that the Earth was too heavy, for it was filled with an abundance of mountains, forests, herds of elephants and beasts of prey. She knew that it needed something to support it. Then in her wisdom Mawu told Aido-Hwedo to lay himself down on the wide waters in a perfect circle with his tail in his mouth (subsequently an African symbol of eternity). On top she set the Earth and the serpent prevents it sinking. In other versions Aido-Hwedo lies around the horizon, binding the top and bottom halves of the calabash.

In some accounts, Mawu made the waters especially for Aido-Hwedo in order to keep him cool – he is known to dislike heat and so lies in the sea. Sometimes he shifts and then the Earth shudders in an earthquake. In one version Aido-Hwedo created rivers and streams: when Mawu first made the Earth there was no running water, only pools, but Aido-Hwedo led the first streams and rivers in a winding path across the land.

Bronze python's head from the West African kingdom of Benin where the cosmic serpent was seen as a divine, creative force. Living both in the trees and under the ground, the python was believed to act as a messenger of the god Olukun and was addressed respectfully as "our king".

Ancestral Snake

The Ngbandi of northern Congo also believed that the snake was the oldest animal. They revered the serpent as their supreme god and the spirit of their tribe. The leopard was also held in awe, and it was said that after death the tribal chief's soul took on the body of a leopard; but the snake had primacy even over this princely animal. Twins – who had widely different significance in Africa, either beneficial or malign – were viewed as human manifestations of the divine snake.

In a number of African cultures the serpent was associated with the primeval ancestor who founded the tribe or led it to its homeland. The Venda took part in the great southwards migration of Bantu-speaking peoples and by the seventeenth century had reached parts of what is now Zimbabwe. They tell a story in which the tribe's founders sprang from a snake's body. In ancient days, they say, a serpent named Tharu stirred on a mountainside that had been baked bone-dry by the sun. He divided into two halves, Thoho ("The Head") and Tshamutshila ("The Tail"), who went their separate ways in search of food.

Tshamutshila settled in a fertile country and became a man. He herded good cattle, raised excellent crops, married fine-boned women of proud bearing and gave issue to a magnificent tribe of children: the Venda. He took the name Ramabulana. His brother Thoho ended up in a dusty land where no crops would grow; he too became a man but he could not settle and had to earn his food as a minstrel.

One day Thoho came to the Venda city where Ramabulana ruled. At the gates he played and sang, managing to attract a large crowd. Even Ramabulana's wives went to watch and they returned in a state of high excitement, clamouring for their husband to venture out and be entertained. Now Ramabulana knew the identity of the minstrel and he feared to meet him – in case, when they stood close, they should once again become a single serpent. But his wives insisted so loudly that he went to see Thoho.

It was precisely as the king had feared. The moment Ramabulana saw his brother he fell to the ground, once again a slithering python. Thoho also reverted to serpent form and the two were fused as of old in the body of the primeval python Tharu. As the Venda people looked on in horror the great snake slipped away into the landscape, to be seen no more. Tshamutshila-Ramabulana's sons quarrelled over the kingship and, with their clans, each went their separate ways as part of the great migration of Venda.

The Kom, whose lands are near Bamenda in northwest Cameroon, also told of an ancestor's transformation into a serpent prior to a migration. After a conflict with Fon tribesmen, the Kom chief told his kinsmen to follow the track of a python when it should appear. Then he took his own life. Sure enough, a python's track appeared – and it led the Kom ancestors to the site of their royal capital. As well as being associated with mythical tribal ancestors, snakes feature in many stories as kingmakers; when they are seen fawning on a warrior or hunter, it is a sure sign that the individual has been fated for greatness.

For many African peoples the long and undulating courses of the Earth's rivers were compelling evidence of the snake's primeval movements. A curving, stylized *a-mantsho-nga-tshol* spirit figure from Guinea's Baga people.

631

The Kings Who Came from the Sky

Myths from both sides of the continent told of gods who came down from the sky to people the Earth – and then stayed to create great kingdoms, including the artistically rich city states of West Africa and the pastoralist realm of Buganda in the east.

The Yoruba people of southwestern Nigeria have one of African's finest artistic legacies, and their historical heritage is just as rich. Although most still make a living as farmers, they also have a long urban tradition, for Yoruba society developed in the form of a number of city states, the best-known being Ile-Ife, Oyo, Owo, Ijebu, Ilorin and Ibadan. Yoruba lived too in the great neighbouring Edo city of Benin. In the cities themselves, the palace of the *oba* or king would be surrounded by the dwellings of shopkeepers, traders and artisans, for the Yoruba were traditionally among the most skilled craftsmen on the continent, excelling in weaving, leatherwork, glass-making and ivory and wood carving.

Ile-Ife occupied a special place in Yoruba myth as the spot where the Earth was created (see pages 626–627). Oduduwa, who was sent down from the heavens to accomplish the task, went on to found the city itself. When the other *orisha*s – the sky-dwelling gods of Yoruba legend – saw that his work was good, they came down to inspect it. One was Orunmila, who taught people the art of divination and founded the city of Benin.

The double-axe motif identifies this as a Yoruba Sango staff linked to the thunder and lightning *orisha*.

The Staff of Oranyan

In time the city's founder Oduduwa died, leaving the realm of Ile-Ife to his son Oranyan. The young man turned out to be an excellent ruler. He was a brave warrior and highly skilled in combat – a necessary prerequisite, because warfare had come to Earth and the *oba*s of other states looked enviously upon the might of Ile-Ife. Yet he remained undefeated, vanquishing every champion who came up against him and routing all the armies sent against the kingdom. As long as he lived, Ile-Ife was safe.

But old age crept up on Oranyan too. Knowing at last that death was near, he called the people together and told them to continue to resist all-comers after he was gone. Grief swept the crowd at his words, and many voices were raised imploring him not to go. But he told them that was not possible. The most he could promise was to come back when danger threatened the city. He said that he would teach the elders of the city secret words by which they could summon him in time of need. And as a pledge of his word and an encouragement to future generations, he planted his wooden staff of office in the centre of the marketplace. It turned miraculously into a column of stone and has stood there ever since, known as Oranyan's Staff to this day.

Oranyan was as good as his word. Upon news of his death, other powers sought to invade Ile-Ife to take advantage of his going. But when their armies approached the city, the elders spoke the secret words. With a noise like thunder the earth opened and the dead king stepped out, fully armed. The mere sight of his weapons flashing in the sun was

Bronzes from Benin

Some of Africa's most beautiful sculptures were created more than 500 years ago by craftsmen in the West African city states of Ile-Ife and Benin.

Some of the works were made in terracotta – fired, unglazed clay – but others were so-called "bronzes" (actually the metal alloy was brass) produced by the lost-wax method. This technique, used by the Yoruba from about the eleventh century, involved covering a sculpted earthenware core with beeswax and an outer casing of clay. The beeswax was then melted out so the space left behind could be filled with molten metal.

The Ile-Ife sculptors' masterpieces were a series of life-size human heads, most probably portraits of rulers of the cities. They are thought to have been used in funerary rites, then either preserved for safe-keeping in the royal palaces or buried at marked spots in sacred groves. The most distinctive feature of the bronzes was their intense naturalism, rare not just in Africa but anywhere in the world at the time when they were produced. When the skills were passed on to Benin – according to tradition, by a famous craftsman called Igueghae late in the fourteenth century – a more stylized tradition developed.

A brass head of an Ile-Ife king, *c.*13th century. Most busts were produced for the royal court of the *oba*, who would dedicate an altar to his predecessor. Such figures were sometimes identified with Olukun, the Yoruba sea god and Benin's most worshipped deity.

enough to spread terror in the enemy ranks, which quickly broke and fled. Then Oranyan returned to the earth from which he had come and the ground closed once more over his regal head.

Word of his miraculous reappearance spread, and for many years Ile-Ife went unmolested. But in time security bred laziness and complacency. The people lost the sense of duty they had had in Oranyan's day and thought only of pleasure. One evening during festival time, when there was much dancing, drumming and drinking of palm wine, some revellers drunkenly called on the elders to summon Oranyan to the celebrations. Shocked at such levity, they at first demurred, but the people insisted. Fearing for their own lives, the old men eventually gave in, summoning the great warrior with the ancient formula that told him that the city of Ile-Ife was in danger.

Oranyan appeared as before in a clap of thunder, gazing around for the foe. But because it was dark he could not tell one face from another. Seeing himself surrounded by what he took to be the enemy, he set about the bystanders, spearing many with his lance and cutting down others with his sword. Soon the marketplace was awash with blood, but the killing went on. Only when dawn broke and Oranyan could at last see the tribal scars on the faces of the dead did he realize that he had been slaughtering

his own people. Then he threw his weapons down in horror, and in anguished tones proclaimed that his fighting days were over. The earth closed around him, and from that day forth Oranyan was never seen in Ile-Ife again. Only his staff remained behind to remind succeeding generations of the city's greatest hero – and the foolish irreverence that had cost them his services for good.

The Trials of Kintu

Approximately 1,900 miles to the east, in Uganda, various peoples were united together by a story which traced another dynasty all the way back to a sky-being who decided to settle on Earth. This person was Kintu, first founder of the royal line of the *kabaka*s (kings) of Buganda.

The stories told how Kintu at first had only a cow for company, and lived off the beast's milk. Then a pretty sky-maiden named Nambi saw him in his loneliness and fell in love with him. But when she told her family about him, they despised him as a mere milksop. To test him, they stole the cow, and for a time he had to grub a living from herbs and leaves.

Eventually Nambi came to tell Kintu that his animal had been taken up to heaven, and he went with her to fetch it back. Nambi's father and brothers were waiting for him. They invited him into the mansion in which they lived, but not as a

Carved ivory cup for ritual and festive drinking, from Owo, *c.*15th century. The city state of Owo was the ancient capital of the Yoruba. Bracelets and boxes were also carved from ivory tusks for the court.

welcome guest. They planned to get rid of him by setting him an impossible task to perform on pain of his life. And so they presented him with a huge meal – enough to feed half a tribe – and told him to eat it all up or else he would be killed. He was left to get on with the task, but could barely digest one-tenth of the food provided. Then he noticed a half-hidden hole in the floor. Quickly he piled all the leavings into it and covered it over. When his hosts came back, they were astonished to find not a crumb remaining.

Nambi's father, Gulu, was not to be appeased so quickly, however, and he at once thought up another, equally daunting challenge. This time Kintu was given a copper axe and told to cut firewood from a rock. Once more he proved equal to the task, finding a boulder that was already deeply fissured and managing to strike splinters from it that he solemnly presented to his prospective father-in-law as fuel for his hearth. In return, he was handed a huge pot and told to fill it with water that came not from any river, lake, pond or well. At a loss, he lay down in a field with the pot beside him – and was delighted to wake up early the next day to find it miraculously filled with morning dew.

By now Gulu was running out of ideas, but he thought he still had one winner up his sleeve. He told Kintu that he could indeed marry Nambi, but only if he could find the cow he had come to seek among his own extensive herds. This too seemed impossible, for Gulu was vastly wealthy and had countless cattle, many of them virtually identical to Kintu's beast. But once more Kintu triumphed, this time with the help of a friendly bumble bee, which promised to alight on the horns of the animal he was seeking.

So, when Kintu was taken out to the first of Gulu's herds the next morning, the first thing he looked for was the bee. He spotted it buzzing around in the shade of a tree, from which it refused to budge; so Kintu, getting the message, told Gulu that his cow was not among the cattle present. The same thing happened when Kintu visited a second herd. The third time, however, the bee at once flew to a large cow, and Kintu claimed it for his own. Then it flew off again, only to settle in turn on three young calves. For a moment Kintu was non-plussed; then he had the presence of mind to insist that they too were his, having been born to his cow during her stay in heaven.

Gulu was amazed. There seemed to be nothing that his daughter's suitor did not know. Convinced of his worthiness as a bridegroom, he finally gave his consent to the match. Married at last, the two returned to Earth to found the royal line of Buganda, which to this day reigns over the kingdom – now part of modern Uganda – on the northern shores of Lake Victoria.

Reminiscent of the tool provided to Kintu, this elaborate copper-handled, iron-bladed axe was carried in a Central African ceremonial rite honouring the ancestors, who are possibly represented by the massed human heads.

635

Learning Lessons from the Animals

Just as people wished to know how humankind and the landscape around them had been created, so they also sought explanations of why the world was ordered the way it was. Many simply observed nature and the result has been a rich body of animal stories.

Among the most popular of all African stories are the animal fables. Those involving the tortoise and the hare are well known, but there are many more, either comic or solemn: some set out to explain how animals gained their characteristics, while others are morality tales aimed at humankind.

Typical of the first kind are the stories describing how the leopard obtained its spots. According to an amusing version from Sierra Leone, it happened when, at his wife's insistence, Leopard foolishly invited his friend Fire round to the house. He no longer had a home left afterwards, but the scorch-marks on his skin have remained to this day.

The Tumbuka of Malawi say that the spots were painted on by Tortoise, who owed Leopard a favour for rescuing him from a tree. In similar vein, Tortoise went on to beautify Zebra by painting on his stripes; but when Hyena, who had originally put him up the tree as a joke, came for the same treatment, he was given the ugly pelt he has retained ever since.

The First Elephant

A curious Kamba tale from Kenya explains the origin of elephants. A poor man who wanted to become rich was sent for advice to a wealthy benefactor called Ivonya-Ngia. This man thought for a while, and then gave him an ointment, telling him to smear it on his wife's canine teeth. They would grow to an unusual size; then he had merely to extract and sell them.

The poor man did as he was told, and was delighted when, in a few weeks' time, her canines turned into tusks of ivory. He pulled them out and got a good price for them, then repeated the process. Soon he was as rich as he had wished.

His success aroused the envy of his neighbour, who asked how he too could make money. The first man directed him to Ivonya-Ngia, who gave him the same ointment but neglected to mention anything about tooth-pulling. As

While renowned and respected for its power and strength, the leopard was also considered by many ordinary people to be a bully, lacking wisdom and intelligence. Snarling leopard plaque that formerly decorated the palace of the *oba*s of Benin.

The Crest and the Hide

A Lega story from Congo points an uncompromising moral about the limits of friendship.

A lizard and a guinea-fowl lived in a village where the people took it in turns to be chief. When the lizard's time came, it did everything possible to ensure that its investiture was suitably splendid. It got a ceremonial drum, a magnificent outfit, a hide to sit on and plenty of beer to refresh the onlookers.

All that remained was a suitable headdress. Wanting a splendid plume to top it, it sent word to its friend the guinea-fowl. The bird presented it with feathers of every shape and size, but none would do, for the lizard had already decided that it would only be satisfied with the guinea-fowl's own splendid crest. Eventually the bird unwillingly had it cut off – leaving guinea-fowl looking shorn ever since.

In time the lizard's term ended and the guinea-fowl's own turn arrived. It too sought to do everything grandly, gathering the necessary drum, drink and finery to wear. But again something was missing – this time a hide. So the bird demanded one from the lizard – and, on a quid pro quo basis, insisted that none would do but the lizard's own. Public opinion sided with the fowl over the request, so the lizard eventually had to agree to be skinned, with fatal results. A Lega proverb spells out the moral: Don't ask a friend for more than he can give.

---

a result, the man let his wife's tusks grow so large that her entire face and body were transformed and she became an elephant. Eventually she went to live in the forest. From her the elephant race descended – and they are still as clever as people.

Two Honey-loving Birds

Some stories straddle the gap between the myth of origin and the moral fable. One example is a Baila tale which explains the different destiny of two bird species: the honey-guide, which is esteemed by humans for showing them where to find honey, and the wheat-ear, which is trapped with birdlime. In early times they lived together, and one day went in search of honey. They found a honeycomb and noted the spot, planning to return the next morning. But in the meantime the wheat-ear slipped out and ate all the honey itself.

When the two returned to the spot the next day, only a few bits of the comb remained. Angrily the honey-guide accused the wheat-ear of having eaten it, but the other bird protested its innocence. When they subsequently found another honeycomb, the wheat-ear, to bolster its story, insisted that they should put birdlime around it to see who

637

the thief really was. The honey-guide agreed, and the two went off to get some from the human beings who made it. Returning home with their purchase, they agreed to lay it the following morning. Only this time the honey-guide stole off to set the lime early. When the wheat-ear then tried to repeat its trick, it got stuck and died.

Next day the honey-guide found the corpse and drew the moral. The wheat-ear would thieve no more; and people would in future cherish honey-guides as helpers, while for wheat-ears they would have only contempt – and birdlime.

Lessons for Humankind

Some Ethiopian fables are similarly bleak in their world-view, but express it wryly. One tells how a leopard cub strayed from home and was killed when an elephant accidentally stepped on it. As soon as news of the tragedy reached the father, he swore revenge. But when he heard that the guilty party was a bull elephant, he momentarily hung back; an image of its huge bulk crossed his mind.

Then, he made his feelings known decisively. "No," he roared. "You're wrong. It was a goat that did this terrible deed!" And he at once rushed off and killed a large number of goats grazing peacefully in the neighbouring hills. The point, needless to say, applies also to the human world: when a man is wronged by a person stronger than himself, he will often seek revenge on someone weaker.

A similar tale recounts what happened when a lion, a leopard, a hyena and a donkey came together to bemoan their condition in the midst of a terrible drought. Food was getting scarce, and between them they tried to work out why. Eventually they decided that it must be divine judgement on their sins, and reckoned it would be best for them all to confess their wrong-doing.

The lion admitted to the heinous offence of killing and eating a young bull near a village, but the other animals, fearing his strength, hastened to assure him that that was no sin. The leopard then said that it had savaged a goat it found wandering away from its herd; once more the consensus was

This ceremonial sword and sheath, known as the *udamalore*, belonged to the ruler of the Owo-Yoruba peoples. It had military and magical prowess because of its powerful animal motifs.

that there was nothing to repent. The hyena had stolen into a village to seize a chicken; but again the animals saw no harm.

Then it was the donkey's turn. The worst fault it could come up with was nibbling a few blades of grass while its owner wasn't looking. But none of the other beasts feared the donkey, so despite the triviality of the offence they all joined in saying, "That is a terrible sin. You have caused all our suffering." And so they killed and ate the inoffensive beast, illustrating the bitter moral that it is usually the powerless who end up getting the blame.

By no means all African animal tales are so pessimistic. A narrative from the Ngbandi people of the Congo region has an upbeat message about the strength that can come from cooperation and community. It describes how an elephant went on a hunting trip with a tiny dudu bird. At the end of the day they wanted to let their respective wives know they were coming home so that each could start getting a meal ready. The elephant trumpeted with all its might, and a great wave of sound swept through the glade. But the bird could only feebly cheep its distinctive *dudu, dudu.*

A second bird nearer home heard the notes, however, and took up the cry. That was picked up by a third, and so on; thus the call passed swiftly through the forest. When the two got back to the bird's house, dinner was ready and waiting.

The bird invited his friend to join him, but the elephant declined, saying that he was expecting a large meal in his own home nearby. Only when he got there, he found nothing at all. Because of the distance, his wife had not heard the trumpeting.

There are many stories in which the weak defeat the strong. One from Malawi's Namwanga people uses the familiar animal-helper theme. It tells how a hunter lifted a shrew across a ditch, for which the profusely grateful animal promised to assist him in return if it ever got the chance. The man and his dogs then killed some guinea-fowl.

Late in the day it rained and the hunter took shelter in a hut. The tiny shrew, which had followed him, hid in the thatch. Before long a lion came along. Scenting the man, it roared out: "Give the guinea-fowl to the dogs to eat – then you eat the dogs and I'll eat you!" The man quaked, thinking his final hour had come. But the shrew had other ideas. In a small but determined voice, it squeaked out: "That's right. Give the guinea-fowl to the dogs to eat, then you eat the dogs, the lion will eat you – and I'll eat the lion!" And with that the lion turned tail and fled.

Living in Terror of Witches

The notion of supernatural power has long excited and frightened people, and even today a belief in witchcraft is widespread in Africa. Unlike Western witches, those in Africa are always malevolent, seeking to kill their victims by secretly consuming their souls.

African concepts of witchcraft draw on the idea that sickness and death are not necessarily natural. Often they may be caused by the intervention of evil spirits – and like as not these will be under the control of a malign individual.

Such people are not always conscious of their powers. Some may simply be born with the evil eye, causing misery around them with no deliberate intent to do harm. Among their ranks are East Africa's *kisirani*, hapless individuals whose mere presence in a room is enough to make valuables lose themselves and send treasured pots tumbling.

An Urge for Evil

More serious misfortunes are likely to be blamed on intentional witchcraft or sorcery, which are used to explain all kinds of tragedy, in particular unexpected deaths. Belief in them stirs many primal fears, for witchcraft is very hard for ordinary people to detect except by its terrible results.

Witches, who may be male as well as female, show no obvious exterior sign of their condition. On the surface they may be likeable and even charming people, only revealing their true nature in private, usually under cover of night. Many stories make the point that they may be found close to home: as neighbours, in-laws or even in one's own family.

Yet underneath their seemingly harmless exterior, witches are entirely evil, driven by an irresistible urge to consume the spiritual strength of their victims – to "eat their soul", as the saying goes. Sometimes they use poison to achieve their ends, but more often the damage is done spiritually. By obtaining objects intimately connected with the targeted individual – such as hairs, nail clippings, or even excreta – they can find a pathway into his or her psyche and transmit a pathogen invisible to the eye of all but a skilled witch-doctor. The affected person will sicken and die for no apparent reason.

Sorcerers and Zombie Slaves

There is no clear line between witchcraft and sorcery, except that sorcerers tend to work on their own. Some can shift shape, taking on the form of birds or animals. Often it is only the soul of the

An array of monkey skulls embedded in a hut wall in Mali decorates the home of a Dogon "spirit master", a curer of witches, who can control the energies released by the process of death itself. Witches themselves live in grave danger from fellow humans who fear them.

sorcerer that inhabits these animal familiars, while his body may be elsewhere altogether. There are many stories of people dying in their beds at the exact moment that a hunter killed the owl, bat, snake, hyena or crocodile sheltering their spirit.

More alarmingly still, some sorcerers dig up dead bodies and bring them back to a terrible half-life as zombies: the word itself comes from the Kongo term for an object of spiritual power. The Zulu of South Africa call these living dead *umkovu* and say that they can only mumble inarticulately, for their tongues are slit to prevent them from talking. The resuscitated corpses then become their animator's slaves.

One tale from Natal describes how a man who had lost his brother to an unexplained illness became convinced that he had fallen victim to sorcery, and set out to find the person responsible. He wandered far and wide, asking everyone he met if they knew anyone who could have caused the young man's death. Eventually he met someone who, although too afraid to speak, pointed him in the direction of nearby hills. There he found his brother at last. He was one of a ghostly host of labourers, all silently hoeing the extensive fields of a sorcerer who had grown rich by exercising his necromantic powers. The seeker led his brother home, but he had lost the power of

A Bellyful of Evil

In many parts of Africa, the stomach is the seat of evil. For the Ngbandi of the northern Congo the spirits that enter it are called li *and the people they possess are* li-men.

Li-men behave like other African witches, doing harm to their victims by obtaining nail clippings or pieces of their clothing. They walk by night, and anyone whose door they knock on is sure to waste away and die in a few days. They are cannibals and dig up corpses to eat the flesh. Some steal children in order to kill and consume them.

Yet by day these terrible creatures are indistinguishable from their neighbours. The only way to identify them is after death, when witchfinders known as "belly-cutters" may be summoned to perform an autopsy. Cutting open the corpse, they will carefully examine the stomach and intestines. If they find a tumour, they will declare it to be the abode of the *li* and will take care to see that it is removed far from the village. As for the dead man's relatives, they will become objects of general suspicion, for the *li* are known to haunt whole families.

A carrier of magic from the land of the spirits, this *nkisi nkondi* **was collected in Congo before 1878. The nails provide protection from spirit forces thought to regulate the world.**

speech and died soon after. His corpse, which had previously remained limp, now stiffened in the normal way, indicating that he was truly dead.

Coven of the Cannibals

Unlike sorcerers, witches assemble in covens to eat the flesh of corpses; each member is expected to provide a body in turn, and these are often the remains of murdered relatives or neighbours. A sense of the terror they inspire comes through strongly in a tale of the Kongo people, who inhabit the lower reaches of the River Congo. This describes how a young woman named Malemba went to visit her lover, little knowing that he was really a witch. She slipped into his hut surreptitiously at twilight, so that the neighbours would not see, then sat quietly in the darkness for him to return.

When he did so, he failed to notice her. Instead, he took down a basket of food left for him by other members of the coven, and Malemba was horrified to see him pick out and eat a human finger. Her disgust turned to terror when he muttered curses at his fellow-witches for leaving him such slim pickings, and promised that they would get no better from him – when the time came for him to kill Malemba.

At that point he lit a torch and saw his intended victim. Malemba tried hard to act as though she had heard nothing, but she could tell that he was not convinced. Muttering some excuse he soon left the hut, and Malemba realized that he must have gone to fetch the rest of the coven.

Panic-stricken, she fled back towards her own village. But the witches took down a fetish – a wooden carving imbued with magical power.

It twisted like a live thing in their hands, seeking the girl as a predator scents its prey. Soon it was pointing out the path that she had taken, and the six members of the coven were running at full pelt in pursuit of their victim.

The girl took refuge in her mother's garden, hiding under a pile of refuse. Her pursuers soon neared and would have found her had an antelope – perhaps a good spirit in disguise – not suddenly leaped out of the undergrowth and thrown the fetish off her track. Confused in the nighttime darkness, the men ran off after the beast. They soon came back, but just as they arrived dawn broke, forcing them to hurry off back to their own village.

The girl was found by her mother more dead than alive. She was able to tell her parents what had happened, but remained desperately weak through the day. The final straw came at dusk that evening when the six witches came to the hut, seemingly on a harmless social visit. The sight of them was more than the sick girl could bear, and she finally passed away.

Her parents saw that her death did not go unpunished. They accused her lover and his five accomplices before the chief's council. The six were condemned to drink the poison of judgement, fatal to witches although supposedly harmless to the innocent. All perished.

An Enduring Fear

Sorcery and the fear of it is still very much a fact of life in parts of the continent, as an internationally publicized spate of witch-killings in South Africa in recent years made apparent. Often the

Late 19th-century *tetela* from Congo made of ivory and metal. This figure was made to rest on top of a fetish gourd filled by a diviner with "medicine" to avert misfortune. The protruding objects may have been added as thanksgivings for its power.

The Talking Bowl of Broth

Sorcerers used poison both to kill their victims and to steal their souls. But in one Hausa tale the potion itself spoke up to thwart its maker.

The witch in question had nine mouths on her body, all invisible to ordinary people, and a ravening appetite for evil that led her to seek to kill her own husband and father-in-law. With murder in mind, she gathered noxious herbs from the forest and boiled them up in a broth. But when the two men sat down to eat and uncovered their bowls, a voice from the first warned them, "Cover me up or else you will die." When the same thing happened a second time, the husband became convinced that witchcraft was afoot. Picking up the bowl, he emptied it over his wife's head. Suddenly the nine mouths became visible, and she was revealed as a witch. She ran away from the village and was never seen again.

true horror lies less in the accusations that are made – real though the fears they represent may be – than in the violence done to the supposed witches. The annals of African justice are full of stories of people weighed down by grief who, crazed by a presentiment of invisible evil all around them, have committed atrocious acts in an attempt to exorcise the demons haunting them.

So, in 1934, a Luba man whose brother had fallen dangerously ill consulted a diviner who suggested to him that one of his four wives must be responsible – without specifying which one. The man took a knife and stabbed one of the wives to death. When his brother's health failed to improve, he killed another. The same scenario was repeated twice more. Then, with all his wives dead and his wits completely gone, the deluded man dragged his brother from his bed and killed him too, raving that he had no reason to be ill after so many had died for him. Fear of witchcraft can bring about deeds quite as horrible as any ever credited to the witches.

THE UNSEEN WORLDS OF AUSTRALASIA

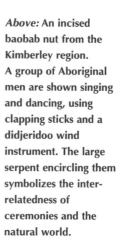

Australasia's two main regions have had very different histories. The continent of Australia has one of the most ancient populations on Earth and has been inhabited by the Aborigine peoples for perhaps 65,000 years. In contrast, the islands of the Pacific Ocean were settled by Polynesians relatively recently – New Zealand, for example, has seen barely 1,000 years of human habitation. The peoples of Australia lived as hunter-gatherers in small groups, developing localized myths influenced strongly by their environment, whereas the Maori of New Zealand were a settled, warlike, sea-going people and evolved a hierarchical society with royal lineages, a pantheon of gods and strict social prohibitions known as *tapu*, or taboos.

Yet for all their differences, these peoples have much in common, mythologically speaking. One widespread idea is the belief in ancestral heroes whose actions remain effective among their descendants today. Another is the concept of a spiritual power that can exist in people or in places, in actions as well as objects, and whoever or whatever possesses it must be respected and feared. This second notion is at its purest in Polynesia, where it is called *mana*, but under different names it resonates across the entire region.

For the Aborigines, there were always two kinds of reality: the everyday life of the world around them and the Altjeringa or "Dreamtime", the age at the world's dawn when a giant ancestor race had walked the land, moulding its contours and stocking it with its familiar wealth of plants and animals. Wherever the ancestors went they left traces of themselves, and these numinous areas, together with the magical songs and objects bequeathed to their human successors, formed the heart of the Aborigines' spiritual heritage.

Myth, then, was the means by which Aborigines and Polynesians comprehended a world in which unseen forces were believed to be shaping people's destinies from day to day. Never simply a thing of the past, the tales had everyday relevance, but once European settlers had arrived and proceeded to destroy much of the indigenous culture, the myths became one of the few means by which native peoples might retain their distinct sense of identity.

Above: An incised baobab nut from the Kimberley region. A group of Aboriginal men are shown singing and dancing, using clapping sticks and a didjeridoo wind instrument. The large serpent encircling them symbolizes the inter-relatedness of ceremonies and the natural world.

Opposite: A bark painting from the Northern Territory depicts goannas drinking from a pool. A Dreamtime story tells of a battle between the land and sea animals which ended with the goanna suffering mortal wounds and turning into Mount Maroon.

645

Dreaming the Earth

Australia's Aborigines possess a body of living myth in which the land is as much part of the spiritual plane as the physical. Mythology is a part of the consciousness by which the world is mapped and the heroic Dreamtime can also be experienced in the here and now.

Arcing and tensing in the infinity of its secret strength, the vast serpent sent a shockwave through the earth. Aroused from endless slumber by some mysterious and intimate signal, it flexed its whole length as it struggled towards wakefulness. Thrusting forwards, tongue flickering and fangs flashing, it exploded upwards through what till that moment had been the blank surface of the world. As rocks and debris showered to the far horizon, the serpent writhed on, bestowing rugged shape on what had been empty indeterminacy. Each corkscrewing twist carved out a valley in the crumbling, quaking earth; every lash of the tail threw up a mountain or a range of hills. Across the entire Australian continent similar serpents were on the move, gouging out deep ravines and pushing up ridges as they went. The ultimate ancestors of the Aboriginal people, these spirits were giving form to a formless world, grinding out the landscape their descendants would inhabit to this day. Other spirits flew down from the heavens to range what had been the smooth surface of the Earth, making all things and giving them their appointed names. They established the different peoples in their allotted lands and gave them their distinct languages, laws and customs.

Such was the violent confusion which conferred order on the Aboriginal world, the incredible cataclysm on which was founded much stability. For the essence of the Aborigine people's existence is its timeless, unchanging mythical and artistic tradition which reinforces the sense of living the same life, in the same landscape, as their forbears. An Aboriginal person knows every inch of his ancestral territory, bleak and monotonous as it might appear to the untutored Western eye. The scrubbiest bush, the barest rock has its established

A bark painting from Arnhem Land depicts the story of the Dreaming Crocodile at Ngalawi. The crocodile and other mythic men had made a sacred hut (represented by the cross) at Blue Mud Bay to store their *rangga* emblems while they danced, but it caught fire and Crocodile had to cover himself with lily grass for protection from the flames.

significance for him; no trickling spring is too puny to escape his notice. Set the Aborigine down far from his native haunts, and his internal compass remains exact; he knows his own land in its every detail. Yet he sees it, not objectively, as external to himself, but as part of a whole of which he himself is another part. Myths such as those of the Altjeringa or "Dreamtime" help to explain the world in these terms, symbolizing the interconnectedness of humanity and nature.

The Dreamtime

The Dreamtime was that moment when the world first came convulsively into being, thrown up in an explosion of energy by ancestral spirits. As much a metaphysical dimension as a cosmological epoch, however, it endured – indeed still endures – as an ecstatic state open to all who would participate. With the right rituals and incantations the Aborigines can gain access to that same primal spark which first quickened the Earth and has since stirred all their forbears into life. Time is abolished on the instant, in that moment of

enlightenment and energy when the Aborigines connect directly with their own creation. An elaborate mythology handed down orally, from generation to generation, helps to maintain the sense that past and present are one.

So strong is the Aborigine peoples' identification with their ancestors that it matches their sense of individual selfhood: they feel they are essentially the same people, from age to passing age. Timeless myths seem to set the same community within the same natural scene, each rehearsal incorporating new events into the same apparently unchanging schema.

The boundaries which Westerners have so painstakingly erected down the millennia to separate themselves from the natural world have never existed in the minds of Aboriginal peoples. Here all – men, women, animals and every living thing – have been called into being by the same sublime and unceasing dream.

Sacred Energy: The Power of *Djang*

The force the ancestors left latent within the earth is accessible to their descendants in the form of **djang**, *a type of stored-up primal power which collects in certain sacred places.*

Held in a particular tree or rock, for instance, this power might be released at a word or a touch to instil strength or confer cunning on the initiate, or to bring much-needed sunshine or rain.

The creative energy by which the world was originally formed, *djang* is literally as old as the hills. The Dreamtime stories tell how spirit beings metamorphosed into things which remain in the landscape. *Djang*'s continued presence allows Aborigines to tap into their people's whole spiritual resource at an instant's notice. *Djang* can also be evoked by the

rituals and dances which reunite the people with the ancestors who inaugurated them.

This gum tree, so distinct in its bare surroundings, is the sort of feature likely to hold supernatural *djang*.

Shaping the Contours

That dream resonates too in the landscape's every rugged contour, crisscrossed as it was in the primal Dreamtime by the originating spirits. In the shape not only of giant snakes but of bounding kangaroos or wallabies, scuttling lizards or creeping crocodiles, the ancestral heroes traversed their terrain, establishing order and inaugurating tribes. The two goanna, or monitor, men, for example, roamed the length and breadth of what is today called the Great Victoria Desert, creating its animals and plants and performing its founding rituals. In the course of their travels, it is reported, they met with other important spirits: the Opossum Woman, the Moon Man and the Mountain Devil. The Djanggawul brother and sisters emerged from the eastern sea in the wake of the rising sun to pace out the northern coastline of the continent. As they went they gave birth to peoples, whom they endowed with eternal rites, finally following the setting sun into the western ocean where they sank gently beneath the waves. Another establisher of the tropical north, Tor Rock, can be seen to this very day. Now no more than a geological feature of the Arnhem Land coast, he once helped to furnish with animals, plants and men, he remains a potent spirit in the mind of the area's indigenous inhabitants.

Wherever they went, these wayfaring spirits marked out the places where they had camped or hunted with features such as caves, creeks or rivers, gleaming saltpans or clumps of trees. Every rock, every dried-up streambed they endowed with sacred significance for all time to come. Sometimes the routes the spirits

In art as in myth and landscape, the Dreaming was the single subject in which all creation was contained. Spoken stories were captured visually in an art which reflected the fluid interaction between human spirit figures and animal heroes, such as those seen here.

Reading the Landscape

The "dreaming tracks" the ancestral spirits followed in their originating journeys across the Australian land have an equivalent in the "song lines" they left behind, connecting the sacred sites.

Audible only to the initiate, "song lines" are stories encoded in the landscape: a tribe's whole history and culture is there for those with eyes to read or with ears to hear. If the Aborigines see their world as essentially static and stable, they for their part are always on the move – not only as hunter-gatherers but as part of their religious observance. Although a big part of their ritual takes the form of collective ceremonies and dancing, the personal pilgrimage is important too. Far from wandering idly and aimlessly the Aborigine on "walkabout" retraces the steps of his ancestors, following "song lines" and "dreaming tracks" in a strenuous bid to ingest the energy and history of his forbears from the dawn of time.

Much Aboriginal knowledge is secret. These boys are being initiated along their tribe's "song line" path – the sacred drawings can only be seen later.

followed were many hundreds of miles long, making paths that might figure in the mythologies of many different peoples; others went on just a few miles and were known only to a number of local tribes. However long or short, though, the routes of their wanderings have remained sanctified in Aboriginal tradition. The spirit's original life-force remains eternally present along these paths, available countless generations on to the initiate in his secret cult. By striking a stone upon which the spirit rested or rubbing the spot at which he entered or emerged from the earth, the Aborigine can draw upon his ancestor's primal energy for strength and skill in hunting or in war.

Much of southwestern Australia was created by a watersnake, the Wagyal, who possessed both masculine and feminine forms, and was simultaneously one and many. Creating mountains, lakes and rivers, such as the Swan on which Perth would one day be sited, his/her form is still discernible in the long escarpment visible from the modern city. A derelict brewery now stands on the site where the Wagyal settled down to lay her eggs: for thousands of years, Aboriginal women from the region would journey to this sacred spot when their time came to give birth. Those born at such sacred places are entrusted with their care and protection: they are, it is said, not just descendants but reincarnations of the ancestral being. Other spirits took up residence within particular birds, animals and insects – honoured still by their Aboriginal descendants, for whom they are important totemic figures (see pages 658–659).

Etched into a rock face, an Aboriginal image becomes part of the very creation it represents; painted in pigments ground up from ashes, earth and bark, it partakes of the natural order it sets out to depict. That such creations tend subsequently to be seen as the work not of human but of spirit artists only underlines the continuity they affirm. So too does the fact that the same stories are painted on the bodies of Aborigines for sacred rituals which help commemorate and celebrate their oneness with the Earth. The great corroborees, or tribal assemblies, at which complicated dances are performed and elaborate rituals staged, recall earlier spirit conventions during the Dreamtime, back at the beginning when the world was being made.

The Serpent and the Rainbow

Water was believed to have been created by the ancestral spirits when the world came into being. The Rainbow Snake, oldest and most universal of the Aboriginal spirit identities, symbolized the water without which life could not continue.

His feet were tough and leathery enough to take the most jagged stones in their stride, and yet the boy winced none the less at the temperature of the rocks he was walking across. Accustomed as he was to the stifling heat of the dry season, he still found himself seized by something approaching panic for a moment as his lungs heaved on the searing desert air. As the twigs crackled, dry and brittle beneath his feet, his nerves seemed only a hair's breadth away from snapping too. All in this arid landscape seemed on the point of burning up: the boy was no exception. Increasingly bored and irritable back in the camp, he had come out here to kill an afternoon, yet the feeling of being slowly cooked was doing nothing whatever for his mood.

As far as the eye could see the sky was an uninterrupted expanse of blue; from horizon to farthest horizon, not a single cloud could be seen. No rain had fallen for weeks; had it really ever rained at all? Moisture was no more than a memory here – or worse, it was a tantalizing mirage, like the heat haze that ringed the sun or the vast lake that seemed to shimmer in the valley bottom: mocking parodies of the water for which all nature was so palpably athirst. Suddenly the boy stood stock still, transfixed by the sight of a snake making its way across a boulder before him, trickling

A waterhole in the Northern Territory's lush and tropical Kakadu National Park. Water, the source of all life, was the gift of the ancestral spirits at the beginning of the world. Some waterholes are sacred and Aboriginal clans act as their custodians; others can be therapeutic or dangerous. The serpent symbolized the wet season and the replenishment of the water.

like liquid over the dry face of the solid stone. In its winding and unravelling coils he could see the meandering of a river; in its lithe languidness he sensed a terrible energy waiting to be unleashed. Most of all, in its inscrutable beauty he felt the presence of unimaginable power: in this mysterious phallic form could be contained all the potency of the world, all the surging strength of water and its capacity to destroy and to save.

The Symbolism of the Snake

The never-ending quest for water in arid conditions defines the rhythm of existence for many Aboriginal peoples; only in the tropical north and temperate south can a ready supply be taken for granted. At the mundane level, the people have a strong positive sense of water's importance, yet they are under no illusions about its immense destructive power. At a more spiritual level, the

Taipan, the Shaman-snake

Among the Wik Kalkan people of the Cape York Peninsula, the story of the snake-deity Taipan is told. Once a man and a powerful magician, he could cure the sick – or kill the healthy – at will.

He could control not only human life and death but the elements: the lightning flashed and the thunder rumbled at his command. For wives he had the watersnakes Uka and Tuknampa, and Mantya the death-adder. Only one child had been born of these alliances, however: a fine son, whom Taipan loved above all things. But one day when the youth went hunting downriver he fell in love with the watersnake Tintauwa, wife of Wala the blue-tongued lizard. She seduced him, and they ran away together into the bush.

Wala gave chase and murdered Taipan's son. The magician was left desolate by his loss. Calling his family together he daubed them all with the blood of his child, before sending them down to take up residence in the earth in whose depths he himself soon joined them. His two sisters,

meanwhile, he sent off to the highest heaven, telling them to add their nephew's red blood to the other colors of the rainbow. It can be seen there to this day, richest color in the spectrum of

the arc of life, in which it stands symbolically for the regenerative blood of menstruation.

summoning of rain by rituals, and the expression of thanks to those spirits which have delivered it, are central preoccupations of religious life.

All this significance, for good and for evil, is invested symbolically in the figure of the snake, whose bite may bring death and yet whose furious coilings carry a suggestion of the quickening impulse of life at creation's heart; whose slender shape suggests the arcing of the rainbow, with all the fertility contained in the gently dropping rain – and with all the latent destructiveness of downpour and sudden flash flood.

It is therefore scarcely surprising that the Rainbow Snake should be one of the oldest and most ubiquitous of all the Aboriginal ancestral figures. It can be seen represented on rocks and cave walls the length and breadth of the Australian continent; it is heard of in the mythology of just about every Aboriginal tribe; and – most important of all, perhaps – its "dreaming presence" is sensed in every waterhole and winding river, of all of which it is at once both creator and proprietary spirit. The Aborigine would never dream of taking water from a billabong without first ritually asking the Rainbow Snake's permission; no more than he would envisage taking the spirit's fish, animals or waterfowl without its authority either. Told by the Djauan people of Arnhem Land, the tale of the black rock-snake Kurrichalpongo is typical in its evocation of the Rainbow Snake's profound – and profoundly ambivalent – power.

Nagacork and Kurrichalpongo

Old man Nagacork, says the story, had searched vainly upriver and down for the special water-shooting fish which was so rare and so dear to his heart. What was wrong with more common fish? the other men asked him, scooping a rich bounty readily from the stream. Their day's hunting done while his was mired in frustration, they laughed and splashed in the shallows and mocked the earnest single-mindedness of his search.

In time Nagacork came to wonder whether they were not right: he had not seen so much as

a scale of the fish he desired – would no other kind really meet his need? Then just as he was despairing of ever finding the water-shooting fish, he saw a column of ants marching up the trunk of a tree. He climbed up to see what they had found, and there, in a hollow cleft, located the blackened bones of the fish he had sought so long and hard. His fellow tribesmen, it seemed, had killed and eaten it, then hidden its bones away from sight. Sadly he climbed down the tree and, seating himself among its roots, he sang a song to the black rock-snake Kurrichalpongo.

The serpent came to his summons, arcing down from the sky, a multi-colored bow in the heavens above his native northern mountains. Where it entered the ground it bored a hole in the bank of a billabong, releasing a torrent of water which inundated the entire area. Nagacork's impious neighbours were either swept away on the angry torrent or escaped by taking on other forms – those of flying birds, for example, or swimming turtles. Now Kurrichalpongo laid eggs which hatched into baby Rainbow Snakes: in every direction they dispersed, their twisting, coiling forms scraping out rivers and billabongs as they went, while the much bigger Kurrichalpongo carved out what is now the Wilton River.

When the black rock-snake reached Luralingi, on the Hodgson River, he reared high into the air, eyes flashing and tongue flickering. The sky grew black and menacing; a great bolt of lightning cleft the sky and the heavens thundered. The mountains trembled at the terrible sound and a rushing wind broke off tree trunks like twigs; rain fell in torrents and the rising water swept violently downriver in a mighty wave, carrying off everything that lay in its path. The Wallipooroo, the Mara, the Yookul, the Karkaringi: all these tribes, and many more, were destroyed en masse, leaving their lands for the sons of Nagacork, the Djauan. Ever mindful of these violent origins, the Djauan would always treat the Rainbow Snake's power with the utmost respect, seeking its permission before drawing its water or wading into its realm in search of fish or turtles.

Ngalyod, as the Rainbow Snake is called in western Arnhem Land, is depicted here with two horns and a crocodile tail. One local story describes Ngalyod eating an orphan who had attracted its attention by crying. Another tells of three birds, one a peewee, that the snake ate. They pecked a hole from which to escape from its belly, emerging as humans and killing their captor as they did so.

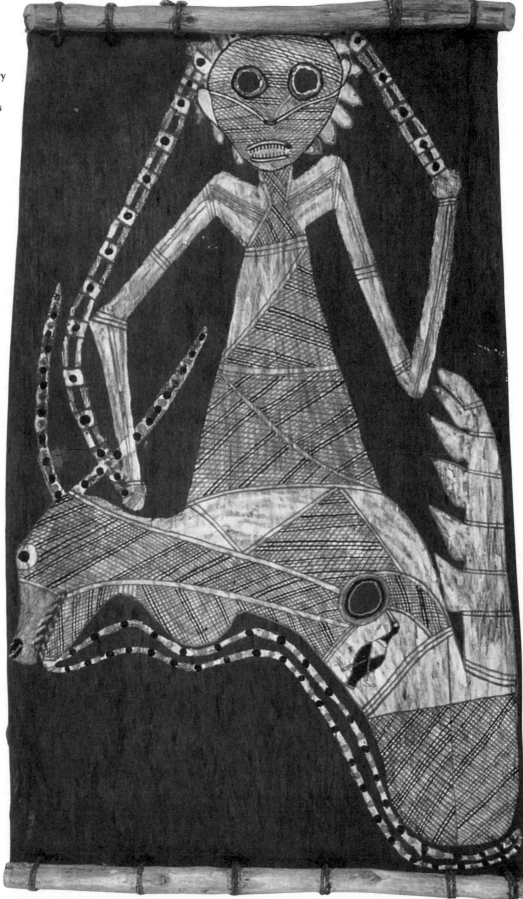

653

Spirit of the Ancestral Sisters

The phallic power of the Rainbow Snake met an opposing feminine force in one of the great founding myths of Aboriginal culture, society and life. The story of the Wawilak sisters emphasized the complementary nature of male and female.

One day during the deepest Dreamtime, two sisters walked side by side together out of the rolling ocean breakers and stepped, dripping wet, onto the Arnhem Land shore at what is now Trial Bay. The older sister was carrying a small baby slung in a little paperbark cradle; the younger was evidently well advanced in a pregnancy of her own. Each was armed with a long spear, and as they struck north into the interior it became abundantly clear that these were no mere ornaments but tools for active – and skilful – use. The sisters killed bandicoots, possums and monitors for their food, supplementing this meat with herbs and fruit which they gathered: they named all the different plants and animals as they made their

Carved representations of the two Wawilak, or Wagilag, sisters. The basic elements of this major ancestral story exist in different Aboriginal cultures with just the names and small details changed.

leisurely way inland, conferring meaning and form on what till then had been an empty waste.

Suddenly one day the younger sister felt the first contractions which signalled that her time was approaching. Her sister prepared her a bed beside the Mirarrmina waterhole. She set up camp, started a fire and went to fetch food for her labouring sister, but every time she killed an animal and tried to cook it, it simply leaped up from the flames and jumped into the pool.

What the women did not realize was that Yulunggur, the Rainbow Snake, lay slumbering beneath the surface of the water. He – for his power was masculine – was the billabong's resident spirit and the owner of all the district's game; no one else had any business, it seemed, taking what belonged to him. Still oblivious, however, to what was going on just a few feet away on the bank beside him, the serpent dozed on unheeding – until the moment when the older sister pursued a fleeing creature to the water's edge. She was menstruating at that time, as it happened, and as she stepped into the shallows, a drop of blood fell into the water and roused the angry serpent from his sleep. He came surging up from the dark depths, the resulting tidal wave flooding the earth; he towered up on his tail and struck furiously at the sky. Then he bore down angrily on the two women who had so violated his privacy. They danced and chanted in the hope of calming his rage, but their efforts were to no avail. Yulunggur spread his jaws wide and swallowed both the sisters and their children; at last, he hoped, he might be left in peace to continue with his sleep. It was not to be, however; awoken themselves by all this turmoil the other snakes started quizzing him about what had been going on. Yulunggur lied, telling his serpent neighbours that he had simply caught and eaten a kangaroo, but not one of them would believe the tale he told. He was finally forced to confess that he had eaten the two women and their children. No sooner had he finished speaking than the monsoon wind blew in: it battered him with its gusting force and with sheets of driving rain. Yulunggur was forced to bow down low before its merciless onslaught; in his agonized thrashings he carved out a river valley, then with a great roar he vomited up the sisters and their children. They fell into a nest of ants, whose angry biting brought them quickly back to life. Yulunggur, meanwhile, crawled ignominiously away, back down to his billabong lair.

The Wawilak, or Wagilag, sisters are, scholars have suggested, the daughters of the "Old Woman", Kunapipi. As original Earth Mother, this figure represented a rival, feminine claimant to the creative power of the archetypally male Rainbow Snake. In some traditions she seems to have been revered as a pre-eminent ancestor, taking the form either of an old woman or her own daughter, a nubile girl. Mostly, however, the woman and the Rainbow Snake are honoured as a duality, as representatives of those eternal masculine and femi-nine principles from whose conjunction all life and creativity must spring. The myth of the Wawilak sisters is typical of this tradition, affirming as it does the profound complementarity of the female and the male. In devouring the old woman's offspring the snake takes to himself their great strength and wisdom: from that time forth men, and not women, will be the custodians of tribal learning and law. Yet the victory, it is clear, is by no means entirely with Yulunggur: he can neither match the women's fertility nor withstand the life-giving abundance of the monsoon rain. Vomited forth from the belly of the serpent, the women are restored to life, and their spirit lives on side by side with his. But where the snake's form can be seen as signifying the male organ, the old woman and her child-bearing daughters represent the productive womb. Both masculine and feminine principles are essential to the continuation of human life: there is a place for both serpent and sisters in the Aboriginal mythic scheme.

This bark painting interpretation of the Wawilak tale, *The Wagilag Sisters Story* by Paddy Dhathangu, shows the richness of plants and animals surrounding the Rainbow Snake, which is coiled to represent the Mirarrmina waterhole.

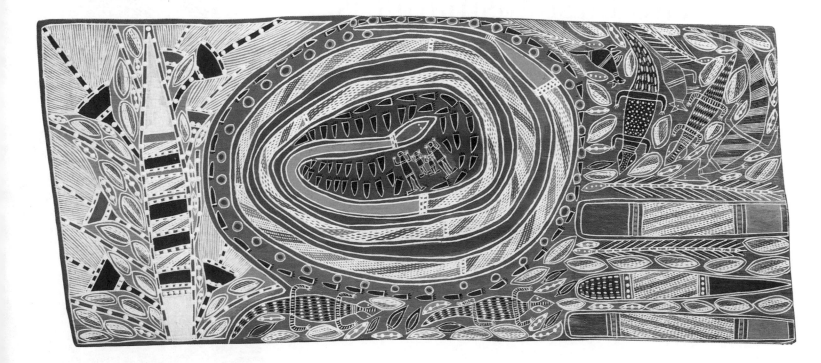

The Making of Humankind

From the Arrente of central Australia comes a creation myth in which humanity is shaped from clay. It differs, however, from Western myths where life is formed from the inert earth. The point is that life inheres in the soil; the "creator" merely releases what is already there.

The making of men and women has no part in most Aboriginal traditions; while creation myths loom large, it is with the landscape and the people's spiritual origins that they are mainly concerned. Snakes, dingoes, monitors, kangaroos – the list of animal ancestors is well-nigh endless, but little is said about how men and women first came to take on their present physical form. This lack of curiosity appears strange to those whose cultural background causes them to place humankind instinctively at the centre of the natural world. But so close were the Aborigines to nature that they were able to see themselves as just another part of the landscape.

Shaping Humankind

From high up among the stars the Numbakulla brothers looked down, divine beings of the utmost benevolence and power. Their heavenly perch commanded a sweeping view of the entire Earth, and they watched its infinite emptiness night and day. No human figure moved, for men and women had yet to be formed. But as they scanned and re-scanned the Earth's vast surface to see what secrets it might yet yield, they were suddenly seized by the sense of certain figures taking form. Far below, by a silent saltlake, scoured by a restless wind, a giant boulder cast its shadow across the clammy clay. The brothers' watching gaze was drawn to

The First Tasmanians

Long ago, the two brightest stars in the firmament were Moinee and Dromerdeener, rivals for supreme mastery of the sky, who resolved to fight it out after epochs of tension and bickering.

Their warcries set the heavens ringing. The other stars looked on helplessly until the duel was over: Moinee was defeated and cast out of the heavenly realm. Dromerdeener stormed across the sky on his victory trail as his defeated rival fell forlornly to Earth. He came to rest off the southern Tasmanian coast, and can still be seen, a large boulder in the sea at Sandy Bay.

Before he died, however, Moinee bestowed a great gift on his earthly home, creating the first Tasmanians to occupy its empty spaces. In his haste, however, he gave them tails like kangaroos – worse still, he neglected to give them jointed knees. They had to spend their whole lives standing up, quite unable to lie or hunker down: soon they cried to the heavens

the spot: they looked more closely, at once astonished and appalled. For there in the sticky mud indeterminate half-outlines could be seen; the shapes were so unformed, it was scarcely surprising they had missed them so many times before. Prisoners of the earth, they simply lay there, unmoving, in the mud. Their stumpy limbs were too short and indefinite for them even to swivel on the spot where they lay, far less to venture out into the world. Lacking all power of movement, they were without physical senses too, with no eyes to see, no ears to hear and no mouths to speak. They could have no social contact with one another, no individual will: none of the things, indeed, which we associate with human life.

From their eyrie in the stars, the brothers saw the suffering of these embryonic half-beings and felt compassion. Descending from the heavens, each clutching a stone knife, they landed where these unhappy creatures lay and promptly set about cutting them free from their muddy bonds. First they shaped their nebulousness into definition, marking out each with a distinct torso and head, the fundamental division of the human body. Then they hacked great Vs to the lower section and to the sides, so that arms and legs might swing loose from the rest. At the end of each extremity they next nicked out little fingers and toes: recognizably human now, the clay beings could stand upright on their own. As yet, however, they could neither hear nor talk, smell nor see: they were still a long way from what we would consider human. The brothers soon saw to that, though, cutting out eyes and mouths with their sharp blades before punching ears and nostrils with their fingers. Finally they fashioned the organs which marked the beings out not merely as people but as male and female: from now on they would be able to reproduce themselves. And so indeed they did, multiplying and spreading out to fill up the land for many days' walking around: the men and women of the Arrente tribe.

to take pity on their plight. Dromerdeener finally heard their call: ruthless though he was, he was moved by what he saw. Descending from heaven, he chopped off their tails and rubbed healing grease upon the wounds. Then to the middle of each leg he added a hinge-like knee: the people were now free to squat or lie down as they wanted.

The Unity of People and Nature

The Aborigines' outlook on the world saw everything as inter-related and fluid, and they expressed their closeness to nature by associating themselves with particular aspects of it. Their use of life-forms as patron spirits, known as totemism, meant they traced their ancestry in the natural things about them: in animals, birds and insects – even the wind.

Many inland Aborigines recall the arrival of their ancestors from overseas – the Djanggawul and his sisters, for example, or the Wawilak women who emerged from the waves – but on Groote Eylandt in the windswept waters of the Gulf of Carpentaria, the people look out daily on the sea from which their forbears first stepped. They paddle their canoes to trade and to fish on the very waters from which their ancestors emerged. The islanders cannot help feeling conflicting pulls, to the continent and to the sea from which they came. Marked out by its distinctly Asiatic monsoon climate, the gulf has the feel of a threshold – whose door remains very much ajar. This ambivalence is only underlined, meanwhile, by the gulf's curious meteorological character and the two opposing winds – Bara and Mamariga – whose alternation measures out the northern year.

The Children of the Wind

Every November when Bara begins to stir, the dry air quickens and grows heavy with moisture. Grey clouds dull the tropic sunshine; the atmosphere seems sluggish, yet tense with expectation. The suspense is not long, for the showers themselves follow quickly: soon these northern regions are being battered by rainstorm after rainstorm. Much as it has needed this inundation, nature seems to buckle before its onslaught: the grass is flattened by its force, and trees bow down as if in surrender. Between each fresh dousing, however, the sun shines down on an explosion of fertility as fresh shoots thrust upwards and new buds burgeon on the dripping trees. Water is everywhere and the landscape glints and twinkles like a tilted mirror.

Through December and January the wind blows on, and nature is extravagant in her bounty. Herbs and cereals grow apace, while the trees offer fruit; amid such plenty, the animals and people find life easy and abundant. By February, however, Bara is already faltering, and in April it is usurped by its rival, Mamariga, blowing from the southeast. An altogether different wind, nature seems to crumple before its hot unforgiving blast as on through the dry days of May, June and July it scours away every trace of fresh green from the scene, leaving a landscape of brittle aridity.

Groote Eylandt's Aborigines see it as a war-like invasion. Their tradition holds that Mamariga has seized Bara and imprisoned it in a giant hollow tree on a headland above the sea. Every year, therefore, as November nears, they assemble before the place of captivity, sing sacred incantations and exhortations, and use their axes to strike deep cuts in the bark. Through these apertures, they believe, the wet wind may once more be released into a welcoming world. They encourage it with rites and offerings, bidding it busy itself on their behalf about restoring the rain. So indeed it inevitably turns out: the damp wind blows and the stormclouds gather; within days the first downpour has come to water the gasping earth. Once more all nature bursts forth in fecundity, all living things have the chance to regenerate – until April, when Mamariga will return to abduct its enemy again.

Tribal Moieties

Some Aboriginal peoples honour totem animals such as reptiles (see pages 662–663), while others invest physical features of the landscape with

sacred energy, but for the people of Groote Eylandt no force could be more powerful than these two rival winds. The opposition of Bara and Mamariga rules all the rhythms of island life, and the cycle of their alternation seems fundamental to the world-view of the people who live there. It is only natural, therefore, that the winds should have come to form the nuclei for their tribal moieties, the complementary halves into which every community is divided and within which men and women must never marry.

The winds which do so much to shape island life are even believed to bring the inhabitants' children, those born into each moiety being blown in on their respective winds. Sailing as spirits down the gusting airways, they put down in the long grass and lurk there until a likely looking woman chances along. Quickly slipping into her body, they settle down in comfort, ready to sit out the long months before their birth in human form. Frank and affirmative as it is about men and women's sexual functions, Aboriginal tradition has tended not to associate sex with reproduction of children. Sexual stimulation from the male may encourage the child growing in the womb, but is not its cause. Rather, human spirits floating free in the air around are "dreamed" into the womb by the mother-to-be, influenced in her turn by watching ancestors.

The Birth of the Djan' Kawu Children at Yalangbara, painted by Wangjuk Marika on bark, is a version of the Djanggawul story whose subject is moieties. The brother stands at the top with his digging-sticks, while below the two sisters give birth to the clans. In the centre this event is shown schematically and at the bottom it is rendered symbolically.

Wonders of the Heavens

Complementing those from the land and the sea, countless more Aboriginal ancestor spirits gaze down from the starry sky. A wondrous show, the Australian heavens shimmer with a lively display of glinting and twinkling from old friends familiar from many tales.

The lone hunter peered into the Outback night trying to orientate himself: he might be anywhere. Far above, in the great vault of the heavens, a throng of starry spirits formed a mass of blazing brilliance. Vast constellations and separate points of light alike, they winked down companionably, reminding him that he need never be alone.

The Southern Cross

At the heart of the night sky are the four stars of the Southern Cross. One tradition among a great many explains that the component stars are the daughters of Mululu, a tribal chief. Fearful as his death approached that he was leaving his girls with no brother to protect them, he asked them to come and join him in the sky. They should go and see a certain medicine-man, he said – they would know him by his long, thick beard – and he would help them make the ascent. Mululu duly died, and his loving daughters set out to honour his instructions. After many days searching they found the man, whose luxuriant beard seemed to go on for ever. He plaited it into a rope, and up it they climbed. Fear gripped the girls, but they kept on going all the way to the sky, where they were reunited with Mululu. Forming a joyous family group, the sisters became the four pointers of the Southern Cross, while Mululu watches over them as the star astronomers call Alpha Centauri.

Spirit of the Moon

Some say the moon is the spirit of Mityan, a native cat who fell in love with and fought for the most beautiful of the wives of Unurginite, of the constellation Canis Major. Driven off in defeat, he has

The Aborigines have a rich astral mythology. The stars and constellations are said to be ancestors who have ascended into the sky and are sitting around their campfires. Many tales associate the moon with the bringing of death into the world.

roamed the skies forlornly ever since, hoping that he may one day be reunited with his lost love.

Another story tells how the moon-man Alinda fell out with the parrot-fish-man Dirima, the two finally fighting so violently that each died of their wounds. Although Alinda ascended into the heavens and Dirima dived into the sea, the two continued with their bickering. Implacable in his hostility, the moon-man ruled that once the parrot-fish died, it might never return to life. All other living things were included in this curse – even Alinda himself, though he managed to contrive a partial reprieve. He only "dies" temporarily before resuming his life-cycle, with the old full moon falling into the sea to become the round nautilus shell.

The Boomerang and the Sun

From the Aborigine people of the Flinders Range of southern Australia comes the story of how the distinction first arose between night and day – for in the world's infancy, it seems, all was light and sunshine, with no intervening darkness.

The trouble started one Dreamtime day when the goanna lizard and the gecko set out to visit neighbours. On arrival, however, they found that their friends had all been massacred: with one voice they vowed vengeance upon those responsible. It had, it soon transpired, been the sun-woman and her dingo dogs who had attacked and killed the defenceless community: she was a formidable foe, but the goanna and the gecko were quite undaunted. As the sun-woman stormed and shouted her defiance, the lizard drew his boomerang and hurled it – and dashed the sun clean out of the sky. It plummeted over the western horizon, plunging the world into total darkness – and now the lizard and the gecko really were alarmed. What would become of them without the sun-woman and her warming, illuminating rays? They must do everything they could to restore her to the heavens. The goanna took another boomerang and hurled it westwards with all his might to where he had seen his target disappearing. It fell ineffectually to ground so he threw two others to the south and north, but they too drifted back without hitting anything. In despair, the

goanna took his last boomerang and launched it into the eastern sky – the opposite direction from that in which he had seen the sun-woman sinking. To his astonishment it returned, driving before it the sun's burning sphere, which tracked westwards across the sky before disappearing. From that day on

the sun maintained this course, rising in the east and setting in the west, lighting up the day for work and hunting and casting the night into shade for sleeping. All agreed this was an ideal arrangement, and the Aborigines of the Flinders have felt a debt of gratitude to the goanna and the gecko ever since.

THE BATTLE OF ULURU

The immense, mountain-sized rock called Uluru, some 1,300 feet in height and with an enormously broad base, occupies a prominent place in the central Australian landscape. Visible from far away, Uluru, or Ayers Rock, dominates the surrounding territory and is the most sacred site of many Aboriginal peoples. At this holy place, potent crossing point of countless dreaming tracks and song lines, legends say that two snake peoples once fought for supremacy during the Dreamtime and the rock itself still bears witness to their epic struggle.

Constantly changing in the light, magical Uluru seems to heave with kaleidoscopic life. It is not hard to imagine it as the hub of a continent-wide network of dreaming tracks and comes as no surprise to learn that it is full of *djang*; nor, come to that, is it difficult to visualize the place as it mythically started – a mass of serpents fighting in the sand.

The Kuniya, or rock-python people, once lived in the desert alongside the Woma, their serpent friends and allies. The Kuniya, however, were restless and questing souls, ever anxious to venture further afield. Their forays took them in the direction of Uluru, although it did not then exist as we know it today, being just another part of the desert's open plain. The Kuniya found it fruitful and liked it so much that they decided to build a new life there. Holding a farewell feast with the Woma, they vowed their enduring loyalty and friendship before striking off for their new home. There they lived contentedly, enjoying the bounty of this rich land – but their idyll was not destined to last long. One day a tribe of venomous Liru –

the deadly carpet-snake – suddenly swept down on the Kuniya camp. A desperate battle began which raged for many hours, and during the seismic upheavals of the conflict, the great rock was born. Marks on its surfaces are said to have been left by weapons or fallen combatants.

Some time after, the Woma decided to pay their old friends a visit. Yet drawing near, and seeing the fate that had befallen their former neighbours, they were quite overcome with grief: they took on snake form, never to return as men.

Born in massacre and shaped in scars, Uluru's appearance marked the end of the creative Dreamtime. At this epoch-making moment the world's creation ceased: from then on the world would be as it was, for better or worse.

Right: Uluru is in the custodianship of the Arrente people. This guide is relating the story of the battle between the Liru and Kuniya, his marks in the sand reminiscent of snake tracks.

Left and above: When the sun starts sinking in the sky the rock transforms as the light works on its hues and coloration, giving the observer an inkling of why this is the most sacred site in the Aborigine's world. The aerial view (above) reveals the immensity of Uluru's base. Visible on the horizon is Katatjuta, a sacred place for female Aborigines that is forbidden to men.

Rangi and Papa, Creators Supreme

In New Zealand, the Maori peoples evolved the concept of two supreme creator beings from whom sprang an orderly pantheon of gods, each with his or her own sphere of responsibility – the sea, the weather, the trees, the fish, the animals and every other aspect of life. The gods also gave birth to humans and ordered the conditions in which they lived.

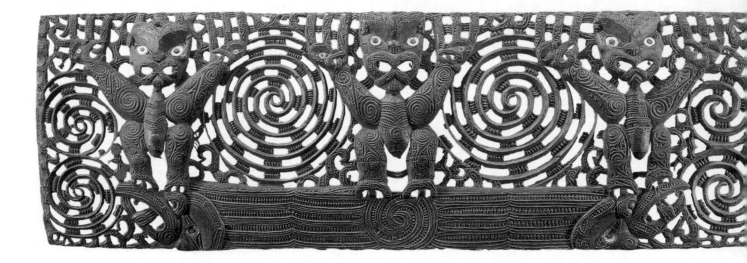

A *pare* or door lintel for a meeting house from the Bay of Plenty, *c.*1840. The three male figures represent Tane and two of his brother gods pushing apart their primal parents, Rangi and Papa.

According to Maori myth, life began with a perfect and absolute void. It was not mere darkness – in itself a source of horror – but something worse, a state of utter emptiness devoid of light, feeling and form. The term used to describe it was *kore*, an expression that later worked its way into the Maori calendar, being used to mark the three nights in each lunar month during which it was supposed to be impossible to obtain food from either land or sea.

Into this state of nothingness emerged two beings, Rangi the sky god and Papa the Earth goddess. They owed their existence to a shadowy parent deity called Io, a name that would later delight Christian missionaries who linked it to Jehovah. Clasped together like a shell, Rangi and Papa produced six children, Tane god of forests, Tangaroa god of the sea, Tu god of war, Rongo god of cultivated plants, Haumia god of wild plants and Tawhiri god of the elements. The space between Rangi and Papa was hot and fecund, giving birth

to trees, ferns, lizards and shellfish. But it was also dark and cramped. Unable to stand, the gods crawled around blindly like lizards, or simply lay on their sides, struggling for breath.

Then a miraculous thing happened. Papa raised her arm and the children caught a brief glimpse of daylight. Immediately they wanted more. Tane suggested they separate their parents, a move which was greeted enthusiastically by all except Tawhiri, who was very attached to his father the sky. But they soon found that speech was easier than action. One by one they struggled to prise the Earth and sky apart. Their efforts were to no avail until Tu had the idea of cutting through Rangi's arms which were clasped tight around Papa. This did the trick and by standing on his head and bracing his feet against the sky Tane was

664

able to split his parents' embrace. With the help of his brothers, Tane used wooden poles to support Rangi in his new position. Forever afterwards Rangi and Papa were immutably divided, expressing their grief with tears that fell as rain from the sky and mists that rose at dawn from the Earth.

Tu's violence not only allowed the Earth and sky to be separated but also gave the world the gift of blood. In many Polynesian myths, blood was an essential part of creation, providing the red hues that islanders associated with kingship and virility. In Tahiti the blood was supplied by Tangaroa, a lesser god in the Maori pantheon who had been elevated there to the status of creator. In Maori stories the blood came from the amputation of Rangi's arms. Falling to the ground, it colored the earth red, creating the ochre with which people and religious objects were daubed.

Tane's prowess made him one of the predominant gods in the pantheon. He was credited with creating light, in the shape of the sun and the moon, and with clothing his father with stars to hide his dark nakedness. In some legends he was also hailed as the first planter of trees, an experiment that was not successful initially. Tane modelled his forestry along human lines, with the trees' legs, or branches, being embedded in the ground while their roots waved in the air like hair. Then, realizing that something was wrong, he reversed them to emulate his own stance when he had divided the Earth and sky. The trees' hair took root and soon they were providing food for birds, animals and humans.

Tane's success at separating his parents led to tempestuous sibling rivalry. A jealous Tawhiri blew down Tane's forests, causing the fish that had previously lived on dry land to flee to the ocean. This in turn caused an everlasting feud between Tane and Tangaroa. Tane supplied the trees with which men made canoes to tame the ocean. In retaliation, Tangaroa launched tidal waves that swept away the forests. It was a cycle of revenge that neatly explained the main elements of Polynesian existence.

Tane was promiscuous, mating with a variety of beings to produce animals, stones and grass. Then, on Rangi's advice, he sculpted a human woman and mated with her. Hine-titama, or Dawn Maiden, was born and Tane slept with her too. When Hine discovered who her father was she was horrified. She fled to the underworld, and vowed to drag all Tane's children down after her. Undeterred, Tane next produced the ancestors of all humankind. But Tane's children could never be immortal like their father. Inexorably they were pulled to their graves by his vengeful daughter.

Tane Mahutia is New Zealand's largest kauri tree, named after Tane, god of the forests. A tall, straight hardwood, it forms a living link between Earth and sky.

The Quarrelsome Elements

After the beginning came the gods, often seen as different personifications of an overall divine force. They were the stars, the winds, the seas and all other natural forces that were beyond human reckoning. Initially, however, they were quarrelsome and it took a series of major conflicts before the Polynesian universe settled into an orderly rhythm.

In New Zealand (Aotearoa), and some other parts of the region, these strife myths told of Tane, the embodiment of light and wisdom, who sought to bring the gift of knowledge to humans. Set against him was Whiro, the god of darkness and evil.

Knowledge was contained within three baskets belonging to Io. In one basket was the knowledge of peace and love, in another the knowledge of prayers and religious ritual, and in the third was the knowledge of survival and war. Io invited Tane to deliver the baskets to the World of Light. In accordance with Io's wishes, Tane scattered their contents across Polynesia, erecting temples to act as repositories for the sacred gift. Jealous that Tane

had been chosen for the task, Whiro did his best to stop him. He sent hordes of centipedes, spiders, moths and ants to attack Tane. The two sides met in a mighty battle from which Tane emerged victorious. But although Whiro's forces were defeated they could not be crushed, and their descendants remained on Earth to plague humankind. Whiro, similarly, could not be killed. He was driven to the underworld, from where he dispensed a destructive legacy of sickness, evil thoughts and death.

The moral of every conflict lay in its aftermath. Against the baleful influence of Whiro could be set Tane's gift of knowledge and the institution of temples that gave men contact with the gods.

On the archipelago of Tuamotu the main protagonists were thought to be Tane and Atea, two gods who inhabited different layers of heaven. As the two battled for supremacy, Tane saw that he was losing and slipped through the layers to seek temporary refuge on Earth.

Tane enjoyed his time among humans and even acquired a taste for cooked food. This was an important change: Polynesians believed that the gods derived sustenance from raw materials and that cooked, spiritless food was anathema.

Tiring of his exile, Tane made his way back to heaven. To his horror he found that most of his family had either been killed by Atea or had fled. All that remained were his father and a number of ancient ancestors. Worse still, heaven did not contain the food to which he had grown accustomed.

Tane was still determined to overcome Atea so he visited the thunder god, Fatutiri, and obtained the gift of lightning. His father warned him not to use it at once; better, he counselled, to wait until Atea was old and weak. In due course, when his father's hair had become silver, Tane,

backed by a band of heavenly allies, met Atea in a duel to determine who was the strongest. The test was to be the power of making fire. Atea rubbed sticks together and produced a flame but Tane blew it out. They changed places and this time Atea tried to blow out Tane's flame. But thanks to Tane's gift of lightning the fire refused to be extinguished. In fact, ironically, the more Atea blew on it the stronger it became.

While the contest was underway one of Tane's followers became jealous of his power and stole a light with which he set fire to the heavens themselves. Tane flew upwards to extinguish it, then returned to deliver the coup de grace to Atea, shooting out a lightning bolt that struck him dead. Then, in recognition of his rival's divinity, Tane set Atea's spirit free on a canoe to float across the southern seas. It came to rest on Tuamotu, where it gave rise to a long line of chiefs.

Otago, in South Island, is home to the tallest mountains in Aotearoa ("Land of the Long White Cloud"), and a place where the elemental powers of nature can be appreciated fully.

First Man Tiki

In some Maori myths humankind was brought into the world by Tane. In others, however, it was Tu, the god of war, who created Tiki, the first man. Tiki's children married both gods and mortals, begetting a chain of descent that led to the royal lineages of Aotearoa (New Zealand).

Tu provided the means whereby humans could survive. He also devised a way in which they could multiply. Seeing how Tane had created a woman from sand, Tu moulded a similar model and breathed life into it. But there were two crucial difference between his and Tane's creation: Tu's model was of a man, not a woman; and it was created not from sand but from powerful red ochre. The result was Tiki, who epitomized procreative power and male sexuality. At the same time Tiki was a trickster, combining various beneficial qualities with an irresistible urge to throw society into disarray.

Tiki himself later made a model of a woman, just as the god Tane had done, and produced a daughter, Tiaki, the first in a line of humans. The concept of Tiki was widespread throughout Polynesia, carrying connotations of power and virility, as well as providing the necessary genealogical link between human rulers and their divine ancestors. The manner in which Tiki and his wife were moulded from earth also reflected the way in which many Polynesians created their own environment. On their travels they often had to ferry cargoes of earth from one island to another to enrich the thin soil. Thus, in reality as in myth, life was moulded out of soil.

Tiki, creator of all children, was the link between humankind and the divine ancestors; carved human figures were called *tiki*. This 19th-century detail from a meeting house's central post represents an ancestor of the tribe that owned the house.

As the first man, Tiki's life bore striking resemblances to that of Tane, the predominant god. His wife was called Hina-one, or Earth Maiden, and she, like Tane's daughter Hine-titama, fled to the underworld after a quarrel with Tiki. Just as Tane slept with his own daughter so, too, did Tiki, causing her to seek refuge with her mother below. So close was the connection that the tales of Tiki and Tane occasionally mingled, with Tiki being portrayed as the son of Tane, or as the husband of Tane's granddaughter.

Unlike Tane, however, Tiki was viewed as a somewhat scurrilous trickster. His voracious sexual appetite was reflected in the name borne by the Maoris' famous *hei-tiki* fertility symbols. In this regard, his behaviour went well beyond all the bounds of decency or social convention. On one occasion he supposedly persuaded his own daughter Tiaki to sleep with him by pretending to be a different person who happened by chance to look like her father. The ruse worked horribly well, earning for Tiki the epithet of *kaikaia*, a title that implied both incest and cannibalism.

Tiki, it was said, could assume two faces. One was so handsome that all women fell in love with him. The other was so disgusting that women wanted to kill him on sight. Rumour had it that he kept his ugly features hidden inside his body, wearing them when the mood came upon him. He was also seemingly indestructible. Once, when Tiki put on his ugly face, the people caught him. They tried to pull out his eyes but without success. The same thing happened when they tried to remove his teeth. They tied his

A green jade *hei-tiki*, c.1840. Female or sexless figures, such pendants were often associated with fertility and childbirth. Many were also sacred clan heirlooms passed down the generations, embodying the *mana* and prestige of the family's links to the gods.

tongue in a knot but the knot untied itself. They cut off his ears, feet, arms and penis but Tiki simply stuck them back on. Finally they sliced him open and unravelled his intestines across the ground. At this indignity Tiki fled in tears and hid under the sand until his pride was restored.

This tale was repeated in many forms. Sometimes narrative tension was heightened by Tiki changing in mid-torture to his beautiful form and then reverting to ugliness once he had been released. Typically, he sought refuge in the sand after surviving prolonged and unsuccessful attempts to destroy him.

In one version his end came while he was recovering in the sand. As he was lying there, with just his eyes showing, an eel seized his heel. He called to his wife to help him but she was reluctant. "I am tired of sleeping with a demon," she said. Nevertheless, she took his head and began a tug-of-war with the eel who was pulling on Tiki's foot. The strain grew greater and greater and then, in mid-contest, Tiki suddenly disappeared.

Perhaps as punishment for his misdemeanours, Tiki was denied the gift of immortality. But he lived on in artistic form, his name being given to the images that Maoris carved from wood and greenstone to represent their ancestors. In this guise he usually appeared with bird-like features – three-taloned hands, ear tufts, slanting eyes and a beaked face – that brought to mind an owl. The likeness was no coincidence, for the owl was associated with Rua, a hero who had won the secret of carving from the gods. Fittingly, the first man was linked to the origins of his portrayal.

A Dynasty of Nobles

To fill the ancestral gap between themselves and Tiki, the Maoris invented a host of human heroes. One of them was Rua, whose gift of carving made canoe-building possible; another was Mataora, who learned the art of distinctive Maori *moko* tattooing from the gods. But the best known heroes were Tawhaki and Rata, whose exploits gave rise to a noble dynasty.

The Tawhaki Cycle comprised the saga of a single family and was popular not only in New Zealand but in most of Polynesia's outlying islands. Passing through the generations, it told of humiliation and revenge, of battles with gods and man, and of a final triumphant sea voyage to establish a community in a new land. Outwardly a tale of heroism, it reflected with startling accuracy the last phase of Polynesian migration in which families dispersed from the central islands to avoid internecine warfare and overcrowding.

The main hero was Tawhaki, a man whose fair hair, golden-red skin and irresistible sex appeal immediately identified him with divinity. He did, in fact, have divine blood being the grandson of Whatiri, a thunder-goddess from whom he inherited the ability to cast lightning bolts from his armpits. On the human side, Tawhaki's family tree was less illustrious. His grandfather, Kai-tangata, was a cannibal who met his end when a latrine collapsed on his head during a visit to the underworld. His father, Hema, meanwhile was so filthy as a child that Whatiri, Hema's mother, deserted her family in disgust. Later, Hema quarrelled with the gods and was imprisoned in an underworld cesspit.

Tawhaki and his brother Karihi determined to rescue Hema. Kahiri, however, was a poor choice of companion. Whereas Tawhaki excelled at everything to such an extent that he was cordially disliked by his fellows, Kahiri was an over-eager incompetent. It was only through Tawhaki's skill and his knowledge of the correct spells needed to

In some stories Tawhaki casts his enemies into the ocean to become sealife. This semi-translucent fish amulet is from Ruapuke Island.

visit the underworld that the two of them survived the trip and successfully rescued their father.

Tawhaki's downfall came when jealous men stripped his golden skin as he slept and threw it into the sea to be devoured by fishes. Now ordinary looking, he no longer attracted women. Eventually he used his divine connections to regain his skin – only one portion was unobtainable, that which covered the soles of his feet – and once more he was an object of desire. But he was full of bitterness at his earlier rejection, and left his homeland to seek a better place.

The epic continued with Rata, Tawhaki's grandson. Like Tawhaki, Rata sought to avenge his father, who had been devoured by a bird-god named Matuku-takotako. At the same time he sought to rescue his mother who had been stolen by Matuku and planted head-down with her feet in the air to act as a food stand for the gods. Unlike Tawhaki, Rata had no divine powers. Although brave and resourceful he was untutored in magic spells. His main skill lay in the construction of war canoes. Fortunately, the underworld in which his mother was captive had risen to the surface and taken the shape of an island. Sailing towards it with a crew of select warriors, Rata battled his way past sea demons and succeeded in defeating the gods who held his mother captive. He also managed to retrieve his father's head from the gullet of Matuku. Rata later married the daughter of a god and their union produced a line from which all later rulers were descended.

670

Hina, the Eel and the Coconut

Hina (translating simply as "young woman") was seen as the divinity of women and women's work. She appeared in different guises throughout Polynesian mythology. In a culture where the composition of love poems and the initiation of courtship were the exclusive province of women, some of Hina's tales were blatantly sexual and others practical.

Hina's favourite bathing spot was a deep, dark sea pool that was full of eels. Normally they fled at her approach, but one eel was larger and more daring than the rest. As Hina relaxed in the water the eel wound itself around her legs. Hina did not discourage it. In fact she let it approach her whenever she went into the pool.

One day, as she was gazing at the eel, it transformed into a handsome young man called Tuna. They became lovers. But Tuna always changed back to an eel after every visit so that nobody would suspect their liaison. Finally, Tuna brought the affair to a close. He announced that a great rain would come, causing a flood that would rise to the door of Hina's house. But she was not to be afraid, for Tuna would swim up to her home and lay his head on the threshold. She was then to cut off his head, bury it on some high ground and see what happened next.

Everything occurred as Tuna had predicted, and Hina duly cut off his head and buried it. The waters subsided and all was normal again. Where the head had been interred, however, two green shoots appeared. The shoots flourished and grew into

coconut trees that provided humankind with milk, flesh and oil, with leaves for baskets, with shells for bowls, with fibre for ropes and with trunks that could be made into house pillars and

canoes. Lest people forget their benefactor all they had to do was remove the husk of a ripened coconut: there they would find markings of the two small eyes and mouth of an eel.

Maui the Trickster Hero

One of the most popular figures in Polynesian mythology was the trickster hero Maui. Rebel, seducer and social iconoclast, Maui flaunted conventions, toppled hierarchies and broke taboos. He was seen as the defender of the weak and the protector of the underprivileged. Such was his fame that one of the Hawaiian islands was named after him.

Even in birth, Maui was different from others. Born prematurely, the result of a miscarriage, he was wrapped in a lock of his mother's hair and thrown into the sea. Many Polynesians believed that discarded embryos became mischievous spirits and Maui was no exception. Rescued by the sun god, this half-human demigod was reunited with his mother and almost immediately began to turn life on its head.

Giver and Creator

One of Maui's first feats was to slow down the passage of the sun by beating it with the jawbone of his dead grandmother so that it was forced to crawl across the sky, thus giving his mother more time in which to beat barkcloth. Some say he achieved this feat by catching the sun in a snare made from the hair of his sister, Hina-ika. Other versions told how he delayed the sun's progress so that humans might have more time for cooking.

Maui provided humans with resources and skills. His name comes from the word for the left, profane side of the body, rather than the sacred, right or *tapa* side. This is reflected in his unconventional behaviour. This oblique profile carving, made for the Rauru meeting house, shows Maui's most spectacular exploit, fishing up the land.

As the hero of the common man it was only natural that Maui should be associated with such everyday tasks as cooking and cloth-making. In the same vein, he was credited with bringing fire to the world. Descending to the underworld, he tricked the goddess Mahui-ike into discarding her burning fingernails, from which fire came. When she had only one fingernail left, she flung it to the ground in anger. Maui called for rain to extinguish the blaze, but the goddess preserved the sacred spark by throwing it onto a nearby stand of trees. She thereby taught Maui a great secret which he bore triumphantly back to humankind: wood could be used to make fire.

Other tales link Maui to features in the landscape – even the creation of land itself. In Tonga there is a great stone trilithon monument more than sixteen feet in height said to have been brought to the island by Maui. In New Zealand it was related that he made the islands surface on a fishing trip. Out on the ocean with his brothers, Maui fell asleep leaving his bait dangling in the water. When he awoke, he hauled up the line

Sentient Creatures

Alongside the gods and their semi-divine or human offspring, Polynesia embraced a body of intermediate spiritual beings. Not quite "fairies" in the European sense, they were usually fair-skinned creatures who lurked in forests or on hills and who interfered for good or evil in human affairs. They were also portrayed as malevolent ogres, enchanted goblins or evil fish.

The *patupaiarehe*, as Maoris called these sentient people, had fair, tattoo-free skin. It is possible they had their origin in tales of the indigenous populace displaced by Polynesian immigration who took refuge in less habitable zones. Either way, the *patupaiarehe* were considered non-human and were shunned as a treacherous and crafty influence – though their plaintive flutes exercised a magnetic effect on women and could result in disruptive inter-marriages.

In parts of Polynesia their fair skin was thought to resemble the pallor of death and they were seen as the lingering spirits of those who had been unable or unwilling to find a final resting place. These spirits could be encountered anywhere – usually at night – but were most often found in remote parts of the forest where they would surprise root-gatherers with a menacing whisper: "You rejoice today, but my turn will come tomorrow."

Spirits were normally viewed as being small to medium sized. Sometimes, though, they assumed the form of mighty humans who could stride from island to island, or of gigantic birds and fish who menaced men and women as they went about their everyday activities.

and found he had caught something so monstrous that it was more the size of an island than a fish. He and his brothers grappled with it but it broke free and fell back into the sea. Maui threw out his hook again – on some islands the hook was said to be the same jawbone with which he had cudgelled the sun – but once more he was unable to control the mighty fish. On his third try he was successful and he set its body in the water where it became New Zealand's North Island. Maui's canoe became the top of the island's highest mountain, Hikurangi, and his hook was immortalized as a crescent-shaped bay called Hawke Bay. As for the fish, its skin began to wither and crinkle in the sun, giving rise to the hilly folds that characterize North Island.

Forever Mortal

Maui was a mythological huckster – his title, Maui of 1,000 Tricks, carried more than a whiff of showmanship – and as such, not everything he did turned out well. Once, he managed to turn his brother-in-law into the first dog. Another time, he tried to achieve immortality by having sex with the goddess of death. The result was disastrous.

It was said that a man approaching death was "creeping into the womb of Sleeping Mother Death", meaning returning to the dark womb of the earth. While wandering through the underworld with his friends, Maui chanced upon the sleeping figure of Hine-nui-te-Po, the giant goddess of death. Maui was delighted, for his mother had told him that should he crawl through Hine's womb and emerge through her mouth then the goddess would die and death would no longer exist. Cautioning silence, Maui stripped off and climbed bodily inside Hine. But halfway through the act he became stuck, a sight that caused his friends much hilarity. In fact, one of them – a bird – laughed so loudly that the goddess woke up. Hine squeezed Maui to death inside her and in return for his impudence she confirmed that humankind would forever remain mortal. From that time every man and woman was doomed to end his or her life in Hine's clutches.

Further Reading

EGYPT'S DIVINE KINGSHIP

Desroches-Noblecourt, C. *Tutankhamun: Life and Death of a Pharaoh*. Penguin Books: Harmondsworth, 1989.

Hart, G. *Egyptian Myths*. British Museum Press: London, 1990.

Hornung, E. *The Valley of the Kings*. Timken: New York, 1982.

Lichteim, M. *Ancient Egyptian Literature*, 3 vols. University of California Press: Berkeley, 1980.

Lurker, M. *The Gods and Symbols of Ancient Egypt*. Thames and Hudson: London, 1980.

Nicholson, Paul and Shaw, Ian., eds. *British Museum Dictionary of Ancient Egypt*. British Museum Press: London, 1995.

Pinch, G. *Magic in Ancient Egypt*. British Museum Press: London, 1994.

Quirke, S. *Ancient Egyptian Religion*. British Museum Press: London, 1959.

Reeves, N. *The Complete Tutankhamun*. Thames and Hudson: London, 1990.

Seton-Williams, M.V. *Egyptian Legends and Stories*. Rubicon Press: London, 1988.

Shafer, B., ed. *Religion in Ancient Egypt*. Routledge: London, 1991.

Silverman, David P., ed. *Ancient Egypt*. Duncan Baird Publishers: London, 1997

Spence, L. *Ancient Egyptian Myths and Legends*. Dover: New York, 1990.

Spencer, A.J. *Death in Ancient Egypt*. Penguin Books: Harmondsworth, 1982.

ANCIENT MESOPOTAMIA

Black, Jeremy and Green, Anthony. *Gods, Demons and Symbols of Ancient Mesopotamia*. British Museum Press: London, 1992.

Brandon, S.G.F. *Creation Legends of the Ancient Near East*. Hodder & Stoughton: London, 1963.

Curtis, Vesta Sarkhosh. *Persian Myths: The Legendary Past*. British Museum Press: London, 1993.

Dalley, Stephanie, trans. *Myths from Mesopotamia*. Oxford University Press: Oxford, 1989.

Eliade, Mircea. *Cosmos and History: the Myth of the Eternal Return*. Harper and Row: New York, 1985.

Gary, J. *Near Eastern Mythology*. Hamlyn: London, 1969.

Hinnells, J.R. *Persian Mythology*. Hamlyn: London, 1973.

Kramer, Samuel Noah. *The Sumerians: Their History, Culture and Character*. University of Chicago Press: Chicago, 1963.

Leick, G. *A Dictionary of Ancient Near Eastern Mythology*. Routledge: London/New York, 1961.

Macqueen, J.G. *The Hittites*. Thames and Hudson: London, 1996.

McCall, H. *Mesopotamian Myths*. British Museum Press: London, 1990.

Pritchard, J.B. *Ancient Near Eastern Texts Relating to the Old Testament*. Princeton University Press: Princeton, 1950.

Roux, George. *Ancient Iraq*. Penguin Books: Harmondsworth, 1992.

Saggs, H.W.F. *The Greatness that was Babylon*. Sidgwick and Jackson: London, 1962.

Willis, Roy, ed. *World Mythology: The Illustrated Guide*. Piatkus: London, 1997.

THE GLORIES OF GREECE AND ROME

Apollodorus. *The Library of Greek Mythology*. Oxford University Press: Oxford, 1997.

Burkert, W. *Greek Religion*. Blackwell: Oxford, 1985.

Carpenter, T. *Art and Myth in Ancient Greece*. Thames and Hudson: London, 1991.

Dowden, K. *Religion and the Romans*. Bristol Classical Press: London, 1992.

Easterling, P.E. and Muir, John V., eds. *Greek Religion and Society*. Cambridge University Press: Cambridge, 1985.

Finley, M.I. *The World of Odysseus*. Penguin Books: Harmondsworth, 1991.

Graf, F. *Greek Mythology*. John Hopkins University Press: Baltimore, Maryland, 1993.

Grant, M. *The Myths of the Greeks and Romans*. Penguin Books: Harmondsworth, 1995.

Graves, Robert. *The Greek Myths*. Penguin Books: Harmondsworth, 1955.

Hoffman, M. and Lasdun, J., eds. *After Ovid*. Faber: London, 1994.

Homer (trans. Rieu, E.V.). *The Iliad*. Penguin Books: Harmondsworth, 1950.

Homer (trans. Cowper, William.). *The Odyssey*. Everyman: London, 1992.

Hornblower and Spawforth. *Oxford Classical Dictionary*. Oxford University Press: Oxford, 1996.

Kirk, G.S. *The Nature of Greek Myths*. Penguin Books: Harmondsworth, 1990.

Lefkowitz, K. *Women in Greek Mythology*. Duckworth: London, 1986.

Morford, M. and Lenardon, R. *Classical Mythology*. Longman, White Plains: New York State, 1991.

Ogilvie, R.M. *The Romans and their Gods*. Chatto & Windus Ltd.: London, 1969.

Perowne, S. *Roman Mythology*. Newnes: Twickenham, 1983.

Rose, H.J. *Handbook of Greek Mythology*. Routledge: London, 1990.

Rose, H.J. *Religion in Greece and Rome*. Harper & Row: New York, 1959.

Scullard, H.H. *Festivals and Ceremonies of the Roman Republic*. Thames and Hudson: London, 1981.

Tripp, E. *Handbook of Classical Mythology*. Harper & Row: New York, 1970.

Virgil (trans. Griffin, J.). *The Aeneid*. Oxford University Press: Oxford, 1986.

CELTIC DEITIES AND HEROES

Ellis, P. B. *Dictionary of Celtic Mythology*. Constable: London, 1992.

Gantz, Jeffrey, trans. *Early Irish Myths and Sagas*. Penguin Books: Harmondsworth, 1981.

Green, Miranda J. *Dictionary of Celtic Myth and Legend*. Thames and Hudson: London, 1992.

Jackson, K.H. *A Celtic Miscellany*. Penguin Books: Harmondsworth, 1971.

Jones, Gwyn and Jones, T., trans. *The Mabinogion*. J.M. Dent (Everyman): London, 1949, revised ed. 1993.

Kinsella, Thomas, trans. *The Táin (The Cattle Raid of Cooley and other Ulster stories)*. Oxford University Press: Oxford, 1970.

Lacy, Norris J., et al., eds. *The New Arthurian Encyclopedia*. Garland Publishing: New York and London, 1991.

Littleton, C. Scott and Malcor, Linda A. *From Scythia to Camelot*. Garland Publishing: New York and London, 1994.

MacCana, Proinsias. *Celtic Mythology*. Hamlyn: London, 1970.

Rees, Alwyn and Rees, Brinley. *Celtic Heritage*. Thames and Hudson: New York, 1961.

Thorpe, Lewis, trans. *The History of the Kings of Britain by Geoffrey of Monmouth*. Penguin Books: Harmondsworth, 1966.

Wood, Juliette. *The Celts: Life, Myth and Art*. Duncan Baird Publishers: London, 1998.

SAGAS OF THE NORSEMEN

Allan, Tony. *Vikings: The Battle at the End of Time*. Duncan Baird Publishers: London, 2001

Crossley-Holland, K. *The Penguin Book of Norse Myths: Gods of the Vikings*. Penguin Books: London, 1980.

Davidson, H.R. Ellis. *Gods and the Myths of Northern Europe*. Penguin Books: Harmondsworth, 1964.

Davidson, H.R. Ellis. *Lost Beliefs of Northern Europe*. Routledge: London, 1993.

Davidson, H.R. Ellis. *Pagan Scandinavia*. Hamlyn: London, 1984.

Magnusson, M. *Viking: Hammer of the North*. Orbis: London, 1976.

Owen, G.R. *Rites and Religions of the Anglo-Saxons*. David and Charles: Newton Abbot, 1981.

Page, R.I. *Chronicles of the Vikings*. British Museum Press: London, 1995.

Page, R.I. *Norse Myths*. British Museum Press: London, 1993.

Todd, M. *The Early Germans*. Blackwell: Oxford, 1992.

Turville-Petre, E.O.G. *Myth and Religion of the North*. Weidenfeld: London, 1964.

INDIA'S ETERNAL CYCLE

Carrithers, Michael. *The Buddha*. Oxford University Press: Oxford, 1984.

Easwaran, Eknath, trans. *The Bhagavad Gita*. Arkana/Penguin: London, 1985.

Easwaran, Eknath, trans. *The Dhammapada*. Penguin Books: London, 1986.

Easwaran, Eknath, trans. *The Upanishads*. Arkana/Penguin: London, 1987.

Flood, Gavin. *An Introduction to Hinduism*. Cambridge University Press: Cambridge, 1996.

Jaffrey, Madhur. *Seasons of Splendour: Tales, Myths and Legends of India*. Puffin: London, 1985.

Jansen, Eva Rudy. *The Book of Hindu Imagery*. Binkey Kok Publications: Holland, 1993.

Mookerjee, Ajit. *Kali, The Feminine Force*. Thames and Hudson: London, 1988.

O'Flaherty, Wendy Doniger, trans. *Hindu Myths*. Penguin: London, 1975.

O'Flaherty, Wendy Doniger, trans. *The Rig Veda*. Penguin: London, 1981.

Pauling, Chris. *Introducing Buddhism*. Windhorse Publications: Birmingham, 1990.

Shearer, Alistair. *The Hindu Vision*. Thames and Hudson: London, 1993.

Trainor, Kevin., ed. *Buddhism: The Illustrated Guide*. Duncan Baird Publishers: London, 2001

CHINA'S HEAVENLY MANDATE

Blunden, Caroline and Elvin, Mark. *Cultural Atlas of China*. Phaidon Press: Oxford, 1983.

Christie, Anthony. *Chinese Mythology*. Paul Hamlyn: London, 1968.

Gernet, Jacques (trans. Foster, J.R.). *A History of Chinese Civilization*. Cambridge University Press: Cambridge, 1985.

Granet, M. *The Religion of the Chinese People*. Blackwood: Oxford, 1975.

Hook, Brian, ed. *The Cambridge Encyclopedia of China*. Cambridge University Press: Cambridge, 1982.

Jianing Chen and Yang Yang. *The World of Chinese Myths*. Beijing Language and Culture University Press: Beijing, 1995.

Lau, D.C., trans. *Confucius: The Analects*. Penguin Classics: London, 1963.

Lau, D.C., trans. *Lao-tzu: Tao te Ching*. Penguin Classics: London, 1963.

Ronan, Colin. *The Shorter Science & Civilisation in China 1* (abridged Joseph Needham). Cambridge University Press: Cambridge, 1980.

Shaughnessy, Prof. Edward L., ed. *China: The Land of the Heavenly Dragon*. Duncan Baird Publishers: London, 2000.

Walls, John and Walls, Yvonne, ed. and trans. *Classical Chinese Myths*. Joint Publishing House: Hong Kong, 1984.

Watson, William. *China*. Thames and Hudson: London, 1961.

JAPAN'S REALM OF THE RISING SUN

Aston, W.G., trans. *Nihongi: Chronicles of Japan from the Earliest Times to AD697*. Charles E. Tuttle: Tokyo, 1978.

Bowring, R. and Kornicki, P., eds. *The Cambridge Encyclopedia of Japan*. Cambridge University Press: Cambridge, 1993.

Colcutt, M., Jansen, M. and Kumakura, I., eds. *Cultural Atlas of Japan*. Phaidon Press: Oxford, 1988.

Earhart, H.B. *Japanese Religion*. Wadsworth Publishing: Belmont, 1983.

Guth, C. *Japanese Art of the Edo Period*. Everyman Art Library: London, 1996.

Hall, J.W. *Japan from Prehistory to Modern Times*. Delacorte Press: New York, 1970.

Knappert, Jan. *Pacific Mythology*. Diamond Books: London, 1995.

Mayer, F.H. *The Yanagita Guide to the Japanese Folktale*. Indiana University Press, 1986.

Ono, S. *Shinto: The Kami Way*. Charles E. Tuttle: Tokyo, 1962.

Piggott, J. *Japanese Mythology*. Peter Bedrick Books: New York, 1991.

Reader, Ian. *Religion in Contemporary Japan*. University of Hawaii Press: Honolulu, 1991.

Tyler, R., ed. and trans. *Japanese Tales*. Pantheon Books: New York, 1987.

NORTH AMERICA'S MOTHER EARTH, FATHER SKY

Bierhorst, J. *The Mythology of North America*. William Morrow: New York, 1985.

Brody, H. *Living Arctic*. Douglas and McIntyre: Vancouver, 1987.

Champagne, D., ed. *Native America: Portrait of the Peoples*. Visible Ink Press: Detroit, 1994.

Deloria, V. *God is Red, a Native View of Religion*. North American Press: Golden, Connecticut, 1992.

Fagan, B. *Ancient North America*. Thames and Hudson: London and New York, 1995.

Hardin, T., ed. *Legends and Lore of the American Indians*. Barnes and Noble Inc.: New York, 1993.

Jonaitis, A. *From the Land of the Totem Poles*. American Museum of Natural History: New York, 1988.

Josephy, A. M. *Five Hundred Nations: An Illustrated History of North American Indians*. Hutchinson: New York, 1995.

Kopper, P. *The Smithsonian Book of North American Indians: Before the Coming of the Europeans*. Smithsonian Institution Press: Washington D.C., 1986.

Niehardt, J. *Black Elk Speaks*. University of Nebraska Press: Lincoln, Nebraska, 1979.

Sturtevant, W.C., gen. ed. *Handbook of North American Indians*. Smithsonian Institution Press: Washington D.C., 1981.

Woodhead, H., series ed. *The American Indians*. Time-Life Books: Richmond, Virginia, 1994.

MESOAMERICA'S GODS OF SUN AND SACRIFICE

Boone, Elizabeth Hill. *The Aztec World: Exploring the Ancient World*. Smithsonian Institution Press: Washington D.C., 1982.

Carter, Geraldine. *The Illustrated Guide to Latin American Mythology*. Studio Editions: London, 1995.

Coe, Michael D. *Mexico: From the Olmecs to the Aztecs*. Thames and Hudson: London, 1994.

Coe, Michael D. *The Maya*, 4th ed. Thames and Hudson: London, 1993.

Laughton, Timothy. *The Maya: Life, Myth and Art*. Duncan Baird Publishers: London, 1998.

Miller, Mary Ellen. *The Art of Mesoamerica: From Olmec to Aztec*. Thames and Hudson: London, 1996.

Miller, Mary Ellen and Schele, Linda. *The Blood of Kings*. George Braziller: New York, 1985.

Miller, Mary Ellen and Taube, Karl. *The Gods and Symbols of Ancient Mexico and the Maya, An Illustrated Dictionary of Mesoamerican Religion*. Thames and Hudson: London, 1993.

Morley, Sylvanus (ed. Robert L. Sharer). *The Ancient Maya*. Stanford University Press: California, 1983.

Taube, Karl. *Aztec and Maya Myths*. British Museum Press: London, 1995.

Townsend, Richard. *The Aztecs*. Thames and Hudson: London, 1992.

Whitecotton, Joseph. *The Zapotecs*. University of Oklahoma Press, 1977.

SOUTH AMERICAN KINGDOMS OF GOLD

Albisetti, Cesar (et al.). *Folk Literature of the Bororo Indians*. UCLA Latin American Center Publications: Los Angeles, 1983.

Burrin, Kathleen, ed. *The Spirit of Ancient Peru*. Thames and Hudson: New York, 1997.

Coe, Michael., Snow, Dean. and Benson, Elizabeth. *Atlas of Ancient America*. Facts on File Ltd.: Oxford, 1993.

Fagan, Brian M. *Kingdoms of Gold, Kingdoms of Jade*. Thames and Hudson: London, 1991.

Hemming, John. *The Conquest of the Incas*. Macmillan: London, 1970.

Lizot, Jacques. *Tales of the Yanomami*. Cambridge University Press: Cambridge, 1991.

MacCormack, Sabine. *Religion in the Andes: Vision and Imagination in Early Colonial Peru*. Princeton University Press: Princeton, 1991.

Morrison, Tony. *The Mystery of the Nasca Lines*. Nonsuch Expeditions Ltd: Woodbridge, 1987.

Morrison, Tony. *The New Larousse Encyclopedia of Mythology*. Hamlyn: London, 1983.

Osborne, Harold. *South American Mythology*. Newnes: Feltham, 1990.

Parks, Donald, ed. *Myths and Traditions of the Arikara Indians*. University of Nebraska Press: Lincoln, 1996.

Stierlin, Henri. *Art of the Incas and its Origins*. Rizzoli: New York, 1984.

THE ANCESTRAL VOICES OF AFRICA

Bacquart, Jean-Baptiste. *The Tribal Arts of Africa*. Thames and Hudson: London, 1998.

Courlander, Harold. *A Treasury of African Folklore*. Marlowe & Company: New York, 1996.

Courlander, Harold. *Gods and Heroes from Yoruba Mythology*. Crown Books: New York, 1973.

Knappert, Jan. *An Encyclopedia of Myth and Legend: African Mythology*. Diamond Books: London, 1995.

Knappert, Jan. *Kings, Gods & Spirits*. Peter Lowe: London, 1986.

Knappert, Jan. *Myths and Legends of the Bantu*. Heinemann: London, 1963.

Knappert, Jan. *Myths and Legends of the Congo*. Heinemann: London, 1971.

Murray, Jocelyn, ed. *Cultural Atlas of Africa*. Checkmark Books: New York, 1998.

Niane, D.T. *Sundiata: An Epic of Old Mali*. Longman: London, 1986.

Parrinder, Geoffrey. *African Mythology*. Hamlyn: London, 1982.

Radin, Paul, ed. *African Folktales*. Schocken Books: New York, 1983.

Schmalenbach, W., ed. *African Art*. Prestel-Verlag: Munich, 1988.

THE UNSEEN WORLDS OF AUSTRALASIA

Alpers, Antony. *The World of the Polynesians*. Oxford University Press: Auckland, 1987.

Berndt, R.M. and Berndt, C.H. *Aboriginal Australian Art*. New Holland Publishers Ltd: Frenchs Forest, New South Wales, 1998.

Craig, R.D. *Dictionary of Polynesian Mythology*. Greenwood Press: New York, 1989.

D'Alleva. *Art of the Pacific*. The Everyman Art Library: London, 1998.

Hiatt, L.R., ed. *Australian Aboriginal Mythology*. Australian Institute of Aboriginal Studies: Canberra, 1975.

Kame'eleiwiha, L. *Native Land and Foreign Desires*. Bishop Museum Press: Honolulu, Hawaii, 1992.

Kirch, P. *Feathered Gods and Fishhooks*. University of Hawaii Press: Honolulu, Hawaii, 1985.

Morphy, H. *Ancestral Connections*. Chicago University Press: Chicago, 1991.

Mudrooroo. *Aboriginal Mythology*. Thorsons: London, 1994.

Orbell, Margaret. *The Illustrated Encyclopedia of Maori Myths and Legend*. Canterbury University Press: Christchurch, 1995.

Starzecka, D.C., ed. *Maori Art and Culture*. British Museum Press: London, 1996.

Thomas, Nicholas. *Oceanic Art*. Thames and Hudson: London, 1995.

675

Index

Page numbers in **bold** indicate major treatment of a subject; page numbers in *italics* indicate illustrations.